The Hidden Origins *of* ISLAM

The Hidden Origins of ISLAM

NEW RESEARCH INTO ITS EARLY HISTORY

EDITED BY KARL-HEINZ OHLIG AND GERD-R. PUIN

Prometheus Books
59 John Glenn Drive
Amherst, New York 14228–2119

Published 2010 by Prometheus Books

Inquiries should be addressed to
Prometheus Books
59 John Glenn Drive
Amherst, New York 14228–2119
VOICE: 716–691–0133
FAX: 716–691–0137
WWW.PROMETHEUSBOOKS.COM

14 13 5 4 3

Library of Congress Cataloging-in-Publication Data

The hidden origins of Islam : new research into its early history / edited by Karl-Heinz Ohlig and Gerd-R. Puin.
p. cm.
ISBN 978–1–59102–634–1 (hardcover : alk. paper)
1. Islam—History. I. Ohlig, Karl-Heinz, 1938– II. Puin, Gerd-R.

BP55.H53 2008
297.09'021—dc22 2008049316

Printed in the United States of America on acid-free paper

CONTENTS

PART II. NEW ASPECTS FOR THE EMERGENCE AND CHARACTERISTIC OF ISLAM

FOREWORD

ISLAM'S "HIDDEN" ORIGINS

Karl-Heinz Ohlig

This volume of collected essays seeks to bring a bit of light into the hidden beginnings of a major world religion, namely, Islam.

This intention, as well as my calling Islam's beginnings "hidden," may well astound many, for the beginnings and later development of only a few religions seem to be as clearly known as those of Islam.

In the early sixth century, the prophet Muhammad (570–632) arose; he proclaimed the revelations of Allah in Mecca and Medina and eventually united all the tribes of the Arabian peninsula into one *umma* under his religious and political leadership. The life of the prophet, his upbringing and marriages, his work, the Hijra from Mecca to Medina in 622, and his battles are narrated in detail in Muslim publications as well as those concerning the academic discipline of Islamic studies.

After his death, the story continued with successes in war and in religion. This early period gave birth to large Islamic empires, beginning with the four "rightly guided" caliphs (632–661), continuing under the Umayyad caliphs, with their capital in Damascus (661–750), and culminating under the Abbasids (beginning in 749), who had their political seat in Baghdad beginning in 762. Why, then, "hidden" origins?

It is well known that there are only a few bits of information to be found in the Qur'an that offer biographical material about the Meccan prophet; however, the consequences of this fact are drawn out by only a few scholars of Islam. All the biographical "information" we have can be found in two types of sources. The first consists of the biographical works of the early ninth and tenth centuries. These include: 1) the "Sira" of Ibn Hisham (d. 834), which claims to be related to a non-extant text of Ibn Is-haq (d. 768); 2) a history of military campaigns by al-Waqidi (d. 822); 3) a book called "Classes" or "Generations" by Ibn Sa'd (d. 845); and 4) a book called "Annals" by al-Tabari (d. 922). The second type of source consists of the six canonical collections of hadith, which date from the late ninth century; these are ascribed to the following redactors: 1) al-Bukhari (d. 870); 2) Muslim (d. 875); 3) Abu Dawud (d. 888); 4) al-Tirmidhi (d. 892); 5) al-Nasa'i (d. 915); and 6) Ibn Maja (d. 886).

Following the canons of historical-critical research, these reports, written approximately two hundred years after the fact, should be taken into consideration only with great reservations.[1] They were collected at a time when Muhammad was the paradigm of identification for a large and powerful empire; consequently, the reports about him were appropriately stylized. Their legendary character forces itself on the reader who comes to the text uncritically; certain questions are asked in ways that become thematic, despite the fact that some of the questions could not have played a role during the suggested lifetime of the prophet; and so on.[2]

Nonetheless, these sources are the first to depict the life of Muhammad and trace the Qur'an back to his proclamations in Mecca and Medina, so that the shape of the Arabian prophet and his life remains historically in shadow. To put the issue more sharply, the problem of the sources casts doubt on the entire question of Muhammad's historicity: "Muhammad is not a historical figure, and his official biography is a product of the age in which it was written."[3] In the same vein, only in the ninth century was it first claimed that the proclamations of Muhammad were brought together into the current, complete text of the Qur'an by a commision of three Meccans under the leadership of Zayd ibn Thabit from Medina. This editorial work is thought to have occurred in the caliphate of 'Uthman (644–656), specifically between 650 and 656—that is, eighteen to twenty-four years after the death of Muhammad.

Rudi Paret writes the following in the introduction to his translation of the Qur'an, and in doing so he gives expression to a consensus practically unanimous among scholars of Islam: "We have no reason to accept the idea that even one single verse in the whole Koran does not stem from Muhammad."[4] But why? How does he know this to be true? On what sources does he build his argument? Such a claim highlights many issues, including: the many tensions within the Qur'an; the placement alongside one another of varying, sometimes even contradictory, traditions; its apparent redactional editorial work; the late date of its emergence as the Qur'an we know (as the earliest manuscript fragments indicate); and the much later date of the ascription of the text to the Arabian prophet.[5] The way that Paret and others simply pass over all these literary-critical problems is, quite frankly, shocking.

The Islamic literature of the ninth century also contributes to current narratives of the later history of the spread of Islam, although only a few "witnesses" from the first two Muslim centuries are extant. Usually, the difficulties these sources create are not mentioned. Josef van Ess is a notable exception. He admits that there are only a few early witnesses and, for the first century after the Hijra, only a few inscriptions, such as those on the Dome of the Rock in Jerusalem, on the Umayyad mosque in Damascus, and in numismatic legends. Further, he admits that all (later) Islamic texts stand "under suspicion of projection."[6] Consequently, he refuses to present the first century at all; rather, he begins with the second, although he also states that the same problems exist for this century, in that there are hardly any "original texts" to be found.[7] In other words, the first two "Islamic" centuries lie in the shadows of history, and it remains inexplicable how the development of a large Islamic empire could have left behind no witnesses whatsoever, even among groups from whom we might expect such traces, such as the enemies of the Arabs, the many Byzantines known for their literary skills and output, and the Jews and Christians living under the alleged Islamic authority.

With help from the few datable and localizable extant witnesses, namely, coins and inscriptions, the contributors to this volume undertake the task of explicating the contours of this development in the first two centuries. It will be proven that the numismatic discoveries from this period, as well as the inscriptions on the Dome of the Rock, actually concern *Christian* texts and symbols, which document Syrian-Arabian theological ideas: that God is one and single, and that the one he has sent (Jesus) is to be praised (*muḥammad*). Such statements were aimed at demarcating the texts' communities from Byzantine conceptions of the Trinity and of Christology. They document the proud attempt of an Arabian Christianity and the empires shaped by it to create and defend their own identity. In addition, it will become clear that, long before the appearance of the idea of a Hijra, there was an Arabian-Christian reckoning of time, which began with the year 622 and was only later "converted" to a Muslim meaning. Until approximately the end of the eighth century, so it seems, Arabian-Christian tribal leaders governed the regions of the Near East and of North Africa—indeed, the Umayyad leaders and even the early Abbasids were Christians.

It was not until the second century after the Hijra that the idea of Muhammad seems to have been loosened from its original connection (namely, to Jesus) and then isolated as a conception unto itself. Further, this process of detachment seems to have experienced both an expansion of the idea, to include a Christian apostle-prophet named Muhammad, and an intermediate stage that served as a conceptual bridge, namely, the worship of a certain ʿAli ("exalted"), who took over normative functions in a more concrete way and in the place of the distant and transcendent Muhammad (Jesus). In the eighth century, and more fully in the ninth, the developing independence of the Muhammad idea made it possible to bind it with (or to establish it as the foundation for) the idea of an Arab prophet of this same name, an idea that had already been transmitted through history to some degree, and through this process gained its own independent shape. This also bound the Muhammad idea to the Arabian holy places of Mecca and Medina. All of this seems to have served the interest of the creation of an Arabian identity for the Abbasid Empire. At this time, then, the biographical works and the collections of Hadith about the Sunna appeared. All of the available traditions concerning earlier Arabian rulers and controversies were then woven into a continuing history of the Islamic religion and the development of its empire. The older veneration of ʿAli was repressed and survives only among the Shiite traditions.

From the perspective of the history of religions, one recognizes here a fascinating process in the emergence of a new religion. The individuals in question, just like the redactors of the Pentateuch, infused their religion into a "canonical" time of beginnings, in which they then grounded and legitimated it.

This interpretation, argued among these contributions most strongly by Volker Popp, and deepened by Christoph Luxenberg (although already suggested by Yehuda D. Nevo and Judith Koren), is not simply a subjective opinion; rather, it is supported here by the only sources able to express themselves in terms of history.

What is the relationship, though, between this thesis and the Qur'an, whose texts[8] are attested—with a few exceptions—only in the early eighth century and in a defective script,[9] and whose Muslim "canonization" was not complete until approximately one hundred years later? One should always remember that the Qur'an appeared in a time and a place (Iraq) when the entire surrounding region was still Christian (and Jewish). Can it have been created as the foundational document of a new religion at that time? Or did it become so only later?

Günter Lüling[10] has most recently argued that, before Muhammad, there was a sort of "Ur-Qur'ān," consisting of hymns arising from an Arian milieu; these hymns were later edited by Muhammad and early Muslim communities. These initially hypothetical arguments have been supported through the work of Christoph Luxenberg, albeit using completely different methodological starting points.[11] Luxenberg has shown the following: 1) the Qur'an emerged in a region that was linguistically Arabic/Syro-Aramaic; 2) a multitude of passages represent Syriac words and sentences written in Arabic letters; 3) that the grammatical structure of the Arabic of the Qur'an betrays Syriac influences throughout; and 4) some original Arabic words were misinterpreted through the development of the "fuller" writing, that is, the fixing of the consonants through diacritical points, a process that took place as much as two hundred years later.[12] Completely new readings and expressions often emerge from these investigations into the Qur'anic text, readings which point to a Christian background.

Luxenberg has also found that the Qur'an not only stems from a region linguistically Syro-Aramaic, but that it is also, at least in large parts, based on an originally Syriac text. He points to four written characters that were either nearly identical or extremely similar in the Syriac and Arabic scripts—and therefore capable of being mistaken for one another—but which served as indicators of *different* consonants in the two written languages. He argues that these characters were preserved in the transfer of the original Syriac text into Arabic, which means that they were *not* then converted into the correctly corresponding Arabic characters. This phenomenon points to the use of a text originally written in Syriac.

If this is correct, then the Qur'an must have had a somewhat longer prehistory in Syro-Aramaic, a possibility also suggested by, for example, the material in the Punishment Stories. Had the Christianized Arabian tribes put together a lectionary or lectionaries—in Syriac, naturally, following the usage of the period—for the validation and certification of the Scriptures (Old and New Testaments), which were then later translated into the Arabic language? And does "later" here mean perhaps only in the time of the Umayyad caliph ʿAbd al-Malik (d. 705) or his successor al-Walid (d. 715), who established Arabic as their new official state language?[13] When did those texts come together which certainly cannot be traced back to Christian roots or that seem to point to an Arabian prophet? There is the famous comment from the ninth century concerning ʿUthman's destruction of all Qurʾanic manuscripts except for the full text that he caused to be put together. Is it possible that this refers much more in reality to the elimination of the foundational Syriac text in the early eighth century?

There are further perspectives, from both linguistics and from the history of religions, that should be considered and will be taken up in the contributions to this volume. Most of these articles were known beforehand to the editors only in the proposals of their topics, not in their content. The authors and their publications allow us to expect, however, that many new aspects of these concerns will be developed, aspects which have not yet received enough attention in the scholarly world. Naturally, though, these perspectives have not yet been drawn together into one over arching concept or even necessarily harmonized; for such to occur, one would need a long symposium.

Consequently, the editors understand this collection as a spur toward discussion and further research, not as a delineation of an already complete idea. Hopefully, though, the collection can make clear that the beginnings of Islam will only be able to be understood on the basis of historical sources, not from later interpretations, and when historical and philological questions are investigated on the basis of those sources.

It may be difficult for the discipline of Islamic studies to call into question rubrics of interpretation hundreds of years in the making. Whether the articles in this volume will be accepted immediately cannot be determined at the present time. In the long run, though, the field will not be able simply to pass over or interpret away the "facts of the case," meaning the historical sources and philological insights.

NOTES

1. Cf. Yehuda D. Nevo and Judith Koren, *Crossroads to Islam: The Origins of the Arab Religion and the Arab State* (Amherst, NY: Prometheus Books, 2003), p.

9: "*Non-contemporary literary sources* are, in our opinion, inadmissable as historical evidence. If one has no source of knowledge of the 7th century except texts written in the 9th century or later, one cannot know anything about the 7th century: one can only know what people in the 9th century or later believed about the 7th."

2. Cf. the author's *Weltreligion Islam: Eine Einführung* (Mainz: Exodus, 2000), pp. 28–41.

3. Nevo and Koren, *Crossroads to Islam*, p. 11.

4. Rudi Paret, *Der Koran* (Stuttgart: Kohlhammer, 1979), p. 5.

5. Ohlig, *Weltreligion Islam*, pp. 42–92.

6. Josef van Ess, *Theologie und Gesellschaft im 2. und 3. Jahrhundert Hidschra: Eine Geschichte des religiösen Denkens im frühen Islam*, vol. 1 (Berlin and New York: Walter de Gruyter, 1991), p. viii.

7. Ibid.

8. It is a scholarly curiosity that, up until the present day, all contemporary Qur'anic exegesis has relied upon the 1924 Cairo edition of the Qur'an and has never, as opposed to all other fields of "book studies," undertaken an attempt to produce a critical edition of at least large portions of the Qur'an with the assistance of the early Qur'an fragments still available. Two requests by the central German Foundation for Research (the "Deutsche Forschungsgemeinschaft" or "DFG") to support such a critical textual analysis have been rejected by experts in Islamic studies, although normally all further exegesis must begin with an attempt at coming closer to the "original" form of the text.

9. The fragments in question, the oldest known fragments of the Qur'an, are available to the public at this time in facsimile editions—one each from Samarkand, from Paris, from St. Petersburg, and from London—as well as in the photographic documentation of the San'a' manuscripts at the University of Saarland. Their script is considered "defective" because it lacks not only the marks of vocalization but also, and nearly throughout, the diacritical points. Although the Arabic script contains twenty-eight consonants (this is also true of the oldest version of the Hijazi script), only seven of them are written unequivocally, while the other characters can refer to more than one consonant—indeed between two and five. Consequently, the characters were clarified and attached firmly to the various consonants through the use of diacritical points (one to three dots under or over the character). See the author's *Weltreligion Islam*, pp. 60–61.

10. Günter Lüling, *Über den Ur-Quran: Ansätze zur Rekonstruktion vorislamischer christlicher Strophenlieder im Quran* (Erlangen: Lüling, 1974 [1st ed.] and 1993 [2nd ed.]). This text has since appeared in an expanded English version: *A Challenge to Islam: For Reformation* (Delhi, 2003).

11. Christoph Luxenberg, *Die syro-aramäische Lesart des Koran: Ein Beitrag zur Entstehung der Koransprache* (Berlin: Das Arabische Buch, 2000 [1st ed.], 2004

[2nd ed.], and 2005 [3rd ed.]). An extended English version has appeared in Berlin: Schiler 2007 with the title *The Syro-Aramaic Reading of the Koran. A Contribution to the Decoding of the Language of the Koran.*

12. The fixing of the many consonants by means of diacritical points, as well as the addition of vocalization points, was achieved by a long process that was not completed until the ninth century, or possibly even later. It is clear that the fixation of the text, which also occurred at a later date, rested upon the interpretations of the individual scribes, which were often wrong. When one places the diacritical points in different locations, the resulting texts give readings that make sense and also fit into their contexts (cf. here, above all, Luxenberg, *Die syro-aramäische Lesart*).

13. It would be most helpful in searching for an answer to this question if the available fragments of the Qurʾān could be dated more precisely. The fragments that until now have been published in facsimile editions are probably to be reckoned to the second half of the eighth century; further, there are good reasons to believe the Sanʿaʾ fragment to be more recent, as was initially accepted.

PART I.

THE EARLY HISTORY OF ISLAM

1

THE EARLY HISTORY OF ISLAM, FOLLOWING INSCRIPTIONAL AND NUMISMATIC TESTIMONY

Volker Popp

THE FICTION OF A UNIFIED HISTORY OF EARLY ISLAM

As early as 1902, Julius Wellhausen brought attention to the fact that the Syrian tradition of the Arabs had been lost.[1] In fact, it was not only the Syrian tradition that was lost, but also the tradition of the eastern regions of the Arabian Empire. One finds references to this loss in Chinese sources.[2] Wellhausen also indicated that the historical reports of the Islamic historians do not satisfy the standards that Theodor Mommsen (1817–1903) established for historical sources.[3] Further, the traditional Islamic historians did not state what the specifically "Arabian" part of the Islamic history was.[4]

Should one desire to reconstruct the historical circumstances in Syria, Mesopotamia, and Iran in the seventh century, this author would *not* suggest turning to the reports of the Islamic historians. Numerous holdings in inscriptions and visual portrayals from this region can be found in both public and private archaeological collections. With these materials at hand—by using the material witnesses that are extant—it is possible to reconstruct the historical contexts in question. As Wellhausen said, "as everyone knows, one must always *construct* history. . . . The only difference is whether one constructs it well or poorly" (my emphasis).[5]

In terms of a *method* of reconstruction, I will follow the path that Michael Bates suggested in 1976. Following this method, the numismatic material will be considered one mint at a time, before proceeding on to consider provinces and then regions as a whole. Only then will I attempt to draw out conclusions which are valid for all the extant material. I also suggest this method of "small steps" for the handling of protocols and titulatures on coins and in inscriptions.[6]

I will not offer here a detailed presentation of the history of pre-Islamic, Christian Arabs in Syria and the western Arabian peninsula, nor will there be a full presentation of the history of Christianity under the Arabs in the eastern peninsula, in Baḥrain, in Qaṭar, and in Oman beginning with the missions of the Syrians in the third century. Of special importance is the history of Christian Arabs in Mesopotamia and in the Jazīra ("the island"). This area in the curve of the Euphrates was a homeland for Arabs quite early, and as a official diocese it was called by contemporaries (in Aramaic) *Bēt ʿArabāyē.*

For the sake of this presentation, it is absolutely necessary to point to the central historical event of the first half of the seventh century, namely, the surprising victory of the Byzantines in 622. The massive political changes that followed were later described by the traditional Islamic literature as the results of the Hijra ("emigration") of the Prophet of the Arabs. This Hijra supposedly took place in 622, and with it supposedly began the Islamic reckoning of time. This is not historical. In reality, though, a new era did begin: the period of the self-government of Christian Arabs.

ON THE PREHISTORY OF "ISLAM"

The Religious War between the Byzantines and the Sassanians

At least as early as 1952, Georg Ostrogorsky could not avoid the conclusion that the drawn-out conflict between New Iran and New Rome had taken on the character of a war of religion, beginning with the government of Chosroes II (591–628).[7] This change in the war was also embodied in its protagonists. Chosroes II had a precise understanding of the structure of the Byzantine system of authority. He knew that the legitimation of the imperial authority rested in its function as protector of the Church. As a young refugee at the imperial court in Byzantium, he had enjoyed the protection of the

Byzantine emperor Mauricius (582–602). After a Byzantine army had helped him in his return to Iran and his achievement of the throne, he later avenged the fate of his previous protector after Mauricius, along with the entire imperial family, was murdered in 602 by the usurper Phocas. Chosroes was married to two Christian women, the Byzantine princess Maria and the Syrian Shīrīn; further, his finance minister, Yazdīn, was a Christian.[8] His relationship to the cult of St. Sergius of Ruṣāfa—not merely as a *dévotion spéciale*—is attested by a report of his donations to the cult and through a note saying that he restored its sacred objects which had been stolen by his ancestors.[9] In the face of the appropriation of Persian traditions by the Nestorian Church of Iran (marriage for priests, its self-understanding as a national church), "people in the Sassanian court had to admit that they could no longer avoid the Nestorians. For a short time, a Nestorian Church stood right next to the royal palace in Seleucia on the Tigris."[10]

The result was a coexistence of two religions, a situation with which we are familiar in contemporary Japan, where the emperor is the chief of the national cult, while all those under him practice their own private religions, which show themselves to be true to the state. Just as in contemporary Japan Shintoism serves as the national religion, and Buddhism and Christianity exist as private religions, so in Iran the Mazdean religion of the Zoroastrian national cult was the official religion of the empire, with the King of Kings as its protector, while all his subordinates including the aristocracy were practitioners of the living religion of Christianity, which remained true to the state. The Arabians connected with the Nestorians of Iran were the kings of al-Ḥīra from the clan of the Lakhmids. Already in the inscription of the Sassanian ruler Narses at Paikuli (293–302), we see one of these Arabian vassals mentioned: *'Amrw lḥm'dyn mlk'* ('Amr, king [*malik*] of the Lakhmids).[11]

With Chosroes' return to the throne in 595, the Arabian ruler in al-Ḥīra was baptized. "That Nu'man became a Nestorian when he decided to become a Christian is completely understandable, not only because his surroundings were Nestorian but also because the Nestorians, alone among the Christian confessional groups, were in any way acceptable to the Persians, as opposed to the 'Roman' Monophysites and Melkites."[12]

The Ghassanids, on the other hand, Arabian rulers of Syria, were supporters of the Monophysite confession. At the end of the sixth century, in questions of Christian doctrine, this group existed in opposition to both their Byzantine overlords and to their enemy Arabian brothers under Sassanian authority. As the local holders of high office, the Ghassanids were part of the aristocracy of Byzantium. Their leader bore the title *Biṭrīq* (from the Latin *patricius*).[13] At the end of the sixth century, then, two Arabian dynasties were pitted against one another, with both serving as the representatives of foreign empires, taking the roles of regional rulers, and defending differing Christian confessions. Both groups' own religions differed from that of their respective national cults (the Zoroastrians in Iran and the imperial church in Byzantium). The war between the two great empires was essentially, in large part, a war of their representatives, led by their Arabian Christian vassals and their successors.

The position of the emperor of Byzantium, Heraclius (610–641), son of the exarch of Carthage, was precarious in ways similar to that of his opponent in the east. Although he was a Christian emperor, he was hated by large parts of Christendom. The western Armenians, the Laz, and other Georgians followed him only under threat. The eastern Armenians had bound themselves to the east Syrians at a 541 synod in Dwīn. The Monophysite Arabs and Copts joined this faction, as well as the Ethiopians, who had accepted missionary preaching from Syria. Even in the emperor's homeland of North Africa, the church of the emperor was in distress. Controversies between the Roman population and the native Numidians played a significant role in these difficulties. The separatist church of the Donatists had made the efficacy of the sacraments dependent upon the holiness of the minister (a catastrophe for every church hierarchy, but St. Augustine had come to the rescue here, developing the rudiments of an official Catholic doctrine of the sacraments).

Also in the West, the western Goths mourned again the loss of their spiritual independence as Arians. In 587, the royal house had chosen to convert from Arian to Catholic Christianity in order to avoid the fate of the eastern Goths in Italy (by 562 the Byzantines had finished annihilating them in battle). The emperor could only be certain of what was happening with the Roman pope as long as the presence of a Byzantine garrison of troops in the fortress of Ravenna constantly reminded the latter of the consequences of the possibility of insubordination.

The Sassanians in the Footsteps of Their Iranian Predecessors in Syria and Egypt

Occupations of Egypt by Iranian overlords took place even in ancient times (525–404 and 343–332 BCE). The Sassanians, in their period, held on to the dream of the previous reach of Iranian authority; indeed, under Shāpūr II (309–379) they had integrated eastern Arabia with the central Arabian landscape of al-Yamāma, and they later advanced as far as the Ḥijāz, overpowering Yemen in 572. Consequently, they made use of the conflicts among Christians in the Byzantine Orient in order to proceed to Syria and Palestine in 614.

As a result of the persecution of Monophysite Christians, the Byzantine emperor Mauricius (582–602) stripped his Arabian vassals in Syria and western Arabia of their power. It was well-known that Arabian Monophysite Christians had already begun to imitate the Byzantine system of authority through the ruling Ghassanids. The connections between the Jacobite Church of Syria and the Ghassanids was a reflection of the relationship between Orthodox Christianity and the imperial palace in Byzantium. At this point, the emperor began seeking to hinder the Monophysites from strengthening their position in the Byzantine east. He accused the Ghassanid phylarchs of treason during a battle against Iran in 581; based on this accusation, he dissolved the Ghassanid buffer state in 584, and the Ghassanid federation broke up again into fifteen tribes. Consequently, one should not be surprised to learn that the Sassanian armies appeared before Antioch as early as 604. One hundred years earlier, Byzantium had withdrawn its military presence from Syria[14] (excepting a few religious centers, like Jerusalem and Ruṣāfa). The border with the area occupied by the Arabian vassals proceeded eastward from Antioch. One further indicator that Byzantium had given Syria over in the sixth century is the fact that the Arabian "barbarians" had erected building inscriptions in their own language.[15]

Consequently, Arabic appeared first as a language of authority. Aramaic remained the language of literature and the church liturgy. One sees evidence of the latter in the reestablishment of the Syrian Church under the Ghassanids. The language of the Jacobite Church remained Aramaic; while the Jacobite Church was supported by the Arabian lords of Syria, it remained a church of Syrians. The Arabian leader ʿAbd al-Malik was the first to found the *Arabian* church in Jerusalem as a foil to the church of the emperor, as a defender of orthopraxy against Orthodoxy.

That Byzantium gave Syria over to the Arabians is further attested in the papyri of Nessana in the northwest Negev. These Greek papyri arise from the period 460–630. Until 601 they reflect the traditions of the imperial chancellery, and the names of the scribes appear in their Greek form. In 601, however, this tradition was given up, and in the eight papyri dated after 601 the scribes no longer used the Greek forms of their names but rather the Arabic forms.[16]

Clear evidence of these changes can be found in the (merely) regional dimensions of the reforms of Heraclius; these dimensions also reflect the self-understanding of Byzantium. After the attempt of Justinian I (527–565) to resurrect the Roman Empire in its former splendor and glory, an attempt that faltered because of an overextension of the empire's means, the results of the intervening catastrophes forced Heraclius into a reform of the empire in a geographically restricted manner. The reorganization of the empire no longer involved Syria, and with the conclusion of the reforms, Syria was excluded from the empire along with the rest of the Byzantine east. One should think here of an exact demarcation. Those regions not included in the reforms no longer belonged to the nucleus of the empire. In other words, whoever was not inside, was outside! Only the ecclesiastical officials of the former Byzantine east now stood in connection with the emperor, and yet Byzantium gave up even these contacts at a later period.[17]

The conquest of Syria and Egypt seems not to have meant much more to the Sassanians than a military exercise. After they had stopped filling episcopal sees in Syria with Nestorians loyal to the state, they contented themselves with pursuing the supporters of the Byzantine Empire and replacing them with Monophysite bishops; it was through this latter action that the Sassanians won over the Syrian population. The Iranian presence consolidated the federation of the oriental Christians against Byzantium. The Jews who had been repressed by the Byzantines were able to make gains under their leader Nehemiah, the son of Hushiel. After the conquest of 614, they were given Jerusalem as their own. The churches of Jerusalem were destroyed, and the Church of the Holy Sepulchre devastated. The majority of the inhabitants of Jerusalem had already been shipped off to Persia, among them the patriarch Zacharias with the reliquary of the True Cross.[18]

The Sassanians had coins minted in Egypt between 617 and 628; these coins show Chosroes II in the form of a Christian ruler. This depiction could have arisen from the fact that the eastern Christians could no longer imagine him in any other way, for he took part as a Christian ruler in the conflict between the Christians of the imperial orthodoxy and those of the supporters of orthopraxy. It could also be that the depiction of a non-Christian ruler was no longer possible in the realm of Sassanian coin-minting in Egypt, and so the Persian ruler was seen as a Christian and as a supporter of the Egyptian Monophysite Christians.[19]

This manner of proceeding on the part of the Persians must have struck the Byzantines right in the heart, for it was an attack on the institution of Empire. The emperor, as the protector of holy places (which he was, as the protector of the *ḥaram* in Jerusalem in the eyes of those Arabians bound in alliance with the Sassanians), had experienced an incalculable loss of legitimacy.[20] Constantinople did not remain quiet. In 622, the emperor set out from Constantinople, with the Church having made its treasures available to the impoverished state.[21] This last appears to be a euphemism for a forced appropriation by the emperor of the church's treasures.

"The war began in a spirit of religious excitement, a spirit unknown in former times. It was the first 'typical' medieval war, reminiscent of the later Crusades. The emperor placed himself at the head of the army and, in his absence, turned over the ruling authority in the capital to the patriarch Sergius and the patrician Bonos, as regents for his son who was at the time still too young to rule. . . . This action was unusual to the highest degree, and as had once been the case with Mauricius, so too Heraclius immediately encountered a great deal of opposition from his advisors, for no emperor had been seen personally on a battlefield since the time of Theodosius the Great. . . . On the second day of the Easter octave, April 5, 622, Heraclius left the capital after a celebratory worship service."[22]

The later history of the battle bore unexpected consequences. The emperor had concerned himself for quite a long time with military theory, and his military leadership defied convention and confused his opponents. For example, instead of using the summertime for battle, he used it simply for training; it was when the season was nearly over that he attacked. Heraclius organized the Byzantine army in such a way as to aim at the strengths of the Persian army. Instead of using infantry, he employed reinforced cavalry, especially emphasizing horses ridden by lightly armored archers. The emperor marched directly toward Armenia, so that the Persians had to follow him "like a dog on a leash. . . . The eventual battle between the two armies on the Armenian landscape ended with a glorious victory for the Byzantines over the great Persian general Shahrwaraz."[23]

The Byzantine victory in 622 was sensational primarily because of its uniqueness. A fifty-year-long portion of the conflict between East and West was ended by one side's surprising conquest, a military victory for the group which had not, throughout the duration of the conflict, been able to enjoy a single convincing success. What is more, this phenomenon is even reflected in the Qur'ān. The Arabian Christians of al-Ḥīra had suffered under Sassanian lordship ever since Chosroes II had pushed the local ruling dynasty of the Lakhmids off to one side. The loss of their high place among the Arabs of Iran must have injured them badly, for, with the events of 622, they saw the Byzantines as their savior in a time of need. Pickthall has translated the beginning of sura 30 (*ar-Rūm*: "the Byzantines") thus: "2) The Romans [author's note: "the Byzantines"] have been defeated 3) In the nearer land, and they, after their defeat will be victorious. 4) Within ten years—Allāh's is the command in the former case and in the latter—and in that day believers will rejoice." The text concerns a loss on the part of the Byzantines, to be followed by a victory.

The final series of Byzantine losses had begun in 613 at Antioch, continued with the Sassanians' conquest of Jerusalem in 614, and ended with the Sassanians' conquest of Egypt in 617. If it is at all possible to understand an event mentioned in the Qur'ān as "historical," then it seems that what we have here concerns a theological mastery of the situation between 617 and 622 from the point of view of the Arabian Christians.

Further, Heraclius avenged the Sassanians' attack on Jerusalem, the attack on the legitimacy of Byzantine authority, with a like reaction. In 623, with the help of the Christian peoples of the Caucasus, he carried out a sort of guerrilla attack on the chief holy place of the Iranian Zoroastrians. He went to Ganzak, the residence of Ardashīr, the first Sassanian overlord, burned its fire-temple to the ground, and thereby took his revenge for the destruction of the Church of the Holy Sepulchre and the attack on the legitimacy of the Byzantine imperial authority as the protector of the Church and its holy places.[24]

The Sassanians' strong resistance led to yet another counterattack, this time by the Persians as far as the Bosporus. The weak point in the Persian attack strategy was again the lack of its own naval fleet, which they could have used to blockade Constantinople. For this, the Persians had to turn to another enemy of the Byzantines, namely, the Avars. Although the Avar Khāqān appeared before Constantinople with a huge mob of Avars, Slavs, Bulgars, and Gepids, and thus besieged the city by land and by sea, the battle with the Byzantine fleet led to the defeat of the Avars at sea. They were likewise defeated on land. With this loss, the Persian attack crashed to the ground in its entirety.[25] The course of the war ultimately led to new confederations. During his stay in the Caucasus, Heraclius cemented new relationships with the empire of the Khazars. "From this point one can date the joint efforts of the Byzantines and Khazars, which over time became an important support for Byzantine politics on its eastern frontier."[26]

After the crushing defeat of the Iranian imperial armies, first in Armenia in 622 and then in Nineveh in 627, Chosroes II was first defamed and then murdered by the courtiers and the Zoroastrian clergy. A controversy over the throne followed these events. One of Chosroes's sons ascended the throne, but just a few months later, on his deathbed, he declared the Byzantine emperor to be regent in the place of his own young son. This son, Ardashīr III, was killed by the famous general Shahrvaraz in 630. The murder of the Sassanian ruler Ardashīr III was already the second and most effective attack on the legitimacy of the authority of the Sassanian dynasty. Chosroes II had lost his throne in 590 to the usurper Bahrām Cobīn and was only able to return to Iran with the help of the Byzantine army in 595. A further pretender to the throne, a certain Wistāhm, who did not belong to the Sassanian dynasty, had coins minted in the north under his own name. A foundational idea of the Sassanian dynasty was thereby cast into doubt, namely, that only the family of Sāsān could rule over the *Erān-Shahr*, because their heritage could be traced back to the original race of gods, and because they consequently possessed the *xvarrah*, the glory of kings. It was because of this doubt that Boran, the daughter of Chosroes II, had good reason to emphasize her own descent from the gods. A gold medallion dating from the second year of her rulership bears the inscription *Borān i yazdān tohm winardār* ("Boran, renewer of the race of the gods).[27] The Arabian Christians, as new rulers in Iran, directly countered this conception with their title *'Abd Allāh* (Servant of God and Christ), in the sense of the old Syrian theology.

At the end of the hostilities a settlement between the Sassanians and the Byzantines was agreed upon. This event saw the return to the emperor of all lands that had once belonged to the Byzantine Empire—Armenia, Roman Mesopotamia, Syria, Palestine, and Egypt. This shows that Heraclius had not planned any sort of conquest to be followed by a long-term occupation; rather, he was interested only in a reestablishment of the legitimacy of the Byzantine imperial authority. Consequently, he visited Jerusalem only once, in 630, when he erected again the True Cross (or rather what was left of it in its reliquary), which had been returned by the Persians.[28]

Heraclius also held to this political policy of settlement concerning the rebellious Christians of the Byzantine East. The attack on the Armenian capital of Dwīn had in short order led to discussions of unification with representatives of the Armenian Church. However, the confederation of Oriental Christians, created by the Sassanians, caused all attempts at unification to go to naught. The Arabs of Iran who remained in the areas held by the Sassanians defended a community of Christians that would not accept the theological possibilities for resolution which Heraclius had suggested. The attempt at bringing the results of the Council of Chalcedon nearer to the eastern Christians (based on a compromise formula) also met with strong rejection. Even the compromise formula of 638 (the *Ekthesis*), defended only grudgingly by the church of the emperor, met with no success among the Christians of the Byzantine east. The text containing the compromise formula, inscribed in the narthex of Hagia Sophia, was answered in writing only later, by ʿAbd al-Malik, when he had his own *Ekthesis* inscribed in the Dome of the Rock in Jerusalem in the year 72 of the Arabian era (691–692 CE).[29]

The local church leaders in the Byzantine east made use of this opportunity. The region had been emptied of Byzantine troops, except for a few merely symbolic contigents. The military's abandonment of the areas formerly occupied by Iran, as well as the presence of the previously Sassanian Arabs, now rulers in their own right, enabled the church officials of the East to effect a total withdrawal of Byzantium from the Byzantine east.

In the year in which Heraclius published his *Ekthesis*, the compromise offered to the Monophysite east, the patriarch of Jerusalem had already caused the Byzantine force occupying the city to withdraw. In addition, the Byzantines also gave up their positions in Mesopotamia, for the mixture of Monophysite and Nestorian Christians living in northern Mesopotamia had developed into a common anti-Byzantine front, which had a natural ally in Armenia. Only the withdrawal from Egypt remained, but there Byzantium had interests to protect. The harbor of Alexandria, with its trade and tolls, was important for Byzantium; and although the empire had already withdrawn its authority from the mainland, it defended its maritime interests in the region that much more passionately. After the war with the Sassanians and the accompanying loss of the last imperial reserves, namely, the treasury of the church, attention to the control of maritime trade in the eastern Mediterranean, and the consequent control of its harbors, was of absolute importance. Only the influx of tolls would be able to supply the means that the imperial palace needed to maintain its power.

The widow of Heraclius, Martina, continued this politic of compromise with the Byzantine east, and consequently encouraged the patriarch of Alexan-

dria to conclude a treaty with the Arab military leaders that would allow the Byzantines to make an orderly retreat from the city. "In carrying out the terms of that treaty which the patriarch Cyrus of Alexandria had signed with the Arabs based on the encouragement of Martina, and which envisioned a total Byzantine withdrawal from the country within a certain period of time, the Byzantine troops left Alexandria on September 12, 642, and sailed to Rhodes."[30] By this point, however, Martina had already been deposed, maimed, and exiled. The period of Byzantine compromise with the Christian Arabs had passed. Consequently, a Byzantine battalion attempted to hem in the path of Arabian expansion, and—again—occupied Alexandria; however, they were not able to maintain the occupation in the face of the opposition of local Christians under the Monophysite patriarch, Benjamin, as the locals preferred the Arabian Christian yoke to that of Byzantium's.[31]

With the deposition of Martina, the attempt to find a compromise on matters of Christology with the Christians of the east ended. The war of religion between the Arabian lords of Iran and the emperor in Constantinople now took on clear contours. In the future, the defender of Orthodoxy, the church of the emperor, would stand against the defenders of the Christian confessional fellowship of the East. Christological questions determined the controversy in large part.

THE PERIOD OF THE FIRST UMAYYAD RULERS

The Arabian Empire at the Time of Mu'āwiya (641–682?)

The dates that concern Mu'āwiya are: 1) After the death of Heraclius in 641, the Arabs began to rule in Syria in 641—that is, year 20 of the Arabian era. 2) 661–662: *Amīr al-Mu'minīn*. 3) 674: Attack on Constantinople. 4) 674: Loss of the East after the failure before Constantinople. 5) Year 53 of the Arabian era: 'Abd Allāh bn al-Zubayr becomes ruler of the East.

Dated coins bearing the name of Mu'āwiya are known only from the mint of Dārābjird, located in ancient Persia. The ruins of the Sassanian city Dārābjird lay in the Iranian province of Fārs, in the district of Fasā. The Sassanian stone relief of Naqsh-i Rustam can be found not far away. That the location is in Old Persia, in the heartland of the Iranian dynasties from the Achaemenids to the Sassanians, as well as the minting activity in Dārābjird,

suggests that the coins should be understood as part of a desire for the continuation of the Persian tradition of authority.

Concerning the naming of Muʿāwiya on the Dārābjird coins, his Aramaic name is written following the East Aramaic (Mandaean) tradition. The question must remain open concerning how much the name *MAAWIA,* that is, "The Weeper," is a *nom de guerre* in the sense of a "malcontent." This type of name is known from the late Sassanian period. For example, the Sassanian general and conquerer of Jerusalem (614) called himself *Shahr-varaz,* that is, "Boar of the State," who inhabited the city in such a way that he lived up to his *nom de guerre*.[32] One should also consider the possibility that the name *MAAWIA* could be a *laqab* (Arabic for a nickname, an epithet, sometimes also in the sense of a conversion name).[33] If this is the case, then we must reckon with the possibility that the true name of the ruler remains unknown to us, and that only a personal characteristic of his, or perhaps the opposite thereof, has been transmitted to us. It is also possible that the nickname "The Weeper" should be considered under the rubric of the *nomina boni auguris*. Behind this derogatory nickname may lie the extremely old, and not only Semitic, conception that a derogatory nickname serves as a deception and provides a protection against the evil eye (cf. Qur'ān sura 113:5). In addition, the lack of a personal name could stand in the old Semitic tradition, in which silence concerning one's actual name can minimize the possibility that someone else can manipulate the bearer of the name.

The coins from Dārābjird are dated to the year 41. The depiction on the coins follows the Sassanian tradition. Muʿāwiya is called *Amīr-i wlwyshnyk'n*[34] on his coins made in Dārābjird.

THE TITLE *AMĪR-I WLWYSHNYK'N*

One notices immediately that the inscriptions on the earliest dated coins of the Arabian Empire are written in the tradition of the Sassanian Empire. The Arabian name of the ruler mentioned on the coin as *MAAWIA* is not given; further, the name *MAAWIA* is not Arabic, but rather Aramaic. In addition, the Aramaic script is used throughout, as was normal at that time for the writing of Middle Persian. The title of the lord is a *mixtum compositum* from the Arabic *Amīr*, and a descriptor of occupation in Pahlavi, which was the official language of the previous Persian dynasty, following the rubric "Emir for/of X."

The expression *wlwyshnyk'n* is clear, at least in its meaning. Formally speaking, it is the plural form of an adjectival derivation from a verbal substantive. The infinitive form of the corresponding Middle Persian verb is *wurroyistan* ("to believe," or perhaps also "to be true/faithful"). The writing of this infinitive is presented in a way unique to Pahlavi, with an Aramaic ideogram bound to a Middle Persian infinitive ending. The Pahlavi heterogram is *HYMNNstn*, which contains the Aramaic root *h-m-n* ("to trust").[35]

The heterogram contains an Aramaic word, which is preserved even today in Arabic. The Arabic word is *amāna,* which corresponds to the Aramaic *HYMN*. This form also appears in the Qur'ān, at sura 49:14: "The Bedouins say, 'We are believers (*āmannā*).' . . ." The institution of *amāna* ("certainty, security") grew from a pre-Islamic institution, namely, the *jiwār*, or "right of asylum." Through this practice, a foreigner who had no protection outside his own tribe or group could receive such from a member of another group to which he did not belong. As a result, the group of the protector committed itself as a whole to the protection of the stranger.[36] This pre-Islamic, institutionalized way of behaving with regard to strangers and their best interests is suggested here by the use of a title that connects with the term *amāna*. The *Amīr-i wlwyshnyk'n* is, therefore, the predecessor of the "Protector," in the sense of the old Arabian tradition.

John Walker has translated the legend on the coin (*MAAWIA, Amīr-i wlwyshnyk'n*) as "Mu'āwiya, Commander of the Faithful."[37] With a great deal of self-confidence, he sees in this person the *Amīr al-mu'minīn* of the later Islamic historiographical literature, and he translates the title following the Islamic understanding. Here it becomes clear how much the later Islamic use of this title in constructing an Islamic, theological historiography has made the recognition of specifically Arabian elements of the early history of Islam difficult.[38] Some two hundred years after the time of Mu'āwiya's reign, a theological function from within a theological understanding of history was given to an institution of Arabian tribal law. In the early period of Arabia's independence, decades before the first historically tangible use of the term *Islām*, there existed no Islamic understanding of history. The practice of authority succeeded much more through the use of Arabian tribal law. This law understood the *Amīr-i wlwyshnyk'n* only as the overlord of those individuals who worked in their own territory for security, in the sense of Arabian tribal law and thereby, very generally speaking, carried out "justice." However, the original conception of "protection" is also preserved in the theological view of the title *Amīr al-mu'minīn*, which is translated today as "prince of the believers":

> Not everyone was authorized to ensure protection. This activity was the responsibility only of those who were considered as *mu'min*. In the understandings of later Islamic theology, Allāh was given the attribute *al-mu'min*. In this perspective Allāh ensures the security (*amāna*) of the believers against unjust treatment.[39]

In this area of former Sassanian rule, Mu'āwiya continued to use the official language of his deposed Persian predecessors. In Arabia, though, he was an Arabian. There we see the Arabic writing of the title *Amīr-i wlwyshnyk'n* in the building inscription dated to the year 58 of the Arabian era (677–678 CE) and found on a dam in the vicinity of al-Ṭā'if.[40] Here the title *Amīr al-mu'minīn* is subjoined to the name *Mu'āwiya*. In Mu'āwiya's Greek inscription in Palestine—an indication of *imitatio imperii* in the former Byzantine east?—we find the Greek writing of the title *Amīr al-mu'minīn*.[41]

THE TITLE *'ABD ALLĀH* IN THE PROTOCOLS OF THE ARABIAN RULERS

1. The complete protocol of Mu'āwiya (41–60? of the Arabian era/661–680?) is found in the Arabic building inscription of al-Ṭā'if. It reads: *li-'Abd Allāh Mu'āwiya Amīr al-mu'minīn*. Furthermore, the protocol is found in the Greek building inscription of Hammat Gader.[42]

2. The complete protocol of 'Abd al-Malik (60–86? of the Arabian era/680–705 CE) is extant in the inscriptions on the coins from the mints at Ba'labakk, Jibrīn, Ḥalab, Ḥimṣ, Sarmīn, 'Ammān, Qinnasrīn, and Qurus.[43] It reads: *li-'Abd Allāh 'Abd al-Malik Amīr al-mu'minīn*. One also finds the variant *'Abd Allāh 'Abd al-Malik Amīr al-mu'minīn*.

3. The complete protocol of al-Walīd (86?–96? of the Arabian era, 705–714/715) is found in the text of the coin inscription from Damascus for the year 87 of the Arabian era (705–706) and reads:

'Abd Allāh al-Walīd Amīr al-mu'minīn.[44] In the text of the building inscription of the Umayyad mosque in Damascus, dated to the year 86 of the Arabian era (705), al-Walīd's protocol reads:

'Abd Allāh Amīr al-mu'minīn al-Walīd. In the text of another building

inscription of the Umayyad Mosque, this one dated to the year 87 of the Arabian era (705–706), the protocol of al-Walīd reads:

ʿAbd Allāh al-Walīd Amīr al-muʾminīn.[45]

4. The complete protocol of Sulaymān (96?–101? of the Arabian era, 714/715–719/720) is found on a lead seal, with which an Umayyad courier's mail sack was sealed. (To my knowledge, approximately one thousand such informative witnesses exist in private and public collections, almost all of which are unpublished.) There one can read:

ʿAbd Allāh Sulaymān Amīr al-muʾminīn.[46]

5. The complete protocol of Hishām (105?–125 of the Arabian era, 723/724–742/743) is found in a building inscription on a fortress (Qasr al-Khayr). It reads:

ʿAbd Allāh Hishām Amīr al-muʾminīn. The inscription is dated to "the year ten-and-one-hundred."[47]

6. The complete protocol of Marwān is extant on a lead seal dated to the year 127 of the Arabian era (744–745). It reads:

ʿAbd Allāh Marwān Amīr al-muʾminīn.[48] The complete protocol of Marwān is also found on the text of a coin inscription, undated and from Atrib (the ancient Atribis in the Nile delta, not far from Benha) in Egypt; it reads:

ʿAbd Allāh Marwān Amīr al-muʾminīn.

The expression *ʿabd Allāh* is translated today as "Servant of God."[49] However, the *Encyclopaedia of Islam* does not yet share the "social-treaty" translation of *ʿAbd* as "Servant." There, in the opening to an extensive article on this topic, one reads the following: "'Abd is the ordinary word for 'slave' in Arabic of all periods (the usual plural in this sense is *ʿabīd*, although the Qurʾān has *ʿibād*: xxiv, 32)."[50] The author of this article protects the possibility of a translation like "servant," in that he emphasizes that in all periods the Arabic word *ʿabd* meant "slave." In the Qurʾān one finds a plural form of the word *ʿabd* that differs from that of the classical High Arabic of the *ʿArabiyya*. The peculiarity of the Qurʾānic use of the word (in the singular *ʿabd*, in the plural *ʿibād*) could be connected with a dialectical or regional peculiarity. This Qurʾānic plural form of the Arabic word *ʿabd* is found only in Mesopotamia, not in the dialect of Mecca. In Mesopotamia there was an Arabian group who used this term for their name: the "tribe" of the *ʿibād*.

THE *'IBĀD*, THE "TRIBE" OF THE ARABIAN SERVANTS OF GOD

The presence of this Mesopotamian form for the plural points to the Arabs living there as the "Arabizers" of the Qur'ānic materials. The most wide-ranging presentation of the relationships of the *'ibād* can be found in the writings of Gustav Rothstein:

> The 'Ibād are tribes made up of different Arabian families that became connected with Christianity in al-Ḥīra . . . that is, they were a *mixtum compositum* made up of various Arabian tribal confederations. The group consisted of members of various tribes; these individuals were called by a common name because of their common religion. . . . It has been said that "being a Christian" was the main characteristic of the 'Ibād, but that does not automatically mean that all Arabian Christians were 'Ibād. The Tamīm, for example, were considered to be Christians in their entirety, but the *'Ibādic Tamīm* were something completely different. The difference which obtained between the 'Ibād and the other Arabian Christians can be seen in the phrase . . . "in al-Ḥīra" in the explanation above: they were the Arabian Christians from al-Ḥīra. . . . These Christians who lived in Ḥīra and came together from different tribes were known by one common name; that is, *al-'ibād*. One can only hypothesize about the source and original meaning of this name. . . . *'bd* is the term used normally, even among pagan Arabians, for the slave (that is, the religious worshiper) of a divinity . . . *al-'ibād* is therefore purely an identifier of religious worshippers. From this the suggestion arises that *al-'ibād* was a term of *self-identification* on the part of the Ḥīra Christians against their pagan surroundings. They understood themselves as the true *viri religiosi*, because they had the true God, etc. Nonetheless, it is noteworthy that the term *al-'ibād* was treated like the name of a tribe, in that the "nisbe" adjective was first built, and the term then became like a proper name—just like, for example, *tamīmī*, etc. Cf., e.g., *'Adī b. Zaid al-'Ibādi*, the name by which a famous poet has always been known. . . . The Ḥīra Christians who came from various tribes thus built up a noticeable unified front toward the outside based on their common religion. What is interesting here, then, is that we have a religious community that reached across boundary lines between tribes. . . . If one places what developed here in Iraq next to what Muhammad (the Prophet of the Arabians) achieved in principle, afterwards and among much more difficult tribal relationships, it is interesting that one finds here a definite analogue.[51]

Such a positive judgment on the achievement of the prophet of the Arabians, namely, the creation of Ḥīra-like conditions in Medina, continues to reverberate in the lines that the eminent scholar of Arabia, Murad Wilfried Hofmann, dedicated to the political abilities of the prophet of the Arabians:

> Beginning in 622, Muhammad and his followers were able to emigrate in small groups to Yathrib, which from then on became known as "Medina," which translated means "the city" (that is, of the prophet). The Islamic calendar began with this key date. Here Muhammad created a federation of states which brought together the Muslim and Jewish tribes of the oasis and for which he published the first written national constitution in the world. This state was revolutionary, in that, for the first time in world history, membership was not determined by clan, race, skin color, or language, but rather by religious affiliation alone. In at least this respect, Medina was an "ideological state."[52]

The Prophet of the Arabians received his revelation when he retreated into the cave with the name Ḥīrā. He made it his practice to return to this cave yearly, spending one month in religious practices.[53] There were approximately two hundred years between the affairs of the *ʿibād* in al-Ḥīra in Iraq, about which Rothstein wrote, and the revelation in the cave Ḥīrā, if one follows the traditional history and Ibn Hishām's (d. 828 or 833, depending on one's source) possibly fictive biography of the prophet. The conception of al-Ḥīra as a place in which revelation was communicated apparently became an independent tradition, and ultimately became the topos of *the* location of *the* revelation, regardless of *which* revelation was intended.

Should one not want to follow this connection of the 'title' *ʿAbd Allāh* to the tradition of the Ḥīra "Servants of God"—for indeed other Arabian Christians called their God *Allāh*—perhaps a note from the Old Testament will provide a further spur; namely, Deuteronomy 9:27: "Think on your servants Abraham, Isaac, and Jacob!" In this way we are squarely in the middle of the Old Testament perspective, which obtains in the Qurʾānic presentations. The rulers saw themselves in the tradition of the prophets. Whoever called himself *ʿAbd Allāh* paid the prophets respect.

THE TITLE *'ABD ALLĀH* AS A SIGN OF ABANDONING A CLAIM OF DESCENT FROM THE GODS FOR THE RULER

Consequently, the term *'Abd Allāh* replaced the Sassanian official titulature *mzdysn bag . . . shāhān shāh ērān kē cihr hac yazdān* in the inscription of Mu'āwiya. The Sassanian titulature read: "The worshipper of [Ahura-] Mazda, the divine . . . , the King of Kings of Iran, whose heritage is from the gods."[54] Against this presentation, Mu'āwiya placed his title: "The servant of God (a human and a Christian), MAAWIA, the leader of the protectors."

The term *'Abd Allāh* thus stands in opposition to the long-standing claim of the Iranian rulers that their heritage was from among the gods. One can see that the question of the term *'Abd Allāh* concerns a title of authority from its use in connection with the naming of the ruler. A brother of the ruler 'Abd al-Malik ordered the building of a canal bridge in Fusṭāṭ in Egypt; the name of the brother was 'Abd al-'Azīz bn Marwān, *al-Amīr*. His function was that of an emir, and so his name was not preceded by any title; the title of *'Abd Allāh* was reserved for the rulers of the Arabian Empire.[55] We can, therefore, take away from the inscriptions that the title of the Arabian rulers in the former Sassanian Empire and in the former Byzantine east was *'Abd Allāh.* The title *caliph/khalīfa,* given in the literature of Islamic studies and in the historical literature of the time of the Abbasids, does not appear in the written witnesses to the early period.

This opposition—divine nature and heritage on the part of the Zoroastrian god-kings of Iran, human nature and heritage on the part of the Arabian Christian leaders of the protectors—is also of interest for the meaning of the term *'Abd Allāh* in the inscription on the Dome of the Rock in Jerusalem. There one reads: *muḥammadun 'Abdullāhi wa-rasūluhu* (= "praised [*sic*] be the servant of God [a human being in the line and the understanding of the prophets] and his apostle").

THE ERA OF THE ARABIANS IN A GREEK INSCRIPTION

The way in which a building inscription of Mu'āwiya in Palestine was carried out reveals how the term *'Abd Allāh* is to be understood during his time. This inscription, from the year 42 of the Arabian era, bears the sign of the cross at the beginning of its first line. This cross is part of the inscription, which then follows in the Greek language and script:

> In the days of Maauia, the servant of God, the leader of the protectors, the hot baths [*clibanus*] were preserved and renovated by the councillor [*emir*] ʿAbdallah, son of Abuasemos, on the fifth of December, on the second day [of the week], in the sixth year of the indiction, in the year 726 from the founding of the city, in the year 42 following the Arabs [662/3], for the healing of the sick, under the supervision of Johannes, the magistrate of Gadara.[56]

The title of "councillor" (*symboulos*) mentioned in the inscription certainly corresponds to the Arabian *emir*. From this correspondence has surely arisen the misunderstanding that Muʿāwiya held the Byzantine title of *protosymboulos*, or "prime councillor." Wellhausen is misunderstood here, in that he invoked only Theophanes as a witness to illustrate the way in which Muʿāwiya had conducted the business of government, namely, as a prime councillor among councillors, or to use Wellhausen's words, "like an old Arabian *sayyid*."[57]

The *emir* who carried out this public building project was named ʿAbd Allāh, as is still the case today among many Christians in Syria. His title shows him to have been a member of a bureaucracy, carried forward from the traditions of Rome and Byzantium, just as the tradition of the Arabian authorities in Syria was carried over from the previous century. Already in the sixth century, officials in the Arabian government in Syria had borne high Byzantine titles. The fact that the inscription was made in Greek is a sign of the *imitatio imperii* (imitation of the Byzantine ideas of "doing empire") employed by Muʿāwiya's government in Syria. In this sense, one can say that Muʿāwiya appears to have also furthered the *Sassanian* practice of government in the East. In Arabia he was an Arabian Arab. There he followed the practice of the Ghassanids, his Arabian predecessors in this region, who tended to make their inscriptions in Arabic.[58]

✝ ЄΠΙΑΒΔΑΛΛΑΜΑΑVΙΑΑΜΗΡΑ
ΛΛΜΥΜЄΝΗΝΑΠЄΛΫΘΗΚϹΑΝЄ
ΝЄШΘΗΟΚΛΙΒΑΝΟϹΤШΝЄΝΤΑV
ΘΑΔΙΑΑΒΔΑΛΛΑVΙϒΑΒϒΑϹЄΜϒ
ϹVΜΒϒΛϒЄΝΜΗΝΗΔЄΚЄΜΒΡΙШ
ΠЄΜΠΤΗΗΜЄΡΑΔЄVΤЄΡΑΙΝΑ῾Ϲ
ЄΤϒϹΤΗϹΚΟΛШΝ͞Ϲ͞ΚΫ ΚΑΤΑΑΡΑΒΑ
ЄΤϒϹΜ̄ΒЄΙϹΙΑϹΗΝΤШΝΝΟϹϒΝ
ΤШΝϹΠϒΔΗΙШΑΝΝϒΜ́ΓΑΔΑΡΗϒ

Fig. 1: "The Greek inscription of Mu'āwiya on the baths of Gadara, with a date following the "Era of the Arabians" (*arabas*)"

PROBLEMS OF DATING

The method of dating the inscription on the baths of Gadara is of great importance for marking off a "historical" history for this region from a theological one, as is handed down, for example, in the Islamic traditional literature. That Mu'āwiya continued Roman traditions by renewing a historical hot bath, and that his inscription (apart from the sign of the cross set at the beginning) contained no elements of religious content, allows some definite conclusions to be drawn concerning his self-understanding and style of life. It is not without good cause that his successor, 'Abd al-Malik, presented him as a "Saul," in the sense of the Old Testament tradition, while presenting himself as a "new David," indeed, naming his own son *Sulaymān* (Solomon).

In the place of a religious opening formula—an element that would not have been uncommon at the time—stands the sign of the cross. Concerning the problem of dating, one notices that first place at the appropriate point in the inscription is given to noting the Roman-Byzantine tax year. Following this method of dating, the era of the city (*colonia*) is given, followed only then by a date giving "the year . . . following the Arabs." The "year . . . following the Arabs," then, does not replace the date following the system of the empire; the era of the Arabs is, one method of dating among many but complementing the traditional date-forms without replacing them.

This pointer to the existence of an era of Arabian authority allows a new evaluation of many datings given in the region of former Sassanian rule. Until now scholars have accepted the thesis that datings given there were to be considered as either still in the era of the last Sassanian ruler, Yazdgard, or else in a "post-Yazdgard era."[59] This acceptance, however, has caused the dates deduced to be off by many years. By means of this (faulty) interpretation, scholars have been able to harmonize the dates given on extant coins with the dates provided in the historicizing Islamic literature. An example of this synchronization with the information given by the historicizing literature (e.g., Balādhurī, Ṭabarī) is the date given for the beginning of the rule of Muʿāwiya's direct successor, ʿAbd al-Malik. A coin in the name of ʿAbd al-Malik from Dārābjird in Iran gives its date as the year 60.[60] Since the discovery of the Greek inscription of Gadara, we know that this dating follows the Arabian era. The historicizing literature of the Abbasid period, though, has ʿAbd al-Malik assuming rule in the year 65 of the Hijra. This was possible in the historicizing presentation of Ṭabarī because, in the meantime, Ibn Hishām's edition of the biography of the Prophet had appeared; consequently, the circumstances of the Hijra of the prophet of the Arabians have become known to the public. In the early period of Arabian self-governance, people were not concerned with such points of connection; since the biography of the prophet of the Arabians was not yet known, and since people had not yet heard of the Hijra of the prophet of the Arabians, they could not name a method of dating after it.

At the time of Muʿāwiya's rulership, the exciting life history of the pugilistic prophet of the Arabians was not yet known. People were content with (and historically correct in) calling their method of dating "of the Arabian era." This method began with the takeover of power in Iran by the Arabs following the battle of 622, a total loss for the Sassanians. Muʿāwiya clearly had no problem with writing his Aramaic name *MAAUIA* in the context of the inscription, for he did not yet have to be an Arab, following the ideal type of "the Arabian Arab from the Arabian peninsula" created by the later historicizing literature of the Abbasid period. In his inscriptions he was still able to embody the Christian Arabs of Mesopotamia, to whom Greek was not a foreign language either (the philosophers of the Athenian Academy had emigrated to the Sassanian Empire after the school was closed in 529 by the order of the Byzantine emperor Justinian I).

How can traditional Islamic numismatics proceed with the dating of a coin of ʿAbd al-Malik to the year 60? Because this dating makes no sense in light of the historicizing literature of the Abbasid period, scholars emphasize that it must be understood in terms of a Persian era, the former is seen as unreliable. With this emphasis, it is possible to understand a number "60" on the coin as the Persian version of the year 72 of the Hijra. Such an understanding would also allow the date to square with the dates of ʿAbd al-Malik's rule as made known by the traditional literature.

To speak clearly: it is from the perspective of the traditional literature that the numbers given on the coins are evaluated. If a date squares with the dates made known by the traditional Islamic literature of later centuries, then scholars consider it to be a dating after the Hijra of the prophet of the Arabians; if it does not, then it is made to fit by adding twelve years and explaining it as following the Persian tradition.[61]

Whoever holds fast to the chronology presented in the theological history has no other choice. Because the literature of the Abbasid period also mentions the reigns of the sons of Muʿāwiya, who were condemned to be destroyed, a period of five years must be added to his reign in the construction of the theological history. As a result, the literature allows ʿAbd al-Malik to enter the scene in the year 65 of the Hijra. However, this is not historically accurate. If there had been a reign of the sons of Muʿāwiya, then this was not of significant length in Syria/Palestine. No coins or inscriptions are known that name any sons of Muʿāwiya as leader of the protectors.

The synchronization of the dates given on the coins with those given in the literary sources demands a high degree of intuition from the editors of those sources. Occasionally, scholars cannot avoid statements of conscience.[62] This phenomenon finds expressions in evaluations of the following type: "The coins dated according to the Hijra would thereby be followed by a 'post-Yazdgard era' dating on the coins here under consideration. Although a clear sequence of coins issues results, it seems incredible that dating would begin by following the Hijra, only to be followed by a switch to a 'post-Yazdgard era' system."[63]

After the dubiousness of this manipulation of dates becomes known to the editor, he consoles himself with a reference to a "last analysis." This scholarly insurance policy results here in a reference to a yet-to-be-created "system of coordination of primary data."[64] This "system" is supposed to become the definitive tool for making clear the "often hidden contours" in the literary sources. By means of this revelation of the hidden contours, the good news will be passed on concerning the connection between literary sources in the (merely) affirmative function of the numismatic texts.[65]

In his attempt to bring light into the darkness of the second civil war, which is purely a dramatic notion on the part of the Abbasid authors in an attempt to master the historical situation of great change after Muʿāwiya, Gernot Rotter suddenly found himself in a difficult situation: "The historians leave us completely in the lurch concerning the first years of the second civil war in the provinces of Fārs and Kirmān; here we are completely dependent upon the numismatic evidence. However, this evidence provides surprising perspectives. The numismatic finds present the information thus. . . ."[66] One immediately recognizes, though, that Rotter's table does not give the numbers found on the coins; rather, it lists numbers for years based on the processing of the numbers in Gaube's work. This processing is at least as questionable as that previously provided by Walker. In Rotter's table, the coins appear following the evaluation of their dates in Gaube, so that it is possible for them to be incorporated into the traditional history—the editing of which was completed in the Abbasid period. The numismatic documents, processed in this fashion, consequently become supports for the literary tradition. This method, were it to be carried over into central European situations, would mean that scholars could use late antique and early medieval coin discoveries to bring together the documentary proofs for Wagner's Bayreuth show, by means of "clear sequences of issue" in terms of a "coordination system for primary data," and thereby take the contours of the festival plays, often hidden by the literary sources, and lay them open in black and white.

In order to meet the standards established by the literary tradition, Rotter synchronizes the coins according to varying eras. The normal places in Iran date their coins after the Hijra of the prophet of the Arabians, but the royal residence in Persia, Dārābjird, always dates its coins following the era of the last Sassanian ruler. Thanks to this game with the Hijra era and the Yazdgard era, one finds the dates in the order previously given by Ṭabarī. Consequently, in order to force the data given on the coins into the procrustean bed of a chronology following Ṭabarī, one must employ the help of these various eras—Yazdgard, post-Yazdgard, and Hijra.

The discovery of Muʿāwiya's inscription on the baths of Gadara, dated to the year 42 of the Arabian era, makes it possible to pass by the commonly accepted chronology and to understand the data on the coins as datings following the era of the Arabians. Followers of the traditional conceptions may want to note that the sign of the cross at the beginning of Muʿāwiya's inscription serves as a sign of "Islamic tolerance." What may be difficult for the followers of the traditional conceptions to explain is the naming of the era as the "era of the Arabians." In the understanding of the traditions of Islam and Islamic studies, Muʿāwiya is hardly an exemplary Muslim, even if he is undoubtedly Muslim, because he belonged to the Quraysh of the theological history, the holy family of the prophet of the Arabians. He is also one of the founders of the *taqiyya*, because he—following the traditional literature—knew how to conceal his support for the prophet of the Arabians for quite a long time.

Even if Muʿāwiya's use of Christian symbols and behavior toward Christians as an extremely Christian ruler may have made obligatory his understanding of the use of *taqiyya*, by naming his own method of dating as an "era of the Arabians" rather than as an "era of Islam" or an "era of the Hijra," he nonetheless betrays the fact that the prophet of the Arabians, as well as the "era of the Hijra," are not yet known to him.

Fig. 2: Reverse of a Christian Arabian coin from Damascus, with the monogram of the emperor Heraclius over the denomination M.

Fig. 3: Obverse of a Christian Arabian coin from Damascus, with a frontal image of the Christian Arabian ruler following the typical depiction of the emperor of Byzantium, and with a bird (of prey?) on the left.

WHY DID MUʿĀWIYA CHOOSE DAMASCUS AS HIS RESIDENCE?

It may have been quite pragmatic considerations that moved Muʿāwiya to choose Damascus as his residence. Rule by Arabians in this area of formerly Sassanian authority was no longer in danger. Further, rule by Arabians in the formerly Byzantine east was not yet ensured for the future, as long as the Byzantines had not yet shared the fate of the Sassanians. In this environment, Muʿāwiya continued the political policies of the Sassanians against the Byzantines. In addition to an army from the formerly Sassanian east, he also took hold of the fleet from the formerly Byzantine east and thereby avoided the earlier weaknesses of the Sassanian plan of attack against Constantinople. It was under Muʿāwiya that such a two-pronged attack was possible for the first time.

However, Muʿāwiya was only able to ensure his authority in the West by returning to an Arabian tradition of the exercise of authority, namely, the connection of authority with the protection of a holy place. As a Christian, he naturally chose a Christian holy place—the tomb of John the Baptist and his basilica in Damascus.

One can already see this traditionally Arabian practice in the exercise of authority during the time of Muʿāwiya's Arabian predecessors in Syria. The Ghassanids sponsored the holy place of the martyr Sergius in Ruṣāfa. Following older Roman tradition, they built up the water supply of this desert locale. Because the emperor and his church still controlled the holy place, they were only able to erect a church of their observance outside the walls. It was only in Ruṣāfa that the Ghassanids would meet with messengers of their Byzantine overlords; this was because the status of the holy place protected them from threats of compulsion.

This type of care for a holy place also led to increased revenue. Pilgrimages to the tomb of the martyr Sergius in Ruṣāfa constituted a thriving business, so much so, in fact, that the Byzantine emperor Anastasius took for himself a portion of the income by bringing one of the martyr's thumbs from Ruṣāfa to Constantinople, and the reputation of the wonder-working power of the reliquary made its way from the capital city as far as distant Gaul, as Gregory of Tours reports in his chronicle of the Franks.

Others went further east quite aggressively and erected a substitute holy place of the same style and size, in order to cut off the flow of pilgrims from the Sassanian Empire in the East and redirect them to a holy place for which they themselves served as *patrones*.[67]

In Damascus, Muʿāwiya was able to put himself forward as the protector of the holy places of the grave of John the Baptist. The holy place of the Baptist lay in a crypt in a former temple district, where the reliquary of the head of the Baptist was kept safe. The Arabs held John the Baptist in their memory as a prophet "who encouraged the Jews to strive toward perfection by exhorting them to practice righteousness toward one another and piety toward God and, thereby, to come to baptism. Only then, as he said, would baptism be pleasing to God, because they practiced baptism for the healing of the body but not for the forgiveness of sins; the soul would then have already been cleansed by means of a righteous life."[68]

Fig. 4: Reverse of a coin with the denomination M (40 nummia); above appears the monogram of emperor Heraclius, to the right 17, the number of the year according to the era of the Arabians (639), and below DAM (Damascus), the name of the mint.

Fig. 5: Obverse of an anonymous coin from Damascus, with the image of the Christian Arabian ruler depicted in the typical manner of a Byzantine emperor.

Such teaching of "right action" must have made a significant impact on the Arabians; it must also have struck a chord with the tenor of their Qur'ānic materials and with their understandings of the *Dīn Allāh*. As a holy place, the crypt with the head of John the Baptist stood in competition with the Church of the Holy Sepulchre in Jerusalem. The emperor in Constantinople served Christology, so to speak, as the representative of Christ on the earth. Without the Baptist, however, the history of Jesus, in terms of prophethood, made no sense. The Baptist was the prophet and the defender of right action. He stood for "prophethood," an institution that would become a central idea of the Arabian Church in the Arabian Empire.[69] Muʿāwiya was able to treat the place of the Baptist's tomb, located in a temple district of Damascus, as a *ḥaram*; the Arabian tribes' control of Syria made it possible for him to protect it.

Fig. 6: Reverse of an anonymous coin from Damascus, with the denomination M; above appears a variant of Heraclius's monogram, to the right information in Arabic concerning the name of the mint (from above right to below right). This type of writing corresponds to the Sassanian tradition, where one finds inscriptions written in the field, to the right and left of the fire-altar, from above to below.

The respect that was paid to the holy place (*iḥtirām*) also passed over to the protector of the location, making it possible for him to turn to tribal law and thus ensure security (*amān*).[70]

Fig. 7: Obverse of an anonymous coin from Damascus, with the image of John the Baptist; to the right appears a reliquary for a head in a container, and to the left appears a globe-cross, with a palm branch above it.

Fig. 8: Reverse of an anonymous Christian Arabian coin with the denomination M; above appears a cross, and to the left a crowned head (of John the Baptist?).

Images of the reliquary of John the Baptist's head appear on coins from the Damascus of this period. On the obverse of the coins, one typically finds the image of the ruler, facing front, with a lance in his right hand. To his right in the portrayal, one sees a bird, perhaps a dove. The left hand of the ruler rests upon a vessel containing the head of the Baptist. The connection between the depiction of the dove and the Gospel narrative of the baptism of Jesus by John is obvious.[71]

There are also many coins that, until now, have been ascribed to the caliph 'Umar and his general Khālid ibn al-Walīd, both known from Islamic historical literature; these coins are most likely also connected with the cult of the Baptist in Damascus. As a destroyer of idols and leader of a military division on its way from Mecca to east Arabia, through Ur in Chaldea to Ḥarrān and Damascus in Syria, General Khālid ibn al-Walīd took the role of an Islamic Abraham in the revival production of the history of Israel as the history of the Arabians.

Fig. 9: Depiction of John the Baptist, preaching on an anonymous Christian Arabian coin of the seventh century, found in Syria.

These coins depict the *agnus Dei* ("lamb of God") and should be connected with the cult of the Baptist, as the lamb was attested as an attribute of the Baptist from as early as the sixth century. The depiction of the lamb in ways other than as a portrait of Christ was forbidden in canon 82 of the Council in Trullo of 692.[72]

In accordance with this canon, Byzantine coins began to depict Christ as *Pantocrator* as early as 692. The answer to this break in tradition was the minting of gold coins by the Arabians in 693–694, the year 74 of the Arabian era.

Fig. 10: Obverse and reverse of a coin of Khālid of Tiberias. This Christian Arabian ruler is depicted along with the lamb of God.

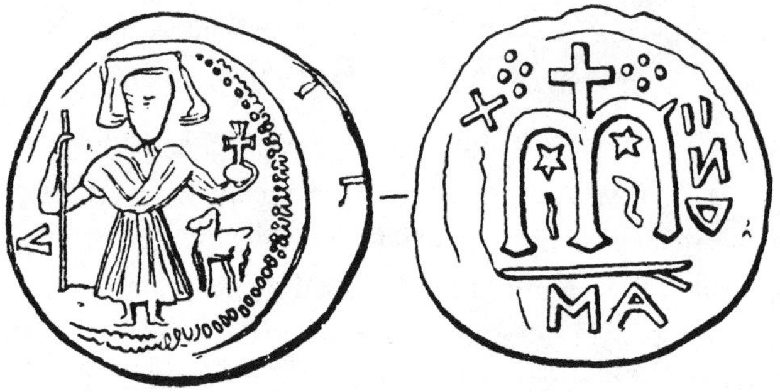

Fig. 11: Obverse and reverse of a Christian Arabian coin from Damascus with the image of a Christian Arabian ruler with the lamb of God, a symbol of John the Baptist.

THE IDEA OF "ZION" AT THE TIME OF MUʿĀWIYA

There is one coin known from Jerusalem at the time of Muʿāwiya. The inscription is in Greek, which shows Muʿāwiya's respect for the heritage of the empire, as the Roman provincial coins of the region also bore Greek legends. The obverse bears the image of a standing ruler, shown frontally, holding the globe-cross in his left hand. On the reverse one sees the denomination M, surrounded by the Greek legend IERO/SOLI/MON, or "belonging to Jerusalem."[73]

Fig. 12: Obverse and reverse of a Christian Arabian coin from Jerusalem with the image of a Christian Arabian ruler and, on the reverse, the indication of the mint surrounding the denomination M.

The main hagiopolite holy place for the Byzantines was the Church of the Holy Sepulchre. Whether Muʿāwiya already had plans for a new sacred building on the Temple Mount is not known. Conjectures that he had already begun erecting the Dome of the Rock are based on accepting particular calculations for the building's construction time. Because the beginning of ʿAbd al-Malik's reign is put at the year 65 (following the Islamic historiography), one often thinks one has to accept the remaining time, that is, until the date "72" from the inscription, as insufficient for the erection of a monument of this type and of imperial size. The construction time of seven years, however, as given in the Islamic literature, may only have symbolic meaning.

Further, because the beginning of ʿAbd al-Malik's reign, following his coinage in Iran, actually occurred in the year 60 of the Arabians (679/80), the number of years during which the building was erected (in this case, twelve) is symbolic once again. Nevertheless, this increases the likelihood that ʿAbd al-Malik was the only erector of the Dome of the Rock, as is conjectured from the gap in the building's inscription (where his name was most likely originally found).

The conception of a "New Zion" was anchored in the Syrian church traditions of the "true Israel." One still sees the results of this in Ethiopia, where the capital city of Axum was called a "New Zion."[74] Further evidence of the continuing influence of this Syrian tradition in Ethiopia can be seen in the "Zion Festival" that began each month in the Ethiopian church. Copper coins found in Palestine and bearing the legend "Zion" are a sign of the self-conception of Arabian Christians at the time of the reign of Muʿāwiya in Palestine. They saw themselves as heirs of the tradition of Israel and considered themselves to be the "true Israel."[75]

Fig. 13: On the obverse of a Syrian coin, a frontal depiction of an enthroned Christian Arabian ruler; on the reverse the denomination M above a defective and retrograde text giving the location of the mint as C(I)ON.

MU'ĀWIYA'S MILITARY VICTORIES

The political policy through which Mu'āwiya was able to bind the Iranians to himself was the continuation of the series of Sassanian conquests of Byzantium, as well as the expectation of a final victory. The eventual loss on the part of the Sassanians at Nineveh in 627 actually helped the Arabian emirs of Iran achieve rulership; however, they were only able to defend this authority by pursuing a project of an Iranian revenge. In the eyes of the Iranians, the dynasty had changed, but the long-term interests of the Iranians had not. The dissolution of the Sassanian dynasty sealed the fate of Zoroastrianism, and the living religion of Iran was from now on only the Nestorian version of Christianity.[76] Buddhism also held a prominent place in eastern Iran.

Fig. 14: Arabic imitation of a copper coin featuring the Byzantine imperial couple Justin and Sophia. On the obverse, under the imperial couple, facing front and enthroned, one sees the Arabian countermark "ṭayyib"; on the reverse there is the denomination M, with the sign of the cross above. The dating follows the Byzantine system of indictions on the right and left, with the location of the mint, namely, CION (Zion) underneath.

Consequently, it may not be shocking that the metropolitan of the Nestorian Christians from Merv caused the last Zoroastrian king of Iran, the Sassanian Yazdgard, to be borne to his grave. The sign of the cross on the Arabo-Sassanian silver coins from Merv amaze only those who follow an Islamic history derived from the literary sources from the ninth century.[77]

When the Lakhmid rulers of al-Ḥīra accepted Christianity, the Arabian Christians from that area saw the completion of the development of their Arabian-Christian state. The great king of the Sassanians, who as overlord was the defender of the Zoroastrian national cult, saw this as well, and he summarily ended the authority of the Lakhmids in al-Ḥīra. The demise of the Sassanian empire also brought the Zoroastrian national cult to an end. The Arabs, defenders of Christianity (the living religion in west Iran),[78] took power in the continuation of the war against Byzantium. The course of this long conflict between Iran and Byzantium had already changed into a war of religion by the time of Chosroes II. This development was aided by the behavior that Byzantium had exhibited for a long time with regard to its Arabian vassals. The resuscitation of the Syrian Church in the mid-sixth century was a project of the Syrian Arabs. When Byzantium learned that the Ghassanids were threatening to succeed in this project of authority, which was (also) ecclesiastically independent, it put them aside as a political player in Syria. The developing alliance of Monophysites in the Byzantine east, which had been under the leadership of the Ghassanids, was greatly hindered by their removal. The full consequences, however (see, for example, the removal of Byzantine troops from Palestine and Egypt in the seventh century, negotiated by the local leaders), did not occur until the time of Muʿāwiya's reign, but they could no longer at this point be reversed.

The dominance of the military during Muʿāwiya's reign is likely one main reason that he implemented no drastic changes in the governmental structures in the areas he controlled. He was not an Arabian Arabizer of freshly conquered regions, but rather an Arabian Iranian in areas already conquered by the Sassanians. His goal must have been the consolidation of the circumstances concerning the tradition of Persian rule. The imperial army of Iran was first defeated in 622 in Armenia, and in 627 it was pushed to the brink of annihilation by the Byzantines at Nineveh. However, the troops of the Arabian vassals of Iran, serving as occupying forces in Syria and Egypt, survived this catastrophe unscathed. The Persians abandoned their posts of authority in Syria in 628, following a truce forced by the Byzantines. There seems to have been no official communication to the Arabian vassals of Iran to the effect that they should pull out of Syria and Egypt.

Muʿāwiya showed himself to be a benefactor to the peoples of the occupied lands by rebuilding many public buildings and institutions. He was able to build on the local populace's aversion to Byzantium. Other than the small minority of Melkites who belonged to the church of the emperor, there was no Christian community or church in the former Byzantine east that had not been made to endure imperial sanctions.

The situation at the time of Muʿāwiya was *not* a conflict between Arabian-Islamic conquerers and a Byzantine-Christian emperor, as the later, historicizing literature of the Abbasid period would have its readers believe. Rather, as shown by documents in the form of inscriptions by the Arabian rulers, the conflict involved the Christians of the former Byzantine east—natural allies of the Nestorian Christians of Iran and under the leadership of Arabian Christians of Iran—on the one side, and the Christians of the emperor in Constantinople (as leader of Greco-Roman Christianity) on the other. The conflict played out as a war of religion between the eastern devotees of a Semitic understanding of Christianity and the defenders of the Hellenistic and Roman counter-development. Questions of Christology were still the central problem. Consequently, the inscription from the year 72 of the era of the Arabians (691–692) inscribed on the Dome of the Rock in Jerusalem, addresses Christianity as a whole: *Yā ahla al-kitāb*, or "Oh, you people of the BOOK!" The Bible is undeniably meant as the "book" in question, and not the messages of the prophet of the Arabians, whose biography would be written one-and-a-half centuries later in the style of an Arabian "savior."

MUʿĀWIYA CONTINUES THE POLITICAL POLICIES OF IRAN IN SYRIA AND ATTEMPTS TO REESTABLISH IRANIAN AUTHORITY IN THE REGION

Muʿāwiya remained in Syria at this time, and he busied his followers with raids into the Byzantine and Armenian borderlands. He also took spoils from Cappadocia. He must also have been active at sea, given his control of the Syrian harbors. Occupied with these affairs, he came to understand the value of a fleet for future undertakings against Constantinople. Joining Iran's military power by land with a Syrian and Egyptian fleet would offer him the possibility of encircling Constantinople by land and blockading it by sea. All Iran's previous military actions had faltered as a result of its inferiority at sea. Muʿāwiya began to systematically bring the islands of the Aegean Sea under his control, so that he might eventually reach the Byzantine imperial capital by "island-hopping." After conquering Cyprus, he took Rhodes in

654. Booty of all kinds was welcome; even the bronze scraps from the colossal statue of Helios at Rhodes' harbor entrance, which had collapsed in 225 BCE, were taken and sold to a scrap-metal dealer in Edessa.

However, the proper time for the action against Constantinople had not yet come. Mu'āwiya first had to secure his leadership among the Arabian emirs. For this reason, he effected a cease-fire in the West and concluded a treaty with Byzantium in 659, although the latter did subject him to the payment of tribute.[79] In Iran, the last Sassanian, Yazdgard III, began to reign in 632, after four years of conflict over the throne—and ten years after the surprising beginning of the decline of the Sassanians as a world power. In the year 20 of the Arabian era, the year Heraclius died, and nine years before Yazdgard met his end in Merv, coins were already being minted for Arabian generals in the Sassanian style. Further, in the year 26 of the Arabian era, the emir Sālim b. Ziyād had coins minted in Dārābjird, the former Sassanian royal residence in the region of Persia. His relative 'Ubayd Allāh b. Ziyād was also minting coins in this year in Zaranj. In the year 41, Ziyād b. Abī Sufyān had coins minted in Dārābjird as well.[80]

The Arabian emirs fought over Dārābjird as the former royal residence of the Sassanians. In the year 41, Samura b. Jundab was able to bring the residence under his control for a short time.[81] Then, however, Mu'āwiya appeared and was acclaimed as the first *Amīr-i wurroyishnigan*.[82]

It is interesting that the names of the Arabian "mint lords" give no indication of a heritage in the Arabian peninsula; among all the names of the Arabian emirs of the Sassanian region, neither a Yamanī, nor a Makkī, nor a Ḥimyarī, nor a Ḥaḍramī, nor a Qaḥṭānī ever appears.

'Abd al-Malik appears to have already been an important person of high social rank before the beginning of his *da'wa* for the *muḥammad*. His descent from the Marwānān shows him to have been a noble among the Arabians.[83] The false understanding of the names of families has long made it easy for scholars of Islamic studies to present the Iranian Arabs as new Islamic citizens of Iran. How else could one explain the readiness of the "Islamic conquerors" to adopt the Iranian traditions of the writing of names? The Arabian family-name *ZUPIL* + (pers.) *-ān* looks like a Pahlavi heterogram. What moved the "Islamic conquerors," then, to give up the Arabian way of writing their names? Reasons for this phenomenon will likely be difficult to find.

MUʿĀWIYA IS A SUCCESSFUL ORGANIZER OF THE WAR AGAINST BYZANTIUM, BUT "GREEK FIRE" IMPEDES AN ULTIMATE VICTORY

After his election as *Amīr-i wurroyishnigan,* Muʿāwiya returned to the West and renewed his military action against Byzantium. "In the year 663 the Arabs reappeared in Asia Minor; from then on, each year for fifteen years, they repeatly pushed forward."[84] The year 663 is also year 42 of the Arabian era, as Muʿāwiya's inscription in Gadara tells us.

Muʿāwiya continued his policies of conquest from just that point at which he had to break it off a decade before. After the relationships of power had been clarified among the emirs, Muʿāwiya was able to work toward his goals as the *princeps inter pares*, following an old Arabian tradition; his principal project was that of the Persians, one that had so often faltered in the past, namely, the attempt to push the Byzantine Empire out through an attack on Constantinople. His goal was now to possess authority over Christendom in the East.[85]

Ostrogorsky describes the course of the attack on Constantinople:[86]

> After the line of islands controlled by the Arabs [Cyprus-Rhodes-Kos] was completed by the taking of Chios, one of Muʿāwiya's generals took power in 670 on the peninsula of Cyzicus, in the immediate vicinity of the Byzantine capital. By this action the Arabs secured a base of operations against Constantinople. However, in 672, before the Arabs made the main attack against the city center, a part of the caliph's fleet besieged Smyrna, while another part occupied the Lycian and Cilician coastlines.
>
> In the spring of 674, the main action began, as a powerful squadron appeared before the walls of Constantinople. The battles lasted through the summer; in the autumn the Arab fleet retreated to Cyzicus. They appeared again the following spring, hoping to hold the Byzantine capital under siege for the entire summer; this sequence of events repeated itself in the coming years. However, all the Arabs' attempts at storming the most well-protected fortress in the entire world of that time remained without success. After suffering severe losses in sea battles fought before the walls of Constantinople, they ultimately had to give up their fight and, in 678, leave Byzantine waters. This was the first time that the famous "Greek fire" was used, a weapon which would from that time on serve the Byzantines in extraordinary ways.

It is not difficult to describe the effects that the introduction of this "super-weapon" of the time had on the hearts of the Arabs. Fire made from a mixture of chalk and sulfur rained down on the attackers from above. So-called siphons were able to cast the incendiary blasts a great distance toward the Arabs' ships. If one were to think of the apocalyptic conceptions current at the time, the expectation of the end-time that was still virulent in the Abbasid period; when the apocalyptic expectations of Ḥimṣ were written down, and the expectation of the Messiah through the *muhājirūn* of the Abbasid literature, then one can begin to imagine how the attacking Arabs thought that they were literally looking into a hell-hole. "In their retreat, the Arab fleet suffered still further losses as a result of a storm on the Pamphylian coast. At the same time, the Arabian army was suffering a major loss in Asia Minor."[87]

As a result of all this, Muʿāwiya conceded with a peace treaty with Byzantium. He sent the emperor a yearly gift of three thousand gold pieces in addition to horses and slaves. The Byzantines considered this to be tribute and registered it appropriately.[88] For Muʿāwiya's true motives for making peace in the West, one can consult the coins minted by the Iranian Arabs.

MUʾĀWIYA LOSES HIS SUPPORT IN THE EASTERN PORTION OF THE REGION OF ARABIAN AUTHORITY

The expectation of a total victory had motivated the Arabs to their maximum expenditure of energy. However, when hell opened up and spewed out fire, all their apocalyptic nightmares of Gog and Magog seemed to be confirmed. Muʿāwiya's opponents used this opportunity to carry out a coup in the East. The legitimation of Muʿāwiya's authority depended upon the continuation of the war against Byzantium. By means of his previous action in this regard, he was able to rally the Persians under his banner. However, getting rid of the humiliation the Sassanians had suffered by losing the battle against their religious enemy was a national problem for many Iranians.

After the unexpected failure at Constantinople and the retreat of autumn 674, the first year of the war, the opposition to Muʿāwiya came together. First, ʿAbd Allāh of the family Āl Zubayr was elected *Amīr-i wurroyishnigan*. His coins minted in Dārābjird begin in the year 53.[89] Following the era of the Arabians, as the inscription from Gadara communicates it to us, this corresponds to the year 672–673.

ʿABD AL-MALIK'S JESUS IS *MUḤAMMADUN*

THE APPEARANCE OF *MUḤAMMADANISM*: ʿABD AL-MALIK'S MISSION THAT JESUS BE UNDERSTOOD AS THE "CHOSEN/PRAISED" (*MUḤAMMADUN*) SERVANT OF GOD (*ʿABD ALLĀH*)

While the Byzantine empire discovered new unity in terms of both authority and confession during these years—those outside its confession in Antioch and Alexandria had been pushed out, and the Roman pope had been marginalized—the authority of the Arabians suffered from a limited legitimacy. This limitation came as a result of a separation of secular and spiritual power. The Iranian national church; the Nestorian version of Christianity, had been rejected in the western portion of the area of Arabian rule. Here, Monophysitism continued to carry the day, practiced by Armenians, Syrian Jacobites, and Egyptian Copts. The church of the emperor was present as well in the midst of the Melkites.

A new Christian movement, intended to unite all the Christians of the Arabian Empire, was announced by the demand that an understanding of Jesus as the *muḥammad* be adopted. This demand was preceded by another, namely, that Jesus be conceived as *ʿAbd Allāh*. The point of this demand was to give Christian theology in the Orient a leitmotif that could be employed over against Byzantium as a unifying program for the Christians in the former Byzantine east and the former eastern Sassanian Empire.

The idea of Jesus as *ʿAbd Allāh* is reminiscent of the position of Arius, who came from Antioch; it also can be found later, in the inscription in the Dome of the Rock, which states, along with a date of 72 following the Arabian era (691–692): *muḥammadun ʿAbdu llahi wa-rasūluhu* (referring to Jesus).[90]

The group surrounding the *Amīr* ʿAbd al-Malik provoked his opponents Muʿāwiya and Ibn al-Zubayr with this demand concerning the *muḥammad*. Muʿāwiya lost power around the year 60 of the Arabian era (679–680), as his loss at Constantinople and the humiliating peace treaty with the Byzantines —especially the renewal of tribute—had discredited him. Ibn al-Zubayr was able to project an image of himself as *Amīr* for another ten years, but his sphere of influence was limited to Kirmān and Persia.[91] The confession of the *muḥammad* formula can be found on many dated and undated coins from the region of Arabian rule in both the East and the West.

THE *MUḤAMMAD* MOTTO IN THE EASTERN PORTION OF THE AREA OF ARABIAN RULE

Gaube has described Arabo-Sassanian drachmas that bear the inscription *muḥammad*; these come from Shīrajān, dated to the year 38 of the Arabian era (658–659); and from Rayy (the ancient Ragae, today a southern suburb of Tehran), dated to the year 52 of the Arabian era (672). He connects the use of the formula *muḥammad* with the name of the prophet of the Arabians.[92] As in the case of the *ʿAbd Allāh* formula, however, this question concerns an inscription that expresses an ideology of authority. The example of Queen Boran's medallion has already made clear that coins can also bear inscriptions that define the idea of authority. This was always the case among the Sassanians, as one sees in their titulature, which emphasized their descent from the gods.

Consequently, it is not necessary that we assign coins with the inscription *ʿabd Allah* to an emir named ʿAbd Allāh b. Amīr. If what appears on a coin is intended as a name of an emir, generally speaking, the name of the father also appears. This is true of Muḥammad b. ʿAbd Allāh, who minted coins in Herat in year 67 of the Arabian era. This is the first time that the personal name Muḥammad appears in historical records. The use of this name became current among the Arabians only after the mission of ʿAbd al-Malik. Further, it is only the coins bearing the name of the *ʿabd Allah* and the *muḥammad* that appear without any names of ancestors. Gaube also recognized this phenomenon in the case of the *muḥammad*; he avoided assigning its meaning to an emir named "Muḥammad b. (name)." While, according to him, it is possible that this title does concern the prophet of the Arabians himself, Gaube's recognition at least remains in the realm of history and not that of speculation.

The coins of the Sassanians were a means of royal propaganda, as they publicly proclaimed their heritage from the gods. Consequently, it should not surprise us that the ideology of the Arabian rulers manifested itself in the same way on their coins. Instead of a note on divine descent, however, one finds here a declaration of the human nature of the ruler and the human nature of the one making the proclamation. The ruler is *ʿabd Allāh*, for Jesus had already been *ʿabd Allāh*. A Christian who saw in Jesus the *ʿabd Allāh* called himself by the name *ʿAbd Allāh*. His tribe called themselves the *ʿIbād* (*Allāh*). However, the Messiah, *al-masīḥ*, was, for the Arabs of the East, not only *ʿabd Allāh*, he was also *muḥammad*.[93] At the end point of his *daʿwa*, where ʿAbd al-Malik erected a shrine as his *ḥaram*, one can read in the cupola of the Dome of the Rock, in the third line on the inside of the octagon, on the south-east side, the following: *muḥammadun ʿabdu llahi wa-rasūluhu* ("The servant of God and his apostle may be praised").

COINS WITH THE *MUḤAMMAD* MOTTO IN THE EASTERN PORTION OF THE AREA OF ARABIAN RULE

The catalog of the Berlin "Sammlung Orientalischer Münzen" ("Collection of Oriental Coins") which appeared in 1898 contains the first mention of an Arabo-Sassanian coin with the inscription *MḤMṬ* in Pahlavi writing using the Aramaic script.[94] Another coin like this one came to light in 1984, the field of which also bears the Arabic inscription *muḥammad* alongside the inscription *MḤMṬ* in Pahlavi.[95]

Scholars until now have rarely understood the inscriptions with the motto *ʿabd Allah* and the motto *muḥammadun* as pointers to Jesus and his status as *ʿabd Allāh* (the "Servant of God" in the sense of East Syrian theology); just as rarely have they understood the categorization of Jesus as *muḥammadun* ("chosen" or "praised"). Consequently, they have typically explained these ascriptions as names of rulers, emirs, or governors who simply forgot to include the names of their fathers when minting coins (*contra* the general practice in the field of Arabo-Sassanian coin minting). For example, Gaube turns the motto *ʿabd Allāh* into the name *ʿAbd Allāh b. Amīr*.[96]

Stuart D. Sears has suggested that scholars should seek the origin of these coins in Azerbaijan, and that they should see their minting history in connection with the activities of Muḥmmad b. Marwān, a brother of ʿAbd al-Malik.[97] Sears distinguishes between four different variants of Arabo-Sassanian drachmas with the motto *muḥammadun*:

- Variant I. Pahlavi inscription *MḤMṬ* in the field, with the Arabic legend *wāfin*;
- Variant II. Pahlavi inscription *MḤMṬ* in the field, with the legend *muḥammadun* in Arabic script;
- Variant III. Pahlavi inscription *MḤMṬ* in the field, with the legend *muḥammad* in Arabic script; a number 60 is given, representing the year 60 of the Arabian era (there are also extant coins with this year given, minted by ʿAbd al-Malik in Dārābjird, and so it was quite natural for Sears to connect

these coins with Muḥammad, the brother of ʿAbd al-Malik, as this would agree with the traditional Islamic literature);

Variant IV. Pahlavi inscription *KhWSRWY* in the field, with the legend *muḥammad* in Arabic script.

He explains the richness of the variants as imitations of various Sassanian examples, namely, the second and third issue of the coins of Chosroes II.[98]

THE MINTING OF COINS WITH THE *MUḤAMMAD* FORMULA IN SYRIA AND PALESTINE

An image of a copper coin with the *muḥammad* motto was published by Sir Alec Kirkbridge in 1947.[99] This coin was part of an issue of irregular, square, poorly-minted copper coins. On their obverse they depict the standing figure of a ruler, crowned with the cross and holding a long cross in his hand. On the left, from top to bottom, there is an inscription that has until now been read as information concerning the mint of origin, namely, ʿAmmān. On the reverse one finds the denomination, a cursive capital M (40 nummia). The denomination also bears a cross, and under the M there appears the motto *muḥammad.*[100]

Another coin from antique Yavneh/Yubna has become known; this coin depicts a ruling figure, facing front. On the right of the figure, on the coin's obverse, the motto *muḥammad* appears, and on the left the motto *bismi llah.* Following our interpretation, the inscription would then read, "He is chosen in the name of God," or "Let him be praised in the name of God." The cursive capital M appears on the reverse as its denomination, surrounded by the inscription *Fulūs Yubnā*, or "money from Yavneh."[101]

THE *MUḤAMMAD* MOTTO AND THE "STANDING CALIPH" IN ḤARRĀN: THE DEPICTION OF THE CROSS IS REPLACED BY THE "STONE" BETH-EL

Along with the followers of ʿAbd al-Malik, the *muḥammad* motto migrated from East to West.[102] Like the battle call of a *daʿwa*, the *muḥammad* motto stood for a change in the inner conditions of the Arabian Empire. If the reign of Muʿāwiya

Fig. 15: Arabo-Sassanian Coin with mention of the *MḤMD* (*muḥammad*) on the right next to the bust, with the Arabic legend *wāfin*.

Fig. 16: Arabo-Sassanian Coin with Pahlavi *MḤMṬ* in the field, on the right next to the bust; the *muḥammad* motto appears in Arabic script as the legend.

Fig. 17: Obverse of a Syrian coin with the *muḥammad* motto; on the left of the standing Christian ruler, from top to bottom, is the inscription *ʿAmmān*.

Fig. 18: Reverse of the Syrian coin with the *muḥammad* motto.

stood for a continuation of Iranian militaristic expansion under the leadership of a new elite and by means of a preservation of the *status quo* in the abilities of religious communities to live together, then the arrival of ʿAbd al-Malik signaled an entirely new perspective. Syrian religious conceptions returned to the place of their birth after a nearly two-hundred-year exile following the flight of their defenders (Barsaumas of Nisibis et al.) into the Sassanian east.

ʿAbd al-Malik wanted to strengthen the Arabian empire from within by erecting an Arabian Church of the Arabian Empire. This church was to be an imperial church in the Iranian sense, following the example of the Nestorian Church in Iran and its role as the Christian imperial church of Iran toward the end of the reign of the Sassanians. To advance this attempted consolidation, he renewed the peace treaty with Byzantium and accepted a significant increase in the tribute demanded. The treaty also allowed its two parties to divide the revenues from Cyprus, Armenia, and the Caucasian Iberia (Georgia).[103]

ʿAbd al-Malik had recognized that further victories against his confessional enemies could only occur if the military efforts were accompanied by an internal consolidation. Thus, he put the emphasis of his own work on the development of ideological armament.[104] His goal was to unify, under the banner of the *muḥammad* motto, the adherents of the old Syrian theology who had been driven into the East. Syrian theology, in its Arabian understanding, was to regain its former homeland under this banner.

One finds connections to the old Syrian theology in an anonymous Jewish work on the history of Jesus (*Toldot Yeshūʿ*). One passage from the last section concerns Nestorius, who was condemned as a heretic at the Council of Ephesus in 431. It is reported here that Nestorius lived in the empire of the Persians, and that in opposition to the apostle Paul, he directed the Christians under his care to follow the Mosaic laws. He is said to have taught that Jesus was no God, but rather a human being inspired by the Holy Spirit, equal to the prophets.[105]

The Muḥammadanism of ʿAbd al-Malik cannot simply be equated with Nestorianism. His Muḥammadanism derives much more from the Arabian understanding of Syrian theology. Further, this Arabian understanding of Syrian theology did not arise in the Nestorian imperial church of Iran; rather, as the tribal religion of the Mesopotamian and Iranian Arabs, it became a constitutive part of their ethnicity.

Just as Syrian theology was manifested among the Arabs in its Arabian understanding—and thus became their tribal religion—so also it existed, even into the modern period, in Ethiopia as a constitutive factor of the Ethiopian kingship. The first missionary work in Ethiopia began at the end of the third century with the work of the Syrian Frumentius and his colleagues. The central dogma of the Ethiopic church is the *täwähedo*, the confession of the unity of the Godhead.[106] On the coast of the Red Sea opposite from Ethiopia, the central dogma of the local Wahhabi teaching is called *tawḥīd*. This group's expression, colored by the Hebrew, can be found in a historically graspable form in the inscription in the Dome of the Rock in Jerusalem. This inscription reads, *Allahu aḥad* [corresponds to Hebrew *adonai eḥad*, which is the ending of the *Shema'*, the Jewish expression of faith], *Allahu 'l-ṣamad*. The meaning and understanding of this formulation appears to have been current among the Arabizers of the Qur'ānic material, as they did not experience it as "un-Arabic."[107]

Following the Mosaic law has not seemed any less "un-Christian" to the Christians of Ethiopia. A custom in the Ethiopic church is notable here, namely, that they read the Song of Songs on Holy Saturday morning, just as it occurs in the synagogue during Passover. This corresponds to the hermeneutical understanding of medieval European Christians in making the Old and New Testaments congruent. The Ethiopian Church still practices circumcision in accordance with the Mosaic law. It is understood as a visible sign of the covenant between God and his people, and it is carried out on the eighth day after birth.[108]

In defending Muḥammadanism, 'Abd al-Malik's autocephalous Arabian Church of the Arabian Empire saw the possibility of keeping the Christological debate open. During this period it had seemed that the emperor and his primary church officer, the patriarch of Constantinople, had fought and directed the Christological controversy; indeed, at the end of the Sixth Ecumenical Council, held in Constantinople in 681, the collection of church leaders had acclaimed Emperor Constantine IV thus: "Many years to the emperor! You have expressed the essence of the nature of Christ. O Lord, protect this lampstand of the world!" However, in 'Abd al-Malik the Tradition of the See (Patriarch) of Antioch reentered the scene. He made the emperor understand that he saw himself as a competitor in the debate over the nature of Christ. He entered the debate with an *Ekthesis* of his own and, in the year 72 of the Arabian era (691–692), had it inscribed in the Temple shrine he had built in Jerusalem called Qubbat al-Ṣakhra ("The Repository of the Rock").

The enemy of the Arabian ruler, Emperor Justinian II (685–695), was a very pious nobleman. On his coin inscriptions he called himself *servus Christi* (servant of Christ), and he was the first among the Byzantine emperors to include the portrait of Christ on his coins' obverse side.[109]

ʿAbd al-Malik answered this practice, calling himself, on his own coins, *Khalīfat Allah*, or "Speaker for God."[110]

Fig. 19: The coin from *Ḥarrān*: the *Beth-El* in the form of the *Yegar Sahaduta* with the *muḥammad* motto on the obverse.

The mistaken belief that the ruler of the Arabian Empire had understood himself as a caliph, and that the title of the caliphs had been *Amīr al-muʾminīn*, arises from the times of the Abbasid caliphs after al-Maʾmūn. This leader called himself *Khalīfat Allāh* as well, but for totally different reasons. In a visit to Jerusalem in the year 217 of the Arabian era, he put his own name into the text in the Dome of the Rock, and he instrumentalized (or interpreted anew) the content of the text in the sense of the Muslim theology, which he himself had initiated.

In a bronze coin from Ḥarrān, one can see ʿAbd al-Malik's competitive stance against the emperor in Constantinople. This type of coin though instead cast in copper, had already been known in Europe for centuries; this particular exemplar, described by Walker, made its way into the Vatican holdings by way of the Borgia collection. The connection between ʿAbd al-Malik and the *muḥammad* motto is made clear from the representation on the coin's obverse of the pile of stones called the *Yegar Sahaduta* יגר שהדותא —Gen. 31:45–47). The anonymous Muḥammad coin from Ḥarrān, bearing the image of the *Beth-El* ("House of God," Gen. 28:15–19) in the form of the *Yegar Sahaduta* as a "witness in stone," points to the later coins from the region bearing the name of ʿAbd al-Malik.

It is interesting that, before the appearance of ʿAbd al-Malik's name and titulature, it is only the movement's *muḥammad* motto that appears on coins of this type. With regard to the order of events of the *daʿwa* of the followers of Muḥammadanism, one sees the following picture by bringing together the sequence of coin-issues:

1. The appearance of anonymous drachma coins in the region of former Sassanian rule, bearing the motto *ʿAbd Allah* from the year 41 of the Arabian era (661–612).
2. The appearance of anonymous, occasionally dated (to the year 60 of the Arabian era [679–680]) drachma coins in the region of former Sassanian rule, bearing the motto *muḥammad*, and:

3. The appearance of the anonymous copper coin from Ḥarrān (the symbolic power of this place-name has been known since the days of the biblical patriarchs) in the region of former Byzantine rule, bearing the motto *muḥammad* and the image of the new national religious symbol, the *Beth-El* in the form of the *Yegar Sahaduta*.
4. These are followed by the appearance of copper and gold coins with the image of the new national religious symbol, the *Beth-El* in the form of the *Yegar Sahaduta*, and of the Arabian ruler with the protocol of ʿAbd al-Malik. The image of the *Beth-El* as *Yegar Sahaduta* spreads toward the West, from which resulted:
5. The appearance of inscribed coins in north Africa with the representation of the new national religious symbol, the *Beth-El* in the form of the *Yegar Sahaduta*.

The spread of this new national religious symbol, the "Stone," also answers the question concerning the absence of the depiction of the cross on the coins from the Arabian Empire. The national religious symbol, the *Beth-El*, in its function as the treaty-guardian *Yegar Sahaduta*, marks a return to the tradition of iconic stone idols. The fixation of ʿAbd al-Malik's movement on the *muḥammad* idea, as a part of its self-understanding as a "true Israel," explains this return to the Semitic tradition.

The disappearance of the sign of the cross in the area of Arabian rule did *not*, therefore, result from an Islamic rejection or prohibition of the figure of the cross, as the historicizing Islamic literature claims. That the cross does appear on the coins of Muʿāwiya and those of the Syrian emirs before ʿAbd al-Malik has equally little to do with a sort of "Islamic tolerance" (as emphasized in the literature) toward those Christians who were necessarily employed in the government as a help to the new rulers.

What scholars of Islamic studies have not yet recognized in this realm is the connection—noted in the Islamic literature—of an Islamic cultural blossoming with a significant percentage of government functionaries being Christian. This blossoming distinguishes the Christian-Arabian early period of Arabian authority from the Mesopotamian-Iranian orientation after al-Maʾmūn's visit to Jerusalem in the year 217 of the Hijra, the era of the Muḥammad who, in the meantime, had been appropriated as the prophet of the Arabians.[111]

The replacement of the sign of the cross with the image of the *Beth-El* in the form of the *Yegar Sahaduta* was a part of the ideological controversy with Byzantium. The return to a symbol reminiscent of the founding of Israel is *not* a suggestion of a Jewish-Christian tradition of the (Christian) Arabian Church of the Arabian Empire; rather, it points to the *Dīn*, the understanding of the interaction between God and his creation as the result of the keeping of a contract.[112]

What follows is the traditional description of the coin from Ḥarrān, which allows far-reaching conclusions of the type described above to be drawn. It is a copper coin with the inscription *muḥammad* on the left, the location of the mint *Ḥarrān* on the right, and in the middle the frontal depiction of the Arabian ruler following the Mesopotamian schema with *kufiya* and the sword of judgment on the obverse. On the reverse one sees a "stepped cross" to its left is a monogram, to its right the motto *muḥammad.* Under the stepped cross is the Greek number *IS* (16).[113]

This traditional description of this coin assumes that the side of the coin with the depiction of the ruler is the coin's obverse. However, in reality, the national religious symbol of the *Yegar Sahaduta* is the most important element and, consequently, adorns the side that should properly be called the obverse. The depiction of the Arabian ruler is the motif for the *reverse*, as was the case on the contemporary coins bearing the image of the Byzantine emperor, which in the same way gave over their obverses to that empire's religious symbol, namely, the depiction of Christ as *Pantocrator*.

Fig. 20: Image of the Arabian ruler on the reverse of the coin from *Ḥarrān*. To the left one sees the inscription *muḥammad*, and on the right the mint location *Ḥarrān*. On the obverse there is the depiction of the "Stone." To the right there is the inscription *muḥammad*, underneath the number 16 using Greek letters, and on the left the depiction of a rhomboid betyl.

Clive Foss held the depiction of the Arabian ruler to be the prophet of the Arabians, just as Gaube believed the motto *muḥammad* to be a mention of the prophet of the Arabians on Arabo-Sassanian coins.[114] It is unquestionable, however, that the coins actually bear a depiction of an Arabian *ruler*. The similarity of the image to that of the Arabian ruler in Khirbat al-Mafjar speaks strongly in favor of this opinion.[115] Further evidence in this regard is the sword of judgment, which is depicted in a pronounced way and is greatly oversized. This long sword is reminiscent of the swords of the guardians at the fire-altar, depicted on the reverse of earlier Sassanian drachmas. Here the ruler is depicted as a guardian over the "contract" between God and humanity. The sword is an indication of the understanding of *Dīn* as a result of a contractual relationship.

The depiction of the Arabian ruler is a reaction to a new type of coin in Byzantium: Justinian II had depicted Christ as the *Rex regnantium* on the obverse of the third type of his gold *solidi*; on the reverse one sees the emperor standing with a long cross in his right hand.[116]

Fig. 21: The Byzantine model of the Arabian gold coin. The obverse has a religious image; the reverse, shown here, bears the image of the standing emperor, Justinian II, with a long cross.

This depiction renders it necessary to view the side of the coin bearing the image of the Arabian ruler as the *reverse* of the coin. Numismatists concerned with Islamic coins have not yet recognized this fact, despite the fact that numismatic conventions dictate that the religious message *always* appears on the obverse. In Byzantium it was the view of Jesus as the Christ, *Rex regnantium*, while in the former Byzantine east it was the depiction of the "witness in stone," the *Yegar Sahaduta*. The depiction of the *Beth-El* in the form of the *Yegar Sahaduta* is found on the obverse of all the coins of ʿAbd al-Malik bearing the image of the Arabian ruler, even in North Africa, in connection with otherwise purely inscriptional types.[117]

Fig. 22: A gold coin of ʿAbd al-Malik following the Byzantine pattern: on the obverse (right in the figure) the national religious symbol (the "Stone" in the form of the *Yegar Sahaduta*), and on the reverse (left in the figure) the depiction of the Arabian ruler with sword (of judgment?).

MUḤAMMADUN RASŪLU ʾLLAH— "PRAISED/CHOSEN IS THE APOSTLE OF GOD"

This expanded definition of the conception of Jesus as the *muḥammad* is found first on Arabo-Sassanian coins in Iran. The earliest known coin from this period is dated to the year 66 of the Arabian era and comes from Bishāpūr in Persia. Coins were also minted at this location during the reign of the Sassanians in Iran.[118] As opposed to the anonymous *ʿAbd Allah* and *muḥammad* coins, this coin was minted by a named leader. The legend on the coin is in Arabic and reads: *Bismi llahi muḥammadun rasūlu llah* ("In the name of God, the apostle of God is chosen/praised").

This expanded formula, which calls the *muḥammad* a *rasūl*, can also be found six years later in the text of the inscription on the Dome of the Rock in Jerusalem. There, in the text on the inner façade of the octagon, one learns that *rasūlaka wa-ʿabdaka ʿĪsā bn Maryam* ("your apostle and servant, Jesus, the son of Mary") is the one whom the preceding Christological explanation concerns. The Qurʾān uses the descriptor *rasūl* alongside that of *nabī* ("prophet").[119] Biblical characters and prophets are called *rasūl*, especially those that carry a special meaning in the Qurʾānic interpretation of history; these include Noah, Lot, Ishmael, Moses, Shuʿayb, Hūd, Ṣāliḥ, and Jesus. These are authorized representatives of God, bearing a mission to save the community of the faithful. Regarding Jesus as the *muḥammad*, one sees here an anti-Pauline view of the community of the faithful; namely, that the Semites—and most especially the Arabs—constituted the community of the faithful because they were relatives of Jesus, of the Aramaic one from Galilee. One sees this expressed in the connection of biblical saviors (Noah—from the flood, Lot—from the fire, and Moses—from the sea) and extrabiblical, Arabian savior-conceptions (the earth will swallow during an earthquake whomever does not accept the God-given order of things, etc.) in the world of the Qur'ānic materials. As the *muḥammad*, Jesus joins the group of the "Seven Saviors." He is the plenipotentiary in the sense of contract law (*walī al-'amr*) and the deputy or representative of God (*walī Allāh*). Here again, the Arabian worldview as a web of contractual relationships becomes visible.

'ALĪ AS THE VIZIER OF THE "PRAISED/CHOSEN ONE"

This assessment is foreign to scholars of Islamic studies. They know the conception of a *walī Allāh* only in connection with the Shī'a, which they (falsely) hold to be a secondary development. The Shī'a know the expression *'Alī walī Allāh*. This shows a specifically Christian Arabian development: the idea of a *MḤMṬ walī Allāh* (from the first centuries of the Arabian era) becomes a general Semitic conception (Aaron/Hārūn) of an *'Alī walī Allāh*, an "Excellent One as Representative of God."

THE PRAISED/CHOSEN ONE AS THE BEARER OF THE LOGOS

The contemporary epigraphic materials allow one to reconstruct the contents of 'Abd al-Malik's *da'wa* (mission), namely, the understanding of Jesus as the *muḥammad*, who as *rasūl* is the apostle of the (Sassanian) Arabs. Because Jesus did not die on the cross (so the Qur'ānic materials claim), he took up the function of a "hidden imām" after his translation into heaven. He is able to appear to the community and, as the authorized representative, protect them from the threatened catastrophe. On this point one should also compare the apocalyptic ideas from Ḥimṣ. These may trace back to Syrian models, but they also show that, among the Arabians, and even in the period of the Abbasids, people were constantly forced to reckon with the appearance of Jesus.

To quote from these apocalyptic texts:

> The Masīḥ ʿĪsā b. Mariam shall descend at the white bridge at the eastern gate of Damascus in the direction of the tree. A cloud will carry him while he will place his hands on the shoulders of two angels. On him will be two white cloths, one of which he will wear as a loin wrap, the other as a loose cloak. When he bows down his head, drops will fall from it like pearls. . . . Then he will come to the gathering of the Muslims, wherever they are. He will find their caliph praying with them. The Masīḥ will stand behind him when he sees him and (the caliph) will say, "O Masīḥ of God, lead the prayer for us." [Here the Messiah's function as imām has become clear.] But he will say, "Rather, you lead the prayer for your companions, for God is pleased with you. I have been sent only as an assistant (*wazīr*); I have not been sent as a commander (*amīr*)."[120]

Then the process of authorization continues. To judge from the inscriptions on the Arabo-Sassanian coins, Jesus is the *muḥammad walī al-ʾamr* ("authorized representative").

The presentation of translations contemporary to ʿAbd al-Malik will simplify the clarification of the expression *rasūl* in this special context. Because ʿAbd al-Malik did not limit his *muḥammad*-mission by using only Arabic terminology, but rather preached in the *lingua franca* of the Near East, the message was also proclaimed in the eastern portion of the lands of the Iranian empire in Middle Persian (Pahlavi). For example, there exists a coin from Sīstān/Sakastan, minted in the year 70 of the Arabian era which bears the inscriptional text *MḤMṬ PTGAMbl Y yazdt*.[121]

Here the expression *Paygambar* appears, a term that depicts the connection between a Persian infinitive form and a related Aramaic expression already in use in the Persian spoken language for centuries. The Pahlavi heterogram contains the Aramaic *PTGM* for *patigama* (message, word).[122] The component *–bar* is the present infinitive of the verb *burdan* (to bear). The Pahlavi term *PTGM-bar* means "bearer of the message/word." Fully translated, the inscription reads, "The bearer of the message/word from God is chosen/is to be praised." It would also be possible to understand the expression *Paygambar* as "bearer of the Word," or the Logos. In this understanding the bearer would be seen as a "vessel," into which God "has cast his

Word and from his Spirit," as it is said of Mary in the inscription on the Dome of the Rock. Here one sees the ancient conception of humans and prophets as vessels of the divine. And once again we find ourselves in the realm of old Syrian theology.

This Middle Persian formulation will be clarified further elsewhere. To avoid misunderstandings, those minting the coins added Arabic legends that precisely defined the function of the *Paygambar* from an Arabian perspective. There is extant a silver coin from a mint in the region of Kirmān in the southeast of Iran, dated to the year 70 of the Arabian era; in addition to the Middle Persian motto *MḤMṬ PGṬAMbl Y Yazd*, this coin has the Arabic legend *bismi llāh walī al-ʾamr* ("in the name of God, he is the authorized representative").[123] Another silver coin, this one from a different mint in Kirmān but also dated to 70 of the Arabian era, has the Middle Persian motto *MḤMṬ PGṬAMbl Y Yazd* and the Arabic legend *bismi ʾllāh walī Allāh* ("in the name of God, he is the representative of God").[124]

FROM THE EPOCH OF ʿABD AL-MALIK UNTIL THE END OF THE REIGN OF HIS SONS IN THE YEAR 125 OF THE ARABIAN ERA (742–743)

THE ARABIAN EMPIRE AND THE SUCCESSION OF THE IMPERIUM (CONSECUTIO IMPERII)

The controversy between ʿAbd al-Malik and the emperor in Constantinople reached a high point when the Arabian Empire began to mint gold coins. Until that time, the Arabs in the former Byzantine east had been satisfied to mint local, copper coins, and also drachmas, following the Sassanian pattern. However, the minting of gold coins threatened the high position of the emperor in Constantinople, who had continued to enjoy the privilege of furthering the tradition of the Roman Empire in the East by means of the minting of gold coins. By releasing his own gold coins, ʿAbd al-Malik ended the monopoly of the emperor and his ability to control the flow of gold coins in the former Byzantine east. At the same time, ʿAbd al-Malik displayed his position as a competitor of the emperor in Constantinople through his own independent ability to mint coins.

Beginning in the year 74 of the Arabian era (693–694), ʿAbd al-Malik's gold coins were totally dedicated to propaganda concerning his Muḥammadanism. These coins set his relationship with the "true Israel" against the Christological relationship indicated by the image on the Byzantine coins: on the one hand, the depiction of the symbol of the founding of Israel through Jacob, the "Stone" in the form of the biblical *Yegar Sahaduta*; and on the other, the depiction of Christ as *Pantocrator*. The inscription on the Arab coins reads: *lā ilaha illā Allah waḥdahu muḥammadun rasūlu llah* ("There is no God but Allāh, him alone, and the apostle of God is to be praised/is chosen").[125]

The introduction of gold coins also visibly illustrates the practice of ʿAbd al-Malik concerning the integration of structures adopted from previous regimes. There were no new and revolutionary practices and methods in the government of the Arabian Empire; rather, the tendency was to fuse what had been inherited from both East and West.

Silver coins were minted in the formerly Sassanian regions of the East, and copper coins were minted in Syria. This situation was supplemented by the independent minting of gold coins, following the tradition of the West, especially of Egypt. In this way, a system of coinage emerged, minted from three different metals, but this system did not lead to a unified use of the minted coins throughout the empire. The eastern portion retained its adopted silver currency, the western regions retained their preference for gold, and Syria continued to use its traditional copper.[126]

This pragmatic approach was necessary to ensure smooth activity at the governmental level in a region that was unified for the first time in a millennium (since Alexander the Great and his Diadochi). It was a land mass from Egypt in the west to central Asia, on the border of China, in the east. This corridor rematerialized as a result of the radical change initiated by the victory of Heraclius over the Persian armies in 622. This victory led to the dissolution of the Sassanian dynasty and, as a result, ended the nearly thousand-year division of the Near East into an Iranian portion and a Hellenistic/Roman portion. The result of this change, which has endured even until today, was the migration of the Arabian Muḥammadanism from the East into the West. This dynamic movement, which according to traditional Islamic scholarship had its origin in the preaching of the prophet of the Arabians, did not spread to Syria from Arabia, in fact, but from Iran. Or rather, Muḥammadanism did not move from south to north, but rather from east to west. The idea of a south to north movement, an idea arising from the early third century of Islam, is actually a portion of the religious history of the movement. The protagonist of this conception is Khālid b. al-Walīd,[127] who understood the connection of Mecca to this historical dynamic. The historical literature of the third century portrays this hero as the leader of a conquering army from Mecca into eastern Arabia. The army continued under his leadership into the homeland of Abraham in Chaldea, and then to al-Ḥīra, the center of the Nestorian Christians in Mesopotamia. From there they proceeded further west to Arrān, the endpoint of Abraham's migration as portrayed in the Bible. Crossing the Jordan River at Yarmūk, they went on into Palestine, which was the "Promised Land" to the Arabians as well—as descendants of Ishmael. Finally, they conquered the Arabian (Nabataean) city of Damascus. It is important to note that victory in battle is a *topos* in this historical literature as divine approval of the conquest.

The religious history actually overtook the historical process. In terms of an Arabian "salvation history," the Mesopotamian-Iranian Arabs became connected with a fictive ancient homeland in Arabia, which gave their entrance into the pages of history added chronological depth. The beginning point for these "salvation-historical" ideas later became Mecca, in the south of the old Nabataean lands. After the year 138 of the Arabian era (756), these salvation-historical ideas replaced the knowledge of the actual historical process: first, that Arabian aristocrats in the Sassanian Empire received their power as military chieftains in occupied Syria and Egypt after the fall of the Sassanian dynasty, which resulted from the defeat of 622; second, that they then remained with their contigents of Arabians in those places rather than returning to their Mesopotamian homelands; and finally, that in concert with the non-Byzantine hierarchs of the formerly Byzantine east, they effected the withdrawal of the Byzantine troops who had stayed behind.

IMPERIAL ACTS: STATUARY, THE BUILDING OF ROADS, A CENTRAL SHRINE OF THE NATIONAL CHURCH, AND THE IDEA OF "ZION"

As a competitor with the emperor in Constantinople, ʿAbd al-Malik did not shy away from the continuation of Sassanian and Roman traditions of authority. Although the nearly life-size statue of an Arabian ruler, found in the vicinity of Jericho in Khirbat al-Mafjar, cannot be unquestionably attributed to him, it shows nonetheless that the traditional ideas concerning the depiction of a ruler, as well as those concerning the construction and erection of statues of a ruler, had not disappeared even by the end of the first century of the Arabian era.[128]

The development and fusion of adopted practices also occurred with regard to palatial architecture among the ruling elite of the Arabian Empire in Syria. In the northern portion of the east wing of the palace in Khirbat al-Mafjar, one sees primarily decorations whose motifs one knows from Sassanian textiles. In the southern portion of the palace, however, decorations from the storehouse of Roman-Byzantine forms dominate. The two types of decoration are not mixed; similarly, as in the minting of coins, the various elements are simply placed side-by-side. People lived in what was first a "country home" in the vicinity of the Dead Sea, but which later became an entire building complex, in which both Roman-Syrian and Mesopotamian-Iranian traditions had been integrated.

Further, in connection with the building of the Dome of the Rock, the road from Damascus to Jerusalem was improved. A milestone bearing an Arabian inscription dating from the year 73 of the Arabian era (692–693) exists.[129] The Dome of the Rock itself is a building of imperial size, competing in its dimensions with the Church of the Holy Sepulchre. The Dome of the Rock embodies the Syrian conception of the church as a structure that follows the plan of the temple of Solomon. This is still the case among the churches of Ethiopia.

The inside of the Ethiopian churches is divided into three concentric areas. The innermost portion is the shrine with the *Tabot* (the Ark of the Covenant), or else the tablets (of stone), which stand in for the *Tabot* as a part for the whole. Only priests and the king are allowed to enter this area. The middle area is reserved for the sacraments and the other sacred rites, while the choir fills the outer area. The faithful stand in the square in front of the church and follow what is happening inside through the open doors.

The division of space in the Dome of the Rock follows this mode of division. The Rock takes the place of the *Tabot*. The innermost portion of the building is fenced in by four massive posts, between which are twelve columns in groups of three. The four posts are reminiscent of Sassanian shrine tradition, the *Chahār Taq*. This building took as its basis the plan of the Persian fire-temple. It is also found in Armenian churches.[130]

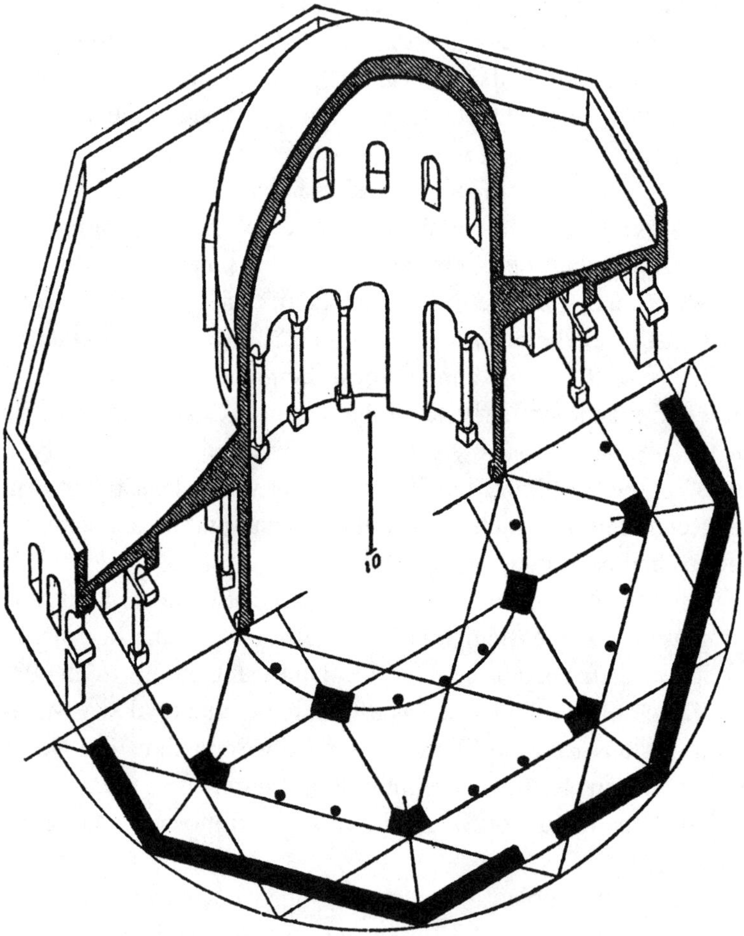

Fig. 23: Cutaway isometric drawing of the Dome of the Rock, showing the arrangement of the four posts and twelve columns in the center under the cupola.

The four posts support a drum, over which stands an arched wooden ceiling, traditional for Syrian shrines. The cupola is essentially a wooden ceiling. There were people at that time with the ability to erect massive cupolas of brick or stone, but their abilities were not employed because of the sacred necessity for a curved canopy (a *baldacchino*) of very temporary material. The reference point of the twelve columns becomes clear from the meaning of the building as the temple of the "New Zion": they are the Twelve, the disciples of Jesus.

TOWARD AN UNDERSTANDING OF THE INSCRIPTION IN THE OCTAGON OF THE DOME OF THE ROCK AS ʿABD AL-MALIK'S *EKTHESIS*

ʿAbd al-Malik had his Christological theses inscribed on the inner octagon of this building. Here, for the first time in a historically verifiable form, one can see a text exhorting the duty of *Islām*.[131] This text corresponds to the procedure followed a half-century before by Emperor Heraclius who had his *Ekthesis* hung on the inner walls of the Hagia Sophia in Constantinople. In Jerusalem, as in Constantinople, the goal of the *Ekthesis* was to have an impact within the congregation. The preservation of Christianity was sworn upon *Yā ahla l-kitāb* ("You people of the Book!").

ʿAbd al-Malik was certain that *Dīn*, as a contractual system for the relationship between God and humanity, had *"Islām"* as its prerequisite. Naturally, this demand did not relate to the *individual* behavior of the faithful, but rather to the behavior of the *community* of the faithful. A community dispersed and divided could not stand before the One God; a contract was not possible with this type of community. Consequently, the conflict over the interpretation of scripture had to end, and agreement had to be reached concerning its understanding. The community of the faithful had to be of a quality that reflected the idea of *Allāh al-ṣamad*. The idea of the One God demanded the One Community as its counterpart in a contractual relationship, and this One Community had to be shaped by a unified understanding of scripture. Consequently, religious duty (*dīn*), as the result of a contract with God, is the restoration of the broken contract and is effected through (renewed) submission (*al-islām*) under the contract. This then would ultimately also lead to a unified understanding of scripture.

However, if one pursues further the meaning of the term *al-islām* given by Horovitz[132] as "to surrender, betray oneself," then the competitive relationship between the Muḥammadanism of ʿAbd al-Malik and the dogmatics of the church of the emperor returns to the foreground. In this conception, the church of the emperor, decorated with images, had fallen to the worship of idols, and its members were *mushrikūn* ("servants of idols, associators"). The reformer, ʿAbd al-Malik, did not shy away from the use of powerful images, just as Luther would do, conceiving of his religious opponents as a "world full of devils." In the light of the characterization found in the Old Testament, the Qurʾānic Abraham/Ibrāhīm had an exemplary function, showing the faithful the way that must be taken: it is only because of the "falling away" of the church of the emperor (who is therefore an "apostate" [Syriac *ḥanpā*]) that one can find the way to the true *Dīn Allāh*, to behavior toward God appropriate under the contract. That Abraham/Ibrāhīm is called *Ḥanīf* in the Qur'ān should be understood theologically, not historically. His betrayal (that is, legitimate opposition) of the servants of idols allowed him to find a new spiritual home. After the act of falling away, he became like a noble, rugged follower of the unfalsified ancient religion, which had existed since the time of Adam. Having escaped from the brainwashing of the servants of idols, he was able to recognize the duty to the *Dīn Allāh*. The Syrian word of contempt *ḥanpā*, in Arabic *ḥanīf* (apostate), becomes a title of honor (in the sense of "resistance"). This call to *islām* makes sense in connection with the exhortations and warnings expressed in the inscription on the Dome of the Rock. These warnings concern the adoration of the "Three," from the perspective of Muḥammadanism: Mary, as "Bearer of God"; Jesus, as "Christ" and "Pantocrator"; and the Holy Spirit, in a form far above the idea of *al-ṣamad* (bound, connected).

THE DEPICTION OF TEMPLE VESSELS FROM THE SOLOMONIC TEMPLE ON THE COINS OF ʿABD AL-MALIK: THE SEVEN-BRANCHED LAMPSTAND WITH AN ISLAMIC INSCRIPTION

In connection with the erection of the Dome of the Rock as the temple of the "New Zion" and as the center of an Arabian-Muḥammadan-Christian imperial church, we must make mention of the depiction of the Solomonic temple's "hardware" on Arabian copper coins of that time. There was a special issue of copper coins concerning ʿAbd al-Malik's *ḥaram*, the Dome of the Rock, which replaced Muʿāwiya's *ḥaram*, the shrine of John the Baptist in Damascus, as the central holy place of the Arabian Empire. The coins from Damascus had pointed to the veneration of John in Damascus by depicting the "Head of the Baptist"; the new coins, however, in depicting the various vessels of the temple, no longer pointed to a single prophet, but quite broadly to the entire "Zion" complex.

Multiple exemplars of these copper coins are known, all coming from finds in Palestine and all bearing the inscription *lā ilaha illā ʾllah waḥdahu*, running from below to above to the right of the depiction of a seven-branched lampstand. The reverse of the coin bears the same inscription in three lines. As early as 1886, J. G. Stickel published the exemplar from the Jena collection, but his publication seems to have been largely ignored.[133] What is most noteworthy is the absence of a mention of the *muḥammad* on these coins with the image of the seven-branched lampstand. Consequently, one could reckon their appearance to the reign of Muʿāwiya. The appearance, however, of an Arabic inscription (*lā ilaha illā ʾllah waḥdahu*) would then contradict the hypothesis of Islamic studies that ʿAbd al-Malik was the one who was the "Arabizer."

In my opinion, Arabic was primarily the language of the ruling Arabian elite at this time. A result of this was the "Arabizing" of the sacral sphere. Educated Syrians would have then conducted themselves just like their ancestors in the Ḥawrān. The languages of all areas of life were current for them: they spoke the Nabataean village dialect at home, Greek at school, Aramaic in church, and Arabic in the military and as the *lingua franca* at court. This functional multilingualism had a long history.

It was only with the development of modern Islamic studies that scholars first sought to definitively establish the use of a unified "national language," in the way that such languages shape modern, centralized nation-states. Here, Islamic studies reveals itself once again as a descendant of colonialism and the nationalistic thought of the nineteenth century. In late antiquity, however, it would not have bothered anyone that well-known and current expressions, like *Allāhu aḥad* (Qurʾān 112:1), although colored by the Hebrew, would have been understood by Arabs as Arabic expressions and used in the presentation of religious concepts.

ʿAbd al-Malik defended the "Zion idea" just as much as his predecessor Muʿāwiya. In doing this, though, ʿAbd al-Malik was not only acting as a zealous supporter of the old Syrian theology, but also as a competitor with Byzantium. The Byzantines had begun to interpret world history from a Christian perspective; they no longer saw themselves as the inheritors of a world empire, but rather as the "chosen people," ringed about by anti-Christian enemies.[134] However, it is important to note that, at the time of ʿAbd al-Malik, the imitation of the Jewish prototype of lampstand (one with seven lights) had begun to decline in favor of a *five*-branched lampstand. The process of adoption and transformation is visible throughout the iconography of the period. First, the Jewish-style lampstand was preserved, but it was

Fig. 24: The five-branched lampstand with Muḥammadan inscription.

transformed into a lampstand of the temple of the "True Israel" and "New Zion." Then, one prime number (seven) was exchanged for another (five): the seven-branched lampstand of the temple became the five-branched lampstand of the "New Zion." The tradition of Israel was thereby continued, but in a Christian-Arabian understanding, rather than in a Jewish one. It would be a mistake to see here a type of Jewish Christianity, for the depiction of the Christian Arabian lampstand was bound up with the naming of the *muḥammad*. In at least this respect the lampstand was also "Islamic," following the stipulations established by scholars of Islamic studies up to now. However, the five-branched lampstand with the naming of Jesus as the *muḥammad* was a part of the Zion-complex, just as much as was the Dome of the Rock, which bears the inscription on the inner portion of its octagon that mentions the word "Islām" for the first time in a historically verifiable manner.[135]

ʿABD AL-MALIK AS THE "NEW DAVID"

If the Byzantine emperor Heraclius had been celebrated as a "new David" a half-century earlier—after the end of the war against Chosroes II[136]—ʿAbd al-Malik presented himself as the father of a new Solomon. By means of his son Sulaymān, then, ʿAbd al-Malik defined himself as a "new David." As such—seen through the lens of the Old Testament—he replaced the regime of a "King Saul." This is yet another example of the competitive behavior between Constantinople and the Arabian Christians from the East, the new rulers of the formerly Byzantine Orient.

The emperor called himself "Servant of Christ" (*servus Christi*) on his gold coins; his opponent in Jerusalem called himself "Speaker for God" (*Khalīfat Allāh*). The emperor was a "new David" as the conqueror of the Persian "Goliath"; in replacing the regime of a King Saul, the Arabian ruler was a "new David," making use of the conceptual world of the Old Testament. Of course, Muʿāwiya was intended in this mention of "Saul": a prince warring and yet erring (in the view of the Arabian Church of the Arabian Empire). Just as for the emperor in Constantinople, so also for the Arabian ruler of the East, the Old Testament was the source for the idea of the role of the emperor.

The definition of the Arabian ruler's authorization as the "Speaker for God" (*Khalīfat Allāh*) presupposes a change in the Byzantine emperor's understanding of his own role. Beginning in 629, Heraclius no longer called himself *autokrator*, in imitation of the idea of the Roman emperor, but rather *basileus*, or "king." This change is only understandable when one brings in the religious background of the new form of legitimation of authority. The use of the title *basileus*, a term in itself connoting a lower rank (rulers had formerly bestowed this title upon their vassals), not only represented a Hellenization of the form, but also an understanding of authority based upon a subordination under the authority of Christ. The (vassal-title) *basileus* was to be understood as that of an earthly, Christian vassal of a heavenly ruler. The Christian background is clear as soon as one quotes the title in its entirety: *pistos en Christoi basileus* ("the king who is faithful in Christ").

It was only as a *mu'min* (Gk. *pistos*) in Christ that Heraclius was equipped for rulership. It was only as a "Speaker for God" (*Khalīfat Allāh*) that ʿAbd al-Malik could rule following the understanding of his Arabian Church of the Arabian Empire. The orthodox emperor was justified in exercising rule by virtue of his subordination to a heavenly ruler; the Arabian lord of orthopraxy, on the other hand, received his legitimation to rule through a defense of the interests of the *muḥammad*. The *muḥammad* stood in the tradition of authorization, which Allāh had distributed since the time of Adam to his representatives (*walī al-ʾamr*) and deputies (*walī Allāh*).

THE SPREAD OF "MUḤAMMADANISM" IN THE WEST AS FAR AS SPAIN

While the ability to mint coins, initiated during the periods of ʿAbd al-Malik and his successors, allowed many mints in the eastern portion of the Arabian Empire (the area of former Sassanian authority) to blossom once again, it is clear that Egypt lost much of this power. No dirhams are known to have been minted during the time of ʿAbd al-Malik and his successors in either Egypt or in the areas of Arabian authority lying further to the west.

Egypt

One of ʿAbd al-Malik's brothers was *emir* in Egypt. An inscription on a bridge over the canal of Fusṭāṭ bears witness to his building activity.[137] The text of the inscription conspicuously lacks a reference to the "Muḥammadanism" of his brother in Jerusalem. The text contains only a plea for divine blessing on the building project, as well as on the project's donor and his family. The inscription, dated to the year 69 of the Arabian era, reads as follows: "This is the bridge-arch (*al-qanṭara*), which ʿAbd al-ʿAzīz bn Marwān, the emir, has had erected. May Allāh bless him in all his efforts, confirm him in his 'sultanate' [that is, "his authority"], and make him to be at peace with himself and his household. Amen. Saʿd Abū ʿUthmān built this; ʿAbd al-Rahmān wrote it in the month of Ṣafar, in the year 69."[138]

Consequently, we should see the religious movement that proceeded under the banner of the *muḥammad* motto in the light of the development of Syrian theology in the eastern portion of the Arabian Empire. Those Arabian tribes which came into contact with Syrian theology quite early (ca. third century) saw a badge of identification in the protection of this theology. Once they had converted to Christianity, they saw the beginning of a new tribal tradition in protecting the form in which Christianity had come to them. The specific type of Christianity at the time of the missionization became the new tribal religion. This phenomenon explains their lack of interest in further developing this theology. The practitioners of the tribal religion were not interested in *orthodoxy*, per se, as much as in *orthopraxy*, in order to ensure security in the legal system as a result of the immovable religious justice of the tribal religion.

Outside of this region of the old Syrian theology, no one was talking at all about narrowing the Christological discourse to focus on the question of whether Jesus was *muḥammad*, that is, one praised/chosen among humans, and consequently also *ʿAbd Allāh*, a servant of God in the sense of a "Christology of worthiness," or a Hellenistic "Son of God" in the sense of the theology of the councils. The continuing discussion of Christological themes at the councils had already left this question aside centuries before. In the eyes of the imperial conciliar theologians, this way of posing the question was already an element of "history."

To the Monophysite Copts in Egypt, the intentions and goals of ʿAbd al-Malik's missionary work—that is, the *daʿwa* for the recognition of Jesus as *muḥammad*—must have seemed like a conflict between two Iranian brothers, one of whom considered the theology known to the Egyptians by the name of its protagonist, Nestorius, as "Arabian," while the other considered it "Iranian" in the sense of the Nestorian Iranian imperial church. This discussion had no effect among the Monophysite Copts. As a result, the Arabian powermonger ʿAbd al-ʿAzīz avoided the fruitless controversy and remained neutral. It was far more important to him that his followers remain united against their common opponent, the emperor of Byzantium, than to find commonalities in Christology.

Tripolitania at the Time of ʿAbd al-Malik

The Tripolitanian copper coins from this period only communicate to us the name of the local ruler; this individual was Mūsā bn Nuṣayr. Just what relationship he had with any overlord cannot be adduced from the coins' inscriptions; one can only come to such an understanding from the image on the reverse of the coins. We find here, again, the national religious symbol of ʿAbd al-Malik—the *Yegar Sahaduta*, the "Stone." Mūsā bn Nuṣayr does not appear to have been a rabid Arabizer, for he preserved the tradition from Roman Africa of using Latin inscriptions. The legend on the obverse of his coins reads *In nomine Domini num(m)us in Tripoli faktus* (*sic*!) ("This nummus was made in Tripoli in the name of the Lord"). The inscription on the reverse reads *Muse Filius Nusir Amir A(fricae)* ("Mūsā, son of Nuṣayr, Emir of Africa"). Mūsā bn Nuṣayr also communicated information useful for learning about his religious convictions, for the obverse of a different issue of coins reads *In nomine Domini Unus Deus* ("In the name of the Lord, [there is] One God").[139]

This evidence clearly shows that, at the time of ʿAbd al-Malik, the Arabic language enjoyed no special authority in this region, either in sacral or in secular areas of life. The religious message was spread in the languages of the various local authorities. In the eastern portion of Iran, in Sīstān/Sakastān and Kirmān, this was Pahlavi, written in the Aramaic script. In Syria the language of rule had been Arabic since the sixth century, for the Ghassanids, having emigrated from Arabia, did not enjoy the background of a Hellenistic education. In the West, however, Latin remained the language of authority.[140]

That the mint in Tripoli belonged to ʿAbd al-Malik's sphere of rule can be deduced from the presence of the image of the *sahaduta*. Where, though, is the confession of Jesus as the *muḥammad*? As was already the case in the Egypt of that period, one does not see the *muḥammad* motto in Tripolitania at the time of ʿAbd al-Malik. Is the explanation that ʿAbd al-Malik did not want to, or could not, achieve the goals of his missionary work in the name of the *muḥammad*?

One must remember that North Africa was primarily an area of retreat for those Arabian powers who had previously been connected with Muʿāwiya. ʿAbd al-Malik could not expect anything more from them than the acknowledgement of his authority. That they took on the national religious symbol of the *sahaduta* satisfied this expectation.

There are coins extant from this region, coins dated to the year 80 with Arabian inscriptions. The governor Nuʿmān did not put his own titulature on his coins. The inscription on the obverse merely gives the date: "in the year 80" (of the Arabian era). The inscription on the reverse begins with the Arabian translation of the phrase *in nomine Domini* ("in the name of the Lord"). It reads as follows: "In the name of Allāh, al-Nuʿmān has ordered it." As a concession to local tradition, the reverse of the coins also bears the image of an imperial bust (Constans II?), while the obverse has the image of the *sahaduta*, in recognition of the balance of power in the region.[141]

The Former Roman Province of Africa, with Its Capital City of Carthage, at the Time of ʿAbd al-Malik

Gold coins with the image of the *sahaduta* were also minted in North Africa. One can ascribe these coins to the time of ʿAbd al-Malik due to their depiction of the national religious symbol of the *sahaduta*. These gold coins communicate a great deal to us concerning the meaning of the dominant religious conceptions of the day. The inscriptions are written as abbreviated coin legends. Here are the texts in their fuller forms:

> NON EST DEUS NISI UNUS CUI NON EST ALIUS SIMILIS.[142]

> NON EST DEUS NISI UNUS CUI NON SOCIUS ALIUS SIMILIS.[143]

Other statements on the nature of God, found in the coin legends from the time of ʿAbd al-Malik, read as follows:

DEUS ETERNUS DEUS MAGNUS DEUS OMNIUM CREATOR.[144]

DEUS ETERNUS DEUS MAGNUS OMNIA NOSCENS OMNIUM CREATOR (dated "in the fourth year of the indiction = the year 87" [of the Arabian era, that is, 705–706]).[145]

Still other coins bear the depiction of the *sahaduta* and an inscription giving the location of the coins' mint:

IN NOMINE DOMINI MISERICORDIS SOLIDUS FERITUS IN AFRICA.[146]

Fig. 25: A north African gold coin with a Latin inscription and the *Yegar Sahaduta* from the time of al-Walīd.

Should one wonder whether the coins can be seen as the work of the "conquering Arabs" under the banner of the *muḥammad*, one must consider the coins' system of dating. Simply put, the dating system follows that of the Byzantine tax year, and the given tax year dates fall during the time of the reign of ʿAbd al-Malik. The rulers were simply not yet as free in the province of Africa as they were in Tripolitania, where the general Nuʿmān was already able at this time to date his coins following the era of the Arabians. The following examples bear this statement out:

IN NOMINE DOMINI MISERICORDIS SOLIDUS FERITUS IN AFRICA INDICTIONE II (that is, in year 84 [of the Arabian era, approx. 703]).[147]

IN NOMINE DOMINI MISERICORDIS SOLIDUS FERITUS IN AFRICA INDICTIONE III (that is, in year 85 [of the Arabian era, approx. 704]).[148]

Analyzing these coins does not allow one to make any conclusions concerning a new religion of a prophet of the Arabians with the name Muḥammad. Not even the *muḥammad* of ʿAbd al-Malik's missionary work is named. The "Islamic" *basmala* appears here as the Christian phrase *IN NOMINE DOMINI MISERICORDIS* ("in the name of the merciful Lord").

Even if the depiction of the *sahaduta* does not appear on the gold coins of the province of Africa (n.b., the traditional name is here appropriated; *"Ifriqiya"* is not in play), this tells us nothing of a connection with the authority of the Arabian Empire in the East. The *muḥammad* motto is nowhere mentioned, and this at a time when the "Muḥammadanizing" carried out by ʿAbd al-Malik had reached it highest point. The coins from the same period that were minted in the eastern portion of the Arabian Empire used the *muḥammad* motto without fail.

What caused the missionaries of the conception of Jesus as the *muḥammad* to fail in North Africa? What hindered them from establishing Muḥammadanism there as well? Was ʿAbd al-Malik simply satisfied to carry out his mission in the homeland of the old Syrian theology? The leadership in the West consisted only of an alliance of Christians opposed to the emperor. The Christians of Egypt and North Africa could not have been opposed to old formulae like the *basmala*.[149] They were also not opposed to the idea of *tawḥīd*, as it appeared in the Latin inscriptions on the coins of ʿAbd al-Malik from the province of Africa.

The sentence *NON EST DEUS NISI UNUS CUI NON SOCIUS ALIUS SIMILIS* ("There is no God but one; there is no other associate like him")[150] not only represents an understanding of Allāh like the one given in the inscription in the Dome of the Rock in Jerusalem, it can also be seen as a pointer to the presence of Monophysites, Monarchians, Nestorians, and Arians among the inhabitants of Africa.[151]

This is also true of the leaders who were ordering the minting of the coins. On their coins one finds legends such as *IN NOMINE DOMINI NON DEUS NISI DEUS SOLUS NON DEUS SIMILIS* ("In the name of the Lord, there is no God but God alone, no God [like him]").[152] The doctrine of a single nature of the God-man had been condemned at the Council of Chalcedon in 451. This condemnation led to an irreparable breach between the church of the emperor and the Monophysites in Egypt (Copts), to be followed soon by parts of Syria (the Jacobites). One can see in the behavior of ʿAbd al-Malik a double role, or perhaps different policies for different places. He defended the mission of the *muḥammad* in his own homeland, the formerly Sassanian East, and in the region that was the source of Syrian theology, in order to emphasize his Arabian understanding of Christianity. Outside of this region, he led the alliance of the emperor's Christian opponents without influencing their theological ideas. This means that he limited the sphere of authority for his Arabian church of the Arabian Empire, with its center in Jerusalem, to the regions of settlement for the Arabian tribes in Iran, Mesopotamia, and Syria. In the areas surrounding this region of missionary work, he accepted the *status quo,* not only in order to keep from stretching his power too thinly, but also in order to make possible opportunistic conquests. This was important because, contrary to an extremely common opinion, what the "conquering Arabs" had in hand was not a wealthy Roman province of Africa. The testator had already consumed the inheritance, so to speak, before the Berberized province was brought within the sphere of authority belonging to ʿAbd al-Malik.[153]

Coins in Maghrib

This flexible use of power made it possible to overlook disturbing details and accept the traditional ideas of the region's inhabitants, both Christian and non-Christian. Among these conceptions can be included the depiction of the bearded Punic Baal, found on contemporary coins from Berber Tlemcen.[154] Coins are also extant from Tangier that bear the following inscription, surrounding the barbarized portrait of an anonymous ruler: *DOMINE DEUS QUI TIBI SIMILIS* ("Lord God, who is like you?"). On the reverse one also finds an Arabic text: *bismi llah fals ḍuriba bi-Ṭanjah* ("in the name of God, [this] copper coin was minted in Tangier").[155]

THE REIGN OF ʿABD AL-MALIK'S SONS

General Characterization

Here we are concerned with a reign, the effects of which can be recognized at two different rates of change. The mission of the conception of Jesus as the *muḥammad* was already an element of the past in Syria, while those carrying the banner of this originally eastern *daʿwa* were still working to establish their ideas in the western portion of the Arabian Empire. We can establish the speed of the western spread of this idea of Jesus as the *muḥammad* of old Syrian theology, a theology which survived in the region of Iran and had enjoyed there a renaissance under the rule of the Arabs, with the help of the dates given in the coin legends that mention the *muḥammad.*

However, concerning the reign in Syria, other emphases have already emerged. After the *muḥammad* idea had been firmly established in the eastern portion of the Arabian Empire and in Syria, the Arabs saw Jesus (as the *muḥammad*) as a patron saint for the ruling dynasty, following the understanding of the Arabian Church. Following Arabian tribal tradition, material and immaterial intervention only counted for blood relatives. ʿAbd al-Malik's efforts concerning the conception of Jesus as the *muḥammad* laid the groundwork for Muḥammad, the prophet of the Arabians, to appear in the Abbasid period as a relative of the Marwānid ruling house, in the eyes of those belonging to the Arabian tribes.[156]

From this time on, the Marwānids enjoyed a status in Syria as at least the spiritual relatives of the "Chosen One." ʿAbd al-Malik was to be seen as the guardian of his shrine. The shrine of the *muḥammad* from the house of David was the *ḥaram* in Jerusalem, which enjoyed the protection of the reign of ʿAbd al-Malik. This authority received its political legitimation by protecting the shrine of the "patron saint." This renders the question moot as to whether the Marwānids acted as kings or caliphs. Their name does not appear on either gold or silver coins of the Arabian empire after the years 77–78 of the Arabian era. The avoidance of this attribute of the "Islamic" ruler—to be named on coins—is unusual; following the general Islamic understanding of the enthroning of the ruler, the practice of authority without exercising the right of the *sikka* (coinage) was unthinkable.

Consequently, one can rightly deduce that a type of authority developed under ʿAbd al-Malik that placed his successors in the role of Arabian Sayyids,[157] whose primary task was to organize pilgrimages to the tombs of the saints and be present at these locations as guardians of the shrines. This portrait accounts for ʿAbd al-Malik's peaceableness: he never went to war against his Christian brothers in Byzantium. It also accounts for the fact that we never hear anything in this period of military action described under the rubric of *jihād*.[158]

Muʿāwiya had already protected the shrine of John the Baptist in Damascus in order to gain influence in Syria. The Marwānid al-Walīd returned to this idea. His reign was associated with the expansion of the "sacred precinct." The tomb of the Baptist was incorporated into the shrine, and the sacred precinct was expanded so that it matched the area enclosed by the old temple. The building inscription that al-Walīd had inscribed, dated to the year 86, informs us of this. Further, the *kanīsa* ("church") of John was partially torn down and replaced with a *masjid* ("place of prayer").[159]

This was a part of al-Walīd's building program. One should not equate this with a mosque-building program. The expansion and improvements of buildings in Jerusalem and Damascus reflect *development*. In place of the emperor's basilica-style church, and the crypt containing the reliquary of the Baptist's head that lay outside the church, al-Walīd built a structure connecting the reliquary with its place of memorialization, in the sense of a "sacred precinct." Further, al-Walīd's brother Hishām took over the protection of the *ḥaram* of the Syrian Christian saint Sergius in Sergiopolis (Ruṣāfa). He expanded the shrine there in the same way as his brother al-Walīd had already done in Damascus. In this way, the Marwānid Sayyids controlled the centers of religious power in Syria and northern Mesopotamia.

After the death of the last of ʿAbd al-Malik's sons, which took place in year 125 of the Arabian era, there was confusion among the Marwānid Sayyids, and a different group of Arabian Sayyids from the east took over the religious leadership of the Arabs. Consequently, the religious centers of the Marwānids fell back a bit in rank. Their center in Damascus began to be ignored, and Jerusalem had to take second place behind the new center in the Ḥijāz, at Medina.

The Coins of ʿAbd al-Malik's Sons in the West

In the western portion of the empire, however, the models from the time of ʿAbd al-Malik continued to have influence. Up to year 98 of the Arabian era, there are half-solidus gold coins from the province of Africa that bear the image of the *sahaduta* and the inscription *SOLIDUS FERITUS IN AFRIKA ANNO XCVNI* (*sic*).[160] At the same time one also finds attempts among the coins of the West to conform to the purely inscriptional forms found in the East. For example, in Damascus, three lines of script had replaced the image of Heraclius with his two sons. The image of the Sassanian fire-altar with two guardians, found on silver coins from the East, had given way to a three-line text. In the same way, the image of the *sahaduta* on the field of the *solidi* in the province of Africa was replaced by one line of text in the center of the field. Behind the text, though, one can still see the old image. This method seems symptomatic of the procedures of the administration of the Arabian Empire. Not including the significant upheaval in the wake of the mission of the *muḥammad*, there were no revolutionary changes, but rather a continuing development toward an Arabian understanding of authority and its exercise.

Solidus coins (their weight does not correspond to that of the dinars from Damascus) from the province of Africa were dated following the Byzantine tax years up to the year 94 of the Arabian era. From the year 84 (703) until the year 94 (712–713), the *solidi* are of the purely inscriptional type and bear Latin legends.

The Latin legend on the coins comes to completion in the middle of the field, so that one quickly learns that one has to deal with one line of text in the middle of the field and also a text *around* the field. The texts read: *DEUS ETERNUS DEUS MAGNUS DEUS OMNIUM CREATOR*. The reverse bears a Latin inscription following the same pattern: *IN NOMINE DOMINI MISERICORDIS SOLIDUS FERITUS IN AFRICA INDICTIONE II* (or *III*, or *IIII*, up to *XIII* for the year 94 of the Arabian era).[161] It was only during the reign of Sulaymān that the leaders attempted to Arabize the coin inscriptions in the province of Africa. The methods of dating were changed in the year 95 of the Arabian era; instead of the dating following the Byzantine tax years, as had been common for the longest time and even under al-Walīd, we find for the first time datings following the Arabian era.[162]

Fig. 26: Arabic-Latin gold coin from North Africa with a Muḥammadan inscription, dated to the year 98 of the Arabian era (716–717).

The eastern portion of the Arabian Empire had known only gold coins that were purely inscriptional and anonymous since the year 77 of the Arabian era; the same was true concerning silver coins beginning in the year 78. All of these coins mentioned the *muḥammad* as *rasūl*. In the West, however, it was only in the year 97 of the Arabian era that gold coins were minted with bilingual legends: Arabic and Latin.[163]

It is also possible to confirm the first mention of the *muḥammad* in an official protocol in the western portion of the Arabian empire. In the year 66 of the Arabian era (685–686), this title had already appeared in Bishāpūr in Iran; thirty-one years later the conception of Jesus as the *muḥammad* found its place in the coin legends of the western portion of the empire. When the mission concerning the *muḥammad* arrived in the province of Africa in the year 97 of the Arabian era (715–716), the spread of the idea of Jesus as the *muḥammad* had finally reached the western portion of the Arabian Empire.[164]

Spanish Coins from the First Century of the Arabian Era

There is only one Spanish coin known from this period: a *solidus* from the year 93 of the Arabian era (711–712).[165] This *solidus* bears a notable inscription: *HIC SOLIDUS FERITUS IN SPANIA ANNO XCIII SIMILIS* ("This *solidus* was made in Spain in the year 93; *similis*"). The word *SIMILIS* belongs to the legend found on the reverse, where one finds a seven-pointed star, not the image of the *sahaduta*. Surrounding the star is the text *IN NOMINE DOMINI NON DEUS NISI DEUS SOLUS NON EST ALIUS* (the text continues on the obverse—"In the name of the Lord, there is no God but God alone; there is no other [like him])."

If one follows the text of the inscription, it becomes clear that the "conquering Arabs" knew that they had reached Spain; they had not yet come into *al-Andalus*. The name *al-Andalus* appears first in coin legends in the year 98 of the Arabian era (716–717). There are extant *solidi* from the year 98 of the Arabian era; in the center of the fields on these coins' obverses appears an eight-pointed star surrounded by the inscription *FERITOS SOLIDUS IN SPANIA ANNO X* ("This *solidus* was made in Spain in the year . . ." [the remainder is lacking]). The inscription on the reverse is written in Arabic. In the center of the field one reads in two lines the following: *muḥammadun rasūl Allah*. Surrounding this text is the following legend: *ḍuriba haḏā l-dīnar bi-l-Andalus sanata thaman wa-tisʿīn* ("this dinar was minted in al-Andalus in the year 98").[166]

The many notable features of the traditional presentation of the "Islamic" conquest of Spain will not be analyzed here. The historically compelling variation on this story, that of a common effort between Christian-Berber North Africans and the non-Catholic population of Spain against the Catholic Visigothic ruling house does not appear in the narratives of the eastern chroniclers. The narrative of the conquerer in the west, Mūsā bn Nuṣayr al-Lakhmī (*sic*!—again, a connection to the Lakhmids, the dynasty from *al-Ḥīra*), mirrors that of the conquerer of the east, Khālid bn al-Walīd.

With a view toward the way of telling the "traditional story" from the Abbasid period, one can see ʿUmar II, who followed the sons of ʿAbd al-Malik, al-Walīd, and Sulaymān, as a pious tradition concerned with mastering the turn of the first century. After overcoming the dangers associated with end-times (ʿUmar II's reign was 99–101 of the Arabian era; no coins or inscriptions are extant bearing his name), the succession of ʿAbd al-Malik's sons could be continued in the traditional literature. In fact, it was never interrupted until it met its end in year 125 of the Arabian era with the death of the last of ʿAbd al-Malik's sons.

THE FURTHER DEVELOPMENT OF THE *MUḤAMMAD* CONCEPT IN THE SECOND CENTURY OF THE ARABIAN ERA

THE DEVELOPMENT OF THE ʿALĪ IDEA: MOSES IS THE PROCLAIMER; MŪSĀ AND HĀRŪN; JESUS IS MUḤAMMAD; ʿĪSĀ AND MUḤAMMAD; MUḤAMMAD IS THE PROCLAIMER; MUḤAMMAD AND ʿALĪ

Moses is mentioned 136 times in the Qurʾān, Jesus (*ʿĪsā*) twenty-four times, and Mary (*Maryam*) thirty-four times, while the term *muḥammad(un)* is used four times.[167]

In 1999, a hoard of treasure was discovered on the island of Gotland, a Swedish county in the Baltic Sea. Among the 14,296 coins, which are primarily Arabian, there is one Arabian silver coin, dated to 766, bearing the inscription *Mūsā rasūl Allāh* ("Moses is the messenger of God"). Alongside the exemplar from the discovery of this treasure, four other exemplars of coins in the name of Moses are extant from finds of Viking coins.[168]

After the death of the last of ʿAbd al-Malik's sons in year 125 of the Arabian era, Marwānid bureaucratic practices continued to function unchanged in Carthage in the western portion of the Arabian empire until the year 137. The same was true in the eastern portion of the empire, in Gharshistān, until the year 138.[169]

The erosion of the theocratic authority of the Marwānids helped to cause ʿAbd al-Malik's Muḥammadanism to be overtaken by an Arabian (Mesopotamian?) conception, which further developed that Muḥammadanism. This development succeeded in a way analogous to the patterns of thought that appear in the Qurʾānic texts. There, Moses asks for support during the audience before Pharaoh. Moses reminds God that he is not rhetorically gifted. Consequently, his brother Aaron is set up alongside him, and Aaron gives forth the message before Pharaoh. This situation—Moses as the prophet and Aaron as his vizier—also comes to expression in the early Arabic rock inscriptions in the Negev. There one finds formulaic petitions to God following this pattern: "You are the Lord of the world, the Lord of Moses and Aaron" (*āmīn rabb al-ʿālamīn rabb Mūsā wa-Hārūn*).[170] The prophet receives a vizier who is responsible for actualizing the revelation given to the prophet.

The further development of Muḥammadanism required the creation of a pairing that would represent the revelation and its actualization. In this process, the Chosen One (*muḥammad*) is a noble (*ʿAlī*) and is given an exalted associate, who is the representative of the prophet and the executor of his will. Consequently, it is no wonder that this exalted one was called the *walī Allāh*. He took shape in connection with late Sassanian conceptions of a prototypical Iranian knight, with elements mixed in from the veneration given to the knightly saint Sergius from Ruṣāfa (whose veneration reached as far as Ḥaḍramawt)[171] and to the Syrian martyrs, who were primarily young members of the Sassanian aristocracy.

This vizier became a martyr in the same way as these others, as did his descendants, for the continued effects of the ideas of the cult of the Syrian martyrs must have caused earthly life to end in catastrophe for him and for his family. The members of the exalted one's family were able to gain influence in the eastern portion of the Arabian Empire; this took place after the family of the Chosen One fell into a crisis of legitimacy in the empire's western portion. The Marwānid Sayyids in the West were not able to successfully maintain their theocratic primacy after the death of ʿAbd al-Malik's sons. As the revolution proceeded, their *maḥrams* were overcome. Pilgrimage practices to Jerusalem and Ruṣāfa were stopped, and the city of the Baptist, Damascus, lost its exalted status as the capital.

Following Arabian tradition, the leadership of the community passed on to the descendants of the nearest relative of the Chosen One. Jesus did not have any male descendants, and his heritage as the son of Mary did not fit into the Arabs' patrilinear system of family relationships. Further, Muḥammad, the form in which he appeared among the Arabs, also did not have any male children. One could work with this situation, but his birth from Mary alone had to be corrected, either through adoption or through an announcement of his earthly father. In the place of a "muḥammad," ʿĪsā bn Maryam, who was an "ʿAbd Allāh," Muḥammad bn ʿAbd Allāh entered the scene. The exalted one became his son-in-law, in order to follow the Arabian understanding of succession in terms of family relationships. The Alid Sayyids directed the veneration of the saints to new places, the shrines of the martyrs from ʿAlī's family in Mesopotamia, in Karbalā and Najaf.

It is astounding that all these religious upheavals had an Iranian background. The *muḥammad* mission of ʿAbd al-Malik began in eastern Iran, and the members of the family following ʿAlī had their center in Fārs and the Jibāl. Further, the powerful figures of the *Āl Muḥammad* could be found further in the east.[172]

The defender of the *Āl Muḥammad* (the family of Muḥammad) called himself *Abū Muslim Amīr Āl Muḥammad* ("the arch-Muslim, the emir of the family-group of Muḥammad") on a coin from al-Rayy dated to the year 131 of the Arabian era. Another coin dated to the year 132, but without giving a location, calls him *Abū Muslim.* These are the first historically verifiable instances of the term *Muslim* being used on coin legends. In the following year other coins appeared, again without a location given, referring to *al-Amīr ʿAbd al-Raḥman bn Muslim.* In the course of this mission, the identity of the leader was further developed. Nonetheless, it will likely prove impossible to pin him down as a historical personage. Again, we may be dealing with a *nom de guerre.*

The uncertainties underlying the ascription of these coins to the family group of Muḥammad become clear when one examines Wurtzel's material. Here we see again an amalgam of early documents understood according to the traditional historiography. Wurtzel describes a coin from *Tawwaj*, dated to the year 132 and allegedly in the name of "(Abū l-Abbās) ʿAbd Allāh al-Saffāḥ." Concerning this coin he notes: "It is the only known coin which bears the name of the first ʿAbbasid caliph." However, on closer inspection one notices that this ascription rests solely upon the legend "*ʿAbd [Allāh A]mīr al-muʾminīn bi-Tawwaj!*" As I have already explained, the term *ʿAbd Allāh* is nothing more than the protocol of the Arabian ruler; the title *Amīr al-muʾminīn* shows that the person involved is one who can guarantee security. What we are then dealing with here is an already post-metaphysical process: the duty of obedience in exchange for the granting of protection. How, then, is all of this to connect with the narratives of the traditional reports concerning a spiller of blood by the name of al-Saffāḥ, named as the first defender of a new dynasty, the Abbasids?

In addition, the building inscription from the year 135 of the Arabian era, found on the shrine in Medina that would later be called the grave of the Prophet, does not point clearly to revolutionary changes in the early period of the Abbasid caliphate, as the traditional reports would have us believe. In the text of this inscription, Jesus is again mentioned as *muḥammadun*, and it repeats the definition of Jesus as "servant of God and apostle" from the inscription on the Dome of the Rock. One can only speak of the idea of Muḥammad as the prophet of the Arabians if the phrase "servant of God" is no longer connected with him in inscriptions. Only then can one proceed with the idea that the Christian understanding of *muḥammadun* has been fully replaced by the Arabian tradition of the understanding of the Prophet. The expression *ʿAbd Allāh* becomes, then, the father of the prophet of the Arabians; the two-fold description of Jesus as "Chosen One" and "Servant of God" becomes Muḥammad, the son of ʿAbd Allāh who died quite early.

Further on in the text of the inscription, one sees for the first time in a historically verifiable way a mention of a *sunna nabawīya*, a "sunna of the prophet." The use of the expression *sunna* points to an understanding in the sense of a "Deuteronomy." The *kitāb Allāh* (the "written text concerning God" [n.b., *not* "the Qur'ān"]) is mentioned here in the same breath as the *sunna nabawīya*. This is a sequence known from the Old Testament: the book of Deuteronomy (from the Greek word meaning "second law") follows upon the four books of Moses. What is to be understood concerning the *sunna* of the prophet only became clear after the instrumentalizing of this term at the time of al-Ma'mūn, after which the *sunna nabawīya* has been understood as an Islamic Mishnah. But at the time that the inscription was created in Medina, the idea was to be understood much more in the sense of the Qur'ānic texts, whose prophet is Moses as the eternal prototype of the "savior." In this understanding, the term would only be a pointer to the validity of the Mosaic law, as is the case in Deuteronomy. Ethiopian Christians still follow the Mosaic law in this sense.

Otherwise, the inscription speaks at length concerning just and unjust taxation, the just exercise of authority; equal distribution of money; and the care of widows, orphans, and the needy—but most especially of respect with regard to family relationships. What a difference between the "public-ness" of ʿAbd al-Malik's *Ekthesis* on the Dome of the Rock, directed toward the "people(s) of the book," and the hermetic position taken by this text! Just how far has one come from the desire to come to an understanding, as found at the time of al-Walīd? From that period one may still read the note in the text found in the shrine of John in Damascus and dated to the year 86 of the Arabian era.

After so many announcements of this kind in the Medina inscription, one would expect to find somewhere the name of the new ruler, the first defender of the Abbasids. However, on the coins from this period one finds only the protocol of the Arabian ruler, *'Abd Allāh*, and the title *Amīr al-mu'minīn*. The new ruler remains anonymous, as was the case before among the Marwānid Sayyids, whose names were not mentioned on the gold and silver coins after 77–78 of the Arabian era.

Fig. 27: Coin from Jayy (Iṣfahān) from the year 116 of the Arabian era (734–735), with Muḥammadan inscription and image of an unknown (regional?) ruler in the style of the Sassanian coins with a Pahlavi inscription.

What is clear is that neither the defenders of the expectations of the members of the *Āl Muḥammad*, whose coin inscriptions (Qur'ān 42:23) point to the meaning of family relationship, nor the adherents of the idea of a theocratic state (*lā hukma illā li-llah*: "there is no authority, unless it be from God") were able to successfully establish their ideas on a wide basis between the years 128 and 135 of the Arabian era. In fact, the victory fell to a third party, one that revived the Sassanian court at its old location and who took over the old Marwānid expressions onto their coin inscriptions with only minor modifications (Christological matters were discarded, as the question whether God had a son or not was no longer important for the continuation of the debate). One notices here that the exhortation to obedience survived this change.

After a decade of religious turbulence, more pragmatic individuals seemed to have gained the upper hand. These individuals limited the practice of their authority to the regions of Sassanian imperial control as of the year 614.

The former Byzantine east again became the object of an aggressive policy of occupation. The Arabian Empire became the heir of the successes and problems of the Sassanian Empire. Among the Sassanians' successes can be numbered their victories over the Romans and Byzantines, as well as the

Fig. 28: Coin with inscription in the style of the Abbasids and dated year 136 (753). Reverse: Muḥammadan inscription with image of the ruler following the mode of the Sassanians.

expansion of their authority as far as Egypt in the footsteps of the Achaemenids. This glorious history of success in the West is balanced by a rather grim set of results in the East, where the victory of Turan stands out. The area of Iranian settlement in the East, formerly reaching as far as the borders of China, had in the meantime fallen into the hands of the Huns, while the oppressive force of Turkish peoples and warlike Tibetans had raised the pressure on the Iranians in the East.

In year 118 of the Arabian era, Badakhshān in the Pamir Mountains was conquered,[173] but the conflict with the Tibetans ultimately led to significant losses reminiscent of the darkest days of the history of the Sassanian dynasty, when the King of Kings himself was taken captive by the Huns. Consequently, it should not be surprising that the court in the new capital of Baghdād, not far from the former Sassanian royal residence in Ctesiphon, should have been founded in connection with powers that were of some weight in the eastern portion of Iran. These were the Iranian Buddhists, defenders of the local nobility. Although they were members of the Iranian aristocracy, they had not been part of the old Sassanian apparatus, which had been open only to members of the Zoroastrian tradition. What we see here, then, is the formation of an alliance between two groups that had been outsiders in the late Sassanian period after 600. Zoroastrians were tolerated in high courtly positions; this, at least, is the position of the traditional Islamic narrative.

THE RULE OF THE VIZIERS

The Buddhist temple leaders' authority as viziers in Baghdād is attested by many numismatic witnesses. The names on these coins allow one to see the descent of the viziers from Buddhist leaders in eastern Iran. For example, the leader of the Buddhist cloister near Balkh called *Nawbahar* (from the Sanskrit *nava vihāra*, or "new temple") bore the title of *parmak*, or "leader, chief." This cloister was known as far away as China; the Chinese pilgrimage literature even mentions it.[174] Incidentally, the statues of Buddha in Bamyian, recently destroyed by the Ṭālibān, were further testimony to the presence of Buddhism in the region of eastern Iran.

The Barmakids emerged onto the stage of history as court officials at approximately the same time as the Abbasids. According to the traditional narrative of the historicizing literature of the Abbasid period, the first Barmakid, named Khālid, was the right-hand man and vizier of the first Abbasid (known only from legend) and his successor al-Manṣūr. These Barmakids were then incorporated into close connections with the Abbasid family by means of "adoptions." Later, Khālid's grandson was named the "stepbrother" of Hārūn. These reports bear witness to the uncertainty concerning the descent of the protagonists of the traditional narrative.

Hārūn al-Rashīd appointed Yaḥyā (John), the son of Khālid, as vizier following his accession to the throne. Khālid's grandsons al-Faḍl and Jaʿfar then followed Yaḥyā in this office. In year 186 of the Arabian era, Hārūn al-Rashīd is supposed to have begun the pilgrimage to Mecca. With this report it is clear that Hārūn was already seen as the protector of the holy places in Mecca, but this is likely a later interpretation. In line with the traditional Arabian practice of authority with regard to control of a *ḥaram*, Hārūn's wife, Zubayda, is supposed to have improved the pilgrim road to Mecca that was named after her. This pilgrimage to Mecca was supposedly the turning point in Hārūn's political policies. This report reveals the event (as described) as a *topos*, for after his return from the pilgrimage to Mecca, Hārūn al-Rashīd is supposed to have put aside his Buddhist viziers and their clan. This event thereby ended one half-century of co-regency in the court on the part of the eastern-Iranian aristocracy. However, the Barmakids did leave behind a legacy that would continue to shape the society: an entire class of scribes and chancery officials that they had developed. Under Hārūn's son al-Maʾmūn, the members of the Barmakid clan returned to some level of influence, as one of their members, al-Faḍl bn Sahl, became al-Maʾmūn's vizier as one who understood the relationships with the powers to the East.

JIHĀD AS A REAPPROPRIATION OF SASSANIAN POLITICAL POLICY TOWARD BYZANTIUM

The reports that follow the conceptions of the traditional narrative point to the importance of Hārūn al-Rashīd as the leader of the *jihād* against the infidels. The reasons for these battles, which were later transformed in meaning to the Islamic *jihād*, may have been of an entirely different sort. It is quite understandable to see these battles as one part of the continuation of the Sassanian political policy toward Byzantium. Considering the inner unrest in wide portions of Iran, this focus on the traditional foreign enemy confirmed the leader in Baghdad in a historically developed leadership role. To attack a Byzantium suffering from inner weakness stood in the tradition of the opportunistic conquests of the time of the Marwānids in North Africa and Spain. That Hārūn was fighting against a woman and had to deal with a woman on the Byzantine side (Empress Irene, ruled 797–802) seems not to have disturbed him at all.

His own wife, Zubayda, had already achieved the right of minting coins. Her coins do not mention Hārūn al-Rashīd at all. Rather, she minted coins for thirteen consecutive years in her own name. Apparently, in the year 185 of the Arabian era, only the regulations concerning succession were of meaning for Hārūn's wife. This granddaughter of al-Manṣūr had sought to ameliorate the dangerous conflict between Hārūn's son, al-Maʾmūn, and her own son (born later), al-Amīn;[175] this she attempted by citing a Qurʾānic text on her coins, namely, sura 15:47–48: "And We remove whatever rancour may be in their breasts. As brethren, face to face, (they rest) on couches raised. Toil cometh not unto them there, nor will they be expelled from thence" (Pickthall's translation). The idea was that the conditions of paradise were to have prevailed in the immediate future. Consequently, it should not come as a surprise that the court in Baghdad welcomed Zubayda's son, al-Amīn, as the successor of Hārūn al-Rashīd.

AL-MA'MŪN

AL-MA'MŪN'S ALLIANCE WITH THE ALIDS

Thanks to a number of his allies, al-Ma'mūn had pushed out Zubayda's son, who had been chosen by the court. In the course of the conflicts, all the parties had been weakened, until only the Alids remained on the scene as opponents of al-Ma'mūn. Al-Ma'mūn freed himself from their opposition by means of a strategy of embrace, for in the year 201 of the Arabian era (817)—the turn from the second to the third century of the Arabian era did not end up being the date of the end of the world, but the end was still seen as possibly near, as the contemporary expectation in Ḥimṣ of the return of the Messiah testifies—al-Ma'mūn decided upon 'Alī bn Mūsā al-Kāẓim as his successor. Silver coins that document this end-time thinking on the part of al-Ma'mūn mention the Alid as *al-Amīr Riḍā walī 'ahd al-muslimīn 'Alī bn Mūsā bn 'Alī bn Abī Ṭālib* ("Emir Riḍā, successor to the throne of the Muslims, 'Alī, son of Moses, son/descendant of 'Alī bn Abī Ṭālib").[176]

In the inscriptions of this issue of coins that name the Alid as the successor, al-Ma'mūn calls himself *Khalīfat Allāh.* Here we again see the caliph's protocol in the form we know from 'Abd al-Malik, albeit under different circumstances. The term *Khalīfa* had by this time already been often used in connection with the Abbasids. The phrase *Khalīfat Allāh*, on the other hand, first appeared in the time of al-Ma'mūn in connection with coins that name the Alid as the successor to the throne. The idea of the *Khalīfat Allāh* as a spokesperson for God was a reaction on the part of the Marwānid 'Abd al-Malik to the claim of the Byzantine emperor in presenting himself as a *servus Christi.* Al-Ma'mūn took this formula up again, but he filled it with new life by using it in contrast to the claims of the Alid. The Alid exchanged roles with al-Ma'mūn; the Alid *imām* became the *amīr*, and the legacy of 'Alī's claims became the legacy of worldly authority. Once he had put the Alid aside, al-Ma'mūn once again took up the title *Khalīfat Allāh.*[177] After this role reversal was complete, only al-Ma'mūn remained as both *Imām* and *Khalīfat Allāh.* John Walker was the first to point to this phenomenon, namely, that the title of *Khalīfat Allāh* reappeared in protocols after an absence of more than a century.[178]

The idea we find in the book *God's Caliph*,[179] that of an understanding of the office from a mythical early period up to that of the Abbasids, is simply not attested by the testimony of the inscriptions. *Khalīfat Allāh* at the time of ʿAbd al-Malik is not the same as *Khalīfat Allāh* at the time of Maʾmūn; the use of the title in a mythical Meccan early period was only current in the historicizing literature of the Abbasid period.

On his way to sole authority, al-Maʾmūn freed himself from al-Faḍl bn Sahl (first his teacher, later his vizier) in the year 202 of the Arabian era. It is reported that the latter was the son of a Zoroastrian. He entered the court as a member of the Barmakids, just one year before the Alid was put aside. His title in the coin inscriptions was *al-amīr*, for al-Maʾmūn had already usurped the title of *imām* in the year 194 of the Arabian era.[180] This move was understandable in that year, given the possibility of the end of the world at the coming turn of the century. We must here remember the seldom-pious ʿUmar II, who is noted in the traditional literature for handling well the change from the first into the second century.

In this way al-Maʾmūn, as *imām* and *Khalīfat Allāh*, embodied from here on the example of the ideal leader in both secular and sacred matters; the literature of the Abbasid period saw this ideal embodied even by the first caliphs in the mythical homeland of the prophet of the Arabians.

Al-Maʾmūn's perspective can be seen in the changes of the coin images beginning in the year 204 of the Arabian era. The reformed type of dirham from Madīnat al-Salām was anonymous. This anonymous coin could also be found later in both the east and west, in both Merv and Miṣr. Al-Maʾmūn indicated his interest in the state of affairs under the Marwānid Sayyids, when the ruler did not rule, but rather was revered as a primary religious thinker and, running an efficient and anonymous government, issued anonymous coins bearing the religious message from many places in the Arabian empire.

AL-MAʾMŪN IN BAGHDAD

At the time of al-Maʾmūn's return in the year 204 of the Arabian era, Baghdad was a magnetic urban area, an intellectual center with a diverse population. "The most characteristic feature of this . . . period is the extreme diversity of people and of doctrines; it is a case of a collection of distinguished individuals, of often 'colorful' personalities, rather than continuous and homogenous associations."[181] An important Jewish community also resided there; they not only studied the Talmud, but they also worked on the development of the Mishnah (in Arabic, *sunna*). Manichaeans had made known the "book" of their founder, Mani. The Zoroastrians were followed by the example of the Christians, who dispersed their own scriptures, namely, a harmony of the New Testament in one book. The author of this edition of the New Testament, Tatian, who came from northern Iraq, had already enjoyed great success in the second century with his harmony of the Gospels, the "Diatessaron." The foundational idea of his theology, of a "divine Truth exclusively understood" (Carsten Colpe), stood behind this text. The early existence of the New Testament in the form of a Gospel harmony—a comprehensive text in one volume—may have justified the later rejection of the translation of all four Gospels into Aramaic in the form of the fifth-century "Peshitta." From then on, the complete translation of all four Gospels was regarded by the Arabians as a falsification of the original one-volume book.

The Zoroastrians had collected and canonized the sacred writings of their faith community. Following their tradition, they gathered together the fragments of the Avesta from the time of the Sassanian ruler Shāpūr I (241–272). The Avesta in this early form was no longer written as a mnemonic construction, intended to help the priest to remember the text. A few centuries later, this form would lead to the creation of an alphabet that was used solely for writing the Zoroastrian religious texts.[182] At the time of al-Ma'mūn, prophetic literature had been committed to writing to such a degree that:

1. The Jews were able to refer to their "book" in a written form. The Talmud supplemented this book, and they were working on the Mishnah.
2. The Zoroastrians could present their "book" in the form of the collected Avesta. There was also current an apologetic literature, represented by the *Shkand-Gumanik Vichar* and the *Denkart*. It is interesting to note that the appearance of the *Denkart* was approximately contemporary to the edition of the Qur'ān, intended to be the final one, in the court of al-Ma'mūn, which should be assigned to the years between 204 and 218 of the Arabian era.
3. The Christians were able, on the one hand, to offer their book in the form of Tatian's Gospel harmony; on the other hand, however, the Aramaic translation of the Gospels was also current and became the foundation of the later Islamic discussion of the "falsification" of the text.

4. The Arabs were only able to testify to their religious tradition, in the realm of the exercise of authority and in that of the court, by means of the Qur'ānic materials. These materials were not yet thought of as a single, independent book; rather, they were still considered to be apocryphal texts (*kitāb Allāh*). The word "Qur'ān," originally Aramaic, is not found anywhere in the early Arabic inscriptions. The only reference in these inscriptions to a commonly known text (*kitāb Allāh*) is that in the inscription from Medina from the year 135 of the Arabian era. As *Imām* and *Khalīfat Allāh*, then, al-Ma'mūn's goal must have been the creation of an independent tradition of his own spiritual authority, a tradition not recognizably derived from the Christian tradition (for this the churches of the future were responsible). His father, Hārūn al-Rashīd, had continued to work on its Arabian foundation, in that he took over the function of the lord of the *ḥaram* of Mecca. Hārūn al-Rashīd's wife did the same, in that she built up the pilgrimage business by improving the pilgrim road. Al-Ma'mūn now turned his eye to the more visible work, which made possible the overcoming of the tribal structure of the society and the calcification of the tribal religion.

The idea of the *umma*, the single community, belonged to this process; the community was no longer the tribal-group-as-religious-group, in which al-Ma'mūn played the roles of *Imām* and *Khalīfat Allāh*. The discovery of traditions had to proceed in such a fashion that all religious movements could be localized with "Arabian" origins, within the panorama of the theological history so that no individuals could become known in the future as relatives of the Prophet, and thereby make claims of their own.[183]

AL-MA'MŪN ON THE ROAD TO EGYPT—LIKE ALEXANDER

Al-Ma'mūn had stayed in the eastern portion of the Arabian Empire, in Khurāsān (Chorasan), for more than ten years before settling down in Baghdad. The conditions there, as reported by the traditional narrative for the years after 127 of the Arabians (729), actually reflect the end of the reign of Hārūn al-Rashīd. The historical prototype of the Abū Muslim of the literature is the *Imām* al-Ma'mūn, who, having come from the east, entered Baghdad with his eastern Iranian-Arabian and Turkish legions in year 204 of the Arabian era. Islam, as it was understood after him, was his own creation.

His time in the east, in regions that reached as far as the borders of China, had given al-Ma'mūn the experience of a new journey on the heels of "Alexander the Great." Just as Alexander had once done, al-Ma'mūn took a trip with an entourage of scholars and philosophers. If Alexander, the student of Aristotle, left his western homeland as a Greek and died in Babylon as a divine king, then al-Ma'mūn, the "son of a Persian woman," after traveling in the east, followed the sun to the west.

Just as Alexander had opened the East to the Hellenistic world, so also al-Ma'mūn opened the West to the members of his school; in addition, during a trip to Egypt, he took the Western tradition of the Arabians into his own possession. Up to the time of this undertaking, the reign of the Abbasids had been a post-Sassanian Arabian-Iranian affair. After al-Ma'mūn's move to the West, though, the tradition of the Syrian Arabs was included again. In addition, their language and theological history was considered in the synthesis of the ideas of the "Arab" and of the "prophet of the Arabians" developed in al-Ma'mūn's Academy.

Along with his scholarly circle, the *Imām* traveled by military escort along Abraham's route to the west. His journey brought him from Mesopotamia to Abraham's new home in Ḥarrān. There he met with the Gnostics of Ḥarrān, whom he considered to be the Sabians mentioned in the Qur'ān. Their abilities and knowledge were well-known, and they provided important services to the Academy in Baghdad.

Fig. 29: Coin in the style of the Abbasids from Bust in the year 209. The reverse shows the name Ṭalḥa, the ruler in Khurāsān. The inscription also mentions his prefect ʿAbd Allāh al-Ṭalḥī. Al-Ma'mūn is not mentioned as *Amīr al-mu'minīn*, nor as *Imām*, nor as *Khalīfa*.

After a military skirmish on Byzantine soil, the *Imām* went on to Damascus and visited the ruins of the Marwānid building complexes, as well as the *masjid al-Walīd*, the prayer location that is today called "the mosque of the Umayyads." It is not difficult to imagine that he would have read both inscriptions carefully, and that he would have accepted them as consonant with his own program. In the text of the Damascus inscription from the year 86 of the Arabian era, he would have read a confirmation of the work of the prophet of the Arabians, "Muḥammad." In the seventh line of the inscription, the text reads *wa-nabiyunā muḥammad* ("And our prophet is Muḥammad"). At the time of al-Walīd, people had understood this quite differently. At that time the term *muḥammad* still referred to Jesus and communicated the idea that "Our prophet (Jesus) is chosen/to be praised."

The expedition continued from there to Egypt. There the *Imām* stood in front of the pyramids, just as Napoleon would do nearly one thousand years later. Napoleon's expedition had enormous consequences for scholarship, which was the religion of the French Republic. As it continued, al-Ma'mūn's expedition was concerned with the Nile and its source. The ruler of Mesopotamia was standing on the banks of the river of strangers, the lifeblood of the second high culture of previous millennia. Here Moses had been set afloat, and here he had been saved. Al-Ma'mūn saw it all with his own eyes.

As the conclusion of his scholarly expedition through the world of the Qur'ān, al-Ma'mūn visited Jerusalem.[184] In al-Quds (Jerusalem), al-Ma'mūn was able to explain the inscription in the Dome of the Rock. The inscription written on the inner portion of the octagon, on the southern side, was read to him as though it concerned a succession of a personal name and the name of a father: "Muḥammad (bn) 'Abd Allāh." This text had formerly been understood as referring to the "chosen/praised servant of God." However, due to the characteristics of Arabic writing, as well as the characteristics of the writing of Arabic names, in which the name of the father always follows one's personal name, it was possible to see this text as proof of the existence of a "Muḥammad, son of 'Abd Allāh."

Al-Ma'mūn sealed this legacy of a proclamation in pure Arabic language. Following old Oriental tradition, he obliterated the mention of 'Abd al-Malik's name. In the midst of 'Abd al-Malik's protocol *'Abd Allāh 'Abd [. . .] Amīr al-mu'minīn*, al-Ma'mūn put his own title and name *'Abd Allāh al-Imām al-Ma'mūn*. With this action he ensured the validity of the *Ekthesis* as he understood it. The dating to the year 72 was preserved. The *Imām* al-

Ma'mūn was then able to understand this number as a indicator of time following the Arabic festival calendar, beginning with the Hijra of Muḥammad, the prophet of the Arabians, from Mecca to Medina.

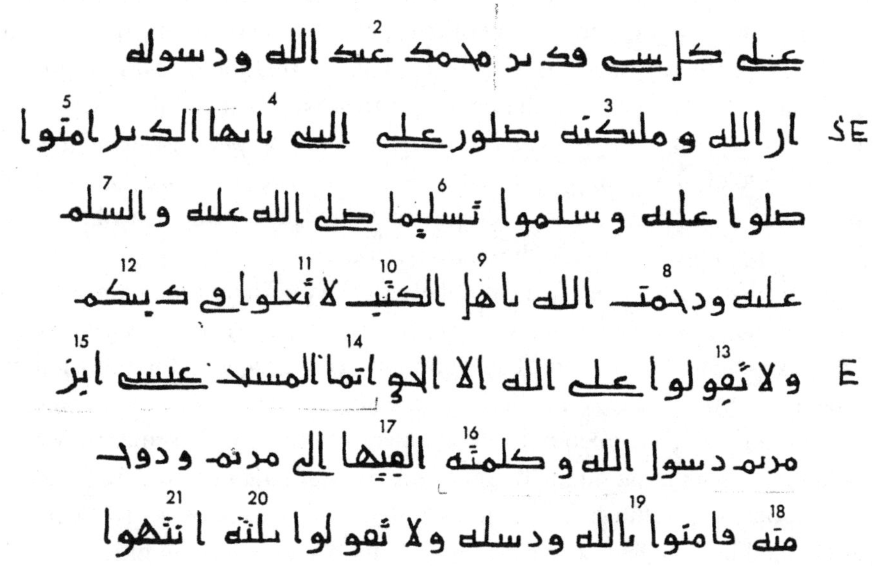

Fig. 30: Excerpt from the inscription in the Dome of the Rock.

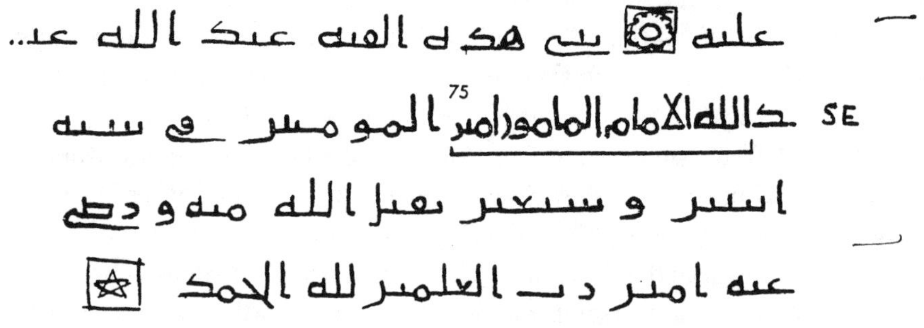

Fig. 31: *Al-Imām al-Ma'mūn Amīr* appears in the inscription in the Dome of the Rock.

SUMMARY

BUILDING INSCRIPTIONS

It is possible to employ a significant number of imperial inscriptions and building inscriptions in order to evaluate the epigraphic witnesses to Arabic rule between the years 664 and 839. These inscriptions have never been comparatively investigated. The inscriptions involved are those of:

1. Maavia, in Hammat Gader, from the year 42 of the Arabian era (664)
2. Mu'āwiya, in the vicinity of al-Ṭā'if, from the year 58 of the Arabian era (680)
3. 'Abd al-Malik, in the Dome of the Rock in Jerusalem, from the year 72 (694)
4. 'Abd al-Malik, on the road from Damascus to Jerusalem, from the year 73 of the Arabian era (692–693)
5. al-Walīd, in the Mosque of the Umayyads in Damascus, from the year 86 of the Arabian era (705)
6. al-Walīd, in the Mosque of the Umayyads in Damascus, from the year 87 of the Arabian era (705–706)
7. al-Hishām, in Qaṣr al-Khayr near Ḥimṣ, from the year 110 of the Arabian era (728–729)
8. The anonymous Arabian ruler, on the house of prayer in al-Madinah, from the year 135 of the Arabian era (753)

In addition, we may add building inscriptions from governors:

9. The bridge of Fusṭāṭ, in the name of 'Abd al-'Azīz bn Marwān, from the year 69 of the Arabian era (688–689)

In each instance these inscriptions give the protocol of the ruler as *'Abd Allah*. Their function is expressed as *Amīr al-mu'minīn*. As *Amīr al-mu'minīn*, the ruler was the leader of the protectors and thereby the highest guarantor of tribal justice. The title had no religious meaning whatsoever. The person next in line to him was the *Amīr*, as the inscription from Fusṭāṭ bears witness. The title *Khalīfa* ("caliph") does not appear in these inscriptions.

TITULATURES

The title *Khalīfat Allāh* ("Speaker for God") first appears in inscriptions on coins from the time of ʿAbd al-Malik. The title functions here as an answer to the Byzantine imperial protocols of the time, which had begun to refer to the emperor as *servus Dei*. ʿAbd al-Malik's successors did not retain this designation.

It is only under al-Ma'mūn that the title next appears in coin inscriptions, namely, in the year 201 of the Arabian era (817). Al-Ma'mūn had also taken on the title *Imām* in the year 194 of the Arabian era (810). Consequently, al-Ma'mūn called himself *Imām* only beginning in the year 194 (810) and *Khalīfat Allāh* beginning in the year 201 (817). The purported early use of these titles and functions in the protocols of the "caliphs" is not supported by the testimony of the inscriptions. The references in the historicizing literature (Ṭabarī et al.) appear then to be later retrojections into a mythical early period.

SYSTEMS OF DATING

The datings follow an "era of the Arabians." This system begins in the year 622, the year of the Byzantine victory over the Sassanians. The self-rule of the Arabians dates from this year forward. In the year 20 of the Arabian era (641), the Christian Arab Maavia (in Arabic, Muʿāwiya) took up the succession after the death of the Byzantine emperor Heraclius as the ruler of the formerly Byzantine east. In his inscription from the baths of Gadara in Palestine, he used the system of dating traditional for that time and place: first he gave the era of the city (*colonia*), then the date following the Byzantine tax year, and finally the date following the era of the Arabians. It is impossible to determine from the inscriptions when the understanding of dating following an era of the Arabians was changed into a dating following the Arabian festival calendar, and thereby the era of the prophet of the Arabians. This impossibility is due to the fact that the Hijra of the prophet of the Arabians, well known from the traditional literature, is nowhere mentioned in the inscriptions.

RELIGIOUS FORMULAE

The inscriptions of Muʿāwiya from the years 42 and 58 of the Arabian era use no religious formulae whatsoever; even the *basmala* does not appear as an opening formula.

THE SERVANT OF GOD

ʿAbd al-Malik's inscription in the Dome of the Rock in Jerusalem from the year 72 of the Arabian era (691–692) gives the first datable reference to a change in the religious state of affairs. In the inner portion of the octagon, the part of the inscription appears which, in the style of an *Ekthesis*, calls for debate concerning an agreement regarding the understanding of the text (duty to Islam). This call is directed to Christendom as a whole: *Yā ahla l-kitāb* (You people of the written text!). Concerning Christology, the text argues that the apostle of God is an *ʿAbd Allāh*, a "servant of God." The "servant of God" is *muḥammadun*, "chosen/praised." The "chosen/praised servant of God" is the *masīḥ ʿĪsā bn Maryam*, "the Messiah, Jesus, the son of Mary, is the apostle of God."

In addition, the inscription of the unknown ruler on the house of prayer in Medina, dated to the year 135 of the Arabian era (753), also speaks of the "praised servant of God" as "apostle." The conception of Jesus as a "servant of God" and "praised/chosen" is first documented in coin inscriptions in the region of Iran between the years 38 and 60 (658/659–679/680).

ISLĀM

In the period under consideration, the movement which stood for the establishment of an understanding of Jesus as the "chosen/praised servant of God" disintegrated. During the rule of the Abbasid caliph al-Maʾmūn, around 217–218 of the Arabian era (832–833), the conception of a Muḥammad bn ʿAbd Allāh ("the Praised One, son of the Servant of God") as a messenger of God became anchored in the realm of a new national-religious movement of the understanding of Islām.

NOTES

1. Julius Wellhausen, *Das Arabische Reich und sein Sturz* (Berlin: G. Reimer, 1902), p. vi: "Without a doubt there *was* a tradition among the Syrians themselves, which is to say among the Syrian Arabs. Unfortunately, it has been lost to us. One finds traces of this tradition in Baladhuri, and possibly also in the Kalbite Avanâ who lived in Kūfa, who was connected to Syria through his tribe, and whom Ṭabarī quite often cited (usually following Ibn Kalbi) as a reporter concerning Syrian matters. One can best get to know the spirit of this Syrian tradition from Christian chronicles, among which the *Continuatio* of Isidore of Hispalis must be mentioned. The Umayyads appear there in a very different and much more positive light than we are used to seeing them. Among the Arabs, their enemies most often had the last word, and so their story suffered significantly."

2. H. Humbach, "New Coins from Fromo Kesaro," in *India and the Ancient World: History, Trade, and Culture before* AD *650 (Festschrift in honor of Professor P. H. L. Eggermont)*, ed. Gilbert Pollet, Orientalia Lovaniensia Analecta, no. 25 (Leuven: Departmente Oriëntalistiek, 1987), p. 83: "Both the fact that Popp's Arabo-Sassanian coins have been overstruck by Fromo Kesaro and the triumphant nature of the text of the overstruck inscription suggest that the coins originated from booty, or rather from a tribute imposed upon the conquered Arabs. Thus, these coins spotlight events of late pre-Islamic and early Islamic history of central Asia (unrecorded by Muslim historians), which took place after 738 but are otherwise difficult to locate."

3. Wellhausen, *Arabische Reich*, iv: "Mommsen once said that uneducated people require no proof that the stories that begin with the statement that the narrator received his information himself from direct participants are, generally speaking, not true."

4. R. B. Serjeant, "Ḥaram and ḥawṭah, the Sacred Enclave in Arabia," in *Mélanges Taha Ḥusain: Offert pàr ses amis et ses disciples à l'occasion de son 70ième anniversaire*, ed Abdurrahman Badawi (Cairo: Dar al-Maaref, 1962), p. 57: "Before looking for Jewish and Christian elements in Islām it would be wise to establish what is specifically Arabian, and I think this will be found to be vastly greater than many western scholars have supposed." Naturally, the expressions "Arabians" and "Arabian" are used here uncritically. We do not know who the *ʿarab* of the Greek and Roman sources were. The Romans tended to refer to the Nabataeans as "Arabians." These groups were portrayed as living in the steppes as Bedouins, enjoying freedom of movement, and forbidding the enjoyment of wine as well as the cultivation of land and the building of fixed houses. See on this topic J. Patrich, *The Formation of Nabatean Art: Prohibition of a Graven Image among the Nabateans* (Jerusalem: Magnes Press, 1990), p. 33.

5. Quoted in Ernst A. Knauf, *Die Umwelt des Alten Testaments* (Stuttgart: Verlag Katholisches Bibelwerk, 1994), p. 20.

6. See M. L. Bates, "The 'Arab-Byzantine' Bronze Coinage of Syria: An Innovation by ʿAbd al-Malik," in *A Colloquium in Memory of George Carpenter Miles (1904–1975)* (New York: American Numismatic Society, 1976), p. 17: "I have become more and more convinced of the uselessness of these three categories [Arab-Byzantine, Arab-Sasanian, post-reform coinage], which I believe ought to be replaced with an organisation of early Islamic coinage based only on the great regional subdivisions of the empire, bringing together all the coins of each mint within each region in chronological order without respect to type. In each region, Muslim coinage began with imitative or derivate types, but the nature of the imitations and the pace of evolution toward purely Islamic coinage was different. Even after the adoption of the new Islamic type, the organization of minting and even the weight standards and fineness of the various denominations varied from region to region. The coinage of the early caliphs and the Umayyads, like the coinage of any large Islamic empire, ought to be studied first mint by mint, then province by province and region by region, before we can think about wide generalized categories encompassing the whole."

7. Georg Ostrogorsky, *Geschiche des Byzantinischen Staates*, Handbuch der Altertumswissenschaft, no. 12 (Munich: C. H. Beck, 1952), p. 81: "The war began in a spirit of religious excitement, a spirit unknown in former times. It was the first 'typical' medieval war, reminiscent of the later Crusades."

8. Gernot Wiessner, "Christlicher Heiligenkult im Umkreis eines sassanidischen Grosskönigs," in *Festgabe deutscher Iranisten zur 2500 Jahrfeier Irans,* ed. Wilhelm Eilers (Stuttgart: Hochwacht Druck, 1971), p. 148.

9. Ibid., p. 144.

10. Franz Altheim, *Entwicklungshilfe im Altertum: Die grossen Reiche und ihre Nachbarn,* Rowohlts deutsche Enzyklopädie, no. 162 (Reinbek: Rowohlt, 1962), p. 113.

11. See line 92 of the inscription; Ernst Herzfeld, *Paikuli: Monument and Inscription of the Early History of the Sasanian Empire,* Forschungen zur islamischen Kunst, no. 3 (Berlin: Reimer, 1924).

12. Gustav Rothstein, *Die Dynastie der Lahmiden in al-Hira: Ein Versuch zur arabisch-persischen Geschichte zur Zeit der Sasaniden* (Berlin: Reuther and Reichard, 1899), p. 143.

13. See the article "Biṭrīk" in the second edition of the *Encyclopaedia of Islam.* Two Ghassanids are mentioned as bearers of this lofty appellation, namely, al-Ḥārith b. Jabala around 540 CE, and his son and successor al-Mundhir around 570.

14. Cf. the presentation of Yehuda D. Nevo and Judith Koren, *Crossroads to Islam: The Origins of the Arab Religion and the Arab State* (Amherst, NY: Prometheus, 2003), pp. 27–46.

15. Cf. here I. Shahid's article "Ghassān" in the second edition of the *Encyclopaedia of Islam* for notes on the dated Arabic inscriptions of the Ghassanids in Syria in the period from 559–578. The architrave of St. Sergius's church (erected in 512) bears the following words in Greek, Aramaic, and Arabic script: "This is a holy place." According to the latest research, this inscription seems to be the oldest extant epigraphical witness of Arabic anywhere. This oldest witness to inscriptional Arabic can be seen without great difficulty in Brussels. The three-meter-long block of gray basalt resides in the exhibit of the Musées Royaux d'Art et d'Histoire, Inventory no. A 1308. Cf. Christian Robin, "L'écriture arabe et l'arabie," *Pour la science (Dossier)* October 2002, pp. 62–69.

16. See the reference to the Arabian Negev in Nevo and Koren, *Crossroads*, p. 47.

17. Ibid., pp. 63–64.

18. Concerning the details of this action, along with the changes in Persian politics that occurred three years later and benefited the Christians in Jerusalem, see M. Avi-Yonah, *Paulys Realencyclopädie der classischen Altertumswissenschaft, Suppl. Bd.* XIII (1973), col. 448.

19. Cf. Cécile Morrisson, *Catalogue des monnaies byzantines de la Bibliothèque nationale* (Paris, 1970), p. 294: "Buste de f. de Chosroes portant le stemma et la cuirasse./IB Au centre, croix potencée au-dessus d'un globe."

20. The role of the emperor against the church has been discussed by many scholars, e.g., Ostrogorsky, *Geschichte,* p. 87, beginning with Justinian I.

21. Ibid., p. 81.

22. Ibid., pp. 81–82: "[The chronicle of] Theophanes 303 (concerning the year 622). . . . This highly important section states that the founding of the *themes* preceded Heraclius' battles against Persia chronologically. After this one must pay attention not only to the perspectives of earlier scholars but also to the outlook of E. Stein, . . . that the establishment of the *themes* 'provides the key to the nearly incredible alteration in the Persian-Byzantine conflict.'" This is disputed by John Haldon and Wolfgang Brandes. Irfan Shahid seems to be among the last supporters of this theory.

23. Ibid., p. 82.

24. Cf. here the study by V. Minorski, "Roman and Byzantine Campaigns in Atropatene," *Bulletin of the School of Oriental and African Studies* 11 (1945).

25. Cf. Ostrogorsky, *Geschichte,* p. 63.

26. Ibid., 83; cf. also the traces of a continuing fear of the Khazars in the apocalyptic prophecies in Ḥimṣ, which were ascribed by later tradents to the time of the Umayyads: "The Turks, including the Khazars, were dangerous warriors, best to be left undisturbed as long as they would cause no trouble. They would, however, eventually erupt and invade Upper Mesopotamia descending on the Euphrates. Then they would be annihilated by divine intervention." This angst was certainly no less potent

at the turn into the third century. Most likely this text concerns a retrojection of present fears into earlier times. See Wilfred Madelung, "Apocalyptic Prophecies in Ḥimṣ in the Umayyad Age," *Journal of Semitic Studies* 31 (1986): 174.

27. T. Daryaee, "The Coinage of Queen Boran and Its Significance for Late Sasanian Imperial Ideology," *Bulletin of the Asia Institute* (1999): 80.

28. Ostrogorsky, *Geschichte,* p. 84.

29. Ibid., pp. 87–88. See also footnote 2 on p. 87, with the literature cited there on the rise of Monotheletism.

30. Ibid., p. 93.

31. Ibid.

32. Richard Nelson Frye, *The Heritage of Persia* (New York: New American Library, 1966), p. 269: "They included the general who had captured Jerusalem, Shahrvaraz, 'the boar of the state' who ruled a few months before he was assassinated."

33. Cf. the article "Laqab" in the second edition of the *Encyclopaedia of Islam.*

34. Cf. Walker, *Catalogue* I, no. 35, p. 25, and the illustration in table V.

35. I am grateful to Prof. Werner Sundermann of Berlin for the suggestion that led to this paragraph. He was so kind as to provide me with both a comprehensive presentation and also detailed information concerning the understanding of *wlwyshnyk'n* and the writing of the infinitive *wurroyistan.* Naturally, though, I alone am responsible for the use of this information.

36. Cf. the article "Amān" in the second edition of the *Encyclopaedia of Islam.*

37. Walker, *Catalogue* I, p. 26.

38. Cf. the presentation of R. B. Serjeant on "Mu'min and Muslim" in "The *Sunnah Jāmi'ah,* Pacts with the Yathrib Jews, and the *taḥrīm* of Yathrib: Analysis and Translation of the Documents Comprised in the So-Called 'Constitution of Medina,'" *Bulletin of the School of Oriental and African Studies* 41 (1978): 12–15. Here one finds a pointer to the practice of Arabian tribal law even today: "I follow Bravmann [M. M. Bravmann, *The Spiritual Background of Early Islam: Studies in Ancient Arab Concepts* (Leiden: Brill, 1972) to some extent in rendering *Mu'min* as 'one who trusts,' but since the *Mu'min* who enjoys the physical security guaranteed to a member of the *Ummat Allāh,* also guarantees that security by his own strong right arm, he is *ipso facto* himself guaranteeing security. *Mu'min* is of course employed in a certain range of senses, but, with the analogy before me of the undertakings that the Ḥaḍrami tribes make to the Manṣab or Lord of a ḥawṭah, it seemed impossible to ignore the fact that *Mu'min* is a person who grants *amān,* i.e., security, safe-conduct, etc."

39. R. B. Serjeant, "The *Sunnah Jāmi'ah,*" p. 18.

40. Adolf Grohmann, *Arabic Inscriptions,* vol. I, part II (Louvain: Publications Universitaires, 1962), no. 268.

41. Joshua Blau, "The Transcription of Arabic Words and Names in the Inscrip-

tion of Muʿāwiya from Hammat Gader," *Israel Exploration Journal* 32, nos. 2–3 (1982): 102.

42. Cf. Y. Hirschfeld and G. Solar, "The Roman Thermae at Hammat Gader: Preliminary Report of Three Seasons of Excavation," *Israel Exploration Journal* 31 (1981): 197–219.

43. Cf. Walker, *Catalogue* II, pp. 32–41.

44. Ibid., p. 253, and table 27.

45. Etienne Combe, Jean Sauvaget, and Gaston Wiet, eds., *Répertoire chronologique d'épigraphie arabe* (Cairo: Impr. de l'Institut français d'archéologie orientale, 1931), text no. 18.

46. Christie's, London, October 16, 2001, Lot 263, no. 5.

47. Nevo and Koren, *Crossroads,* p. 410.

48. Christie's, London, October 16, 2001, Lot 263, no. 12.

49. Cf. Rudi Paret's translation of the Qurʾān at sura 4:172: "Diener Allāhs."

50. Second edition of the *Encyclopaedia of Islam,* I:24.

51. Rothstein, *Dynastie der Laḫmiden*, pp. 20–21, *passim.*

52. Murad Wilfried Hofmann, *Der Koran: das heilige Buch des Islam* (München: Diederichs, 1999), pp. 15f.

53. Cf. the article on Ḥīra in the second edition of the *Encyclopaedia of Islam,* III:462, where the sources of this tradition are given, namely, Ibn Hishām and Ṭabarī.

54. Robert Göbl, *Sasanidische Numismatik,* Handbücher der mittelasiatischen Numismatik, no. 1 (Braunschweig: Klinkhardt and Biermann, 1968), table XV.

55. Combe, Sauvaget, and Wiet, *Répertoire chronologique,* inscription no. 8.

56. J. Green and Y. Tsafrir, "Greek Inscriptions from Hammat Gader: A Poem by the Empress Eudocia and Two Building Inscriptions," *Israel Exploration Journal* 32, nos. 2–3 (1982): 94–95.

57. Wellhausen, *Arabische Reich,* p. 87.

58. The following are the known Arabic inscriptions in Syria from the sixth century: (1.) the inscription on St. Sergius' church in Ruṣāfa; (2.) the inscription of al-Ḥārith b. Jabala on the tower of the cloister of Qaṣr al-Khayr al-Gharbī, dated to 559; (3.) the inscription on the house of Flavius Seos in al-Hayāt in the region of Ḥawrān, dated to 578; and (4.) the fortress of Dumayr with an Arabic inscription from al-Mundhir (569–82). Cf. here the second edition of the *Encyclopaedia of Islam,* II:1021.

59. Heinz Gaube, *Arabosasanidische Numismatik*, Handbücher der mittelasiatischen Numismatik, no. 2 (Braunschweig: Klinkhardt and Biermann, 1973), p. 136.

60. Walker, *Catalogue* I, no. 3, p. 28.

61. Cf. here ibid., pp. 27–29.

62. Walker was aware of the dubiousness of this practice (ibid., p. xxxvii):

"The importance of the coins lies in their providing us with contemporary data for corroborating, supplementing, or at times correcting the historians. Even so, there are numerous cases where the coin evidence cannot be reconciled with the historical tradition."

63. Gaube, *Arabosasanidische Numismatik*, p. 137; pp. 136–41 *passim* offer numerous data concerning the synchronization of coin datings with the dates given in the historicizing literature of the Abbasid period. My own sarcasm with regard to this activity should be obvious, both here and in the paragraphs that follow.

64. Ibid., p. 135: "In the previous chapters we have used primarily the Islamic 'Hijra' system for the reckoning of dates, and when we have spoken of dates on coins, we have restricted our comments to the terms 'year' or 'minting year,' without also indicating to which system of dating these 'years' belong. Our procedure is well-founded, for our concerns are primarily the coins as such, and also a wide-ranging employment of the data to be found thereupon. The chronological ordering and historical evaluation of individual numismatic documents can only be undertaken once they are anchored in a system of coordination of primary data." We do not understand how this system will look and how the data will be processed, so that they are usable as "primary data." The "clear sequence of coin-issues" which Gaube produced is not necessary at all, for researchers avoid taking into consideration the consequences of his datings. As soon as the consequences of the "post-Yazdgard era" on the Hijra era come into his thoughts, he lets the topic drop like a hot potato. A withdrawal from a dating following the Hijra of the prophet of the Arabians could potentially give the impression of a withdrawal from Islām and signify a return to the traditions of Iran.

65. Ibid., p. 7.

66. Gernot Rotter, *Die Umayyaden und der zweite Bürgerkrieg (680–692).* (Wiesbaden: Kommissionsverlag F. Steiner, 1982), p. 85 and n. 568: "I begin here with the mint table in Gaube's *Numismatik,* which surpass the corresponding data in Walker's *Catalogue*."

67. Wiessner, "Christlicher Heiligenkult," p. 146: "It is known from the life of the Monophysite metropolitan Aḥū-d-emmeh that this church leader made attempts to limit the flow of pilgrims from the Sassanian Empire into the city of Sergiopolis in the Byzantine Empire. For this purpose he is reported to have built a basilica of St. Sergius on the pilgrim road into the Byzantine Empire. Fiey has identified this church with a building of the current Qaṣr Serēj, approximately 21 km west of Balad. As Fiey's illustrations in *Sumer* 14 (1958) show, the St. Sergius church west of Balad exhibits surprising similarities with the large basilica of St. Sergius of Ruṣafa."

68. Flavius Josephus, *Antiq.* XVIII.5.

69. On the relationship of Jesus and John, see also J. Hämeen-Antilla, "John

the Baptist and Early Islamic Polemics concerning Jesus," in *Acta Orientalia* (Lund, 1999), pp. 72–87.

70. Cf. here the considerations of Serjeant in his "Ḥaram and ḥawṭah."

71. A. Berman, *Islamic Coins: Exhibition, Winter 1976, L. A. Meyer Memorial Institute for Islamic Art* (Jerusalem: L. A. Meyer Memorial Institute for Islamic Art, 1976), no. 1. Further exemplars with this depiction are known: see Münzenhandlung F. Sternberg, Zürich, Auction of 1978, nos. 1010 and 1011; idem, Auction of 1983, no. 1181; Spink and Son Ltd., Zürich, Auction 31 (1989), no. 204; and in R. Milstein, "Hoard of Umayyad Damascus Coins," *Israel Numismatic Journal* 10 (1988–1989), nos. 132 and 133. Milstein refers to the existence of an unpublicized lot of approximately 500 coins from the same find in Hawrān; these are to be found in the Bibliothèque Nationale in Paris.

72. Walker, *Catalogue* I, pp. 15–16.

73. S. Qedar, "Copper Coinage of Syria in the Seventh and Eighth Century AD," *Israel Numismatic Journal* 10 (1988–1989): 33, plate 6.

74. Enno Littman, *Deutsche-Aksum Expedition,* 4 vols., vol. 1 (Berlin: G. Reimer, 1913), p. 50.

75. An exemplar of a copper coin with this mint location can be found in the Pontifical Biblical Institute in Jerusalem (see also W. Andrew Oddy's incorrect reading of the inscription "CION" on this coin in "The Early Umayyad Coinage of Baisan and Jerash," *ARAM* 6, no. 4 [1994]: 405–18); a second exemplar, of the type of Constans II, exists in a private collection in Germany.

76. Wiessner, "Christlicher Heiligenkult," p. 142: "The closing off of Christians living in the central regions of Iran into the Nestorian 'state church' brought these Christians into theological and political opposition against the inherited enemy of New Iran, that is, New Rome; further, this isolation served as an example of how individuals can hold their ground in a world inimical to their own, namely, by means of deep partisanship for the tasks of *Realpolitik* that the enemy state prescribes, even if this results in theological and religious isolation." On the historical continuity of national Iranian Christianity, see Gernot Wiessner, "Zu den Subskriptionslisten der ältesten christlichen Synoden in Iran," in *Festschrift für Wilhelm Eilers: Ein Dokument der internationalen Forschung zum 27. September 1966,* ed. by Gernot Wiessner (Wiesbaden: O. Harrassowitz, 1967), pp. 288–98.

77. Gaube, *Arabosasanidische Numismatik,* p. 12: "We see a similar and quite curious alteration of a crescent moon (F) into a cross on a series of coins minted by Salm b. Ziyad of Merv and bearing the year 63. H. This is an important detail, because it can hardly be accepted that a cross was inscribed onto coins minted in the time of the Islamic conquests and in a city with a population that was in large proportion Christian simply 'by accident.'"

78. Geo Widengren, *Die Religionen Irans,* Die Religionen der Menschheit, no.

14 (Stuttgart: Kohlhammer, 1965), pp. 274–83, has strengthened the following thesis, formerly proposed by H. S. Nyberg: "We should not doubt at all that the Islamic conquest of Iran put an end to the developing circumstances of the time which could have led to the full Christianization of Iran. It is clear that Zoroastrianism was no equal opponent of Christianity as a living religion."

79. Ostrogorsky, *Geschichte*, n. 1, p. 95: Franz Dölger, Regesten der Kaiserurkunden des Oströmischen Reiches von 565–1453, 5 vols., Corpus der griechischen Urkunden des Mittelalters und der neueren Zeit, Reihe A, Abt. I:1–5 (München: R. Oldenbourg [vols. 1–3] and C. H. Beck [vols. 4–5], 1924–1965), Reg. 230.

80. Walker, *Catalogue* I, p. 40, no. 58.

81. Ibid., p. 46, M. 26.

82. Ibid., nos. 35–37, pp. 25–26; cf. the coins from Dārābjird in the year 41 with his name and with this title. It is clear that Mu'āwiya allowed himself to be called this without suggesting that he descended from the Sufyanids. Ziyād, as the strongman in the region, minted coins in Dārābjird in the year 41; thereupon he gave his heritage as ABU ZUPIL + (pers.) -ān. Scholars should give up the conception of Mu'āwiya as one of the Sufyanids, for nowhere does he call himself such. Further, his successor 'Abd al-Malik called himself, on his Iranian coins, by the following name: APDULMLIK-I MRWAN + (pers.) -ān. This is only a claiming of heritage from a clan, namely, the Marwānān, not descent from a father (or ancestor) named Marwān.

83. Cf. Walker, *Catalogue* I, no. 1, p. 29.

84. Ostrogorsky, *Geschichte,* p. 101.

85. Here one should not overlook a reference to a characterization of Mu'āwiya's position, as provided by Theophanes. Wellhausen took this up and quoted it on p. 86 of his *Arabisches Reich.* According to this report, Mu'āwiya behaved toward his ruling colleagues as a prime councillor among many councillors. M. A. Shaban, *Islamic History* (Cambridge: Cambridge University Press, 1971), p. 57, misunderstood this statement, concluding from the behavior described there that Theophanes translated the title *Amīr al-mu'minīn* as *protosymboulos.*

86. Ostrogorsky, *Geschichte,* p. 101.

87. Ibid., p. 102.

88. Ibid., p. 102, n. 1; Dölger, *Regesten,* Reg. 239.

89. Cf. Walker, *Catalogue* I, ANS 7, p. 33. This dating to the year 53 of the Arabian era has been continually manipulated so that the result is the year 65 of the Hijra. This occurs according to the following method: (1.) what Ṭabarī says, and (2.) what date Ṭabarī gives. Then, one calculates a number X that must always be added to the number given on a set of coins, until one comes to a dating that is possible within the chronology supplied by Ṭabarī. In this way one finds that, in the literature of Islamic studies, the coins of Ibn Zubayr as *Amīr-i mu'minīn* are always dated

according to the fictional "Yazdgard era." To illustrate, by adding this number X (in this case, 12) to a pagan system of dating, the year 53 on a coin becomes the year 65 of the Hijra, and the year 54 on a coin becomes the year 66 of the Hijra. However, as soon as Ibn Zubayr loses power and returns to "Kirmān" (so Gaube) as a pious Muslim, there is no longer any need for a corrective number X in dating his coins. That is, as soon as Ibn Zubayr takes over his benefice in Kirmān as retired *Amīr-i wurroyishnigan,* the numbers given on his coins are understood without any correction as datings following the era of the Hijra (a system, incidentally, that did not even exist at that time). Having become pious, Ibn Zubayr can do nothing other than to give up his pagan style of dating. This account is not credible, but it is accepted nonetheless; see Walker, *Catalogue* I, nos. 28–41, pp. 30–32.

90. Cf. the coins, mainly those dated around the year 41 of the Arabian era. The *ʿAbd Allāh* formula appears on coins with indications of eight different original mints (Gaube, *Arabosasanidische Numismatik,* p. 59).

91. Cf. his coins from this time period in Walker, *Catalogue* I, pp. 30–32, 36.

92. Gaube, *Arabosasanidische Numismatik,* p. 36: "The name of the prophet Muḥammad is found on coins of the Chusro type . . . ."

93. If one does archaeology on the dictionary, one finds the term *muḥammad* already in Ugarit: *mḥmd arzh,* or, the "most desired" or "excellent" gold. Cf. here also Cyrus H. Gordon, *Ugaritic Manual* (Rome: Pontificium Institutum Biblicum, 1955), text 51: V.78 and 51: V.10.

94. H. Nützel, *Katalog der orientalischen Münzen,* vol. 1 (Berlin: W. Spemann, 1898), no. 93, table 2; this coin is also mentioned in Walker, *Catalogue* I, plate XXXXVII, no. 8, p. 124, where Walker reads the number on the coin as "40," therefore as "year 40" (of the Arabian era).

95. F. Timmerman, "An Unpublished Arab-Sasanian Dirham of the Hitherto Unidentified Governor Muḥammad," *Oriental Numismatic Society Newsletter* 92–93 (1984). The same exemplar appears in *Arabian Coins and Medals,* Islamic Coin Auction, London no. 3, 2001, no. 1. The coin is undated.

96. Gaube, *Arabosasanidische Numismatik,* p. 59: "There is no doubt that this person ʿAbd Allāh, who had coins minted in both Bishapur and also Merv, is ʿAbd Allāh b. Amīr." This mention of doubt suggests concerns about the traditional, authoritative account. One can already see something similar in the Qurʾān, at sura 2:2: "This is the Scripture whereof there is no doubt . . ." (Pickthall's translation).

97. "While much is unknown about the history of Azerbaijan during this time, the 'Muhammad' mentioned on the coinage may refer to Muḥammad b. Marwān." The whole article can be found in S. D. Sears, "The Sasanian Style Coins of 'Muhammad' and Some Related Coins, *Yarmouk Numismatics* 7 (AH 1414/1995): 7–17.

98. One can also find Arab-Sassanian coins with the *muḥammad* motto among coin dealers. Cf. Morton & Eden, London (auction) 2003, Lot no. 180, which

includes two different exemplars, the one undated and the other with the number 47 (?). Cf. also Stephen Album, *A Checklist of Islamic Coins* (Santa Rosa, CA: S. Album, 1998), p. 19: "Arab-Armenian [this series has been described in a forthcoming article by A. Nikitin, to be published in the proceedings of a 1993 conference at Tübingen]: E97, In the Name of Muhammad (unidentified), AR zuzun, RR, With Arabic *muḥammad* before bust, *waf* ("full") in margin. . . . F97: AR zuzun, similar but Pahlavi *MḤMṬ* before bust, Arabic *muḥammad* in margin, RRR."

99. A. S. Kirkbridge, "Coins of the Byzantine-Arab Period," *Quarterly of the Dept. of Antiquities in Palestine* 62 (1947). The same coin is also described in Walker, *Catalogue* II, p. 52, ASK. 6.

100. Clive Foss, "Anomalous Arab-Byzantine Coins—Some Problems and Suggestions," *O.N.S. Newsletter* 166 (London, 2001): 7, no. 9: "The Qedar coin shows that the obv. figure bore a cross on its crown and that another cross appeared above the M of the rev. It and the present example both reveal the rev. legend clearly. Mr. Qedar plausibly reads this mintmark, bi-ʿAmman." The coin mentioned can currently be found in the Israel Museum in Jerusalem. In the meantime, other exemplars have come to light. Cf., e.g., *Islamic Coin Auction in London,* Baldwin's Auction Ltd., 12 October 2004, nos. 3117 and 3118, with commentary: "The issue was probably issued by a minor chief named Muhammad rather than in the name of the prophet." In this statement the commentator does not betray knowledge of the fact that the personal name Muḥammad does not appear in the realm of the mission for religious politics until the reign of ʿAbd al-Malik. The earliest date of such usage appears in a coin legend for the year 67 of the Arabian era (686–687); cf. Walker, *Catalogue* I, p. 95, no. 5 (Muḥammad ibn ʿAbd Allāh, Dirham from Herat). Here one also finds the name of the father, which was typical when giving a personal name.

101. Cf. Bank Leu AG, Zürich, *Auction 29,* 1981, no. 6, p. 6.

102. Patricia Crone and Martin Hinds, *God's Caliph: Religious Authority in the First Centuries of Islam* (Cambridge: Cambridge University Press, 1986), pp. 24–25: "It is a striking fact that such documentary evidence as survives from the Sufyanid period makes no mention of the messenger of God at all. The papyri do not refer to him. The Arab inscriptions of the Arab-Sasanian coins only invoke Allāh, not his rasūl; and the Arab-Byzantine bronze coins on which Muḥammad appears as rasūl Allāh, previously dated to the Sufyanid period, have now been placed in that of the Marwānids. Even the two surviving tombstones fail to mention the rasūl, though both mention Allāh; and the same is true of Muʿāwiya's inscription at Ṭaʾif."

103. Ostrogorsky, *Geschichte,* p. 106; cf. also his reference there to Dölger, *Regesten,* p. 257.

104. E. Ullendorf, "Hebraic-Jewish Elements in Abyssinian (Monophysite) Christianity," *Journal of Semitic Studies* 1 (London, 1956): 253: "To the Semites'

unified conception of life, it would appear, social, political, and religious institutions are one and have no separate existence."

105. Samuel Krauss, *Das Leben Jesu nach jüdischen Quellen* (Berlin: S. Calvary, 1902), pp. 48f., 85f.

106. The Ethiopic church calls itself, even to this day, *yä-Itopeya täwahedo orthodox betä Krestiyan.*

107. M. B. Schub, "True Belief—A New Translation and Commentary on Sûra 112," *Zeitschrift für Arabische Linguistik* 22 (1990): 81: "Verse 1: (a) ʾaḥadun: The rules of the ʿArabiyya require wāḥidun here."

108. Ullendorf, "Hebraic-Jewish Elements," p. 249: "With the strong consciousness among Ethiopians of being the heirs of Israel as the Chosen People, circumcision has become to Ethiopians a religious as well as national duty, the symbol of their status as a New Zion."

109. Ostrogorsky, *Geschichte,* p. 111.

110. Walker, *Catalogue* II, pp. 30–31; he ascribes the provenance of these coins to North Syria due to the appearance of the national religious symbol, the "Stone."

111. Rudolf Sellheim, *Der zweite Bürgerkrieg im Islam (680–692): Das Ende des mekkan.-medines. Vorherrschaft* (Wiesbaden: F. Steiner, 1970), p. 95: "The region's population was, as we have said, loyal to the government. The leadership tolerated a not insignificant Christian minority in many cities, and yes even a Christian *majority* in several locations. Further, the rulers had left intelligent Christians at their governmental posts, as a result of a lack of Muslims with skills appropriate for the jobs; they had even on occasion recruited Christians *into* such positions." This author connects this period of blossoming in Islām with the presence of Christians, as well as the appropriation of Byzantine institutions, such as mail service (as though such an institution had not already existed in ancient eastern empires). Such descriptions of the circumstances of the time, written by scholars of Islamic studies, are nonetheless numerous and completely unhistorical.

112. Cf. the article on "Dīn" in the second edition of the *Encyclopaedia of Islam.*

113. Walker, *Catalogue* II, no. 1, p. 25.

114. Foss, "Anomalous Arab-Byzantine Coins," p. 9: "This raises the curious possibility that these coins portray not the caliph, but the prophet Mohammed. At first sight, this seems highly implausible, for Islam is well known for its prohibition of images, and the Prophet himself is never portrayed until the late Middle Ages, and then veiled. Yet so little is known of early Islamic iconography, that the possibility may remain open. As Prof. Oleg Grabar informs me, there was apparently no formal prohibition against representing the Prophet in early Islam, but a general avoidance of images begins under ʿAbd al-Malik."

115. Cf. R. W. Hamilton in *Quarterly of the Department of Antiquities in Pales-*

tine 14 (Jerusalem, 1950): plate XLV, 2. Nonetheless, George C. Miles, "The Earliest Arab Gold Coinage," *ANS Museum Notes* 13, no. 36 (1967): 216, points to the similarities between the depiction of the Arabian ruler on the Islamic coins and the depiction of Christ on the Byzantine coins: "his long hair and beard resemble those of Christ on the Byzantine coin." Should one follow Miles's conception, the depiction no longer concerns an Arabian ruler but rather an Arabian Jesus in his role as *walī al-ʾamr* (authorized representative) and *walī Allāh* (representative of God).

116. Morrisson, *Catalogue des monnaies byzantines,* 404, 15 Cp/AU/04–09, plate LXI. The reasons Morrisson gives here for the minting of the coins with the depiction of the standing ruler and the national religious symbol, the "Sone," the *Yegar Sahaduta,* have already been expressed by Miles, "Earliest Arab Gold Coinage," p. 215: "Most important in this connection is the obvious relationship between the Standing Caliph motif and the solidi of Justinian II portraying the Byzantine emperor standing and hoilding the cross on steps. Certainly it was this latter issue that inspired the Standing Caliph type, the Arab response in the ideological and iconographical war between Byzantium and the Arabs."

117. Recently, an Islamic explanation for this symbolic depiction that replaced the cross was offered by Nadia Jamil, "Caliph and Qutb: Poetry as a Source for Interpreting the Transformation of the Byzantine Cross on Steps on Umayyad Coinage," in *Bayt al Maqdis,* vol. 2, *Jerusalem and Early Islam,* ed. Jeremy Johns, Oxford Studies in Islamic Art, no. 9:2 (Oxford: Oxford University Press, 1999).

118. Walker, *Catalogue* I, p. 97, Sch. 5; cf. also the footnote to this entry: the auction of the Strauss collection, Schulman, Amsterdam, auction of Jan. 1913, no. 1005, plate V.

119. A. J. Wensinck, "Rasūl," in *Handwörterbuch des Islam,* ed. A. J. Wensinck and J. H. Kramers (Leiden: Brill, 1941), p. 611: "Concerning the close relationship between the *rasūl* and his *ʾumma,* one can compare the teaching of the apocryphal Acts of the apostles, in which the twelve apostles are supposed to have divided the entire world among themselves, so that each apostle was to preach the gospel to a specific people. . . . The expression *rasūl Allāh* was more often used in its Syriac form (*shelīḥeh d'Alāhā*) in the apocryphal Acts of Thomas."

120. Madelung, "Apocalyptic Prophecies," p. 167.

121. M. I. Moshiri, "A Pahlavi Forerunner of the Umayyad Reformed Coinage," *Journal of the Royal Asiatic Society* 113 (1981): 168–72.

122. Cf. G. R. Driver, *Aramaic Documents of the Fifth Century B.C.,* abridged and revised edition (Oxford: Clarendon Press, 1965), pp. 23, 29, and 50.

123. *Islamic Coin Auction 9 in London,* Baldwin's Auctions Ltd. 2004, Lot no. 3172, with illustration.

124. S. Eshragh, "An Interesting Arab-Sasanian Dirhem," *O.N.S. Newsletter* 178 (2004): 45–46, with illustration.

125. The aforementioned study by Miles, "Earliest Arab Gold Coinage," although from 1967, remains the richest presentation of the beginnings of the minting of gold coins in the Arabian Empire.

126. Cf. S. Heidemann, "The Merger of Two Currency Zones in Early Islam: The Byzantine and Sasanian Impact on the Circulation in Former Byzantine Syria and Northern Mesopotamia," *Iran* 36 (1998): 95–112.

127. See the corresponding article by Patricia Crone in the second edition of the *Encyclopaedia of Islam,* IV: 928–929.

128. In the second edition of the *Encyclopaedia of Islam,* V: 14, it says: "The caliph is clad in a long coat trimmed with Iranian-type pearls, worn over wide trousers, and holds a short sword."

129. M. Sharon, "An Arabic Inscription from the Time of the Caliph ʿAbd al-Malik," *Bulletin of the School of Oriental and African Studies* 29 (1966): 367–72; the stone is catalogued in the Israel Museum, Jerusalem, as Inventory no. IAA 63-428.

130. This is true for the ground level of the fifth-century cathedral in Etchmiadzin, where four posts bear the weight of the cupola. The previous building had been a basilica (cf. P. Paboudjian, *La cathédrale d'Etchmiadzine* [Beyrouth, 1965], p. 359). One can compare the building activity under al-Walīd in Damascus, where the local basilica dedicated to John the Baptist was replaced with a building reminiscent of the Syrian tradition.

131. Christel Kessler, "'Abd al-Malik's Inscription in the Dome of the Rock: A Reconsideration," *Journal of the Royal Asiatic Society* (1970): 6.

132. Josef Horovitz, *Koranische Untersuchungen* (Berlin and Leipzig: Walter de Gruyter, 1926), p. 55.

133. J. G. Stickel, "Noch einmal die omajjadische Askalon-Münze und ein Anhang," *Zeitschrift der Deutschen Morgenländischen Gesellschaft* 40 (1886): 81–87. After exactly one hundred years of absolutely no attention, the first reference to this article by the professor from Weimar appeared in 1986 in the apparatus of the (at that time) standard publication by D. Barag on the theme of "Islamic lampstands." That Islamic studies scholars have ignored the complex of holy vessels from the Solomonic temple—including other objects besides the lampstand—seems to me symptomatic of the attention typically given to other subdisciplines in this area of scholarship. For an opposite example, one may consider the method of Th. Mommsen concerning research on Roman history; he was not at all above a wide-ranging consideration of both numismatics and national law. It is only in Islamic studies that one sees such hubris as to allow philology and literary studies alone to influence one's statements about history.

134. Peter Brown, *The World of Late Antiquity 150–750* (New York: Harcourt Brace Jovanovich, 1971), p. 174.

135. D. Barag, "The Islamic Candlestick Coins of Jerusalem," *Israel Numismatic Journal* 10 (1988–1989): 40–48, tables 7–9.

136. H. A. Pohlsander, "Herakleios, byzantinischer Kaiser," in *Biographisch-bibliographisches Kirchenlexicon,* XIX (2001), col. 654: "Heraclius must also be mentioned in connection with Byzantine art. Nine beautiful silver platters stem from the period of his reign, most likely from the years 628–630; these platters were discovered in 1902 in Lambousa (Lapethos) on the northern coast of Syria. Three of the nine now reside in the Cyprus Museum in Nicosia, and the other six can be found in the Metropolitan Museum of Art in New York City. The platters are decorated with depictions from the life of the biblical King David. It is known that Constantine I, Marcianus, and Justin I were celebrated as "new Davids," fully in line with Byzantine conceptions of emperor and empire, and that such acclamations were also in use in later periods. Heraclius was called *basileus* beginning in 629 and had good reason to identify himself with David, especially after the end of the war against Khosrau. These platters, whose programmatic character is unmistakable, should be understood in this light. It must be added as well that, shortly after the return of the True Cross to Jerusalem, Heraclius and his empress Martina bore a son whom they named David; he was crowned emperor in 638."

137. Fusṭāṭ is today a part of the city of Cairo. The name derives from the Latin *fossatum.* This canal is the body of water behind which western Roman troops in enemy territory retreated.

138. Cf. Nevo and Koren, *Crossroads,* p. 410: RCEA inscription no. 8; no line divisions are given.

139. Walker, *Catalogue* II, pp. 59–60.

140. Concerning the prevalence of Latin in the court of the Fatimid caliphs of North Africa, a prevalence able to be shown to be in force even centuries later than the time of ʿAbd al-Malik, cf. H. Halm, "Les arabes et l'héritage byzantin en Afrique du nord," *Revue des études islamiques* 55–58 (1987–1989): 288–89: "In 947, after the defeat of the famous Berber rebel Abū Yazīd al-Khārijī, the young caliph undertook a campaign that led him into the heart of the central Maghreb, up to the borders of the Sahara. . . . Our caliph, always eager to recognize Roman ruins, climbed the little hill; near the biggest of the three burial mounds, he found an inscription 'bi-r-rūmiya' ('in Latin'), and demanded that one of his companions translate for him the text, which read as follows: 'I am Solomon the general, and this town is called Mauritania.' . . . What emerges from this episode is that there was, in the entourage of the caliph, someone who was capable not only of translating an inscription from Latin into Arabic, but also of correctly rendering the term *magister militium* with the corresponding Arabic term, *as-sardaghus* (Gk. *strategos*)."

141. Walker, *Catalogue* II, p. 61f.

142. Ibid., p. 65: "There is no God but one; there is no other like him."

143. Ibid., p. 67: "There is no God but one; there is no other associate like him."

144. Ibid., p. 66, no. 170: "God is eternal; God is great; God is the creator of all."

145. Ibid., p. 71, no. 179: "God is eternal; God is great; he knows all things; he is the creator of all things."

146. Ibid., p. 65, no. 169; p. 67, no. 173; p. 68, no. 177: "In the name of the merciful Lord, this *solidus* was made in Africa." It is important that the Latin form of the *basmala* is followed by the coin-name "solidus." This shows that there was no consistent, unified terminology for coins at the time of ʿAbd al-Malik.

147. Ibid., p. 70, no. C.(ambridge) [hereafter, C.], 11: "In the name of the merciful Lord, this *solidus* was made in Africa, in the second year of the indiction."

148. Ibid., p. 71, no. 178: "In the name of the merciful Lord, this *solidus* was made in Africa, in the third year of the indiction."

149. Cf. Nevo and Koren, *Crossroads,* p. 310, on the Arabs' use of their predecessors' formulae, e.g., the Greek *en onomati tou theou* in use in the Greek chancellery. The Arabs developed a corresponding phrase in Arabic, the *basmala.*

150. Walker, *Catalogue* II, p. 73, no. C., 12.

151. Altheim, *Entwicklungshilfe,* p. 37: "One needs only to say it out loud, and it will become clear that these Monophysites were the continuation of the Syrian and Egyptian Neoplatonists. Both were zealous defenders of the principle of the divine unity. They suppressed only incompletely what had been given to them: neither the Neoplatonists the multiple gods of antiquity, nor the Monophysites the Logos alongside the Father. But they reduced the value of what opposed the unity, in that they exalted it *in* the unity. The Neoplatonists and the Monophysites took the same action, and it was hardly coincidental that both groups recruited new members from Egypt and Syria. This passionate striving for divine unity shaped the thought of both countries."

152. Walker, *Catalogue* II, p. 73, B.(erlin) [hereafter, B.], 12.

153. Cf. here Halm, "Les arabes," 292.

154. Walker, *Catalogue* II, p. 240, no. P.(aris) [hereafter, P.], 127.

155. Ibid., p. 63, no. P., 28.

156. A. Elad, "Why Did ʿAbd al-Malik Build the Dome of the Rock? A Re-examination of the Muslim Sources," in *Bayt al-Maqdis,* vol. 2, *Jerusalem and Early Islam*, ed. Johns: "He ends his report by saying that no one in Syria had ever doubted that the Banū Umayya were the sole representatives of the Prophet. In this context it is worth noting the report that, immediately after the 'Abbasids' victory, a delegation of Syrian notables visited the first ʿAbbasid caliph, Abu ʾl-ʿAbbas al-Saffāḥ, and swore that they had been unaware that the Prophet had any other relatives or a family worthy of succeeding him except the Umayyads, until after the

ʿAbbasids had seized power." This report is found in the writings of al-Ḥasan ibn Aḥmad al-Muhallabī. It is a reflection of the further development from the conception of Jesus as the *muḥammad* to Muḥammad, the prophet of the Arabians, which took place in the second century of the Arabian era.

157. Cf. the publication of R. B. Serjeant, "Hud and Other Pre-Islamic Prophets of Hadramawt," *Le Muséon* 67 (1954): 121–79, *passim.*

158. Wellhausen, *Arabische Reich,* p. 217: "He [Hishām bn ʿAbd al-Malik] was not intolerant concerning his Christian subordinates. Indeed, he made it possible for them [the Melkites?] to retake the see of Antiochia, which they had not been able to do for the previous forty [*sic*] years; this was, though, under the condition that they not elect as patriarch any educated or prominent individual, but rather a simple monk, his friend Stephanus, a condition to which they agreed." See also Wellhausen's footnote 1 here: "Theophanus *A.M.* 6234; cf. 8236."

159. Cf. Nevo and Koren, *Crossroads,* p. 419: "*masjid* is a common Aramaic term for 'place of worship.' The word 'mosque' can translate it, provided it is not taken to imply a *miḥrāb*-oriented structure; there is no archeological evidence that the type of structure we today call a 'mosque' existed in Walid's time."

160. Walker, *Catalogue* II, no. 182, p. 76: "This *solidus* was made in Africa in the year 98."

161. Ibid., pp. 70–73, nos. C., 11–C., 14: "God is eternal; God is great; God is the creator of everything"; "In the name of the merciful Lord, this *solidus* was made in Africa in the second (or third, or fourth, etc.) year of the indiction."

162. Ibid., p. 76, no. P., 49.

163. Ibid., p. 78, no. 184.

164. Ibid.

165. Ibid., p. 77, no. P., 47.

166. Ibid., p. 79, no. C., 17.

167. Nevo and Koren, *Crossroads,* p. 258: "For although the terms 'the Prophet' and 'the Messenger of God,' alone or in combination, are all-pervasive in the Qurʾān, its central named religious figure is not Muḥammad, who is mentioned only four times, but Moses."

168. The coins are unpublished. They can be found in Swedish museums and have been falsely ascribed by the specialists there to the Khazars on the lower Volga. They allegedly serve as proof that the Khazars of this period had become Jewish. But if the Khazars had truly felt a need to document their appropriation of Judaism in this way, one wonders why they did not mint silver coins with *Hebrew* inscriptions. Their God did not announce himself in pure Arabic, nor did he command them to write in Arabic. On the other hand, the Viking traders certainly did not care at all as to who put what in coin inscriptions, for they made what is known as "hacksilver" out of the coins and sent them to the grave along with their illiterate princes.

In the medieval period Polish Jews minted silver coins, with Hebrew inscriptions to use for trade. These coins were gladly accepted by the adherents of all religions and confessions because the silver content of the coins was high. What would have held these Khazars back, having become Jewish, from confessing Moses as their prophet in Hebrew?

169. Cf. the silver coin from Ifriqiya, dated to 137 and struck in the style of the Marwānids, in Sotheby's, London, *Coins, Medals, Decorations, and Banknotes, 2&3 May 2001,* Lot no. 912 (Dirham, Ifriqiya 137). Two dirhams from Gharshistān in the S. E. Sheikh Ḥamad bn ʿAbd Allāh Āl Thānī collection in Doha, Qaṭar, bear witness to the continuing activity in the east of minting coins in the style of the Marwānids.

170. Yehuda D. Nevo, Zemira Cohen, and Dalia Heftman, *Ancient Arabic Inscriptions from the Negev,* vol. 1 (Jerusalem: IPS Ltd., 1993), p. 142.

171. Cf. R. B. Sergeant, "Saint Sergius," *Bulletin of the School of Oriental and African Studies* 22 (1950): 574f.

172. See C. Wurtzel's overview of the minting of coins among these parties in the years 127–33 of the Arabian era in "The Coinage of the Revolutionaries in the Late Umayyad Period," *ANS Museum Notes* 23 (1978): 161–99.

173. Cf. the dirham from this mint and this year in Sotheby's (London), Auction from April 25th and 26th, 1996, Lot no. 414.

174. The article "al-Barāmika" in the second edition of the *Encyclopaedia of Islam,* I:1033–36, offers the following concerning the name of the dynast: "1. Origins—The name Barmak, traditionally borne by the ancestor of the family, was not a proper name, according to certain Arab authors, but a word designating the office of a hereditary high priest of the temple of Nawbahar, near Balkh."

175. Cf. here the dirham from Spink's 185th auction in London, March 31, 2005, lot no. 337.

176. Lavoix, *Catalogue des Monnaies Musulmanes de la Bibliothèque Nationale,* vol. 1, *Khalifes orientaux* (Paris: Imprimerie nationale, 1887), p. 223, no. 913.

177. The Baldassari collection, Leu Numismatics, Zürich 1995, p. 47, no. 501 (Samarkand 210).

178. Walker, *Catalogue* II, no. 4, p. xxxvi: "For example on the coins of Maʾmūn (see Lavoix, ibid., nos. 604 and 613; Miles, N. H. R., nos. 103, 104, and 106)."

179. Crone and Hinds, *God's Caliph,* pp. 4–21 *passim.*

180. Cf. here a silver coin from the year 194 from Madinat Samarkand. The stamp for the mint had been altered, with the word *al-imām* engraved over the title *al-amīr.* Cf. the Baldassari collection, Leu Numismatics, 47, no. 491.

181. Second edition of the *Encyclopaedia of Islam,* VII:784.

182. Frye, *Heritage*, p. 251.

183. Second edition of the *Encyclopaedia of Islam,* VI:337: "Furthermore, with the object of wooing the support of the Shiʿis, ʿAlī was proclaimed 'the best of the Companions, after the Prophet' (in 211/826, reaffirmed in 212/827)."

184. Cf. here the notable coin from the mint of al-Quds which names al-Maʾmūn. The coin is dated to the year 217. (Is this of the Arabian era, or perhaps of the Hijra? N.b.: The point in time in which the era of the Hijra was introduced during the rule of al-Maʾmūn cannot be determined with certainty from the inscriptions. There is no specific reference to the Hijra in the datings of the coin inscriptions.) See N. G. Nassar, "The Arabic Mints in Palestine and Trans-Jordan," *Quarterly of the Department of Antiquities in Palestine* 13 (Jerusalem, 1948): 119.

BIBLIOGRAPHY

Standard Works

EI^2 = *The Encyclopaedia of Islam.* New edition. Leiden: Brill, 1960.

Handwörterbuch des Islam. (Following the first edition of the *Encyclopaedia of Islam.*) Leiden, 1941.

Walker, *Catalogue* I = Walker, John. *A Catalogue of the Arab-Sassanian Coins.* London, 1941.

Walker, *Catalogue* II = Walker, John. *A Catalogue of the Arab-Byzantine and Post-Reform Umaiyad Coins.* London, 1956.

Journals

INS 10 = *Israel Numismatic Journal.* Published by the Israel Numismatic Society, vol. 10. Jerusalem, 1988–89.

INS 13 = *Israel Numismatic Journal.* Published by the Israel Numismatic Society, vol. 13. Jerusalem, 1994–99.

Secondary Literature

Altheim, Franz. *Entwicklungshilfe im Altertum.* Hamburg, 1962.

Der Qurʾān. Translated by Rudi Paret. Stuttgart, 1979.

Gaube, Heinz. *Arabosasanidische Numismatik.* Braunschweig, 1973.

Lavoix, Henri. *Catalogue des Monnaies Musulmanes de la Bibliothèque Nationale,* vol. 1, *Khalifes Orientaux.* Paris, 1887.

Nevo, Yehuda, and Judith Koren. *Crossroads to Islam: The Origins of the Arab Religion and the Arab State*. New York, 2003.
Ostrogorsky, Georg. *Geschichte des byzantinischen Staates*. München, 1952.
Rothstein, Gustav. *Die Dynastie der Laḫmiden in al-Ḥīra*. Berlin, 1899.
Rotter, Gernot. *Die Umayyaden und der Zweite Bürgerkrieg (680-692)*. Wiesbaden, 1982.
Serjeant, R. B. *Studies in Arabian History and Civilization*. London, 1981.
Wellhausen, Julius. *Das Arabische Reich und sein Sturz*. Berlin, 1902.

Illustrations

(All figures in the text are not according to scale)

1. The inscription of Muʿāwiya on the baths of Gadara. *Israel Exploration Journal* 32 (1982): 94.

2. Reverse of a coin from Damascus before 642. H. Lavoix, *Catalogue*, vol. 1, no. 1, p. 1.

3. Obverse of a Christian Arabian coin from Damascus. Leu, Zürich, auction no. 56 (1992), no. 7.

4. Reverse of a Christian-Arabian coin, giving the monogram of the emperor Heraclius and a date. Leu, Zürich, auction no. 56 (1992), no. 7.

5. Obverse of an anonymous coin from Damascus with the image of the Christian-Arabian ruler in the manner of Byzantine depictions of the emperor.

6. Reverse of the same coin, with the name of the mint given in Arabic. The Arabic inscription runs from above to below in the manner of the Pahlavi texts on Sassanian coins. Spink, Zürich, auction no. 18 (1986), no. 84, p. 29.

7. Obverse of an anonymous Christian-Arabian copper coin from Damascus, bearing the image of the ruler with a globe-cross on the left and a reliquary of a head (of John the Baptist?) on the right. Frank Sternberg, Zürich, auction no. 8 (1978), no. 1011.

8. Reverse of an anonymous Christian-Arabian copper coin with the denomination *M* (40 nummia); above is a cross, and to the left a crowned head (of John the Baptist?). Leu, Zürich, auction no. 35 (1985), no. 412.

9. Obverse of an anonymous Christian-Arabian copper coin of the seventh century from Syria; it bears the image of a Christian preacher. Leu, Zürich, auction no. 35 (1985), no. 411.

10. Obverse and reverse of a coin of Khālid from Tiberias/Ṭabariyya. The Christian ruler is depicted with the *agnus Dei*. Walker, *Catalogue* II, p. 47.

11. Obverse and reverse of a copper coin from Damascus, bearing the image of the Christian-Arabian ruler and with the *agnus Dei* on the right. Walker, *Catalogue* II, p. 50.

12. Obverse and reverse of a copper coin from Jerusalem. On the obverse, the image of the standing Christian-Arabian ruler. On the reverse, the mint location *HIEROSALEMON* ("in Jerusalem"). Spink, Zürich, auction no. 31 (1989), no. 189.

13. Obverse and reverse of a Christian-Arabian copper coin from *C(I)ON* ("Zion"). *Israel Numismatic Journal* 10, no. 152, p. 26.

14. Obverse and reverse of a Christian-Arabian copper coin. The mint location of *CION* ("Zion") is given on the reverse, under the denomination *M*. Pontifical Biblical Institute Collection, Jerusalem.

15. Arabo-Sassanian drachma with the motto *MḤMD* (*muḥammad*) in Pahlavi script on the right of the obverse, next to the bust, with an Arabic legend *wāfin*. Morton and Eden, London, auction in May 2003, ex. no. 180.

16. Arabo-Sassanian drachma with the Pahlavi inscription *MḤMṬ* on the right, next to the bust. There is an Arabic version of the *muḥammad* motto as a legend on the obverse. Arabian Coins and Medals, Dubai, auction no. 3 (2001), no. 1.

17. Obverse of a copper coin depicting the standing Christian-Arabian ruler; to the left appears the inscription *bi-ʿAmman*, written from above to below in the Sassanian manner. Israel Museum, Jerusalem, inventory no. 88454.

18. Reverse of the same coin, bearing the denomination *M*, a cross above, and the *muḥammad* motto below. Israel Museum, Jerusalem, inventory no. 88454.

19. The *Beth-El* in the form of the *Yegar Sahaduta*, with the *muḥammad* motto, on the coin from Ḥarrān. Walker, *Catalogue* II, fig. 1, p. 26.

20. Image of the eastern type of the Christian-Arabian ruler on the reverse of the coin from Ḥarrān; to the left appears the *muḥammad* motto, written from above to below in the Sassanian manner, and to the right the location of the mint, also written from above to below parallel to the image of the ruler. This coin, depicting a ruler between two lines of text, corresponds to the type of image found on Sassanian drachmas, where the fire-altar appears between two guardian-figures. Hess, Lucerne, auction no. 255 (1984), table 1, p. 7.

21. The Byzantine model for the earliest Arabian gold coins. The obverse depicts Christ, and the reverse Emperor Justinian II as a *servus Christi*. Baldwin's, London, auction no. 3 (1995), no. 152, plate VII.

22. A gold coin of ʿAbd al-Malik according to the Byzantine exemplar. The obverse depicts the national religious symbol, the "Stone," that is, the *Beth-El* in the form of the *Yegar Sahaduta,* while the reverse depicts the Eastern type of the Christian-Arabian ruler with a sword. Private French collection.

23. Cutaway isometric drawing of the Dome of the Rock. Clearly recognizable are the four posts in the area under the cupola.

24. Obverse of a copper coin bearing the image of a five-branched lampstand, surrounded by an Arabic inscription. Walker, *Catalogue* II, 208, no. 805.

25. North African gold coin from the time of al-Walīd, bearing a Latin inscription and the *Yegar Sahaduta*.

26. Bilingual (Arabic-Latin) gold coin from North Africa, from the year 98 of the Arabian era (716/717).

27. Copper coin from the year 116 of the Arabian era from Jayy (Iṣfahān). Sotheby's, London, auction of April 1982, no. 206.

28. Anonymous copper coin without a mint location, from the year 136 of the Arabian era (753), minted in the Sassanian style.

29. Copper coin bearing the image of a ruler in Sassanian style, from the mint of Bust and dated to the year 209 of the Arabian era (825). The governor Ṭalḥa is mentioned, but not the *caliph*, al-Ma'mūn.

30. Selection from the inscription on the Dome of the Rock, mentioning Jesus as a "Servant of God" and "Chosen One." Text provided by Christel Kessler, *Journal of the Royal Asiatic Society,* 1970.

31. Selection from the inscription on the Dome of the Rock, mentioning *al-Imām al-Ma'mūn* in the place of ʿAbd al-Malik. Text provided by Christel Kessler, *Journal of the Royal Asiatic Society*, 1970.

2

A NEW INTERPRETATION OF THE ARABIC INSCRIPTION IN JERUSALEM'S DOME OF THE ROCK

Christoph Luxenberg

This present essay is concerned with the inscription on the inner side of the octagon on the Dome of the Rock in Jerusalem. The inscription is over 240 meters long, was written in Arabic using the Kufic monumental script, and was created with gold-colored mosaic stones on a green background. According to an inscription on the outer side of the octagon,[1] this sacred building, which has heretofore been considered the earliest Islamic building, was erected in the year 72 (if this number does not have merely a symbolic character) of the Arabian era (beginning in 622 CE and later called "Hijra") by ʿAbd al-Malik ibn Marwān, the fifth caliph of the Umayyad dynasty (and ruling 685–705 CE, following Arabian historiography).[2] This article presents a new attempt to analyze the text of this inscription in a historico-linguistic way, following the methods first developed in the work *Die syro-aramäische Lesart des Koran*.[3] Besides using Arabic, this book began foundationally from the Aramaic language, which was the *lingua franca* in the entire Near East region for more than a millennium preceding Arabic. The translation of the Bible into Syro-Aramaic (ܦܫܝܛܬܐ /*Pšiṭṭā*/Peshitta), which was already current in the second century, determined (as in other cultures) the place of Aramaic as the language of cult and culture before the rise of Islam for the Arabs who lived between the Tigris, the Nile, and the Arabian peninsula. This study achieved fundamentally new results with the help of investigations into individual passages of the Qur'ān. In light of these linguistic analyses, the results allow one to expect new semantic content from the inscription inside the Dome of the Rock. Further, this content will open the way for conclusions relevant in the fields of theology, the history of religions, and the history of linguistics. That this dated inscription is older than the oldest Qur'ānic manuscripts known to us does not, nevertheless, allow us to recognize any linguistic structure that varies from the Qur'ānic language, because the majority of the inscription can also be found in the canonical text of the Qur'ān. This phenomenon provides another reason why the methods mentioned above are to be employed in the following textual analysis.

The accurate photographic reproductions that appear in Oleg Grabar's book on the Dome of the Rock will serve as the textual basis for this study.[4] The text will be reprinted here in modern Arabic script, supplemented by the diacritical markings that are, for the most part, lacking in the inscription; in the main, these markings agree with those in the Qur'ān of today, insofar as the passages match with Qur'ānic texts. In addition, the very occasional passages that do bear diacritical markings will be underlined; most notable among these instances are the double-points that appear above one another rather than next to one another. If these points are original, then the inscription would be a witness to an earlier usage of diacritical markings in Arabic writing than has been accepted heretofore. Two criteria, however, make it more probable that they were added later as a result of a subsequent restoration: a) the replacement of the name of the inscription's sponsor, ʿAbd al-Malik, by that of the caliph al-Maʾmūn in year 216 of the Hijra[5]; and b) the hyper-correct writing of the word اولوا (*ʾūlū*) against the more authentic form اولا (*ʾūlā* /*ʾūlē*), as found in the facsimile of the Qur'ānic codex BNF 328a (fol. 2b, l. 12). For the purposes of the textual analysis, this Kufic inscription, which runs in one line up to a sentence divider (three vertical points, which could relate to the following ـشـ of the word شهد as diacritical markings), will be divided in sections bearing Arabic numerals. The transliteration into Latin characters, which occasionally varies from the traditional Qur'ānic reading, is based on the philological analyses that will follow; their results will be anticipated in the translations that accompany the texts given here. Finally, the sura numbers that precede some texts in parentheses indicate that the texts which follow also appear in the Qur'ān in the places given.

THE KUFIC INSCRIPTION ON THE INSIDE OF THE DOME OF THE ROCK: TEXT IN MODERN ARABIC SCRIPT,[6] TRANSCRIPTION IN LATIN CHARACTERS, AND TRANSLATION

بسم الله الرحمن الرحيم / لا اله الا اللـه وحده لا شريك له / له الملك وله الحمد/ يحيي
ويميت وهو على كل شى قدير / (1

1. *bi-sm(i) llāh(i) r-raḥmān(i) r-raḥīm* / *lā ilāh(a) illā llāh(a) waḥdah(ū) lā šarīk(a) la-h(ū)* / (sura 64:1) *la-h(ū) l-mulk(u) wa-la-h(ū) l-ḥamd(u)* / (sura 57:2) *yuḥyī wa-yumīt(u) wa-hu(wa) ʿalā kull(i) šay(yin) qadīr* /

1. In the name of the gracious and merciful God (or, "In the name of the *loving* and *beloved* God") / There is no god but God alone; he has no associate / (sura 64:1) To him (belongs) sovereignty and to him (belongs) praise / (sura 57:2) He gives life (or, "He restores to life") and makes (people) die, He is almighty. /

محمد عبد اللـه ورسوله / ان اللـه ومليكته يصلون على النبي / يايها الذين امنوا صلوا
عليه وسلموا تسليما / صلى اللـه عليه والسلام عليه ورحمت اللـه / (2

2. *muḥammad(un) ʿabd(u) llāh(i) wa-rasūluh(ū)* / (sura 33:56) *ʾin(na) llāh(a) wa-malāykat(a)h(ū) yuṣallūn(a) ʿalā n-nabī(yi)* / *yā-ʾayyuhā l-laḏīn(a) ʾāmanū ṣallū ʿalayh(i) wa-sallimū taslīmā* / *ṣallā llāh(u) ʿalayh(i) wa-s-salām(un) ʿalayh(i) wa-raḥmat(u) llāh* /

2. Praised be [*muhammad(un)*] the servant of God and his messenger (or, "May the servant of God and his messenger be praised") / God and his angels bless the prophet / O you who believe, implore (God's) blessing and grace upon him! / God bless him, and (may there be) God's grace and mercy (or "love") upon him./

ياهل الكتب لا تعلوا في دينكم ولا تقولوا على اللـه الا الحق / انما المسيح عيسى ابن
مريم رسول اللـه وكلمته القيها الى مريم وروح منه / فامنوا باللـه ورسله ولا تقولوا
ثلثه / انتهوا خيرا لكم / انما اللـه اله وحد / سبحنه / ان يكون له ولد / له ما في
السموت وما في الارض / وكفى باللـه وكيلا / (3

3. (sura 4:171) *yā-ʾahl(a) l-kitāb(i) lā taʿlū fī dīnikum wa-lā ta-qūlū ʿalā llāh(i) ʾillā l-ḥaqq(a)* / *ʾin(na)mā l-Masīḥ(u) ʿĪsā bn(u) Maryam rasūl(u) llāh(i) wa-kalimat(u)h(ū) alqayhā ʾilā Maryam wa-rūḥ(un) minh(ū)* / *fa-ʾāminū bi-llāh(i) wa-rusul(i)h(i) wa-lā ta-qūlū ṯ(a)lāṯa* / *ʾintahū ḫayra(n) la-*

kum / ʾin(na)mā llāh(u) ʾilāh(un) wāḥid(un) / subḥān(a)h(ū) / ēn yakūn(u) la-h(ū) walad(un) / la-h(ū) mā fī s-samaw(ā)t(i) wa-mā fī l-ʾarḍ(i) / wa-kafā b-l-lāh(i) wakīlā /

3. (sura 4:171) O people of the Scripture, *do not go astray in your exegesis* (*exegetical interpretation of scripture*), and do not tell anything but the truth about God / For (verily) the Messiah Jesus, son of Mary, (is) the messenger of God and his Word (Logos), (which) he has infused into Mary, along with His Spirit. / So, believe in God and his messengers, and do not say "three"; / cease (doing that); (it would be) better for you. / For (verily) God is a unique God—may he be praised!—*how* could he then have a child! (Rather, all) belongs to him that (is) in the heavens and on the earth! / For God (alone) is sufficient as a Helper (for mankind).

4) لن يستنكف المسيح ان يكون عبد اللـه ولا المليكه المقربون / ومن يستنكف عن عبدته
ويستكبر فسيحشرهم اليه جميعا /

4. (sura 4:172) *lan yastankif(a) l-Masīḥ(u) ʾan yakūn(a) ʿabd(a) llāh(i) wa-lā l-malāykē l-muqarrabūn / wa-man yastankif ʿan ʿibādat(i)h(i) wa-yastakbir / fa-sa-yaḥš(u)r(u)hum ʾilayh(i) jamīʿā /*

4. The Messiah would not disdain to be God's servant, nor (would) the angels standing near (to God). / Whoever disdains it, however, to serve him, and himself behaves haughtily, such people he will (one day) call together in his presence (lit.: to himself).

5) اللهم صلي على رسولك وعبدك عيسى ابن مريم / والسلم عليه يوم ولد ويوم يموت
ويوم يبعث حيا / ذلك عيسى ابن مريم قول الحق الذى فيه تمترون / ما كان للـه ان
يتخذ من ولد / سبحنه / اذا قضى امرا فانما يقول له كن فيكون / ان اللـه ربي وربكم
فاعبدوه / هذا صرط مستقيم

5. *allāh(u)m ṣallī ʿalā rasūl(i)k(a) wa-ʿabd(i)k(a) ʿĪsā (i)bn(i) Maryam /* (sura 19:33–36) *wa-s-salām(u) ʿalayh(i) yawm(a) wulid(a) wa-yawm(a) yamūt(u) wa-yawm(a) yubʿaṯ(u) ḥayyā / ḏālik(a) ʿĪsā (i)bn(u) Maryam qawl(u) l-ḥaqq(i) l-laḏī fīh(i) tamtarūn / mā kān(a) li-llāh(i) ʾan yattaḫiḏ min walad(in) / subḥānah(ū) / ʾiḏā qaḍā amra(n) fa-ʾin(na)mā yaqūl(u) la-h(ū) kun fa-yakūn /* (sura 43:64) *ʾin(na) allāh(u) rabbī wa-rabb(u)kum fa-ʿbudūh(ū) / hāḏā ṣirāṭ(un) mustaqīm /*

5. O God, bless your messenger and servant Jesus, son of Mary! / (sura 19:33–36) Grace (be) upon him on the day on which he was born, on the day

on which he will die, and on the day on which he will be resurrected! / Such is Jesus, son of Mary, the word of truth (as to his christological relevance), about whom you fight with one another. / It does not become God to *adopt* a child—may he be praised! When he decides something, he only needs in this regard to say: "Be!"—and it comes into being. / (sura 43:64; 5:117) God is my lord and your lord, so serve him—this is a straight *line*.

(6 شهد اللـه انه لا اله الا هو / والمليكه واولوا العلم قيما بالقسط لا اله الا هو العزيز الحكيم /

6. (sura 3:18) *šahhad(a) llāh(u) 'annah(ū) lā 'ilāh(a) illā hu(wa) / wa-l-malāykē wa-'ūlū l-'ilm(i) qayyāmē bi-l-q(i)sṭ(i) lā 'ilāh(a) illā hu(wa) l-'azīz(u) l-ḥakīm /*

6. God has *warned* (us), that there is no other god besides Him. / And the angels as well as the learned people (i.e., the *theologians*, the *authorities on the Scriptures*) *confirm according to the truth*: There is no god besides him, the Powerful, the Wise!

(7 ان الدين عند اللـه الاسلم / وما اختلف الذين اوتوا الكتب الا من بعد ما جاهم العلم بغيا بينهم / ومن يكفر بايت اللـه فان اللـه سريع الحساب /

7. (sura 3:19) *'in(na) d-dīn(a) 'ind(a) llāh(i) l-'islām / wa-mā (i)ḫtalaf(a) l-laḏīn(a) 'ūtū l-kitāb(a) illā min ba'd(i) mā jā('a)hum(u) l-'ilm(u) bāġyē bay-nahum / wa-man yakfur bi-āyayt(i) llāh(i) fa-'in(na) llāh(a) sarī'(u) l-ḥisāb /*

7. The *right interpretation of Scripture* (*dîn*) (is) with God the *conformity/agreement/concord* (*islâm*) (with the *Scripture*). For those to whom the Scritpure was given only fell into *disagreement/discord* (with the Scripture) after the (revealed) Knowledge (i.e., the *Scripture*) had come to them while *disputing* with each other. / Whoever denies the Signs (i.e., the letters/characters) of God [i.e., the *written* words of God in the revealed *Scriptures*], however, God will swiftly call (such people) to account (cf. sura 43:65).

PHILOLOGICAL TEXTUAL ANALYSES

1. The text begins with the doxology that is called *basmala* in Arabic. This doxology is traditionally understood thus: "In the name of the gracious

and merciful God. . . ." If one transcribes this phrase into Syro-Aramaic (ܒܫܡ ܐܠܗܐ ܪܚܡܢܐ ܘܪܚܝܡܐ / *b-šem allāhā raḥmānā wa-rḥīmā*), the following understanding results: "In the name of the *loving* and *beloved* God. . . ." What follows causes no difficulties: "There is no god but God alone; he has no associate; (sura 64:1) to him (belongs) sovereignty and to him (belongs) praise; (sura 57:2) he gives life (or, "he restores to life) and makes (people) die; he is almighty."

2. In the sequence that follows, one can see the second portion of the *Šahāda*, the Islamic creed (so to speak), but only if one takes the gerundive محمد / *muḥammad(un)* ("the one who should be praised" or "the one who is to be praised") as a personal name. In its context the sentence reads: محمد عبد اللـــه ورسوله *muḥammad(un) ʿabd(u) llāh(i) wa-rasūluh(ū)*. According to the traditional conception, one can understand this sentence only thus: "Muhammad (is) the servant of God and his messenger!" However, when connected with the preceeding nominal doxology derived from the same verbal root له الحمد / *la-h(ū) l-ḥamd(u)* (to him [belongs] praise), which relates to God, the *gerundival participle* محمد / *muḥammad(un)*, which is connected thereunto, should be read as "*praised be* the servant of God and his messenger!" Therefore, by using this gerundive, the text here is not speaking of a person named *Muhammad*, which was made only later metaphorically into a personal name attributed analogically to the prophet of Islam. This is true not only because the supposed copula "*is*" does not appear in the text but even more because the gerundive here, as a *verbal form*, makes an additional copula superfluous. Syntactically, then, the sentence should be understood thus: "*Praised be* the servant of God and his messenger!" The synonymous expressions ممجد / *mumajjad(un)* and مبارك / *mubārak(un)*, meaning "praised (be), blessed (be)," are still current in Arabic (including Christian Arabic) as, for example, in the well-known biblical and and liturgical hymn: مبارك الآتي باسم الرب / *mubārak(un) al-ʾâtī bi-smi r-rabb* "*Blessed be* he who comes in the name of the Lord!" (Psalm 118:26/Matthew 21:9). If one were to create the parallel expression محمد الأتي باسم الرب / *muḥammad(un) al-ʾātī bi-smi r-rabb*, one would certainly *not* understand it as "Muhammad (is the one) who comes in the name of the Lord!"

EXCURSUS: THE USE OF THE GERUNDIVAL PARTICPLE محمد / *MUḤAMMAD* (THE PRAISED ONE, THE ONE TO BE PRAISED) AS A METAPHORIC APPELLATION FOR JESUS CHRIST AMONG THE PRE-ISLAMIC CHRISTIAN ARABS

The context of the fifth section of the inscription makes clear that this blessing does not concern the name of the prophet of Islam, but rather Jesus, son of Mary, for indeed, this section, which expressly relates to Jesus, follows directly upon the theological-christological statement quoted in sura 4:171–72. The text reads: اللهم صلي على رسولك وعبدك عيسى ابن مريم /*allāh(u)m ṣallī ʿalā rasūl(i)k(a) wa-ʿabd(i)k(a) ʿĪsā (i)bn(i) Maryam* ("O God bless your messenger and servant Jesus, son of Mary!") Here, the double expression of the introductory blessing, الله ورسوله / *ʿabd(u) llāh(i) wa-rasūluh(ū)* "the *servant* of God and his *messenger*," is taken up again and irrefutably connected with *Jesus, son of Mary*.

DEEPER ANALYSIS

The "Servant of God" عبد الله / ʿabd(u) llāh(i) *as a Theological Terminus Technicus from Pre-Nicene Syrian Christology*

The Qurʾānic identification of Jesus as عبد الله / *ʿabd(u) llāh(i)*, or "servant of God," is connected with a Syrian Christian tradition that reaches back into early Christianity and has its roots in the sixth-century BCE "Servant Songs," found in the book of Isaiah but composed by a prophet of the exile about whom nothing else is known.[7] The Christology of the letter commonly called 1 *Clement*, written to the Christian community in Corinth around the end of the first century CE, seems to correspond to this understanding; according to this text, there is one God, creator of the universe, and "his beloved *servant* Jesus Christ, our Lord."[8] The *Didache*, compiled in the first quarter of the second century CE, also speaks of the "servant of God," as does the *Martyrdom of Polycarp*, which appeared in the second half of the same century. This latter text reads (14): "Lord, God Almighty, Father of this beloved and *praised servant* Jesus Christ. . . ."[9] With this expression "*praised servant*," we would have the exact correspondence to محمد عبدالله / *muḥammad(un) ʿabd(u) llāh(i)*, "*praised be the servant of God!*" (cf. the well-known Latin expression "*laudetur Jesus Christus = praised be Jesus Christ!*"). Consequently, this blessing from the Dome of the Rock makes a connection with a Christological tradition that we find already attested in the second Christian century.

Qur'ānic Parallels to the Expression عبد اللـه / ʿabd(u) llāh(i) ("*Servant of God*").

Two especially striking passages in the Qur'ān illustrate the central meaning of this ancient Christian expression, "*Servant of God*":

1. The Qur'ān portrays the infant Jesus as speaking miraculously from his cradle just after his birth; the function of this speaking is to free his mother from suspicion on the part of her family members of having given birth illegitimately. In sura 19:30 it reads: قال اني عبد اللـه اتيني الكتب وجعلني نبيا "He said, 'I am the *servant of God*; he gave me the scripture and made me a prophet.'" We also see this last term in the inscription of the Dome of the Rock, as it follows upon the blessing which relates to the "*servant of God*."

2. Scholars of the Qur'ān, even until today, have completely misunderstood the following passage from sura 72:18–20, which I will show to be of central importance when it is understood rightly:

وان المسجد للـه فلا تدعوا مع اللـه احدا / وانه لما قام عبد اللـه يدعوه كادوا
يكونون عليه لبدا / قل انما ادعوا ربي ولا اشرك به احدا

The most important translators of the Qur'ān have understood this set of three verses thus:

Paret: "(18) And, 'The *cultic places* (*masājid*) are (exclusively) there for God. Consequently, do not call upon anyone (else) besides God!'

(19) And, 'When the *servant of God* [n.: "i.e., Muhammad"] *raised himself up* in order to call upon him [n.: "or, 'to pray to him'"] they would have nearly *crushed* him (for blatant meddling?) (? *Kādū yakūnūna ʿalaihi* libadan)' [n.: "The meaning of this verse is very unclear."].

(20) *Say*: 'I will call upon my Lord (alone) [n.: "or, 'I will pray to my Lord alone"], and I will associate no one with him.'"[10]

Blachère: "(18) The [sacred] *mosque* is for Allah. Therefore do not pray to any person besides Allah! (n.: "*The [sacred] mosque*: cf. sura 9:17").

(19) When the Servant of Allah *got up*, praying, [the infidels] failed to be *against him* in *masses* (?). [n.: "*The Servant of God* = Muhammad; concerning *Kâdû yakûnûna ʿalay-hi libadâ* (var. *lubada* and *lubbâda*), 'the infidels, etc.,' the subject is uncertain—the commentators say that they are the *jinn*, but this is hardly probable."]

(20) *Say*: 'I will not pray to anyone but my Lord, and I will not associate anyone with Him.'"[11]

Bell: "(18) And that, the *places of worship* belong to Allah; so along with Allah call not ye upon anyone.

(19) And that, when a servant of Allah stood calling upon Him, they were upon him almost in *swarms*. (n. 3: "The meaning is uncertain. The 'servant of Allah' is usually taken to be Muhammad, and 'they' to refer to jinn, which is possible if angels now speak.")

(20) *Say*: 'I call simply upon my Lord, and I associate not with Him any one.'"[12]

Concerning verse 18, Paret and Bell remained faithful to the canonical understanding of this verse, that is, that the *rasm* مسجد *msjd* should be read in this context as the plural *masājid*; consequently, they were able to understand the word only as "cultic places" and "places of worship," respectively. Blachère dared to see the term in the singular, translating it as "the [sacred] mosque." This reading is fundamentally correct, but not in the Arabic sense in which Blachère understood it. If our Qurʾānic translators had incorporated some elementary rules of Syro-Aramaic grammar into their considerations, they could quite easily have recognized the logical context of this simple verse. The *rasm* مسجد (*msjd*) corresponds morphologically to the Syro-Aramaic infinitive ܡܣܓܕ / *mesgaḏ* ("to pray to someone, worship someone"). In fact, one sees here and there in Arabic such Aramaic substrata, which the Arab grammarians call مصدر ميمي / *maṣdar mīmī* ("infinitive with the 'm-prefix'"); however, their use is restricted to specific verbal forms, for such an infinitive form belongs to the Syro-Aramaic paradigm, not the Arabic. In the case of مسجد *msjd*, if one follows the Syro-Aramaic vocalization, it would be read in Arabic as *misjad* (or *masjad*), and not *masjid* (as a *nomen loci*); however, one cannot even imagine an Arabic infinitive having such a form, which would in fact be سجود / *sujūd*. If the verse were to be understood as وان السجود لله / *wa-ʾanna s-sujūda li-llāh*, the sense of the verse would become immediately clear: "Worship belongs (only) to God; you should not, therefore, call upon anyone besides God!"

Concerning verse 19, our Qur'ānic translators make manifest a further dificiency, this time of religio-historical dimension, by trusting to the Arab commentators and relating the Christological term عبد الله / *'abd(u) llāh(i)* ("servant of God") to Muhammad, the prophet of later Islam. If they had simply realized that the Muhammad to whom this text refers was not "Muhammad II" but rather "Muhammad I," that is, Jesus, son of Mary, the religio-historical significance of this verse would have become clear. The correct understanding in its context of the verb قام / *qāma* is a crucial part of this sense; the aforementioned translators understood this verb in its normal meaning of "to stand, to stand up," for they did not see the common context of all three verses. This context only becomes clear with an adequate understanding of the individual expressions. If an expression does not fit, then the proposed context fails as a logical unity. In the case of قام / *qāma*, scholars of Arabic know that it (like the Syro-Aramaic ܩܡ / *qām*) can carry the meaning of "to arise" (from the dead) in addition to the normal meaning of "to stand, to stand up." This understanding only becomes apparent, however, when one unpacks the meaning of the puzzling Arabic word لبدا (traditionally pronounced as *libadan*), whose difficulty all three translators admit.

It is unnecessary to reproduce the attempts of the Arab exegetes, philologists, and lexicographers to interpret this misread word, as these explanations, working from mistaken assumptions, do not get us any closer to the word's content. The mistaken reading of this difficult word, however, cannot in this case be attributed to a misplaced diacritical marking. The only point below the word لبدا cannot be refuted. Rather, the element that has led to the misreading does not reside in the Arabic system of writing at all, but rather in another system; the following explanation will show why it may have served as the basis for the misreading.

CONFUSION CONCERNING SYRO-ARAMAIC LETTERS

Confusion concerning Syro-Aramaic letters within the Syriac system of writing is a phenomenon sufficiently well known to Syriacists. One can see such confusion in the example of لبدا. If this word is transcribed into Syro-Aramaic, the Arabic لبدا becomes the Syriac ܠܒܕܐ (*LBDA*). The initial letter (*L*), in Arabic ـا and in Syro-Aramaic ܠ, can be distinguished in the two writing systems only in that the vertical stroke leans gently toward the left in the latter. The Syro-Aramaic alphabet also has a second, similar letter, distinguished from ܠ by a somewhat shorter vertical stroke: the guttural ܥ *'ayn*. If one were to put two words together that are otherwise identical except for these letters—for example, ܠܒܕܐ *LBDA* and ܥܒܕܐ *'BDA*—then one could well imagine how easily the two letters could be confused, especially in texts copied by hand—and not always very carefully. It is relatively easy, then, to recognize such confusion within the Syro-Aramaic writing system; however, if we transfer such cases into another writing system, such as the Arabic, the situation often becomes more difficult to recognize. In the case just explained, the Syriac word ܥܒܕܐ *'BDA*, misread as ܠܒܕܐ *LBDA*, could easily be transferred into Arabic as لبدا *LBDA*, instead of the correct Arabic عبدا (*'BDA*). Here the mistranscription is no longer visible within the Arabic writing system, for ـلـ (*L*) and ـعـ *'ayn* are easily distinguishable from one another. Consequently, one can discover the mistake only by postulating a transfer from the Syro-Aramaic writing system.

This is the case in sura 72:19, in the writing of the Arabic word normally transliterated as لبدا / *libadan*. This *rasm* must trace back to a transcription of the Syro-Aramaic ܥܒ̈ܕܐ / *'āḇdē*, which should have been written in Arabic as عبدا *'abadē*, or, because of the rhyme, *'ibādā*. Consequently, we have a new reading of sura 72:19:

/ وانه لما قام عبد الله يدعوه كادوا يكونون عليه عبدا /*wa-anna-h(ū) lammā qām(a) 'abd(u) llāh(i) ya-d'ū-h(ū) kādū ya-kūnūn(a) 'alay-h(i) 'ibādā.*

Following the explanation given above, then, this verse should be understood as follows: "And that, after the servant of God was *resurrected*, they (the people) would have almost *worshiped*[13] him (as God)." In verse 20, then, the servant of God (Christ) defends himself, and he speaks (*qāla* and not *qul*): "(thereupon) *he said*: 'I call indeed upon my Lord and associate no other with him!"

I would then reconstruct the logical connection between the three verses thus: (verse 18) you should worship the one God; (verse 19) when the servant of God was resurrected, the people would have worshiped him, practically as God (cf. sura 5:116); (verse 20) the servant of God defends himself and emphasizes that he calls upon (worships) only the one Lord (cf. sura 5:117).

The three verses, then, sura 72:18–20, should be understood thus:

(The Jinn, the invisible beings, spirits, claim:)

18. And that *worship* (belongs) to God, so you should call upon no other besides God;

19. And that, when the *Servant of God* was *resurrected, all the while calling* Him (that is, *continuing to worship God*), they (the people) would almost have *worshiped* him (as God);

20. (Upon which, defending himself,) He *said* (*not* "say"): 'I call indeed upon my Lord, and I associate no other with him!"

With the disclosing of verse 19, the Qur'ān speaks for the first time of a *resurrected Servant of God* who spent some period of time among human beings, according to the Gospels, before his ascension. This detail does not emerge from the other four places in which the Qur'ān speaks of the death, resurrection, and ascension of Jesus (suras 3:55; 4:158; 5:117; 19:33). In addition, verse 19 contributes to a new interpretation of the only Qur'ānic passage that alludes to the crucifixion (sura 4:157).

A forthcoming contextual and philological analysis will show that the Qur'ān does not deny the crucifixion as a historical fact; it refutes more precisely the claim of Jesus' opponents انا قتلنا المسيح عيسى ابن مريم رسول الله "We have <u>killed</u> the Messiah Jesus, son of Mary, the messenger of God." The Qur'ān answers: وما قتلوه "But they did not *kill* him," وما صلبوه "and (in this sense) they did not crucify him" (i.e., the crucifixion did not result in the *definitive death*), ولكن شبه لهم "rather it <u>appeared</u> to them" (as if they had *killed* him through crucifixion); وان الذين اختلفوا فيه لفي شك منه " "those who dispute about this are in doubt (as to his death)"; ما لهم به من علم الا اتباع الظن "they have in this regard no (revealed) knowledge, but just conjectural considerations" وما قتلوه يقينا "for they did not really <u>kill</u> him" (and not "they did not really <u>crucify</u> him"); (158) بل رفعه الله اليه "rather God raised him to Himself" (after his resurrection, as now attested in sura 72:19). A deeper founded philological analysis of these passages will follow elsewhere.

In this way, setting individual stones into a larger mosaic, one can slowly reconstruct a coherent picture of Qur'ānic Christology.

CONTINUATION OF THE TEXTUAL REVIEW OF THE INSCRIPTION INSIDE THE DOME OF THE ROCK

2. "God and his angels bless the *prophet*." The Qur'ān itself testifies that this last expression relates to Jesus, son of Mary; one sees this testimony in sura 19:30, where the infant Jesus, while still in the cradle, says of himself, اني عبد اللــــه اتيني الكتب وجعلني نبيا ("I am the servant of God; he gave me the scripture and made me a prophet"). The inscription then continues: "O You who believe, implore (God's) blessing and grace upon him! God bless him, and (may there be) God's grace and mercy (or "love") upon him!"

3. (Sura 4:171) "You People of the Scripture, do not astray in your judgment (concerning the interpretation of the Scripture)." Paret (p. 85) rightly casts doubt upon his own translation ("Do not go *too far* in your *religion*"); he shows this by transliterating the sentence (*lā taġlū fī dīnikum*). The point over the *ġ* is secondary and does not appear in the inscription on the Dome of the Rock. This sentence is an Arabic rendering of the Syro-Aramaic idiom ܐܥܠܝ ܒܕܝܢܐ / *aʿlī b̲d̲īnā*, "to err in one's judgment, to make a mistake."[14]

The text continues: "And do not tell anything but the truth about God. For the Messiah Jesus, son of Mary, (is) the messenger of God and his Word (Logos), (which) he infused into Mary along with His spirit (lit.: Spirit from him). So, believe in God and his messengers, and do not say "three"; cease (doing) that; (it would be) better for you. For (verily) God is a unique God—may he be praised!—how[15] could he then have a child? (Rather, all belongs) to him that (is) in the heavens and on the earth! For God (alone) is sufficient as a Helper (for mankind)."

4. (Sura 4:172) "The Messiah would not disdain to be God's servant, nor (would) the angels standing near (to God). Whoever disdains it, however, to serve him, and himself behaves haughtily, such people he will (one day) call together in his presence (lit.: to himself)."

5. "O God, bless your messenger and servant Jesus, son of Mary! (sura 19:33–36) Grace (be) upon him on the day on which he was born, on the day on which he will die, and on the day on which he will be resurrected! Such is Jesus, son of Mary, the word of truth (as to his Christological relevance), about whom you all fight with one another. It does not become God to adopt[16] a child—may he be praised! For when he decides something, he only needs in this regard to say: "Be!"—and it comes into being. (Sura 43:64) God is my lord and your lord, so serve him—this is a straight line."[17]

Paret's translation agrees for the most part with this one, except for the expression اتّخذ ولدا / *ittaḫaḏa waladan*, which he translates as "to acquire a child for oneself," and the word صراطا / *ṣirāṭ*, which he translates as "way," following the scholarship current up to this time.[18]

6. (Sura 3:18) "God has warned (us)[19] that there is no other god besides him; and the angels as well as the learned people[20] (i.e., the *theologians*, the *authorities* on the Scriptures) *confirm*[21] (lit.:) in the truth (i e., in accordance with the truth): "There is no god besides Him, thc Powerful, the Wise!"

Apparently, Paret was not able to grasp the syntactic relationship of this two-part sentence, as he turned it into five independent sentences. His translation reads thus: "God *testifies* that there is no other god besides him. Likewise, the angels and those who possess the knowledge (of revelation). *He maintains righteousness* (*qā'iman bil-qisti*). There is no God besides him. He is the powerful and wise one."[22]

7. (Sura 3:19) "The *right Interpretation of Scripture*[23] (*dīn*) (is) with God the *conformity / agreement / concord* (*islām*) (with the *Scripture*).[24] For those to whom the Scripture was given only fell into *disagreement / discord* (with the Scripture) after the (revealed) Knowledge (i.e., the Scripture) had come to them, while disputing[25] with each other. / Whoever denies the *Signs* (i.e., the *letters / characters*) of God (i.e., the written words of God in the revealed *Scriptures*), however, God will swiftly call (such people) to account."

In this verse, Paret overlooks the decisive context concerning the "Scripture"; he translates, following the Arabic understanding: "*Islam* counts with God as the (*only true*) *religion*. And those who have received the Scripture, became—*in mutual revolt*—at odds with one another only after the knowledge came to them. However, if one does not believe in the signs of God, God comes quickly for an accounting."[26]

Richard Bell (I 46b) renders this verse in quite similar manner:

> 17. Verily the *religion* in Allah's sight is *Islam*; and those to whom the Book has been given did not differ until after the knowledge (i.e., of revealed religion) had come to them, out of *jealousy* among themselves; if anyone disbelieves in the signs of Allah, Allah is quick to reckon.

SUMMARY

RELEVANCE FOR THE HISTORY OF LINGUISTICS

The foregoing philological analyses of the earliest known Arabic inscription in a cultic building have again made clear the decisive role which philology, as applied to historical linguistics, plays in the analysis of materials relevant for the history of culture and religions. All of the previous attempts at deciphering this earliest stratum of written Arabic, to which the language of the Qur'ān belongs and which supposedly served as the foundation for later "classical Arabic," have consequently led to serious misrepresentations of historical facts. This has occurred because scholars in the Western schools of Arabic and Islamic studies, arriving rather late on the scene, have uncritically put their trust in the traditional Arabic philology, despite the well-known principles of the historical-critical methods. These scholars have been deeply influenced by the strict classical rules of Arabic grammar, which in fact began around the end of the eighth century CE, and by the imposing quality of the Arabic lexicography and literature which appeared thereafter.

Consequently, they saw in this literary Arabic, which only appeared after the Qur'ān, the continued life of an "Old Arabic," whose roots naturally must have reached back into the pre-Aramaic period. They even argue that the Arabic philologists succeeded in creating a normative artificial language that served as a bridge between the various Arabic dialects and has stood the test of time. However, anyone who studies in-depth the Arabic commentators on the Qur'ān or the Arabic lexicographers must surely wonder at the philological incompetence of certain of the "authorities" when there is a question concerning an etymological explanation of one of the many "Arabic" words borrowed from the Aramaic. Here the currently existing shortfalls of Western scholars of Oriental studies can be seen; their ability to work in comparative Semitics and their competence, which far exceeds that of the traditional Arabic philologists, could have enabled them to offer help in this regard. As a result, foundational philological works such as a historical grammar of post-Qur'ānic classical Arabic, as well as historico-linguistic and etymological Arabic lexica, remain major desiderata. The realization of these works is just as pressing as the production of a critical edition of the Qur'ān; however, the necessary philological instruments, as well as a new generation of competent, well-trained scholars, are prerequisites for the evaluation of this edition. If this insight can work its way into the leading research institutions, perhaps this call will encourage them to carry out a sensibly coordinated research project on a historical-critical analysis of the Qur'ān in the near future.

RELEVANCE FOR THE HISTORY OF RELIGIONS

The text examined in this essay is concerned with the theological teaching of ʿAbd al-Malik, who was at the same time the Arabic caliph and the religious commander of the faithful (or, "of those entrusted to his care"; Arabic: *Amīr al-mu'minīn*). This doctrine contains Christological material throughout and is directed exclusively to those Christians who had defended an alternative conception of Jesus since the Council of Nicaea (325). This conclusion springs clearly from the context. Consequently, we may come to a number of conclusions.

PRE-NICENE SYRO-ARABIAN CHRISTIANITY[27]

The inscription is directed to the "People of the Scripture" (*ahl al-Kitāb*). Indeed, in the Qur'ān this description can refer to both Jews and Christians; however, according to the context, it is clear that Christians are the intended audience. By this teaching ʿAbd al-Malik defends his faith both in Christ as the "servant of God" (*ʿabd Allāh*) and also in the one God, over against the Trinitarian teaching of the followers of Nicaea. ʿAbd al-Malik is defending hereby a pre-Nicene Syrian Christianity, a version of Christianity that one should not refer to generally as "Jewish Christianity" but rather, more accurately, as "Syrian-Arabian Christianity." Further, this religious-theological symbiosis is accompanied by a linguistic symbiosis, as we see in this inscription and in the language of the Qur'ān, whose original version was put together entirely in the Syriac script (a way of writing Arabic called "Garshuni" or "Karshuni").[28] Consequently, without Syro-Aramaic we cannot understand this "mixed language" at all in the way it was to be understood.

"MUHAMMAD I" AND "MUHAMMAD II"

This textual analysis has shown that the gerundival participle *muḥammad* was not originally a personal name, but rather a commendation ("praised be") connected with the servant of God, namely, Jesus, son of Mary. It is only because later individuals understood this commendation as a personal name and assigned it to the prophet of Islam in the later "*Sīra*," the biography of "the Prophet," that we must distinguish in the future between a "Muhammad I" and a "Muhammad II." This distinction raises new historical problems. The inscription on the Dome of the Rock cannot be used to defend the position that "Muhammad II" lived from 570 to 632 CE, as the "Muhammad" named there was entirely referring to Jesus, son of Mary—that is, "Muhammad I." It is the task of historians to discover whether "Muhammad II," about whom the "*Sīra*" has so much to report, actually lived shortly before the appearance of the biography of the Prophet (ca. mid-eighth century), or whether he should be seen merely as a symbolic figure. The first name of his father, "*ʿAbd Allāh*," which may in fact be similarly symbolic, reflecting the expression "servant of God" from the Dome of the Rock, helps to suggest this latter possibility.

"ISLAM I" AND "ISLAM II"

This textual analysis has also made clear that, by the expression "*islām*," no proper name is intended, but rather a conformity with "the Scripture." Because this "Scripture," following the Christological content of the inscription, refers to the Gospel, it cannot then also refer to the Qur'ān, even if we find portions of the exact wording of the inscription reproduced in the Qur'ān. Consequently, it is a historical error to see in this expression ("*islām*") and in this context the beginning of "Islam" as we know it. Therefore, the speculation is confirmed that historical Islam began at the earliest in the middle of the eighth century. However much the Qur'ān may have existed partially before the rise of historical Islam—a possibility that the inscription on the Dome of the Rock suggests—it seems to have been the liturgical book of a Syrian-Arabian Christianity. Even if written Christian sources from the first half of the eighth century speak of a "Muhammad" as the "prophet of the Arabs," this phenomenon is to be explained as that this Arabian name for Christ was simply not current among

Aramaic- or Greek-speaking Christians. Therefore, this metaphor, which would have sounded strange to them, must have seemed to be the name of a new prophet. Regardless, there was no talk at this time of "Islam." Consequently, over against the practice of Islamic historiography up to this time, we must also distinguish in the future between "Islam I" and "Islam II."

CONCERNING THE CHRISTIAN SYMBOLISM OF THE DOME OF THE ROCK

According to Christian legends, which are connected with Jewish legends concerning the meaning of the Temple Mount, Jesus Christ was supposedly crucified at that place. In concert with his interpretation of sura 23:20, Heinrich Speyer has offered the following informative references:

> Therefore, according to the Book of the Cave of Treasures (*Schatzhöhle*, ed. Bezold,[29] p. 14), Adam was created in Jerusalem at the location of the Savior's crucifixion; there he gave the animals their names. There also Melchizedek functioned as priest (ibid., p. 254), Abraham nearly offered up Isaac as a sacrifice,[30] and *Christ was crucified*; this place is the midpoint of the world. Ephrem the Syrian, in his commentary on Ezekiel (Opp. II, 171A), also called Jerusalem "the middle of the earth."[31]

Jerome and Theodoret, taking as their text Ezekiel 5:5 ירושלים בתוך הגוים, explain the same thing, namely, that Jerusalem is the midpoint of the earth.[32] The "Book of Enoch" (ed. Dillmann, ch. 26) contains a description of the "middle of the earth," a place where there is to be a holy mountain; the author apparently had Jerusalem—more specifically, the Temple Mount—in mind. In that place Adam was also buried.[33]

The clearest indication of this is in the Book of the Cave of Treasures itself:

> And Isaac was twenty-two years old, when his father took him and climbed up the mountain Yabōs to Melchizedek, the servant of the most high God. The mountain Yabōs is actually the mountain range of Amoraea; at this location the cross of the Messiah was erected. There grew a tree which bore the lamb that saved Isaac. This place is the center-point of the earth—the grave of Adam, the altar of Melchizedek, Golgotha, the "Place of the Skull," and Gabbatha. There David saw the angel bearing the fiery sword.

There Abraham presented his son Isaac as a burnt offering; there he saw the *Messiah and the cross* and the salvation of our lord Adam.[34]

This wealth of legendary detail concerning the Temple Mount as the location of the crucifixion in the Syrian Christian tradition certainly provided ʿAbd al-Malik with the suggestion to associate this symbolic place with this originally Syrian-Christian sacred building. However, the following facts also testify that, according to tradition, this location was not only the place of Jesus' crucifixion but was also bound up with those of his entombment, resurrection, and ascension:

1. The expression "Dome of the Rock" (or "Cupola of the Rock"), still current today, comes from the Arabic form in which it has come down to us: قبة الصخرة / *qubbat aṣ-ṣaḫra*. This expression contains two pieces of information. First, the Arabic قبة / *qubba* derives from the Syro-Aramaic ܩܘܒܬܐ / *qubbṯā*, to which word belongs the variants ܐܩܒܘܬܐ, ܩܒܘܬܐ / *qebbūṯā* ("cupola"). The *Thesaurus*, II:3452, gives the meaning for this word as "*de arca in qua corpus sancti repositum est*" ("the cupola in/under which the body of a saint is stored"). The Arabic قبة / *qubba* corresponds to this term in the Islamic tradition as the word for a mausoleum dedicated to a ولي / *walī* ("friend of God" = "saint"). Second, the word الصخرة / *aṣ-ṣaḫra* ("the rock") refers to the stone that lies in the Dome of the Rock under the cupola, surrounded by a low railing. This stone, under which lies a *crypt*, symbolizes the *tomb of Christ*, which was reported in at least three of the Gospels (according to the Syriac Peshitta) to have been hewn out of a rock (Mt. 27:60; Mk. 15:46; Lk. 23:53; in Jn. 20:1 the text is concerned with the stone that had been rolled away from the tomb).

2. The Church of the Resurrection, also known as the Church of the Holy Sepulchre, which stands in the middle of the Old City of Jerusalem, is called in Christian Arabic both كنيسة القيامة / *kanīsat al-qiyāma* ("Church of the Resurrection") and also, especially in the area of Mesopotamia, قبر الخلاص / *qabr al-ḫalāṣ* ("Tomb of Salvation"). Both of these (Christian) conceptions, bound up with the burial location of Christ, were categorically cast aside by post-Qurʾānic Islamic theology (i.e., in the sense of "Islam II"); this occurred because later Islamic exegetes, consciously or unconsciously, misunderstood the Qurʾān's sporadic references to Christ's crucifixion, death, and resurrection in a Christian docetic sense. Consequently, Islamic tradition (i.e., "Islam II") was unable to link the Dome of the Rock to these core questions of Chris-

tian doctrine. "Islam I," rejecting the Hellenistic understanding of what it means for Christ to be the "Son of God," and also the corresponding doctrine of the Trinity, was still bound to these ideas, as the Christian symbolism associated with this sacred building inherently communicates.

3. Finally, the later Islamic exegetes believed that they saw a reference in the misunderstood passage in sura 4:157–58 to the direct ascension of Christ to heaven (not noticing the other Qur'ānic passages that contradicted this understanding); as a result, they connected this ascension, at least in Islamic folk belief, with a reminiscence that had its origin in a Christian story. This story goes as follows: If one visits the Holy Land and wants to see the place atop the Mount of Olives (east of Jerusalem) from which Christ ascended to heaven, one will be let into a walled courtyard, in the middle of which a medium-sized stone rises up just a bit from the ground. There one will be pointed to two depressions hewn into the rock, which are supposed to be the footprints that Christ left behind at his ascension. Incidentally, this same legend is told to the visitor to the Dome of the Rock. There, though, the footprints are supposedly those of the white horse "*Burāq*," on whose back "the Prophet" (Muhammad II) is to have made his journey to heaven.

This legend is important for the history of religions, in that it reveals a reminiscence of Christ stemming from the Christian period and yet still present in Islamic folk belief. Further, the transfer from "Islam I" to "Islam II," and that from "Muhammad I" to "Muhammad II," become apparent in that the Islamic tradition, in agreement with the later theology of "Islam II," reinterpreted the original Christian ("Islam I") symbolism of the Dome of the Rock. This reinterpretation took place in two stages. In the first step, the Dome of the Rock, which previously had been known as the site of Christ's burial and resurrection, was also said to be that of his ascension (as "Muhammad I"). Only later did the second step occur, by which the ascension, to which both the Gospel and the Qur'ān bear witness and which they both relate to Christ, was transferred legendarily to "Muhammad II."

My conclusion, then: according to the foregoing philological analyses of the inscription on the Dome of the Rock, "Islam I" was a pre-Nicene, Oriental Christian, Syrian-Arabian form of Christianity. This form of Christianity most likely survived in the region of Mesopotamia until the end of the Umayyad dynasty (ca. 750), and perhaps even longer. This explains why Jerusalem was the destination for pilgrimage before Mecca enjoyed the same honor. This also explains the spacious precinct that lies around the Dome of the Rock and served to receive these pilgrims. With the Christological doctrine presented in the inscription on the Dome of the Rock, "Islam I" desired to bear witness to its own orthodoxy with regard to Christian theology, against the opinions of Nicaea that were defended in the nearby Constantinian Church of the Holy Sepulchre. It is in this way that we can speak of the fidelity to the "Scripture" on the part of "Islam I."

"Islam II" refers to the turn from the (Christian) "Islam I" and, consequently, from the "Scripture." Other changes that resulted included the turn from Jerusalem to Mecca and the replacement of the "Scripture" (i.e., *Bible*)with the (Arabic) Qur'ān. These changes can only be explained in political terms. When the Abbasids took power, they wanted nothing more to do with their Umayyad opponents or with their religion. From this perspective, and from this point in time (ca. 750), "Islam II" slowly appeared as an exercise in "community building" ("Gemeindebildung") and was then put through politically. It is only because the Abbasids made "Islam II" their national ideology that one can explain historically why Christianized Arabian tribes were suddenly forced to submit to "Islam II." In this reconstruction, the meaning of the inscription on the Dome of the Rock has now become clear in its relations to historical linguistics and the history of religions; ironically, by means of its misunderstood expressions "Muhammad" (I) and "Islam" (I), the understanding of this inscription seems to have provided the parameters for "Muhammad II" and "Islam II."

The lack of a trustworthy literature from this period in order to explain the historical phenomena in question does not make life easy for the historian attempting to discover "truth." The enlightening inscription on the Dome of the Rock, however, is far more valuable; its language, which has been misunderstood up until today, has protected it from manipulation. Historians should be thankful for this situation, because it has "revealed" to us, in the truest sense of the word, a bit of historical truth by means of this new historico-linguistic interpretation.

NOTES

1. This inscription is reproduced in modern Arabic script in Oleg Grabar, *The Shape of the Holy: Early Islamic Jerusalem* (Princeton, NJ: Princeton University Press, 1996), p. 184.

2. This year would correspond to 694 CE (following a solar calendar) or 692 CE

(following a lunar calendar). The latter may have been introduced only at a later period by later Arabian historiographers, as a separate study will show. It seems to have been transmitted faithfully that the name of ʿAbd al-Malik was removed from the memorial inscription and replaced by that of the caliph al-Maʾmūn in the Hijra-year 216 (ca. 835 CE), as the current outer inscription testifies.

3. Christoph Luxenberg, *Die syro-aramäische Lesart des Koran: Ein Beitrag zur Entschlüsselung der Koransprache* (Berlin: Das Arabische Buch, [1st ed] 2000, [2nd ed.] 2004). In this article I will not consider other interpretations that I have presented heretofore.

4. Grabar, *Shape of the Holy*, pp. 92–99. Cf. p. 60 for an English translation of the inscription following its understanding up to that point.

5. Ibid., p. 186, for a reproduction of this later text in modern Arabic script.

6. Ibid., p. 185, for a reproduction of the original text in modern Arabic script with a few discrepancies.

7. Cf. Karl-Heinz Ohlig, *Ein Gott in drei Personen? Vom Vater Jesu zum "Mysterium" der Trinität* (Mainz: Matthias-Grünewald Verlag, 1999 [1st ed.] and 2000 [2nd ed.]), p. 41. Cf. also pp. 40ff., the section "4.2: Die zentralen Varianten des Gottdenkens bis gegen Ende des 2. Jahrhunderts; 4.2.1: Judenchristliche Traditionen; 4.2.1.1: Das Bekenntnis zum monotheistischen Gott nach jüdischer Art."

8. Ibid., p. 41, n. 90.

9. Ibid., p. 40, n. 86.

10. Rudi Paret, *Der Koran: Übersetzung*, 2nd ed. (Stuttgart: Kohlhammer, 1982), p. 486. The original German is as follows: "(18) Und: 'Die *Kultstätten* (*masājid*) sind (ausschließlich) für Gott da. Daher ruft neben Gott niemand (anders) an!' (19) Und: 'Als der *Diener Gottes* [Anm.: d.h. *Mohammed*] sich *aufstellte*, um ihm anzurufen [Anm.: Oder: zu ihm zu beten], hätten sie ihn (vor lauter Zudringlichkeit?) beinahe *erdrückt* (*? Kādū yakūnūna ʿalaihi libadan*)' [Anm.: Die Deutung des Verses ist ganz unsicher.] (20) *Sag*: Meinen Herrn (allein) rufe ich an [Anm.: Oder: Ich bete allein zu meinem Herrn] und geselle ihm niemand bei."

11. Régis Blachère, *Introduction au Coran* (Paris: G. P. Maisonneuve, 1947), p. 620. The original French is as follows: "(18) La *Mosquée* [*sacrée*] est à Allah. Ne priez donc personne à côté d'Allah! (n.: "La mosquée [*sacrée*]. V. sourate IX, 17.") (19) Quand le Serviteur d'Allah *s'est levé*, priant, [les Infidèles] ont failli être *contre lui* des *masses* (?). [n.: "*Le serviteur d'Allah* = Mahomet. / / *Kâdû yakûnûna ʿalay-hi libadâ* (var. *lubada* and *lubbâda*), 'les Infidèles etc.' Le sujet est incertain. Les commt. disent que c'est *djinns*, mais c'est peu probable."] (20) *Dis*: 'Je ne prie que mon Seigneur et ne Lui associe personne.'"

12. Richard Bell, *The Qurʾān: Translated with a Critical Re-arrangement of the Surahs*, vol. 2 (Edinburgh: T&T Clark, 1939), pp. 611ff.

13. The accusative usage of the preposition عليه / *ʿalay-hi* in place of له / *la-*

hū, in connection with the participial form of عبد / *'abada* (to pray to, to worship), as in sura 3:79 (عابدين لي = كونوا عبادا لي), should be considered with the parallel, alternating usage of the synonymous عكف / *'akafa*, as in suras 20:91 (لن نبرح عليه عاكفين) and 26:71 (نعبد اصناما فنظل لها عاكفين). This exchange of usage of the preposition على / *'alā* shows the process of its deteriorating use; this process included the obscure East Aramaic/Babylonian preposition إلى / *'ilā* and ended with its reduction to the simple لـ / *la*: على / *'alā* > إلى / *'ilā* > لـ / *la*.

14. *Mannā*, p. 544, provides the following definition for ܐܥܠܒ ܒ / *a'līb-*: أثم. أذنب / *aṯima, aḏnaba* (to transgress, to commit a moral error). The differing semantics of the Syro-Aramaic ܕܝܢܐ / *dīnā* must be considered in usages of the Arabic دين / *dīn*, depending on the context. The *Thesaurus* (I: 843) gives as definitions of the Syriac the following under (5), among others: "*modus interpretandi*" ("manner of interpretation, of assigning meaning"). At II: 2832, under ܐܥܘܠ / *a'-wel*, "*iniquum esse fecit, pervertit*," ܡܥܘܠ ܕܝܢܐ / *ma'wel dīnā* ("to pervert or warp justice").

15. ان is here the defective version of اين / *ayna*, which appears as the miswritten and misread انى / *annā* twenty-eight times in the Qur'ān. The fuller version اين / *ayna* becomes clear as a loan-word from the Syro-Aramaic ܐܝܟܐ / *aykā* in the form ܐܝܟܘ / *aykaw* ("how?"), which has been intensified by the enclitic ܗܘ / *(h)ū*. Cf. the definition in the *Thesaurus* (I: 148, 10): *quomodo fit?* Cf. also *Mannā*, 16: ܐܝܟܘ / *aykaw* (2) لماذا. كيف / *li-māḏā, kayfa* ("why, how?").

Paret, p. 85, was not able to explain this usage of ان / *'an* and paraphrased it thus: "May he be praised! (*He is far too exalted*) to have a child. To him belongs (even more, all). . . ."

Blachère, p. 130, translates it thus: "O keepers/possessors of the Scripture! Do not be *extravagant* in your *religion*!" Concerning this translation he notes, p. 169, "This very important verse is handed on with the absolute literalness which it demands." Concerning ان / *'an*, he defines it as "God forbid, etc." The text is: "Glory be to him *that he* had a child."

Bell, I: pp. 90, 169, translates it thus: "O People of the Book, do not go *beyond bounds* in your *religion*, . . . Allah is only one God; glory to him (*far from*) His having a son!"

Here we see that all three translators have overlooked a parallel passage in the Qur'ān that makes it clear that this ان is a defective version of انى (ostensibly *'annā* = اين / *ayna* = "how?"). The passage is sura 6:101 بديع السموت والارض انى يكون له ولد ولم تكن له صحبة وخلق كل شي وهو بكل شي عليم.

(Pickthall's translation): "The Originator of the heavens and the earth! *How* can he have a child, when there is for Him no consort, when he created all things and is Aware of all things?"). The Arabic بديع / *badī'* (the passive participle with an active meaning) seems to have arisen here by metathesis from the Syro-Aramaic ܥܒܕ / *'ābeḏ* ("maker, creator") in a literal translation from ܥܒܕ ܫܡܝܐ ܘܐܪܥܐ / *'ābeḏ šmayyā w-arʿā* (“creator of heaven and earth”) (cf. *Thesaurus*, II: 2766). The defective version of انى (ostensibly *ʾannā* = اين / *ayna*, *ayn*) points to the monophthongization of *ayn* to *ēn*. This is not the only place in the Qurʾān where ان is to be pronounced as *ēn*.

16. The Arabic اتخذ ولدا / *ittaḫaḏa waladan* reflects the Syro-Aramaic ܢܣܒ ܠܗ ܒܪܐ / *nsab̲ leh brā* (*Thesaurus*, II: 2394, “adoptavit filium”).

17. Cf. the same words in the mouth of Jesus at sura 5:117. On the word صراط / *ṣirāṭ* (“line”), cf. *Die syro-aramäische Lesart des Koran*, 2nd ed., p. 18, n. 6.

18. Blachère, p. 332, n. 35, believes this passage to be a later insertion and relates it to Muhammad. Bell, I: 287, translates اتخذ ولدا / *ittaḫaḏa waladan* as “to take to Himself any offspring.”

19. The Arabic شهد / *šahida* does not mean “to testify” but rather شهد / *šahhada*, which corresponds to the Syro-Aramaic ܣܗܕ / *sahheḏ*, for which *Mannā*, p. 480a, gives under (3): ناشد. استحث نبه. حذر. / *nabbaha*, *ḥaḏḏara*, *nāšada*, *istaḥaṯṯa* (“to caution, to warn, to swear by oath, to urge on”).

20. Literally, اولوا العلم / *ʾūlū l-ʿilm* means “members/possessors of knowledge,” that is, of the text. Elsewhere I will provide more information on the hyper-correct form اولو as the plural of آل / *ʾāl*, or as a secondary form of اوليا / *awliyā*, which is itself the plural of ولي / *walī*.

21. Morphologically, قيما corresponds to the Syro-Aramaic plural *nomen agentis* ܩܝ̈ܡܐ / *qayyāmē* and here should be understood as verbal in the sense of قيمين / *qayyāmīn*. For a lexicographical meaning, one should consult *Mannā*, pp. 663a / b, ܩܝܡ / *qayyem*, under (5): حقق. قرر. ثبت. أكد. مكن / *ḥaqqaqa*, *qarrara*, *ṯabbata*, *akkada*, *makkana* (“to make real, to conclude, to make firm, to confirm, to strengthen”). Cf. also C. Brockelmann, *Lexicon Syriacum*, p. 654a, under “Pa.: 4”: “*confirmavit*.”

22. His original German, found on p. 45, is: “Gott *bezeugt*, dass es keinen Gott gibt außer ihm. *Desgleichen* die Engel und diejenigen, die das (Offenbarungs)wissen besitzen. *Er sorgt für Gerechtigkeit* (*qāʾiman bil-qisti*). Es gibt keinen Gott außer ihm. Er ist der Mächtige und Weise.”

Blachère, pp. 77ff., desiring to clear some of the shadows away from this verse, makes three separate suggestions in the following translation: “1) He has *attested* (with regard to) Allah, as well as the angels and the possessors of knowledge; 2) Allah *attests* [*sic*] along with the angels and the possessors of knowledge; 3) Witnesses of Allah as well as the angels and the possessors of knowledge, that there is no divinity besides Him, arraying himself *with justice*, no divinity besides him, the Powerful, the Wise.”

Bell, I: 45ff., proposes a lacuna in the second portion of the sentence and translates it thus: “Allah hath *testified* that there is no god but He, *likewise* the angels and the people of knowledge; . . . *dispensing* justice, there is no god but He, the Sublime, the Wise.”

23. The understanding of this word results from its antonym, which immediately follows: اختلف / *'iḫtalafa* (to be in disagreement). The Arabic اسلام / *islām* reproduces the Syro-Aramaic ܫܠܡܘܬܐ / *šalmūṯā*. Cf. *Thesaurus*, II:4190ff.: *consensus, concordia*. Cf. also the *Ap.*, lexx. الاتفاق. الموافقة. / *al-ittifāq, al-muwāfaqa, ijmā'*, for which ܠܐ ܫܠܡܘܬܐ / *lā šalmūṯā* = خلاف / *ḫilāf* is given as the antonym. Cf. especially Michael Sokoloff, *A Dictionary of Jewish Palestinian Aramaic*, Bar Ilah University Press, first published 1990, second printing 1992, p. 147a/b, under דין (dīn): 8. "exegetical interpretation of scripture."

24. The first meaning of the Syro-Aramaic word ܕܝܢܐ / *dīnā* is "what is true, right"; cf. *Mannā*, 142b, which gives ten semantic meanings in total; the Arabic understanding of "religion" is secondary. The codex of Ibn Mas'ūd, following sura 18: 1–2, gives the reading دينا / *dīnan* instead of قيما / *qayyiman* ("straight") as the opposite of عوجا / *'iwajan* ("deviation"): عوجا بل دينا / *'iwajan bal dīnā*; cf. Arthur Jeffery, *Materials for the History of the Text of the Qur'ān* (Leiden: Brill, 1937), p. 55. In its context sura 18: 1 must read:

الحمد لله الذي انزل على عبده الكتب ولم يجعل له عوجا بل دينا

("Praise be to God, who has sent the Scripture down to his *servant* and who has not made it diverging (from what is right), but rather *straight*." In this Scripture ولم يجعل له / *wa-lam yaj'al* la-hū represents the Syro-Aramaic ܘܠܐ ܥܒܕ ܠܗ / *w-lā 'ḇaḏ leh* ("and did not make *it* [*al-kitāb* = "the Scripture"]) and should be understood as accusative in meaning. Concerning the use here of the expression "servant," which we have discussed above, Paret, p. 237, n. 1, notes, "that is, Muhammad." The text, however, certainly has in mind here "Muhammad I," insofar as the infant Jesus in sura 19: 30 calls himself عبد الله / *'abd Allāh* ("servant of God") and says of himself that اتيني الكتب / *'ātānī l-kitāba* ("he [God] has given me the Scripture").

25. Here as well, the Arabic بغيا represents morphologically the Syro-Aramaic plural present participle ܒܥܝܐ / *bā'yē* = *bā'ēn* ("[some plural group] disputing"). Cf. *Mannā*, p. 73a, ܒܥܐ ܥܡ / *b'ā 'am*: باحث. جادل. ناقش / *bāḥaṯa, jādala, nāqaša* ("to dispute, to discuss, to debate"). Cf. also what was said above at note 21 concerning قيما (falsely transmitted into Arabic as *qā'iman* = Syro-Aramaic ܩܝܡܐ / *qayyāmē*).

26. Paret, p. 45. Blachère, p. 78, translates الدين / *ad-dīn* in the same way: following the Arabic understanding, he has "religion" here. He also understands الاسلام / *al-islām* as a proper noun: "Islam." He gives بغيا بينهم / *baġyan* (= *bā'ēn*) *baynahum* as "by *mutual rebellion*."

Bell, I: pp. 46,17, understands the same expression in the same way; he translates the phrases in question "religion," "islam," and "out of *jealousy* among them."

27. Cf. here the article by Karl-Heinz Ohlig in the present volume.

28. I will give the graphological proof of this claim in a soon-to-be-published work.

29. The edition Speyer refers to is that of Carl Bezold, *Die Schatzhöhle (syrisch und deutsch)* (Leipzig: J. C. Hinrichs, 1883–1888). The English edition is that of E. A. Wallis Budge, *The Book of the Cave of Treasures: A History of the Patriarchs and the Kings, their Successors, from the Creation to the Crucifixion of Christ* (London: Religious Tract Society, 1927).

30. Cf. footnote 2: "Aphrahat (ed. Wright, p. 400) also explained that the mountain on which Abraham was to have offered up his son was the later Temple Mount. There is a shadowy memory of the role of Moriah in the Adam legend preserved in Ephrem the Syrian (*Opp. Bened.* I, p. 100 17C); cf. Louis Ginzberg, "Die Haggada bei den Kirchenvätern und in der apokryphischen Literatur (Fortsetzung)," *Monatschrift für Geschichte und Wissenschaft des Judentums* 43 (1899): 72: "Adam's body was buried in this place. . . . God pointed this place out to Abraham for the sacrifice, in order to show him that his own son as well—Jesus—would there be given over to death."

31. Heinrich Speyer, *Die biblischen Erzählungen im Qoran* (Gräfenhainichen: Schultze, 1931; reprint ed. in Hildesheim: Olms, 1961), pp. 63ff.

32. Ginzberg, "Die Haggada," p. 68, n. 3.

33. See Bezold's edition of the *Schatzhöhle*, p. 40, and Ephrem the Syrian, *Opp.* I:171. [Translator's note: I have not been able to find the edition of Ephrem referred to in both the quotation from Speyer and in this footnote. That they give "II: 171" and "I: 171," respectively, seems to suggest that there is a mistake in one of these; unfortunately, as the edition is not available to me, I cannot confirm the correctness of either reference.]

34. Bezold, *Schatzhöhle*, p. 146.

BIBLIOGRAPHY

Bell, Richard. *The Qur'ān Translated, with a Critical Re-arrangement of the Surahs.* 2 vols. Edinburgh: T&T Clark, 1937–1939.

Blachère, Régis. *Le Coran, traduit de l'arabe*. Paris: Librairie orientale et américaine, 1957.

Brockelmann, Carl. *Lexicon Syriacum.* 2nd ed. Halle: Sumptibus M. Niemeyer, 1928.

———. *Syrische Grammatik.* 8th ed. Leipzig: Verlag Enzyklopädie, 1960.

Déroche, François, and Sergio Noja Noseda, eds. *Sources de la transmission du texte coranique, I: Les manuscrits de style ḥiǧāzī*, vol. 1, *Le manuscrit arabe 328(a) de la Bibliothèque Nationale de France*. Paris: Bibliothèque Nationale de France, 1998.

Jeffrey, Arthur. *Materials for the History of the Text of the Qur'ān*. Leiden: Brill, 1937. Arabic portion: كتاب المصاحف ، للحافظ أبي بكر عبد الله بن أبي داود سليمان بن الأشعث السجستاني

(*Kitāb al-maṣāḥif li-l-ḥāfiẓ abī Bakr ʿAbd Allāh b. abī Dāwūd Sulaymān b. l-Ašʿaṯ as-Siǧistānī*). Cairo, 1936.

Manna, Jacques Eugène. *Vocabulaire chaldéen-arabe*. Mosul: Imprimerie des pères dominicains, 1900. Reprint ed. by Raphael J. Bidawid, with a new appendix: Beirut: Markaz Babil, 1975.

Ohlig, Karl-Heinz. *Ein Gott in drei Personen?: Vom Vater Jesu zum "Mysterium" der Trinität*. Mainz: Matthias-Grünewald Verlag, 1999 [1st ed.] and 2000 [2nd ed.].

Paret, Rudi. *Der Koran: Übersetzung*. 2nd ed. Stuttgart: Kohlhammer Verlag, 1982.

Smith, R. Payne, ed. *Thesaurus Syriacus*. 2 vols. Oxford: Clarendon Press, 1879–1901.

Sokoloff, Michael. *A Dictionary of Jewish Palestinian Aramaic*. Ramt-Gan: Bar Ilan University Press, 1990.

Speyer, Heinrich. *Die biblischen Erzählungen im Qoran*. Gräfenhainichen: Schultze, 1931. Reprint: Hildesheim: Olms, 1961.

Syriac Bible (63DC). London: United Bible Societies, 1979.

3

ON THE ORIGIN OF THE INFORMANTS OF THE PROPHET[1]

Claude Gilliot

INTRODUCTION[2]

The topic of the so-called Informants of the Prophet ultimately begs the question of a *qurʾān* ("lectionary"), or of the *qurʾān* before the Qurʾān (*al-qurʾān*), or rather of the various versions or stages of the Qurʾān *qua* text. This is so because, as time has gone on, we have been personally convinced that the Qurʾān is at least partially the work of a group[3] or of a community.[4] In this essay we will not treat of the topic of the informants in its entirety (that has already been done),[5] even though we have found more material in the meantime. What interests us most specifically here is the origin and the language of the informants.

The *locus classicus* of this topic in the Qurʾān is sura 16 (*al-Naḥl*): 103.[6] The text reads as follows: *Wa-la-qad naʿlamu annahum yaqulūna innamā yuʿallimuhu basharun. Lisānu l-ladhī yulḥidūna ilayhi aʿjamiyyun wa-hādhā lisānun ʿarabiyyun mubīnun.* Rückert's translation of this text is as follows: "We know as well, that people say that a person is teaching him. The tongue of that person whom they are talking about is foreign, but it is a pure Arabian tongue."[7]

The difference between *aʿjamī* and *ʿajamī*, according to Thaʿlabī and others before him,[8] is as follows:[9]

> The difference between the person who cannot speak good Arabic and the non-Arabian (on the one hand), and the Arabian and the nomad (on the other), is as follows. The one who cannot speak good Arabic, cannot speak correct Arabic, even if he lives in a Bedouin area; the non-Arabian comes from a non-Arabian land, even if he can speak correct Arabic. The Arabian nomad is the Bedouin; the Arabian belongs among the Arabians. (*al-farqu bayna l-aʿjamiyyi wa-l-ʿajamiyyi, wa-l-ʿarabiyyi wa-l-aʿrābiyyi*[10] *anna l-aʿjamiyya lā yafṣuḥu wa-in*[11] *kāna nāzilan bi-l-bādiyati, wa-l-ʿajamiyya mansūbun ilā l-ʿajamiyyi, wa-in kāna faṣīḥan, wa-l-aʿrābiyya*[12] *al-badawiyyu, wa-l-ʿarabiyya mansūbun ilā l-ʿarabi, wa-in lam yakun faṣīḥan*).

One sees immediately that a part of Rückert's translation is influenced by the Islamic quasi-dogma of the purity of the Qurʾānic Arabic,[13] for *mubīn* is the active participle of the causative or declarative fourth stem *afʿala*, which is here *abāna*. Consequently, *mubīn* does not here mean "pure" or "clear," but rather "making (the things) clear."[14] Muḥammad answers here that what he announces is an understandable (definite) Arabic language. This is a very unique and not very convincing style of argumentation on the part of the Qurʾān (or "of Muḥammad"; the reader can decide). Most likely the speaker intended to show that the things he was saying were not simply a reproduction of what foreigners had spoken to him, "but rather a repetition and confirmation of those things, based upon direct revelation."[15]

The language of the informant(s) was not Arabic, "good Arabic" (*aʿjamī*), or a foreign language, which could indicate that the informants were not Arabians.

WHAT CAN BE SAID ABOUT THE ORIGIN OF THE INFORMANTS?

It is possible that these informants were Christians of Aramaic origin. According to ʿUbayd (or ʿAbd) Allāh b. Muslim al-Ḥaḍramī,[16]

> We had two slaves from ʿAyn al-Tamr; the one was named Yasār (his *kunya* was Abū Fakīha [or Abū Fukayha][17]),[18] and the other was named Jabr. They

made sabres in Mecca, and they read in the Pentateuch (*al-Tawrāt*) and in the Gospel. Occasionally the Prophet would go over to them when they would read, and he would remain, in order to listen to them.[19]

In the texts of Ṭabarī[20] or Wāḥidī[21]:

According to ʿUbayd Allāh b. Muslim al-Ḥaḍramī, "we had (or, in Ṭabarī, "they had"), two Christian slaves (Ṭabarī: *ʿabdāni*; Wāḥidī: *ghulāmāni*) from ʿAyn al-Tamr; the one was named Yasār, and the other was named Jabr, and they polished sabres (*wa-kānā ṣayqalayni).*[22] They read a book that they had, which was in their language (following Wāḥidī; or, "they read the Pentateuch," following Ṭabarī and Māwardī),[23] and the Messenger of God went to them and listened to what they read (following Wāḥidī; or, "the Messenger of God sat down with them," following Ṭabarī), and the heathens said that he learned from them (following Wāḥidī; or, following Ṭabarī, "the unbelieving Qurayshis said that he sat with them and learned from them").

Or, in another place:

Jabr, the servant/slave (*ghulām*) of al-Fākih b. al-Mughīra (b. ʿAbd Allāh al-Maḫzūmī).[24] Jabr, the slave of al-Ḥaḍramī, the father of ʿAmr, ʿĀmir, and al-ʿAlāʾ, the sons of al-Ḥaḍramī. The name of al-Ḥaḍramī was ʿAbd Allāh b. ʿAmmār.[25]

It is said in yet another place that Ibn al-Ḥaḍramī possessed two young Christian servants: they read a book that they had, and this book was in either the Hebrew or the Byzantine script (*bi-l-rūmiyya*; does this reference more likely mean Aramaic than Greek?).[26]

ʿAyn al-Tamr[27] lay 130 kilometers southwest of Karbala; the city boasted a Christian population and church, and it also possessed a Jewish community and synagogue. ʿAyn al-Tamr, along with Ḥīra, Anbār, and other places,[28] was a part of the kingdom of Jadhīma al-Abrash.[29]

Most likely, we are concerned here with an Aramaic context, for according to the hypothesis of Jean Starcky, the archaic Arabic script derived from the Syrian branch of the Aramaic script:

The most likely prototype of this Arabic script was a Syriac cursive, one which would have developed from the Estrangela script in the chancery of

> the Lakhmids of al-Ḥīra. In this reconstruction, the cursive in question would then also have been used for the common Arabic speech in use in the region. It would only be from this point that the Arabic alphabet would have come into contact with the Roman provinces and with the Ḥijāz.[30]

Adolph Grohmann has expressed concerns about Starcky's arguments; nevertheless, in a 1991 article Gérard Troupeau accepted Starcky's hypothesis.[31]

The mention of Ḥīra arises from the relationships obtaining between Mecca and Ḥīra; these relationships are not only known historically[32] but also appear in some of the exegetical texts. For example, in a report of Muqātil b. Sulaymān (d. 150/767),[33] concerning sura 31 (*Luqmān*):6, he says: "Al-Naḍr b. al-Ḥārith made a merchant trip to Ḥīra; there he found the stories of Isfandiyār and Rustam. He bought them and brought them to the Meccans; he said, 'Muḥammad told you the stories of ʿĀd and Thamūd; in reality, they are like the stories of Rustam and Isfandiyār.'"[34] Onc finds more information from the reports of Muqātil and al-Kalbī (Abū l-Naḍr M. b. al-Sāʾib, d. 147/763)[35] in Thaʿlabī: ". . . I told them the stories of Rustam, of Isfandiyār, of the Persians (*al-aʿājim*) and of their kings (*al-akāsira*). These stories pleased them, and they no longer listened to the recitation of the Qurʾān."[36]

As is so often the case in such reports, these texts have to do with reversal of roles. Just as was the case with Musaylima, who was also a dangerous opponent of Muḥammad, his adversary al-Naḍr was ridiculed. Al-Naḍr b. al-Ḥārith most likely said that he had already heard or even read the "Punishment Stories" (probably only concerning ʿĀd and Thamūd) in Ḥīra, for it is said elsewhere that he "kept company with Christians and Jews" in Ḥīra.[37] Naḍr was probably well versed in legends from the Bible and other sources. Sprenger has written that "if he had not been dangerous to Muḥammad because of his knowledge, he certainly would not have had him executed. There was nothing that Muḥammad feared more than talent, and so he had people assassinated who did not carefully hide their opinions."[38]

Whether al-Naḍr b. al-Ḥārith had a hand in exposing Muḥammad is another matter, as one sees in Balādhurī: "Al-Naḍr said, 'The ones who are helping him to recite what is in his book (*innamā yuʿīnuhu ʿalā mā yaʾtī bihi fī kitābihi*) are Jabr, the servant (*ghulām*) of al-Aswad b. al-Muṭṭalib, and ʿAddās, the servant of Shayba b. Rabīʿa; it is said that the servant of ʿUtba b. Rabīʿa is also involved, as well as others.'"[39]

We are familiar with at least two versions of Ibn Isḥāq (d. 150/767) concerning the informants of Muḥammad. In Ibn Hishām (Ibn Hishām, Abū M. ʿAbd al-Malik, d. 218/833) it is said that Muḥammad "often sat on Merwa before the booth (*mabīʿa*) of a young Christian who was named Djebr and was a slave of the Benu-l-Hadrami, so that people used to say that Djebr taught Muḥammad much of what he revealed."[40] The other version is that of Ṭabarī, who says through his chain of tradents, M. b. Ḥumayd/Salama/Ibn Isḥāq: "The messenger of God often sat, according to what has been transmitted to me, on the hill of Marwa with a young Christian servant whose name was Jabr. He was a slave of the banū al-Ḥaḍramī, and the people used to say, 'By God, much of what Muḥammad teaches comes merely from Jabr the Christian, the servant of the banū al-Ḥaḍramī.'"

There is still a third version, but one that does not come from Ibn Isḥāq; rather, it comes from ʿAbd Allāh b. Kathīr, the famous Iranian reader of the Qurʾān who was also a *qass*:[41] "The people used to say, 'a Christian is teaching Muḥammad on the hill of Marwa; he is a Byzantine (*rūmī*),[42] whose name is Jabr.' He possessed writings (*kana ṣāḥiba kutubin*); he was a slave of Ibn al-Ḥaḍramī."[43] One finds a similar text according to Mujāhid b. Jabr (d. 104/722): "A slave of Ibn al-Ḥaḍramī, a Byzantine (*rūmī*) and the possessor of a book."[44]

Another place of origin that would have had to do with the Aramaic language would be Nineveh, as, for example, in a recension that goes back to ʿUrwa b. al-Zubayr: Ibn Lahīʿa (d. 174/790) / Abū l-Aswad (Yatīm ʿUrwa, M. b. ʿAr, d. 131/748 or later) / ʿUrwa b. al-Zubayr (d. ca. 94/712)[45] (or perhaps with the chain of tradents [?]: Mūsā b. ʿUqba [d. 141/758] / al-Zuhrī [d. 124/742]): after Muḥammad had spoken with Khadīja about his first revelation, she went to "a servant of ʿUtba b. Rabīʿa b. ʿAbd Shams, who was a Christian from Nineveh and whose name was ʿAddās." After she had explained the situation to him, ʿAddās was supposed to have said that Gabriel is "the one assigned (*amīn*) between God and the prophet, and he is the companion of Moses and Jesus."[46]

This ʿAddās is also named in another apologetic report. According to this text, when he told Muḥammad that he came from Nineveh, Muḥammad answered him, saying, "From the city of the pious man Jonah, the son of Amittai (Yūnus b. Mattā) . . . ."[47]

Elsewhere it is said that Muḥammad was taught by people from Babylon,[48] or that it was transmitted to him from them (*yarwīhi ʿan ahli Bābil*).[49]

Another possibility would be that the informers were of Jewish heritage. According to Muqātil b. Sulaymān, there was "a young servant (*ghulām*) of ʿĀmir b. al-Ḥaḍramī al-Qurashi who was a Jew and who spoke the 'Byzantine language' (*rūmiyya*; better would be 'a language of Byzantium'); his name was Yasār Abū Fakīha (or Abū Fukayha). When the unbelievers from Mecca saw that the prophet spoke with him, they said, 'Yasār Abū Fakīha is teaching him.'" Muqātil interprets *aʿjamī* from sura 16:103 thus: "*rūmī yaʿnī Abā Fakīha* (or: *Fukayha*)."[50]

Mujāhid's comment on sura 25 (*Furqān*):4–5 provides similar information, only without names: "That is nothing but a fraud that he concocted and concerning which other people helped him. . . . And they say, 'Stories (or probably 'written texts') of the aged (*asāṭīr al-awwalīn*)[51] that he wrote down for himself.'" Mujāhid adds to this comment, "Jews."[52]

Yet another possibility is that the informants were of Persian heritage. According to Ibn ʿAbbās, "They meant slaves of the Arabs, who were Persians" (*ašārū ilā ʿabīd kānū li-l-ʿArab min al-Furs*).[53]

NEW INFORMATION CONCERNING THE CASE OF THE SO-CALLED ʿUBAYD B. AL-KHIḌR AL-ḤABASHĪ, THE SOOTHSAYER (OR: "A MISTAKE IN SOME MANUSCRIPTS PRESERVED IN MOST OF THE EDITED TEXTS")

Sprenger mentions another possibility according to al-Ḥasan al-Baṣrī (d. 110/726): "Hasan (Baçry) names the Abyssinian ʿObayd al-Chidhr, who was a Kahin."[54] One still finds this reading in the modern, uncritical editions of Baghawī's commentary: "*wa-qāla* l-Ḥasan: *huwa* ʿUbayd b. al-Khiḍr al-Ḥabashī, the soothsayer (*al-kāhin*)."[55] In the poorly edited commentary of Thaʿlabī, one reads, "*qāla al-Ḥasan b. ʿUbayd b. al-Khiḍr: al-Ḥabashī al-kāhin,*"[56] where it should read, "*qāla al-Ḥasan: ʿUbayd b. al-Khiḍr al-Ḥabashī al-kāhin.*"

In Qurṭubī's commentary, he has that people had said that Muḥammad was instructed by (*wa-qīla ʿan*) ʿAdī (this should be "ʿabd") al-Ḥaḍramī, the soothsayer.[57]

In the opinion of the present author, none of these texts actually presents the correct reading. The reason for this is that Hūd b. Muḥakkam (fl. mid-third/tenth century), whose commentary is an Ibadi synopsis of the commentary of the Basrian Yaḥyā b. Sallām (d. 204/819) (who in his turn knew the exegesis of Ḥasan al-Baṣrī very well), gives the following interpretation of Ḥasan al-Baṣrī: *wa-fī qawli l-Ḥasani: huwa ʿabdun li-bni l-Ḥaḍramiyyi, wa-kāna kāhinan fī l-jāhiliyyati.*[58] One finds the same in Ibn a. l-Zamanīn (d. 399/1008), whose commentary is also a synopsis of that of Yaḥyā b. Sallām: *yuʿallimuhu ʿabdun li-banī l-Ḥaḍramiyyi, wa-kāna kāhinan, fī tafsīri l-Ḥasani.*[59]

In Yaḥyā b. Sallām's commentary itself (concerning sura 16:103), one finds the following: *wa-fī qawli l-Ḥasani: huwa ʿabdun li-bni l-Ḥaḍramiyyi, wa-kāna kāhinan fī l-jāhiliyyati* ("he was a slave of the Ibn al-Ḥaḍramī, a soothsayer from before Islam").[60] Further on, one reads (concerning sura 25:4), *wa-qāla l-Ḥasanu: yaʿnūna ʿabdan li-bni l-Ḥaḍramiyyi*[61]—here, notably, without "*al-Ḥabashī*."

OTHER POSSIBLE INFORMANTS

Among other possible informants, we would like to mention here only Waraqa b. Nawfal and Khadīja. We will first treat of Waraqa b. Nawfal, of whom we have made some remarks in another work, on the topos of "Holy, holy."[62] According to Ṭalha b. ʿAmr,[63] "I heard through the grapevine (lit. *balaghanī*), that Khadīja consorted a good deal with Khayr[64] (probably to be read "Jabr"), and that the Qurayshis said, 'Look, a slave of the banū al-Ḥaḍramī is teaching Khadīja, and Khadīja is teaching Muḥammad, and God revealed this verse (i.e., sura 16:103).'"[65]

Zayd b. Thābit, the secretary of Muḥammad, especially concerning his revelations, is another possibility.[66] He was most likely a Jew (according to multiple statements of Ibn Masʿūd, who says, for example, that "Zayd b. Thābit was still a Jew with his pair of side-curls"), or he had at least attended the Jewish school in Yathrib,[67] where he probably learned Aramaic or Hebrew (or the Aramaic script) or both. In a famous traditional statement with many versions or variants, Muḥammad is supposed to have said to Zayd b. Thābit, "I do not want to depend upon the Jews for my correspondence; therefore, you must learn Hebrew" (or, according to another reading, "Syriac")[68] or "the written text of the Jews (*kitāb Yahūd*)." We are dealing here, once again, with a reversal of roles, for Zayd b. Thābit already knew Aramaic or Hebrew.

We are not the first to have formulated the situation in this way—at least up to our own interpretation of the reversal of roles. The famous Muʿtazilī and theologian Abū l-Qāsim al-Balkhī al-Kaʿbī (d. 319/931)[69] held forth about this topic long ago, in his book on the critique of traditions and the tradents. He first introduced the following tradition concerning the Kufi al-Shaʿbī:[70] Qays[71]/Zakariyyā[72]/al-Shaʿbī, and Shaybān[73] and Qays/Jābir[74] and Firās[75]/al-Shaʿbī: "The Qurayshis were able to write, but the Helpers (*anṣār*) could not; consequently, the messenger of God commanded those who had no herds (or "property": *man kāna lā mala lahu*) to teach the script to ten Muslims; to these belonged Zayd b. Thābit." Al-Balkhī continued: "I questioned people who knew about the *Sīra*: Ibn a. l-Zinād,[76] M. b. Ṣāliḥ,[77] and ʿAbd Allāh b. Jaʿfar.[78] They negated this definitively and said, 'How could they have taught him the script, for Zayd b. Thābit had already learned it before the messenger of God came to Medina. When Islam arose, there were approximately ten people in Mecca who could write; when Islam came to Medina, there were twenty men who could write, among them Zayd b. Thābit, who could write both Arabic and Hebrew, as well as Saʿd b. ʿUbāda,[79] al-Mundhir b. ʿAmr,[80] Rāfiʿ b. Malik,[81] so-and-so, and so-and-so."[82]

We would go even further, for when it is said that Zayd b. Thābit was able to recite seventeen or ten suras of the Qurʾān,[83] even before Muḥammad came to Yathrib, the question inevitably arises: "Just what kind of 'suras' were they?" Would that not be yet another reversal of roles? For *sūra* is a word like *qurʾān*[84]—not of Arabic heritage, but rather from the Aramaic.[85] One can well imagine that the young Zayd knew by heart sections of Jewish writings that pleased Muḥammad, and which he then made his own.[86]

REMINISCENCES OF WRITTEN TEXTS OF THE INFORMANTS IN THE QUR'ĀN ITSELF, AS WELL AS IN THE EXEGETICAL TRADITION

Here we will concern ourselves with the *asāṭīr al-awwalīn*,[87] a phrase used in the Qurʾān that is normally translated as the "fairy tales," "stories," or "fables" "of the elders." This expression appears nine times in the Qurʾān. Aloys Sprenger recognized long ago that the root *s-ṭ-r* in the Qurʾān means "to write";[88] he thought, however, that Muḥammad had a teacher who had a book with that title, a conclusion that we cannot accept, especially with regard to the title. *S-ṭ-r* most likely came from the Aramaic and referred to something written.[89] According to Ibn ʿAbbās, *usṭūra* came from the Himyaritic and meant a written text or book (*kitāb*).[90] Or, *mā saṭara l-awwalūna fī kutubihim*.[91] It was also sometimes understood as *asājīʿ al-Ḥīra* (according to al-Suddī).[92]

Cultural memory still held a few traces of or references to a reminiscence of the time when Muḥammad and those who were helpful to him in the manufacture of the Qurʾān were instructed. As Christoph Luxenberg has elsewhere shown,[93] this applies to one particular sura, namely, 108 (*Al-Kawthar*), a text that to me makes almost no sense whatsoever. The theologian and exegete al-Māturīdī[94] expresses quite clearly his embarrassment at the first word of this sura. To be sure, he mentions the fabulous reports of the so-called River of Paradise, which God is to have given to his Messenger. He says, however, that "there is nothing fundamentally special (*takhṣīṣ*) in the giving of a river—no particular honor (*tashrīf*) or gift (*ʿaṭiyya*)—for God has promised more than that to his community, as is shown in the traditional sayings handed down from the Prophet: the people of Paradise have what no eye has seen, what no ear has heard, what has not come into the thought (*qalb*) of any human (*wa-lā khaṭara ʿalā qalbi bashar*)."[95] Apparently, al-Māturīdī preferred the first interpretation he mentions, namely, *al-khayr al-kathīr*. He mentions another possibility which he considered: something that God gave his Messenger, and of which we know nothing.[96] However, at the end of his presentation, he notes, "It has been said that *al-kawthar* is a word taken from the old books (*ḥarf ukhidha min al-kutub al-mutaqaddima*)." In this context he could have meant only Jewish or Christian books.

When I read this report, I thought to myself that it would be hopeless to try to find an older authority for this last interpretation. However, employing the virtue of perseverance,[97] I sought further and found what I was looking for in Thaʿlabī's commentary.[98] This older authority is Ibn Kaysān Abū Bakr al-Aṣamm,[99] an outsider under the Muʿtazilis, who interpreted *kawthar* thus: *huwa kalimatun mina l-nubuwwati l-ūlā wa-maʿnāhā al-īthr* (it reads thus in the published text;[100] but in the Ahmet III manuscript, it reads: *huwa kalimatun mina l-kutub al-ūlā maʿnāhā al-īthār*).[101] Qurṭubī mentions the interpretation of Ibn Kaysān, but he leaves out the sentence before *al-īthār*, simply writing "*al-īthār*."[102] The interpretation of *al-īthār* appears in another context, concerning sura 74 (*Muddaththir*):24: "And he said, 'That is nothing but sorcery that is handed down ("magie apprise" or "magie d'emprunt": *fa-qāla: inna hāḏā illā siḥrun yu'thar*).'" Here, though, *al-īthār* would seem to have to do with the selection (choice, preference) of a prophet, as in the Old Testament (?). However, it is noteworthy that *īthār*, like *kawthar*, has a rhyme with *rā*', like the sura that is called "*al-Kawthar*" itself.

There are other passages in the Qur'ān that Luxenberg has treated in various essays and articles, some of which are not yet published.[103] Among these is the verse of the veil (sura 24:31), which he has translated ". . . that they fasten their girdles around their waists. . . ."[104] Luxenberg has also written on "Christmas in the Qur'ān," concerning sura 97 (*al-Qadr*). (Incidentally, the end of this article, Luxenberg explains the differences between his own method and that of Lüling.) His translation of sura 97 reads:

1. We caused him (the infant Jesus) to descend on the Night of Destiny (of the star of the Nativity).
2. What do you know concerning what the Night of Destiny is?
3. The Night (the night office) of Destiny (of the star of the Nativity) is more beneficial than a thousand vigils.
4. The angels, (accompanied by) the Spirit, with the permission of their Lord, caused all sorts of hymns to come down to that place.
5. This (this night with these hymns) is peace, until the break of dawn.[105]

As is well know, Richard Bell long ago noted the word *salām* in verse 5 means something slightly different in the context of this sura than it normally does: "*salām* in the Qur'ān is usually a greeting. The idea of the night being 'peace' recalls descriptions of the Eve of the Nativity."[106]

THE INFORMANTS AND "MUḤAMMAD'S GOSPEL"[107]

When the Qur'ān cites the New Testament, it mentions the *Injīl*, as though there were only one single Gospel. The topic in the Islamic tradition of falsifying the Scriptures, and especially the New Testament or the Gospel, reminds one of specific critics of early Christianity from the pagan world, including Celsus (who wrote ca. 178), Porphyry, the Emperor Julian (ruled 361–363), and the Manichaeans. Tatian (ca. 120–173) and Marcion (ca.

85–160) reacted to these criticisms, in that they sought to present a single Gospel text. Consequently, Tatian's *Diatessaron* was the only translation of the gospel in Syriac until the beginning of the fourth century. Further, it remained for centuries the only Gospel text that was used in the liturgy.[108] There are a few places in the Qur'ān where one finds similarities with the *Diatessaron*, such as the parable of the sower (sura 48:29);[109] passages concerning the youth of Mary, John, and Jesus (suras 3:35–48; 19:3–36);[110] and a section on the crucifixion of Jesus (sura 4:157).[111]

Van Reeth offers a possible solution to the relationship between the Paraclete and *aḥmad* (sura 61:6). In his commentary on the *Diatessaron*, St. Ephrem identifies the Paraclete with Jesus on multiple occasions. In this case the Qur'ān is much closer to the *Diatessaron* and to Manichaeanism, in both of which the Paraclete possesses a prophetic function.[112] The identification of Muḥammad with the Paraclete was explicitly discussed in the Islamic tradition, including by Ibn Ishāq, who used the Syriac word *mênaḥḥemânâ* (which corresponds to the Arabic *qā'im*, from *naḥem*, "to raise from the dead").[113] In this tradition, Muḥammad is the prophet of the end of the world.[114] Supposedly, Muḥammad gave himself five names, in this order: "I have multiple names: I am *muḥammad*; I am *aḥmad*; I am the Eliminator (*al-māḥī*), for through me God will eliminate the unfaithful; I am the Gatherer (*al-ḥāshir*), for the people will be gathered to my feet; I am the Last (of the Prophets) (*al-'āqib*)."[115] One can even ask whether the name "Muḥammad," which was most likely not his original name,[116] does not come from a type of "*mimétisme concurrentiel*," or a competition with the Paraclete, who was understood as the "last Prophet."

In connection with the *Diatessaron*, Mani, and the Manichaeans—who wanted to emphasize the unity of the Gospel message—the topic of the "Informants" is a suggestion to us that a Syriac lectionary (*qeryān*), or at least portions thereof, was known in Mecca.

SUMMARY

Many of the reports in the Qur'ān did not sound particularly new to the minds of many of the Quraysh, as the Qur'ān itself, the "most strongly self-referential holy text in the history of religion,"[117] states (sura 25 [*Furqān*]:4–5). One can see this in its style, for the rhyming prose of the text is very noticeable when one leaves out the *iʿrāb* endings in order to hear how the texts were probably originally spoken. Consequently, people like Musaylima and others were ridiculed in the early Islamic traditions. This is also the reason that Muḥammad and his companions fought against some poets.[118] The soothsayers and the poets were able to do similar things: ". . . they say: We have heard. If we wish we can speak the like of this" (sura 8 [*Anfāl*]:31, in Pickthall's translation).[119] This self-referential character of the Qur'ān reflects not only a process of communication, as Angelika Neuwirth has often emphasized,[120] but also the fact that the Quraysh do not seem to have been much impressed early on by the Qur'ān's language and style. This only seems to have happened when Muḥammad became so strong that he nearly succeeded in gaining an authoritative position over the tribes.[121]

What interests us here, though, is the actual content of these reports or statements in the Qur'ān. The Arabian peninsula was no *terra deserta et incognita*; its people lived in relationship with their surroundings, most especially with the Aramaic, Jewish, and Christian cultures nearby (e.g., Syria, Ḥīra, Anbār). Much of what the Islamic tradition has handed down concerning the informants of Muḥammad is not absolutely historical, for the so-called occasions of revelations[122] (or "cause of revelations,"[123] *asbāb al-nuzūl*) also contain apologetic strands, and this impacts directly on"the informants of Muḥammad." Nearly all of these people became Muslim and confirmed, from the Islamic standpoint, the truth of the Muḥammadan revelation. Those surrounding Muḥammad also had a hand in this, including Khadīja, Waraqa b. Nawfal, and then the Jew Zayd b. Thābit.

If we were to take, however, Christoph Luxenberg's book[124] and combine it with the material presented above, we would have good reason to accept that the "*piste araméenne*," the Aramaic trail, is one of the possible (and also written) trails to follow that lead to the *one* lectionary (*qeryān*) that existed before *the* Arabic-Islamic lectionary (*al-qur'ān*), or better yet, before the various stages of this lectionary.

Luxenberg's book stands in the tradition of the "variant readings" of the Qur'ān, if we distinguish between three types of variations: 1) "the minor variation," comprising various readings of the same consonantal structure; 2) "the major variation," comprising variations in the consonantal structure, such as those in the so-called non-ʿUthmānic codices; and 3) "the very major variation," which involves an Arabic-Aramaic transformation of the consonantal structure.[125] Before Luxenberg, G. Lüling[126] had noticed something of the same thing with his theory concerning hymnology (as did Tor Andrae[127] and others before him, including Aloys Sprenger, Wilhelm Rudolph, et al.),[128] even if his method was not wholly convincing. Unfortunately, his book was almost completely ignored, especially in Germany, perhaps not only because his method and his theory concerning hymnology did not always convince people, but probably also because of the "Nöldeke-ian," and "Spitaler-ian" dogma of the "classical language" of the Qur'ān, a dogma that was so strongly influenced by the Islamic imagination concerning the language of the Qur'ān. Our Orientalist forebears did not allow themselves to be so influenced by this dogma; for example, Friedrich Leberecht Fleischer wrote, "We do not share the exclusively philological and religious perspective of the Arabian lexicographers. Our question does not concern the purest Arabic, the most correct, and the most beautiful; our question is simply 'What is Arabic at all?'"[129]

The neo-Romantic school of Orientalism, with its motto of "God is beautiful!" was not awakening at that time—neither on the Rhine, nor on the Spree, nor on the banks of other rivers, at least not in the field of Qur'ānic studies.

NOTES

1. This essay is an expanded version of a paper I gave in German at the symposium "Historische Sondierungen und methodische Reflektionen zur Koranexegese: Wege zur Rekonstruktion des vorkoranischen Koran," held in Berlin, January 21–25, 2004. An English version of the same paper appeared in 2005 in the published proceedings of the symposium.

2. For more references, cf. Claude Gilliot, "Les 'informateurs' juifs et chrétiens de Muḥammad: Reprise d'un problème traité par Aloys Sprenger et Theodor Nöldeke," *Jerusalem Studies in Arabic and Islam* 22 (1998): 84–126, and idem, "Informants," *Encylopedia of the Qur'ān* (Leiden: Brill, 2001–2006), II: 512–18.

3. Cf. Gilliot, "Informants," 517b; idem, "Le Coran, fruit d'un travail collectif?" in *Al-Kitāb: La sacralité du texte dans le monde de l'Islam (Actes du Symposium international tenu à Leuven et Louvain-la-Neuve du 29 mai au 1 juin 2002*, ed. D. de Smet, G. de Catallaÿ, and J. M. F. van Reeth, Acta Orientalia Belgica, Subsidia III (Bruxelles: Belgisch Genootschap voor Oosterse Studiën/ Société belge d'Études orientales, 2004), *passim*, but especially pp. 222–23.

4. Karl-Heinz Ohlig, "Der Koran als Gemeindeprodukt," in "Neue Wege der Koranforschung," ed. Hans-Caspar Graf von Bothmer, Karl-Heinz Ohlig, and Gerd-Rüdiger Puin, *Magazin Forschung* (Universität des Saarlandes) 1 (1999): 33–37;

Claude Gilliot, "Une reconstruction critique du Coran," a paper given at the First World Congress of Middle Eastern Studies (WOCMES), Mainz, Germany, September 8–13, 2002, concerning the working group organized by Manfred Kropp (director of the Institut der Deutschen Morgenländischen Gesellschaft in Beirut) called "Results of Contemporary Research on the Qur'ān," §§1 and 23.

5. Gilliot, "Informateurs," and idem, "Informants."

6. Even if they do not contain as many specific details, one can consult the various commentaries on the Qur'ānic passage sura 25 (*Furqān*):4–5: Muqātil b. Sulaymān (d. 150/767), *Tafsīr*, III:226–27; Rāzī (Fakhr al-Dīn, d. Shawwāl 1, 606 [March 29, 1210]), *Tafsīr*, XXIV:50, where he answers with the challenge (*taḥaddī*) and the Qur'ān's "inimitability" (*i'jāz*) and "insurpassibility of correctness" (*nihāyat al-faṣāḥa*); Qurṭubī (d. Shawwāl 9, 671 [April 29, 1273]), *Tafsīr*, XIII:3–4; Ibn 'Ādil (Sirāj al-Dīn a. Ḥafṣ 'Umar b. 'Alī b. 'Ādil al-Dimashqī al-Ḥanbalī, writing 880/1475), *Lubāb* XIV:478. Concerning sura 26 (*Shu'arā'*):192–98: Muqātil, *Tafsīr*, III:279–80. Concerning sura 41 (*Fuṣṣilat*):44: Muqātil, *Tafsīr*, III:745, cited by Tha'labī, *Tafsīr*, VIII:298. Concerning sura 44 (*Dukhān*):14: Muqātil, *Tafsīr*, III:819; Tha'labī (Abū Isḥāq A. b. M., d. Muḥarram 427 [November 5, 1035]), *Tafsīr*, VIII:350, but without giving names of the informants of Muḥammad. Concerning sura 74 (*Muddaththir*): 24–25, cf. Hūd b. Muḥakkam, *Tafsīr*, IV:436; Tha'labī, *Tafsīr*, X:73; Qurṭubī, *Tafsīr*, XIX:76–77.

7. Rückert's German is: "Wir wissen wohl auch, daß sie sagen: es lehret ihn ein Mensch. Die Zunge dessen, den sie meinen ist eine fremde, aber dies ist rein arabische Zunge." Cf. Hartmut Bobzin, ed., *Der Koran in der Übersetzung von Friedrich Rückert*, 3rd ed. (Würzburg: ERGON, 2000).

8. Farrā' (d. 207/822), *Ma'ānī*, II:283, concerning sura 26:198: *wa-l-a'jamiyyu al-mansūbu ilā aṣlihi ilā l-'ajami wa-in kāna faṣīḥan*; Naḥḥās (d. 338), *I'rāb*, III:192, concerning sura 26:198, has a somewhat more developed comment than that of Farrā'; Ṭabarī (d. 310/923), *Tafsīr*, XIX:113, concerning sura 26:198.

9. Tha'labī, *Tafsīr*, VI:44.

10. In the edited text, VI:44, it says "*al-'irābī*" where it should read "*al-a'rābī*."

11. In the edited text, it says "*wa-annahu*" where it should read "*wa-in*."

12. In the edited text, it says "*al-'irābī*" where it should read "*al-a'rābī*."

13. Cf. John Wansbrough, *Quranic Studies: Sources and Methods of Scriptural Interpretation*, London Oriental Series no. 31 (Oxford: Oxford University Press, 1977) pp. 98–99, concerning *a'jamī* and *'ajamī* and their use by the exegetes in the interests of an idea of a *lingua sacra* (99ff.); cf. Claude Gilliot and Pierre Larcher, "Language and Style of the Qur'ān," *Encyclopedia of the Qur'ān*, III:113–15.

14. Cf. Gilliot and Larcher, "Language and Style," p. 114b, as well as the whole section on pp. 113–15 bearing the title "The Qur'ān on His Own Language and Style: Does the Qur'ān Really Say It Is in 'A Clear Arabic Tongue'?"

15. Frants Buhl, *Das Leben Muhammeds*, 3rd ed. (Heidelberg: Quelle & Meyer, 1961), p. 164.

16. Ibn a. Muslim al-Ḥaḍramī; cf. Mizzī, *Tahdhīb*, XII:267, no. 4268. Ibn Ḥajar, *TT*, VII:47–48 and VI:31, no. 50, under "'Al.," refers to 'Ubayd Allāh. The expression "we had" appears to refer to the fact that this particular tradent is of the family of al-'Alā' b. 'Abd Allāh b. 'Ammār b. al-Ḥaḍramī (d. 21/642; cf. Sam'ānī, *Ansāb*, II:230), who had two brothers, 'Amr and 'Āmir.

17. Qurṭubī, *Tafsīr*, X:178, has *Nabt* (or *Nabit*) *wa-yuknā Abā Fukayha* (or *Abū Fakīha*), in Zabīdī, *Tāj*, XXXVI:462a.

18. This parenthetical comment is not in the published text, but it appears in the Ahmet III manuscript.

19. Cf. Tha'labī, *Tafsīr*, VI:43–44, sura 16 (Naḥl):103; Abū l-Muẓaffar al-Sam'ānī (d. 489/1096), *Tafsīr*, III:202; Qurṭubī, *Tafsīr*, X:178; Ibn 'Ādil, *Lubāb*, XII:108; Aloys Sprenger, *Das Leben und die Lehre des Moḥammad*, 3 vols (Berlin: Nicolaische Verlagsbuchhandlung, 1869), II:388; Gilliot, "Informateurs," pp. 91–93, §14.

20. Ṭabarī, *Tafsīr*, XIV:178, ll. 21–26.

21. Wāḥidī (Abū l-Ḥasan 'Alī b. A. al-Nīsābūrī, d. Jumādā II 468 [January 11, 1076]), *Wasīṭ*, III:84–85.

22. In the edition of Ṭabarī, "*ṭiflayni,*" where it should read "*ṣayqalayni.*"

23. Māwardī (d. 450/1058), *Nukat*, III:215, where it should read "*Ḥusayn 'an 'Abd Allāh,*" or "*'Ubayd Allāh b. Muslim,*" not "*Ḥusayn b. Abd Allāh b. Muslim.*"

24. Suhaylī (d. 581/1185), *Ta'rīf*, p. 173 (where it should read *al-Fākih*, not *al-Fākiha*; cf. Zabīdī, *Tāj*, XXXVI:463a), pp. 95–96. His wife was Hind Bint 'Utba b. Rabī'a al-Hāshimiyya. She married Abū Sufyān and became the mother of Mu'āwiya. Cf. Ibshīhī, *Al-Mustaṭraf*, trans. by G. Rat, II:172–75.

25. Suhaylī, *Ta'rīf*, 173, 96, according to the exegete Abū Bakr al-Naqqāsh (M. b. al-Ḥasan b. Ziyād al-Mawṣilī, d. 351/962), in his Qur'ānic commentary *Shifā' al-ṣudūr*, also cited by Qurṭubī, *Tafsīr*, X:177, on sura 16:103.

26. Bayhaqī (Abū Bakr, d. 458/1066), *Dalā'il*, I:17.

27. Cf. Saleh A. El-Ali's article in *EI*, I:812; cf. also Guy Le Strange, *The Lands of the Eastern Caliphate: Mesopotamia, Persia, and Central Asia, from the Moslem Conquest to the Time of Timur* (Cambridge: Cambridge University Press, 1905; reprint edition, London: Cass, 1966), pp. 65, 81.

28. Cf. Alfred-Louis de Prémare, *Les fondations d'Islam: Entre écriture et histoire* (Paris: Seuil, 2002), pp. 242–60, concerning Ḥīra and Anbār.

29. Ṭabarī, *Annales*, I:750; *The History of al-Ṭabarī*, IV:132.

30. Gerhard Endress, "Herkunft und Entwicklung der arabischen Schrift," in *Grundriss der arabischen Philologie*, vol. 1, *Sprachwissenschaft*, ed. Wolfdietrich Fischer (Wiesbaden: Ludwig Reichert Verlag, 1982), p. 170.

31. Gérard Troupeau, "Réflexions sur l'origine syriaque de l'écriture arabe," in

Semitic Studies in Honor of Wolf Leslau, 2 vols., ed. Alan S. Kaye (Wiesbaden: Otto Harrassowitz, 1991), pp. 1562–70. In "L'écriture arabe et l'Arabie," p. 66, Christian Robin presents both of these hypotheses but actually supports neither the former (that of a Nabataean origin) nor the latter (a Syrian origin): "Cette écriture dérive d'une écriture araméene de Syrie, soit le nabatéen, soit le syriaque," *Pour la science (Dossier)* (October 2002): 66.

32. Michel Tardieu, "L'arrivée des manichéens à al-Hira," in *La Syrie de Byzance à l'Islam: VIIe-VIIIe siècles*, ed. Pierre Canivet and Jean-Paul Rey-Coquais, Actes du colloque international, Lyon—Maison de l'Orient méditerranéen, Paris—Institut du monde arabe, 11–15 Septembre 1990 (Damas: Institut français de Damas, 1992), pp. 15–16, confirms what Ibn Qutayba wrote, namely, that there were Manichaeans among the Qurayshis who had taken on this religion from Ḥīra: "*kānat al-zandaqa fī Quraysh akhadhahā min al-Ḥīra*" (*Ibn Coteibas Handbuch der Geschichte*, ed. Wüstenfeld, p. 299; *Maʿārif*, ed. ʿUkkāsha, p. 621).

33. Concerning Muqātil b. Sulaymān, cf. Gilliot, "Muqātil, grand exégète, traditionniste et théologien maudit," *Journal Asiatique* 279 (1991): 39–92.

34. Muqātil, *Tafsīr*, III:433; Yaḥyā b. Sallām, *Tafsīr*, ed. Ḥammādī Ṣammūd, *al-Juzʾ al-sādis ʿashar wa-l-thāmin ʿashar min Tafsīr Yaḥyā b. Sallām*, p. 131: *wa-fī tafsīr al-Kalbī annahā nazalat fī l-Naḍr b. al-Ḥārith min banī ʿAbd al-Dār wa-kāna rajulan rawiya li-aḥādīth al-jāhiliyya wa-ashʿārihā* (taken over from Hūd b. Muḥakkam, *Tafsīr*, III:3322–23).

35. Concerning him, cf. the article by Josef van Ess in *Theologie und Gesellschaft im 2. und 3. Jahrhundert Hidschra: Eine Geschichte des religiösen Denkens im frühen Islam*, 6 vols. (Berlin: Walter de Gruyter, 1991–97), I:298–301. Concerning the similarities between his exegesis and that of Muqātil, cf. Gilliot, "La théologie musulmane en Asie Centrale et au Khorasan," *Arabica* 49, no. 2 (2002): 133.

36. Thaʿlabī, *Tafsīr*, VII:310, concerning sura 31:6 (taken over from Baghawī, *Tafsīr*, III:489); Wāhidī, *Wasīṭ*, III:19; cf. Sprenger, *Leben*, II:393.

37. Balādhurī, *Ansāb al-ashrāf*, I:139–42; cf. Gilliot, "Informateurs," p. 98, §25. Or: *yamurru bi-l-Yahūdi wa-l-Naṣārā fa-yarāhum yarkaʿūna wa-yasjudūna wa-yaqraʾūna l-Tawrāta wa-l-Injīla, fa-jāʾa ilā Makkata fa-wajada rasūla Llāhi yuṣallī wa-yaqraʾu l-Qurʾāna, fa-qāla l-Naḍru: "qad samiʿna law nashāʾu la-qulnā mithla hādhā"* (sura 8 [*Anfāl*]:31); Baghawī, *Tafsīr*, II:245, taken over with additions from Thaʿlabī, *Tafsīr*, IV:350.

38. Aloys Sprenger, "Über eine Handschrift des ersten Bandes des Kitáb Ṭabaqát al-kabyr vom Sekretär des Wáqidy," *Zeitschrift der Deutschen Morgenländischen Gesellschaft* 3 (1849): 455. Cf. Claude Gilliot, "Poète ou prophète? Les traditions concernant la poésie et les poètes attribuées au prophète de l'islam et aux premières générations musulmanes," in *Paroles, signes, mythes: Mélanges offerts à Jamal Eddine Bencheikh*, ed. Floréal Sanaugustin (Damas: Institut français d'études arabes de Damas, 2001), pp. 382–88 (against the prophet).

39. Balādhurī, *Ansāb al-ashrāf*, I:140–41, no. 291; cf. Gilliot, "Informateurs," p. 99, §26.

40. *Sīra* (Wüstenfeld), 260/ I:393; Sprenger, *Leben*, II:388. This text is based on the translation of Gustav Weil, *Das Leben Mohammeds nach Mohammed Ibn Ishak und Abd el Malik Ibn-Hischam*, Die fünfzig Bücher no. 14 (Berlin: Ullstein, 1916), p. 194. Cf. also Gilliot, "Informateurs," p. 91, §13.

41. Abū Maʿbad al-Dārī al-Kinānī al-Makkī, b. 48 in Mecca, d. after 122/740; Dhahabī, *Siyar*, V:318–22; cf. *GdQ*, III:166: "al-Dārī (i.e., the spice-dealer)"; most of the sources, however, say that he was a *mawlā* of the *banū al-Dār*, etc., and that he was a *ʿaṭṭar* (spice-dealer). Samʿānī, *Ansāb*, II:443, following the *ʿIlal al-qiraʾāt* of Abū Naṣr Manṣūr b. M. al-Muqriʾ al-ʿIrāqī, has "*al-dārī bi-lughat ahl Makka al-ʿaṭṭār.*"

42. *Rūm* can mean the Greeks from the Byzantine Empire or from Asia, but it most likely refers also to Aramaeans or Christians of Aramaic language in the Byzantine Empire.

43. Ṭabarī, *Tafsīr*, XIV:178, II: 15–18.

44. Hūd b. Muḥakkam, *Tafsīr*, II:389.

45. Bayhaqī, *Dalāʾil*, II:145, where the chain of tradents follows the report; cf. Gregor Schoeler, *Charakter und Authentie der muslimischen Überlieferungen über das Leben Mohammeds* (Berlin: Walter de Gruyter, 1996), p. 81, according to Bayhaqī, whose *isnād* Schoeler claims was misunderstood by Suyūṭī, *Khaṣāʾiṣ*, I:93. Suyūṭī has: Mūsā b. ʿUqba (d. 141/758)/al-Zuhrī (d. 124/742), according to al-Bayhaqī and Abū Nuʿaym al-Iṣfahānī (d. 430/1038). The problem, however, is that we do not have the text of Abū Nuʿaym. It is not in his *Dalāʾil al-nubuwwa*; it was most likely in his *Maʿrifat al-ṣaḥāba*. Consequently, we cannot be certain whether Schoeler is right. Bayhaqī, *Dalāʾil*, II:145, writes: "*wa-qad dhakara Ibn Lahīʿa ʿan Abī l-Aswad ʿan ʿUrwa b. al-Zubayr hādhihi l-qiṣṣata bi-nahwi hādhā wa-zāda fīhā.*" This could be understood as saying that ʿUrwa b. al-Zubayr gave approximately the same report (as Mūsā b. ʿUqba?), but that he also added to it. The sure tradent in his report seems to be al-Zuhri; cf. Bayhaqī, *Dalāʾil*, II:143, l. 1. Cf, nevertheless, Gilliot, "Informateurs," p. 102, n. 120, following Dhahabī (but the reference should be to p. 129, not p. 149).

46. Bayhaqī, *Dalāʾil*, II:143; Gilliot, "Informateurs," p. 101, §29; cf. also Suyūṭī, *Khaṣāʾiṣ*, I:93; M. Bāqshīsh Abū Mālik (collected by him), *Al-Maghāzi li-Mūsā Ibn ʿUqba*, 64 (only according to Ibn Ḥajar, *Iṣāba*, IV:467, and consequently without a chain of tradents); Sprenger, *Leben*, II:389, following Ibn Ḥajar, *Iṣāba*.

47. With a chain of tradents that traces back to ʿUrwa b. al-Zubayr (d. ca. 94/712): Ibn Lahīʿa (d. 174)/Abū l-Aswad (Yatīm ʿUrwa, M. b. ʿAr., d. 131/748 or later)/ʿUrwa, in Abū Nūʿaym al-Iṣfahānī, *Dalāʾil al-nubuwwa*, p. 296; Gilliot, "Informateurs," pp. 104–105, §32 and n. 133. Concerning this chain of tradents, cf. Schoeler, *Charakter und Authentie*, p. 81.

48. Qurṭubī, *Tafsīr*, XIX:77: "*qīla: arāda annahu talaqannahu min ahli Bābil.*" Also, according to al-Suddī (Abū M. Ismāʿīl b. a. Karīma al-Kūfī, d. 128/745; *GAS*, I:32–33): "Yasār, a slave of the banū al-Ḥaḍramī who sat with the prophet" (p. 76); cf. also p. 77: "*wa-qila ʿan Musaylima.*" In Ibn ʿĀdil, *Lubāb*, XIX:515: "Sayyār [*sic*; it should read here "Yasār"], a slave of the banū al-Ḥaḍramī, or of someone who claimed in front of him that he was a prophet."

49. Thaʿlabī, *Tafsīr*, X:73, concerning sura 74:24–25, with Yasār and Jabr, and also Musaylima, the lord of Yamāma (*ṣāḥib al-Yamāma*).

50. Muqātil, *Tafsīr*, II:487, ll. 8–18; Gilliot, "Informateurs," pp. 90–91, §12. The following should be to references Abū l-Muẓaffar al-Samʿānī, *Tafsīr*, V:56–57, concerning sura 41:44.

51. See below, in the section entitled "Reminiscences of Written Texts . . . ."

52. Ṭabarī, *Tafsīr*, XVIII: 181, II: 20–22; Thaʿlabī, *Tafsīr*, VII:123; Thaʿlabī adds to this: "*wa-qīla*: Yasār wa-ʿAddās *mawlā* Ḥuwayṭib b. ʿAbd al-ʿUzzā." Mujāhid also says, "*ashārū ilā qawmin min al-Yahūdi*"; Ibn ʿAṭiyya, *Muḥarrir*, IV:200, concerning sura 25:4. Mujāhid, *Tafsīr* (Ādam/Warqaʾ/Ibn a. Najīh/Mujāhid), however, has "*Yahūdun taqūluhu*" (concerning 25:4).

53. Ibn ʿAṭiyya, *Muḥarrir*, IV:200, concerning sura 25:4. In Abū Ḥayyān (Athīr al-Dīn M. b. Yūsuf b. ʿAlī al-Andalusī al-Nifzī, d. Ṣafar 18, 745 [July 1, 1344]), *Baḥr*, VI:481, according to Ibn ʿAbbās: Persian slaves of the Arabians: Abū Fakīha, *mawlā* of both al-Haḍramī or the banū al-Ḥaḍramī, Jabr, Yasār, and others; cf. Gilliot, "Informateurs," p. 91, n. 52.

54. Sprenger, *Leben*, II:389, according to Baghawī, *Tafsīr*, concerning sura 25:4.

55. Baghawī, *Tafsīr*, III:361, concerning sura 25:4

56. Thaʿlabī, *Tafsīr*, VII:123, concerning sura 25:4, where it should read in the edited text, "*qāla l-Ḥasan: ʿUbayd b. al-Khiḍr al-Ḥabashī al-kāhin,*" not "*qāla l-Ḥasan b. ʿUbayd b. al-Khiḍr: al-Ḥabashī al-kāhin.*" Unfortunately, this appears thus in Gilliot, "Informants," p. 513b.

57. Qurṭubī, *Tafsīr*, XIX:77, concerning sura 74 (*Muddaththir*):24–25.

58. Hūd b. Muḥakkam, *Tafsīr*, II:389.

59. Ibn a. l-Zamanīn (Abū ʿAbd Allāh Muḥammad b. ʿAbd Allāh b. ʿĪsā al-Murrī al-Andalusī al-Ilbīrī, d. Rabīʿ II 399 [in 1008]), *Tafsīr*, IV:200, concerning sura 44:14.

60. Al-Bashīr al-Mkhīnīnī, *Taḥqīq al-juzʾ al-thālith ʿashar wa-l-juzʾ al-sābīʿ ʿashar min Tafsīr Yaḥyā b. Sallām*, p. 19.

61. Ibid., p. 94. The editor of Ibn ʿĀḍil, *Lubāb* XIV:478 (concerning sura 25:4), chose the reading "*wa-qāla l-Ḥasan: ʿUbayd b. al-Ḥaṣr* [*sic*] *al-Ḥabashī al-kāhin,*" and he wrote in the critical apparatus, "*ka-dhā bi-l- Baghawiyyi,*" adding further, however, that one can read in the manuscript of Ibn ʿĀḍil the text "*al-Ḥaḍramī.*" He made the wrong choice.

62. Gilliot, "Informateurs," pp. 99–104, §§27–30; this section is summarized in Gilliot, "Le Coran," pp. 188–90. Cf. also Schoeler, *Charakter und Authentie*, passim. On Waraqa himself, cf. Sprenger, *Leben*, I:124–34.

63. This person is most likely Ṭalha b. ʿAmr b. ʿUthmān al-Ḥaḍramī al-Makkī (d. 152/769), one who had a bad reputation from the standpoint of Islamic "tradent criticism." Cf. Dhahabī, *Mīzān*, II:340–42, no. 4008; Mizzī, *Tahdhīb*, IX:2612, no. 2962; Ibn Ḥajar, *TT*, V:23–24.

64. The name appears thus in the Ahmet III manuscript and in the edited text of Thaʿlabī's commentary.

65. Thaʿlabī, *Tafsīr*, VI:43, concerning sura 16:103. One should read here "Ṭalha b. ʿAmr," not "Ṭalha b. ʿUmar," as in the edited text.

66. *GdQ*, II:54.

67. Michael Lecker, "Zayd b. Thābit, 'a Jew with two sidelocks': Judaism and Literacy in Pre-Islamic Medina (Yathrib)," *Journal of Near Eastern Studies* 56 (1997): 259–73; now also in idem, *Jews and Arabs in Pre- and Early Islamic Arabia* (Aldershot, Ashgate: Variorum, 1999), no. III.

68. Cf. Gilliot, "Le Coran," §9, with varying versions; Cf. also idem, "Langue et Coran: une lecture syro-araméenne du Coran," *Arabica* 50 (2003): 390–91. Cf. also Sprenger, *Leben*, I:130–31.

69. Abū l-Qāsim ʿAbd Allāh b. A. b. Maḥmūd al-Balkhī (al-Kaʿbī for the anti-Muʿtazilis); *GAS*, I:622–23; van Ess, *TG*, *passim* (cf. index, IV:1068).

70. Abū ʿAmr ʿĀmir b. Sharāḥīl al-Kūfī, d. 103/721 (or 105, 106, 107, etc.); *GAS*, I:277; Mizzī, *Tahdhīb*, IX:349–57, no. 3026; Dhahabī, *Siyar*, IV:294–318.

71. Abū Muḥammad Qays b. al-Rabīʿ al-Asadī al-Kūfī, d. 165/781; Mizzī, *Tahdhīb*, XV:306–12, no. 5489.

72. Abū Yaḥyā Zakariyyā b. a. Zāʾida Khālid b. Maymūn b. Fayrūz al-Hamdānī al-Wādiʿī al-Kūfī, d. 147 or 148/764; Mizzī, *Tahdhīb*, VI:309–11, no. 1975.

73. Abū Muʿāwiya Shaybān b. ʿAbd al-Raḥmān al-Tamīmī al-Baṣrī al-Muʾaddib, who lived in Kūfa and died 168 or 169/784; Mizzī, *Tahdhīb*, VIII:415–18, no. 2768.

74. Abū ʿAbd Allāh (or Abū Yazīd) Jābir b. Yazīd b. al-Ḥārith al-Juʿfī al-Kūfī, d. 128/745; Mizzī, *Tahdhīb*, III:304–309, no. 863.

75. Abū Yaḥyā Firās b. Yaḥyā al-Hamdānī al-Khāriqī al-Kūfī al-Muktatib, d. 129/746; Ibn Ḥajar, *TT*, VIII:259.

76. He cannot be ʿAbd al-Raḥmān b. a. l-Zinād b. ʿAbd Allāh b. Dhakwān, who died in Baghdad in 174/790; cf. Ibn Mākūlā, *Ikmāl*, IV:200–201; Mizzī, *Tahdhīb*, XI:182–86, no. 3779; Ibn Ḥajar, *TT*, VI:170–73. The Ibn a. l-Zinād whom al-Kaʿbī questioned could have been a son of ʿAbd al-Raḥmān b. a. l-Zinād, for we know that Abū l-Zinād (ʿAbd al-Raḥmān's father), who came from Medina, had a good reputation with regard to the traditions, along with his son and grandson; Mizzī, *Tahdhīb*,

XI:184. In addition, ʿAbd al-Raḥmān, who counted al-Wāqidī among his listeners (he is one of Wāqidī's authorities in the *Annals* of Ṭabarī) appears in a chain of tradents which introduces the report that Muḥammad commanded Zayd b. Thābit to learn the script of the Jews; cf. Balādhurī, *Futūḥ al-buldān*, p. 664. ʿAbd al-Raḥmān b. a. l-Zinād had one brother, Abū l-Qāsim Ibn a. l-Zinād, who was older than he; Mizzī, *Tahdhīb*, XXI:458–59, no. 8167.

77. Abū ʿAbd Allāh or Abū Jaʿfar b. al-Naṭṭāḥ Abū l-Tayyāḥ Muḥammad b. Ṣāliḥ b. Mihrān al-Qurashi al-Baṣrī (*mawlā* of the banū Hāshim), d. 252/866; Mizzī, *Tahdhīb*, XVI:364–65, no. 5884; he was a famous tradent of the historical traditions concerning the wars and people of early Islam (*rāwiya li-l-siyar*). He wrote a *K. al-Dawla*, of which al-Khaṭīb al-Baghdādī said that he was the first to have collected those traditions into a book ("*awwal man ṣannafa fī akhbārihā kitāban*"); Baghdādī, *TB*, V:357–58.

78. Not identified.

79. Cf. Balādhurī, *Futūḥ al-buldān*, p. 663, according to Wāqidī. Saʿd b. ʿUbāda b. Dulaym al-Anṣārī al-Khazrajī al-Sāʿidī was a syndic (*naqīb*) of the banū Sāʿida; he became the standard-bearer of the Helpers (*anṣār*); Bayhaqī, *Dalāʾil*, II:448; Ibn al-Athīr, *Usd*, II:256–58, no. 2012.

80. Ibid.; al-Mundhir b. ʿAmr b. Khunays al-Anṣārī al-Khazrajī al-Sāʿidī was also a syndic of the banū Sāʿida; Bayhaqī, *Dalāʾil*, II:448; Ibn al-Athīr, *Usd*, V:269–70, no. 5107.

81. Balādhurī, ibid.; Rāfiʿ b. Malik b. al-ʿAjlān al-Anṣārī al-Khazrajī was syndic of the banū Zurayq (Zurayq b. ʿĀmir); Ibn al-Athīr, *Usd*, II:197–98, no. 1598.

82. Balkhī/Kaʿbī, *Qābūl al-akhbār*, I:202; Gilliot, "Le Coran," pp. 198–99, §12; cf. also idem, "L'embarras d'un exégète musulman face à un palimpseste: Māturīdī et la sourate de l'Abondance (*al-Kawthar*, sourate 108), avec une note savante sur le commentaire coranique d'Ibn al-Naqīb (m. 698/1298)," in *Words, Texts and Concepts Cruising the Mediterranean Sea: Studies on the Sources, Contents and Influences of Islamic Civilization and Arabic Philosophy and Science (Dedicated to Gerhard Endress on his Sixty-fifth Birthday*, ed. Rüdiger Arnzen and J. Thielmann, Orientalia Lovaniensia Analecta no. 139 (Leuven: Peeters, 2004), §17; cf. also idem, "Une reconstruction critique," §22.

83. Ibn ʿAsākir, *Taʾrīkh madīnat Dimashq*, XIX:302, nos. 4453–54; Ibn Ḥanbal, *Musnad*, V:186/ XVI:41, no. 21510; Ibn Saʿd, *Ṭabaqāt*, II:358–59; Dhahabī, *Siyar*, II:428; Sprenger, *Moḥammad*, III:xxxix, n. 1; de Prémare, "Les textes musulmans dans leur environnement," *Les usages de Coran: présupposés et méthodes*, ed. Claude Gilliot and Tilman Nagel (*Arabica* 47, nos. 3–4 [2000]): 393–94; Gilliot, "Le Coran," p. 196, §9.

84. *Qurʾān* comes from the Syriac *qeryān*, meaning a "lectionary," a book that consists of a selection of texts of holy scripture; cf. Arthur Jeffery, *The Foreign*

Vocabulary of the Qur'ān (Baroda: Oriental Institute, 1938), pp. 233–34; cf. John Muehleisen-Arnold, *The Koran and the Bible, or Islam and Christianity*, 2nd ed. (London: Longmans, Green, Reader and Dyer, 1866), p. 99, n. 49 (*lectio, liber lectionis*); Christoph Luxenberg, *Die syro-aramäische Lesart des Koran: Ein Beitrag zur Entschlüsselung der Koransprache*, 1st ed. (Berlin: Das Arabische Buch, 2000), pp. 79ff.

85. Siegmund Fraenkel, *Die aramäischen Fremdwörter im arabischen* (Leiden: Brill, 1886), pp. 272–73; Jeffery, *Foreign Vocabulary*, p. 201; Ahmed Hebbo, *Die Fremdwörter in der arabischen Prophetenbiographie des Ibn Hischām (gest. 218/834)*, Heidelberger orientalistische Studien no. 7 (Frankfurt: Peter Lang, 1984), pp. 252–55.

86. Gilliot, "Le Coran," §10.

87. See above, at the end of the section entitled "What Can Be Said . . . ?"

88. Sprenger, *Leben*, II:390, and the excursus "Asatyr alawwalyn, d. h. die Märchen der Alten," pp. 390–97.

89. Fraenkel, *Fremdwörter* (Aramaic), p. 250; Jeffery, *Foreign Vocabulary* (Aramaic and Akkadian), pp. 169–70.

90. Suyūṭī, *Itqān*, cap. 37 (ed. Sprenger et al., p. 311, II.: 11–15; ed. M. Abū l-Faḍl Ibrāhīm, II:108). Also according to Juwaybir in his *Tafsīr 'an Ibn 'Abbās*, concerning sura 17:58 (*Al-kitāb al-masṭūr*); Sprenger, *Leben*, II:295; Ibn Kathīr, *Tafsīr*, III:588, concerning sura 8 (*Anfāl*):31, says "i.e., (*asāṭir*) plural of *usṭūra*, i.e., their writings (*kutubuhum*), from which (Muḥammad) took over (*iqtabasahā*) material."

91. Wāḥidī, *Wasīṭ*, II:455, concerning sura 8:31.

92. Ibn a. Ḥātim al-Rāzī (Abū M. 'Abd al-Raḥmān, d. Muḥarram 327 [October 29, 938]), *Tafsīr*, V:1689; Ṭabarī, *Tafsīr*, ed. Shākir, XIII:504, no. 15978; Tha'labī, *Tafsīr*, IV:350, concerning sura 8:31.

93. Luxenberg, *Die syro-aramäische Lesart*, pp. 271–76.

94. Abū Manṣūr M. b. M. b. Maḥmūd al-Samarqandī al-Ḥanafī, d. 333/944; cf. Ulrich Rudolph, *Al-Māturīdī und die sunnitische Theologie in Samarkand*, Islamic Philosophy, Theology, and Science no. 30 (Leiden: Brill, 1996).

95. Māturīdī, *Āyāt wa-suwar min Ta'wīlāt al-Qur'ān*, pp. 43–44; cf. Gilliot, "L'embarras," §8, "La piste du palimpseste et l'embarras d'al-Māturīdī."

96. Māturīdī, ibid., p. 74.

97. Cf. Luxenberg, *Die syro-aramäische Lesart*, p. 275, for his back-translation into Aramaic of *kawthar*.

98. This discovery rebuts the statement of Harris Birkeland in *The Lord Guideth: Studies on Primitive Islam,* Skrifter Utgitt av det Norske Videnskaps-Akademi i Oslo, Hist.-Filos. Klasse II (Oslo: I kommisjon hos H. Aschehoug [W. Nygaard], 1956), p. 137, concerning the development of Qur'ānic exegesis, for there is much to find, not only in Ṭabarī, Zamakhshari, Rāzī, etc., but also in Qurṭubī,

Thaʿlabī, Wāḥidī, Māturīdī, et al.; cf. Walid A. Saleh, *The Formation of the Classical* Tafsīr *Tradition: The* Qurʾān *Commentary of al-Thaʿlabī (d. 427/1035)*, Texts and Studies on the Qurʾān no. 1 (Leiden: Brill, 2004), p. 15, n. 26.

99. ʿAbd al-Raḥmān b. Kaysān, d. 200/816 or 201/817. This comes from Ibn al-Nadīm, *Fihrist*, ed. Tajaddud, p. 214; in the translation of Dodge, I:414–15. He did not die ca. 190/805, as in Saleh, *Formation*, p. 246, no. 12 (following *GAS*, I:614). Concerning Ibn Kaysān, his ontology and his commentary, cf. van Ess, *TG*, II:396–417 and V:193–211.

100. Thaʿlabī, *Tafsīr*, X:310, II:8–9.

101. Gilliot, "L'embarras," §8; Saleh, *Formation*, 119–24, has studied Thaʿlabī's exegesis of sura 108, but he did not remark upon the specific interpretation of Ibn Kaysān (al-Aṣamm).

102. Qurṭubī, Tafs*īr*, XX:217, I:18—the eighth interpretation in Qurṭubī. Cf. Gilliot, "L'embarras," §4. This also appears in newer commentaries, e.g., Shawkānī, *Tafsīr*, V:502: *wa-qāla Ibn Kaysān: huwa l-īthār.*

103. We are very grateful to Mr. Luxenberg; he has both shared these works with us and allowed us to mention or cite them.

104. Christoph Luxenberg, "Le voile islamique," in *Cités* (Paris, PUF), March 2004; the original French is "Qu'elles s'attachent leur ceinture autour de la taille."

105. One can find a French translation of Luxenberg's article in his "Noël dans le Coran," in *Enquêtes sur l'Islam: en hommage à Antoine Moussali* (Paris: Desclée de Brouwer, 2004); it is also in the original German in his "Weihnachten im Koran," in *Streit um den Koran: Die Luxenberg-Debatte: Standpunkte und Hintergründe*, 2nd ed., ed. Christoph Burgmer (Berlin: Schiler, 2004), pp. 35ff.

106. Richard Bell, *The Qurʾān*, II:669; idem, *A Commentary of the Qurʾān*, ed. Clifford Edmund Bosworth and M. E. J. Richardson, Journal of Semitic Studies Monographs no. 14 (Manchester: University of Manchester Press, 1991), II:564 (the quotation comes from this commentary).

107. We are dependent in this section on the important article of Jan M. F. van Reeth, "L'evangile du Prophète," in *Al-Kitāb*, ed. de Smet et al., pp. 155–74. One can find another essay by the same author in *Arabica* 2005 under the title "Le vignoble du paradis: La these de Luxenberg et les sources du Coran."

108. Van Reeth, "L'Évangile," pp. 158–59.

109. Ibid., pp. 161–62 (here compared with the text of the *Diatessaron* in Middle Dutch from Liège). Cf. C. C. de Bruin, *Het Luikse Diatesseron* (Leiden: Brill, 1970), which was translated in the thirteenth century from a lost Latin edition; cf., however, Karl Ahrens, "Christliches im Koran: Eine Nachlese," *Zeitschrift der Deutschen Morgenländischen Gesellschaft* 84 (1930): 165, although he does not refer to the *Diatessaron*, and Heinrich Speyer, *Die biblischen Erzählungen im Qoran* (Gräfenhainichen: Schultze, 1931), p. 457.

110. Van Reeth, "L'Évangile," pp. 162–66; cf. Heikki Räisänen, *Das koranische Jesusbild: Ein Beitrag zur Theologie des Korans* (Helsinki: Missiologian ja Ekumeniikan, 1971), pp. 23–37; idem, *Marcion, Muhammad, and the Mahatma: Exegetical Perspectives on the Encounter of Culture and Faith* (London: SCM Press, 1997), pp. 87–91, but without reference to the *Diatessaron.*

111. Van Reeth, "L'Évangile," pp. 167–69; cf. Räisänen, *Das koranische Jesusbild*, pp. 65–67.

112. Van Reeth, "L'Évangile," pp. 169–72.

113. Ibn Isḥāq, *Sīra*, 150/Ibn Hishām, *Sīra*, I:233/Alfred Guillaume, *The Life of Muhammad* (Oxford: Oxford University Press, 1987), p. 104.

114. Van Reeth, "L'evangile," p. 173.

115. Bukhārī, *Ṣaḥīḥ*, p. 65; *Tafsīr*, p. 61 (concerning sura 61 [*Ṣaff*]:6), ed. Krehl, III:352/*Les traditions prophétiques*, III:472; Zabīdī, *Tāj*, III:400a: according to Abū ʿUbayd, "the last Prophet." This is translated following Otto Pautz, *Muhammeds Lehre von der Offenbarung quellenmässig untersucht* (Leipzig: J. C. Hinrichs, 1898), p. 126, n. 2. Cf. Ibn Saʿd, *Ṭabaqāt*, I:105; Räisänen, *Das koranische Jesusbild*, pp. 52–56; Theodor Nöldeke, *Geschichte des Qorāns*, vol. 1, *Über den Ursprung des Qorāns*, 2nd ed., ed. Fr. Schwally (Leipzig: T. Weicher, 1909), p. 9, n. 1.

116. The idea that "Muḥammad" was not actually called by that name comes from our colleague and friend Dr. Abdallah Cheikh Moussa of the Sorbonne. We have discussed this question for over ten years, for the way in which Ibn Ḥabīb, *Muḥabbar*, p. 130 (also Ibn Saʿd, *Ṭabaqāt*, I:169; Qāḍī ʿIyāḍ, *Shifāʾ*, ch. 13, I:445–47; Sprenger, *Leben*, pp. 155–62 [translator's note: the reference to Sprenger is unclear in Gilliot's original]) sought nearly hopelessly for a few bearers of the name "Muḥammad" from before Islam is likely a clue that he was not actually called by that name, or, if anything, that he bore a theophoric name. In addition, it is passed down that his father's name was "ʿAbd Allāh."! One can legitimately doubt both names, however. Edward Jabra Jurji, "Pre-Islamic Use of the Name Muḥammad," *MW* 26 (1936): 389–91, speaks from the realm of philology and calls it a "noun-verb concept."

117. Stefan Wild, *Mensch, Prophet, und Gott im Koran: Muslimische Exegeten des 20. Jahrhunderts und das Menschenbild der Moderne* (Münster: Rhema, 2001), p. 33. Angelika Neuwirth often emphasized this aspect of the Qurʾān, most recently in "Qurʾān and History—A Disputed Relationship: Some Reflections on Qurʾānic History and History of the Qurʾān," *Journal of Qurʾānic Studies* 5 (2003): 3: "the striking extent of self-referentiality."

118. Cf. Gilliot, "Poète ou prophète?"

119. Matthias Radscheit, *Die koranische Herausforderung: Die* taḥaddī *Verse im Rahmen der Polemikpassagen des Korans*, Islamkundliche Untersuchungen no. 198 (Berlin: Klaus Schwarz, 1996), pp. 14–23 and 35–60 (on "pseudo-prophecy").

Pickthall's translation can be found in Mohammed Marmaduke Pickthall, *The Glorious Qurʾān: Translation* (Elmhurst, NY: Tahrike Tarsile Qurʾān, 2000).

120. Neuwirth, "Qurʾān and History," p. 3.

121. Hermann Reckendorf, *Mohammed und die Seinen*, Wissenschaft und Bildung no. 2 (Leipzig: Quelle & Mayer, 1907), pp. 40–41 and 55 (see his comments on war as a means of intimidation and as a lure).

122. Ignaz Goldziher, *Die Richtungen der islamischen Koranauslegung* (Leiden: Brill, 1920), p. 305, translates the phrase "Anlässe der Offenbarungen."

123. Nöldeke/Schwally, *GdQ*, vol. 2, *Die Sammlung des Qorans* (Leipzig: T. Weicher, 1909), p. 182, translate the phrase "Veranlassung der Offenbarungen."

124. The best thing one could do with the review of Luxenberg's book (see the bibliography for a list of reviews of his book) which appeared in a journal probably very much valued by the *filii Fortunati* (banū Suʿūd) (vol. V/1 [2003], pp. 92–97) would be to ignore it totally. Among other things, it contains (on p. 97) comments that some people would likely consider to be "thoroughly racist." On the other hand, it is at least a bit surprising that an irresponsible statement concerning Luxenberg's identity was made in Beirut shortly thereafter by a colleague. There is a French proverb: "Qui veut noyer son chien l'accuse de la rage." Roughly translated into English, it means "He who wishes to drown his dog accuses it of having rabies" (i.e., makes false accusations against it). Lüling's book was ignored; do such people then wish that Luxenberg will simply be assassinated by the new "Defenders/ Anṣār"? Do they thereby wish to imitate Muḥammad, who had poets (both male and female) executed (*āmiran bi-ḍarbi ʿunuqihi*; cf. Gilliot, "Poète ou prophète?" p. 383, n. 306), in order to preserve their own unique theses concerning the language and history of the Qurʾān?

125. Cf. Gilliot and Larcher, "Language and Style," p. 131b; Gilliot, "L'embarras," §9.

126. Günter Lüling, *Über den Ur-Qurʾān: Ansätze zur Rekonstruktion vorislamischer christlicher Strophenlieder im Qurʾān* (Erlangen: Lüling, 1974) (now translated into English, expanded, and newly edited as *A Challenge to Islam for Reformation: The Rediscovery and Reliable Reconstruction of a Comprehensive Pre-Islamic Christian Hymnal Hidden in the Koran under Earliest Islamic Reinterpretations* [Dehli: Motilal Banarsidass Publishers, 2003]).

127. Tor Andrae, *Der Ursprung des Islams und das Christentum* (Uppsala: Almqvist & Wiksells, 1926), pp. 149ff.; *Les origins de l'islam et le christianisme*, trans. J. Roche, Initiation à l'Islam no. 8 (Paris: Adrien-Maisonneuve, 1955), pp. 9ff.

128. Wilhelm Rudolph, *Die Abhängigkeit des Qorans von Judentum und Christentum* (Stuttgart: W. Kohlhammer, 1922).

129. Friedrich Leberecht Fleischer, "Ueber arabische Lexicographie und Thaʿâlibī's Fiqh al-lughah," in *Berichte für die Verhandlungen der Königlich Säch-*

sischen Gesellschaft der Wissenschaften zu Leipzig (Leipzig: Breitkopf & Härtel, 1854), p. 5; idem, *Kleinere Schriften*, 3 vols. (Leipzig: S. Hirzel, 1885–1888; reprint edition, Osnabrück: Biblio Verlag, 1968), III:156; cf. Gilliot and Larcher, "Language and Style," pp. 121b–122a.

BIBLIOGRAPHY

Translations of the Qur'ān

Der Koran. Translated by Max Henning. Reprint edition, Stuttgart: P. Reclam, 1960.

Der Koran in der Übersetzung von Friedrich Rückert. 3rd ed. Edited by Hartmut Bobzin. Würzburg: ERGON, 2000.

The Glorious Qur'ān: Translation. Translated by Mohammed Marmaduke Pickthall. Elmhurst, NY: Tahrike Tarsile Qur'ān, 2000.

Other Works

Abū l-Muẓaffar al-Sam'ānī (Manṣūr b. M. b. 'Abd al-Jabbār b. Aḥmad al-Tamīmī al-Marwazī al-Ḥanafī, then: Al-Shāfi'ī, b. 426, d. Rabī' I 23, 489 [March 21, 1096]). *Tafsīr*. 6 vols. Edited by Abū Tamīm Yāsir b. Ibrāhīm. Riyadh: Dār al-Waṭan, 1418/1997.

Abū Nu'aym al-Iṣfahānī (Aḥmad b. 'Abd Allāh b. Aḥmad b. Isḥāq, d. Muḥarram 20, 430 [October 22, 1038]). *Dalā'il al-nubuwwa*. 2 volumes in one publication. Edited by M. Rawwās Qal'ajī and 'Abd al-Barr 'Abbās. Beirut: Dār al-Nafā'is, 1406/1986.

Ahrens, Karl. "Christliches im Koran: Eine Nachlese." *Zeitschrift der Deutschen Morgenländischen Gesellschaft* 84 (1930): 15–68, 148–90.

Andrae, Tor. *Der Ursprung des Islams und das Christentum*. Uppsala: Almqvist & Wiksells, 1926. Reprinted as *Les origins de l'islam et le christianisme*. Translated by J. Roche. Initiation à l'Islam, no. 8. Paris: Adrien-Maisonneuve, 1955.

Baghawī Muḥyī al-Sunna a. M. al-Ḥusayn b. Mas'ūd. b. M. al-Farrā' al-Shāfi'ī (d. Shawwāl 516 [December 3, 1122]). *Tafsīr al-Baghawī al-musammā bi-Ma'ālim al-tanzīl*. 4 vols. 3rd ed. Edited by Khālid 'Abd al-Raḥmān al-'Ak and Marwān Sawār. Beirut: 1992.

Baghdādī (al-Khaṭīb Abū Bakr Aḥmad b. 'Alī b. Thābit, d. Dhū l-Ḥijja 7, 463 [September 5, 1071]). *TB = Ta'rīkh Baghdād*. 14 vols. Edited by M. Sa'īd al-'Irāqī. Cairo: 1931–1949. Reprint edition: Beirut, 1970–1980.

Balādhurī (Aḥmad b. Yaḥyā, lived 3rd/9th centuries). *Ansāb al-ashrāf*. Edited by M. Hamīdullāh. Cairo: 1959.

———. *Futūḥ al-buldān*. Edited by ʿAbd Allāh and ʿUmar Anīs al-Ṭabbāʿ. Beirut: 1407/1987 (1st edition, Beirut: 1377/1957).

Bāqshīsh: see below, Mūsā b. ʿUqba.

Bayhaqī (Abū Bakr Aḥmad b. al-Ḥusayn b. ʿAlī b. Mūsā al-Khusrawjirdī al-Khurasānī, d. Jumādā I 10, 458 [April 8. 1066]). *Dalāʾil al-nubuwwa*. 7 vols. Edited by ʿAbd al-Muʿṭī Qalʿajī. Beirut: 1405/1985.

Bell, Richard. *A Commentary of the Qurʾān*. Edited by Clifford Edmund Bosworth and M. E. J. Richardson. *Journal of Semitic Studies* Monographs, no. 14. Manchester: University of Manchester Press, 1991.

Birkeland, Harris. *The Lord Guideth: Studies on Primitive Islam*. Skrifter Utgitt av det Norske Videnskaps-Akademi i Oslo, Hist.-Filos. Klasse II. Oslo: I kommisjon hos H. Aschehoug (W. Nygaard), 1956.

Buhl, Frants. *Das Leben Muhammeds*. 3rd ed. Heidelberg: Quelle & Meyer, 1961.

Bukhārī (a. ʿAbd Allāh Muḥammad b. Ismāʿīl al-Juʿfī, d. Shawwāl 1, 256 [September 1, 870]). *Ṣaḥīḥ*. 4 vols. Edited by L. Krehl and Th. W. Juynboll. Leiden: 1862–1908. [Or, with the numbering of the traditions, cf. below, Ibn Ḥajar, *Fatḥ*.]

———. *Les traditions islamiques*. 4 vols. Translated and edited by Octave Houdas and William Marçais. Paris: Imprimerie Nationale, Leroux, 1903–1914. Reprint edition, Paris: Librairie d'Amerique et d'Orient, 1977.

Burgmer, Christoph, ed. *Streit um den Koran: Die Luxenberg-Debatte: Standpunkte und Hintergründe*. 2nd ed. Berlin: Schiler, 2004.

De Smet, Daniel, and J. M. F. van Reeth. "Les citations bibliques dans l'oeuvre du *dāʿī* ismaélien Ḥamīd ad-Dīn al-Kirmānī." In *Law, Christianity and Modernism in Islamic Society (Proceedings of the Eighteenth Congress of the Union Européenne des Arabisants et Islamisants, Held at the Katholieke Universiteit Leuven (September 3–9, 1996)*, ed. Urbain Vermeulen and J. M. F. van Reeth, 147–60. Orientalia Lovaniensia Analecta, no. 86. Leuven: Uitgeverij Peeters, 1998.

De Smet, Daniel, G. de Catallaÿ, and J. M. F. van Reeth, eds. *Al-Kitāb: La sacralité du texte dans le monde de l'Islam (Actes du Symposium international tenu à Leuven et Louvain-la-Neuve du 29 mai au 1 juin 2002)*. Acta Orientalia Belgica, Subsidia III. Bruxelles: Belgisch Genootschap voor Oosterse Studiën/Société belge d'Études orientales, 2004.

Dhahabī (Shams al-Dīn M. b. A. b. ʿUthmān b. Qāymāz al-Turkumānī al-Fāriqī al-Dimashqī al-Shāfiʿī, d. Dhū l-Qaʿda 3, 748 [February 4, 1348]). *Mīzān al-ʿitidāl fī naqd al-rijāl*. 4 vols. Edited by ʿAlī M. al-Bijāwī. Cairo: 1963. Reprint edition, Beirut: Dār al-Maʿrifa (no year given).

———. *Siyar aʿlām al-nubalāʾ*. 25 vols. Edited by Shuʿayb al-Arnaʾūṭ et al. Beirut: 1981–1988.

EI = *The Encyclopaedia of Islam*. 11 vols. New ed. Edited by H. A. R. Gibb et al. Leiden: Brill, 1960–.

Endress, Gerhard. “Herkunft und Entwicklung der arabischen Schrift.” In *Grundriss der arabischen Philologie*, vol. 1, *Sprachwissenschaft*, ed. Wolfdietrich Fischer, 165–97. Wiesbaden: Ludwig Reichert Verlag, 1982.

EQ = *Encyclopaedia of the Qurʾān*. 5 vols. Edited by Jane Dammen McAuliffe. Leiden: Brill, 2001–2006.

Ess, Josef van. *TG* = *Theologie und Gesellschaft im 2. und 3. Jahrhundert Hidschra: Eine Geschichte des religiösen Denkens im frühen Islam*. 6 vols. Berlin: Walter de Gruyter, 1991–1997.

Farrāʾ (a. Zakariyyāʾ Yaḥyā b. Ziyād b. ʿAbd Allāh b. Manṣūr al-Daylamī al-Asadī al-Kūfī al-Naḥwī, d. 207/822). *Maʿānī l-Qurʾān*. 3 vols. Edited by M. ʿAlī al-Najjār et al. Cairo: 1955–1973.

Fatḥ: see below, Ibn Ḥajar.

Fischer, Wolfdietrich, and Helmut Gätje, eds. *GAP* = *Grundriss der arabischen Philologie*. 3 vols. Wiesbaden: Ludwig Reichert Verlag, 1982–1992.

Fleischer, Friedrich Leberecht. *Kleinere Schriften*. 3 vols. Leipzig: S. Hirzel, 1885–1888. Reprint edition, Osnabrück: Biblio Verlag, 1968.

———. “Ueber arabische Lexicographie und Ṯaʿâlibī's Fiqh al-luġah.” In *Berichte für die Verhandlungen der Königlich Sächsischen Gesellschaft der Wissenschaften zu Leipzig*. Leipzig: Breitkopf & Härtel, 1854. [Reprinted in idem, *Kleinere Schriften*, III: 152–66.]

Fraenkel, Siegmund. *Die aramäischen Fremdwörter im Arabischen*. Leiden: Brill, 1886.

GAP: see above, Fischer.

GAS: see below, Sezgin.

GdQ: see below, Nöldeke.

Gilliot, Claude. *Exégèse, langue, et théologie en islam: L'exégèse coranique de Ṭabarī (m. 311/923)*. Paris: Libr. J. Vrin, 1990.

———. “Informants.” In *Encylopedia of the Qurʾān*, edited by Jane McAuliffe, II:512–18. Leiden: Brill, 2001–2006.

———. “Langue et Coran: une lecture syro-araméenne du Coran.” *Arabica* 50 (2003): 381–93.

———. “La théologie musulmane en Asie Centrale et au Khorasan.” *Arabica* 49, no. 2 (2002): 135–203.

———. “Le Coran, fruit d'un travail collectif?” In De Smet, De Catallaÿ, and van Reeth, *Al-Kitāb: La sacralité du texte dans le monde de l'Islam*, pp. 185–231.

———. “L'embarras d'un exégète musulman face à un palimpseste: Māturīdī et la sourate de l'Abondance (*al-Kawthar*, sourate 108), avec une note savante sur le commentaire coranique d'Ibn al-Naqīb (m. 698/1298).” In *Words, Texts and Concepts Cruising the Mediterranean Sea: Studies on the Sources, Contents and Influences of Islamic Civilization and Arabic Philosophy and Science (Dedicated *to Gerhard Endress on his Sixty-fifth Birthday*, edited by Rüdiger Arnzen and J. Thielmann. Orientalia Lovaniensia Analecta, no. 139. Leuven: Peeters, 2004.

———. "Les 'informateurs' juifs et chrétiens de Muḥammad: Reprise d'un problème traité par Aloys Sprenger et Theodor Nöldeke." *Jerusalem Studies in Arabic and Islam* 22 (1998): 84–126.

———. "Muqātil, grand exégète, traditionniste et théologien maudit." *Journal Asiatique* 279 (1991): 39–92.

———. "Poète ou prophète? Les traditions concernant la poésie et les poètes attribuées au prophète de l'islam et aux premières générations musulmanes." In *Paroles, signes, mythes: Mélanges offerts à Jamal Eddine Bencheikh*, edited by Floréal Sanaugustin, 331–96. Damas: Institut français d'études arabes de Damas, 2001.

———. "Une reconstruction critique ou Coran ou comment en finir avec les merveilles de la lampe d'Aladin?" A paper given at the First World Congress of Middle Eastern Studies (WOCMES), Mainz, Germany, September 8–13, 2002, as a part of the working group organized by Manfred Kropp (director of the Institut der Deutschen Morgenländischen Gesellschaft in Beirut) published as "Results of Contemporary Research on the Qurʾān: The Question of a Historical-Critical Text of the Qurʾān. Edited by Manfred S. Kropp. Würzburg: ERGON, 2007.

———. "Un verset manquant du Coran ou réputé tel." In *En hommage au Père Jacques Jomier, o.p.*, edited by Marie-Thérèse Urvoy, 73–100. Paris: Cerf, 2002.

Gilliot, Claude, and Pierre Larcher. "Language and Style of the Qurʾān." *Encyclopedia of the Qurʾān*, edited by Jane McAuliffe, III:113–15. Leiden: Brill, 2001–2006.

Goldziher, Ignaz. *Die Richtungen der islamischen Koranauslegung*. Leiden: Brill, 1920. Reprint edition, Leiden: Brill, 1970.

Hebbo, Ahmed. *Die Fremdwörter in der arabischen Prophetenbiographie des Ibn Hischām (gest. 218/834)*. Heidelberger orientalistische Studien, no. 7. Frankfurt: Peter Lang, 1984.

Horovitz, Josef. *The Earliest Biographies of the Prophet and Their Authors*. Edited by Lawrence I. Conrad. Studies in Late Antiquity and Islam no. 11. Princeton, NJ: Darwin Press, 2002.

Hūd b. Muḥakkam/Muḥkim (al-Huwwārī, lived mid-3rd/9th centuries). *Tafsīr*. 4 vols. Edited by Belḥājj Saʿīd Sharīfī. Beirut, 1990.

Ibn Abī Ḥātim al-Rāzī (Abū Muḥammad ʿAbd al-Raḥmān b. Abī Ḥātim M. b. Idrīs al-Tamīmī al-Ḥanẓalī, d. Muḥarram 327 [October 29, 938]). *Tafsīr al-Qurʾān al-ʿaẓīm*. 10 vols. Edited by Asʿad M. al-Ṭayyib. Mecca and Riyadh, 1417/1997.

Ibn Abī l-Zamanīn (a. ʿAbd Allāh M. b. ʿAbd Allāh b. ʿĪsā al-Murrī al-Andalusī al-Ilbīrī, d. Rabīʿ II 399 [December 3, 1008]). *Tafsīr*. 5 vols. Edited by Abū ʿAbd

Allāh Ḥusayn b. ʿUkkāsha and M. b. Muṣṭafā al-Kanz. Cairo: al-Fārūq al-Ḥadītha li-l-Ṭibāʿa wa-l-Nashr, 1423/2002.

Ibn ʿĀdil (Sirāj al-Dīn a. Ḥafṣ ʿUmar b. ʿAlī b. ʿĀdil al-Dimashqī al-Ḥanbalī, 880/1475). *Al-Lubāb fī ʿulūm al-Kitāb*. 20 vols. Edited by ʿĀdil A. ʿAbd al-Mawjūd and ʿAlī M. Muʿawwaḍ. Beirut: Dār al-Kutub al-ʿIlmiyya, 1419/1998.

Ibn ʿAsākir (Thiqat al-Dīn Abū l-Qāsim ʿAlī b. a. Muḥammad al-Ḥasan b. Hibat Allāh al-Dimashqī al-Shāfiʿī, d. Rajab 11, 571 [January 25, 1176]), *TD* = *Taʾrīkh madīnat Dimashq*. 8 vols. Edited by Muḥibb al-Dīn al-ʿAmrawī. Beirut, 1995–2000.

Ibn al-Athīr (ʿIzz al-Dīn Abū l-Ḥasan ʿAlī b. M. al-Shaybānī al-Jazarī al-Shāfiʿī, d. Shaʿbān 25, 630 [June 6, 1233]). *Usd al-ghāba fī maʿrifat al-ṣaḥāba*. 7 vols. Edited by Maḥmūd Fāyid et al. Cairo, 1963 (2nd ed., 1970).

Ibn ʿAṭiyya (Abū Muḥammad ʿAbd al-Ḥaqq b. Ghālib al-Gharnāṭī, d. Ramaḍān 25, 541 [February 28, 1147] or 542). *Al-Muḥarrir al-wajīz*. 5 vols. Edited by ʿAbd al-Salām ʿAbd al-Shāfī Muḥammad. Beirut: Dār al-Kutub al-ʿIlmiyya, 1413/1993.

Ibn Coteiba: see below, Ibn Qutayba.

Ibn Ḥajar al-ʿAsqalānī (Shihāb al-Dīn Abū l-Faḍl Aḥmad b. Nūr al-Dīn ʿAlī M. al-Kinānī al-Shāfiʿī, d. Dhū l-Ḥijja 28, 852 [February 22, 1449]). *Fatḥ al-bārī bi-sharḥ Ṣaḥīḥ al-Bukhārī*. 13 vols. and *Muqaddima*. Edited by ʿAbd al-ʿAzīz b. ʿAl. Bāz (numbering of the traditions by M. Fuʾād ʿAbd al-Bāqī, under the direction of Muḥibb al-Dīn Khaṭīb). Cairo, 1390/1970. Reprint edition, Beirut (no year given).

———. *Al-Iṣāba fī tamyīz al-ṣaḥāba*. 4 vols. Edited by Ibr. b. Ḥ. al-Fayyūmī. Cairo: Maṭbaʿat al-Saʿāda, 1328/1910. Published with Ibn ʿAbd al-Barr, *Al-Istīʿāb fī maʿrifat al-aṣḥāb*. Reprint edition, Beirut: Dār Iḥyāʾ al-Turāth al-ʿArabī (no year given). Published alone in 8 vols., edited by ʿAlī M. al-Bijāwī, in Cairo: Dār Nahḍat Miṣr, 1970–1972.

———. *TT* = *Tahdhīb al-tahdhīb*. 12 vols. Hyderabad, 1325–1327/1907–1909. Reprint edition, Beirut (no year given).

Ibn Isḥāq (M. b. Isḥāq b. Yasār al-Qurashī al-Muṭṭalabī al-Madanī, d. 150/767 [or 151/2]). *Sīrat rasūl Allāh* (*Das Leben Muḥammed's nach Muḥammed b. Isḥāq), bearbeitet von Abd el malik b. Hischam*. 2 vols. Edited by F. Wüstenfeld. Göttingen: Dieterichs, 1858–1860. Also in Ibn Hishām (revised edition of the *Sīra* of Ibn Isḥāq). *Al-Sīra al-nabawiyya*. 2 vols. 2nd ed. Edited by Muṣṭafā al-Saqqā, et al. Cairo, 1375/1955. Translated in Alfred Guillaume. *The Life of Muhammad: A Translation of Ibn Isḥāq's Sīrat rasūl Allāh*. 5th ed. Karachi, 1978. Also translated in Ibn' Isḥāq. *Muhammad*. 2 vols. Translated and edited by ʿAbdurrahmân Badawī. Beirut/Paris, 2001.

Ibn al-Nadīm (a. l-Faraj M. b. a. Yaʿqūb Isḥāq al-Warrāq, d. 380/990 or 385/995). *Al-Fihrist*. Edited by Riḍā Tajaddud. Tehran, 1393/1973. Translated in *The Fihrist of Ibn al-Nadīm: A Tenth-Century Survey of Muslim Culture*. Translated and edited by Bayard Dodge. New York: Columbia University Press, 1970.

Ibn Qutayba (a. M. ʿAbd Allāh b. Muslim al-Dīnawarī, d. Rajab 1, 276 [October 30, 889]). *Ibn Coteibas Handbuch der Geschichte* (Kitāb al-Maʿārif). Edited by Ferdinand Wüstenfeld. Göttingen: Vandenhoeck and Ruprecht, 1850. Also in *Kitāb al-Maʿārif*. 2nd ed. Edited by Tharwat ʿUkkāsha. Cairo, 1388/1969.

Ibn Saʿd (a. ʿAl. M. b. Saʿd b. Manīʿ al-Baṣrī al-Zuhrī, d. Jumādā II 4, 230 [February 16, 845]). *Al-Ṭabaqāt al-kubrā*. 9 vols. Introduction by Iḥsān ʿAbbās. Beirut, 1957–1959. Also in *Al-Qism al-mutammim li-tābiʿī ahl al-Madīna wa-man baʿdahum*. 2nd ed. Edited by Ziyād M. Manṣūr. Medina, 1408/1987.

Ibshīhī (Bahāʾ al-Dīn Abū l-Fatḥ M. b. Aḥmad b. Manṣūr, d. after 850/1446). *Al-Mustaṭraf fī kull fann mustaẓraf*. See also below, Rat, *Al-Mostaṭraf*.

Kaʿbī, al-Balkhī (Abū l-Qāsim ʿAbd Allāh b. A. b. Maḥmūd, d. 319/931). *Qābūl al-akhbār wa-maʿrifat al-rijāl*. 2 vols. Edited by M. Abū ʿAmr al-Ḥusayn b. ʿUmar b. ʿAbd al-Raḥīm. Beirut, 1421/2000.

Lecker, Michael. *Jews and Arabs in Pre- and Early Islamic Arabia*. Aldershot, Ashgate, UK: Variorum, 1999.

———. "Zayd b. Thābit, 'a Jew with two sidelocks': Judaism and Literacy in Pre-Islamic Medina (Yathrib)." *Journal of Near Eastern Studies* 56 (1997): 259–73. Reprinted in idem, *Jews and Arabs*, no. III.

Le Strange, Guy. *The Lands of the Eastern Caliphate: Mesopotamia, Persia, and Central Asia, from the Moslem Conquest to the Time of Timur*. Cambridge: Cambridge University Press, 1905. Reprint edition, London: Cass, 1966.

Lüling, Günter. *Über den Ur-Qurʾān: Ansätze zur Rekonstruktion vorislamischer christlicher Strophenlieder im Qurʾān*. Erlangen: Lüling, 1974. (The 3rd ed. is entitled *Über den Urkoran* . . . [Erlangen: Lüling, 2004].) (Reviews are available in Maxime Rodinson, *Der Islam* 54 [1977]: 321–25; Claude Gilliot, "Deux etudes sur le Coran," *Arabica* 30 [1983]: 16–37.)

———. *A Challenge to Islam for Reformation: The Rediscovery and Reliable Reconstruction of a Comprehensive Pre-Islamic Christian Hymnal Hidden in the Koran under Earliest Islamic Reinterpretations*. Dehli: Motilal Banarsidass Publishers, 2003.

———. *Die Wiederentdeckung des Propheten Muhammad: Eine Kritik am "christlichen Abendland."* Erlangen: Lüling, 1981. (See also Claude Gilliot, "Deux etudes sur le Coran," *Arabica* 30 [1983]: 16–37.)

Luxenberg, Christoph. *Die syro-aramäische Lesart des Koran: Ein Beitrag zur Entschlüsselung der Koransprache*. 1st ed., Berlin: Das Arabische Buch, 2000. 2nd ed., Berlin: Schiler, 2004. (Reviews are available in Rainer Naibielek, "Weintrauben statt Jungfrauen: Zu einer neuen Lesart des Korans," *Informationsprojekt Naher und Mittlerer Osten* 23/24 [Autumn/Winter 2000]: 66–72;

R. R. Phenix and C. B. Horn, in *Hugoye: Journal of Syriac Studies* 6 [January 2003]; Mona Naggar, "Wie aramäisch ist der Koran? Ein provokatives Buch zur Deutung 'unklarer' Stellen," *Neue Zürcher Zeitung*, April 3, 2001, p. 54; Karl-Heinz Ohlig, "Eine Revolution der Koran-Philologie," available at http://www.phil.uni-sb.de/projekte/imprimatur/2000/imp000510.html [accessed May 2007]; Claude Gilliot, "Langue et Coran"; Rémi Brague, "Le Coran: sortir du cercle?" *Critique* 671 [April 2003]: 232–51; François de Blois, *Journal of Qurʾāic Studies* 5 [2003]: 92–97; pages 7–10 of Angelika Neuwirth's article "Qurʾān and History" [see below] are on the Internet at http://www.islamic-awareness.org/Quran/ Text/luxreview1.html.)

———. "Weihnachten im Koran." In *Streit um den Koran*, edited by Christoph Burgmer, 62–68. Berlin: Schiler, 2004.

Māturīdī (Abū Manṣūr M. b. M. b. Maḥmūd al-Samarqandī al-Ḥanafī, d. 333/944). *Āyāt wa-suwar min Taʾwīlāt al-Qurʾān*. Edited by Ahmet Vanlioğlu and Bekir Topaloğlu, with a Turkish translation by Bekir Topaloğlu. Istanbul: Acar Matbaacılık (Imām Ebû Hanîfe ve Imām Mâtürîdî Araştirma Vakfi), 2003.

Māwardī (Abū l-Ḥasan ʿAlī b. Muḥammad b. Ḥabīb, d. 450/1058). *Al-Nukat wa-l-ʿuyūn (fī l-tafsīr)* [corrected a *Al-Nukat wa-l-ʿuyūn fī tafsīr al-Māwardī*; it should be, *Al-Nukat wa-l-ʿuyūn fī l-tafsīr li-l-Māwardī*]. 6 vols. Edited by al-Sayyid b. ʿAbdmaqṣūd b. Abdarraḥīm. Beirut: Dār al-Kutub al-ʿIlmiyya/ Muʾassasat al-Kutub al-Thaqāfiyya, 1412/1992.

Mkhīnīnī: see below, Yaḥyā b. Sallām.

Mingana, A. "Syriac Influence on the Style of the Kuran." *Bulletin of the John Rylands Library* 11 (1927): 77–98. Reprinted in Ibn Warraq, *What the Koran Really Says*, pp. 171–92.

Mizzī (Jamāl al-Dīn Abū l-Ḥajjāj Yūsuf b. al-Zakī ʿAr. al-Dimashqī al-Shāfiʿī, d. Ṣafar 12, 742 [July 28, 1341]). *Tahdhīb al-kamāl fī asmāʾ al-rijāl*. 23 vols. Edited by Aḥmad ʿAlī ʿAbīd and Ḥasan Aḥmad Āghā. Beirut, 1414/1994.

Muehleisen-Arnold, John. *The Koran and the Bible, or Islam and Christianity*. 2nd ed. London: Longmans, Green, Reader and Dyer, 1866.

Mujāhid (b. Jabr al-Makkī, d. 104/722). *Tafsīr*. 2 vols. Edited by ʿAr. b. Ṭāhir b. M. al-Sūratī. Qaṭar, 1976.

Muqātil b. Sulaymān (d. 150/767). *Tafsīr*. 5 vols. Edited by ʿAl. Maḥmūd Shaḥḥāta. Cairo, 1980–89.

Mūsā b. ʿUqba (d. 141/758). *Al-Maghāzi li-Mūsā Ibn ʿUqba*. A set of fragments collected by M. Bāqshīsh Abū Mālik. Silsilat al-Uṭrūḥāt wa-l-Rasāʾil. Agadir: Jāmiʿat Ibn al-Zuhr Kulliyyat al-Adab wa-l-ʿUlūm al-Insāniyya, 1994.

Naḥḥās (a. Jaʿfar A. b. M. b. Ism. al-Murādī al-Miṣrī, d. Dhū l-Ḥijja 338 [May 22, 950]). *Iʿrāb al-Qurʾān*. 5 vols. 2nd ed. Edited by Zuhayr Ghāzī Zāhid. Beirut: ʿĀlam al-Kutub and Maktabat al-Nahḍa al-ʿArabiyya, 1405/1985.

Neuwirth, Angelika. "Qur'ān and History—A Disputed Relationship: Some Reflections on Qur'ānic History and History of the Qur'ān." *Journal of Qur'ānic Studies* 5 (2003): 1–18.

Nöldeke, Theodor. *Geschichte des Qorāns*. Vol. 1, *Über den Ursprung des Qorāns*, 2nd ed., edited by Friedrich Schwally; Vol. 2, *Die Sammlung des Qorāns*, 2nd ed., edited by Friedrich Schwally; Vol. 3, *Die Geschichte des Qorantexts*, 2nd ed., edited by Gotthelf Bergsträsser and Otto Pretzl. Leipzig: T. Weicher, 1909–1938.

Ohlig, Karl-Heinz. "Der Koran als Gemeindeprodukt." In von Bothmer, Ohlig, and Puin, "Neue Wege der Koranforschung," pp. 33–37.

Pautz, Otto. *Muhammeds Lehre von der Offenbarung quellenmässig untersucht*. Leipzig: J. C. Hinrichs, 1898.

de Prémare, Alfred-Louis. *Les fondations d'Islam: Entre écriture et histoire*. Paris: Seuil, 2002.

———. "Les textes musulmans dans leur environnement." In *Les usages de Coran: présupposés et méthodes*, edited by Claude Gilliot and Tilman Nagel. *Arabica* 47, nos. 3–4 (2000): 391–408.

Puin, Gerd-R. "Über die Bedeutung der ältesten Koranfragmente aus Sanaa (Jemen) für die Orthographiegeschichte des Korans." In von Bothmer, Ohlig, and Puin, "Neue Wege der Koranforschung," pp. 37–40.

Qurṭubī (Shams al-Dīn Abū ʿAbd Allāh M. b. A. b. a. Bakr al-Mālikī, d. Shawwāl 9, 671 [April 29, 1273]). *Tafsīr = al-Jāmiʿ li-aḥkām al-Qur'ān*. 20 vols. 2nd ed. Edited by Aḥmad ʿAbd al-ʿAlīm al-Bardūnī et al. Cairo, 1952–1967. Reprint edition, Beirut, 1965–1967.

Radscheit, Matthias. *Die koranische Herausforderung: Die* taḥaddī *Verse im Rahmen der Polemikpassagen des Korans*. Islamkundliche Untersuchungen, no. 198. Berlin: Klaus Schwarz, 1996.

Räisänen, Heikki. *Das koranische Jesusbild: Ein Beitrag zur Theologie des Korans*. Helsinki: Missiologian ja Ekumeniikan, 1971.

———. *Marcion, Muhammad, and the Mahatma: Exegetical Perspectives on the Encounter of Culture and Faith*. London: SCM Press, 1997.

Rat, Gustave, trans. *Al-Mostaṭraf: Recueil de morceaux choisis çà et là dans toutes les branches de la connaissance reputes attrayantes, par l'Imâm, l'unique, le savant, le très érudit, le disert, le perspicace, le Šaïk Šihâb-ad-Dīn Aḥmad al-Abšīhī: Que Dieu le couvre de sa Miséricorde et lui accorde les marques de sa satisfaction! Amen! Ouvrage philologique, anecdotique, littéraire et philosophique*. 2 vols. Paris: Ernest Leroux (and Toulon: Th. Isnard and B. Brun), 1899–1902.

Rāẕī (Faḫr al-Dīn Abū ʿAbd Allāh Muḥammad b. ʿUmar b. al-Ḥusayn, d. Shawwāl 1, 606 [March 29, 1210]). *Tafsīr = Mafātīḥ al-ghayb*. 32 vols. Edited by M. Muḥyī l-Dīn ʿAbd al-Ḥamīd, ʿA. I. al-Ṣāwī et al. Cairo, 1933–1962.

Reckendorf, Hermann. *Mohammed und die Seinen*. Wissenschaft und Bildung, no. 2. Leipzig: Quelle & Mayer, 1907.

Robin, Christian. "L'écriture arabe et l'Arabie." *Pour la science (Dossier)* (October 2002): 62–69.

Rudolph, Ulrich. *Al-Māturīdī und die sunnitische Theologie in Samarkand*. Islamic Philosophy, Theology, and Science no. 30. Leiden: Brill, 1996.

Rudolph, Wilhelm. *Die Abhängigkeit des Qorans von Judentum und Christentum*. Stuttgart: W. Kohlhammer, 1922.

Saleh, Walid A. *The Formation of the Classical* Tafsīr *Tradition: The* Qur'ān *Commentary of al-Tha'labī (d. 427/1035)*. Texts and Studies on the Qur'ān no. 1. Leiden: Brill, 2004.

Sam'ānī (a. Sa'd 'Abd al-Karīm b. M. b. Manṣūr al-Tamīmī al-Khurāsānī al-Marwazī, d. Rabī' I, 562 [December 26, 1166]). *Al-Ansāb*. 5 vols. Edited by 'Abd Allāh 'Umar al-Bārūdī. Beirut: Dār al-Jinān, 1988.

Ṣammūd: see below, Yaḥyā b. Sallām.

Schoeler, Gregor. *Charakter und Authentie der muslimischen Überlieferungen über das Leben Mohammeds*. Berlin: Walter de Gruyter, 1996.

Sezgin, Fuat. *Geschichte des arabischen Schrifttums*. 9 vols. Leiden: Brill, 1967–1984.

Shawkānī (Abū 'Abd Allāh Muḥammad b. 'Alī b. M. b. 'Abd Allāh al-Ṣan'ānī, d. Jumādā II 27, 1250 [October 31, 1834]). *Tafsīr = Fatḥ al-qadīr al-jāmi' bayna fannay r-riwāya wa-d-dirāya fī 'ilm at-tafsīr*. 5 vols. Cairo: Muṣṭ. l-Bābī l-Ḥalabī, 1349/1930. 3rd reprint edition, Beirut: Dār al-Fikr, 1973.

Speyer, Heinrich. *Die biblischen Erzählungen im Qoran*. Gräfenhainichen: Schultze, 1931. Reprint editions, Hildesheim: Olms, 1961, 1971.

Sprenger, Aloys. "Foreign Words Occurring in the Qôran." *Journal of the Asiatic Society of Bengal* 21, no. 226 (1852): 109–14.

———. *Das Leben und die Lehre des Moḥammad*. 3 vols. 2nd ed. Berlin: Nicolaische Verlagsbuchhandlung, 1869.

———. "Aus Briefen an Prof. Fleischer." *Zeitschrift der Deutschen Morgenländischen Gesellschaft* 7 (1853): 412–15.

———. "Ueber eine Handschrift des ersten Bandes des Kitáb Ṭabaqát al-kabyr vom Sekretär des Wáqidy." *Zeitschrift der Deutschen Morgenländischen Gesellschaft* 3 (1849): 450–56.

———. "Ueber den Ursprung und die Bedeutung des arabischen Wortes Nâmûs." *Zeitschrift der Deutschen Morgenländischen Gesellschaft* 13 (1859): 690–701.

Suhaylī (a. l-Qāsim 'Abd al-Raḥmān b. 'Abd Allāh b. A. b. a. l-Ḥasan al-Andalusī al-Mālikī, d. Sha'bān 26, 581 [November 22, 1185]). *Al-Ta'rīf wa-l-i'lām fī-mā ubhima fī l-Qur'ān min al-asmā' al-a'lām*. Edited by 'Al. M. 'A. al-Naqrāt. Tripoli, 1401/1992. Also edited by 'Abd Allāh 'Alī Muhannā. Beirut: Dār al-Kutub al-'Ilmiyya, 1407/1987 (following the Cairo edition of 1938).

Suyūṭī (Jalāl al-Dīn Abū l-Faḍl ʿAbd al-Raḥmān b. a. Bakr al-Khuḍayrī al-Shāfiʿī, d. Jumādā 19, 911 [October 18, 1505]). *Al-Khaṣāʾiṣ al-kubrā (Kifāyat al-ṭālib al-labīb fī khaṣāʾiṣ al-ḥabīb al-maʿrūf bī . . .)*. 2 vols. Hyderabad: Dāʾirat al-Maʿārif al-Niẓāmiyya, 1320–1321/1902–1903. Reprint edition, Beirut: Dār al-Maʿrifa (no year given).

———. *Al-Itqān fī ʿulūm al-Qurʾān (Soyuti's Itqan)*. Edited by A. Sprenger et al. Calcutta, 1852–1854. Reprint edition, Osnabrück: Biblio Verlag, 1980. Second, improved edition, *Al-Itqān fī ʿulūm al-Qurʾān*. 2 vols. in one. Edited by M. Abū l-Faḍl Ibrāhīm. Cairo, 1974–1975.

Ṭabarī (a. Jaʿfar M. b. Jarīr b. Yazīd, d. Shawwāl 27, 310 [February 17, 923]). *Tafsīr*. Edited by Maḥmūd M. Shākir and A. M. Shākir (as far as sura 14 [*Ibrāhīm*]:27). 16 vols. Cairo, 1954–1968 (a second edition was published in 1969). The remainder of the Qurʾān's commentary was edited by A. Saʿīd ʿAlī Muṣṭ. al-Saqqā et al., beginning at XIII:231, sura 14 (*Ibrāhīm*):28, through vol. XXX. Cairo, 1373–1377/1954–1957.

———. *Annales*. 3 vols. (16 vols.). Edited by M. J. de Goeje et al. Leiden: Brill, 1879–1901. Also in *Taʾrīḫ al-rusul wa-l-mulūk*. 11 vols. Edited by M. Abū l-Faḍl Ibrāhīm. Cairo, 1960–1969.

———. *The History of al-Ṭabarī*, vol. IV, *The Ancient Kingdoms*. Translated by Moshe Perlmann. Albany: State University of New York Press, 1987.

———. *Al-Kashf wa-l-bayān ʿan tafsīr al-Qurʾān*. In a manuscript in Istanbul, Ahmet III 76 (from sura 5 to the end of the Qurʾān).

Tardieu, Michel. "L'arrivée des manichéens à al-Hira." In *La Syrie de Byzance à l'Islam: VIIe-VIIIe siècles*, edited by Pierre Canivet and Jean-Paul Rey-Coquais. Actes du colloque international, Lyon—Maison de l'Orient méditerranéen, Paris—Institut du monde arabe, 11–15 Septembre 1990: 15–24. Damas: Institut français de Damas, 1992.

TB: see above, Baghdādī.

Thaʿlabī (Abū Isḥāq Aḥmad b. Muḥammad b. Ibrāhīm, d. Muḥarram 427 [November 5, 1035]). *Al-Kashf wa-l-bayān ʿan tafsīr al-Qurʾān*. 10 vols. Edited by Abū M. ʿAlī ʿĀshūr Abū M. b. ʿĀshūr. Beirut: Dār Iḥyāʾ al-Turāth al-ʿArabī, 2002.

Troupeau, Gérard. "Réflexions sur l'origine syriaque de l'écriture arabe." In *Semitic Studies in Honor of Wolf Leslau*. 2 vols., edited by Alan S. Kaye, II:1562–70. Wiesbaden: Otto Harrassowitz, 1991.

TT: see above, Ibn Ḥajar.

van Reeth, Jan M. F. "L'evangile du Prophète." In *Al-Kitāb: La sacralité du texte dans le monde de l'Islam*, edited by Daniel De Smet, Daniel, G. de Catallaÿ, and J. M. F. van Reeth. Acta Orientalia Belgica, Subsidia III. Bruxelles: Belgisch Genootschap voor Oosterse Studiën/Socieété belge d'Etudes orientales, 2004, pp. 155–74.

Von Bothmer, Hans-Caspar Graf, Karl Heinz Ohlig, and Gerd-Rüdiger Puin, eds.

"Neue Wege der Koranforschung." *Magazin Forschung* (Universität des Saarlandes) 1 (1999): 33–46.

Wāḥidī (Abū l-Ḥasan ʿAlī b. A. al-Nīsābūrī, d. Jumādā II 468 [January 11, 1076]). *Al-Wasīṭ fī tafsīr al-Qurʾān*. 4 vols. Edited by ʿĀdil A. ʿAbd al-Mawjūd et al. Beirut, 1415/1994.

Wansbrough, John. *QS* = *Quranic Studies: Sources and Methods of Scriptural Interpretation*. London Oriental Series no. 31. Oxford: Oxford University Press, 1977.

Weil, Gustav. *Das Leben Mohammeds nach Mohammed Ibn Ishak und Abd el Malik Ibn-Hischam*. Die fünfzig Bücher no. 14. Berlin: Ullstein, 1916.

Wild, Stefan. *Mensch, Prophet, und Gott im Koran: Muslimische Exegeten des 20. Jahrhunderts und das Menschenbild der Moderne*. Münster: Rhema, 2001.

Yaḥyā b. Sallām (Abū Zakariyāʾ Yaḥyā b. Sallām b. a. Thaʿlaba al-Taymī al-Baṣrī, d. Ṣafar 200 [September 10, 815]). *Tafsīr*. Edited by Ḥammādī Ṣammūd, *al-Juzʾ al-sādis ʿashar wa-l-thāmin ʿashar min Tafsīr Yaḥyā b. Sallām*. Master's thesis, Tunis, ca. 1969–1970. Also edited by al-Bashīr al-Mkhīnīnī, *Taḥqīq al-juzʾ al-thālith ʿashar wa-l-juzʾ al-sābiʿ ʿashar min Tafsīr Yaḥyā b. Sallām*. Master's thesis, Tunis, ca. 1970.

Zabīdī (al-Sayyid Murtaḍā M. b. M. al-Ḥusaynī, d. 1205 [September 10, 1790]). *Tāj al-ʿarūs min jawāhir al-Qāmūs*. 40 vols. Edited by ʿAbd al-Sattār Aḥmad Farāj et al., al-Turāth al-ʿArabī no. 16. Kuwait: al-Majlis al-Waṭanī li-l-Thaqāfa wa-l-Funūn wa-l-Ādāb, 1385–1422/1965–2001.

4

ʿABD AL-MALIK B. MARWĀN AND THE PROCESS OF THE QURʾĀN'S COMPOSITION

Alfred-Louis de Prémare

The process by which the Qurʾān was composed has been the subject of long and detailed studies, beginning with the German Orientalists during the second half of the nineteenth century and the first half of the twentieth century. However, some more recent works have profoundly questioned, in ways that themselves are almost entirely different and even opposed to each other, a certain number of assumptions and conclusions that had heretofore been generally accepted.[1] This article must, therefore, be limited in its scope and not violate its modest intentions. Knowing the composite nature of the texts, which are collected in the Qurʾānic corpus, and the uncertain character of the *akhbār* concerning their "gathering" (*jamʿ al-Qurʾān*) I would like straightaway to ground my study in certain accepted facts, or historical givens, that lay outside of that material which constitutes the *akhbār*. Such données all belong to the period of the Marwānid Umayyad Caliphate, beginning with the reign of ʿAbd al-Malik b. Marwān (AH 65–86 /685–705 CE).

ACCEPTED FACTS

Epigraphy and Numismatics

The first Islamic religious writings that have been dated thus far and attested to by external documents are the mosaic inscriptions in the Dome of the Rock, founded by ʿAbd al-Malik in Aelia (*Īliyā*), the Roman name for Jerusalem that was still used at the time. They are located on the ceiling of the building; their golden cubes decorate both the interior and the exterior surfaces of the octagonal arcade that divides the ambulatory into its inner and outer sections; the inscription on the outer surface, east and southeast, mentions the name of the Caliph responsible for the structure, and the year since the Hijra when it was built: AH 72 (692–693 CE). The text of the inscriptions, which was published in the 1930s and has been the subject of many studies subsequently, was the object of a "*Reconsideration*" in 1970 by Christel Kessler, who edited the inscriptions anew and reproduced them in their graphic configuration, illustrated with plates containing detailed photographs.[2]

The contents of the inscriptions are made up of formulaic statements, a number of which exist in parallel and in various passages and places in the Qurʾān, most noticeably the *basmala* and the *shahāda*, the latter being lengthened by eulogies dedicated to the Prophet (*al-taṣliya*).[3] The *basmala* and the *shahāda*, repeated at regular intervals, frame different short texts one after the other, as if one were looking at a series of short, successive suras. Only in the latter do we find a few diacritical marks meant to distinguish particular letters, but almost none, with only a few exceptions, correspond precisely to the ones belonging to later Arabic script.

The subjects of these texts are polemical. They are addressed directly to the "People of Scripture [*ahl al-kitāb*]," referring to the Christians, as the polemic concerns mainly Jesus and the Trinity. We find those passages again in the Qurʾān, both in complete lines and in fragments of lines, organized in different ways and with grammatical variants due to different arrangements or to a different syntactical context.[4]

Within such texts we find the definition of divine uniqueness: *qul huwa Allāh aḥad, Allāh l-ṣamad, lam yalid wa-lam yūlad, wa-lam yakun la-hu kufuwan aḥad*. This text exists in isolation in the Qurʾān, where it comprises the entirety of the short sura 112 (*al-Ikhlāṣ*). This is a "definition" in the theological-canonical sense of the term, in the style and in the image of

Christian conciliar definitions on points of dogma. In the context of the Dome of the Rock, such a lapidary formulation is also polemic in nature: the statement that Allāh "does not generate, nor is he generated," and that "He has no equal," are expressed in formulae just as obviously crafted, in response to the definition issued during the Council of Nicaea (325 CE) condemning Arianism and declaring that Jesus Christ must be called "τὸν υἱὸν τοῦ θεοῦ, γεννηθέντα ἐκ τοῦ πατρὸς μονογενῆ ... γεννηθέντα οὐ ποιηθέντα, ὁμοούσιον τῷ πατρί. . . ."[5]

John of Damascus, who was active in the Umayyad administration at the time of ʿAbd al-Malik, was of the opinion, in "Heresy no. 100," that the doctrine of the prophet of the new religion had been influenced by an Arian monk.[6]

The eastern and northern doors of the building also contain a certain number of inscriptions on copper plates that are considered as dating from the Umayyad period. On the northern door, the supremacy of the "religion of truth" is stated in the same words with which it is declared to be so, three times, in the Qurʾān.[7]

This motif or theme is immediately followed by a collective profession of faith: "We believe in Allāh, in that which came down to Muḥammad, and in that which the Prophets received from their Lord, without making any distinction among them, and it is to Him that we are beholden." Two lengthy parallels exist within the Qurʾān, with the following variant: "in that which has come down upon/towards us" (instead of "towards Muḥammad"), and where we also find a list of names of the biblical characters Abraham, Ishmael, Isaac, Jacob, *al-Asbāṭ*, Moses, and Jesus.[8] The supremacy of the "religion of truth against the liking of the "associators" (that is, Christians who "associate" others—meaning Jesus—with God), and the refusal to "distinguish" between the various prophets are here again proclaimed in opposition to the Christians, as "associators." The designation of "associators" as applied to Christians was the object, at that time, of a polemical discussion in "Heresy no. 100" by John of Damascus.[9]

Some religious formulas identical to those in the Dome of the Rock are found on Arabic coins that were struck and put into circulation by the monetary reform of ʿAbd-al Malik beginning in AH 77 (696–697 CE). On certain silver coins we find either the partial or the complete polemical-dogmatic "definition" of Divine uniqueness already to be found in the Dome of the Rock (*Allāh Aḥad, Allāh l-Ṣamad. . . .*).[10] This definition seems to become a sort of leitmotif of the new religious identity as against that of the peoples newly conquered and subjected to the Islamic empire. We find it again, blended in with other formulae, inside an Umayyad inscription placed to the right of the al-ʿUmarī mosque in Buṣrā in the Ḥawrān, founded by ʿUmar II b. ʿAbd al-ʿAzīz (AH 99 [717–718]).[11]

The inscription on the base of the Umayyad mosque in Damascus, built by al-Walīd I, son of ʿAbd al-Malik (AH 86–96 [705–715 CE]), consists, just after the *basmala*, of a short text that we find as a verse of the Qurʾān (*lā ikrāha fī l-din*).[12] This text is followed by a lengthy *shahāda* attesting that God is unique, and without associates, and that "our religion is Islam and our prophet is Muḥammad." The mention, in conclusion, of the founding Caliph and of the date of construction (AH 86 [705 CE]) points out that the mosque was built "on the location, and after the destruction of, the church that was previously there."[13] That church was the Cathedral of Saint John the Baptist: as the Christians had obstinately refused to give it up, al-Walīd, it is said, struck the first blow in its demolition, and then ordered that the Jews come to complete it.[14]

Given such circumstances, and in its textual surroundings, placing the mention of the demolished church with the text "*lā ikrāha fī l-dīn*" (there is no compulsion in religion) appears to be paradoxical: the Christians, although they have not given up serving the *ṭāghūt*, are not forced to embrace Islam, but Islam shows nonetheless its essential superiority (it is the "good direction" as opposed to the "errant" one), and its supremacy is testified to by the fact of the destruction of the cathedral and its replacement by a mosque, by order of the Muslim caliph.

The passage *lā ikrāha fī l-dīn*, as a Qurʾānic verse (2, 256) is a text without a real literary context: it is preceded by the verse of the Throne, which is a piece "in itself," and it is followed by short narratives about Abraham and the resurrection of the dead. The literature of the *Asbāb al-nuzūl* tried to find the circumstances of the transmission of *lā ikrāha fī l-dīn* in the framework of Medina, generally around the theme of the "votive" children, linked to the expulsion of the Jewish tribe of the Banū l-Naḍīr. It would appear that the damascene framework of the Umayyad mosque might apply just as well, if not more so.[15]

The geographer al-Muqaddasī (writing in AH 375 /985 CE) later recalled, in relevant fashion, the psycho-historical context of the construction of this mosque, one of a mimetic rivalry with Christians.[16]

A historian studying these texts might envisage three hypotheses concerning the content of the inscriptions on these monuments, which have parallels within the Qurʾān:

1. the texts were composed directly for the monuments in question, and were reused later, with some slight modifications, in the final composition of the Qurʾānic text;
2. they represent fragments that were still scattered, attesting to the existence of a sort of Ur-Qurʾān, still being drafted, selected, and assembled, some of which at the same time could have been used in the inscriptions on the monuments;
3. they were actual "quotations," taken from a fully formed Qurʾān that is the one we now have today.

Although none of these hypotheses seems sufficient to prevail over the others, based only on the inscriptions, it seems to me, based on the analyses offered below (II, III), that one can exclude the third hypothesis. It is in Jerusalem, in any case, in the place that stood as the symbol of eastern Christianity, where the Islamic anti-trinitarian and Christological polemic, as expressed in the inscriptions in the Dome of the Rock, has its true *sitz im leben*. We might be able to extend such an affirmation to the *lā ikrāha fī l-dīn* text that appears in the foundation inscription of the Damascus mosque.

PALEOGRAPHY AND THE STUDY OF THE CODICES

I shall not dwell on the problems that the oldest, and fragmentary, manuscripts we possess of the Qurʾān pose for scholars, for these are not my field of expertise. I shall limit myself to mentioning a few elements that I am familiar with, and which seem relevant to my argument, and which concern exclusively those manuscripts which are considered the oldest, because of the style of their lettering.[17]

We are always dealing with fragmentary texts, despite the fact that some of them may be quite lengthy. Their dates are only approximate, as the margin of uncertainty was still considerable between the end of the seventh century of the modern era and the first half of the eighth century (the end of the first century AH); these documents still belong to the same Marwānid period attested to by the epigraphic and numismatic evidence mentioned above. The writing of these texts is defective, and the orthography often tentative. The systems with which the verses are separated are very variable, and no title is given for those units of the text which are now considered the suras. Yet such units seem to be set—and they are indicated by the *basmala*—by a white line of separation, or by some decorative element. Finally, a number of these manuscript fragments positively attest to an arrangement of the texts different from the one we find in the definitive corpus, something that we have only known, thus far, from literary sources.[18] Thus, we are dealing with a period when not only the writing of the Qur'ān, but also the organization of its contents, were not yet stabilized.

EXTERNAL LITERARY SOURCES

Two Christian works of that same period refer to Islamic writings known to be the authoritative scriptures for the new religion.

The Monk of Beth Ḥalé

In a *Disputatio* composed in Syriac by an anonymous monk from the Beth Ḥalé Monastery in Mesopotamia, the author conducts a dialogue, in a fashion reminiscent of some Iranian texts, with a Muslim notable from the entourage of the emir Maslama (d. 120/738), son of ʿAbd al-Malik, and the governor of the Jazīra in 91/710. This detail, together with other information, allows us to assign the composition of the work to the first two decades of the eighth century.[19]

The Christian apologist makes a clear distinction between the writings he attributes to Muḥammad (*Mḥmd*); a distinction is made between 1) the laws and commandments to be found "in the *Qur'ān* that Muḥammad has taught you," and 2) other laws and commandments to be found in three different writings by Muḥammad, including "the writing of the Cow [*sūrat al-Baqara*].[20] He does not provide any more details on the content of this text. On the other hand, the Arabic word *sūra*, as its Syriac counterpart *sūrṭā*, from which it is probably derived, may refer, as is generally the case in the Qur'ān itself, to a fragmentary "writing," rather than what we now call "suras."[21] Further, the title of the suras as we know them are late, and are thus not present in the oldest manuscript fragments of the Qurʾān. It is therefore likely that the writings referred to by the monk do not correspond completely to what we now know as the sura called "the Cow." It appears, in any case, that around 710, there did exist, among other writings, a "writing on the Cow" distinct from the Qurʾān.

John of Damascus

The second work is the "Book of Heresies," written in Greek around 735 by John of Damascus, one of the Fathers of the Church. He had followed his father in the service of the Umayyad administration between 700 and 705 (AH 81–85), during the last years of the reign of ʿAbd al-Malik.[22] It would appear that "Heresy 100" [Περι αιρέσεως ρ'], which concludes his work and concerns "the cult of the Ishmaelites" (θρησκεια των Ισμαηλιτων), or Islam, is the product of knowledge he had acquired at the time from existing Islamic writing.[23]

The Arabic word Qurʾān is not mentioned, rather the Greek word "βιβλος," a "book" composed by Muḥammad (Μαμεδ) based on a writing "γραφή/συγγραφή" (so-called coming from Heaven) in the words of the polemicist, who discusses its origin and content, essentially in a theological context. What he mentions about this βιβλος in relation to the polemic against Christian christology is summarized with precision, and we also have parallels existing between certain passages in the inscriptions on the Dome of the Rock and in the Qurʾān.[24]

He also refers to various texts written by Muḥammad, and it is difficult to say whether he considers them as part of the βιβλος mentioned above. They have different names (προσηγορία), which correspond to their respective subjects (e.g., "The Cow," "God's She-Camel," "the Table," "The Woman"); these are not, properly speaking, "titles" (ἐπιγραφή). "The woman's writing (ή γραφή τῆς γυναικός) concerns, among other things, the laws regarding polygamy[25] and repudiation, the latter being illustrated by the story of Zayd's repudiation of his wife for the benefit of Muḥammad. It is "in the same writing" ('Εν αύτῇ δὲ τῇ γραφῇ), he reports, that there appears there the commendation to go unto one's wife in such-and-such a way, as one plows a field.[26] We know now that, in the definitive text of the Qurʾān, this image occurs in sura 2, al-Baqara, together with the legal norms governing repudiation,[27] and that mention of Zayd and his wife occurs in sura 33, *al-Aḥzāb*.[28] These themes, gathered in "one same writing," titled "Woman," leads us to think that we are dealing with a text that is organized quite differently from the current sura 4, titled "Women."

Another text is referred to at length; it is titled "God's she-Camel" (ἡ γραφὴ τῆς καμήλου θεοῦ), and it, too, is attributed to Muḥammad. The subject of the she-camel, in the definitive text of the Qur'ān, is spread out among various passages, far from one another, without leading to a single grouping within a particular sura under the heading "God's she-Camel."[29] Further, the writings to which John refers include, on the subject of the she-camel, some elements that are not found in the pages of the Qur'ān on the same subject, including the fact that a she-camel cannot pass between two mountains because there is not enough space; that she is without a father and a mother; that she nurses people with her milk, that she has a baby camel; and that following the murder of her mother the young camel cries to God and is raised to Heaven. The polemicist discusses all these details—and mocks them.[30]

We have spoken of the "extremely succinct character" shown by the author of "Heresy 100" in his knowledge of Islam, or even of "mistakes that are more intentional than involuntary."[31] At best, and without meaning to question his "solid information," these variations from the Qur'ān have been perceived as "imprecisions in the details,"[32] or a blending with oral sources in the development of the stories of Zayd or of God's she-camel,[33] whereas John says explicitly that such elements are to be found in some of Muḥammad's "writings." Such judgments are a projection onto the information provided by John in his own time, of which we now know from the current textual corpus of the Qur'ān, as if the latter were the measure of everything on the historical and literary level. We do have, in places other than the work of John of Damascus, and essentially in the same period, visible traces of what he says concerning the "writing about God's she-camel."

Such traces exist most notably in what was transmitted by Muqātil b. Sulaymān (d. 150/767), as an explanation (*tafsīr*) of those Qur'ānic passages where there is mention of "God's she-camel" (*nāqat Allāh*). We find here the following themes: the she-camel has neither father nor mother (*min ghayri nasl*); she is close to giving birth (*'usharā'*); she emerges from a stony cliff (*ṣakhra*); people feed on her milk (*fī laban*) when she is standing still, drinking the water given to her; the young camel (*faṣīl*) cries for help after the murder of its mother, it is saved, and it mysteriously disappears.[34]

An analysis of these texts, as they have reached us,[35] allows us to easily perceive within them, due to their disorganized character, what is a *tafsīr* of Muqātil, introduced most frequently by *yaʿnī, yaqūlu*, or *innamā*, or by *qāla Muqātil*. On the other hand, a certain number of themes are not introduced by such openings, and these appear without an obvious link with the contents of a text that they do not intend to explain, but that forms a part of the same text. The most significant passage concerns verses 155–58 of sura 26, *al-Shuʿarāʾ*.[36] In the light of what is said by John of Damascus, and taking into careful consideration that which is reproduced from Muqātil, the hypothesis that the latter contains traces of a text earlier than the various current Qurʾānic passages on the she-camel of the Thamūd, acquires a clear shape. According to such a hypothesis, this text is not an exegetical gloss added after the Qurʾānic passages, as one might surmise; rather, the Qurʾānic passages can be seen as the later result of mental labor aimed at the redaction, selection, and stylistic reorganization of the text, and carried out during the final composition, based on various preexisting texts not yet formally fixed and rendered immutable.

On the other hand, Muqātil is not the only one in whose writings we find the different motifs referred to by John of Damascus concerning the text about God's she-camel. But he is the earliest, and he shows it to us in what is, effectively, a raw first state. Al-Ṭabarī (d. 310/923) later gives us a well-composed sampling of ancient Arab legends in his Qurʾānic commentary titled *Jāmiʿ al-bayān*. He refers each time to transmitting sources that are all contemporaneous with John of Damascus: al-Suddī (Kūfa, d. 127/745), Ibn Iṣḥāq (Medina, al-Ḥīra, Baghdad, d. 150/767) and, to a lesser extent, al-Ḥasan al-Baṣrī (Baṣra, d. 110/728).[37] All this would lead one to think that such narratives were no longer just orally transmitted, but that some had been set down in writing, on the model of the γραφὴ τῆς καμήλου τοῦ θεοῦ, which, according to John of Damascus, was attributed to Muḥammed.

INTERNAL HISTORICAL AND LITERARY SOURCES

Based on the elements presented and analysed above, the period between the very end of the seventh century and the beginning of the eighth century constitutes a key moment in the history of the Qurʾān. It is in the light of such elements that we must view what is said by the Arab historical and literary sources of the time.[38] Ibn Abī Dāwud al-Sijistānī, in his *Kitāb al-maṣāḥif*, places himself squarely in the camp of the traditionists, who believe that the Qur'ān was entirely formed and officially sanctioned at the time of 'Uthmān, and by his fiat. Yet he dedicates a number of pages of his work to the scriptural work carried out under the direction of al-Hajjāj b. Yūsuf, governor of Iraq, a liege of Caliph 'Abd al-Malik (AH 65–85 [685–705 CE]), then of his son and successor, al-Walīd (AH 86–96 [705–715 CE]). This is one of the first indications of its importance.

In the field of Arab historiography, however, there are sources of information other than those specifically concerning the study of the Qur'ān, and these are generally less conditioned by the attitudes typical of the traditional, and freer in the transmission of their *akhbār*. This applies, in particular, to biographical and genealogical works, works of *adab*, and historical-geographical works.[39] I shall rely in particular on such literary sources, exercising the necessary critical caution, as one should do when viewing the information being transmitted and the nature of the works in which we find them.

'ABD AL-MALIK B. MARWĀN (AH 65–86/685–705 CE)

The Theological and Political Background

The caliph is necessarily involved in scriptural issues, first of all in his institutional role, as political power is indissolubly linked to its religious legitimacy. All Umayyads, beginning with 'Uthmān, are not only aware of their role, but they also bestow upon themselves the title of "God's Caliph," *khalīfat Allāh*. References and quotations provided by P. Crone and M. Hinds on this matter, beginning with 'Uthmān, are of particular significance. The attestations concerning 'Abd al-Malik are especially striking.[40]

The title *khalīfat Allāh* does not appear following his name on the inscription in the foundation stone of the Dome of the Rock, only the epithet of *amīr al-mu'minīn*. Some coins of the period, however, do contain that title, although such numismatic use of "*khalīfat Allāh*" does not appear to have lasted for long.[41] We also have some evidence of the attribution of that title to 'Abd al-Malik by the main poets of the time: al-Farazdaq, Jarīr, and al-Akhṭal; we even find it in Ibn Qays al-Ruqayyāt, despite the latter's having been linked for a certain period with the Zubayrids, the principal opponents of the Umayyad dynasty.[42]

This might be explained by taking into account the larger context, as marked by a number of significant events, such as the foundation of the Dome of the Rock, a symbol of Islam's prestige and triumph over the Christians; the imposition of the *jizya* on the non-Muslim population as a whole;[43] the Arabization of the administration; the creation of a currency that was clearly Arab and Muslim;[44] and, finally, the recognition of the legitimate role of ʿAbd al-Malik as caliph. The traditionists have dated this legitimization process to the time of his victory over ʿAbd Allāh Ibn al Zubayr, in the year AH 73, now referred to as "the year of unity" *(ʿām al-jamāʿa)*.[45]

In the circumstances of a *fitna* which was undergoing a continuous renaissance, particularly in Iraq, al-Ḥajjāj b. Yūsuf, the governor of that region, was particularly keen to praise the stature of ʿAbd al-Malik as "God's Caliph." He is viewed as the principal author of a sort of theologico-political doctrine aimed at justifying the actions and decisions of the caliph:

> He [al-Ḥajjāj] had a pure Arabic language, he was eloquent and well-versed in the law [*kāna faṣīḥan balīghan faqīhan*], wrote Ibn Hajar about him; he said that obedience to the Caliph in his every demand was compulsory [*farḍ*] for the population, and he even debated that very point.[46]

Numerous letters by al-Ḥajjāj have been quoted by historians. In one of these, addressed to Muṭarrif b. al-Mughīra, governor of al-Madāʾin (Ctesiphon) in Iraq, who was making peace with those who took part in the *khārijite* revolt of Shabīb b.Yazīd, in 77/696, he wrote: "ʿAbd al-Malik is God's caliph concerning His servants, and he is more greatly honored by Him than Muḥammad and the other messengers."[47]

Another of his letters is quoted, this one addressed to ʿAbd al-Malik, "in which he praised the stature of the Caliphate, and he said that the Caliph, in the eyes of God, was better than the angels, closest (to God), even closer than the Prophets who were sent. . . . ʿAbd al-Malik, says the informer, was surprised, and said 'I would have liked it if some *khārijite* had been present, to be able to oppose him at least through this letter!'"[48]

One might think that the caliph is here being depicted almost as a pawn in the hands of the powerful governor, and some of these *akhbār* could simply be a reflection of the anti-Umayyad propaganda of the Abbassids. Other *akhbār* show, on the other hand, that ʿAbd al-Malik remains the master of the game. We have many examples of this, which I cannot dwell upon at length here. It shows, essentially, that al-Ḥajjāj is merely a servant of the caliph, the object of his favor due to his effectiveness in repressing the dissidents in Iraq, yet he is just as likely, under different circumstances, to incur the caliph's displeasure or simply be "put back in his place."[49] Further, ʿAbd al-Malik, in Syria, has other very influential advisors: Rajāʾ b. Ḥaywa, the administrator of, and "spiritual advisor" for, the construction of the Dome of the Rock; his personal secretary, Qabīṣa b. Dhuʾayb, in charge of the mint and the postal systems; and finally, Ibn Shabīb al-Zuhrī, who was to become the principal mentor of his successors in the recording of the collections of religious traditions. These three personages were not only high officials, they were also scholars working in Syria in the service of the caliph and advising him on important matters, such as the construction of the Dome of the Rock, the creation of the new currency, and the management of the writings and Traditions that were circulating. They could not have been unaware of the composition of the religious scriptures. Yet a careful study of each of these three would require going beyond the scope of the present article.

ʿAbd al-Malik and the Religious Scriptures

ʿAbd al-Malik, just as al-Ḥajjāj does, appears in the most authoritative biographic dictionaries of the Islamic tradition as a transmitter of *ḥadīths*, as an expert in Qurʾānic texts, and as a *faqīh*, with the chain of transmission extending back to a number of Muḥammad's Companions, including ʿUthmān. Thus, he was recognized as having a role in religious affairs because of the unusual abilities attributed to him, even in the Abbasid period.[50]

Such considerations must necessarily contain some fictitious elements, as they tend to project onto the period of ʿAbd al-Malik some categories established later in the history of Islamic religious science.[51] Yet it is true that, even though after the fact, they constitute a sort of posthumous recognition of his fulfillment, not only of his official responsibilities, but of what in fact he managed to achieve beyond that. Thus, in order to properly highlight the juridical knowledge of ʿAbd al-Malik, the testimony of al-Aʿmash is often invoked as that of one of the recognized specialists of the "readings" of the Qurʾān.[52]

Were the authors thinking more particularly about interventions (by ʿAbd al-Malik), or about decisions made about the composition of the Qurʾān? ʿAbd al-Malik, it is said, made the following remark: "I am afraid of dying during the month of Ramaḍān. That is the month in which I was born, it is the month in which I was weaned, it is the month in which I gathered together the Qurʾān [*jamaʿtu l-Qurʾān*], and it is the month in which I was sworn allegiance [as the caliph]." And he died at mid-Shawwāl, when he no longer was worried about the possibility of dying (during Ramaḍān).[53]

This information has been used as an indication of the role played by ʿAbd al-Malik in the composition of the Qurʾānic texts, quite apart from its anecdotal and literary aspects, which deserve to be analyzed in themselves.[54] Yet, as the verb *jamaʿa*, "to gather" (in a *muṣḥaf*), is also used with the meaning of "memorizing/learning by heart," one may also understand it as a reference to his memory of learning, as a child, after he had been weaned. In any case, we would still need to establish the nature of the "Qurʾān" he learned by heart when he was a child. Thus we must rely on other information in order to try to understand the role assigned in the ancient texts to ʿAbd al-Malik in the matter of the Qurʾān.

An early indication may be found in Ibn Saʿd. It is quite interesting, especially if we keep in mind his habitual reserve concerning the actual writing down of the Qurʾān.

The Silences of Ibn Saʿd

Ibn Saʿd, in fact, is obstinately silent about a "gathering-up of the Qurʾān" in pages (*ṣuḥuf*) or in a codex (*muṣḥaf*), done supposedly first at the time of Abū Bakr, and later at the time of ʿUthmān. All the more reason for his silence, not only concerning the Ḥafṣa sheets, but also, apart from a brief allusion, concerning the role of Zayd b. Tābit as the sole creator of a *muṣḥaf*. In his view, Zayd is solely an expert on legal (succession-related) matters (*farāʾiḍ*). If there were *akhbār* about these two collections already in circulation in the first half of the eighth century, beginning with accounts attributed to Ibn Shihāb al-Zuhrī, Ibn Saʿd, who knew them, did not take them into account.[55] Whatever the intentions of Ibn Saʿd, this does not surprise, given the diversity of the contradictory *akhbār* concerning this question; the canonical version of al-Bukhārī, on the other hand, chose to ignore the existence of real competing Qurʾānic collections, which he was content to mention only very vaguely. The narrative by Ibn Saʿd concerning his teacher al-Wāqidī can be found in the long biographical note he dedicates to ʿAbd al-Malik.

The Speech to the People of Medina

Al-Wāqidī attributes the direct transmission to Muḥammad b. Kaʿb al-Quraẓi, the *qāṣṣ* at the Medina mosque and a member of the household of the Umayyads.[56] Ibn Saʿd places him in the context of the official pilgrimage to the holy places of the Ḥijāz, led by ʿAbd al-Malik in the year 75/695. The caliph, passing through Medina on that occasion, made a conciliatory speech to the people of Medina concerning both their *muṣḥaf* and their particular corpus of legal prescriptions.[57]

The caliph, according to this account, appeared to wish to put an end to the stormy relationship that had arisen between the people of Medina and the Umayyads since the caliphate of Yazīd I, and, in particular, the secession by the caliph of Mecca, ʿAbd Allāh Ibn al-Zubayr, which had ended two and a half years earlier by al-Ḥajjāj b. Yūsuf. The pilgrimage of 75/695 marked the solemn conclusion of that second and long civil war. The memory of the letter is all the more alive for the people of Medina, as they suffered greatly in 63/683, following their revolt, their defeat at the *ḥarrat Wāqim* (*al-Ḥarra*, near Medina), and the massacre that followed in the town itself. During his visit with them, ʿAbd al-Malik does not shy away from reminding them sternly about those events, and he shows himself to be intransigent concerning the legitimacy of his power as well as that of "the people of his house."[58] His last speech is altogether different in tone:

> Muḥammad b. ʿUmar [al-Wāqidī] spoke to us, and said: "Ibn Abī Sabra[59] reported to me, the supporter of Abū Mūsā al-Ḥannāṭ, the supporter of Ibn Kaʿb [al-Quraẓī], who said: I heard ʿAbd al-Malik b. Marwān say:
>
> 'People of Medina, you had the greatest right to be linked to the first work;[60] whereas there have flowed over you from the East some *ḥadīths* which we do not know,[61] but we only know the reading of the Qurʾān. So you should cling to what is in your *muṣḥaf*, around which the *imām* so unjustly treated[62] has gathered you; and observe the *farāʾiḍ*,[63] around which your *imām*, so unjustly treated, has gathered you. May God have mercy on him, as he had consulted Zayd b. Tābit about this, and he was an excellent advisor for Islam, may God have mercy on him. They both firmly established what they established, and they abolished that which they diverged from.'"[64]

The authenticity of this speech has been doubted in the light of later developments in the juridical tradition, and of what it says concerning the *ḥadīths* from Iraq and the *farāʾiḍ* of Zayd.[65] Personally, I would envisage things in another way, beginning with what is said in the *muṣḥaf*, and placing myself in the framework of the narrative as a literary text not without data of a "historical" nature. Four important elements are worthy of note:

1. Apart from the *ḥadīths*, the caliph speaks of that which, in Iraq, concerns "the reading of the Qurʾān," and that he knows (and recognizes?).
2. He mentions a *muṣḥaf* belonging to the people of Medina (*muṣḥaf-kum*), supported by ʿUthmān, and he urges them "to cling to that which in found in" that codex.
3. He refers to a body of *farāʾiḍ*, the substance of which he attributes to Zayd b. Thābit, advisor to ʿUthmān, and which is distinct from the Qurʾānic *muṣḥaf*, and he declares those prescriptions to be "good for Islam."
4. ʿAbd al-Malik, in any case, in his role as caliph exercises his decision-making authority.

Furthermore, what we know both from the external information noted above, and from external literary sources and internal information of a historiographical nature, corresponds, in general, to the contents of the speech of ʿAbd al-Malik, namely, the existence of different "Qurʾānic" traditions in different parts of the empire, in Ḥijāz, in Syria, and in Iraq; the existence, alongside a Qurʾān which had not yet stabilized, of other writings attributed to Islam's Prophet, which are distinct from that Qurʾān; and, finally, the fact that ʿAbd al-Malik, certain of his own legitimacy and of his role as *khalīfat Allāh*, decides and intervenes as the unifier of the community.

Ibn Saʿd has gathered these elements in the general framework of the pilgrimage in the year AH 75. Such framing is doubtless a symbolic one. Yet, in that case, it is intended to show that the reign of ʿAbd al-Malik, the legitimate caliph beginning in the year 73, and the one who presided over the pilgrimage of the year 75, was a significant moment in the composition of an official corpus called the Qurʾān, consisting of writings that at the time were still dispersed.

AL-ḤAJJĀJ B. YŪSUF (AH 41–95/661–714 CE)

Al-Ḥajjāj b. Yūsuf is credited by traditional sources with a certain number of "technical" interventions of the ʿUthmān codex (diacritical marks, corrections, division of the text). But such indications are often contradictory and uncertain.[66]

Information of this kind, much like the criticism that has been levied against it, is based on various assumptions, to wit: that the basic Qurʾānic codex was put together under ʿUthmān; that that codex was entire, having been completed and officially divulged beginning at this time; and, finally, that the current *muṣḥaf* is evidence of an "ʿUthmānian text."[67] As long as a *muṣḥaf* that can be proven to be that of ʿUthmān remains out of our grasp, such assumptions must be reexamined in the light of the current status of historical research on the Umayyad period; there have been, in fact, new elements gathered from the updating and publication of texts that were previously either unknown or unpublished. These texts make it clear that the information known thus far concerning the history of the *maṣāḥif* were the result of a conditional selection, which left aside many aspects liable to turn one's views in a completely different direction.

THE SENDING OF THE *MUṢḤAF* TO THE CAPITALS OF THE EMPIRE

The first question to arise concerns the nature and content of the *muṣḥaf* allegedly compiled in Medina on the initiative of ʿUthmān, and supposedly set out to the capitals to unify the readings and to "officialize" the texts. Ibn Shabba, in his *History of Medina*, reports the following *khabar*: "ʿAbd al-ʿAzīz b. ʿAmrān told us, according to Muḥriz Ibn Thābit, *mawla* of Maslama b. ʿAbd al-Malik, who had it from his father, who said: I was one of the guards of Ḥajjaj b. Yūsuf. Al-Ḥajjāj wrote the *muṣḥaf*. Then he sent them to the military capitals (*al-amṣār*). He sent one to Medina. The members of ʿUthmān's family disapproved of that. They were told: "Get out the *muṣḥaf* of ʿUthmān b. ʿAffān, so that we may read it! They answered: it was destroyed on the day when ʿUthmān was killed."[68]

The distribution of the *maṣāḥif* in all the military capitals by al-Ḥajjāj is evoked in a similar manner by the Egyptian historian Ibn Duqmāq (d. 809/1406):

> Al-Ḥajjāj b. Yūsuf al-Thaqafī wrote *maṣāḥif* and sent them to all the military capitals [*al-amṣār*]. One he had sent to Egypt. When he saw that, ʿAbd al-ʿAzīz b. Marwān went into a rage, for at the time he was serving as governor of Egypt for his brother ʿAbd al-Malik. He says: "He permits himself to send a *muṣḥaf* to the very military district [*jund*] where I am serving, me!"[69]

The author then recounts that the Umayyad governor ordered that a special *muṣḥaf* be written for him and placed in the Great Mosque, yet he does not tell us what the work he ordered was based upon, other than to say that, once it was completed, he submitted it to to be vetted by the *qurrāʾ*.

Al-Samhūdī (d. 911/1506) quotes the *khabar* of Ibn Sabba, with a mistake in the name of Maslama.[70] This quotation appears in a chapter in which the author is asking himself highly critical questions about ʿUthmān's *muṣḥaf*. The latter, brought from Egypt, was allegedly kept in Medina, and he resists crediting the pious legend reported by the Andalusian traveler Ibn Jubayr on that subject,[71] mentioning three items of information based on the account of Mālik b. Anas (d. 179/796), the *imām* of Medina:

> Mālik said: "Reading from the *muṣḥaf* at the Mosque was not done by people in the past. It was al-Ḥajjāj b. Yūsuf who first instituted it. . . ." Ibn Zabāla[72] said: "Mālik b. Anas reported to me: 'Al-Ḥajjāj b. Yūsuf sent the *muṣḥaf* to the capitals. He sent a large one to Medina. He was the first to send *maṣāḥif* to the cities. . . .'" Concerning al-Shāṭibī,[73] he said the following: "Mālik also said: ʿUthmān's *muṣḥaf* has disappeared [*taghayyaba*]. And we have found no information about it among the authoritative writers [*al-ashyākh*].'"[74]

The latter remarks were already present in the *Kitāb al-Maṣāḥif* of Ibn Abī Dāwud, quoted from ʿAbd Allāh Ibn Wahb (d. 197/813), one of the most ancient disciples and transmitters of Mālik:

> Ibn Wahb reported back to us, and said, "I interrogated Mālik concerning ʿUthmān's *muṣḥaf*, and he said to me: 'It has disappeared [*dhahaba*].'"[75]

These indications, rooted in the Medina tradition of Mālik from quite early on regarding the role of al-Ḥajjāj in Qurʾānic affairs, and in particular concerning the first shipment of an official *muṣḥaf* to the capital cities, occurred when such pride of place is usually attributed to ʿUthmān. They further emphasize the fact that, even in very early times, there had been a vain search of the latter's *muṣḥaf*.

All this allows us to bring back to proper perspective what has been told concerning a *muṣḥaf* that was completed and officially sanctioned in ʿUthmān's day: there had been at that time, or possibly later, a collection of "Qurʾānic" writings in Medina, for which he had been considered responsible, just as there had been others elsewhere, under the names of other Companions. Concerning a *muṣḥaf* that had been completed and officially sanctioned for the purposes of unification, that was, doubtless, the result of further work and later political decisions, at a time when both the calligraphy and the orthography of the texts were acquiring forms that were better defined, and when (even more importantly) the status of an *umma* which was evolving with a new environment, internally rent by different and opposing currents, required the revising and then the clear establishment of a version of scriptures that could serve as a fixed reference.

AL-ḤAJJĀJ B. YŪSUF AND THE CONTENTS OF THE QURʾĀN

Some information leads us to believe that, beyond the purely technical textual issues of the kind normally discussed (such as diacritical marks, corrections, divisions of the text, etc.), al-Ḥajjāj was dealing with a different kind of problem—the "composition" of the Qurʾān:

> According to a *ḥadīth* reported by al-Bukhārī and Muslim, al-Aʿmash, a recognized expert on the variant "readings" of the Qurʾān, recounted the following:[76]
>
> "I heard al-Ḥajjāj b. Yūsuf say, in a speech delivered from the pulpit (*minbar*), 'compose the Qurʾān as Gabriel composed it [*allifū l-Qurʾān kamā allafa-hu Jibrīl*]: the writings that include the mention of the cow [*al-sūra llatī yudhkaru fīhā l-baqara*], and the writings that include mention of women [*al-sura llatī yudhkaru fīhā l-nisā*], and the writings that include mention of the family of ʿImran [*al-sūra llatī yudhkaru fīhā Al ʿImrān*].'"

Al-A'mash then went to visit a colleague who, upon being informed of that statement, countered it with an earlier saying by ʿAbd Allāh b. Masʿūd, according to which, in speaking of the Prophet about one of the rites within the pilgrimage, he used the expression "He upon whom has descended the sura of the Cow" (*alladhī unzilat ʿalay-hi sūrat al-Baqara*).[77]

The statement of al-Ḥajjāj no doubt was intended for the scribes in charge of the *taʾlīf* al-Qurʾān, heard and then transmitted by a "reader" of the Qurʾān, and ultimately discussed by a traditionist, indicating that, at that time, the *taʾlīf* was not yet fixed but being worked on, or at least that certain parts of the corpus still presented some problems for the "composition." A further indication of that is the fact that al-Ḥajjāj does not mention the themes of "the cow," "the women," and "Imran's family," in the order of the suras that we know under such titles, something which created later problems for the commentators on the *ḥādīth*.[78]

The word *sūra*, in the Qurʾān itself, does not mean "*sūra*" in the sense that is now accepted. Rather, it is a written text, however limited. The word *taʾlīf*, it should be noted, is ambiguous.[79] It may mean "a linked assemblage." However, unlike a similar collection of scattered pieces (*jamʿ*), it implies a deliberate composition, and it may even designate something originally composed by one author. This is the case in a narrative attributed to ʿUmar b. al-Khaṭṭāb, in which he recounts his conversion: having heard Muḥammad as he began to recite al-Ḥāqqa (sura 69), "I started to marvel at the composition of the Qurʾān [*fa-jaʿaltu uʿjabu min taʾlīf al-qurʾān*] and I said to myself 'By God, he is a poet!'"[80]

Thus, what is truly in play, what is at stake in the *ḥādīth*, is the "composition" of the texts and their being organized into a whole. We know that at the time of the monk of Beth Ḥalé and of John of Damascus, contemporaries of al-Ḥajjāj, there existed some parallel writings that were not yet a part of the Qurʾān/βιβλος, including "the text of the Cow" and that of "the Woman."[81]

It appears, on the other hand, according to the *Maghāzī* literature, that the expression *sūrat al-Baqara* referred for a time to a distinct and particular piece of ancient writing. Qatāda b. Diʿāma (d. ca. 117/735) conveys an epic narrative of the Battle of Ḥunayn (8/630), where the words *yā aṣḥāb sūrat al-Baqara* were a rallying cry that was supposedly made in a loud voice by al-ʿAbbās, uncle of Muḥammad, to rally troops in danger of becoming demoralized. The same anecdote is recounted by Ibn Kathīr (d. 774/1373), beginning with some *akhbār* of the same period, concerning the battle of Yamāma against Musaylima and the Banū Ḥanīfa (12–13/633).[82] If these narratives tell true stories, one may hypothesize that the older "writing about the Cow" included verses 63–74 of the future sūra 2, on the same theme of the Cow, recycled from biblical and para-biblical texts,[83] as the remaining components were added later.

Taking into account all these facts, one can surmise that the suggestion by al-Ḥajjāj to the scribes signifies a particular moment of the *taʾlīf*, when the issue arose of whether to revise and add one or the other such writings in "composing" them, so as to fold them into larger works. It seems clear that such a conclusion goes against the canonical version of the history of the Qurʾān, which holds that Zayd b. Thābit, at the time of ʿUthmān, was the only author of that kind of "composition."

Ibn Masʾūd and His Bedouin Rajaz

Another public statement by al-Ḥajjāj b. Yūsuf is quoted, and in this he is supposed to have vigorously condemned "the *qirāʾa*" of Abd Allāh b. Masʾūd; it is referred to by the *akhbār*, in which this statement is reported as a whole, not as one or more particular and limited variants: "This concerns the *rajaz* of the Bedouin [*rajaz ka-rajaz al-Aʿrāb*]. By God, if I can find someone who will read it, I will kill him, and I will even rub his *muṣḥaf* with a side of pork."

The direct sources of such information (*samiʿtu l-Ḥajjāj*) are not only an extreme *shiʿite* traditionist from Kūfa, Sālim b. Abī Ḥafṣa, but also, according to Ibn ʿAsākir, two important "readers" of the Qurʾān, also from Kūfa, ʿĀṣim and his disciple al-Aʿmash. The latter is alleged to have stated: "I then told myself: by God, I will read it despite you!" But, he added, "I kept that to myself." We know that the textual tradition of al-Aʾmash later became regarded as authoritative, although it involved many variants (*qirāʾāt*) deriving from Ibn Masʿūd.[84] The codex of Ibn Masʿūd was definitively proscribed in the tenth century, although some variants, generally minor ones in relation to the received texts, and deriving from his codex, have, despite everything, filtered into certain traditional texts, and they especially can be seen in the commentaries. Just like variants deriving from other sources, they represent, no doubt, only what survived from such collections after a selection that was more drastic than has been acknowledged. In fact, the Qurʾānic commentator Abū Ḥayyān al-Gharnāṭī, putting forward many of the best known *qirāʾāt*, said that he had omitted those which diverged too much from the definitive received text.[85]

The official *muṣḥaf*, according to historiographical sources, was not only the product of a "composition," it was also the result of a selection, of which we have, in any case, many echoes at various times in the history of the Qur'ān.[86] One might think that a further selection must have occurred at the time of ʿAbd al-Mālik; it is likely that some texts described by al-Ḥajjāj as part of the "the *rajaz* of the beduin," although Ibn Mas'ūd, according to a famous *khabar*, stated that he had heard the Qur'ān "from the mouth of the Messenger of God."[87]

Al-Ḥajjāj and Inspiration

The governor of Iraq is presented to us not only as a political decision maker on Qur'ānic matters, but also as someone who knew the Arabic language well and was an active participant in the scribes' work: "When I heard al-Ḥajjāj reading, said one of his contemporaries, I realized that he had long studied the Qur'ān."[88] A *khabar* reported by Ibn Abī Dāwud places him at the scene, and in the act of dividing the texts of the corpus into reading portions *(tajzi'at al-Qur'ān)*: "According to Muṭahhar b. Khālid, Abū Muḥammad al-Ḥimmānī said, "we worked on that project for four months, and al-Ḥajjāj read it every night."[89]

One last *khabar* deserves mention. Around that same time a pious legend began to circulate. It was said that after Muḥammad's death, his slave Umm Ayman would not stop crying. Abū Bakr and ʿUmar went to see her, and asked her, "What makes you cry so? The Messenger of God has reached a place where everything is better for him than anything in this sublunar world." She answered, "that is not why I am crying. I know well that God's Messenger has left for something better than this lowly world. I am crying because the inspiration has stopped [*abkī alā l-waḥy inqaṭaʿa*]." This story reached the ears of al-Ḥajjāj, who is said to have stated "Umm Ayman lied: I only work by inspiration [*kadhabat Umm Ayman: ma aʿmalu illa bi-wahy*]."[90]

The general framework within which Ibn ʿAsākir has placed this *khabar* is interesting to consider. The author-compiler begins by briefly recalling a reflection of al-Ḥajjāj on the caliph as superior to the prophets; he then places his statement concerning his "inspired" work at the center of the various versions of his speech in violent denunciation of the "*rajaz* of the Bedouin" of Ibn Mas'ūd. His statement about inspiration, therefore concerns mainly, in his eyes, the governor's work on the Qur'ānic *muṣḥaf*. Al-Ḥajjāj could have believed that his work on the composition of the *muṣḥaf*, in the service of one of "God's Caliphs," was superior both to angels and to prophets, especially in opposition to the Qur'ān of Ibn Mas'ud, even though it might have been heard from the very mouth of Muḥammad. As such, it deserved to be considered to have been inspired: the *waḥy* had not stopped with the death of Muḥammad. Is this not an implicit criticism, and a rejection of the Umayyad claims to superiority in relation to the Prophet? Or is it, rather, a recognition, also implicit, of the "imagined" role that they played in the composition of the Qur'ānic *muṣḥaf*? We might think that, in the case of Ibn 'Asākir, it was both things at once.[91]

Al-Ḥajjāj and the Caliph

In this collection of *akbār* about the scriptural activities of Al-Ḥajjāj, the role of 'Abd al-Mālik seems to be rather downplayed. The governor of Iraq would appear to be acting of his own initiative: he has his own team of scribes; he decides what needs to be done; and, ultimately, it is he who sends the *maṣāḥif* to the great military centers of his empire.

A number of *akhbār* show a desire to correct such an impression. Al-A'mash confirmed that he had heard al-Ḥajjāj's speech about the "*rajaz* of Beduin" while attending Friday Prayers with him, and he specifies that the governor had added, "Listen, therefore, and obey God's Caliph, and to his chosen one, 'Abd al-Mālik b. Marwān."[92] So it is in the service of God's caliph that he worked in Iraq, most particularly on Qur'ānic matters. The speech attributed to 'Abd al-Mālik concerning the *muṣḥaf* of the people of Medina and on their *farā'iḍ* follows the same line: it is the caliph's role to endorse that which he considers good "for Islam." In addition to the fact that "'Abd al-Mālik had his own experts in Syria, it is unthinkable that if, according to Mālik b. Anas, it was al-Ḥajjāj who first sent out the official *maṣāḥif* to the various capitals, he would have done so without the approval of the caliph. We have no information about the date when the distribution of such codices might have been made. What Ibn Duqmāq says about the negative reaction of the governor of Egypt, 'Abd al-'Azīz, brother of the caliph, might suggest a hypothesis. We know that 'Abd al-Mālik thought seriously about relieving his brother of his status as heir to the throne in favor of his own sons. According to al Madā'inī, al-Ḥajjāj had written to him to encourage him to do it, while, according to al-Wāqidī, Qabīṣa b. Dhu'ayb, the private secretary of the caliph in Syria, was against it. In any case, the governor of Egypt died before the decision could be made (AH 85/704 CE).[93] We may have, in this, an indication of the fact that the formal refusal by ʿAbd al-ʿAzīz to accept the *muṣḥaf* sent to Egypt by al-Ḥajjāj may have played a role in the incitement by the latter, which led to his removal from office, and that this may have occurred during the last years of the reign of ʿAbd al-Mālik.

If we juxtapose the totality of the *akhbār* from different sources, we can at the very least notice a certain consistency. The role and function of "God's Caliph" remain central and decisive. ʿUthmān, first legitimate representative of the Umayyad family, is its symbolic figure, even though all tangible trace of his *muṣḥaf* "has disappeared," and even though, in fact, ʿAbd al-Mālik was the real decision maker. In any case, this is the framework within which the Iraqi compilers of the *akhbār* wished to place the control exercised by al-Ḥajjāj over the work of the scribes. The latter, here represented by ʿĀṣim and al-Aʿmash, who lived on long after the death of al-Ḥajjāj, remain at the center of the scriptural work, as the history of the Qurʾānic corpus does not stop at the time of ʿAbd al-Mālik.

NOTES

1. Weil (1844 and 1872), Nöldeke, Schwally, Bergsträsser and Pretzl (1860, 1919, 1938), Blachère (1947, 1949–1950), Burton (1977), Wansbrough (1977).

2. See bibliography. The question of knowing whether the mention of the year 72 signifies the date of the beginning or that of the end of construction is still being debated. There is a tendency to lean towards the second hypothesis.

3. 57 *al-Hadī*, 2b; 33 *al-Ahzāb*, 56, etc.

4. *Al-Nisāʾ*, pp. 171–72; 19 *Maryam*, pp. 33–36; 3 *Āl ʿImrān*, pp. 18–19; 17 *al-Isrāʾ*, p. 111.

5. Concerning the gradual elaboration of the Islamic "Unitarian" definition before the inscription in the Dome of the Rock and sura 112, see de Prémare, "*Quelques questions*," pp. 44–48.

6. John of Damascus, *Écrits*, pp. 210–13.

7. 9 *al-Tawba*, 33; 48 *al-Fatḥ*, 28; 61 *al-Ṣaff*, 9.

8. 2 *al-Baqara*, p. 136 and 3 *Āl ʿImrān*, p. 84; Grabar, *Formation*, pp. 87–89.

9. John of Damascus, *Écrits*, pp. 216–19.

10. Lavoix, *Catalogue*, p. 60, n. 61–62, n. 172. Cf. photographic reproductions in Sourdel, *Islam Classique*, p. 104, illustration n. 25; comp. n. 23 and 24.

11. Ory, "*Mosquée al-ʿUmarī*." p. 374 and pl. 50a.

12. 2, *al-Baqara*, p. 256.

13. *Amara bi-bunyan l-masjid wa-hadm al-kanīsa llati kānat fi-hi*. Combe-Sauvaget-Wiet, *Répertoire*, n. 18.

14. See Nasrallah, "*Mosquée omayyade*," pp. 141–42.

15. Qurʾān, 2 al-Baqara, 255–60; al-Suyūṭī, *Durr*, II, pp. 19–23, which synthesizes the different imagined *asbāb* in order to explain verse 2, 256.

16. *Dhālika anna-hu [=al-Walīd] raʾā l-Shām balada l-naṣārā wa-raʾā la-hum fī-hā biyaʿan ḥasana qad aftana zakhārifu-ha wa-ntashara dhikru-hā . . . fa-ttakhada li-l-muslimīn masjidan ashgala-hum bi-hi ʿan-hunna wa-jaʿala-hu aḥada ʿajāʾib al-dunyā*. The same thing was later said about ʿAbd al-Mālik apropos the Dome of the Rock: al-Muqaddasī, *Aḥsan al-taqāsim*, p. 159.

17. Cf. in particular Adolf Grohmann (1958), François Déroche and Sergio Noseda (1998 and 2001), Yūsuf Rāghib (1990 and 1994), Gerd-Rüdiger Puin (1996), Hans-Caspar Graf von Bothmer, Karl-Heinz Ohling, and Gerd-Rüdiger Puin (1999).

18. Von Bothmer et al., *"Neue Wege"*; Puin, *"Observations,"* pp. 110–11.

19. This "Disputatio," as yet unpublished, has come down to us in two late manuscript copies. The one from Diyarbakir, from the early eighteenth century, comprises 85 folios. There were two monasteries by the name of Beth Ḥalé: one near Mosul, the other near Ḥīra. See Crone-Cook, *Hagarism*, pp. 12–13, and p. 163, note 23; pp. 17–18, and p. 167, note 14; Hoyland, *Seeing*, pp. 465–72.

20. The titles of the two other texts that are mentioned could not be properly identified.

21. A. T. Welch, "Sūra," *EI* IX: 921a–25a, p. 921b–22; Jeffery, *Foreign*, p. 182; Payne Smith, *Compendious*, p. 370b, sūrtā.

22. Vassa S. Conticello, "Jean Damascène," in *Dictionnaire des philosophes antiques*, ed. Richard Goulet (Paris: CNRS Éditions, III, 2000), pp. 1001–1003.

23. Concerning the text of "*Heresy no. 100*," see Kotter, *Die Schriften*, IV (PTS 22, 1981), pp. 60–67. This "heresy" bore the number 100 in the earlier edition of the works of John of Damascus, edited by M. Lequien (Paris, 1712); John of Damascus, *Écrits*, "Hérésie 100," text and French translation by B. Kotter, pp. 210–27. Concerning the authenticity of the attribution of these writings to John of Damascus, see B. Kotter; Khoury, *Théologiens byzantins* I, pp. 53–59, Glei-Khoury, *Johannes Damaskenos*, pp. 38–43.

24. Kessler, "Dome," pp. 4–6; Qurʾān 4 *al-Nisāʾ*, 171–72; Jean Damascène, *Écrits*, "Hérésie 100," pp. 212–13.

25. Cf. Qurʾān, 4 *al-Nisāʾ*, 3.

26. John of Damascus, *Ècrits*, "Hérésie 100," pp. 222–23.

27. 2, *al-Baqara* 223; 226–32; See also 65, *al-Ṭalāq*, 1–7.

28. 33, *al-Aḥzāb*, pp. 37–38.

29. Cf. Qurʾān, 7 *al-Aʿrāf*, pp. 73; 11, *Hūd*, pp. 61–68; 26, al-*Shuʿarāʾ*, pp. 141–59; 91, *al-Qamar*, pp. 11–15.

30. John of Damascus, *Écrits*, "Hérésie n. 100," pp. 222–25.

31. Abel, "Chapitre CI," pp. 6 and 12.

32. Khoury, *Théologiens byzantins*, pp. 59–60.

33. Hoyland, *Seeing*, p. 489.

34. Muqātil, *Tafsīr,* III:276 (on Qurʾān 26, *al-Shuʿarāʾ*, 154–57: the she-camel is full, she emerges from a rock, she gives milk); II:46 (on Qurʾān 7, *al-Aʿrāf*, 73, where there appears the young camel (*al-faṣīl*); IV:712–13 (on Qurʾān 91, *al-Qamar*, 12–14: the detailed story of the young camel, its prayer, and its disappearance).

35. Concerning the problems related to the transmission of the Muqātil texts, which form the oldest known complete *tafsīr*, see Gilliot, "*Muqātil*," pp. 40–50; Goldfeld, "*Muqātil*."

36. Muqātil, *Tafsīr*, III:276. The Muqātil texts on this subject will be presented and analyzed in an upcoming work, currently in preparation for Éditions du Seuil in Paris.

37. Al-Ṭabarī, *Jāmiʿ*, V.8, pp. 224–29, Commentary to the Qurʾān, 7 *al-Aʿrāf*, 73; VII:12, pp. 64–65, Commentary on the Qurʾān, 11; *Hūd*, 65.

38. Concerning the Umayyad Caliphate, and, in particular, the reign of ʿAbd al-Mālik, see Hawting, *The First Dynasty*, chap. 4–5.

39. *Al-Ṭabaqāt* of Ibn Saʿd (d. 230/845), *Ansāb al-ashrāf* of al-Balādhurī (d. ca. 279/892), *Taʾrīkh al-Madīna* of Ibn Shabba (d. 262/876), *Taʾrīkh madīnat Dimashq* of Ibn ʿAsākir (d. 571/1176), *al-ʿIqd al-farīd* of Ibn ʿAbd Rabbih (d. 328/940), *al-Intiṣār* of Ibn Duqmāq (d. 790/1388), *Wafāʾ al-Wafāʾ* of al-Samhūdī (d. 911/1506).

40. Crone-Hinds, *God's Caliph*, in particular chapters 2 and 3.

41. Ibid., pp. 7, 11–12; Hoyland, *Seeing*, p. 699, n. 36 and references.

42. Crone-Hinds, *God's Caliph*, p. 8 and references; about Ibn Qays al-Ruqayyāt, *EI,* III:843a–844a (by J. W. Fück).

43. Pseudo-Denys, p. 116.

44. Ibn Saʿd, *Ṭabaqāt*, V:229; Ibn Qutayba, *Maʿārif*, p. 357, which places this creation in 76/695–696; al Yaʿqūbī, *Taʾrīkh*, II:281, says that al-Ḥajjāj was the instigator; al-Thaʿālibī, *Laṭāʾif*, p. 31 (English translation pp. 47–48), says, instead, that it was the caliph who ordered him to supervise its execution. The person in charge of currency, as well as of the postal service, was Qabīṣa b. Dhuʾayb, personal secretary to the caliph: *kāna l-khātam ilay-hi wa-kānat al-sikka ilay-hi*; al-Ṭabarī, *Taʾrīkh*, III, year 85, p. 664.

45. *Kānat al-jamāʿa ʿalā ʿAbd al-Malik b. Marwān sanat thalāth wa-sabʿīn, Ibn ʿAsākir*, TD, XXXVII:132.

46. Ibn Ḥajar, *Tahdhīb*, II: 185 (n. 388).

47. *Inna ʿAbd al-Malik khalīfat Allāh fī ʿibādi-hi, fa-huwa akram ʿalay-hi min*

Muḥammad wa-ghayri-hi min al-rusul, al-Balādhurī, *Ansāb al-ashrāf*, VII:2, p. 289, concerning the rebellion of Muṭarrif b. al-Mughīra b. Shuʿba in 77/696, see al-Ṭabarī, *Taʾrīkh*, III:592–601 (year 77); concerning Shabīb b. Yazīd, see EI, IX:169b–70a (1996); Hawting, *The First Dynasty*, pp. 66–67.

48. . . . *idh atā-hu kitāb min al-Ḥajjāj yuʿaẓẓimu fī-hi amr al-khilāfa wa-yaẓʿumu anna l-samāwāt wa-l-ʾarḍ mā qāmatā illā bi-hā, wa-anna l-khalīfa ʿinda Llāh afḍal min al-malāʾika l-muqarrabīn wa-l-ʾanbiyāʾi l-mursalīn . . . fa-uʿjiba ʿAbd al-Mālik bi-dhālika wa-qāl: la-wadidtu anna ʿindī baʿḍ al-khawārij fa-ukhāṣim-hu bi-hādā l-kitāb:* Ibn ʿAbd Rabbih, *ʿIqd*, V:51–52, according to al-Haytham b. ʿAdī.

49. See, in particular, al-Balādhurī, *Ansāb al-Ashrāf*, VII:2, pp. 255–56, according to al-Madāʾinī.

50. Ibn Ḥajar, *Tahdhīb*, VI:373–74 (n. 781).

51. See Crone-Hinds, *God's Caliph*, chap. 5.

52. Ibn ʿAsākir, *TD*, XXXVII:120.

53. *Akhāfu l-mawt fī shahr ramaḍān; fī-hi ūlidtu, wa-fī-hi fuṭimtu, wa-fī-hi jamaʿtu l-Qurʾān, wa-fī-hi bāyaʿa lī l-nas, fa-māta li-l-niṣf min shawwāl ḥīna amina l-mawta fī niṣf-hi:* al-Balādhurī, *Ansāb al-Ashrāf*, IV:2, p. 586; the information is mentioned again in the same terms by Ibn al-ʿIbrī, *Tārīkh mukhtaṣar*, p. 194; ; it is broadened and modified by al-Thaʿālibī: *ūlidtu fī shahr ramaḍān, wa-fuṭimtu fī shahr ramaḍān, wa-khatamtu l'Qurʾān fī shahr ramaḍān, wa-balaghtu l-ḥulum fī shahr ramaḍān, wa-wullītu fī shahr ramaḍān, wa-atat-ni l-khilāfa fi shahr ramaḍān, wa-akhshā an amūta fī shahr ramaḍān: Laṭāʾif*, p. 110, English transl. p. 109.

54. Mingana, *Transmission*, pp. 32–33; Sharon, "*Umayyads*," p. 131, note 37; Prémare, *Foundations*, p. 297.

55. Concerning the canonical version of the composition of the Qurʾān, as presented in the version of al-Bukhārī and its parallels, see Motzki, "Collection"; de Prémare, *Origines*, pp. 70–80.

56. Concerning Muḥammad b. Kaʿb al-Quraẓī (d. 117/735), Ibn Ḥajar, *Tahdhīb* IX:373–74, n.691; Ibn Saʿd, *Ṭabaqāt*, V:370. Biographers note that his father, Kaʿb al-Quraẓī, was one of the prepubescent Jewish boys who, together with their mothers, had been spared and sold as slaves at the time of the execution of the men from the Banū Qurayẓa tribe in the year 5 of the Hijra (617 CE). The name of Muḥammad b. Kaʿb al-Quraẓī appears regularly in the chains of transmission of the authors of Maghāzī-Siyar (Ibn Isḥāq, Ibn Bukayr, Ibn Hishām, Ibn Saʿd, al-Wāqidī, al-Balādhurī).

57. Ibn Saʿd, *Tabaqāt*, V:231–33.

58. Some parallel accounts of these intransigent speeches exist in other works, such as, for example, Ibn Shabba, *Madīna*, III:1084–88.

59. Concerning Abū Bakr b. ʿAbd Allāh b. Muḥammad b. Abī Sabra, d. 162/778–79, Ibn Hajar, *Tahdhīb*, XII:31–32 (notice n. 138). In general, not consid-

ered very highly on the subject of the *ḥadīth*, he is, nonetheless, a link in the chain of an important transmitter such as Ibn Jurayj, and he is quoted by Ibn Māja. In a historiographical context, Ibn Abī Sabra is one of al-Wāqidī's constant references.

60. The phrase *al-amr al-awwal* can be understood as an allusion to the support lent by the Anṣār to Muḥammad at the time of the Hijra. However, in this context, it appears rather like an allusion to the composition of a first *muṣḥaf.*

61. A reference to Iraq.

62. ʿUthmān b. ʿAffān, the third successor to Muḥammad, was assassinated in his home in Medina in 35/656.

63. The term *farīḍa* (pl. *faraʾiḍ*), in its general meaning, refers to all religious prescriptions that are compulsory by law; see Ibn Manẓūr, *LA*, rac. *FRḌ*; Wensinck, *Concordance*, V:115–17, *sub voc. farīḍa*. In its specific meaning, of "compulsory part/portion" (of a dowry, of an inheritance, of alms, of a tithe), the Qurʾān wavers between the general meaning and the specific meaning. At a later time, *ʿilm al-farāʾiḍ* referred to part of the *fiqh* concerning the distribution in a succession. In the Ḥadīth, Zayd b. Thābit is described as *afraḍ al-nās*, "the most knowledgeable in *farāʾiḍ*," without specifying the nature of these *farāʾiḍ*: Ibn Ḥanbal, *Musnad*, III:281.6; al-Tirmidhī, *Jāmiʿ*. 50 *Manāqib* 33 [V:664–65]; Ibn Māja, *Sunan, Muqaddima* 11 [I: 67–68]. The Qurʾān contains precise dispositions concerning succession (4, 7–12, but where the final term *farīḍa* maintains the very general meaning of "obligation/prescription"). These, as well as others, could form part of an independent collection, before being included in the definitive Qurʾān. At the time of the battle and massacre of al-Ḥarra, in year 63/683, ʿUrwa b. al-Zubayr, it is said, took care to burn "the *fiqh* writings that were his (or "belonging to him"?) *aḥraqa kutuba fiqh kānat la-hu*: Ibn Saʿd, *Ṭabaqāt*, V:179.

64. Ibn Saʿd, *Ṭabaqāt*, V:233. This speech is mentioned in the same terms by Ibn ʿAsākir, *TD*, XXXVII:134–35. Mention of Ubayy b. Kaʿb as a transmitter in place of Ibn Kaʿb [al-Quraẓī] is without a doubt a copyist's mistake that was not corrected by the publisher.

65. Crone-Hinds, *God's Caliph*, pp. 71–72.

66. Ibn Abī Dāwud, *Maṣāḥif*, pp. 117–22, and passim; Ibn al-Nadīm, *Fihrist*, p. 63 sq.; Ibn Khallikān, *Wafayāt*, II:32. A summarized presentation and critical analysis of these data is in Régis Blachère, *Introduction*, pp. 71–102.

67. See, for example, François Déroche, *Le livre manuscript arabe. Preludes à une histoire* (Paris: Bibliothèque Nationale de France, 2004), p. 15.

68. Ibn Shabba, *Madīna,* I: 7. Concerning ʿAbd al-ʿAzīz b. ʿAmrān al-Aʿraj (d. 197/812–813), who appears not be particularly highly valued by official traditionalists, see Ibn Saʿd, *Ṭabaqāt,* V:436; Ibn Ḥajar, *Tahdhīb*, VI:312–13, n. 674. Maslama, son of Caliph ʿAbd al-Mālik, was one of the great Umayyad generals of his day (d. 121/738).

69. Ibn Duqmāq, *Intiṣār*, 4th part, pp. 72 sq. On Ibrāhim Ibn Duqmāq, *EI*, III: 779b (by J. Pedersen).

70. Al-Samhūdī, *Wafā'*, II:667; he omits the name of ʿAbd al-ʿAzīz b. ʿAmrān, the direct source of Ibn Shabba. The error concerning the name of Maslama (which became Salama), also appears in other eastern editions of *Wafā'*. We should mention that the name of Maslama also appears in the *Disputatio* of the monk of Beth Ḥalé.

71. Ibn Jubayr (540–614/1145–1217), *Riḥla*, p. 164.

72. Ibn Zabāla (d. end of the 2nd/beginning of the 3rd century), a disciple of Mālik, and the author of a *Kitāb al-Mādina wa-akhbāri-hā*, now lost, but from which al-Samhudi, among others, quotes long passages in various parts of his work; See Fuat Sezgin, *Geschichte des Arabischen Schrifttums*, Band I (Leiden: E. J. Brill), 1967, pp. 343–44.

73. Abū l-Qāsim al-Ruʿaynī, from Jativa, in Spain (538–590/1144–1194), an expert in Qur'ānic studies; *EI*, IX:376b–378a (by Angelika Neuwirth).

74. Al-Samhūdī, *Wafā'*, II:667, 668, 669. The list of the *ashyākh* of Medina that figure prominently in the chains of transmission of Mālik includes what was best known at the time. See Ibn Ḥajar, *Tahdhīb*, X:5–8 (n. 3).

75. Ibn Abī Dāwud, *Maṣāḥif*, p. 35, lines 18–19; concening ʿAbd Allāh Ibn Wahb, *EI*, III: 978b (by J. David-Weill).

76. Concerning al-Aʿmash (60–148/679–765), *EI*, I:443b–444a (by Carl Brockelmann/Charles Pellat); Ibn Ḥajar, *Tahdhīb*, IV:195–97 (n. 386), and see Blachère, *Introduction*, *passim*.

77. Muslim, *Ṣaḥīḥ*, *Ḥajj* 306, (V.9, 42–44); al-Bukhārī, *Ṣaḥīḥ*, 25 *Ḥajj* 138 (II: 234, n. 1750); cf. Ibn Ḥajar, *Tahdhīb*, II:186.

78. See the commentary by al-Nawawī (d. 676/1277), in the margin of the *Ḥadīth* of Muslim, *Ṣaḥiḥ*, pp. 43–44.

79. Concerning the term *ta'līf*, and the diverse contexts in which it appears in the literature about the *ḥadīth* regarding the Qur'ān, see Gilliot, "Traditions." About the word *sūra*, see note 21.

80. Ibn Hanbal, *Musnad*, I:17.8. This short narrative constitutes one of the many elaborations on the theme of the conversion of ʿUmar. It appears as a brief commentary on sura 69 *al-Ḥāqqa*: hearing this sura convinced ʿUmar that this *ta'līf* was not the work of a prophet nor of a soothsayer, but rather a revelation coming from the Lord of the Universe (verses 38–43).

81. See above, II: External Literary Sources.

82. Ibn Saʿd, *Ṭabaqāt*, II:151, IV:19; Ibn Kathīr, *Tafsīr*, I:63–64 (end of the introduction to sura 1); it is generally recognized in the *Maghāzī* literature: al-Suyūṭī, *Durr*, IV:160 (commentary to the Qur'ān 9, *al-Tawba* 25).

83. Cf. Numbers, 19:1–3; Deuteronomy, 21:1–9.

84. Al-Balādhuri, *Ansāb al-ashrāf*, VII: 2, pp. 300–301; Ibn ʿAsākir, *TD*, XII:

159–60. On Sālim b. Abī Ḥafṣa al-ʿIjlī (d. ca. 140/757), Ibn Saʿd, *Ṭabaqāt,* VI:336; Ibn Ḥajar, *Tahdhīb*, III, 374–75 (n. 800); on ʿAṣim (d. 127/744), *EI*, I 728a–b (by Arthur Jeffery); Ibn Ḥajar, *Tahdhīb*, V, 35–36 (n. 67); on al-Aʿmash (d. 148/765), see above, note 76.

85. *Baḥr*, VII:268, quoted by Arthur Jeffery, *Materials*, p. 10. About Abū Ḥayyān al-Gharnāṭī (654–745/1256–1344), *EI*, I:129b–130a (by S. Glazer, 1954). His commentary *al-Baḥr al-muḥīṭ*, published in Cairo in 1911, was reprinted in Beirut, Dār al-Fikr, 1983.

86. Summarized in de Prémare, *Origines*, pp. 83–89.

87. Ibn Shabba, *Madīna*, III:1006; the disdain toward the Bedouin language of Ibn Masʾūd is generally acknowledged in the traditions concerning the *qirāʾāt*; cf. al-Bukhārī, *Ṣaḥiḥ*, 62. *Faḍāʾil aṣḥāb al-nabī*, 20 (IV:258–59, n. 3742–43), which tries to circumscribe the debate within limits acceptable to the people of the *Ḥadīth.*

88. Ibn ʿAsākir, *TD*, XII:116; remarks by ʿAbd Allāh b. ʿAwn b. Arṭabān (66–151/685–767), from Baṣra; see Ibn Saʿd, *Ṭabaqāt*, VII:261–68; Ibn Ḥajar, *Tahdhīb*, V:303–305, n. 600.

89. Ibn Abī Dāwud, *Maṣāḥif*, p. 120; referred-to by Ibn ʿAsākir, *TD*, XII:116. Concerning the source, Abū Muḥammad Rāshid b. Najīḥ al-Ḥimmānī from Baṣra, transmitter of Anas b. Mālik, see Ibn Ḥajar, *Tahdhīb*, III, n. 43.

90. Ibn ʿAsākir, *TD*, XII:160. The transmitter of this *khabar* is ʿAṭāʾ b. al-Sāʾib (d. ca. 136/753), who came from the *Thaqīf*, the tribe of al-Ḥajjāj. He tells the story of Umm Ayman, according to one of the Prophet's companions, ʿAttāb b. Usayd, a member of the Umayyad family, and a late convert. Concerning the story of Umm Ayman, apart from the reflection attributed to al-Ḥajjāj, see Ibn Saʿd, *Ṭabaqāt*, VIII: 226.

91. The way in which the *akhbār* concerning delicate subjects are arranged often show an intentional "opacity," in the sense attributed to that term by experts in the narrative.

92. *Ismaʿū wa-aṭīʿū li-khalīfat Allāh wa-li-ṣafiyyi-hi ʿAbd al-Mālik b. Marwān*: Ibn ʿAsākir, *TD*, XII:159.

93. Al-Ṭabarī, *Taʾrīkh*, year 85, III:664–66; cf. Ibn Saʿd, *Ṭabaqāt*, V:233–34; al-Yaʿqūbī, *Taʾrīkh* II:279–80, says that he actually did depose him; he acknowledges, however, some contradictory information, according to which ʿAbd al-ʿAzīz was not deposed, rather, he was poisoned, in 85/704.

BIBLIOGRAPHY

Abel, Armand. "Le chapitre CI du Livre des Hérésies de Jean Damascène: son inauthenticité." *Studia Islamica* 19 (1963): 5–25 ["Chapitre CI"].

al-Balādhurī, Aḥmad. *Ansāb al-ashrāf*, IV.2, edited by ʿAbd al-ʿAzīz al-Dūrī and ʿIṣām ʿUqla. Bibliotheca Islamica no. 28 e. Beyrouth, 2001; VII.2, edited by Muḥammad al-Yaʿlāwī. Bibliotheca Islamica, no. 28 j. Beyrouth, 2002 [*Ansāb*].

Blachère, Régis. *Introduction au Coran*. Paris: Maisonneuve et Larose, 1947; repr., 1991 [*Introduction*].

von Bothmer, Hans-Caspar Graf, Karl-Heinz Ohlig, and Gerd-Rüdiger Puin. "Neue Wege der Koranforschung." Universität des Saarlandes: *Magazin Forschung* 1 (1999): 33–46 ["Neue Wege"].

al-Bukhārī, Muḥammad. *Al-Ṣaḥīḥ*, edited by ʿAbd al-ʿAzīz b. ʿAbd Allāh b. Bāz. 8 parts in IV vols. + Indices. Beyrouth: Dār al-Fikr, 1994 [*Ṣaḥīḥ*].

Combe, Étienne, Jean Sauvaget, and Gaston Wiet. *Répertoire chronologique d'épigraphie arabe* (*RCEA*). Le Caire: Institut Français d'Archéologie Orientale, 1931 [*Répertoire*].

Conticello, Vassa S. "Jean Damascène." In *Dictionnaire des philosophes antiques*, edited by Richard Goulet. Paris: CNRS Éditions, vol. 3, 2000, pp. 989–1012 [*"Jean Damascène"*].

Crone, Patricia, and Michael Cook. *Hagarism. The Making of the Islamic World*. Cambridge: Cambridge University Press, 1977 [*Hagarism*].

Crone, Patricia, and Martin Hinds. *God's Caliph. Religious Authority in the First Century of Islam*. Cambridge: Cambridge University Press, 1986 [*God's Caliph*].

Déroche, François. *Le livre manuscrit arabe. Préludes à une histoire*. Paris: Bibliothèque Nationale de France, 2004 [*Livre manuscrit arabe*].

EI = *Encyclopédie de l'Islam*. New edition, Leiden: Brill [*EI*].

Gilliot, Claude. "Muqātil, grand exégète, traditionniste et théologien maudit." *Journal Asiatique* 279, no. 1–2 (1991): 39–92 [*"Muqātil"*].

———. "Les traditions sur la composition / coordination du Coran (*taʾlīf al-Qurʾān*)." In *Das Prophetenḥadīṯ*, edited by C. Gilliot and T. Nagel, 14–39 [*"Traditions"*].

Gilliot, Claude, and Tilman Nagel, eds., *Das Prophetenḥadīṯ*. Göttingen, 2005. Nachrichten der Akademie der Wissenschaften zu Göttingen. I. Philologisch-Historische Klasse, Nr 1 [*Das Prophetenḥadīṯ*].

Glei, Reinhold, and Adel-Théodore Khoury. *Johannes Damaskenos und Theodor Abū Qurra. Schriften zum Islam* (Corpus Islamo-Christianum, series graeca 3). Würzburg and Altenberg, 1995 [*Johannes Damaskenos*].

Goldfeld, Isaiah. "Muqātil Ibn Sulaymān." In *Arabic and Islamic Studies*, volume 2, edited by Jacob Mansour. Bar-Ilan University Press, 1978, XIII–XXX (1–18) [*"Muqātil"*].

Grabar, Oleg. *La formation de l'art islamique* (1973). French translation by de Yves Thoraval. Paris: Flammarion, 2000 [*Formation*].

Hawting, Gerald R. *The First Dynasty of Islam. The Umayyad Caliphate AD 661–750*. Carbondale: Southern Illinois University Press, 1987 [2nd ed. London: Routledge, 2000] [*The First Dynasty*].

Hoyland, Robert G. *Seeing Islam as Others Saw It. A Survey and Evaluation of Christian, Jewish and Zoroastrian Writings on Early Islam*, Princeton, NJ: Darwin Press, 1997 [*Seeing*].

Ibn ʿAbd al-Barr, Yūsuf. *Al-Istīʿāb fī maʿrifat al-aṣḥāb*, edited by ʿAlī Muḥammad al-Bijāwī. VI vols. Beyrouth: Dār al-Jīl, 1992 [*Istīʿāb*].

Ibn ʿAbd Rabbih, Aḥmad. *Al-ʿIqd al-farīd*, edited by Aḥmad Amīn *et alii*, VI vols. + Indices. Cairo: Maṭbaʿat Lajnat al-Taʾlīf wa l-Tarjama wa l-Nashr, 1948–1973 [*ʿIqd*].

Ibn Abī Dāwud al-Sijistānī, ʿAbd Allāh. *Kitāb al-maṣāḥif*, edited by Arthur Jeffery. Cairo: al-Maṭbaʿa al-Raḥmāniyya, 1936 [*Maṣāḥif*].

Ibn ʿAsākir, ʿAlī. *Taʾrīkh madīnat Dimashq*, edited by Muḥibb al-Dīn ʿUmar al-ʿAmrāwī. LXXX vols. Beyrouth: Dār al-Fikr, 1995–2000 [*TD*].

Ibn al-Athīr, ʿAlī. *Usd al-ghāba fī maʿrifat al-ṣaḥāba*. VI vols. Beyrouth: Dār al-Fikr, 2003 [*Usd*].

Ibn Duqmāq, Ibrāhīm. *Al-Intiṣār li-wāsiṭat ʿaqd al-amṣār*, partially edited by Karl Vollers, *Description de l'Égypte par Ibn Doukmak*. Cairo: Imprimerie Nationale, 1893, + Indices par Muḥammad ʿAlī al-Biblāwī, 1898; repr. Frankfurt am Main [Islamic Geography, vol. 51], 1992 [*Intiṣār*].

Ibn Ḥajar al-ʿAsqalānī, Aḥmad. *Tahdhīb al-Tahdhīb*. XIV vols. Beyrouth: Dār al-Fikr, 1984–1985 [*Tahdhīb*].

Ibn Ḥanbal, Aḥmad. *Al-Musnad*, edited by Muḥammad al-Zuhrī al-Ghamrāwī. VI vols. Cairo: al-Maymaniyya, 1313 / 1895; repr. Beyrouth: Dār al-Fikr, n.y. [*Musnad*].

Ibn al-ʿIbrī, Ghrīghūrius = Bar Hebraeus. *Taʾrīkh mukhtaṣar al-duwal*, edited by Anṭūn Ṣalḥānī. Beyrouth: Imprimerie Catholique, 1890 [*Taʾrīkh mukhtaṣar*].

Ibn Jubayr, Muḥammad. *Riḥla*, edited by Mohammed Zeinhom, Cairo: Dār al-Maʿārif [Dhakhāʾir al-ʿArab no. 77] [*Riḥla*].

Ibn Kathīr, Ismāʿīl. *Tafsīr*. VII vols. Beyrouth: Dār al-Andalus li-l-Ṭibāʿa wa-l-Nashr wa-l-Tawzīʿ, n.y. [*Tafsīr*].

Ibn Khallikān, Aḥmad. *Wafayāt al-aʿyān wa-anbāʾ abnāʾ al-zamān*, edited by Iḥsān ʿAbbās. VIII vols. Beyrouth: Dār Ṣādir, 1977–1978 [*Wafayāt*].

Ibn Māja, Muḥammad. *Sunan*, edited by Muḥammad al-Albānī. IV vols. Maktabat al-Maʿārif li-l-Nashr wa-l-Tawzīʿ, 1997 [*Sunan*].

Ibn Manẓūr, Muḥammad. *Lisān al-ʿArab*, different editions [*LA*].

Ibn al-Nadīm, Muḥammad. *Al-Fihrist*, edited by Yūsuf A. Ṭawīl. Beyrouth: Dār al-Kutub al-ʿIlmiyya, 1996 [*Fihrist*].

Ibn Qutayba, ʿAbd Allāh. *Al-Maʿārif*, edited by Tharwat ʿUkāsha [1960]. 6th ed. Cairo: al-Hayʾa al-Miṣriyya al-ʿĀmma li-l-Kitāb, 1992 [*Maʿārif*].

Ibn Saʿd, Muḥammad. *Al-Ṭabaqāt al-kubrā*, edited by Iḥsān ʿAbbās. VIII vols. + Indices. Repr., Beyrouth: Dār Ṣādir, 1985 [*Ṭabaqāt*].

Ibn Shabba, ʿUmar. *Taʾrīkh al-Madīna al-munawwara*, edited by Fahīm Muḥammad Shaltūt. IV vols. Mecca, 1979 [*Madīna*].

Jean, Damascène. *Écrits sur l'Islam*, Présentation, Commentary and translation by Raymond Le Coz. Paris: Cerf [Sources chrétiennes no. 383] [*Écrits*].

Jeffery, Arthur. *Materials for the History of the Text of the Qurʾān. The Old Codices*, Leiden: Brill, 1937 [*Materials*].

———. *The Foreign Vocabulary of the Qurʾān*. Baroda: Oriental Institute, 1938 [*Foreign*].

John of Damascus, see above Jean Damascène.

Kessler, Christel. "ʿAbd al-Malik's Inscription in the Dome of the Rock: A Reconsideration." *Journal of the Royal Asiatic Society of Great Britain & Ireland* (1970): 2–14 [*"Dome"*].

Khoury, Adel-Théodore. *Les théologiens byzantins et l'Islam*. Université de Lyon, I–II, 1966 [*Théologiens byzantins*].

Kotter, Bonifaz. *Die Schriften des Johannes von Damaskos*. V vols. (Patristische Texte and Studien 7, 12, 17, 22, 29.) Berlin: 1969–1988 [*Die Schriften*].

Lavoix, Henri. *Catalogue des monnaies musulmanes de la Bibliothèque Nationale. Khalifes orientaux*. Paris: Imprimerie Nationale, 1887 [*Catalogue*].

Mingana, Alphonse. "The Transmission of the Kurʾān." *Journal of the Manchester Egyptian and Oriental Society* (1916): 25–47 [*"Transmission"*].

Motzki, Harald. "The Collection of the Qurʾān. A reconsideration of Western Views in Light of Recent Methodological Developments." *Der Islam* 78 (2001): 1–34 [*"Collection"*].

al-Muqaddasī. *Aḥsan al-taqāsīm fī maʿrifat al-aqālīm*, edited by Michael J. De Goeje (*B.G.A.* no. 3. Leiden: E.J. Brill, 2nd ed., 1906 [*Aḥsan al-taqāsīm*].

Muqātil Ibn Sulaymān. *Tafsīr*, edited by ʿAbd Allāh Maḥmūd Shaḥāta. V vols. Cairo: al-Hayʾa al-Miṣriyya al-ʿĀmma li-l-Kitāb, 1979–1989 [*Tafsīr*].

———. *Kitāb tafsīr al-khams miʾat āya min al-Qurʾān. A Compendium of Qurʾānic Law*, edited by Isaiah Goldfeld. Bar-Ilan University. Printed by Al-Mashriq Press Shfaram, 1980.

Muslim b. al-Ḥajjāj. *Al-Ṣaḥīḥ*, with commentary by al-Nawawī. 18 parts in IX vols. Beyrouth: Dār al-Fikr, n.y. [*Ṣaḥīḥ*].

Nasrallah, Joseph. "De la cathédrale de Damas à la mosquée omayyade." In *La Syrie de Byzance à l'Islam*, edited by Pierre Canivet and Jean-Paul Rey-Coquais. Institut Français de Damas, 1992 [Actes du Colloque international Lyon-Maison de l'Orient Méditerranéen, Paris: Institut du Monde Arabe, 11–15 décembre 1990], 139–44 [*"Mosquée omayyade"*].

Ory, Solange. "L'inscription de fondation de la mosquée al-ʿUmarī à Buṣrā." Deutsches Archäologisches Institut, Orient-Abteilung. *Sonderdruck aus Damaszener Mitteilungen* 11 (1999): 371–78 [*"Mosquée al-ʿUmarī"*].

Payne Smith, Jessie, and Mrs. Margoliouth. *A Compendious Syriac Dictionary Founded Upon the Thesaurus Syriacus of R. Payne Smith*. Oxford: Oxford University Press, 1902; repr., New York: Wipf and Stock Publishers, 1999 [*Compendious*].

de Prémare, Alfred-Louis. "Quelques questions sur le *musnad* de Tamīm al-Dārī et sur les informations le concernant." In C. Gilliot and T. Nagel, eds., *Das Prophetenḥadīṯ*, 40–49 [*"Quelques questions"*].

———. *Les fondations de l'islam. Entre écriture et histoire*. Paris: Éditions du Seuil, 2002 [*Fondations*].

———. *Aux origines du Coran, questions d'hier et approches d'aujourd'hui*. Paris: Téraèdre, 2004 [*Origines*].

Pseudo-Denys = *Chronicon anonymum Pseudo-Dionysianum vulgo dictum*, French translation by Robert Hespel. *CSCO*, Scriptores Syri, t. 213, Lovanii, E. Peeters, 1989 [Pseudo-Denys].

Puin, Gerd-R. "Observations on Early Qurʾān Manuscripts in Ṣanʿāʾ." In *The Qurʾan as Text*, edited by Stefan Wild, 107–11. Leiden: E. J. Brill, 1996 [*"Observations"*].

al-Samhūdī, ʿAlī. *Wafāʾ al-Wafāʾ bi-akhbār dār al-Muṣṭafā*, edited by Muḥammad Muḥyī l-Dīn ʿAbd al-Ḥamīd. (Le Caire 1955); repr., Beyrouth: 4 parts in III vols., Dār al-Kutub al-ʿIlmiyya, 1984 [*Wafāʾ*].

Sharon, Moshe. "The Umayyads as *Ahl al-Bayt*." *Jerusalem Studies in Arabic and Islam* [*JSAI*] 14 (1991): 115–52 [*"Umayyads"*].

Sourdel, Dominique et Janine. *La civilisation de l'Islam classique*. Paris: Arthaud, 1968 [*Islam classique*].

al-Suyūṭī, ʿAbd al-Raḥmān. *Al-Durr al-manthūr fī tafsīr al-maʾthūr*. VIII vols. Beyrouth: Dār l-Fikr li-l-Ṭibāʿa wa-l-Nashr wa-l-Tawzīʿ, 1983 [*Durr*].

al-Ṭabarī, Abū Jaʿfar. *Jāmiʿ al-bayān ʿan taʾwīl āy al-Qurʾān*, edited by A. Saʿīd ʿAlī, M. al-Saqqāʾ *et alii*, 30 parts in XV vols., repr. Beyrouth: Dār al-Fikr, 1984 [*Jāmiʿ*].

———. *Taʾrīkh al-rusul wa l-mulūk*. V vols. + Indices. Beyrouth: Dār al-Kutub al-ʿIlmiyya, 1987 [*Taʾrīkh*].

al-Thaʿālibī. *Laṭāʾif al-maʿārif*, edited by Muḥammad Ibrāhīm Salīm. Cairo: Dār al-Ṭalāʾiʿ, 1992; English transl., introd., and notes by Clifford Edmund Bosworth, Edinburgh: Edinburgh University Press, 1968 [*Laṭāʾif*].

al-Tirmidhī, Muḥammad. *Al-Jāmiʿ al-ṣaḥīḥ / Sunan*, edited by Aḥmad Muḥammad Shākir et al. V vols. Beyrouth: Dār ʿImrān, n.y. [*Jāmiʿ*].

Wensinck, A. J., et al. *Concordance et indices de la tradition musulmane*. VII vols. Leiden: E. J. Brill, 1936–1969 [*Concordance*].

al-Yaʿqūbī, Aḥmad. *Taʾrīkh*. Dār Ṣādir, vols. I–II, Beyrouth, 1960 [*Taʾrīkh*].

PART II.

NEW ASPECTS FOR THE EMERGENCE AND CHARACTERISTICS OF ISLAM

5

A PERSONAL LOOK AT SOME ASPECTS OF THE HISTORY OF KORANIC CRITICISM IN THE NINETEENTH AND TWENTIETH CENTURIES[1]

Ibn Warraq

SKEPTICISM AND KORANIC RESEARCH

It was Gustav Weil, in his *Mohammed der Prophet, sein Leben und seine Lehre* (Stuttgart 1843), who first applied the historico-critical method to the writing of the life of the Prophet. However, his access to the primary sources was very limited, though he did manage to get hold of a manuscript of the oldest extant biography of the Prophet by Ibn Hishām. It was only some years later, with the discovery and publication of the works of Ibn Sa'd, al-Ṭabarī and the edition of Ibn Hishām in 1858 by G. Wüstenfeld, that scholars had the means for the first time to critically examine the sources of the rise of Islam and the life of its putative founder, Muḥammad. Weil translated Ibn Hishām into German in 1864. Al-Wāqidī's *Kitāb al-Maghazi* was edited in 1856 by Alfred von Kremer and printed in Calcutta. An abridged translation of the latter work by Julius Wellhausen appeared in Berlin in 1882. Parts III and IV of al-Ṭabarī were published in the 1880s. The *Tabaqat* of Ibn Sa'd (vols. I & II) was edited by a team of Orientalists; Mittwoch, Sachau, Horovitz and Schwally, at the beginning of the twentieth century.

The biography of the Prophet made great advances in the writings of Sir William Muir, Aloys Sprenger, and Theodor Nöldeke.

Muir's *Life of Mahomet* appeared in four volumes between 1856 and 1861. It is worth examining Muir's methodological assumptions, since they seem to have been shared by many Islamologists up to the present time. Muir brought a highly critical mind to bear on the hitherto recalcitrant material on the life of the Apostle of God. He recognized the purely legendary nature of much of the details, he realized the utter worthlessness of the tales contributed by the storytellers, and he was equally skeptical of the absolute value of the Traditions: "Even respectably derived traditions often contained much that was exaggerated and fabulous." Muir continues by quoting Weil approvingly:

> Reliance upon oral traditions, at a time when they were transmitted by memory alone, and every day produced new divisions among the professors of Islam, opened up a wide field for fabrication and distortion. There was nothing easier, when required to defend any religious or political system, than to appeal to an oral tradition of the Prophet. The nature of these so-called traditions, and the manner in which the name of Moḥammad was abused to support all possible lies and absurdities, may be gathered most clearly from the fact that Al-Bukhari, who travelled from land to land to gather from the learned the traditions they had received, came to the conclusion, after many years' sifting, that out of 600,000 traditions, ascertained by him to be then current, only 4,000 were authentic! And of this selected number, the European critic is compelled without hesitation to reject at least one-half. (Weil, *Gesch. Chalifen,* II:290; *I. Kh.* II:595)[2]

A little later, Muir passes an even more damning judgement on traditions. Written records would have fixed "the terms in which the evidence was given; whereas tradition purely oral is affected by the character and habits, the associations and the prejudices, of each witness in the chain of repetition. No precaution could hinder the commingling in oral tradition of mistaken or fabricated matter with what at the first may have been trustworthy evidence. The floodgates of error, exaggeration, and fiction were thrown open; . . ."[3]

Muir even takes Sprenger to task for being too optimistic about our ability to correct the bias of the sources. "It is, indeed, the opinion of Sprenger that 'although the nearest view of the Prophet which we can obtain is at a distance of one hundred years, and although this long vista is formed of a medium exclusively Moḥammadan, yet our knowledge of the bias of the narrators' enables us to correct the media, and to make them almost achromatic.' The remark is true to some extent; but its full application would carry us beyond the truth."[4] One would have thought that these considerations would have induced extreme skepticism in Muir about our ability to construct a life of Muḥammad out of such crooked timber. Not a bit of it! Instead, through "a comprehensive consideration of the subject, and careful discrimination of the several sources of error, we may reach at least a fair approximation to the truth."[5] Muir also accepted uncritically the absolute authenticity of the Qur'ān as a contemporary record; and he had unbounded confidence in the accuracy of the early historians, particularly Ibn Isḥāq, Ibn Hishām, al-Wāqidī, Ibn Sa'd, and al-Ṭabarī. The result was the massive four-volume *Life of Mahomet.* Even a cursory glance at Muir's labors makes one wonder just what he has discarded from the traditions, since he seems to have taken at face value, and included in his biography of the Prophet, countless details, uncritically garnered from al-Wāqidī, that are of dubious historical value, from long speeches to the minutiae of Muḥḥammad's appearance and dress.

Julius Wellhausen, in his pioneering work on the Old Testament, which he began publishing in 1876, showed that the Pentateuch was a composite work in which one could discern the hand of four different "writers," usually referred to by the four letters J, E, D, and P. A century later, his biblical higher criticism is still considered valid and very influential. Wellhausen then turned his critical mind to the sources of early Islam. Towards the end of the nineteeth century, Wellhausen tried to disentangle an authentic tradition from the snares of a deliberately concocted artificial tradition—the latter being full of tendentious distortions. The authentic tradition was to be found in Abu Mikhnaf, al-Wāqidī, and al-Mada'ini, while the false tradition was to be found in Sayf b. 'Umar. For Wellhausen, the "value of the *isnad* depends on the value of the historian who deems it reliable. With bad historians one cannot put faith in good *isnads*, while good historians merit trust if they give no *isnad* at all, simply noting that 'I have this from someone whom I believe.' All this permits a great simplification of critical analysis."[6]

As Patricia Crone says:

> One might have expected his *Prolegomena zur ältesten Geschichte des Islams* to have been as revolutionary a work as was his *Prolegomena zur ältesten Geschichte Israels*. But it is not altogether surprising that it was not. The biblical redactors offer us sections of the Israelite tradition at different stages of crystallisation, and their testimonies can accordingly be profitably compared and weighed against each other. But the Muslim tradition was the outcome, not of a slow crystallisation, but of an explosion; the

> first compilers were not redactors, but collectors of debris whose works are strikingly devoid of overall unity; and no particular illuminations ensue from their comparison. The Syrian Medinese and Iraqi schools in which Wellhausen found his J, E, D, and P do not exist: where Engnell and other iconoclasts have vainly mustered all their energy and ingenuity in their effort to see the Pentateuch as a collection of uncoordinated hadiths, Noth has effortlessly and conclusively demonstrated the fallacy of seeing the Muslim compilers as Pentateuchal redactors.[7]

The next great step in the critical examination of our sources for Muḥammad and the rise of Islam was taken by the great scholar Ignaz Goldziher in his *Muhammedanische Studien* (Halle 1889, 1890). Goldziher showed that a certain amount of careful sifting or tinkering was not enough, and that the vast number of *hadiths* were total forgeries from the late second and third Muslim centuries. This meant, of course, "that the meticulous *isnads* which supported them were utterly fictitious."[8] Faced with Goldziher's impeccabilly documented arguments, conservative historians began to panic and devised spurious ways of keeping skepticism at bay, by, for instance, postulating *ad hoc* distinctions between legal and historical traditions. But as Humphreys says, "In terms of their formal structures, the *hadith* and the historical *Khabar* [Arabic, pl. *akhbar*, "discrete anecdotes and reports"] were very similar indeed; more important, many 2nd/8th and 3rd/9th century scholars had devoted their efforts to both kinds of text equally. Altogether, if *hadith isnads* were suspect, so then should be the *isnads* attached to historical reports."[9]

In 1905, Prince Caetani, in his introduction to his monumental ten-folio volumes of *Annali dell' Islam* (1905–1926), came to "the pessimistic conclusion that we can find almost nothing true on Mahomet in the Traditions, we can discount as apocryphal all the traditional material that we possess."[10] Caetani had "compiled and arranged (year by year, and event by event) all the material that the sources, the Arab historians, offered. The resultant conclusions based on the facts, which took into account the variant forms in which they were found in the sources, were accompanied by a critical analysis that reflected the methodological skepticism that Langlois and Seignobos[11] had just set forth as absolutely indispensible for the historian."[12] But, like Muir, Weil, and Sprenger before him, Caetani failed to push to their logical conclusion the negative consequences of his methodology, and, like his predecessors, he thought it was all a matter of critically sifting through the mass of traditions until we arrived at some authentic core.

The methodological skepticism of Goldziher and the positivist Caetani was taken up with a vengeance by Henri Lammens, the Belgian Jesuit. Though born in Ghent in 1862, Lammens left for Beirut at the age of fifteen to join the Jesuit order there, and he made Lebanon his home for the rest of his life. During the first eight years of his studies, Lammens "acquired an exceptional mastery of Arabic, as well as of Latin and Greek, and he appears also to have learnt Syriac. In 1886 he was assigned to teach Arabic at the Beirut Jesuit College, and he was soon publishing his own textbooks for the purpose. His first work of Orientalist scholarship appeared in 1889: A dictionary of Arabic usage (*Kitāb al-farā'iḍ fi 'l-furuq*), containing 1,639 items and based on the classical Arabic lexicographers."[13] He travelled for six years in Europe and twice edited the Jesuit newspaper, *al-Bashir.* He taught Islamic history and geography at the College, and he later used his lectures notes when he came to publish his studies on pre-Islamic Arabia and the Umayyads. "With the establishment of the School of Oriental Studies at the Jesuit College in 1907, Lammens began his career as an Orientalist in earnest; and his appointment as professor at the newly founded school enabled him to devote his whole effort to study and research. His well-known works on the *sira* appeared during the first seven years following his appointment."[14]

Though he had what Rodinson[15] calls a "holy contempt for Islam, for its 'delusive glory' and its works, for its 'dissembling' and 'lascivious' Prophet," and despite his other methodological shortcomings (to be discussed below), Lammens, according to F. E. Peters, "*whatever his motives and style . . . has never been refuted.*"[16] Lawrence Conrad makes a similar point that despite Lammens' well-known hostility to Islam, he offers a "number of useful insights."[17] Rodinson also concedes Lammens' partiality, but once again realizes that Lammens's "colossal efforts at demolishing also had constructive results.[18] They have forced us to be much more highly demanding of our sources. With the traditional edifice of history definitively brought down, one could now proceed to the reconstruction."[19] Finally, al-Salibi summarizes, "although the *sira* thesis of Lammens did not remain unquestioned, it continues to serve as a working principle. The modern reaction in favor of the authenticity of the *sira*, represented by A. Guillaume and W. Montgomery Watt, has modified this working principle in some details without seriously affecting its essence. Lammens certainly provided *sira* scholarship with an important clue to the riddle of Muḥammad, and many of his own conclusions, as well as his technique, have been adopted and developed by later scholars."[20]

In the first of the three works translated in 2000[21] for the first time into English, Lammens, influenced both by Goldziher's analysis of *hadith* and Snouck Hurgronje's emphasis on the importance of the Qur'ān for the *sira*, "asserted that the traditional Arabic *sira*, like the modern Orientalist biographies of the Prophet, depended mainly on *hadith*, whereas the Quran alone can serve as a valid historical basis for a knowledge of the Prophet's life and career. The historical and biographical *hadith*, far from being the control of the *sira* or the source of supplementary information, is merely an apocryphal exegesis of the historical and biographical allusions of the Quran. The value of an *hadith* regarding the Prophet's life or career, he argued, would lie in its independence from the Quran, where such independence can be clearly demonstrated. As a rule, he adds, a *hadith* which is clearly exegetical of the Quran should be disregarded."[22]

Lammens is often criticized for accepting uncritically any material that disparaged the Prophet, and, conversely, for applying rigorous criticism when the source material tended to praise the Prophet. In his defense, Lammens pleaded that "pious Traditionists and *sira* writers could not have invented information that reflected poorly on Muḥammad; and therefore, any such information which may have slipped in must be true."[23] But at other times, Lammens adhered to the principle that we ought not to judge Muḥammad from modern European standards of right and wrong, since traits in the Prophet's character found to be unacceptable by Europeans may have been highly thought of by the early Muslims.

In the third of his works, *Fatima et les Filles de Mahomet* (*Fatima and the Daughters of Muhammad*), "Lammens set out to prove that Fatima was not the favourite daughter of Muḥammad, and that the Prophet had never planned his succession through her progeny. All *hadith* and *sira* material favourable to Fatima, 'Ali, and their sons, al-Hasan and al-Husayn, is subjected to a searching criticism, with interesting and often valid results."[24] But, rather inconsistently, Lammens accepted uncritically all the anti-'Alid material that showed that Muḥammad cared neither for Fatima nor 'Ali. Given Lammens's hostility to Islam and the character of Muḥammad, one is inclined to accept the argument that a biography of the Prophet completed by Lammens was never published by express orders from Rome, for its publication would have caused considerable embarrassment to the Holy See. In any case, in this post-Rushdie world, there is probably only one publisher in the world who would risk it, and if it is ever published, it should be, as Jeffery puts it, "epoch-making."

The ideas of the positivist Caetani and the Jesuit Lammens were taken up by a group of Soviet Islamologists, whose conclusions sometimes show a remarkable similarity to the works of Wansbrough, Cook, and Crone. N. A. Morozov propounded the theory that until the Crusades, Islam was indistinguishable from Judaism, and that only then did Islam receive its independent character, while Muḥammad and the first caliphs were mythical figures. Morozov's arguments, first developed in his *Christ* (1930), are summarized by Smirnov:[25] "In the Middle Ages Islam was merely an offshoot of Arianism evoked by a meteorological event in the Red Sea near Mecca; it was akin to Byzantine iconoclasm. The Qur'ān bears the traces of late composition, up to the eleventh century. The Arabian peninsula is incapable of giving birth to any religion—it is too far from the normal areas of civilization. The Arabian Islamites, who passed in the Middle Ages as Agars, Ishmaelites, and Saracens, were indistinguishable from the Jews until the impact of the Crusades made them assume a separate identity. All the lives of Muḥammad and his immediate successors are as apocryphal as the accounts of Christ and the Apostles."

Under the influence of Morozov, Klimovich published an article called "Did Muḥammad Exist?" (1930), in which he makes the valid point that all the sources of our information on the life of Muḥammad are late. Muḥammad was a necessary fiction, since it is always assumed that every religion must have a founder. Whereas another Soviet scholar, Tolstov, compares the myth of Muḥammad with the "deified shamans" of the Yakuts, the Buryats, and the Altays. "The social purpose of this myth was to check the disintegration of the political block of traders, nomads, and peasants, which had brought to power the new, feudal aristocracy." Vinnikov also compares the myth of Muḥammad to 'shamanism,' pointing to primitive magic aspects of such ritual as Muḥammad having water poured over him. While E. A. Belyaev rejects the theories of Morozov, Klimovich, and Tolstov, who argued that Muḥammad never existed, he does consider the Qur'ān to have been concocted after the death of the Prophet.[26]

Ignaz Goldziher's arguments were followed up nearly sixty years later by another great Islamicist, Joseph Schacht, whose works on Islamic law are considered classics in their field. Schacht's conclusions were even more radical and perturbing, and their full implications have not yet sunk in.

Humphreys has summed up Schacht's theses as: "(1) that *isnads* going all the way back to the Prophet only began to be widely used around the time of the 'Abbasid Revolution—that is, the mid-2nd/8th century; (2) that, ironically, the more elaborate and formally correct an isnad appeared to be, the more likely it was to be spurious. In general, he concluded, no existing *hadith* could be reliably ascribed to the Prophet, though some might ultimately be rooted in his teaching. And though he devoted only a few pages to historical reports about the early Caliphate, he explicitly asserted that the same strictures should apply to them."[27]

Here is how Schacht sums up his won thesis:

> It is generally conceded that the criticism of traditions as practiced by the Muhammadan scholars is inadequate and that, however many forgeries may have been eliminated by it, even the classical corpus contains a great many traditions that cannot possibly be authentic. All efforts to extract from this often self-contradictory mass an authentic core by "historic intuition," as it has been called, have failed. Goldziher, in another of his fundamental works [*Muh. St.,* II: pp. 1–274] has not only voiced his "skeptical reserve" with regard to the traditions contained even in the classical collections, but shown positively that the great majority of traditions from the Prophet are documents not of the time to which they claim to belong, but of the successive stages of development of doctrines during the first centuries of Islam. This brilliant discovery became the cornerstone of all serious investigation of early Muhammadan law and jurisprudence, even if some later authors, while accepting Goldziher's method in principle, in their natural desire for positive results were inclined to minimize it in practice . . .
>
> This book [Schacht's own work, *The Origins of Muhammadan Jurisprudence*] will be found to confirm Goldziher's results, and to go beyond them in the following respects: A great many traditions in the classical and other collections were put into circulation only after Shafi'i's time [al-Shafi'i died 820 CE]; the first considerable body of legal traditions from the Prophet originated toward the middle of the second [Muslim] century, in opposition to the slightly earlier traditions from Companions and other authorities, and to the "living tradition" of the ancient schools of law; traditions from Companions and other authorities underwent the same process of growth, and are to be considered in the same light, as traditions from the Prophet; the study of isnads often enables us to date traditions; the isnads show a tendency to grow backwards and to claim higher and higher authority until they arrive at the Prophet; the evidence of legal traditions carries us back to about the year 100 AH [8th century CE] only.[28]

Schacht proves that, for example, a tradition did not exist at a particular time by showing that it was not used as a legal argument in a discussion that would have made reference to it imperative if it had existed. For Schacht, every legal tradition from the Prophet must be taken as an inauthentic and fictitious expression of a legal doctrine formulated at a later date: "We shall not meet any legal tradition from the Prophet which can positively be considered authentic."[29]

Traditions were formulated polemically in order to rebut a contrary doctrine or practice; Schacht calls these traditions "counter traditions." *isnads* "were often put together very carelessly. Any typical representative of the group whose doctrine was to be projected back on to an ancient authority, could be chosen at random and put into an isnad. We find therefore a number of alternative names in otherwise identical *isnads* . . ."[30] Another important discovery of Schacht's that has considerable consequences only appreciated recently by Wansbrough and his followers is that "Muḥammadan [Islamic] law did not derive directly from the Koran but developed . . . out of popular and administrative practice under the Umaiyyads, and this practice often diverged from the intentions and even the explicit wording of the Koran . . . Norms derived from the Koran were introduced into Muḥammadan law almost invariably at a secondary stage."[31]

The distinguished French Arabist Régis Blachère, translator of the Qur'ān and historian of Arabic literature, undertook the writing of a critical biography of the Prophet taking fully into account the skeptical conclusions of Goldziher and Lammens. His short study appeared in 1952, two years after Schacht's pioneering work. Blachère takes a highly critical view of the sources, and he is particularly pessimistic about our ability to reconstruct the life of Muḥammad prior to the Hijra in 622 CE.[32] His preliminary reappraisal of the sources ends on this very negative note:

> The conclusions to be drawn from this survey will appear disappointing only to those more smitten with illusion than truth. The sole contemporary source for Muhammad, the Koran, only gives us fragmentary hints, often sibylline, almost always subject to divergent interpretations. The biographical Tradition is certainly more rich and more workable but suspect by its very nature; it poses, in addition, a problem of method since, for Muhammad's apostolate, it originates from the Koran which it tries to explain and complete at the same time. In sum, we no longer have any sources that would allow us to write a detailed history of Muhammad with a rigorous

> and continuous chronology. To resign oneself to a partial or total ignorance is necessary, above all for everything that concerns the period prior to Muhammad's divine call [ca. 610 CE]. All that a truly scientific biography can achieve is to lay out the successive problems engendered by this pre-apostolate period, to sketch out the general background atmosphere in which Muhammad received his divine call, to give in broad brushstrokes the development of his apostleship at Mecca, to try with a greater chance of success to put in order the known facts, and finally to put back into the penumbra all that remains uncertain. To want to go further is to fall into hagiography or romanticization.[33]

And yet the biography that emerges, despite Blachère's professed skepticism, is dependent upon the very traditions that Goldziher, Lammens, and Schacht had cast into doubt. Blachère's account of the life of the Prophet is far less radical than one would have expected—it is full of the recognisable events and characters familiar from the traditional biography, though shorn of the details.

Some of the most discussed works published in the 1950s were the three publications of Harris Birkeland, a Swedish Orientalist: *The Legend of the Opening of Muhammad's Breast*; *Old Muslim Opposition against Interpretation of the Koran*; and *The Lord Guides, Studies on Primitive Islam*, which examines five *suras* that he considers the earliest stratum of the Qur'ān, and which expresses, so he contends, the early ideas of Muḥammad. In *The Lord Guides*, Birkeland argues, "Goldziher's method to evaluate traditions according to their contents is rather disappointing. We are not entitled to limit our study to the texts (the so-called 'matns'). We have the imperative duty to scrutinize the *isnads* too . . . and to consider the matns in their relation to the *isnads*. . . . For it is very often the age of the contents that we do not know and that we, consequently, wish to decide. The study of the *isnads* in many cases gives us valuable assistance to fulfill this wish, despite the fact that in principle they must be held to be spurious. However fictitious they are, they represent sociological facts."[34]

Birkeland expends a vast amount of energy "in collecting, differentiating and thoroughly scrutinizing all traditions and comments concerning a certain passage of the Quran or some legend about the Prophet."[35] But the German scholar Rudi Paret, for one, finds the results "rather diasppointing."[36] Birkeland maintains that "the Muslim interpretation of the Quran in the form it has been transmitted to us, namely in its oldest stage as *hadith*, does not contain reliable information on the earliest period of Muḥammad in Mecca." Nevertheless, Birkeland continues, "The original *tafsīr* of Ibn 'Abbas and possibly that of his first disciples must, however, have contained such information. . . . An exact, detailed and comparative analysis of all available materials, of *isnads* and matns and exegetical-theological tendencies, in many instances enables us to go behind the extant texts and reach the original interpretation of Ibn 'Abbas, or at least that of his time, thus obtaining a really authentic understanding of the Koranic passage."[37] Rudi Paret remains very skeptical: "To tell the truth: I cannot make this optimistic outlook my own. Nor can I quite agree with Birkeland as to his evaluation of the so-called family *isnads*."[38]

Even the most conservative scholars now accept the unreliability of the Muslim sources, but an increasing number also seem to confirm, however indirectly, the more radical conclusions of Wansbrough, Cook, and Crone. One of the most remarkable of the latter was Dr. Suliman Bashear, a leading scholar and administrator at the University of Nablus (West Bank). His generally radical and skeptical views about the life of the Prophet and the history of early Islam often got him into trouble, not only with the university authorities but also with the students, who, on one occasion, threw him out of a second story window (luckily, he escaped with minor injuries). Bashear lost his post at the university after the publication of his *Introduction to the Other History* (in Arabic) in 1984, whereupon he took up a Fulbright fellowship in the United States and returned to Jerusalem to a position in the Hebrew University in 1987. He fell seriously ill in the summer of 1991, was told to rest, but continued his research nonetheless. He died of a heart attack in October 1991, just after completing *Arabs and Others in Early Islam*.[39]

In one study, Bashear[40] examines verses 114–16 of *sura* 2 of the Qur'ān and their exegesis by Jalal al-Din al-Suyuti (d. 911/1505) and others. Qur'ān 2:114 reads, "Who is more wicked than the men who seek to destroy the mosques of God and forbid His name to be mentioned in them, when it behooves these men to enter them with fear in their hearts? They shall be held up to shame in this world and sternly punished in the hereafter." Qur'ān 2:115–16, reads, "To God belongs the east and the west. Whichever way you turn there is the face of God. He is omnipresent and all-knowing. They say: 'God has begotten a son.' Glory be to Him! His is what the heavens and earth contain; all things are obedient to Him."

Bashear was intrigued by verse 114 and al-Suyuti's claim that it was revealed concerning the barring of Muslims by the Byzantines from the Jerusalem sanctuary. "Such a remarkable commentary in itself justifies further investigation. Moreover, 2:114 is followed by two verses (2:115–16) that could be taken as referring to the abrogation of the Jerusalem *qibla* and the argument surrounding the nature of the relation between God and Christ."[41]

He continues:

> Two main questions are tackled here concerning the occasion of revelation of the verse [2:114]: who are those it blames, and where and when was the act of barring from, or destroying, the mosques committed? The answers are split between four notions current in exegetical traditions and commentaries:
>
> 1. The Jerusalem—Christian/Byzantine context
> 2. The Meccan-Qurashi context
> 3. A general meaning without specific reference to any historical context
> 4. It was the Jews who tried to destroy the Ka'ba or the Prophet's mosque in Medina in reaction to his change of *qibla* . . .[42]

After a meticulous examination of the commentaries, Bashear concluded:

> Up to the mid-second [Muslim] century a clear anti-Christian/Byzantine sentiment prevailed in the exegesis of 2:114, which overwhelmingly presented it as referring to the Jerusalem sanctuary-temple. We have also seen that no trace of sira material could be detected in such exegesis and that the first authentic attempt to present the occasion of its revelation within the framework of Muhammad's sira [biography] in Mecca is primarily associated with the name of Ibn Zayd, who circulated a tradition to that effect in the second half of the second [Muslim] century. Other attempts to produce earlier traditional authorities for this notion could easily be exposed as a later infiltration of sira material simply by conducting a cross-examination of sira sources on the occasions of both Quraysh's persecution of Muhammad before the hijra and their barring of him at Hudaybiyya. . . . [T]he notion of an early Meccan framework cannot be attested before the first half of the second [Muslim] century.
>
> All in all, the case of verse 2:114 gives support to Wansbrough's main thesis, since it shows that from the mid-second [Muslim] century on Quranic exegesis underwent a consistent change, the main "impulse" behind which was to assert the Hijazi origins of Islam.[43] In that process, the appearance and circulation of a tradition by the otherwise unimportant Ibn Zayd slowly gathered prominence. Simultaneously, other ingenuous attempts were made to find earlier authorities precisely bearing Ibn 'Abbas's name

for the same notion, while the more genuine core of the original tradition of Ibn 'Abbas was gradually watered down because it was no longer recognized after the "legend of Muhammad" was established.[44]

Bashear also indirectly complements the work of G. Hawting[45] and M. J. Kister[46] when he claims that, "on yet another level, literary criticism of the traditional material on the position of Jerusalem in early Islam has clearly shown that the stress on its priority was not necessarily a function of the attempt to undermine Mecca but rather was independent of the position of the latter since Islam seems not to have yet developed one firmly established cultic centre."[47]

Bashear then, towards the end of his analysis, remarks: "The present inquiry has shown how precisely around this period (mid-second [Muslim] century), elements of a Hijazi orientation made their presence felt in the exegetical efforts to fit what became the canon of Muslim scripture into the new historical framework of Arabian Islam. From the literary scrutiny of the development of these efforts it becomes clear how such exegetical efforts affected the textual composition of 2:114–16 in a way that fitted the general orientation, attested from other literary fields, towards a Hijazi *sira*, sanctuary and, with them, scriptural revelation."[48]

In his study of the title "fārūq," and its association with 'Umar I Bashear confirms the findings of Crone and Cook[49] that "this title must be seen as an Islamic fossilization of a basically Jewish apocalyptic idea of the awaited messiah,"[50] and a little later Bashear says that certain traditions give "unique support to the rather bold suggestion forwarded by Cook and Crone that the rise of 'Umar as a redeemer was prophesied and awaited."[51] Again, as in his discussion of Qur'ān 2:114, Bashear thinks his analysis of the traditions about the conversion of 'Umar to Islam and Qur'ān 4:60 has broader implications for our understanding of early Islam. Bashear tentatively suggests that certain traditions were fabricated to give an Hijazi orientation to events that probably took place outside it.[52]

In *Abraham's Sacrifice of His Son and Related Issues*,[53] Bashear discusses the question as to which of the two sons was meant to be sacrificed by Abraham: Isḥāq or Ismail. He concludes, "In itself, the impressively long list of mainly late scholars and commentators who favored Ismail confirms Goldziher's note that this view eventually emerged victorious. In view of the present study, however, one must immediately add that such victory was facilitated only as part of the general process of promoting the position of

Mecca as the cultic center of Islam by connecting it with the biblical heritage on the story of Abraham's trial or, to use Wansbrough's terminology, the reproduction of an Arabian-Hijazi version of Judeo-Christian 'prophetology.'"[54] Bashear once again brings his examination to a close with the observation that it was only later traditionists who consciously promoted Ismail and Mecca for nationalist purposes to give an Hijazi orientation to the emerging religious identity of the Muslims:

> For, our attempt to date the relevant traditional material confirms on the whole the conclusions that Schacht arrived at from another field, specifically the tendency of isnads to grow backwards.[55] Time and again it has been demonstrated how serious doubts could easily be cast not only against traditions attributed to the Prophet and Companions but a great deal of those bearing the names of successors too. We have actually seen how the acute struggle of clear national motive to promote the positions of Ismail and Mecca did flare up before the turn of the century, was at its height when the Abbasids assumed power, and remained so throughout the rest of the second [Muslim] century.
>
> Though we did not initially aim at investigating the development of Muslim *hajj* rituals in Mecca, let alone its religious position in early Islam in general, our enquiry strongly leads to the conclusion that such issues were far from settled during the first half of the second [Muslim] century. While few scholars have lately arrived at similar conclusions from different directions,[56] it is Goldziher who must be accredited with the initial note that Muslim consecration of certain locations in the Hijaz commenced with the rise of the Abbasids to power.[57] Indeed we have seen how "the mosque of the ram" was one of such locations.[58]

Bashear continues his research with his article "Riding Beasts on Divine Missions: An Examination of the Ass and Camel Traditions,"[59] where he tentatively suggests that "prominence of the image of the camel-rider was a function of the literary process of shaping the emergence of Arabian Islam."[60] Thus, much of Bashear's work seems to confirm the Wansbrough/Cook/Crone line that Islam, far from being born fully, fledged with a watertight creed, rites, rituals, holy places, shrines, and a holy scripture that was a late literary creation, as the early Arab warriors spilled out of the Hijaz in such dramatic fashion and encountered sophisticated civilizations—encounters which forced them to forge their own religious identity out of the already available materials, which were reworked to fit into a mythical Hijazi framework. This is further underlined by Bashear's last major work, published posthumously in 1997, *Arabs and Others in Early Islam*.[61]

The core of the latter work was adumbrated in chapter VIII, *Al-Islam wa-l-'Arab*, of his work published in Arabic in 1984, *Muqaddima Fi al-Tarikh al-'Akhar.* In *Arabs and Others in Early Islam*, Bashear questions the *a priori* acceptance of the notion that the rise of the Arab polity and Islam were one and the same thing from the beginning.[62] Furthermore, he doubts the Hijazi origins of classical Islam:

> "The proposition that Arabia could have constituted the source of the vast material power required to effect such changes in world affairs within so short a span of time is, to say the least, a thesis calling for proof and substantiation rather than a secure foundation upon which one can build. One may observe, for example, that in spite of all its twentieth-century oil wealth, Arabia still does not possess such material and spiritual might. And at least as extraordinary is the disappearance of most past legacies in a wide area of the utmost diversity in languages, ethnicities, cultures, and religions. One of the most important developments in contemporary scholarship is the mounting evidence that these were not simply and suddenly swallowed up by Arabian Islam in the early seventh century, but this is precisely the picture that the Arabic historical sources of the third [Muslim]/ninth [CE] century present."[63]

A little later, Bashear explicitly endorses the revisionist thesis that "the first/seventh century witnessed two parallel, albeit initially separate, processes: the rise of the Arab polity on the one hand, and the beginnings of a religious movement that eventually crystallized into Islam. It was only in the beginning of the second/eighth century and throughout it, and for reasons that have yet to be explained, that the two processes were fused, resulting in the birth of Arabian Islam as we know it, that is, in the Islamization of the Arab polity and the Arabization of the new religion."[64] This Arabization of the new religion and the Islamization of the Arab polity is reflected in the attempts to stress the national Arabian identity of the prophet of Islam, and of Arabic as the divine tool of revelation.[65]

How can we characterize the situation in the year 2000? Even in the early 1980s, a certain skepticism of the sources was fairly widespread; M. J. Kister was able to round off his survey of the *sira* literature, which first appeared in 1983, with the following words: "The narratives of the *sira* have to be carefully and meticulously sifted in order to get at the kernel of historically valid information, which is in fact meager and scanty."[66] If we can consider the new edition of the *Encyclopaedia of Islam* as some kind of a yardstick of the prevailing scholarly opinion on the reliability of our sources for the life of the Prophet and the rise of Islam, then the situation is clearly negative. W. Raven in the entry for *SIRA* (Vol. IX), written in the mid-1990s, comes to this conclusion in an excellent survey of the *sira* material:

> The *sira* materials as a whole are so heterogeneous that a coherent image of the Prophet cannot be obtained from it. Can any of them be used at all for a historically reliable biography of Muhammad, or for the historiography of early Islam? Several arguments plead against it:
>
> 1. Hardly any *sira* text can be dated back to the first century of Islam.
> 2. The various versions of a text often show discrepancies, both in chronology and in contents.
> 3. The later the sources are, the more they claim to know about the time of the Prophet.
> 4. Non-Islamic sources are often at variance with Islamic sources (see P. Crone and M. Cook, *Hagarism*).
> 5. Most *sira* fragments can be classed with one of the genres mentioned above. Pieces of salvation history and elaborations on Kuranic texts are unfit as sources for scientific historiography.[67]

FOR AND AGAINST WANSBROUGH

John Wansbrough, despite his meager output, more than any other scholar has, as Berg says, undermined all previous scholarship on the first three centuries of Islam. Many scholars continue as though nothing changed, and they carry on working along traditional lines, taking the historical reliability of the exclusively Islamic sources for granted. Others, sometimes known as the revisionists, find Wansbrough's methodology, at least, very fruitful. Thus, we are left with an ever-widening gap between the two camps, a gap nowhere more apparent than when those opposed, or even hostile, to Wansbrough's work refused to contribute to a collection of essays devoted to the implications and achievements of his work.[68]

Space forbids devoting too much time to those scholars who have extended or been influenced by Wansbrough's work, such as Hawting, Calder, Rippin, Nevo, van Ess, Christopher Buck, and Claude Gilliot, among others, since their work is well represented in my collection *What the Koran Really Says*.[69] It would be just as well to interject a word of caution here: the scholars who have been influenced by Wansbrough do not necessarily and uncritically endorse every aspect of his theories—not all would agree with Wansbrough's late date for the establishment of the canonical Qur'ān, for instance. The so-called disciples of Wansbrough, far from being epigones, are formidable and original scholars in their own right; and in true Popperian fashion they would be prepared to abandon this or that aspect of the master's theories should contrary evidence materialize. Nor do the scholars who do not accept Wansbrough's conclusions necessarily blindly accept the traditional Muslim account of the *sira*, the rise of Islam, or the compilation of the Qur'ān; John Burton, Gerd-R. Puin, and Günter Lüling are some of the scholars in this latter category.

But now perhaps I should say something about recent articles or books challenging Wansbrough's basic assumptions. One debate revolves round the person of Ibn 'Abbas, the cousin of the Prophet and a source of a great deal of exegetical material. Rippin sums up the arguments on both sides with admirable clarity:

> Wansbrough drew attention to a series of texts ascribed specifically to Ibn 'Abbas, all of them of a lexicographical nature. One of the roles of the figure of Ibn 'Abbas within the development of *tafsīr,* according to Wansbrough's argument, was bringing the language of the Quran into alignment with the language of the 'Arabs' . . . Identity of the people as solidified through language became a major ideological stance promulgated in such texts.
>
> Such an argument, however, depended upon a number of preceding factors, including the emergence of the Quran as authoritative, before it could be mounted. Such an argument could not have been contemporary with Ibn 'Abbas, who died in 687 CE, but must stem from several centuries later. The ascription to Ibn 'Abbas was an appeal to authority in the past, to the family of the Prophet, and to a name that was gathering an association with exegetical activity in general.

Issa Boullata examines one such text attributed to Ibn 'Abbas and argues "that the tradition that aligns Ibn 'Abbas with lexicographical matters related to the Quran is early, although it was clearly subject to elaboration as time went on . . ." But Boullata raises the crucial issue: "J. Wansbrough believes that the reference of rare or unknown Quranic words to the great corpus of early Arabic poetry is an exegetical method which is considerably posterior to the activity of Ibn 'Abbas."[70] While the activity may have been limited, Boullata admits, "if there was anybody who could have dared to do it (or have such activity ascribed to him) it was Ibn 'Abbas, the Prophet's cousin and Companion, because of his family relationship and authoritative position."[71] Oral tradition would have been the means by which these traditions from Ibn 'Abbas were transmitted down to later exegetical writers. Just because poetical citations are not found in early texts (as Wansbrough pointed out) does not mean, for Boullata, that such an exegetical practice did not exist: "One cannot determine which of these materials is authentic and which is not, but everything points to the possibility that there existed a smaller core of materials that was most likely preserved in a tradition of oral transmission for several generations before it was put down in writing with enlargements."[72]

"Possibility" and "most likely" are the key methodological assumptions of this historical approach, and certainly all historical investigations proceed on the basis of analogy of processes that underlie these assumptions. But Boullata underestimates the overall significance of what Wansbrough has argued. The debate is not whether a core of the material is authentic or not. By underemphasizing issues of the establishment of authority of scripture and bringing into comparison profane texts with scripture, Boullata avoids the central crux. Ultimately, the assertion is that it would have been "only natural" for the Arabs to have followed this procedure within exegesis. Boullata asserts that there is an "Arab proclivity to cite proverbs or poetic verses orally to corroborate ideas in certain circumstances. This is a very old Arab trait that Ibn 'Abbas . . . could possibly have had."[73] For Wansbrough, nothing is "natural" in the development of exegetical tools. The tools reflect ideological needs and have a history behind them.

Substantial evidence in favor of the overall point that Wansbrough makes in this regard stems from Claude Gilliot's[74] extensive analysis of the *tafsīr* of al-Ṭabarī (d. 923 CE). It is surely significant that al-Ṭabarī would still be arguing in the tenth century about the role and value of the Arabic language in its relationship to the Qur'ān, and that his own extensive *tafsīr* work is founded upon an argument to make just that case for language. The relationship of the sacred to the profane in language was not an issue that allowed itself to be simply assumed within the culture. It was subject to vigorous debate and a back-and-forth between scholars.[75]

Another scholar whose views and methodological assumptions differ radically from John Wansbrough's is C. H. M. Versteegh. Essentially, Versteegh has a vision of the rise of Islam that is no longer accepted by a number of historians: he is convinced that "after the death of the Prophet the main preoccupation of the believers was the text of the Quran. This determined all their efforts to get a grip on the phenomenon of language, and it is, therefore, in the earliest commentaries on the Quran that we shall have to start looking for the original form of language study in Islam."[76] However, by contrast, Wansbrough and others "have argued that 'Islam' as we know it took a number of centuries to come into being and did not spring from the desert as a mature, self-reflective, defined entity. The idea that Muḥammad provided the community with its scripture and that after his death all focus immediately turned to coming to an understanding of that scripture and founding a society based upon it simply does not match the evidence that we have before us in Wansbrough's interpretation. Nor does it match the model by which we have come to understand the emergence of complex social systems, be they motivated by religion or other ideologies."[77]

Versteegh has a totally different conception of "interpretation": where he sees it as "a process somewhat abstracted from society as a whole, an activity motivated by piety and a dispassionate . . . concern for the religious ethos and which took place right at the historical beginnings of Islam," Wansbrough sees it as "a far more interactive and active participant within the society in which it takes place. . . . The pressures of the time and the needs of the society provide the impetus and the desired results of the interpretative efforts."[78] However, as Rippin concludes, it is not simply a question of skepticism about texts, but also a question of our understanding of how religious and other movements in human history emerge and evolve, and finally of the "interpretative nature of human existence as mediated through language."[79]

Estelle Whelan, in a 1998 article, challenges Wansbrough's conclusions. She is perfectly aware of the rather devastating implications of Wansbrough's analysis, that is, "that the entire Muslim tradition about the early history of the text of the Quran is a pious forgery, a forgery so immediately effective and so all-pervasive in its acceptance that no trace of independent contemporary evidence has survived to betray it. An important related issue involves the dating of early manuscripts of the Quran. If Wansbrough is correct that approximately a century and a half elapsed before Muslim scripture was established in 'canonical' form, then none of the surviving manuscripts can be attributed to the Umayyad or even the very early Abassid period; particularly, one controversial manuscript discovered in San'a in the 1970s . . . for which a date around the turn of the eighth century has been proposed, would have to have been copied at a much later period."

Whelan devotes considerable space to examining the inscriptions at the Dome of the Rock in Jerusalem, since they represent the primary documents for the condition of the Qur'ānic text in the first century of Islam, having been executed in the reign of 'Abd al-Malik in year 72 (691–692 CE). Her main arguments are that these inscriptions "should not be viewed as evidence of a precise adherence to or deviation from the 'literary form' of the Koranic text; rather, they are little sermons or parts of a single sermon addressed to an audience that could be expected to understand the allusions and abbreviated references by which 'Abd al-Malik's particular message was conveyed." Thus, the apparent deviations from the Qur'ānic text only show that there was conscious and creative modification of the text for rhetorical or polemical purposes, namely, to declare the primacy of the new religion of Islam over Christianity. But for this device to work well depends on the listener or reader being able to recognize the text or references, which in itself is a strong indication, according to Whelan, that the Qur'ān was already the common property of the community in the last decade of the seventh century.

Whelan also argues that there is enough evidence for "the active production of copies of the Qur''''''ān from the late seventh century, coinciding with and confirming the inscriptional evidence of the established text itself. In fact, from the time of Mu'āwiya through the reign of al-Walid the Umayyad caliphs were actively engaged in codifying every aspect of Muslim religious practice. Mu'āwiya turned Muḥammad's minbar into a symbol of authority and ordered the construction of *maqsuras* in the major congregational mosques. 'Abd al-Malik made sophisticated use of Quranic quotations on coinage and public monuments, to announce the new Islamic world order. Al-Walid gave monumental form to the Muslim house of worship and the service conducted within it. It seems beyond the bounds of credibility that such efforts would have preceded interest in codifying the text itself." Thus for Whelan, the Muslim tradition is reliable in attributing the first codification of the Qur'ānic text to 'Uthman and his appointed commission.[80]

Whelan's arguments are by no means terribly convincing, and they will certainly not appease the skeptics. First, one cannot argue from a part to a whole; the fact that there are *some* late seventh-century inscriptions at the Dome of the Rock that can be identified as being from the 'Qur'ān' as we know it today does not mean that the whole of the 'Qur'ān' already existed at the end of the seventh century. Because a part of the Qur'ān exists does not mean that the whole of it does; what we know is that the Qur'ān has a long history, and that it did not materialize out of nowhere, fully formed, but emerged slowly over time. We would expect the Qur'ān to have some authority in the community, and there is no evidence that that is the case as early as the first Muslim century.

To assert that the deviations from the Qur'ān that are apparent in the inscriptions at the Dome of the Rock are not really deviations but rather sermons seems a little *ad hoc* to say the least; one could just as easily argue that the inscriptions and the "sermons" are similar because they are drawing on the same not-yet-canonical body of literature. In fact, Wansbrough himself allows for the early existence of "qur'ānic logia" that precedes the canonized Qur'ān, and that would account rather well or even better for the inscriptions at the Dome of the Rock.

Whelan also blithely sidesteps all the skepticism that has been directed against all the sources of our "knowledge" of early Islam, and in the section on "the copying of the Quran," she takes for granted that these sources are totally reliable as history. We do not have independent sources for the biographical material that she uses, and she is reduced to using the very sources at which so much criticism has been levelled for over a century, from at least Goldziher onwards. The reliability of these sources is precisely the issue. The same forces that produced the literature about the formation of the canon are at work on these other materials used by Whelan, and they therefore suffer from the same limitations (e.g., these sources are late, tendentious, they all contradict each other, and they are literary fictions rather than history).

Fred Donner is another very distinguished scholar who takes issue with Wansbrough and the revisionists. In *The Early Islamic Conquests* (1981),[81] Donner—although he is, like so many historians in the past, very cautious about the sources—is nonetheless very confident that a reliable account of the early Muslim conquests can be reconstructed. However, as Hawting[82] points out in his review of Donner, "when contradictions between different accounts cannot be resolved, broad generalization is resorted to . . . and there is a tendency to accept information that is consistent with the thesis being argued while rejecting or even ignoring that which is inconsistent." While Donner's account may be plausible, contradictory ones are no less so.[83]

More recently, Donner[84] has argued that the language of the Qur'ān and the language of *hadith* are different, and that this suggests a chronological separation between the two, with the Qur'ān preceding the *hadith*. He also argues for a Hijazi (Arabian) origin of the Qur'ān. Again, skeptics find Donner's arguments less than compelling. Even the revisionists, on the whole, do not deny that there are differences between the two; the language of the Qur'ān is like nothing else, and it obviously does not come from the same context as *hadith*. The question is, what are the sources of those differences? We certainly cannot legitimately jump to the chronological conclusion in the way that Donner does; and in any case why make the Qur'ān first? We need additional arguments whereas Donner has simply accepted the traditional Muslim account, which, as we have seen, is precisely what the skeptics are skeptical about. For a certain number of scholars, the most plausible hypothesis is that much[85] if not all of the Qur'ānic material predates Muḥammad, and that it is liturgical material used in some community of possibly Judeo-Christian, and certainly monotheist, Arabs, and that is why the Muslims, by the time they got around to writing their commentaries on the Qur'ān, did not have the faintest idea what large parts of this material meant.[86] They were then forced to invent some absurd explanations for these obscurities, and it all eventually got collected together as the Arabian book of God, in order to forge a specifically Arabian religious identity. This scenario, of course, only makes sense if we accept the revisionists thesis that "Islam," as such, did not emerge fully fledged in the Hijaz as the Muslim traditions would have us believe. Even Lüling's and Puin's ideas make more sense if we do not try to fit these ideas into the Meccan/Medinan procrustean bed that the Muslim's traditions have prepared for us; but rather accept that the Arabs forged their religious identity only when they encountered the older religious communities *outside* the Hijaz, since the thought that Mecca in the late sixth and early seventh centuries was host to such a Judeo-Christian community seems highly improbable.

Juynboll once said that Wansbrough's theories were so hard to swallow because of the obvious disparity in style and contents of Meccan and Medinan *suras*.[87] There is indeed a difference in language, style, and even message between the so-called Meccan and Medinan *suras*. But all that shows is that there are two quite different styles in the Qur'ān, and of course, Muslim exegetes solved this problem by assigning one set to Mecca and the other to Medina, with considerable tinkering (verses from the "Medinese" *suras* assigned to Mecca, and *vice versa*). But why should we accept the Medinan and Meccan labels? What is the source or sources of this difference? To accept these labels is simply to accept the entire traditional Muslim account of the compilation of the Qur'ān, the biography of the Prophet, and the Rise of Islam. Again, this is precisely what is at stake: the reliability of the sources. The differences, if anything, point to a history far more extensive than the short life of Muḥammad as found in the *sira*, and they do not have to be interpreted biographically through the history of the life of Muḥammad in Mecca and Medina. There is nothing natural about the Meccan-Medinan separation. It is clear from Lammens, Becker, and others, that large parts of the *sira* and *hadith* were invented to account for the difficulties and obscurities encountered in the Qur'ān, and these labels also proved to be convenient for the Muslim exegetes for the same reason. The theory of abrogation also gets the exegetes out of similar difficulties and obviates the need to explain the embarrassing contradictions that abound in the Qur'ān.

It is Muslim tradition that has unfortunately saddled us with the fiction that such and such a verse in the Qur'ān was revealed at such and such a time during Muḥammad's ministry. As early as 1861, the Reverend Rodwell, in his preface to his translation of the Qur'ān wrote:

> It may be considered quite certain that it was not customary to reduce to writing any traditions concerning Muhammad himself, for at least the greater part of a century. They rested entirely on the memory of those who had handed them down, and must necessarily have been colored by their prejudices and convictions, to say nothing of the tendency to the formation of myths and to actual fabrication, which early shows itself, especially in interpretations of the Koran, to subserve the purposes of the contending factions of the Umayyads and 'Abbasids.

Even the writings of historians, such as Ibn Isḥāq, are, according to Rodwell,

> necessarily colored by the theological tendencies of their master and patron. . . . Traditions can never be considered as at all reliable, unless they are traceable to some common origin, have descended to us by independent witnesses, and correspond with the statements of the Koran itself—always of course deducting such texts as (which is not unfrequently the case) have themselves given rise to the tradition. It soon becomes obvious to the reader

> of Muslim traditions and commentators that both miracles and historical events have been invented for the sake of expounding a dark and perplexing text; and that even the earlier traditions are largely tinged with the mythical element.[88]

The above passage is a remarkable anticipation of the works of not only Goldziher but also Henri Lammens. The former had shown by 1890 the entirely spurious and tendentious nature of the *hadith*, and the latter should that, "on the fabric of the Koranic text, the *hadith* has embroidered its legend, being satisfied with inventing names of additional actors presented or with spinning out the original theme." It is the Qur'ān, in fact, that has generated all the details of the life of the Prophet, and not *vice versa*: "One begins with the Koran while pretending to conclude with it." Muslim Tradition has often been able to do this because of the often vague and very general way events are referred to, such that they leave open the possibility of any interpretation that the Muslim exegetes care to embroider.

Michael Schub[89] shows that the traditional interpretation of *sura* IX, verse 40 is suspect, and that it is probably derived from the Old Testament, I Samuel 23, verses 16 ff.: "Faithful Muslims will forever believe that Quran IX. 40: 'If ye help him not, still Allah helped him when those who disbelieve drove him forth, the second of two; when they two were in the cave, when he said unto his comrade: Grieve not. Lo! Allah is with us. Then Allah caused His peace of reassurance to descend upon him and supported him with hosts ye cannot see, and made the word of those who disbelieved the nethermost, while Allah's word it was that became uppermost. Allah is mighty, wise' refers to the Prophet Muḥammad and Abu Bakr, although not one word of the Quranic text supports this."

Rippin has also argued that certain passages in the Koran that are traditionally interpreted as referring to Muḥammad are not necessarily historical. Citing *sura* 93, Rippin states that "there is nothing absolutely compelling about interpreting [*sura* XCIII] in light of the life or the lifetime of Muḥammad. The 'thee' [in verse 3: "The Lord has neither forsaken thee nor hates thee"] of this passage does not have to be Muḥammad. It certainly could be, but it does not have to be. (I might also point out that Arberry's translation also suggests the necessity of 'he' as God [or 'He'], which is also not necessarily compelling). All the elements in the verses are motifs of religious literature (and indeed, themes of the Qur'ān) and they need not be taken to reflect historical 'reality' as such, but, rather, could well be understood as the foundational material of monotheist religious preaching."[90] One of Rippin's conclusions is that

> the close correlation between the sira and the Qur'ān can be taken to be more indicative of exegetical and narrative development within the Islamic community rather than evidence for thinking that one source witnesses the veracity of another. To me, it does seem that in no sense can the Qur'ān be assumed to be a primary document in constructing the life of Muhammad. The text is far too opaque when it comes to history; its shifting referents leave the text in a conceptual muddle for historical purposes. This is the point of my quick look at the evidence of the "addressee" of the text; the way in which the shifts occur renders it problematic to make any assumption about the addressee and his (or her) historical situation. If one wishes to read the Qur'ān in a historical manner, then it can only be interpreted in light of other material.[91]

In his *Qur'ānic Studies*, John Wansbrough had expressed the view that *asbab* material had its major reference point in the so-called halakhic works—that is to say, works concerned with deriving laws from the Koran. Andrew Rippin,[92] however, examined numerous texts, and concluded that the primary purpose of the *sabab* material was in fact not halakhic, but rather haggadic, "that is, the *asbab* functions to provide an interpretation of a verse within a broad narrative framework." This puts the origin of the *asbab* material in the context of the *qussas,* "the wandering storytellers, and pious preachers and to a basically popular religious worship situation where such stories would prove both enjoyable and edifying." He also notes that the primary purpose of such stories is to historicize the text of the Koran in order to prove that "God really did reveal his book to humanity on earth," and that in arguments over conflicting *asbab* reports, isnad (chain of transmission) criticism was a tool that could be "employed when needed and disregarded when not."

As Hawting points out,

> The very diversity of these "occasions of revelation" (*asbab al-nuzul*), the variety of the interpretations and historical situations the tradition provides for individual Koranic verses, is an argument for the uncertain nature of the explanations that are provided. One often feels that the meaning and context supplied for a particular verse or passage of the Koran is not based on any historical memory or upon a secure knowledge of the circumstances of

> its revelation, but rather reflect attempts to establish a meaning. That meaning, naturally, was established within a framework of accepted ideas about the setting in which the Prophet lived and the revelation was delivered. In that way, the work of interpretation also defines and describes what had come to be understood as the setting for the revelation.[93]

Given the above examples of some of the difficulties, any critical reading of the Koran should prompt the exasperated but healthy response, "What on earth is going on here?" The fact that so many, but thankfully not all, scholars of the last sixty years have failed to even ask this question, let alone begin to answer it, shows that they have been crushed into silence out of respect for the tender sensibilities of Muslims, by political correctness, postcolonial feelings of guilt, and dogmatic Islamophilia, and that they have been practising "Islamic scholarship" rather than scholarship on Islam.

Some scholars have posed pertinent questions, however, and given us important insights. And yet so often their keen and just observations have been vitiated by a faulty chronology—that is, they have all accepted the traditional historical framework fabricated by Muslim tradition. It seems to me that their work makes far more sense within a broad revisionist structure provisionally constructed by Wansbrough and his disciples.

To give a plausible account of the rise of Islam, we must put back the last of the three monotheist religions in its Near Eastern geographical, religious, historical, and linguistic (Hebrew, Aramaic, and Syriac) context. Scholars have been well aware of the influences of Talmudic Judaism, heretical Christianity, and now even Essenians, on Islam, but relying on the fictive chronology of Muslim tradition has often meant the invention of ingenious—but ultimately far-fetched—scenarios of how Christian monks, Jewish rabbis, or Essenians fleeing Romans had whispered their arcane knowledge into the ears of an Arabian merchant.

Many scholars have also uncritically accepted the traditional account of the compilation of the Koran. But this account is, in the words of Burton, "a mass of confusion, contradictions, and inconsistencies,"[94] and it is nothing short of scandalous that Western scholars readily accept "all that they read in Muslim reports on this or that aspect of the discussions on the Qur'ān."[95] Given that so much of the Koran remains incomprehensible despite hundreds of commentaries, surely it is time to look for some more plausible historical mechanism by which the Koran came to be the Koran, and to restore the original text.

Barth and Fischer's important work on emendations and interpolations, though it did influence Richard Bell in the writing of his commentary on the Koran, was unfortunately not followed up. Even Bell, on the whole, is unwilling to accept emendations too readily, and most scholars seem to agree with Nöldeke that the Koran is free of omissions and additions. But as Hirschfeld says, "Considering the way in which the compilation was made, it would have been a miracle had the Qoran been kept free of omissions, as well as interpolations."[96] Some scholars did question the authenticity of certain verses: Antoine-Isaac Silvestre de Sacy was doubtful about *sura* III 138; Weil of *sura* III 182, XVII 1, XXI 35–36, XXIX 57, XLVI 14, XXXIX 30; and Sprenger of LIX 7.[97]

Another scholar who has dared to question the authenticity of the Koran is Paul Casanova, whose ideas are rather perfunctorily dismissed by Watt and Bell. Casanova finished his study, *Mohammed et la fin du Monde*, in 1921, but in recent years his work has been, I believe, unjustly ignored.[98] I suspect one reason for this neglect has nothing to do with the force of his arguments or the quality of his scholarship, but the simple unavailability of all three volumes of his work, with volume three being particularly difficult to come by.[99]

Casanova wrote:

> It is generally admitted that the text of the Koran, such as it has come down to us, is authentic, and that it reproduces exactly the thought of Muhammad, faithfully gathered by his secretaries as the revelations gradually appeared. We know that some of his secretaries were highly unreliable, that the immediate successor of the Prophet made a strict recension, and that, a few years later, the arrangement of the text was altered. We have obvious examples of verses suppressed, and such a bizarre way in which the text is presented to us (in order of the size of the chapters, or *sura*) shows well the artificial character of the Koran that we possess. Despite that, the assurance with which Muslims—who do not refrain from accusing Jews and Christians of having altered their scriptures—present this incoherent collection as rigorously authentic in all its parts has imposed itself upon the Orientalists, and the thesis that I wish to uphold will seem very paradoxal and forced.
>
> I maintain, however, that the real doctrine of Muhammad was, if not falsified, at least concealed with the greatest of care. I shall set out soon the extremely simple reasons which led first Abu Bakr, then 'Uthman, to alter thoroughly the sacred text, and this rearrangement was done with such skill that, thenceforth, it seemed impossible to reconstitute the Ur-Koran or the

> original Koran. If, however, my thesis was accepted, it could serve as a point of departure for this reconstitution, at least for everything that concerns the original revelations, the only really interesting ones from my point of view, and the only ones, moreover, that there was any advantage in reworking, by means of either very light changes of the text, or by deplacements. There is abundant evidence that the first Muslims, despite the undoubtedly powerful memories of the Arabs, were profoundly ignorant of the Koran, and one could, with Muhammad dead, recite them verses of which they had not, at their own admission, the slightest idea. A rearrangement that did not change the exterior forms of the verses was thus the easiest. Sprenger, who had had a vague intimation of the thesis that I advocate, accuses Muhammad of having thrown the incoherence into his text himself, in order to get rid of the trace of imprudent words.[100] I say in fact that it is for a reason of this kind that the incoherence was introduced, but not by the author—by his successors.[101]

According to Casanova, Muḥammad, under the influence of a Christian sect, put great emphasis on the imminent end of the world in his early proclamations. When the approaching end failed to take place, the early followers of the Prophet were forced to refashion or rework the text of the Koran to eliminate that doctrine from it. Casanova provides some very convincing arguments for the presence of interpolations in the Koranic text, and he further points up its general incoherence. Whether they prove what he wanted to prove is another matter. But it is certainly unfair of Watt and Bell to pronounce dismissively that Casanova's thesis is "founded less upon the study of the Qur'ān than upon investigation of some of the byways of early Islam."[102] Casanova has anticipated just such a criticism, and we can see the following as an implicit answer to these types of accusations:

> Already, at this period [Caliph 'Abd al-Malik, reigned 685–705 CE] the book [Koran] was hardly understood. "If obscurity and lack of coherence with the context in our modern Koran ought to be considered as proof of nonauthenticity, I fear that we ought to condemn more than one verse" says Nöldeke.[103]
>
> I confess that as for me I accept these premises and this conclusion. Obscurity and incoherence are the reasons, not to deny absolutely, but to suspect the authenticity [of the Koran], and they permit all effort to restore a more clear and more coherent text.
>
> Permit me some characteristic examples. I have collected them by a

careful study of the Koranic text, I could have multiplied them but that would have uselessly padded out this book. Besides, in most cases, all the while feeling the strangeness and obscurity of terms, that the naive exegesis of the commentators only brings out the better, one is very perplexed to propose a rational solution, a credible restoration. I ought to be on my guard the more so because people will not fail to accuse me (which has already been done) of declaring falsified such and such passages because they go counter to my theories. To defend myself from this reproach, I shall add to this list of alterations a short analysis of those which have been noted before me by scholars totally unaware of my aforementioned thesis.[104]

There then follow examples of interpolations, displacement of verses, and other textual evidence of the general incoherence of the Koran.

Watt and Bell's defense depends completely on tightly linking the Koran to the biography of the Prophet. This linkage is, of course, entirely derived from Muslim tradition:

> As to [Casanova's] main thesis, it is true that the Qur'ān proclaims the coming Judgement and the end of the world. It is true that it sometimes hints that this may be near; for example, in XXI 1 and XXVII 71–3 f. In other passages, however, men are excluded from knowledge of times, and there are great differences in the urgency with which the doctrine is proclaimed in different parts of the Qur'ān. All this, however, is perfectly natural if we regard the Qur'ān as reflecting Muhammad's personal problems and the outward difficulties he encountered in carrying out a task to which he had set his mind. Casanova's thesis makes little allowance for the changes that must have occurred in Muhammad's attitudes through twenty years of ever-changing circumstances. Our acceptance of the Qur'ān as authentic is based not on any assumption that it is consistent in all its parts, for this is not the case, but on the fact that, however difficult it may be to understand in detail, it does, on the whole, fit into a real historical experience, beyond which we discern an elusive but, in outstanding characteristics, intelligible personality.[105]

It requires little reflection to see, once again, the circularity of Watt and Bell's argument. If by "authentic" we mean that the Koran was the word of God, as passed onto—either directly from God or through the intermediary of an angel—a historical figure called Muḥammad, supposedly living in Arabia, then clearly we need some independent confirmation of this extraordinary claim. We cannot say the Koran is authentic because "it does fit . . . into a real historical experience." This circular reasoning would give us the following tautology: The Koran is authentic—that is, it fits into a real historical experience—because it fits into a real historical experience.

Some scholars have, of course, been trying to prise the Koranic text away from the supposed historical fit with the *sira*, the life of Muḥammad, including Lammens,[106] Tor Andrae,[107] and (more modestly) Andrew Rippin[108] and Michael Schub.[109] But perhaps the most radical thesis is that of Günter Lüling, who argues very persuasively that at least a third of the Koran pre-dates Islam, and thus, of course, has nothing whatsoever to do with someone called Muḥammad. A third of the Koran was originally a pre-Islamic Christian hymnody that was reinterpreted by Muslims, whose task was made that much easier by the ambiguity of the *rasm*, the unpointed and unvowelled Arabic letters. Thus, both Casanova and Lüling point to the present incoherence of the Koranic text as evidence for its later editing, refashioning, emending, reinterpretation, and manipulation. It is interesting to note that although he finds Lüling's evidence "unsound, and his method undisciplined,"[110] Wansbrough nonetheless thinks that the "recent conjectures of Lüling with regard to the essentially hymnic character of Muslim scripture are not unreasonable, though I [Wansbrough] am unable to accept what seems to me [Lüling's] very subjective reconstruction of the text. The liturgical form of the Qur'ān is abundantly clear even in the traditional recension, as well as from the traditional literature describing its communal uses. The detection of strophic formation is certainly not difficult, and the theological (as opposed to rhetorical) nature of orthodox insistence upon the absence from scripture of poetry and even (though less unanimous) of rhymed prose must be acknowledged."[111]

Lüling is reviving a theory first put forward by H. Müller,[112] according to which it was possible to find in the Koran, as in the Bible, an ancient poetical form, the strophe or stanza. This form was present in seventeen *sura*, particularly *sura* LVI and XXVI. For Müller, composition in strophes was characteristic of prophetic literature. Rudolph Geyer[113] took up the theory and thought he had proved the presence of a strophic structure in such *sura* as *sura* LXXVIII. These ideas were dismissed at the time, but perhaps make more sense now, if we see, as Lüling does, pre-Islamic Christians texts in the Koran.

Lüling's thorough grounding in Semitic languages enables him to show that we cannot hope to understand the Muslim tradition's reworking of the Koranic text without an understanding of Hebrew and Syriac. Following in the footsteps of Mingana, Jeffery, and Margoliouth, but going way beyond them, is Christoph Luxenberg,[114] who also tries to show that many of the obscurities of the Koran disappear if we read certain words as being Syriac and not Arabic. In order to elucidate passages in the Koran that had baffled generations of scholars, Muslim and non-Muslim, Luxenberg used the following method:

1. He went carefully through al-Ṭabarī's great commentary on the Koran, and also consulted Ibn Manzur's celebrated dictionary of the Arabic language, *Lisan al-'Arab*, in order to see if Western scholars had not omitted any of the plausible explanations proposed by the Muslim commentators and philologists.
2. If this preliminary search did not yield any solutions, then he tried to replace the obscure Arabic word in a phrase or sentence that had hitherto mystified the Muslim commentators, or that had resulted in unconvincing, strained, or far-fetched explantions with a Syriac homonym that had a different meaning (though the same sound), but that made more sense in the context.
3. If the preceding step did not yield a comprehensible sentence then, he proceeded to the first round of changes of the diacritical points that, according to Luxenberg's theory, must have been badly placed by the Arabic readers or whoever was the original redactor or copier of the Koran, and that had resulted in the actual obscurity of the passage concerned. In this way, he hoped to obtain another more logical reading of the Arabic.
4. If his third approach also failed to give any results, Luxenberg then proceeded to a second round of changes of the diacritical points in order to eventually obtain a more coherent Syriac reading, and not an Arabic one.
5. If all these attempts still did not yield any positive results, Luxenburg tried to decipher the real meaning of the Arabic word, which did not make any sense in its present context, by retranslating it into Syriac to deduce from the semantic contents of the Syriac root the meaning best suited to the Koranic context.

In this way, Luxenberg was able to explain not only so-called obscure passages, but also a certain number of passages he considers to be misunderstood, and whose meaning up until now no one had doubted. He was also able to explain certain orthographic and grammatical analomies that abound in the Koran.

This method allows Luxenberg, to the probable horror of all Muslim males dreaming of sexual bliss in the Muslim hereafter, to conjure away the wide-eyed houris promised to the faithful in *suras* XLIV 54 and LII 20. According to Luxenberg, the new analysis yields "white raisins" of "crystal clarity" rather than doe-eyed and ever-willing virgins. Luxenberg claims that the context makes it clear that it is food and drink that is being offered, not unsullied maidens. Similarly, the immortal, pearl-like ephebes or youths of *suras* such as LXXVI 19 are really a misreading of a Syriac expression meaning "chilled raisins (or drinks)" that the just will have the pleasure of tasting, in contrast to the "boiling drinks" promised the unfaithful and damned.

NOTES

1. The following contribution is a portion of a more extensive investigation into the discussion of the Qur'an.

2. Muir, *The Life of Mahomet*, 3rd. ed., Indian Reprint (New Delhi, 1992), pp. xli–xlii.

3. Ibid., p. xlvi.

4. Ibid., p. xlviii (quoting Sprenger's Mohammad, p. 68).

5. Ibid., p. xlviii.

6. J. Wellhausen, Prolegomena, 4, quoted by R. S. Humphreys, *Islamic History: A Framework for Inquiry* (Princeton, 1991), p. 83.

7. Patricia Crone, *Slaves on Horses: The Evolution of the Islamic Polity* (Cambridge, 1980), p. 13.

8. Humphreys, *Islamic History: A Framework for Inquiry*, p. 83.

9. Ibid.

10. Quoted by R. Blachère, *Le Probleme de Mahomet* (Paris, 1952), p. 9.

11. C. V. Langlois and C. Seignobos, *Introduction aux études historiques* (Paris, 1898); English translation: *Introduction to the Study of History* (London, 1898; 5th ed., New York, 1932).

12. M. Rodinson, "A Critical Survey of Modern Studies on Muhammad," in *Studies on Islam*, ed. M. Swartz (New York, 1981), p. 24.

13. K. S. Salibi, "Islam and Syria in the Writings of Henri Lammens," in *Historians of the Middle East*, ed. B. Lewis and P. M. Holt (Oxford, 1962), p 331.

14. Ibid.

15. M. Rodinson, "A Critical Survey of Modern Studies on Muhammad," in *Studies on Islam*, ed. M. Swartz (New York, 1981).

16. F. E. Peters, "The Quest of the Historical Muhammad," *International Journal of Middle East Studies* 23 (1991): 291–315.

17. Lawrence Conrad, "Abraha and Muhammad: Some Observations Apropos of Chronology and Literary Topoi in the Early Arabic Historical Tradition," *Bulletin of the School of Oriental and African Studies* 1 (1987): 225.

18. Cf. A. Schweitzer, *The Quest of the Historical Jesus*, trans. W. Montgomery (London, 1945) [1st Eng. ed., 1910], pp. 4–5, "For hate as well as love can write a Life of Jesus, and the greatest of them are written with hate: that of Reimarus, the Wolfenbuttel Fragmentist, and that of D. F. Strauss. . . . And their hate sharpened their historical insight. They advanced the study of the subject more than all the others put together. But for the offence which they gave, the science of historical theology would not have stood where it does to-day."

19. Rodinson, "A Critical Survey of Modern Studies on Muhammad," pp. 26–27.

20. Salibi, "Islam and Syria in the Writings of Henri Lammens," p. 335.

21. Ibn Warraq, ed., *The Quest for the Historical Muhammad* (Amherst, NY: Prometheus Books, 2000), pp. 169–329.

22. Salibi, "Islam and Syria in the Writings of Henri Lammens," p. 335.

23. Ibid.

24. Ibid., p. 336.

25. N. A. Smirnov, *Russia and Islam* (London, 1954).

26. E. A. Belyaev, *Arabs, Islam and the Arab Caliphate in the Early Middle Ages* (New York, 1969).

27. Humphreys, *Islamic History: A Framework for Inquiry*, p. 83.

28. Schacht, *The Origins of Muhammadan Jurisprudence* (Oxford, 1950), pp. 4–5.

29. Ibid., p. 149.

30. Ibid., p. 163.

31. Ibid., p. 224.

32. R. Blachère, *Le Problème de Mahomet: Essai de biographie critique du fondateur de l'Islam* (Paris, 1952), pp. 11, 15.

33. Ibid., pp. 17–18.

34. H. Birkeland, *The Lord Guides, Studies on Primitive Islam* (Oslo, 1956), pp. 6 ff.

35. R. Paret, "Researches on the Life of the Prophet Muhammad," *Journal of the Punjab Historical Society* (1958): 81–96.

36. Ibid., p. 89.

37. Birkeland, *The Lord Guides, Studies on Primitive Islam*, pp. 133–35.

38. Paret, "Researches on the Life of the Prophet Muhammad," p. 89.

39. S. Bashear, *Arabs and Others in Early Islam* (Princeton, 1997).

40. S. Bashear, "Quran 2:114 and Jerusalem," *Bulletin of the School of Oriental and African Studies* (1989): 215–38.

41. Ibid., p. 215f.

42. Ibid., p. 217.

43. J. Wansbrough, *Quranic Studies* (Oxford, 1977), pp. 58, 179.

44. Bashear, "Quran 2:114 and Jerusalem," pp. 232–33.

45. G. Hawting, *The First Dynasty of Islam* (London, 1986), pp. 6–7; also his "The Origins of the Muslim Sanctuary at Mecca," in *Studies in the First Century of Islam*, ed. G. H. A. Juynboll (Illinois, 1982).

46. M. J. Kister, "On 'Concessions' and Conduct: A Study in Early Hadith," in *Studies in the First Century of Islam*, ed. G. H. A. Juynboll (Illinois, 1982), pp. 89–108.

47. Bashear, "Quran 2:114 and Jerusalem," p. 237.

48. Ibid., p. 238.

49. P. Crone and M. Cook, *Hagarism* (Cambridge, 1980), s. index 'Umar al- Faruq.

50. S. Bashear, "The Title 'Faruq' and Its Association with 'Umar I," *Studia Islamica* 72 (1990): 69.

51. Ibid.

52. Ibid., p. 70.

53. S. Bashear, "Abraham's Sacrifice of His Son and Related Issues," *Der Islam* 67 (1990): 243–77.

54. Wansbrough, *Quranic Studies*, pp. 58, 179.

55. J. Schacht, *Origins . . .* (London, 1950), pp. 107, 156.

56. [Bashear's note: "G. R. Hawting has lately argued that Islam does not seem to have one firmly established cultic center in the first [Muslim] century," *The First Dynasty of Islam* (London, 1986), p. 6 f. Before that Kister has shown how the struggle between Mecca and Jerusalem over primacy in Islam goes to the first half of the second [Muslim] century. "You Shall Only Set . . ." *Le Museon* 82 (1969): 178–84, 194.

57. Goldziher, *Muslim Studies* (New York, 1971), 2:279–81.

58. Bashear, "Abraham's Sacrifice of His Son and Related Issues," p. 277.

59. S. Bashear, "Riding Beasts on Divine Missions: An Examination of the Ass and Camel Traditions," *Journal of Semitic Studies* 37, no. 1 (Spring 1991): 37–75.

60. Ibid., p. 75.

61. S. Bashear, *Arabs and Others in Early Islam*, Studies in Late Antiquity and Early Islam 8 (Princeton, 1997).

62. Ibid., p. 3.

63. Ibid., p. 113.

64. Ibid., p. 116.

65. Ibid., p. 118.

66. M. J. Kister, "The Sirah Literature," in *Arabic Literature to the End of the Umayyad Period*, ed. Beeston, Johnstone, et al. (Cambridge, 1983), p. 367.

67. W. Raven, art. SIRA in the second edition of *Encyclopaedia of Islam*, vol. 9, p. 662.

68. Which eventually appeared with only the contributions of the advocates of Wansbrough, *Islamic Origins Reconsidered: John Wansbrough and the Study of Early Islam*, in *Method & Theory in the Study of Religion*, volume 9–1, ed. Herbert Berg (Berlin: Mouton, de Gruyter, 1997): with articles by H. Berg, G. R. Hawting, Andrew Rippin, Norman Calder, and Charles J. Adams.

69. Ibn Warraq, *What the Koran Really Says* (Amherst, NY: Prometheus Books, 2002).

70. Issa Boullata, "Poetry Citation as Interpretive Illustration in Quran Exegesis: Masa'il Nafi' ibn al-Azraq," in *Islamic Studies Presented to Charles J. Adams*, ed. Wael B. Hallaq and Donald P. Little (Leiden: Brill 1991), p. 38.

71. Ibid.

72. Ibid., p. 40.

73. Ibid., p. 38.

74. Claude Gilliot, *Exégèse, langue et théologie en Islam. L'exégèse coranique de Tabari* (Paris: Vrin, 1990).

75. A. Rippin, "*Quranic Studies*, Part IV: Some Methodological Notes," in *Islamic Origins Reconsidered: John Wansbrough and the Study of Early Islam*, ed. Herbert Berg, in: Method & Theory in the Study of Religion, Volume 9–1, ed. Herbert Berg (Berlin: Mouton, de Gruyter, 1997), pp. 41–43.

76. C. H. M. Versteegh, *Arabic Grammar and Quranic Exegesis in Early Islam* (Leiden: Brill, 1993), p. 41.

77. Rippin, "*Quranic Studies*, Part IV: Some Methodological Notes," p. 44.

78. Ibid.

79. Ibid., p. 45.

80. E. Whelan, "Forgotten Witness: Evidence for the Early Codification of the Quran," *Journal of the American Oriental Society* (January–March 1998).

81. F. Donner, *The Early Islamic Conquests* (Princeton, 1981).

82. G. R. Hawting, review of *The Early Islamic Conquests*, by F. Donner in *Bulletin of the School of Oriental and African Studies* 47 (1984): 130–33.

83. Humphreys, *Islamic History: A Framework for Inquiry*, p. 70.

84. F. Donner, *Narratives of Islamic Origins: The Beginnings of Islamic Historical Writing* (Princeton, 1998).

85. G. Lüling asserts that a third of the Koran is of pre-Islamic Christian origins, see *Über den Urkoran* (Erlangen, 1993) [1st ed., 1973], p. 1.

86. Gerd-R. Puin is quoted as saying in the *Atlantic Monthly*, January 1999,

"The Koran claims for itself that it is 'mubeen' or 'clear.' But if you look at it, you will notice that every fifth sentence or so simply doesn't make sense. . . . The fact is that a fifth of the Koranic text is just incomprehensible."

87. G. H. A. Juynboll, review of *Quranic Studies*, by John Wansbrough. *Journal of Semitic Studies* 24 (1979): 293–96.

88. Rev. J. M. Rodwell, *The Koran Translated* (London: Dutton, 1921) [1st ed., 1861], p. 7. Emphasis added by Ibn Warraq.

89. M. Schub, "Dave and the Knave in the Cave of the Brave," *Journal for Arabic Linguistics* 38 (2000): 88–90.

90. A. Rippin, "Muhammad in the Qur'an: Reading Scripture in the 21st Century," in H. Motzki, ed., *The Biography of Muhammad: The Issue of the Sources*, ed. H. Motzki (Leiden: Brill 2000), pp. 299–300.

91. Ibid., p. 307.

92. A. Rippin, "The Function of the Asbab al-nuzul in Qur'anic Exegesis" *Bulletin of the School of Oriental and African Studies* 51 (1988): 1–20, also in Ibn Warraq, ed., *The Quest for the Historical Muhammad* (Amherst, NY: Prometheus Books, 2000), pp. 392–419.

93. G. R. Hawting, *The Idea of Idolatry and the Emergence of Islam: From Polemic to History* (Cambridge, 1999), pp. 31–32.

94. John Burton, *The Collection of the Qur'an* (Cambridge, 1977), p. 225.

95. Ibid., p. 219.

96. H. Hirschfeld, *New Researches into the Composition and Exegesis of the Quran* (London, 1902), p. 137.

97. S. de Sacy, *Journal des savants* 1832, p. 535 sq.; G. Weil, *Historisch–kritische Einleitung in den Koran*, 2nd ed., (Bielefeld, 1878), p. 52; A. Sprenger, *Das Leben und die Lehre des Mohammad* (Berlin 1861–1865), p. 164.

98. I hope to publish extracts in English in an anthology in the near future.

99. I was lucky enough to obtain a photocopy of the third volume at New York Public Library. Two of the greatest modern scholars of the Qur'an did not possess the third volume, and were happy to receive a photocopy from me. What I have called volume 3 is, in fact, *Notes Complémentaires II*, of Deuxième Fascicule.

100. Sprenger, *Das Leben und die Lehre des Mohammad*, p. 533.

101. P. Casanova, *Mohammed et la Fin du Monde* (Paris 1911–1921), pp. 3–4.

102. Watt/ Bell, pp. 53–54.

103. Nöldeke, *Ceschichte des Qorans*, p. 202.

104. Casanova, *Mohammed et la Fin du Monde*, pp. 147ff.

105. Watt/Bell, pp. 53–54.

106. H. Lammens, "Koran and Tradition," in Ibn Warraq, ed., *The Quest for the Historical Muhammad*, pp. 169–87.

107. T. Andrae, "Die Legenden von der Berufung Muhammeds," *Le Monde Oriental* 6 (1912): 5–18.

108. Rippin, Muhammad in the Qur'an: Reading Scripture in the 21st Century," pp. 299–300.

109. Schub, "Dave and the Knave in the Cave of the Brave," pp. 88–90.

110. J. Wansbrough, *The Sectarian Milieu* (Oxford, 1978), p. 52.

111. Ibid., p. 69.

112. H. Müller, *Die Propheten in ihrer ursprünglichen Form* (Vienna, 1896).

113. R. Geyer, "Zur Strophik des Qurans," *Wiener Zeitschrift für die Kunde des Morgenlandes* 22 (1908): 265– 86.

114. C. Luxenberg, Die Syro-Aramäische Lesart des Kroan (Berlin: Verlag Hans Schiler, 2000). An enlarged English translation titled *The Syro-Aramaic Reading of the Koran: A Contribution to the Decoding of the Language of the Koran* was published in Brlin by Verlag Hans Schiler in 2007.

6

PRE-ISLAMIC ARABIC—KORANIC ARABIC—CLASSICAL ARABIC

*A Continuum?**

Pierre Larcher

Translated by Susan Emanuel

The question for us is not which is the purest, or the most correct or the most beautiful Arabic, but what is Arabic at all?

Heinrich Leberecht Fleischer, 1854

PRE-ISLAMIC ARABIC

Before Islam, Arabic was known only by inscriptions and graffiti. This is why one might call it pre-Islamic epigraphical Arabic. This Arabic can be classified into three groups, according to a dual criterion of language and writing.

The first group is written in northern Arabic languages—the group from which Arabic directly comes—and southern Arabic writing. It is a matter of Dedanite, Lihyanite (today regrouped as simply Dedanite), Hasaitic, Safaitic, and Thamudic inscriptions. Unlike the first four groups, the fifth is itself heterogeneous, today divided into five subgroups—A, B, C, D, and E—of which only A (Taymanic) and E (Hismaic) are decoded, with B, C, and D remaining in the course of being deciphered.[1]

The second group is written in Arabic, but in a heterogeneous Arabic (where Aramaisms of the north and Sabeisms of the south meet) and in writing systems, whether northern Semitic or southern Arabic. The two most famous inscriptions of this group are those of al-Ḥijr (Madā'in Ṣāliḥ) and al-Namāra, respectively dated 267 and 328 CE. Recent additions to this group are three inscriptions discovered in Qaryat al-Fāw (3rd to 1st centuries BCE?) and the inscription of 'En 'Avdat (end of 1st to start of 2nd century CE?).[2]

The third and last group is written in Arabic, from both the standpoint of language and writing. To this group belong three graffiti (today considered as one and the same) of the Wādī Ramm (300 CE?) and the inscription of Umm al-Jimāl (5th or 6th century CE?) and two dated inscriptions, from Zabad, near Aleppo (512 CE) and from Ḥarrān (568 CE). In 1964, an inscription was added to this group. This long misrecognized inscription from Jabal Usays (*Ses* in Syrian dialect) will serve as an example of pre-Islamic epigraphical Arabic.

This inscription was first published (drawing without photo) by Muḥammad Abū l-Faraj al-'Ushsh in the journal *al-Abḥāth* in Beirut in 1964. It was republished (drawing plus photo) by Alfred Grohmann in 1971.[3] Grohmann reads the fourth line as giving the date in Nabatean figures (4 x 100 + 20 +3), namely, 423. If one takes as a signpost the creation of the Roman province of Arabia (105 CE), this means 528–529. Jabal Usays's inscription is thus the oldest inscription that is simultaneously in Arabic, in Arabic writing, and perfectly dated. Zabad's inscription, which might claim this title, is in effect an addition in Arabic (which might be contemporaneous, but also later) to a Greco-Syriac inscription dated 512 CE. Taking the date into account, Grohmann interprets *al-Ḥārith al-malik* of the second line as the Ghassānid al-Ḥārith ibn Jabāla, victor in 528 over the Lakhmid king Mundhir III.

Apart from the fact that it is perfectly dated, this inscription has been the object of a recent and decisive rereading by Christian Robin and Maria Gorea,[4] who now read the first word of the third line as *Usays,* meaning the very name, right up until today, in the Arabic of that site. Until now, this word was read as *Sulaymān* and interpreted either as an anthroponym or as a toponym, which did not ensure the reading of the following word (even if the latter, from the beginning, was recognized as a word of the SLḤ group). Thus, viewing *Usays* as a toponym, Robin and Gorea read *maslaḥa*. This is a place-name, whose definition, in the *Lisān al-'Arab* (art. SLḤ) by Ibn Manẓūr (d. 711/1311) perfectly suits the place *ka-l-thaghr wa-l-marqab*, and this is indeed an observatory (*marqab*) situated on the border (*thaghr*) of the Ghassānid and Lakhmid kingdoms, even if the term might apply, by metonymy, to soldiers who find themselves as *qawm fī ʿudda bi-mawḍiʿ raṣad qad wukkilū bihi bi-ʾizāʾ thaghr* (men equipped in a place of observation, of which they are in charge, facing a frontier). Finally, the first line, which was read until now as *Ibrāhīm b. Mughīra al-Awsī*, is now read as *ʾanā Qutham b. Mughīra al-Awsī*—that is, as the topic (*mubtadaʾ* in Arabic) of a sentence, the rest of which is the comment (*khabar* in Arabic), which is syntactically satisfying. The whole is now interpreted as "Me, Qutham son of Mughīra, of the tribe of Aws, al-Ḥārith the king sent me to Usays as garrison in the year 423."[5]

Such an inscription suggests some thoughts to a linguist. First of all, on the syntactical plane, recognizing the thematic structure, if it does not allow us to say that the language written by this soldier has or does not have case endings (declension), it at least allows us to say that if there is one, it serves no purpose. In such a structure, in effect, the function of elements is indicated either by their position (the case of the topic), or by the suffix pronoun *–nī*, which could only be the object of *ʾarsala*, automatically designating *al-Ḥārith al-malik* as the subject of the verb.

On the phonological level, the fact that al-Ḥārith is known in Byzantine sources under the name Arethas (with a *theta*)[6] suggests that the interdental is maintained, which is perhaps not always the case: we have previously an Aretas (with a *tau*), the king of the Arabs in the second book of the Maccabees (II, 5:8) of the Septuagint.[7] For the vocalism, the fact that we have an *epsilon* suggests that Greek ears did not hear an i, which resembles the current pronunciation in Eastern Arabic al-Ḥāreth (linked to both the brevity of the vowel and the absence of inflection).

The construction of the verb *ʾarsala* with *ʿalā*, rather than *ʾilā* (*ʿalā* or *ʿa-* being employed in the sense of *ʾilā* in many current dialects),[8] is surely justified here by the fact that Usays is a mountain and that the inscription was found at the summit of the inside crater.

On the graphical level, we find a fundamental trait of archaic writing, which is not to note the long *ā* inside a word, al-Ḥārith being represented in script by ḤRṮ.

Finally, on the level of phonic-graphic relations, Robin and Gorea note that if one accepts the hypothesis of *maslaḥa* reading, one must then conclude that the *tāʾ marbūṭa* existed already before Islam (whereas its existence is not elsewhere assured in the pre-Islamic epigraphical material). This conclusion goes too far: if one observes, as they do (p. 507), that one has a "long" *t* in liaison within *snt* (*sanat, sint?*), while in so-called classical Arabic one would have a *tā' marbūṭa* in both cases, it would be judicious to conclude that the soldier writes as he pronounces: a *t*- in liaison, but a *–h* in the pause, whereas the *tā' marbūṭa,* a hybrid of the two graphemes *t* and *h,* testifies to the double pronunciation possible at the end of the same phoneme.

If indeed one has to read *maslaḥah* with an *–h,* this means that archaic writing explicitly notes a pausal pronunciation, exactly as it does it, with the final *'alif,* the pausal pronunciation of *tanwīnan* (in the inscription of Umm al-Jimāl with a word read successively by Littmann in 1929 and 1949 as *ghiyāran* and *ghafran*), which underlines the importance of the phenomena of pauses in Arabic and makes a link with Koranic Arabic.

KORANIC ARABIC[9]

Koranic Arabic is the Arabic of the Koran (if I can be forgiven my triviality). But for a linguist, the Koran is nothing other than a text which has a history. As we know, this history is recounted very differently by Muslim tradition and by Islamologists. For Muslim tradition, the Koran contains solely the preaching of Mohammed from Mecca and then Medina. This preaching goes along orally, even it was able to be partially put into writing on heteroclite materials, until the era of the third caliph 'Uthmān (23–35/644–656), who had it transcribed (what is called in Arabic the *muṣḥaf 'Uthmān* or 'Uthmān's codex). Among Islamologists, there are at least three hypotheses, two marginal and one central. The two marginal ones are those of John Burton and John Wansbrough. For Burton,[10] a written Koran existed from Mohammed's period in Medina. For Wansbrough,[11] on the contrary, the constitution of the Koranic corpus was a long-running labor extending over three centuries. For most Islamologists, the *muṣḥaf 'Uthmān* is the "conventional" name of the official version imposed by the Umayyad caliph 'Abd al-Malik (65–86/685–705).[12] The first material attestation of the Koran—the polemical verses of the cupola of the Dome of the Rock in Jerusalem—date from this era. The first dated manuscripts, in Kūfic writing, do not appear before the first half of the second (eighth) century.[13] Manuscripts in *ḥijāzī* or *māʾil* writing also exist. They are not dated but are paleographically datable to the second half of the first (seventh) century. The discovery of fragments of Ṣanʿāʾ[14] has confirmed what one knew from tradition: the existence alongside the codex called "of ʿUthmān" of other non-ʿUthmānic codices, in particular those of Ibn Masʿūd and of Ubayy and, thereby, with what one could call "great variation," the variation in the very ductus and in its arrangement of the Surahs. The history of the Koranic text is thus of a tendency to unity (of ductus and order) from a situation of plurality.

In its most ancient epigraphical and manuscript attestations, the Koran is not presented very differently from pre-Islamic epigraphical material: a ductus (*rasm*) without diacritical points for the letters—even if they start to appear in the *ḥijāzī* manuscripts—without vocalization, not necessarily noting the long vowels, and so on. But unlike this epigraphical material, whose deciphering is random, the deciphering of the ductus is here signposted by reading traditions, the famous *qirāʾāt*. The history of these *qirāʾāt* is long and complicated.[15] Just like the history of the ductus, it moves in the direction of restriction, but, unlike the ductus, without reaching unification. In the fourth (tenth) century, they were fixed at the number of "seven" canonical ones (which we call the "small variation").[16] Nevertheless, unification was under way. From these seven readings, essentially two remain in use today: those of Ḥafṣ ʿan ʿĀṣim (Koran of Cairo) and that of Warsh ʿan Nāfiʿ (Koran of the Maghreb). The globalization of the Muslim world privileges the former. One anecdote: to illustrate an archaic point of syntax, often ignored by Arabists themselves, to wit, the possible use of *lā* + apocopate, not only in the protasis (in the form *ʾillā*), but even the apodosis of hypothetical systems in *ʾin* (while classical Arabic systematically uses *lam yafʿal*), I had cited in the classroom sura 3:120: *Wa-ʾin taṣbirū wa-tattaqū lā yaḍirkum kaydu-hum shayʾan*—"And if you are patient and you fear [Allah], their cunning will not harm you." A (Maghrebi!) student corrected "my" *yaḍirkum* to *yaḍurru-kum*, visibly ignorant that I had cited the reading of Warsh ʿan Nāfiʿ, whereas he was citing that of Ḥafṣ ʿan ʿĀṣim!

Obviously, one must not project backwards into the past this number one reading of one ductus! On the contrary, the fact that one might add three to seven, and again four to the ten, the existence of the *qirāʾāt shawādhdha* ("exceptional readings") reminds us that the *qirāʾāt* constitute an impressive variation, essentially phonological and morphological (the unity of the ductus being maintained), but sometimes also syntactical and semantic, as we shall see. The interpretation of these *qirā'āt* is frightfully delicate; one constantly hesitates between grammatical speculation or reflection of a linguistic reality. Thus, if Warsh ʿan Nāfiʿ reads *lā yaḍir-kum* it is because it is syntactically more satisfying, but he does so at the price of a weak verb, *ḍāra—yaḍīru,* not attested elsewhere in the Koran, but where one finds the geminate verb *ḍarra—yaḍurru.* And if Ḥafṣ ʿan ʿĀṣim reads *lā yaḍurru-kum* (in the indicative), it is syntactically less satisfying, but he cannot do otherwise: in the Koran the third person of the apocopate of a geminate verb has the form *yamsas*, not *yamassa* (the difference being visible in script: *ymss* versus *yms*).

Taking into account the uncertainty that we have just recalled, what might a linguist say about the Koranic language? The first thing that strikes one (and strikes the eye, since there is a graphic trace of it) is the importance of the phenomena of pause (*waqf*). The pause is necessary to the rhyme between segments (which is one of the fundamental traits of the Koranic style). Of course, with the Koran one does not use the word *qāfiya*, but *fāṣila* ("separator"). But this is jargon that fools only those who want to be so in any case, not the *Lisān al-ʿArab*, which defines (in art. FṢL) *wa-'awākhir 'ayāt kitāb Allāh fawāṣil bi-manzilat qawāfī al-shiʿr*—"The ends of the verses of Allah's book are the *fawāṣil*, the analogue of the rhymes in poetry." One can nevertheless say that the rhymes metonymically draw their name from their function of segmenting the text into verses, even if there are more rhymes than verses (cf., for example, sura 20:63).[17]

Rhyme is so important that it explains some of the violence done to the syntax, as in sura 80:11–12:

(11) *kallā 'innahā tadhkirah*—"No! This is a reminder:

(12) *fa-man shā'a dhakarah*—Who wants to will be reminded."

Dhakarahu, pronounced *dhakarah*, rhymes with *tadhkiratun*, pronounced *tadhkirah*, while the feminine gender of this noun (contextually attested by *'innahā*) should have led to the reading *dhakarahā*, *tadhkira* being the sole antecedent possible for the anaphoric suffixed pronoun.

Very generally, the Koran practices the equivalent of the *qāfiya muqayyada*, that is to say, the suppression of the short final vowel, with or without *tanwīn,* except in the case of *tanwīnan,* realized as a long *–ā* (and written with an *'alif*). This objectively makes the Koran approach what one may observe in the meager epigraphical material that has been conserved.

On the other hand, this separates the Koran from the rules of the pause in archaic poetry, which practices very generally the *qāfiya muṭlaqa*, or the realization of the short final vowel, with or without *tanwīn*, uniformly like a long vowel ū, ā, ī. The particular rules of poetic language might possibly constitute an argument for seeing in this a language that is in some manner artificial, a *Kunstsprache,* as the Germans say.[18] Still, the Koran sometimes even practices not the suppression of the short vowel *–a* but its lengthening into *–ā*, as in sura 33:66 and 67, where one finds *al-rasūlā* and *al-sabīlā*. It is sufficient to observe that an *'alif* is inscribed (which is the case in poetry) to conclude that this is an exception due to rhyme (one has *naṣīran* > *naṣīrā* in 33:65, *kabīran* > *kabīrā* in 33:66). I would only like to point out here a syntactical consequence of the pause.

The rules of the pause have the effect of deleting all the short final vowels, and hence, among these vowels, those that mark the case. Such a deletion evidently makes illusory the existence of a pertinent declension in Koranic Arabic. Let us take the example of sura 85:21–22:

(21) *bal huwa qur'ānum majīd*

(22) *fī lawḥim maḥfūẓ*

Six readers out of seven read *fī lawḥin maḥfūẓin*—that is to say, they read *maḥfūẓ* as an epithet (*ṣifa*) of *lawḥ,* and so interpret it "Nay, this is a glorious Koran, on tablets preserved [understood: from demons]." A single reader, Nāfiʿ (as transmitted by Warsh) reads *fī lawḥin maḥfūẓun*—that is to say, *maḥfūẓ* as an epithet of *qur'ān*, and so interprets it "Nay, this is a glorious Koran, preserved on tablets,"[19] If one forgot for an instant the rules of the pause, one might be tempted to say that declension is pertinent here, which distinguishes not only between meanings but also has as a correlate the displacement of phrases. Unfortunately, these are purely theoretical readings, for whether one reads *maḥfūẓin* or *maḥfūẓun*, one still says *maḥfūẓ*. It is clear here that the *qirā'āt* are variants of reading of a written text (and not of recitation of an oral text). Six out of seven readers have chosen the principle *potius lectio facilior*—that is to say, they are governed by the (visible) position of elements and not by the declension (in fact, not realized).

If great attentions had been paid to phenomena of pause,[20] less attention has been paid to linking. By linking, I do not mean the traditional *waṣl*, but in fact the phenomena of assimilation between the final consonant of a word and the initial consonant of the following word, ranged under the *idghām* when it is total, and in the *qalb* when it is partial. Thus, if one prolongs

80:11–12, mentioned above, to 13, *fī suḥufin mukarramatin* ("on venerated pages"), pronounced *fī ṣuḥufim mukarramah* (this type of assimilation is signaled by a *shadda* on the *mīm* of *mukarrama* in the Koran of Cairo); and to 16, *kirāmin bararatin* ("[in the hands of the scribes] noble, pure"), pronounced *kirāmim bararah* (this type of assimilation is signaled by a small *mīm* under the final consonant of the first word in the Koran of Cairo). In Arabic grammar, *idghām* means, in fact, two things: on the one hand, the contraction of two similar consonants into a geminate (consonant), or else the total assimilation of two consonants close to each other (which is obligatory, possible, or forbidden according to whether it occurs inside a word or between two words), and whether the first consonant is not vocalized and the second is, or the inverse, or else both are vocalized. But here there is a remarkable divergence between grammarians and readers.[21] The *idghām* of grammarians is in fact the *idghām ṣaghīr* ("minor *idghām*") of readers, because at least one reader, Abū ʿAmr, hence perfectly canonical, practices the *idghām kabīr* ("major *idghām*"); that is to say, he allows the total assimilation between the final consonant of a word and the initial one of the following word, both consonants being vocalized and "near to one another," so that sura 2:284 *yuʿadhdhibu man yashāʾu* ("He will torment whom he wants to") is to be read as *yuʿaddim-man yashāʾ*.[22]

Recently, Owens (2002) has shown, I think very convincingly, that the *idghām kabīr* did not imply linguistically the loss of a final vowel of the first word, but only its lack. Let us observe in the previously cited example that there is no *idghām kabīr* at all unless one starts from *yuʿadhdhibu man yashāʾu*. But if one starts from the *yuʿadhdhib man yashāʾ*, there is only a very ordinary *idghām*. So let us go back to the memory of all the traditions recommending reciting the Koran with *iʿrāb*, which presupposes, as Kahle noted,[23] that there were people who recited it without this. But whereas Kahle saw this as the sign, if not of rewriting, as Vollers[24] supposed, at least of an adaptation of Koranic language to poetic language, Owens sees in the *idghām kabīr* a confirmation of the existence, inside the tradition of recitation, of a *caseless* variant of the Arabic. For us, whether one follows Owen's interpretation or not, the result is the same: with the *idghām kabīr*, there are no short vowels at the end of words, which confirms the functional uselessness of vowels of declension and makes the link with the third part of this exposition: Classical Arabic.

Before moving on to that, I would like to turn to a remark made by

Diem,[25] who places himself in the traditional framework of historical linguistics dear to German Arabists and who, after Fleischer,[26] conceived the history of Arabic as one of changes from an Old Arabic type (inflected, and hence more synthetic and with a freer word order) to a neo-Arabic type (non-inflected, and hence more analytical and a less free word order).[27] In this context, Diem[28] correctly recalls that the triptote declension, marked by three short vowels *u/a/i,* is not the only inflection. There also exists a "visible" inflection, case-endings (diptote declension of the masculine plural *-ūn/īn,* to which one might add the dual *-ān/ayn*), and mood-endings (*-ī/ū(n)*): the presence/absence of *–n* in the second person of the feminine singular and in the second and third persons of the masculine plural of imperfect makes the difference between the free form (indicative) and linked forms (subjunctive/apocopate). But in this relation, the Koran presents some "bizarre" traits, among which the best known is obviously sura 20:63 *'in(na) hādhāni la-sāḥirāni*—"there are two magicians."

Only two readers, Ibn Kathīr and Ḥafṣ, read *'in,* all the others read *'inna.* Among the latter, only one, Abū ʿAmr, "corrects" the ductus in *hādhayni.*[29] In other words, four out of seven readers adopt a reading formally contravening a "rule" of Classical Arabic, according to which *'inna* is an operator applying to a sentence with a nominal head that it governs in the accusative, whereas *hādhāni* is the nominative. How to interpret this fact? Is this a variant (*lugha*) of the *ʿarabiyya,* as suggested by the *Tafsīr al-Jalālayn*[30] "that conforms to the manner of speaking of those who produce, for the dual, an *'alif* in three cases" (*wa-huwa muwāfiq li-lughat man ya'tī fī l-muthannā bi-l-'alif fī aḥwālihi al-thalāth*), which amounts to saying that there are no more cases? Is it a stylistic effect (the violence done to the syntax has the effect of introducing an internal rhyme *hādhāni/sāḥirāni*, the latter itself followed by *yurīdāni*)? Or else a "linguistic error,"[31] and in this case, is it to be interpreted historically as the index of an evolution under way, or else socio-linguistically as a pseudo-correction (neo-Arabic retaining only the case regime of the diptote declension of the old Arabic)?

The same uncertainty is found with the mood endings, for example, in sura 6:80 all readers read *a-tuḥājjūnnī*—"Would you dispute with me?" except for two, Nāfiʿ and Ibn ʿĀmir, who read *a-tuḥājjūnī,*[32] that is, an assimilation in the first case (< *tuḥājjūn(a)-nī*), but a suppression of one of the two *nūn* in the second case (both readings are compatible with the ductus, which bears only one *nūn*): *Tafsīr al-Jalālayn* p. 113, indicates that for the grammarians it is the *nūn* of the indicative (hence < *tuḥājjū(na)-nī*) but for the readers the *nūn* constitutes part of the suffix of the first person *–nī*, hence <*tuḥājjūn(a)-(n)ī*). The bother is that one wonders why the same thing is not produced in sura 2:139 in almost the same context, where we have *a-tuḥājjūna-nā*—"Will you dispute with us?," with two *nūn* in the ductus! Here again, how to interpret this fact? Historically, as index of an evolution, or socio-linguistically as the coexistence of variants, wondering about what governs their appearance? If one observes 1. that prior to Arabic, other Semitic languages do not have this *nūn,* and 2. that later down the line, although many Arab dialects today do not have it, a certain number of others do, one is led to doubt that the history of Arabic can be summarized, on this point, by a uniform evolution of an old Arabic type toward a neo-Arabic type *–ūn(a)* > *ū* . . .

CLASSICAL ARABIC

The reader will have understood from what I have said about pre-Islamic epigraphical Arabic on the one hand, and Koranic Arabic on the other hand, that classical Arabic is not for me a state of Arabic in the sense of historical linguistics, and more particularly is not the state of Arabic beginning around 500 CE (an era when there appeared the first inscriptions in Arabic and in Arabic writing), following a periodization widespread among the Arabists.[33]

Generally speaking, "classical" is not a historical label, but rather a socio-linguistic label, even if the appearance of a "classical" variety can be located chronologically in the history of a language.

Classical comes in effect from the Latin *classicus*, which is an adjective corresponding to the noun *classis* (*classe* in French, *Klasse* in German). What is "classical" in Latin is what belongs to the first class of citizens. Classical Latin is understood as that of the Roman aristocracy. So it is a "classist" label that perhaps suits Roman society, but surely not Arab society, which knows neither "classes" nor "citizens"![34] By a first extension of the meaning, *classical* means of "the first class" (hence prestigious), and by a second extension of the meaning, "what is taught in the classes" (hence scholastic). To define classical Arabic as a variety of prestige and the scholastic norm seems to me quite adequate.

In Arabic itself, classical Arabic is called *al-lugha al-fuṣḥā*. If the two expressions designate the same thing, they do not signify it in the same way. *Al-lugha al-fuṣḥā* is an expression that appears in the fourth/tenth century as a rewriting of an older expression that is *ʾafṣaḥ al-lughāt al-ʿarabiyya* (approximately "the most refined way of speaking Arabic") and recalls the concept that the most ancient Arabic grammarians, Sībawayhi (died 177/793?) and al-Farrāʾ (d. 207/822), had of Arabic: as a language that was at a time singular *(al-ʿarabiyya, lisān al-ʿArab*) and plural, a *lugha* (sg.) made of *lughāt* (pl.), the *lughāt* not being autonomous varieties (and still less dialects as opposed to a *koine!*), but only variants, good or bad, of one and the same language.

For theological reasons, the *lugha fuṣḥā* will be definitively identified in the fourth/tenth century with the *lughat Quraysh* ("language of the Quraysh"), the latter being considered as the language of the Koran.[35] But philologically, we find in the Arabic sources all the evidence that allows us to consider this double identification as purely dogmatic. The features of the *lugha fuṣḥā*, quite often, are in no way those reported of the *lughat Quraysh* or, more generally, the *lugha ḥijāziyya*. Let us recall some famous examples. In the phonological order, the people of the Ḥijāz were said to practice "the alleviation of the hamza" (*takhfīf al-hamza*), unlike other Arabs who practiced its "realization" (*tahqīq al-hamza*). The classical feature is the effective realization of the *hamza,* not its weakening—in other words, the *muʾmin* ("believing") pronunciation, and not the *mūmin* one, even if the two variants belong to "the language of the Arabs." In the morphological order, there exist two variants of the jussive mood (apocopate and imperative) of geminate verbs like *yardud/urdud* and *yarudda/rudda,* labeled, respectively, by Arabic grammar as "Ḥijāzian" or "Tamīmite" pronunciation (that is to say, West-Arabic and East-Arabic). And although the former, appearing in the Koran, is characterized by Ibn Jinnī (d. 392/1002) as *al-lugha al-fuṣḥā al-qudmā*—"the most refined and most ancient way of speaking"[36]—one cannot ignore that the classical language has in fact retained the "tamīmī" variant (nobody in fact writes *yardud/urdud*). Similarly, in the syntactical order, the *mā al-ḥijāziyya* that appears in the Koran and has the construction and meaning of *laysa* (e.g., sura 12:31: *mā hādhā basharan*—"this is not a man!") has remained a "Ḥijāzism," *laysa* only being the "classical" negation of the sentence with a nominal head. We have already seen the use of *lā yafʿal* in the hypothetical systems in *ʾin,* attested in the Koran and in archaic poetry (and maybe in the inscription of ʿEn ʿAvdat!)[37] and considered by Fischer[38] as one of the traits of what he calls "pre-classical Arabic," but forgotten by classical Arabic.[39] These are only a few examples: one finds a list of the particularities of the Koranic language in relation to classical Arabic in Talmon.[40]

Classical Arabic is thus not the whole *ʿarabiyya* as it was described by the grammarians, but only a part. And to the extent that it is the product of a selection,[41] this part cannot be identified with a sector of the reality. We saw above that the identification with the *lughat Quraysh* was dogmatic. We would now like to do justice to another identification, the one made by many Arabists with a common language (*koine*), a vehicle of poetry, among other things. If such a poetic *koine* existed, one wonders why Ibn Fāris, in the *Ṣāḥibī*[42] illustrated "blameful" features (*madhmūma,* i.e., nonclassical) by the verses of poets, who are not all anonymous poets of the Jāliliyya, but among whom at least one is a great poet of the Umayyad era: Dhū l-Rumma (died 117/735–736?) from whom one verse serves as example of the *ʿanʿana* (i.e., the fact of pronouncing the *ʿayn* like the *hamza*) of the Tamīm:

ʾa-ʾan [= ʾan] tarassamta min kharqāʾa manzilatan
māʾu ṣ-ṣabābati min ʿaynayka masjūmun (< ū)
"Is it because you observed a camp of Kharqāʾ
That the water of tears flows from your eyes?"[43]

Note that these data are not in the rough state. And when the *kashkasha* is illustrated, still by Ibn Fāris, by the (anonymous) verse *fa-ʿaynā-shi ʿaynāhā wa-jīdu-shi jīdu-hā*—"your eyes are her eyes, your neck her neck . . ."—it is clear that it is not a matter here of pronunciation, free or conditioned, of the *k* as a palatoalveolar fricative *ch* or an affricative *tch* and in general a phenomenon known in many dialects (*kīs* "sack," spoken as *tchīs*), and in many languages (*Caesar/Cesare*), but precisely of the suffixed pronoun of the second person of the feminine singular—*ki* as in an affricate. But such a pronunciation has no sense unless the short vowels of these pronouns are suppressed, the realization of the *k* into *tch* allowing a distinction to be made between the two genders (*ʿalayk/ʿalayts* versus *ʿalayka/l ʿalayki*).[44] The form mentioned thus represents an approximation of the effective form, a classisization (on the phonological not morphological plane)—in short, a true hybrid form. Classical Arabic acts everywhere as a filter: thus we noted above that of the two variants of the jussive, it was the "tamīmī" that imposed itself. But Arab sources indicate that the vowel is variable, according to place and context, whereas classical Arabic retained the vowel

–a.[45] And so we see that *(ya)-rudda* is all that remains of a double variation: variation of form, variation of final vowel of one of the two forms. Classical Arabic is indeed a selection, a restriction, a fixing. The poetic *koine* is thus a myth: it represents a retroprojection of standardized Arabic onto the history of the language.

It is time to conclude. Classical Arabic is a construction, even if it is not a construction *ex nihilo*. At the center of this construction was put the *iʿrāb,* whereas the epigraphical material conserved does not allow us to deduce the existence of such an inflection (except for the pausal pronunciation of *tanwīnan* into *–ā*) but that there seems indeed to have been, among the *qirāʾāt*, a caseless variant. The question of the *iʿrāb* therefore remains open. Even if for my part I think that it might be a feature of high antiquity, which was maintained for reasons, not syntactical but metric and prosodic, in the poetic register of the language, before being retained by reason of the prestige attached to this register by classical Arabic, still, other hypotheses cannot be excluded, notably the one that sees it as an innovation, an internal development in classical Arabic, consisting in a reinterpretation in case inflection of vowels of liaison (*waṣl*). This position, which originates in Arab grammatical tradition itself with Quṭrub, died 206/821,[46] was defended in the nineteenth century by Wetzstein;[47] it is defended today, with a very great technical refinement, by Owens.[48]

A final example to illustrate both the concept proposed here of classical Arabic and the alternative that follows for the history of the language: The treatises of Arabic grammar generally open with a definition of the utterance (*kalām*), and of its constituents (*kalimāt*, plural of *kalima*). About the latter, the grammarians note[49] that there exist three variants (*lughāt*): one, *kalima,* given as "ḥijāzī" and which is the one retained by classical Arabic; and two others, given as "tamīmī," namely, *kilma* and *kalma*. If we observe that 1. these three variants evidently coexisted a long time ago in the Arab domain, and 2. many Arabic dialects today (for example, the Arabic of Damascus *kalme*) prolong no less evidently the variant *kilma*, then classical Arabic is not a point of departure, but of arrival—not the base, but the result of a long and slow process of constitution (assuredly comparable to that of any other "classical" or "literary" or "standard" language). Hence, we must go back to Fleischer's program,[50] that is to say, apprehend Arabic in its totality: *als Gesammtsprache*.[51]

NOTES

* A first version of this text was the subject of a lecture at Zürich University on April 21, 2005. I thank my colleagues of the Orientalisches Seminar for their comments. Thanks also to Jonathan Owens (University of Bayreuth, Germany) for his reading and comments and to my colleague of Hebrew Philippe Cassuto for the details in note 7.

1. Christian Julien Robin, "Les inscriptions de l'Arabie antique et les études arabes," *Linguistique arabe: Sociolinguistique et histoire de la langue* (Pierre Larcher, dir.), in *Arabica* 48, no. 4 (2001): 509–77; in this example, pp. 537–43.

2. Ibid., pp. 545–50.

3. Alfred Grohmann, *Arabische Paläographie*. II. Teil, pp. 15–17.

4. Robin and Gorea. "Un réexamen de l'inscription arabe du Djébel Usays (528-9 è. Chr.)," *Arabica* 48, no. 2 (2002): 503–10.

5. One can still wonder if this reading does not amount to projecting a collocation from French ("sent as garrison") onto Arabic. It would be necessary to be sure of the possibility of such a construction in Arabic and the syntactical category of *maslaḥa.*

6. Procopius of Caesarea (died 562?), *De Bello persico,* I 18, vol. 1, p. 96, l. 25: Αρέθας.

7. Αρέτας: nothing can be concluded from the transliteration. The original Hebrew/Aramaic of these books is lost and the double pronunciation of the *taw* as "occlusive" (dental) and spirant (interdental), given by the grammars of biblical Hebrew (e.g., Lettinga, 1980: 9) seems to be a late phenomenon, hence the influence of Arabic is not excluded. Evidently, if one could show that the variant Aretas/Arethas from Greek is the reflection, even indirect, of a variant of Arabic itself, of just as ancient a date, this would be an additional argument in favor of the vision of classical Arabic proposed in 3: It is not Arabic dialects who maintain or lose interdentals, it is (inversely) classical Arabic that retains the interdentals in an ensemble of dialects, of which some have them and others don't.

8. But this is a matter, on both the formal and semantic levels, of an ancient phenomenon, see Fleisch (1961, 152).

9. For a recent overview, see Gilliot and Larcher (2003).

10. John Burton, *The Collection of the Qur'ān* (London, New York, Melbourne: Cambridge University Press, 1977).

11. John Wansbrough, *Quranic Studies—Sources and Methods of Scriptural Interpretation*. ([London Oriental Studies, vol. 31] Oxford: Oxford University Press, 1977).

12. For a recent overview of this question, cf. Prémare (2004).

13. A copy dated 94/712–13 and two respectively from 102/720 and 107/725 according to Grohmann (1958, note 18).

14. Gerd-R. Puin, "Observations on Early Qur'ān Manuscripts in Ṣan'ā'," in *The Qur'ān as Text*, ed. Stefan Wild. Leiden, New York, Köln: Brill, 1996.

15. For an overview, see Leemhuis (2001).

16. If one calls "small variation" the variants of reading of the ductus and the "great variation" the variants of the ductus itself, one might then call "very great variation" the Arabic/Aramaic transliteration of the ductus by Luxenberg (2000).

17. See art. FĀṢILA in *EI* (H. Fleisch).

18. On rhymes in poetry and in the Koran, cf. the detailed exposition of Zwettler (1978), ch. 3.

19. Cf. *Taysīr* by Dānī [d. 444/1052–1053], p. 179, and *Tafsīr al-Jalālayn* of Maḥallī [d. 864/1459] and Suyūṭī [d. 911/1505], p. 507.

20. I refer here to the now classic work by Birkeland, 1940.

21. This divergence is unfortunately not signaled in the article IDGHĀM in *EI* (H. Fleisch).

22. Henri Fleisch, *Traité de Philologie arabe*. Vol. I: *Préliminaires, Phonétique, Morphologie nominale*. Vol. II: *Pronoms, morphologie verbale, particules*. (Beyrouth: Imprimerie catholique, 1961, 1979), p. 83.

23. Paul Kahle, *The Cairo Geniza* (Oxford: Basil Blackwell, second ed., 1959). p. 145, n. 1.

24. Karl Vollers, *Volksprache und Schriftsprache im alten Arabien* (Strassburg, 1906 [repr. Amsterdam: APA-Oriental Press, 1981]).

25. Werner Diem, "Vom Altarabischen zum Neuarabischen—Ein neuer Ansatz," in *Semitic Studies in Honor of Wolf Leslau on the occasion of his eighty-fifth birthday* ed. Alan S. Kaye (Wiesbaden: Harrassowitz, 1991), vol. I, pp. 297–308.

26. Heinrich Fleischer, "Ueber arabische Lexicographie und Tha'ālibī's Fiqh al-lugah," in *Berichte über die Verhandlungen der Königlich Sächs. Gesellschaft der Wissenschaften. Philol.-histor. Cl.* (Leipzig, 1854, pp. 1–14 [repr. in *Kleinere Schriften,* 1885–1888, vol. 3, ch. 9, pp. 152–66]).

27. The classic formulation of this thesis is found in Fück (1955 [1950]). Today it is illustrated by Blau (e.g., 2002, p. 16).

28. Diem, "Vom Altarabischen," pp. 299, 307, n. 30.

29. *Taysīr,* p. 123.

30. *Tafsīr al-Jalālayn*, p. 264.

31. John Burton, "Linguistic Errors in the Qur'ān," *Journal of Semitic Studies* 33 (1988): 181–96.

32. *Taysīr,* p. 86.

33. Cf. art. 'ARABIYYA in *EI*.

34. For a recent overview on the history of Latin, cf. Dubuisson (2004).

35. Cf. *Ṣāḥibī*, pp. 52–53, of Ibn Fāris (died 395/1004). For a commentary, see Larcher (2004b).

36. Abū l-Fatḥ, ʿUthmān Ibn Jihnī, *al-Khaṣāʾiṣ*, 3 vols., ed. Muḥammed ʿAlī -l-Najjār (Beyrouth: Dār Lisān al-ʿArab, n.y.), vol. 1, p. 260.

37. See, in particular, Kropp (1994).

38. Wolfdietrich Fischer, "Die Perioden des Klassischen Arabisch," *Abr Nahrain* 12 (1970–71): 15–18.

39. Fischer does not note that *lā yafʿal* is also employed in the apodosis. The fact that *lā yafʿal* is elsewhere a negation of the jussive (imperative and injunctive) is an argument for seeing in the conditional use of the apocopate an avatar of the jussive, not of the former perfect of the Semitic.

40. Rafael Talmon, "Grammar and the Qurʾān," in *The Encyclopaedia of the Qurʾān,* ed. Jane Dammen McAuliffe (Brill: Leiden, 2001), vol. II, pp. 345–69.

41. Ibn Fāris, and before him al-Farrāʾ, were not unaware that the *lugha fuṣḥā* is a selection. While identifying it with the *lughat Quraysh,* they made this latter the basis of a process of koineization justified by the fact that Mecca was the center of an intertribal pilgrimage (for details, see Larcher 2004b).

42. P. 53.

43. See also Raḍī al-Dīn al-Astarābādhī (died 688/1289), *Sharḥ Shāfiyat*, vol. 3, p. 203, reference 160, and ʿAbd al-Qādir al-Baghdādī (died 1093/1682), *Sharḥ Shawāhidihi,* vol. 4, p. 427, reference 205.

44. As suggested by the fact that the dialects that do not practice this type of *kashkasha,* for example, Arabic of Damascus, have *ʿalēki* (f.) versus *ʿalēk* (m.). For a recent overview of the *kashkasha*, ancient and modern, see Holes (1991).

45. Fleisch, *Traité de Philologie* (1979), p. 350, n.1.

46. Cf. Versteegh (1981 [1983]).

47. Johann Wetzstein, "Sprachliches aus den Zeltlagern des syrischen Wüste," *Zeitschrift der Deutschen Morgenländischen Gesellschaft* 22 (1868): 69–194.

48. Jonathan Owens, "*Idġām al-kabīr* and history of Arabic language," in *"Sprich doch mit deinen Knechten Aramäisch, wir verstehen es!" 60 Beiträge zur Semitistik für Otto Jastrow zum 60. Geburtstag*, ed. Werner Arnold and Hartmut Bobzin (Wiesbaden: Harrassowitz, 2002), pp. 503–20.

49. For example, Ibn Hishām al-Anṣārī (died 761,1361), *Sharḥ shudhūr al-dhahab,* p. 11.

50. " Ueber arabische Lexicographie," p. 155.

51. On Fleischer's concepts, cf. Larcher (2001).

BIBLIOGRAPHY

Astarābādhī, Raḍī al-Dīn al-. *Sharḥ Shāfiyat Ibn al-Ḥājib ma'a Sharḥ Shawāhidihi li-l-Baghdādī*. 4 vols. Cairo, 1939–1958 [repr. Beyrouth: Dār al-Kutub al-'Ilmiyya 1395/1975].

Birkeland, Harris. *Altarabische Pausalformen.* Oslo: Det Norske Videnskaps-Akademi, 1940 (Skrifter utgitt av det Norske Videnskaps-Akademi i Oslo, II. Hist.-filos. klass, no. 4).

Blau, Joshua. *A Handbook of Early Middle Arabic*. Jerusalem: Max Schloessinger Memorial Foundation and the Hebrew University, 2002. (The Max Schloessinger Memorial Studies Monographs 6, Institute of Asian and African Studies, Faculty of Humanities).

Burton, John. *The Collection of the Qur'ān*. London, New York, Melbourne: Cambridge University Press, 1977.

———. "Linguistic Errors in the Qur'ān." *Journal of Semitic Studies* 33 (1988): 181–96.

Dānī (al-). *Taysīr* = Abū 'Amr 'Uthmān b. Sa'īd al-Dānī, *Kitāb al-Taysīr fī l-qirā'āt al-sab'*. Beyrouth: Dār al-Kutub al-'Ilmiyya, 1416/1996.

Diem, Werner. "Vom Altarabischen zum Neuarabischen—Ein neuer Ansatz," in *Semitic Studies in Honor of Wolf Leslau on the occasion of his eighty-fifth birthday,* edited by Alan S. Kaye. Wiesbaden: Harrassowitz, 1991, vol. I, pp. 297–308.

Dubuisson, Michel. "Le pouvoir et la langue: le cas du latin "classique." In *Le discours sur la langue sous les régimes autoritaires*, edited by P. Sériot et A. Tabouret Keller. Université de Lausanne (2004), *Cahiers de l'ILSL*, no. 17, pp. 33–43.

*EI*² = *Encyclopaedia of Islam*, new edition, Leiden: Brill, 1960.

Fischer, Wolfdietrich. "Die Perioden des Klassischen Arabisch," *Abr Nahrain* 12 (1970–71): 15–18.

Fleisch, Henri. *Traité de Philologie arabe*. Vol. I: *Préliminaires, Phonétique, Morphologie nominale.* Vol. II: *Pronoms, morphologie verbale, particules*. Beyrouth: Imprimerie catholique 1961, 1979.

Fleischer, Heinrich. "Ueber arabische Lexicographie und Tha'ālibī's Fiqh al-lugah." In *Berichte über die Verhandlungen der Königlich Sächs. Gesellschaft der Wissenschaften. Philol.-histor. Cl.,* Leipzig, 1854, pp. 1–14 [repr. in *Kleinere Schriften,* 1885–1888, vol. III, ch. IX, pp. 152–66].

Fück, Johann. *'Arabīya. Recherches sur l'histoire de la langue et du style arabe*. Paris: Didier, 1955 [French transl. of *Arabīya. Untersuchungen zur arabischen Sprach- und Stilgeschichte*. Berlin: Akademie Verlag, 1950 (Abh. d. sächs. Akademie der Wissenschaften zu Leipzig, Phil.-hist. Kl., Band 45, Heft 1)].

Gilliot, Claude, and Pierre Larcher. "Language and Style of the Qur'ān." In *The Encyclopaedia of the Qur'ān*, edited by Jane Dammen McAuliffe. Brill: Leiden, 2003, vol. III, pp. 109–35.

Grohmann, Alfred. *Arabische Paläographie*. II. Teil *Das Schriftwesen. Die Lapidarschrift*. Wien: Hermann Böhlaus Nachf, 1971.

———. "The Problem of Dating Early Qur'āns," *Der Islam* 33 (1958): 213–31.

Holes, Clive. "Kashkasha and the fronting and affrication of the velar stops revisited: a contribution to the historical phonology of the Peninsular Arabic dialects." In *Semitic Studies in Honor of Wolf Leslau on the occasion of his eighty-fifth birthday*, edited by Alan S. Kaye. Wiesbaden: Harrassowitz, 1991, vol. I, pp. 652–78.

Ibn Fāris. *Ṣāḥibī* = Abū l-Ḥusayn Aḥmad Ibn Fāris. *Al-Ṣāḥibī fī fiqh al-lugha wa-sunan al-ʿarab fī kalāmihā*, edited by Moustafa El-Chouémi. Beyrouth: A. Badran & Co., 1383/1964. (Coll. Bibliotheca philologica arabica, publiée sous la direction de R. Blachère et J. Abdel-Nour, vol. 1).

Ibn Hishām al-Anṣārī. *Sharḥ shudhūr al-dhahab fī maʿrifat kalām al-ʿArab,* edited by Muḥammad Muḥyī al-Dīn ʿAbd al-Ḥamīd. Kairo, n.y. Ibn Jinnī, *Khaṣāʾiṣ* = Abū l-Fatḥ ʿUthmān Ibn Jinnī, *al-Khaṣāʾiṣ*. 3 vols, edited by Muḥammad ʿAlī al-Najjār. Beyrouth: Dār al-Hudā li-l-Ṭibāʿa wa-l-Nashr, n.y.

Ibn Manẓūr. *LA* = Muḥammad b. Mukarram b. ʿAlī b. Aḥmad al-Anṣārī al-Ifrīqī al-Miṣrī Jamāl al-Dīn Abū l-Faḍl Ibn Manẓūr, *Lisān al-ʿArab al-muḥīṭ*. 4 vols., ed. by Yūsuf Khayyāṭ. Beyrouth: Dār Lisān al-ʿArab, n.y.

Kahle, Paul. *The Cairo Geniza*. Oxford: Basil Blackwell. First ed., 1947, second ed., 1959.

Kropp, Manfred. "A puzzle of Old Arabic Tenses and Syntax: The Inscription of ʿEn ʿAvdat." *Seminar for Arabian Studies* 24 (1994): 165–74.

Larcher, Pierre. "Moyen arabe et arabe moyen." *Linguistique arabe: sociolinguistique et histoire de la langue* (Pierre Larcher, dir.), *Arabica* 48, no. 4 (2001): 578–609.

———. "Du jussif au conditionnel en arabe classique: une hypothèse dérivationnelle." In *Romano-Arabica* III Arabic Linguistics. Bucharest: Center for Arab Studies, 2004a, 185–97.

———. "Théologie et philologie dans l'islam médiéval: relecture d'un texte célèbre de Ibn Fāris (Xe siècle)." In *Le discours sur la langue sous les régimes autoritaires*, edited by P. Sériot and A. Tabouret Keller. Université de Lausanne, *Cahiers de l'ILSL,* no. 17 (2004b): 101–14.

Leemhuis, Frederik. "Readings of the Qur'ān." In *The Encyclopaedia of the Qur'ān*, edited by Jane Dammen McAuliffe. Brill: Leiden 2004, vol. IV, pp. 353–62.

Lettinga, Jan P. *Grammaire de l'hébreu biblique*. Brill: Leiden, 1980.

Littmann, Enno. *Arabic Inscriptions*. Brill: Leiden, 1949 (Syria: Publications of the Princeton University Archaeological Expedition to Syria in 1904–1905 and 1909. Division IV, Section D).

———. "Die vorislamisch-arabische Inschrift aus Umm ij-Jimāl." *ZS* 7 (1929): 197–204.

Luxenberg, Christoph. *Die syro-aramäische Lesart des Korans. Ein Beitrag zur Entschlüsselung der Koransprache*. Berlin: Das Arabische Buch, 2000.—An enlarged English version *The Syro-Aramaic Reading of the Koran. A Contribution to the Decoding of the Language of the Koran* has been published in Berlin: Schiler, 2007.

Owens, Jonathan. "Case and Proto-Arabic." *Bulletin of the School of Oriental and African Studies,* part I, 61, no. 1 (1998): 51–73 and part II, 61, no. 2, pp. 215–27.

———. "*Idġām al-kabīr* and History of Arabic Language." In *"Sprich doch mit deinen Knechten Aramäisch, wir verstehen es!" 60 Beiträge zur Semitistik für Otto Jastrow zum 60. Geburtstag*, edited by Werner Arnold and Hartmut Bobzin. Wiesbaden: Harrassowitz, 2002, pp. 503–20.

Prémare, Alfred-Louis de. *Aux origines du Coran. Questions d'hier, approches d'aujourd'hui*. Paris: Tétraèdre, 2004 (Coll. L'Islam en débats).

Procopius of Caesarea. *Procopii Caesariensis opera omnia in aedibus B. G. Teubneri, Bibliotheca scriptorum graecorum et romanorum Teubneriana*, 3 vols., Leipzig, 1905–1913.

Puin, Gerd-R. "Observations on Early Qur'ān Manuscripts in Ṣanʿāʾ." In *The Qurʾān as Text*, edited by Stefan Wild. Leiden, New-York, Köln: Brill, 1996.

Rabin, Chaïm. *Ancient West-Arabian*. London: Taylor's Foreign Press, 1951.

Robin, Christian Julien. "Les inscriptions de l'Arabie antique et les études arabes." In *Linguistique arabe: Sociolinguistique et histoire de la langue* (Pierre Larcher, dir.), in *Arabica* 48, no. 4 (2001): 509–77.

Robin and Gorea. "Un réexamen de l'inscription arabe du Djébel Usays (528-9 è. Chr.)." *Arabica* 49, no. 2 (2002): 503–10.

Tafsīr al-Jalālayni = *Tafsīr al-imāmayn al-jalīlayn* Jalāl al-Dīn al-Maḥallī (and) Jalāl al-Dīn al-Suyūṭī. Cairo: Maktabat al-Jumhūriyya al-ʿArabiyya, n.y.

Talmon, Rafael. "Grammar and the Qurʾān." In *The Encyclopaedia of the Qurʾān*, edited by Jane Dammen McAuliffe. Brill: Leiden, 2001, vol. II, pp. 345–69.

ʿUshsh, Muḥammad Abū l-Faraj al-. "Kitābāt ʿarabiyya ghayr manshūra fī Jabal Usays." *Al-Abḥāth* 17, no. 3 (1964): 227–316.

Versteegh, Kees. "A Dissenting Grammarian: Qutrub on Declension." *Historiographia Linguistica* 8, nos. 2–3 (1981 [1983]): 403–29 [repr. in Cornelis H. M. Versteegh, Konrad Koerner, and Hans-J. Niederehe, eds. *The History of Linguistics in the Near East*. Amsterdam/Philadelphia: Benjamins, 1983 (Studies in the History of Linguistics 28), pp. 167–93].

Vollers, Karl. *Volksprache und Schriftsprache im alten Arabien*. Strassburg, 1906 [repr. Amsterdam: APA-Oriental Press, 1981].

Wetzstein, Johann. "Sprachliches aus den Zeltlagern des syrischen Wüste." *Zeitschrift der Deutschen Morgenländischen Gesellschaft* 22 (1868): 69–194.

Wansbrough, John. *Quranic Studies—Sources and Methods of Scriptural Interpretation*. Oxford: Oxford University Press, 1977 (London Oriental Studies, vol. 31).

Zwettler, Michael. *The Oral Tradition of Classical Arabic Poetry—Its Character and Implications*. Columbus: Ohio State University Press, 1978.

7

FROM SYRIAC TO PAHLAVI

The Contribution of the Sassanian Iraq to the Beginning of the Arabic Writing

Sergio Noja Noseda

THE AVERSION AND CONTEMPT FOR WRITING OF THE NORTHERN ARABS AT THE TIME OF THE JĀHILIYYAH

In the light of many new studies[1] it is highly probable that the two very famous phrases of Abū Bakr and of Zayd, son of Thābit, outbursts prompted by the proposal to collect the Koran in written form:[2] "What? Do you want to embark on what the Prophet never did?" and "Why do you want to undertake what the Prophet had never done?"[3] should not be read with slavish monotony, as has been for 1,500 years in the Muslim and our own world, as a refusal, or at least an expression of surprise focused on the text of the Revelation, but rather, generally, as a reluctance to put in writing a text of such importance—of such dimensions—and above all of that kind.

An examination of the substantial extra material that is now in our hands, compared to a hundred years ago, written in Arabic in the days of "ignorance" and in the early years of Islam shows that the Arabs undoubtedly *knew* how to write. What emerges, and what is important to us, is that they *did not want* to write. This negative attitude was not generalized but was specifically focussed on everything that we might define as a literary work. I have sometimes compared this attitude with the contempt that noblemen of the past displayed regarding details of the administration of their own lands!

As to "the ability to write" there is no doubt: the Koran uses the root "write" hundreds of times, but it is interesting to observe what the purpose of this "writing" was. On one hand there is a nuanced vision of "heavenly writings"[4] but in human reality only receipts and treaties.[5]

It therefore seems there was a reluctance to "write down" any literary work, or rather, and this is the point, anything that was living, and especially poetry. Displaying the contempt described above, they could psychologically bury the probably detested statements of debit and credit along with the writing. The traditional idea of beautiful poems hanging on the Kaʿbah in the pre-Islamic era really has to be dropped today.[6]

On this point it is interesting to note that even today we find an almost identical attitude in the North African desert,[7] so that, without returning to lost worlds like those of the bards in Celtic mists, we would do well to delve into this world that has survived to our own times, a situation that may well represent what the habits and the mentality of the pre-Islamic northern Arabs were.[8]

The political and social conditions have always been such that, so far as we know, the Berbers have never developed a "civilization of writing" in their language. There is nevertheless a Berber script, whose origin is still unknown, that only the Tuareg currently use and which they call tifinaγ. If we overlook a few letters, they use this for brief writings on objects such as buckles and bracelets or on rocks, or for silent conversation during amorous encounters.[9]

This script too, like Arabic, is consonantal. The writings are always brief and, generally, it is this lack of spacing, rather than handwriting errors, of which we have glaring examples, that gives rise to the main difficulties in reading them. If the problems that this causes are greatly reduced because of the usual brevity of the texts, these same problems are offset by this same brevity.

All in all one can say that the Tuareg make relatively little use of writing: during evenings in company, characteristic of Tuareg society, girls and boys, in a kind of *cour d'amour* entertain each other by writing with their fingers on the palm of the other's hand. Simple spaced writing or the composition of a single character is specific to this mode of writing.[10] Texts of a certain size, chronicles, and genealogies are traditionally committed to memory, while brief texts for immediate use were entrusted to tifinaγ, such as inscriptions, letters, dedications, and names on objects, without any specialization in terms of specific writing materials like parchment, making the most of any suitable surface,[11] writing in the sand[12] for their own pleasure, for example, or to discuss the form of a word.

And it is here that one may try to catch a glimpse of this aversion of the northern Arabs of the past, and of the Tuareg even today, for putting literary works in writing. There seems to be a concept of "castration" as described by Géza Róheim[13] of the concepts freely expressed by the spoken word each time that they are substituted with writing. Such an idea, albeit in different terms, had also been entertained by the Greeks in the teaching of Plato: "We now have to consider the suitability and unsuitability of writing, when it is appropriate and when on the other hand it is not."[14]

Certainly it can also be seen in this reluctance, in this resistance to the "theft of imagination," or rather to the "theft of the imaginary" by the desert civilizations, from the northern Arabs in the period of the birth of Islam to the Tuaregs.

Why *theft*? Because—without even mentioning the third element in play today, namely, pictures—if we reflect a little on the current relationship between the spoken and the written word, one can say that, all in all, it is the spoken word that has kept its prestige. In the written word there is a lack of liberty, a fading of imagination-based initiative. In other words, the rigidity of writing results in a blunting of the expressive will, of the impulse to let your imagination wander, which is the first springboard toward the formation of a "collective imagination" and even more toward the formation of one's own private imaginary embryo.

Yet while the preeminence of the spoken word (let us call it "logocentrism") compared to any other form of communication is perfectly obvious, we also have to realize that precisely what slips from the grasp of the spoken word is what constitutes the first embryo—an imaginary one, of course—of our thought, perhaps of a thought that is not conceptualized but laden with possible aesthetic factors. This is not yet a matter of the spoken word, but rather of that combination of images (visual, auditory, but also tactile, olfactory, coenaesthetic . . .) that exist beyond the realm of verbal language and which may turn into concepts and words only later, as they often do.[15]

And so why should we not believe that even the primeval "logos"—the primordial human word—was not at first an articulated language, but rather an all-encompassing image charged with smells and tastes, lights and shadows, shapes and gaps? All this is the antithesis of the ideas of those who think that thoughts cannot exist without words, and cognitive activity is only possible when expressed in words, or even that—as Chomsky claims—language is innate to human beings.[16] Nothing forbids us to suppose that the thinking of northern Arab society at the time of the Jāhiliyyah was structured in this way.

As far as the beginning is concerned, Arabic writing would appear to have experienced freedom. No matter what efforts of imagination I make, I cannot visualize the highest Shanfarā sitting down to write, then correcting and recorrecting his verses.[17] The writings were a characteristic sign of the system. How can one avoid thinking of contempt for writing in the comparison of Labīd:

> and the torrent-beds of el-Raiyán—naked shows their trace,
> rubbed smooth, like letterings long since scored on a stony slab;[18]
> . . .
> Then the torrents washed the dusty ruins, until they seem
> like scrolls of writing whose text their pens have revised . . .[19]

and of their silence:

> So I stood and questioned that site; but how should we question rocks
> Set immovable, whose speech is nothing significant?[20]

This attitude could also have represented a true drive for freedom against the structures of the southern Arabs, perhaps against the same Nabataeans or their cousins of Hatra distinguished by their monumental inscriptions, a decided wish to be able to alter the texts handed down "by memory."

Here, there is a sense of "liberty" coupled with a rejection of writing that must in some way be innate to human nature in that it has been constantly repeated in the history of humankind right up to the "Slam Poetry" of our times, the poetry that one must not write down. In this idiom the voice of the poet and the listening of his audience create a community, or rather a TAZ (Temporary Autonomous Zone) in which words, thought, criticism, dialogue, and debate, coupled with the tolerance and willingness to listen of the other party are fundamental values.[21]

Such an atmosphere could well explain why the prophet of Islam did not want to be the one to put the text of the Revelation into writing, although he frequently ordered his secretaries[22] to write letters and small treaties. One need only recall the one with the Quraysh people and the reply by Suhayl son of ʿAmr at the time of dictating the terms of the armistice "if I witnessed that you were God's apostle I would not have fought you."[23]

As regards "dictating" this may be considered something normal. The Koran gives orders to "dictate" to write the debt statements,[24] and indeed the fact that the Revelation orders or recommends "writing" a document supports the idea that it was not a matter of habit or desire to do so. Even the sense of the root *k-t-b* may be understood as "dictating"[25] and in this his behavior should not surprise the Western world, in which this was the current practice in ancient times (the example of Pliny the Elder is famous) and one supposes that Saint Jerome, at the end of the fourth century, did not write some of his works with his own hand, and neither did Saint Augustine[26] for that matter. Something of this tradition must have remained in the air, at least in the East, if a painter of the fifteenth century chose to paint in the church of St. Paraskevi at Geroskipou, on the island of Cyprus, the Apostle Paul, on foot, bent over the shoulder of his secretary, watching him write what he dictated.

The prophet of Islam was in no way opposed to the verses of the Revelation, such as those collected by ʿUmar's sister, being written.[27]

Yes, writing existed, but on a "tablet kept" in Heaven.[28] And the word "heaven" has always made me think of the laws of the southern Arabian kings written in enormous characters on the walls of the gigantic clefts between the wadis in an incredible Official Gazette.[29] It is only worth noting that even today this custom persists at the border between the two Koreas.[30]

Opposition to the "book" as a concept was not so complete, as it had been known at least since the times of the Syriac world—the oldest Syriac manuscripts are pre-Islamic[31]—given that the word kitāb appears in Zuhayr's verse: "and either it's postponed, and put in a book, and stored away"[32] although this verse is accused of containing a "Koranic echo that is clearly understood,"[33] an echo that I personally do not hear.

THE SASSANID ERA IN IRAQ: THE COEXISTENCE OF SYRIAC AND PAHLAVI

On September 26, 226, Ardashir made his triumphal entrance into the conquered Ctesiphon and, having declared the Arsacid dynasty defunct, began a new one that, in the name of the founder, is known as "of the Sassanids."

In 614 the King of Kings' army arrived to devastate and sack Jerusalem, a huge event that reverberated around the whole of Arabia to the point that it found a remarkable echo in the Koran:

> A.L.M. * The Roman Empire, has been defeated *
> in a land close by . . .[34]
>
> ... الم * غلبت الروم * فى أدنى الارض

One need only think of the conquest of the Persian Gulf[35] and of Yemen to realize how completely this immense empire covered the areas that we are mainly interested in. The western borders of the empire reached well beyond the Euphrates and the many cities of Iraq, like al-Ḥīrah,[36] which are mentioned repeatedly in the Arab chronicles of the years that precede Islam, should nearly all be regarded as being in territory dominated by the Sassanids.[37] The chancellery of this immense empire, in a continuous exchange of correspondence—not only with the Byzantine Empire to the west, but also with the peoples beyond Samarkand and Pamir toward the Celestial Empire[38]—had to greatly increase its size while the missionary thrust of the Nestorians and of the Manichaeans[39] transformed many languages from "domestic tongues" or from *langue véhiculaire* into written languages. Given that, according to what contemporary writers said, one certainly cannot claim that the Persian had a "vocation" for writing, what occurred in this context in territories dominated by the Aryans was truly incredible.

While the Annals of King Assurbanipal tell us that the Semitic king learned to ride, to shoot with a bow, and "the entire art of writing according to the traditions of the teachers," Herodotus wrote that the Persians "taught their sons only three things: to get on a horse, to shoot with a bow, and to tell the truth," an education manifestly different from that of the King of Mesopotamia.

In reality Herodotus could have added, had he known it, that the art of writing had always implied something Satanic, and "Satanic," in ancient Persian, was equivalent to "non-Iranian" (anêrân). In practice the types of writing used by the Persians throughout their religious-literary history were of non-Aryan origin, but they wrote with different scripts and alphabets over the centuries and it is difficult not to suppose that this fact of writing so much in the Persian world suggests that the Persians owed a real debt to *Babilonia capta*.[40]

The ability to write in Persia, where entire families of the minor nobility dedicated themselves entirely to this pursuit, is very widely known and many of these families continued for at least two centuries after the victory of Islam to provide the "scribes" of the new empire.[41] But there were also Arab families in loco who dedicated themselves to translating and presumably to writing.

Among these characters there was ʿAdī son of Zayd, the famous poet. It is known that, because of hatreds within the court, he was killed at the behest of Nuʿmān III, king of the Lakhmids.

His son, Zayd son of ʿAdī, his heart burdened with unquenchable hatred for Nuʿmān, moved to Ctesiphon where he took up his father's occupation and became a translator-scribe regarding the Arab affairs of the Persian court. The work of translation of texts was continuous. Relations with the Arabs were very important.

As he was in continuous contact with the King of Kings, one day he suggested that the latter should ask for the hand of Nuʿmān's daughter. It was the same Zayd son of ʿAdī who dealt with the matter, and the king of al-Ḥīrah's reply was altered by him—an ancient reminder of the continual work and importance of the translators in the Persian court?—to the point of that he put in evidence the expression "the wild cows" as the translation of the Arabic word *ʿīn* which, meaning "with large eyes," usually refers to "gazelles," a very common word in Arabic poetry used to mean "girls." And Nuʿmān was killed on the orders of the emperor![42]

Apart from these few examples of the vast work of the Department of Foreign Affairs of the court of the King of Kings and of the Arabic Affairs Office—the deliberately wrong translation by Zayd son of ʿAdī could have been limited to an exchange of pleasantries—writing "in Arabic" might seem normal to us, to judge from a very important episode in the history of those times: the peace treaty of 561 between Byzantium and Sassanid Persia.

The special precautions taken for the translation of the treaty from Greek into Persian and from Persian into Greek, described by the Greek historian Menander, who speaks of no less than six Persian and six Greek translators, are highly significant.[43]

Although we do not have the document, one would be right to think that a copy was made of the treaty in Arabic for the use of or as a warning to the Ghassānids and the Lakhmids.[44] These were involved in the treaty in a special way and it would not have made sense to give them a copy in Greek or Persian, a text that they would have translated freely at home with unforeseeable consequences. Bearing in mind that, as Menander relates, the copies in Greek and Persian bore the twelve seals of the translators, it is hard to imagine that less care was taken over the copies intended for the Arabs.[45]

The Arabs felt a certain aversion to Greek writing and to the Greeks in particular.[46] It seems common sense to suppose that the Byzantine governments used Aramaeans who were already close to the Arabs in language terms for their relationships with the Ghassānids, something that the caliphs then did with the family of Ḥunayn son of Isḥāq for classic translations in Arabic. These Aramaeans were Christians and Syriac was their mother tongue, although they also knew Greek. In the other court, the Kings of Kings used Arabic-speaking families in their offices for the translation and writing of documents, and these families, too, were Christians who knew Syriac quite well. And it was in these families of translators of the two great empires that, for reasons of work such as the preparation of translations, of copies of them, and of some correspondence, one might reasonably suppose that Arabic writing both began and developed.

With the great treaty of 561 still in mind, the following question arises: In what script was the Arabic version of this treaty written? One thinks of the writing that is even now the script of the Arabs, of which we have a contemporary epigraphic example in the writing of Jabal Usays, which predates the treaty because it was written in 528.[47]

This writing of Usays is immediately followed, in the evidences that archaeology has brought to light, by another dated entry in Arabic, that of Ḥarrān, in 568, which moreover also includes a text in Greek and one in Syriac.[48]

And then, if that is not enough, we have the evidence provided by a great inscription placed by Hind in his monastery in al-Ḥīrah between 561 and 569, an inscription that was still remembered at the time of Hārūn al-Rashīd almost two hundred years later.[49]

Islamic tradition relates[50] that, shortly before the Prophet, three men of the Ṭayy tribe (and the Ṭayy were partly Christian) met at Baqqah, identified as a place near al-Ḥīrah and, adopting and modifying the Syriac script (*al-suryāniyyah*), composed Arabic writing. These people taught Arabic writing to various people of Anbār, and its use also spread among the inhabitants of al-Ḥīrah.

It is also Arab tradition that tells us that Bishr son of ʿAbd al-Malik, brother of the prince of Dūmat al-Jandal,[51] who was Christian by religion, came at that time to stay in al-Ḥīrah and learned Arabic writing there. Bishr then went to Mecca for the wedding[52] and often had occasion to meet Sufyān son of Umayyah[53] and Abū Qays son of ʿAbd Manāf.[54] Noticing that he used a script, they asked him to teach it to them.

Bishr taught the two Quraysh men the art of reading and writing Arabic with the new characters, and when the three men went to al-Ṭāʾif on business they also taught the art of writing to others.[55]

Subsequently Bishr left Mecca and went to the Muḍar tribes of central Arabia, where he taught the script to ʿAmr son of Zurārah[56] who took the name of ʿAmr *al-Kātib.* Finally Bishr went to Syria and had various pupils there too.

Bearing in mind the missionary vocation of Christianity, may we not think that the name of the brother "Bishr" was a nickname linked to the root *b-š-r* or "herald," bearer of the novelty of writing? It would seem to be a precursor of the nickname of *Kātib* given to the character of his successor ʿAmr son of Zurārah. It turns out that in Jāhiliyyah there existed Christian names used as adjectives or Arabicized, either by altering the form or by reproducing the meaning. Among these both Bishr and Bashir[57] figure in the *Onomasticon arabicum.*

"Bishr" means "joy, communication, annunciation." It is not certain that the name was given to him by Islamic tradition. It could be that it was given by the Christians and he was a messenger. Adam is called *Abū al-Bashar*, the Gospel *Bishārah* and *ʿīd al-bishārah* is the feast of the annunciation of Mary. And he was not the only one of this name, a name that was in any case linked to Christianity. In subsequent times Theophane spoke of βησηρ (Bishr), a Syrian Christian who had converted to Islam.[58]

This word seems to have a certain background. The biblical מבשר would seem to be very clear, as it is in other Semitic languages.[59] In Syriac this meaning is expressed by ܣܒܪ ,[60] but Leslau suggests that the Syriac verb *sbar* which in the doubled (intensive) form *sabbar* means "to herald," is connected to the root, having undergone a metathesis.[61]

As I wish to record this matter with care, it may also be worth observing the move of the population from Mesopotamia to Dūmat al-Jandal shortly before the beginning of Islam, as well as the movement to found a second Dūmah, after the defeat in the year 9 in the principality of al-Ḥīrah. There is undoubtedly a link with al-Ḥīrah in both senses.

Tradition says that the inhabitants of this fortress-city were *ʿIbād,* or "Christians," and that Ukaydir and his people remained faithful to the Christian religion. This observation tallies with the fact that the inscriptions in Arabic of the years before the Prophet of Islam were produced in a Christian context.

Caskel, in his edition of the *Ǧamharat an-nasab*,[62] under the heading dedicated to our Bishr, placed amid seventy-six people of the same name, raises strong doubts in presenting a résumé of his history, wondering whether it would have been possible for the brother of a prince to travel around acting as a "*magister peregrinus*."[63] Apart from the fact that teaching the writing of a new alphabet is not like being a *fahrender Schulmeister*, if we dare to think that this was a process of starting an evangelization, it would not have been in any way a degrading or dishonorable activity for the brother of a princeling of a run-of-the-mill Arabian oasis. After all St. Cyrill and St. Methodios were the sons of an imperial deputy governor!

Arabic writing must therefore have been born in Sassanid territory between the rivers of Mesopotamia, a long way to the west, around 200 kilometres, which is equal to the distance between Medina and Mecca. Seleucia-Ctesiphon faces al-Anbār and is only a few tens of kilometres[64] away.

We also know that at that time Pahlavi was in use among the Persians as was Syriac, and it is the Syriac in this equation that emerges triumphant as a root.

But Pahlavi involved a factor that was very similar to Arabic writing without the diacritical points. Apart from the fact that as an Indo-European language it indicated the vowels, unlike Semitic languages, many symbols had sounds that were very different. One of these could be read from /a/ to /h/ and to /ḥ/, while another indicated both /p/ and /f/.

Iranian tradition, probably referring to Aramaic but perhaps also taking account of the so-called heterograms, spoke of a script that had 365 characters taught by a demon. These were then reduced in number, probably following a general rule, with the aim of producing ever more fluent writing, until they came down to the 18 characters of Pahlavi.[65] Speaking of the sameness of these characters, Cohen tells us: "Adaptation to the non-Semitic Iranian language was not achieved by creating new characters, with the result that certain letters were used with more than one value."[66]

In this case, the most striking aspect is that at some undetermined time the Persians wanted to put in writing the ancient version of the sacred texts known as Avesta and which had been preserved orally by innovating a script whose base was Pahlavi, but changed the letters to make the reading unequivocal, a change to which imitation of Greek contributed, in some cases.[67] This aim was achieved not by the addition of diacritical points external to the letters but by changing the letters, just as is done in our world with the modern script of certain non-Latin languages written with the Latin alphabet, such as the /č/ in Czech, distinct from the /c/.[68]

If we look at table 1,[69] in which the characters of the Pahlavi script are shown on the left and those of the Avesta on the right, the mechanism of adding diacritical marks seems obvious, beginning from the character  which indicated a, x^v, and x^l, which is elongated, in the direction of the writing, toward the left, changing into  to indicate the <ā> and changing into  for <x^l> and into  for <x^v>. The character  that indicated both /p/ and /f/ was divided into two with the elongation of the stroke  to indicate the /f/ and the other characters were modified in the same way.

While keeping in mind the lack of a definite source indicating when this work of adding diacritical marks began, one now usually thinks of the reign of Shapur II (309–379 AD) because there is the dated inscription on a famous sarcophagus in Istanbul, prior to 430 AD, which leads one to think that it was invented in the fourth century.[70]

It is highly probable that like many movements whose origin is unknown—nearly always the alternative to Islam has been represented by Byzantium, and on this matter see the magnificent study by Ugo Monneret de Villard[71] of the reciprocal influences—imitation comes into play, as in the case of the iconoclasm and the veil for women. The phenomenon of imitation, common to all peoples and eras, is exemplified by women's fashion, or by the continual imitation over the centuries of the military uniforms of one army or another.

This idea of guaranteeing the sound values of the letters with precision may have come to those who were creating the Arabic writing that was emerging or had just emerged from the clouds that crossed Iraq at the time, in a world that has been lucidly described as one of "*splendid confusion.*"[72]

The *Fihrist* says that one of the languages of the Persians was Syriac, not neglecting to repeat this, and especially referring to the Sawād, or lower Iraq, when it says, "they speak Syriac writing it in a type of Syriac-Persian."[73] It was precisely between the two rivers that the two scripts were side by side, if they were not mixed. At this point it would seem wise on one hand not to broaden the issue to include the Jews, even if traces of a certain confusion between "Syriac" and "Hebrew" writing remain in Islamic tradition, and on the other not to let one's imagination roam regarding the unproven theory, suggested by Bausani, that the mechanism of heterograms of Aramaic origin was so widespread as to make one think of a closed caste of Iranian scribes in league with Aramaic scribes to make Pahlavi "a matter of class, difficult."[74]

The fact that Arab tradition speaks of three inventors, almost a committee—let us not forget that the modification of Pahlavi to extend the alphabet of the Avesta had been the work of an ad hoc committee—seems to be ignored by Western scholars. Why not calmly suppose that the three people mentioned by tradition really were a committee and that deliberately, imitating the Persians or following the trend that was emerging at that time, they decided to perfect the Arabic script taking the *ductus* of Syriac—which is something about which there does not seem to be any doubt—and adding diacritical points following the example of the transition Pahlavi → Avesta, but using the points already in use in Syriac to distinguish between <r> and <d>? These points had been in use for centuries because they sometimes appear in Palmyrene inscriptions,[75] bringing into being diacritical points together with the Arabic letters that were already contemporary.

While we are in this geographical area, we should emphasize the movement that led to the *ductus* of Syriac and the alignment of the consonants on a single horizontal line, even if sometimes interrupted. The bottom link had already emerged from western Aramaic in the Aramaic Hatran[76] and is typical of the *estrangelā*. . . . From its earliest manifestations, this oldest Syriac writing displays a marked predisposition toward italic forms and the linking of the characters. A fact that conflicts with the current hypothesis that Arabic writing emerged in the Syrian area is that this tendency toward linking would be typical of the scripts of the area beyond the Euphrates, which appear in highly evolved forms while to the west of the Euphrates the development occurred more slowly because of slower penetration adapted from those innovations coming from the East that traveled along the commercial and military routes of the Roman lines.[77] It is true that in the area of Iraq the first scripts of the south-Mesopotamian family always had links too, but here the story is complicated by the *vexata questio* of the origin of the Mandaean script.[78]

The information that tradition gives regarding the specializations of the three personalities, namely, that

1. Murāmir, son of Marwah conceived the shape of the letters,
2. Aslam, son of Sidrah defined the way of writing them, separately or joined, and
3. ʿĀmir, son of Gadarah invented the diacritical points (*iʿjām*),

may also be an indication of a very modern think tank that could not be grasped in the real-life situation, made up of free discussions, and was understood neither by the Arabs of the second Islam when they committed these traditions to writing, nor by the nineteenth-century Leone Caetani.

Among other matters the anarchic mentality of the Bedouins and more generally of the pre-Islamic northern Arabs and of the first Islam was highly compatible with a *think tank* approach, with free expression of one's own ideas and creativity, very different to the rigid structures of the society that followed, and it seems sensible to think that perhaps that society was no longer capable of understanding these matters. It should not be forgotten that even the writing of the Vulgate had been the work of a *think tank* directed by Zayd son of Thābit.

It is not for nothing that Islamic tradition places the emergence of the diacritical points in Iraq, where the melting pot was on the boil, even if it was postponed to the times of al-Ḥajjāj. This information is highly questionable given that the latter, born at al-Ṭā'if in the year 41 of the Hijrah (661 AD), was seventeen years old when the Caliph Mu'āwiyah erected, on the dam that he had had built close to his native city, an epigraph dated 58 h (677 AD) in which certain diacritical points appear.[79]

In this field we have to admit that there must have been a little confusion in the records of Islam, because we cannot forget that in the manuscripts of ancient times small strokes are used and not points (those on the al-Ṭā'if dam are points) and the vowels are shown with colored points in exactly the opposite way: Points stand for diacriticals and small strokes for vowels.

THE VERTICAL ALIGNMENT OF ARABIC WRITING AT THE BEGINNING

It is known that humankind has developed scripts in all directions including not just horizontal and vertical ones, or spiralling ones like the magic goblets of Mesopotamia,[80] continuing to modern times,[81] but also—and this is much less well known—three-dimensional writing.[82] The script of the Berbers is an example of this kind of possibility. There can be vertical lines from bottom upward or from top downward, or horizontal from right to left or from left to right, with all the lines in the same direction, or *boustrophedon*. The writing can also be in columns. The lines are anything but regular; instead they deviate or zigzag, often curved in relation to the object about which one is writing, so that the direction of the writing is understood, and with ease, only from the way in which certain letters are orientated.[83]

To come to the period that interests us, it is as well to be guided by the conclusions that science has currently reached regarding cuneiform writing. The reigning view of the past among Assyriologists has been overtaken. That view held that there must have been a remarkable ambivalence that allowed one to write and read both vertically and horizontally without distinction. This misinterpretation had strange consequences, such as the claim that one had to bend over sideways to read an inscription on a monument.[84]

The first discoveries concerned Assyrian monumental writings that, in relation to the various iconographic items that accompanied them, displayed a type of writing that was unequivocally horizontal. The inscriptions, relatively late, belong to the first millennium before Christ. The fact that they were written horizontally now seems normal to us, for that period. But the first scholars, whose deduction was understandable, thought that cuneiform writing must have been horizontal from the beginning, and this view did not change when the vertical inscriptions of the legends of the cylindrical seals were discovered.[85]

On the contrary, when the system, having crossed its own national boundaries, came into contact with populations speaking different languages, it gave the writing, which was originally vertical, a character that was at first ambivalent and then clearly horizontal.[86] Something of the kind was moving and developing, after the Second World War, in the Chinese and Japanese world, where vertical writing tended, in episodes that became ever less sporadic, to become horizontal writing, and for an identical reason, namely, the comparison with invading scripts of other languages. However, there are habits and traditions that remain in the air.

It is difficult to ignore the fact that the Syriac script comes from Palmyran, in which there is no lack of evidence of vertical writing. This habit is clear in the monumental inscriptions in this alphabet.[87] Vertical writing in Syriac, well established by the monuments,[88] including the Nestorian stele of 781 in which the lines of writing in this alphabet are aligned in a similar way to those in Chinese characters,[89] and which survived over the centuries because of the Syriac manuscripts,[90] was not only not unknown; it was practiced with a certain regularity in the area—one need only think of the graffiti of the Thamud tribes. Apart from that, even Pahlavi is not without vertical writing, as witnessed in the writings found at Derbend at the outer limit of civilization, as well as in the coins.[91]

But it would not be so easy to think of vertical writing if there were not now, perhaps, the hopefully correct translation of the phrase of the *Fihrist* that regulary crops up in our studies, beginning with Silvestre de Sacy, passing on to the old Nabia Abbott, and continuing to the contemporary Déroche. The phrase is the following:[92]

قال محمد بن اسحاق: فأول الخطوط العربية، الخط المكي وبعده المدني ثم البصري ثم الكوفي. فأما المكي والمدني ففي الفها تعويج الى يمنة اليد وأعلا الأصابع وفي شكله انضجاع يسير.

In Silvestre de Sacy's translation it appears as: "les élifs sont fortement inclinés vers le côté droit de la main, et la figure des lettres est en peu cuché."[93]

Nabia Abbott then gives this interpretation: "The alif bends to the right and lower end, the extended vertical strokes (*al-aṣâbi*ʿ, i.e., *alif*, *lâm*, *lâm-alif*, *ṭâ*ʾ, and sometimes *kâf*) are high, and the script has a moderate downward slant to left,"[94] and this observation is followed by Dodge's translation: "for the alifs of the scripts of Makka and al-Madīna there is a turning of the hand to the right and lengthening of the strokes, one form having a slight slant," and in a note: "The Arabic phrase translated as 'lengthening of the strokes' is literally 'raising of the fingers.' See Abbott."[95]

Finally, Déroche says: "Leurs alifs sont tordus vers la droite de la main et étiré en hauteur, et leur apparence est légèrement incliné"; he continues this translation with an observation linked to Abbott's translation: "La partie centrale de cette description . . . fait référence aux *aṣâbi*ʿ, littéralement: 'doigts,' mot que N. Abbott a compris comme désignant de manière analogique les hastes des *alifs*, un sens que n'est pas attesté par ailleurs mais qui semble plausible dans ce contexte," adding:

> Une autre interprétation pourrait être avancé, qui ne remet pas fondamentalement en cause la signification du texte: au lieu de voir dans ce passage une description en quelque sorte statique de la forme de la lettre, on pourrait penser à une évocation du mouvement de la main du copiste qui élève (*iʿlā*ʾ) *les doigts* tenant le calame en direction de la partie supérieure du feuillet pour tracer un *alif*; l'absence du suffixe possessif—renvoyant aux *alif*s—serait alors plus compréhensible.[96]

At this point we need to go back to the writing of the Syriac manuscripts and quote the *Fihrist* yet again, where it says that the Persians wrote in Syriac,[97] speaking in a particular manner of the Sawād—once again Sassanid Iraq—which had a huge importance linked to the Christians who were there in large numbers. Describing someone who is preparing to make a sheet ready for vertical writing, with the sheet then to be rotated through ninety degrees for the reading, one may read the following text:

> In its *alifs* there is a curving (the dictionaries say "bend") towards the right side of the hand and there is a raising of the fingers and in its shape there is a slight lying down (to lie down).

If one thinks of the vertical writing of Arabic in the early years as imitating the Syriac, this expression of the *Fihrist*—"a raising of the fingers"—becomes clear. Anyone who saw the manuscript rotated through ninety degrees and written vertically would realize that the *alifs* had been written with the quill coming down at forty-five degrees from the top left toward the bottom right in writing the longer part of the *alif*, and they would moreover notice a smudge produced by the "raising of the fingers" that the scribe would have produced by bringing the quill from the bottom to the top vertically.

And it is again the *Fihrist* that speaks of the Christians to whom the order for the writing of the Koran[98] was given. They must have been professional scribes, and therefore accustomed to writing in Syriac. It should be said, in corroboration of this theory, that Arabic written vertically is found on the coins of the first Islam in Persia alongside Pahlavi writing (table 2),[99] like the ones imitating Byzantine practice minted in Palestine in early times.[100] It was the same in this case, too. Having passed through the era of the conquest there was a transition to horizontal writing.

This phenomenon of vertical Arabic writing may have only lasted for a very short time, and writing may have become horizontal for the same reasons that caused the change of direction of cuneiform writing, if we reread what was said before: "when the system . . . , having crossed its own national boundaries, came into contact with populations speaking different languages, it gave the writing, which was originally vertical, a character . . . that was clearly horizontal."[101]

If we want to refute *una tantum* the words of the sublime poet, "Per la contradizion che nol consente," we can say that there is no contradiction between the inclined *alifs* of the vertical writing of the Ḥijāzī manuscripts and the perfectly vertical *alifs* of the epigraphy, because the difference in the writing material is clear. Furthermore, in my view, when the Arabs began writing on stone, the vertical writing had already evolved, becoming horizontal.

But there is more to be said. The originally vertical writing of Arabic was preserved, in keeping with the constant rule of the archaism of forms, in marginal areas of Africa. This was noted by M. Marcel Cohen, who mentioned it in 1931 concerning the vertical writing of Arabic in Harar,[102] and he returned to the subject during the *Groupe Linguistique d'études chamito-sémitique* in 1951.[103] A few years later, in 1954, in the same *GLECS* context, Gérard Troupeau took up this subject again, referring not only to Cohen but also speaking of his personal experiences, and he was greeted by a chorus of general agreement. Troupeau said he had seen Arabic students writing in an absolutely vertical mode, just as he had seen the copyists writing in an identical way in Syriac. He added that he had not noticed the faithful having any problems in reading the vertical writings in Syriac on the walls of the churches, and he said that the habit of reading Syriac from all directions was a "*pratique nécessitée par la position des chantres à l'église, qui forment un cercle autour du livre liturgique posé à plate sur un pupitre placé au milieu d'eux.*" The latter observation may not be unavoidable, given that in general the texts are committed to memory, as in the בעל קורא of the Synagogal world.

One of those who attended this meeting said he had written in this way on tablets when he was a young student in Egypt, while another noted that this direction of the writing in the Jacobite outline of Syriac explained the Greek letters used for vocalization, such as the "capital ἦτα." These speakers were followed by two others. One pointed out that with the writing medium resting on the thigh, vertical writing permitted longer lines than horizontal writing, while the other observed that this phenomenon of vertical Arabic writing could explain why certain Arabic figures appeared to be *basculé* (toppling over) compared to Indian figures, such as the 3 of the Arabs ٣ compared to the ३ of the Sanskrit.[104] It seems to me that, in truth, this observation could be extended, as it would appear that something identical also occurred as regards the figure 2 among the Arabs ٢ from the Nagari २ and for 8 among the Arabs ٨ and in India ८.

Attracted by this argument and by a photograph in *National Geographic*,[105] having mentioned it in my report to the Istituto Lombardo, Accademia di Scienze e Lettere in Milan on October 17, 2002,[106] I was able to send an expedition from the Fondazione Ferni Noja Noseda in the summer of 2004 to the oasis of Fachi in Niger, where a DVD report on vertical writing on wooden tablets was made.[107] While I was preparing the above-mentioned report, I mentioned this idea of vertical writing to my friend Déroche, and he was favorably impressed because, probably at his request, his teacher Troupeau had inserted a comment on the matter in his review.[108]

Now, this process of becoming aware of the vertical writing of Arabic—first with surprise and then with naturalness—has recently made me think again of *Rhinoceros* by Ionesco. If we replace "*rhinoceros*" with "vertical writing," we seem to hear the same words of the first act:

> JEAN: Oh! a rhinoceros!
> (The noise made by the animal dies away swiftly and one can already hear the following words. The whole of this scene must be played very fast, each repeating in swift succession: Oh! a rhinoceros!)
> WAITRESS: Oh! a rhinoceros!
> GROCER'S WIFE (sticks her head out of her shop doorway): Oh! a rhinoceros! (To her husband still inside the shop): Quick, come and look; it's a rhinoceros!

CONCLUSIONS

The Arabic of the northern central region used various scripts until it felt the need to have its "own" script, just as not long afterward it felt the need to have its "own" sacred book in its "own" language, as the Koran shows.[109] How could these Arabs, who were so proud, use the scripts of others?

The parallel with the Slavic world seems impelling: every Slav (or rather "he who speaks") calls the Germans "dumb" because they do not speak Slavonic, and St. Cyril and St. Metodius created an alphabet of their own to evangelize the Slavs.

At the same time, both the attempt by the Syriac Church to spread Christianity κατά πόλεις and the rejection of this attempt must have had a massive impact: Syriac could not be adopted in toto.

The journey through time seems to emerge clearly:

1. The epigraphs in Liḥyānite and Dedanite must be regarded as one being among of many *faute de mieux* attempts.

2. The upsurge of the southern Arabian in relation to the north seems clear. Beyond Fāw it could have reached as far as Mecca. Tradition, recounted by al-Fākihī, handed down the text in the southern Arabian characters of Maqām Ibrāhīm.[110]
3. King Imru' al-Qays made use of Nabataean in the Nemara inscription because he wanted to proclaim his victory and his glory in that area at that time[111] and Nabataean was the available script. Then the Nabataean world was extinguished.
4. Finally, southern Arabian was definitely rejected, and there is no lack of rejections such as this, even in recent history, ranging from that of the Weimar Republic in Germany concerning the so-called Gothic of Imperial Germany to that of Atatürk regarding the Arabic script! One cannot rule out the possibility that there was a reaction by the emigrants toward the world from which they had come, and in fact it was mainly tribes of southern origin who were involved in the new script that was emerging. At the time, these Arabs were struck by the sight of two major systems, the Christian Church and the Empire of the King of Kings. Sassanid Iraq, where Syriac and Pahlavi were side by side, became the melting pot.
5. A self-appointed committee of sages met with the intention of creating a truly Arabic script, and with much goodwill, to provide their own people and language with a different script to that of nearby peoples. If for a moment we dare to substitute the word "script" for the word "language" in the Koranic text (XVI, 103), we hear the following verse: "The 'script' of he to whom they wickedly point to is notably foreign, while this is Arabic, pure and clear!"
6. The *ductus* was certainly that of Syriac. Starcky's observation on the upper alignment of Nabataean and the lower alignment of Syriac and of Arabic is of fundamental importance.[112] The validity of the thesis has now been confirmed by a further conclusive study, the recent one by Gérard Troupeau, which resolves the problems that no one had tackled until now arising not only from the script but also from the phonetic of the adaptation of certain letters of the Syriac alphabet to those of the emerging Arabic script.[113]
7. Faced with many letters that were the same, they noted that the Persians were modifying or had modified the characters of Pahlavi in order to record the Avesta accurately. Modification of the letters as

> implemented by the Persians seemed difficult from the graphical standpoint, and the diacritical point of Syriac for distinguishing between *r* and *d* was fundamental in prompting the big idea: It was in this way that the "diacritical points" were developed.

This process of the emergence of Arabic writing was very similar to the process used by those who returned from the Babylonian exile. Wanting to distinguish themselves from those who had remained in the Land of Israel, and not being able to make them change the script, the veterans from Babylonia invented square Hebrew, imitating, in general, the square and rectangular shapes of the cuneiform.[114]

It should be recalled that the fact that ʿAbd Allah son of Mālik al-Khuzaʿ and Yaḥyā son of Khālid the Barmekid (the teacher of Hārūn al-Rashīd) read the inscription of Hind in his monastery without difficulty would seem to demonstrate the identity of Arabic writing at the time when Islam emerged with what triumphed then, and existed over the centuries, within Islam.

Table 1: The addition of diacritical modifications to the Pahlavi script and the resulting writing of the Avesta

Pahlavi			Avesta	
𐬐	= k	→	𐬐	= k
	= ɣ	→	𐬖	= ɣ
𐬞	= p	→	𐬞	= p
	= f	→	𐬟	= f
	= β	→	𐬡	= β
𐬙	= t	→	𐬙	= t
	= t̲	→	𐬝	= t̲
𐬀	= a	→	𐬀	= a
	= ā	→	𐬁	= ā
	= x^v	→	𐬓	= x^v
	= h	→	𐬵	= h
	= x^l	→	𐬒	= x^l

*Table 2: Sassanid coins of early Islam**

1. *Recto* on the right in Pahlavi writing, from top down:
   'wbyt'l'/ Y / zyy't'n = Arabic *ʿUbaydallāh ibn Ziyād*

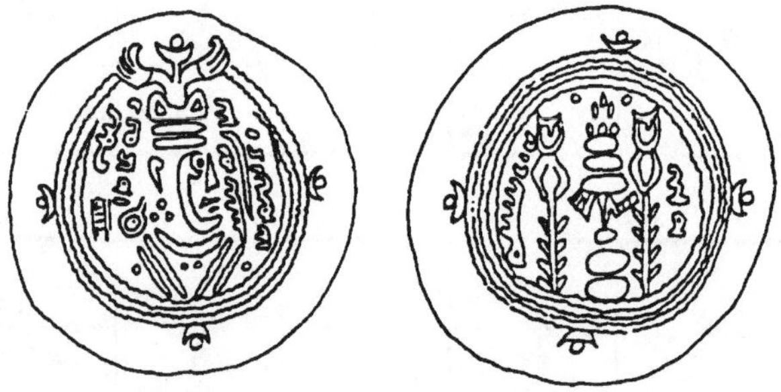

2. *Recto* on the right in Arabic characters, from top down:
   Khālid bin ʿAbbād

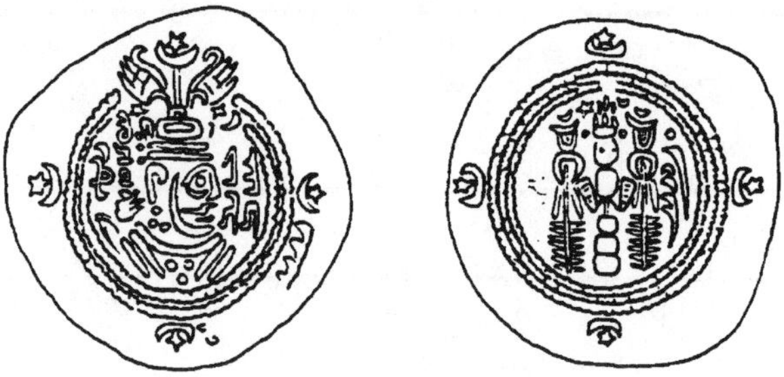

3. *Recto* on the right in Arabic characters, from top down:
   jāʾiz ('current')

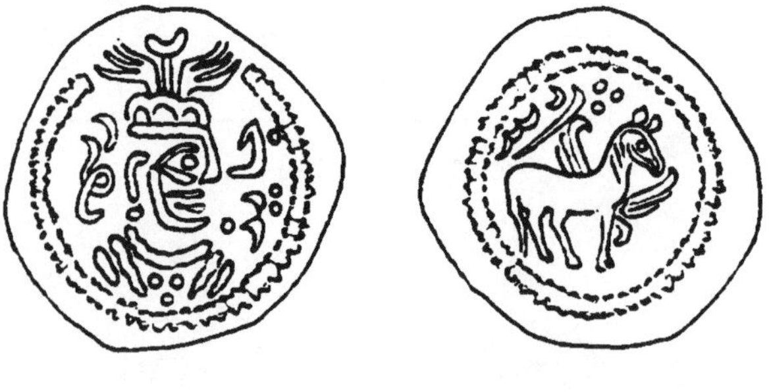

*From Rika Gyselen, *Arab-Sasanian Copper Coinage* (Wien, 2000), pp. 117–19.

NOTES

1. "Depuis une trentaine d'années, l'histoire de la formation de l'islam a connu un extraordinaire regain d'intérêt. Deux ouvrages de John Wansbrough, qui appliquent au Coran les méthodes de l'exégèse biblique, et concluent que le recueil coranique que nous connaisons s'est constitué tardivement (après 200 h.) à partir de matériaux hétérogènes, ont été le point de départ d'une réorientation radical des recherches, caractérisée par une suspicion systématique de 'l'histoire traditionelle.'" Christian Julien Robin, "La réforme de l'écriture arabe, à l'époque du califat médinois," in *IV International Conference on codicology and paleography of middle–eastern manuscripts* (Bologna, 2002).

2. Tradition has it that Zayd son of Thābit also knew Syriac, see Régis Blachère, *Introduction au Coran* (Paris, 1947), p. 31.

3. O. Houdas, *El-Bokhāri*, *Les traditions islamiques*, III (Paris, 1984), p. 522.

4. Koran XIII, 39; XLIII, 4; LII, 2–3; LVI, 78, 79; LXXX, 13–16.

5. "O ye who believe! When ye deal with each other, in transactions involving future obligations in a fixed period of time, reduce them to writing. Let a scribe write down faithfully as between the parties: let not the scribe refuse to write: as God has taught him, so let him write. Let him who incurs the liability dictate, but let him fear his Lord God, and not diminish aught of what he owes" (II, 282).

6. Daniela Amaldi, *Le Muʿallaqāt. Alle origini della poesia araba* (Venice, 1991), p. 21.

7. Luigi Serra, "I Berberi come preesistenza e persistenza indigena in Nord Africa," in *L'Africa Romana, Atti del VII Convegno di studio, Sassari, 15–17 dicembre 1989* (Sassari, 1990), pp. 309–22.

8. M. V. McDonald, "Orally Transmitted Poetry in Pre-Islamic Arabia and Other Pre-Literate Societies," *Journal of Arabic Literature* 9, pp. 15–31.

9. Charles Fossey, *Notices sur les caractères étrangers anciens et modernes rédigés par un groupe de savants et réunies par Charles Fossey* (Paris, 1948), p. 135.

10. Marcel Cohen, *La grande invention de l'écriture et son évolution*, vol. I (Paris, 1958), p. 334; Lionel Galand, "Les alphabets libyques," *Antiquités africaines*, t. 25 (1989): 69–81; Lionel Galand, "Lecture et décifrement des inscriptions sahariennes," *Sahara* 4 (1991): 53–58; Paulette Galand-Pernet, "Le poème oral et ses marges: prologues berbères," *Lalies* 6 (1988): 149–66.

11. Giorgio Raimondo Cardona, *Storia universale della scrittura* (Milan, 1986), p. 153.

12. There is a good example in the same book by Cardona in photo number 27 where the writing is vertical (see chap. 3).

13. Géza Róheim, *Animism, Magic and the Divine King* (London, 1972).

14. Plato, *Phaedrus*, V.

15. Carlo Severi, *Il percorso e la voce* (Torino, 2004).

16. Noam Chomsky, *On Nature and Language* (Cambridge, 2002); *Ideas and Ideals* (Cambridge, 2004); *Linguaggio e problemi della conoscenza* (Bologna, 1998).

17. R. A. Nicholson, *A Literary History of the Arabs* (Cambridge, 1968), pp. 79–83.

18. Arberry, *The Seven Odes* (London, New York, 1957), p. 142.

19. Ibid.

20. Ibid.

21. Lello Voce, *L'avventura dello slam (in Italia e nel mondo). Un dialogo con Marc Kelly Smith e Rayl Patzack. Con una postilla sul PJ-Set*, http://www.lellovoce.it; Henry Burt Stevens, *Poetry*, http://www.authorsden.com/henrybstevens; *3.11.2003*, *A live performance of Monte Smith*, http://www.33third.com/monte/soapbox.html; *Gotpoetry?* http://www.gotpoetry.com/FAQ/—.

22. The names of the 65 in Muḥammad Muḥṭafā Al-Aʿẓamī, *The History of the Qur'ānic Text* (Leicester, 2003), p. 68.

23. A. Guillaume, *The life of Muhammad. A Translation of Isḥāq's* Sīrat Rasūl Allah, *with Introduction and Notes* (London, 2nd ed., 1968), p. 504.

24. See note 5.

25. This meaning is certain in Ibn Saʿd, II (1), 73, "When the Prophet had the pact stipulated between him and the Meccani written (*kataba*), on the day of Ḥudaybiyyah, he said: Write . . . ."

26. Frédéric Barbier, *Histoire du livre* (Paris, 2000), p. 34.

27. Régis Blachère, *Introduction au Coran* (Paris, 1947), pp. 15, 29.

28. See note 4.

29. Inscriptions RES 3688 and RES 3689 in the Wadi Labakh. My transparency is a kind gift by Jaqueline Pirenne.

30. Philippe Pons, "L'ultimo confine," *Internazionale* 577 (February 11, 2005): 56.

31. Françoise Briquel Chatonnet, "Les manuscrits syriaques d'Antioche," *Topoi* Suppl. 5 (2004): 543–53.

32. Arberry, *The Seven Odes*, p. 116.

33. Daniela Amaldi, *Tracce consunte come graffiti su pietra* (Naples, 1999), p. 19.

34. Koran XXX, 1–3.

35. Geo Widengren, "The Establishment of the Sasanian Dynasty in the Light of New Evidence," in Accademia Nazionale Dei Lincei, *La Persia nel Medioevo* (Rome, 1971), pp. 711–84.

36. M. J. Kister, "Al-Ḥīra. Some Notes on Its Relations with Arabia," in *Studies in Jāhiliyya and Early Islam* (London, 1980), pp. 143–69.

37. Malise Ruthven and Azim Nanji, *Historical Atlas of the Islamic World*

(Oxford, 2000), p. 25; William C. Brice, *An Historical Atlas of Islam* (Leiden, 1981), T. 15, 19.

38. Janos Harmatta, "The Middle Persian—Chinese Bilingual Inscription from Hsian and the Chinese—Sāsānian Relations," in *La Persia nel Medioevo* (Rome, 1971), pp. 363–76; Paolo Daffina', "La Persia Sassanide secondo le fonti cinesi," *Rivista di Studi Orientali* 57 (1983): 121–70.

39. G. Gnoli, *Il Manicheismo* (Milan, 2003), vol. 1, p. XXI.

40. Gherardo Gnoli, "Babylonian Influences on Iran," in *Encyclopaedia Iranica*, http://www.iranica.com/articlenavigation/search/, *Politica religiosa e concezione della regalità sotto gli Achemenidi in Gururājamañjarika* (Naples, 1974), vol. 1, pp. 23–88.

41. Geoffrey Khan, "Arabic Documents from Early Islamic Khurasan, Islamic Documents," in *From Andalusia to Khurasan* (2007).

42. Tabarī, *The History of al-Ṭabarī*, vol. V (New York), p. 354; Masʿudi, *Les Prairies d'or*, vol. II (Paris, 1965), p. 404; R. A. Nicholson, *A Literary History* (Cambridge, 1968), p. 48.

43. Irfan Shahid, *Byzantium and the Arabs in the Sixth Century* (Dumbarton Oaks, 1995), p. 280.

44. Ibid.

45. Ibid., p. 281.

46. Antonio Panaino, "Greci e Iranici: confronto e conflitti," in *I Greci. Storia, Cultura, Arte, Società*, vol. 3: *I Greci oltre la Grecia*, ed. Salvatore Settis (Torino, 2001), p. 135.

47. Christian Julien Robin, *La réforme de l'écriture arabe*. Ta. 2.

48. Ibid., Ta. 3.

49. Shahid, *Byzantium and the Arabs in the Sixth Century*, p. 481, the Arabic text in YĀQŪT, *Muʿjam al-buldān*, II (Beirut, 1999), p. 5164. A popularization (freehand drawing) in Christian Julien Robin, "Monde arabe. Une écriture réformée à l'aube de l'Islam," in *Science et vie, Comment est née l'écriture* (Paris, 2004), p. 113.

50. What follows is taken from Leone Caetani, *Annali dell'Islam,* vol. II, tomo I (Milan, 1907), p. 692ff., where there are all the references to the Arab sources.

51. Ukaydir son of ʿAbd al-Malik.

52. With al-Ṣahyā daughter of Ḥarb, sister of Sufyān son of Ḥarb.

53. Son of ʿAbd Shams.

54. In turn son of Zuhrah.

55. Ghaylan son of Salamah of the Thaqīf.

56. In turn son of ʿUdas.

57. Leone Caetani and Giuseppe Gabrieli, *Onomasticon arabicum*, vol. 1, p. 76.

58. Carolus de Boor, *Theophanis Chronografia*, II (Hildesheim, 1980), p. 584.

59. David Cohen, *Dictionnaire des racines sémitiques ou attestées dans les langues sémitiques*. Louvain, sub BSR, 1.

60. J. Payne Smith, *A Compendious Syriac Dictionary* (Oxford, 1903), sub SBR.

61. Wolf Leslau, *Comparative Dictionary of Geʿez* (Wiesbaden, 1987).

62. Werner Caskel, *Ǧamharat an-nasab, das genealogische Werk des Hišām ibn Muḥammad al-Kalbī* (Leiden, 1966), vol. 2, p. 226.

63. Ibid., pp. 226–28.

64. William C. Brice, *An Historical Atlas of Islam* (Leiden, 1981), where "Anbar" is written on pp. 15 and 22, but "Ambar" on p. 19.

65. Henrik Samuel Nyberg, *A Manual of Pahlavi* (Wiesbaden, 1974).

66. Marcel Cohen, *La grande invention de l'écriture*, p. 166.

67. Antonio Panaino, "Philologia Avestica V, The Origin of Avestan Letters ý and v," *Münchener Studien zur Sprachwissenschaft* 57 (1997): 81–96.

68. K. Hoffmann, Zum Zeicheninventar der Avesta-Schrift, in W. Eilers (Hrsg.), *Festgabe deutscher Iranisten zur 2500 Jahrfeier Irans. Stoccarda 1971*, pp. 64–73 (also in K. Hoffmann, *Aufsätze zur Indoiranistik*. Bd. 1 [Wiesbaden, 1975], pp. 316–25); J. Kellens, "Avestique" in R. Schmitt, *Compendium Linguarum Iranicarum* (Wiesbaden, 1989), pp. 32–55; W. Sundermann, *"Partisch,"* ibid., pp. 114–37; W. Sundermann, *"Mittelpersisch,"* ibid., pp. 137–64.

69. Taken from R. Hoffmann, "Avestan language, i, The Avestan script," in *Encyclopaedia Iranica*, available at http://www.iranica.com/articlenavigation/search/.

70. Philippe Gignoux, "Glossaire des inscriptions pehlevies et parthes," in *Corp. Inscr. Iran., Suppl. Ser. I* (London, 1972), p. 14.

71. Ugo Monneret de Villard, *Introduzione allo studio dell'archeologia islamica, le origini ed il periodo omayade* (Venezia, 1968), p. 250.

72. The Sassanian Empire was a meeting point of religions and cultures. Although the official religion of the ruling dynasty was Zoroastrianism, Judaeo-Christian sects and Semitic pagan cults jostled with each other in splendid confusion in Mesopotamia. To these was added a strong Jewish presence in Babylonia and Adiabene. It had been established since the first century. The victories of Shāpūr I brought large numbers of captive Romans to residence in the Sassanian Empire and many of them were Greek-speaking Christians from conquered cities like Antioch. Furthermore, Buddhism had also exerted considerable influence on the cultural and religious life of eastern Iran, especially areas conquered by the Sassanians from the Kushan Empire. It was as a "Buddha" that Mani was received by the shah of Tūrān. S. N. C. Lieu, *Manichaeism in Mesopotamia and the Roman East* (Leiden, 1999), p. 25.

73. Bayard Dodge, *The Fihrist of al-Nadīm*, vol. 1, p. 24.

74. Alessandro Bausani, "La scrittura pahlavica frutto di bilinguismo aramaico-iranico?" in *Vicino Oriente, III, 1980* (Rome, 1980), pp. 269–76.

75. Jutta Meischner and Eleonora Cussini, "Vier palmyrenische Grabreliefs im Museum von Antakya," in *Archäologischer Anzeiger* 2 (Halbband, 2003), pp. 97–105.

76. Fabrizio A. Pennacchietti, "Iscrizioni aramaiche hatrene su un sostegno fittile," *Mesopotamia* 33 (1998): 286.

77. Marco Moriggi, *La lingua delle coppe magiche siriache* (Florence, 2004), pp. 68–69.

78. A. Klugkist, "The Origin of the Mandaic Script," in AA.VV. *Scripta signa vocis* (Groningen, 1986), pp. 111–19.

79. Christian Julien Robin, *La réforme de l'écriture arabe*, fig. 14.

80. Marco Moriggi, *La Lingua delle*, pp. 1–34.

81. There is a modern example in Martin Kuckenburg, *Wer sprach das erste Wort?* (Stuttgart, 2004), p. 119.

82. D. E. Ibarra-Grasso, "La escrittura indigena andina," *Annali Lateranensi* 12 (1948): 9–124.

83. Charles Fossey, *Notices*, p. 136.

84. Sergio Angelo Picchioni, "La direzione della scrittura cuneiforme e gli archivi di Tell Mardikh Ebla," *Orientalia* 49, no. 3 (1980): 234.

85. Ibid.

86. Ibid., p. 249.

87. Pierfrancesco Callieri, "Il rilievo palmireno di BTMLKW e ḤYRN nel Museo Nazionale di Arte Orientale di Roma," *Arte Orientale in Italia* 6 (1980): 5–18; Eleonora Cussini, "Two Palmyrene Aramaic Inscriptions in American Collections," *Syria* 69, nos. 3–4 (1992): 423–29.

88. Marcel Cohen, *La grande invention* (see note 10) plate 42.

89. Paul Pelliot, *L'inscription nestorienne de Si-ngan-fou* (Kyoto, 1996).

90. Françoise Briquel Chatonnet, "La mise en page dans les manuscrits Syriaques d'après les plus anciens manuscrits," *Manuscripta Orientalia* 9, no. 4, p. 3.

91. W. B. Henning, "Mitteliranisch," in *Handbuch der Orientalistik*, Erste Abteilung, Vierter Band: Iranistik, Erster Abschnit: Linguistik (Leiden, 1958), p. 48; *Il Medioiranico* (Naples, 1996), p. 35.

92. Gustav Flügel, *Kitāb al-Fihrist mit Anmerkungen hereausgegeben*, published with Anmerkungen (Leipzig, 1872), p. 6.

93. A. Silvestre de Sacy, "Mémoire sur l'origine et les anciens monuments de la litterature parmi les Arabes," *Mémoires de la littérature tirés des registres de l'Académie royale des inscriptions et belles lettres* 50 (1808): 253–54, 297; now also in F. Déroche and S. Noja Noseda, *Sources de la transmission manuscrite du texte coranique, I, Les manuscrits de style ḥiǧāzī*, vol. 1 (Lesa, 1998), pp. XXVII–XCII, with the scientific transcription of the words and of the Arab names.

94. Nabia Abbott, *The Rise of the North Arabic Script and Its Qur'ānic Development* (Chicago, 1939).

95. Bayard Dodge, *The Fihrist*, vol. I, p. 10.

96. François Déroche, "Les manuscrits du Coran en caractères Ḥigāzī," in *Quinterni 1* (Lesa, 1996); F. Déroche and S. Noja Noseda, *Sources de la transmission manuscrite du texte coranique, I, Le manuscrits de style ḥiǧāzī*, 1 (Lesa, 1998), p. XVI.

97. See note 76.

98. Sergio Noja Noseda, "La mia visita a Sanaa e il Corano palinsesto," Istituto Lombardo Accademia di Scienze e Lettere: *Rendiconti, Classe di lettere e Scienze Morali e Storiche* 137, no. 1 (2003): 43–60.

99. Rika Gyselen, *Arab-Sasanian Copper Coinage* (Vienna, 2000).

100. Ariel Berman, *Islamic Coins* (Jerusalem, 1976), p. 19; David Diringer, *L'alfabeto nella storia della civiltà* (Florence, 1969), table LIII.

101. See note 88.

102. Marcel Cohen, *Études d'Éthiopien Méridional* (Paris, 1931), p. 330.

103. Marcel Cohen "Communication," *Comptes rendus du Groupe linguistique d'études chamito-sémitiques (GLECS)* 5 (1951): 98.

104. Gérard Troupeau, "Sur l'écriture verticale," *Comptes rendus du Groupe linguistique d'études chamito-sémitiques (GLECS)* 7 (1954–1957): 6–8.

105. Donovan Webster and George Steinmetz, "Journey to the Heart of the Sahara," *National Geographic Magazine* 195, no. 3 (March 1999): 2–33.

106. See note 88.

107. Roberto and Cecilia Baratelli, "Viaggio all' oasi di Fachi," in *Quinterni 2* (Lesa, 2004).

108. G. Troupeau, review of François Déroche, "Manuel de codicologie des manuscrits en écriture arabe," *Arabica* 49, no. 1 (2002): 123–24.

109. Koran XVI, 103; XLI, 44.—Efim A. Rezvan, *Koran i ego mir* (St. Petersburg, 2001), Q.2, G.1, s. 171; Robert G. Hoyland, *Arabia and the Arabs* (London, 2003), p. 229; Jan Retsö, *The Arabs in Antiquity* (London, 2003), p. 24.

110. M. J. Kister, "Maqām Ibrāhīm, a Stone with Inscription," *Le Museon* 84, pp. 477–91.

111. Christian Julien Robin, "Linteu inscrit: AO 4083," in *Arabie heureuse, Arabie déserte* (Paris, 1997), pp. 265–69.

112. J. Starcky, "Pétra et la Nabatène," in *Supplément au Dictionnaire de la Bible* (Paris, 1964), col. 886–1017.

113. Gérard Troupeau, "Écriture et phonétique arabes," in *Mélanges David Cohen* (Paris, 2003), pp. 707–10.

114. Sergio Noja Noseda, "L'assunzione di forme quadrate nella scrittura aramaica e il proto-arabo," *Istituto Lombardo, Rend. Lett.* 125 (1991): 269–75.

8

EARLY EVIDENCES OF VARIANT READINGS IN QUR'ĀNIC MANUSCRIPTS

Alba Fedeli

I have seen a number of Qur'ānic manuscripts, which the transcribers recorded as manuscripts of Ibn Mas'ūd. No two of the Qur'ānic copies were in agreement and most of them were on badly effaced parchment. I also saw a Qur'ānic manuscript transcribed about two hundred years ago which included the opening of the Book.

Al-Nadīm[1]

THE ABSENCE AND THE BLINDNESS

In 1895, during her third journey in Egypt,[2] Mrs. Agnes Smith Lewis bought a manuscript from a commercial antiquary in Suez.[3]

It was a palimpsest. In the *scriptio superior* she could read a few Homilies of early Christian Fathers, written in Arabic, while the material recycled by the scribe came from different manuscripts. The scribe who wrote the Homilies on the effaced parchment put various leaves together: eighty-four leaves in Syriac, forty-four leaves in Arabic, and one leaf in Greek.[4]

The *scriptio inferior* of these leaves in Arabic contains part of the Qur'ānic text—there were twenty-three leaves in vertical format, and they were rewritten perpendicularly to the older script. The former leaves were assembled in new quires of a smaller size: they were folded in half and some of them were cut out (e.g., 152a–149b). Mrs. Lewis cut—with a natural reluctance, she admitted—the binding cords which held the book together and smoothed out the pages to read the text of the *scriptio inferior* of the palimpsest.

After 1902, the year of the publication of *Studia Sinaitica*, XI, *Apocrypha Syriaca: The Protevangelium Jacobi and transitus Mariae*, with texts from the Septuagint, the Coran, the Peshitta, and from a Syriac hymn in a Syro-Arabic palimpsest of the fifth and other centuries, and with an appendix of Palestinian Syriac texts from the Taylor-Schechter collection,[5] Mrs. Lewis entrusted the manuscript into the hands of expert binders, Messrs. Eyre and Spottiswoode, who restored the leaves.[6]

In 1913 Mrs. Lewis met Alphonse Mingana in Cambridge and showed him her book, *Apocrypha Syriaca*, and the manuscript, which was her own property. The parchment was reexamined and the transcription of the Qur'ānic text was edited in its entirety, with an introduction and a list of its variants.[7]

Soon afterward in 1914, the manuscript was sent to an international exhibition of books and manuscripts at Leipzig, but at the outbreak of the European War it disappeared. It was subsequently traced by Dr. Oman, of Westminster College in Cambridge, aided by Professor Huene, of Tübingen, and finally in 1936[8] (April 20) the manuscript was returned to the University Library of Cambridge,[9] in accordance with the will of Agnes Lewis,[10] who had been dead for ten years.

One year later, in 1937, Arthur Jeffery deflated the importance that Lewis and Mingana attached to the manuscripts.[11] After great expectations, the scholars met with disappointment. Moreover, the relentless[12]—and sometimes justifiable[13]—criticism of Blachère shattered Lewis and Mingana's hypothesis, and the value of the palimpsest was, at the same time, destroyed. Since then—though Blachère was invited to study the manuscript again[14]—no one has written any more about the leaves. Far from being extraordinarily important, as Mingana and Lewis thought,[15] at the beginning of the last century these leaves were at least the only extant evidence of variant readings of the Qur'ānic text.

Now, one century later, a Muslim scholar tore the study "Leaves from three ancient Qurâns" to shreds;[16] nevertheless, sometimes his words are unfounded as Mingana's words.[17] An inexplicable omission ensued as a consequence. The article of Mingana and Lewis was criticized, but at the same time the manuscript was forgotten.

In 1937, Arthur Jeffery attempted an assembly of all the material that had survived from the "rival texts"—that is, rivals for the standard text of ʿUthmān. In his *Materials*,[18] Jeffery collected a list of the Qurʾānic variants,[19] such as those survived from Ibn Masʿūd, but his collection of variants "is void from the start because none of his references even cites a *Muṣḥaf* of Ibn Masʿūd."[20] The materials are only quotations, a reconstruction derived from the literature on the readings, because of the absence—at the beginning of the twentieth century—of a written manuscripts' tradition of the Qurʾānic text dated from the first years of Islam.

The scholar himself, when speaking about the quotations of the older variants, said: "This in the absence of any direct manuscript evidence gives us our sole witness to the types of text which ʿUthmān's standard text superseded."[21]

Ten years later, in 1947, in his *Introduction to the Qurʾān*, Régis Blachère complained about the lack of the materials available to him for a critical edition of the Qurʾān, and he wished for a joint effort, "une collaboration internationale, une mise en commun de toutes les ressources en manuscrits existant dans le monde."[22] Therefore, it seems to be illogical to complain about the absence of evidence of variant readings and at the same time to be blind in front of a witness for a critical edition of the Qurʾān, the ignored manuscripts of Lewis and Mingana.[23]

THE EVIDENCE OF VARIANT RADINGS IN QUR'ĀNIC MANUSCRIPTS

Evidence in Bonhams' Palimpsest

When I started working on the "Amari Project,"[24] aimed at the publication of the early Qurʾānic manuscripts,[25] I could not even imagine that I would see two leaves that could have delighted Jeffery and Blachère and anyone who was looking for the former text, *al-ḥarf al-ʾawwal*.[26]

It was possible to study these two leaves thanks to the kindness of the antiquarian Sam Fogg and the Bonhams auction house,[27] and to the stubbornness of Professor Noja Noseda who got their photographs.[28] Currently, the reproduction of "an important early Qur'ān leaf in Hijazi script. Western Arabia, probably Medina, early to mid-1st century AH" is in Catalogue 27 of Sam Fogg, "Islamic Calligraphy,"[29] but it is not possible to trace the present whereabouts of Bonhams' palimpsest.[30]

Bonhams' fragment is a palimpsest in Ḥijāzī script on parchment. The *scriptio superior* consists of twenty-four verses from the sūra *al-Nisā'*: from the word *naṣībahum* (Q 4:33) to the word *kafarū* (Q 4:56). The *scriptio inferior* consists of part of the sūra *al-mā'idah*, from the word *yuṭahhira* (Q 5:41) to the word *yujāhidūna* (Q 5:54).

The text of the *scriptio inferior* is different from the standard text of ʿUthmān. The variant readings of the Qur'ānic text, through the direct manuscript evidence and not by quotations, are listed below.

A Different Sequence of Words

Q 5:41, at the beginning of line 2 on the recto, it is possible to read Tā' marbūṭah and assume *fī l-'ākhirati* before *lahum*: *wa-fī l-'ākhirati lahum ʿadhābun ʿaẓīmun*, rather than *wa-lahum fī l-'ākhirati ʿadhābun ʿaẓīmun*, which is the standard reading.

Q 5:48, *li-kullin minhum jaʿalnā shirʿatan*, whereas the rest reads *li-kullin jaʿalnā minkum shirʿatan*.

Q 5:50, *wa-man* [*'aḥsanu ḥukm*]*an min allahi*, instead of the standard *wa-man 'aḥsanu min allahi ḥukman*.

Omissions

It is possible to note also the omission of certain words or whole phrases:

Q 5:42, *fa-'in jā'ūka* is missing. The words *fa-'in jā'ūka* are present in the standard reading, but they are missing in the *scriptio inferior* of the palimpsest (fig. 1).

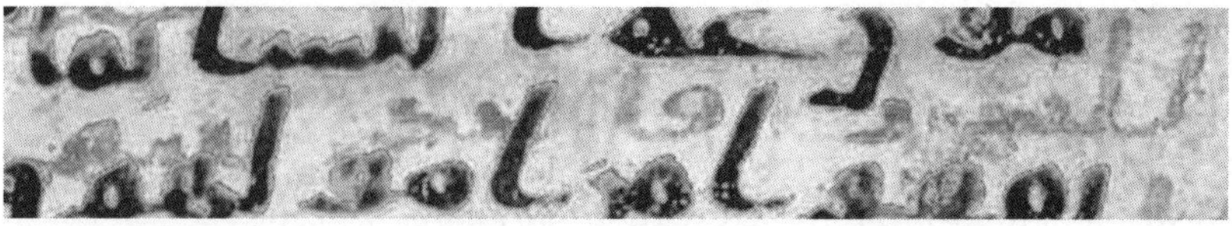

Fig.1: *Islamic and Indian Works of Art: Auction of October 11, 2000*, lot 13, recto l. 3 © Bonhams.

Q 5:42, *ʿanhum* is missing: the leaf shows *ʾaw ʾaʿriḍ* instead of the standard *ʾaw ʾaʿriḍ ʿanhum.*

Q 5:49, *fa-ʾannamā*, as opposed to *fa-ʿlam ʾannamā* of the standard reading.

Different Words

Through our comparison, it should be noted that there are different words:

Q 5:42, *yasmaʿūna*, as opposed to *sammāʿūna*, which is the reading of the others. In the same verse we can find *lā* instead of the standard *lan* for the negative sentence *fa-lan yaḍurrūka*.

Q 5:43, we come across *fa-mā* with a Fāʾ and not with a Wāw—that is *wa-mā*, as in the standard text.

Q 5:44, we read *wa-ʾanzalnā*, as opposed to *ʾinnā ʾanzalnā.*

Q 5:44, from line 7 to 11, on the recto, is the most different from the standard text.

The variant opposed to *al-tawrāta* is unreadable; *ʾalladhīna ʾas*[*lamū*] *wa-ʾalladhīna hādū* is opposed to *ʾalladhīna ʾaslamū li-lladhīna hādū*; the sentence *yaḥkumūna bi-mā nazala allahu fī-hā* is added, *wa-ʾillā bi-mā* is opposite to *bi-mā*.

The standard text is: *ʾinnā ʾanzalnā al-tawrāta fī-hā hudan wa-nūrun yaḥkumu bi-hā al-nabiyyūna ʾalladhīna ʾaslamū li-lladhīna hādū wa-l-rabbāniyyūna wa-l-ʾaḥbāru bi-mā ʾstuḥfiẓū min kitābi allahi,*

"It was We who revealed / The Law (to Moses): therein / Was guidance and light. /

By its standard have been judged / The Jews, by the Prophets / Who bowed (as in Islam) / To God's will by the Rabbis / And the Doctors of Law: /

For to them was entrusted / The protection of God's Book,"

whereas in the palimpsest the text is:

line 7. *wa-ʾanzalnā al-m* [. . .]

line 8. *fī-hā nūrun wa-hud*[*an . . .*]*kumu bi-hā ʾillā shayʾan ʾalladhīna ʾas*[*lamū*]

line 9. *ʾwa-ʾalladhīna hādū yaḥkumūna bi-mā nazala allahu fī-hā*

line 10. *yaḥkumu bi-hā al-* [. .] *ūna wa-ʾillā bi-mā ʾstuḥfiẓū min kitābi ʾa*

line 11. *llahi.*

Q 5:54, the future tense is introduced by *sa-*; that is, *sa-yaʾtī* instead of *fa-sawfa yaʾtī* which is the reading of the others.

Furthermore, we get a singular form instead of a plural one—and the other way around; the second person plural instead of the third person singular; the personal pronouns *hum* instead of the substantive *al-nās*, which we can read in the ʿUthmānic text. Therefore, in Q 5:44 we read *fa-lā takhshawū-hum* as opposite to *fa-lā takhshawū al-nāsa.*

Q 5:45 (fig. 2) we can read *ʿalā banī ʾisrāʾīl* as opposed to the standard text *ʿalayhim*. The end of line 13, on the recto, is an unreadable lacuna, but it should be supposed that it was *wa-ʾanzala allahu:* [*wa-ʾanzala allahu*] *ʿalā banī ʾisrāʾīl*, which is the same reading of ʾUbayy b. Kaʿb,[31] rather than *wa-katabnā ʿalayhim*, which is the reading of the others.

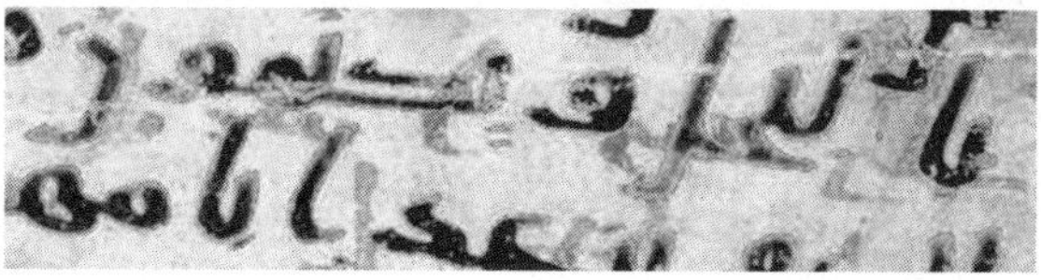

Fig. 2: *Islamic and Indian Works of Art: Auction of October 11, 2000*, lot 13, recto l. 14 © Bonhams

Q 5:46, we can read *li-qawmin yū*[*q*]*inūna* (like the end of Q 5:50 "For a people whose faith / is assured") or *li-qawmin yuʾ*[*m*]*inūna*, whereas the standard text is *li-l-muttaqīna*, "to those who fear God."[32]

Q 5:54, whereas the standard text is *ʾaʿizzatin ʿalā al-kāfirīna*, the manuscript is damaged, but before the preposition *ʿalā* we can see three vertical strokes, whereas in the word *ʾaʿizzatin* (Alif, ʿAyn, Zāʾ, Tāʾ marbūṭah) there is only one stroke.[33]

Orthographical Variants

Another type of variants is the orthography of the words.[34]

a) Sometimes, the long vowel *ā* is not written with an Alif (*scriptio defectiva*).[35]

Fig. 3: Ms. or. fol. 4313, Preussische. Staatsbibliothek, Berlin

b) The long vowel *ā* is written with a Yāʾ in the middle of the word, such as in (Q 5:44) *bi-ʾāyātī*, namely, by the letters Bāʾ, Alif, Yāʾ, Tāʾ, that is, three teeth after the Alif: The first tooth is the usual semi-vowel Yā', whereas the second one stands for the long *ā*; the third one is for the Tā', then final Yā'—instead of the standard text, with one Yā', only (fig. 3)

The same spelling (with *a* Yā' for long *ā*) is found in the same part of the sūra *al-Mā'idah* in the Qur'ānic fragment[36] of the Berlin Library, (fig. 4).[37] These orthographic features can help to date the manuscripts.

Fig. 4: Islamic and Indian Works of Art: auction October 11, 2000, lot 13, recto l. 12. © Bonhams

c) The orthography of the article: *bi-l-'anfi* in Q 5:45 is written without the Alif of the article, whereas the standard is *bi-(')l-'anfi* with an Alif.[38]
d) In Q 5:48, the preposition *'an* is in the separate form, *'an-mā* whereas the standard text has *'ammā.* In the same verse it should be noted *fī-mā* whereas the others read the separate form *fī mā.*

To sum up, apart from the orthographic variants, the variant readings in Bonhams are about thirty, where the Tradition reports only one of them: Q 5:45, *'alā banī 'isrā'īl,* which is in part the same reading of 'Ubayy b. Ka'b.

EVIDENCE IN FOGG'S PALIMPSEST

The Relation between the Texts

The *scriptio superior* of the palimpsest consists of ten verses from the sūra *al-Baqarah,* from verse 277 to verse 286. The *scriptio inferior* keeps part of the same sūra, from verse 206 to verse 223. The text of *scriptio inferior* is different from the standard text, but sometimes the *lectiones* are simply conjectured readings, because the variants are more thoroughly erased than the rest of the *scriptio inferior* and the text is unreadable, but we can read the corrections added by another copyist with a different ink (fig. 5).

Fig. 5: *Catalogue 27, Islamic Calligraphy,* no. 1 © Sam Fogg

Such as in Bonhams' fragment, the parchment hands down the old marks of different words,[39] added expressions, and omitted words (fig. 6).

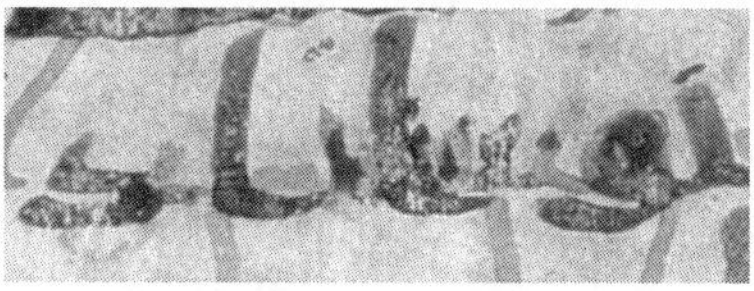

Fig. 6: *Catalogue 27, Islamic Calligraphy*, no. 1 © Sam Fogg

Variants

Apart from the orthographic variants, the *lectiones* are about fifteen, where the Tradition reports only two of them, namely, Q 2:217 and Q 2:222.

In Q 2:217, the standard text is [*yas'alū*]*naka 'an al-*[*sha*]*hri al-ḥarāmi qitālin fī-hi*, whereas in the palimpsest the text is *yas'alūnaka 'an al-shahri al-ḥarāmi wa-'an qitālin fī-hi*, like the *qirā'ah* of Ibn Mas'ūd, al-Rabī', Ibn 'Abbās, al-A'mash, and 'Ikrima: *yas'alūnaka 'an al-shahri al-ḥarāmi 'an qitālin fī-hi*.[40]

In Q 2:222, instead of the standard *fa-'tazilū al-nisā'a fī l-maḥīḍi wa-lā-taqrabūhunna ḥattā yaṭhurna*, "So keep away from women / In their courses, and do not / Approach them until / They are clean," it is possible to read (fig. 7) (*lā-taqra)bū al-nisā'a fī maḥīḍihinna hattā yataṭahharna*, which is the same reading that the Tradition traces back to Ibn Mas'ūd,[41] without *wa-'tazilū-hunna*.

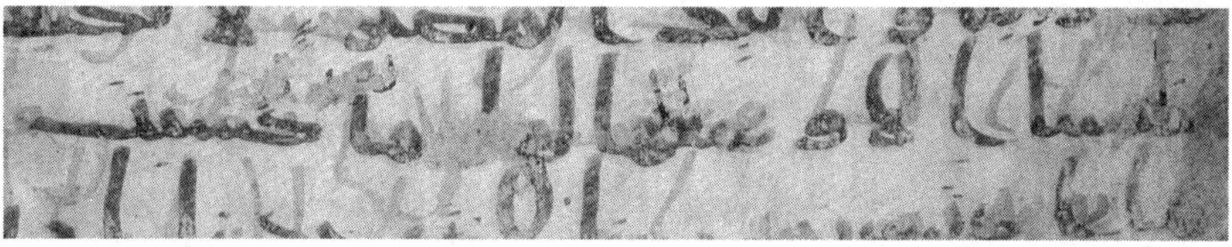

Fig. 7: *Catalogue 27, Islamic Calligraphy*, no. 1 © Sam Fogg

The variant was later corrected according to the standard reading. The end of line 19, on the verso, is an unreadable lacuna, whereas at the beginning of line 20 the writing kept a vertical stroke added as continuation to the Bā' (fig. 7): Bā', Wāw, and Alif—the final part of *taqrabū*—become Lām, Wāw, and Alif—the final part of *fa-'tazilū*. The article *al-* was added later to *maḥīḍi* and the final pronoun *hunna* was rubbed out. Before *hattā*, the sentence *wa-lā-taqrabūhunna* was amended such, as in the standard text (see table 1).

Table 1: Q 2:222, Fogg, verso, line 20

Reading of Ibn Mas'ūd	يتطهرن	حتى	واعتزلوهن	محيضهن		فى	النساء	تقربوا		ولا
	⇩			⇩				⇩		
Pal. Fogg, *scriptio secunda*	يتطهرن	حتى		محيضهن		فى	النسا	بوا	-	-
Pal. Fogg, *scriptio prima*			ولا تقربوهن	محيض	الـ			لوا		
			⇧		⇧			⇧		
Standard Text	يطهرن	حتى	ولا تقربوهن	المحيض		فى	النسا	فاعتزلوا		

The *scriptio prima* of the Fogg palimpsest was scrapped . . . out or adjusted in favour of the "correction" according to the so-called text of 'Uthmān, which has now become the "standard text" since 1924, but the original wording of it corresponds well with the Reading of Ibn Mas'ūd, except for his واعتزلوهن .

Error and Corrections[42]

The written transmission of texts necessarily implies mistakes, if nothing else, due to errant human nature. In the knowledge transmission of the ḥadīth-literature, for example, we can notice that a standard typology of manuscript corrections took shape early.

Certainly as to what concerns the Qur'ān, because it was a Holy Book, whose careful copying would attract many blessings for the believer, copies made of its *textus receptus*—that is, the 'Uthmānic text—largely excluded the possibility of corruption.[43]

However, human mistakes are unavoidable, and this also applies to a scribe's hand,[44] even if he is writing a copy of Qur'ānic text. Mistakes, and above all their corrections, are very common, even in the Qur'ānic text,[45] as it appears in some of the most ancient manuscripts.[46]

There are two kinds of corrections added to the text. On one hand, we can find corrections due to different variants with textual significance, be they canonical readings or noncanonical variants.[47] On the other hand, corrections can be related to copyists' mistakes, be they due to the orthography of the Arabic writing and its reform[48] or to corrections to a perhaps minor kind of mistake—a scribe's *lapsus calami*.[49]

A classical example of corrections due to the orthographic reform is the tendency to spell a long *ā* with an Alif as a *mater lectionis*.[50]

The tradition of the two thousand Alifs added by the governor of Iraq, ʿUbaydallāh ibn Ziyād, is reported by Ibn Abī Dāwūd in his *Kitāb al-Maṣāḥif*.[51] Even if two thousand letters are a remarkable quantity,[52] the added Alifs present in the manuscripts are indeed a great number. We can find them in the "Qurʾān of ʿUthmān," kept in the Institute of Oriental Studies, Russian Academy of Sciences,[53] where missing Alifs were added in red ink during the first stage of the text's revision.[54] In the papyrus of Leiden[55] there seems to be a particular mix-up to correct the lack of the Alifs.[56]

These early manuscripts are full of corrections,[57] not only added words, but also rubbed-out words. An amusing example is in the manuscript of the Staatsbibliothek zu Berlin, where we can read *qālū* (Q 5:14) without an Alif, in *scriptio defectiva*, and few lines below, on the same leaf[58] (3b), we can read *qālū* (Q 5:17) with an Alif, in *scriptio plena*.[59] But the first *qālū* was corrected and an Alif was added (fig. 8), while the second *qālū* too was corrected and the Alif was rubbed out (fig. 9).[60] This is a sign of a complete lack of a standard rule.[61]

Fig. 8: Ms. or. fol. 4313, Preussische Staatsbibliothek, Berlin, f. 3 verso, l. 7

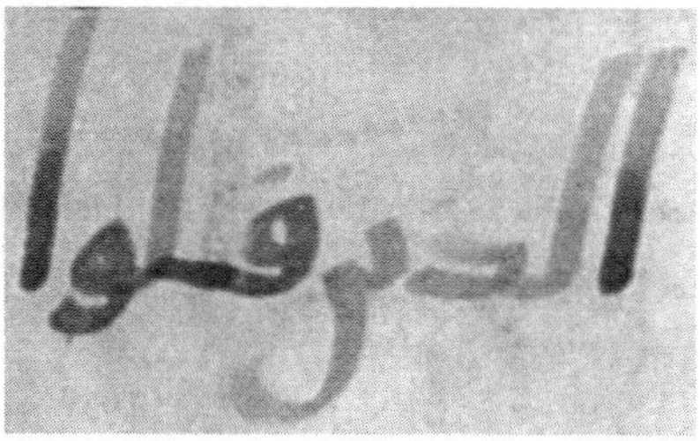

Fig. 9: Ms. or. fol. 4313, Preussische Staatsbibliothek, Berlin, f. 3 verso, l. 13

In the fragments collected in volume 5, I of the *Sources de la transmission manuscrite du texte coranique* of the Amari Project, I have come across corrections in the parchment kept in the Oriental Institute of the University of Chicago (A. 6959),[62] as on the verso, line 4, the Alif al-wiqāyah in *sh r k w ʾ* (Q 68:41)[63] was added later. A whole part of a verse (Q 10:109) is added in black ink at the end of the sūra in the parchment kept in the Biblioteca Apostolica Vaticana.[64]

In the manuscript of Berlin there are some missing words added later, such as *li-llahi* (Q 4:139) in line 3, fol. 1a; *'ilay-hi* (Q 4:175) in line 7, fol. 2a; *dhālikum fisqun al-yawma ya'isa 'alladhīna* (Q 5:3) in lines 6–7, fol. 2b (fig. 10); *'illā 'alladhīna* (Q 5:34) in line 13, fol. 4b; *allahu ('ilay-ka)*[65] (Q 5:49) in line 18, fol. 5b; *min-hum yusāri'ūna* (Q 5:62) in line 6, fol. 6a.[66]

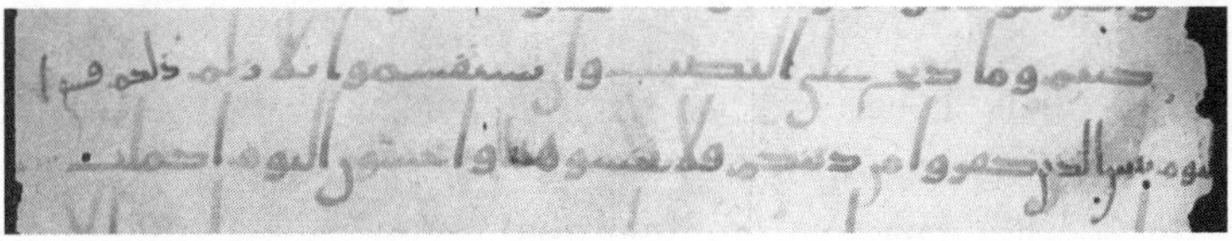

Fig. 10: Ms. or. fol. 4313, Preuβische Staatsbibliothek, Berlin

In the same manuscript, some letters are rubbed out or added: in *yurā'ūna* (Q 4:142; fol. 1a, l. 12) an original Yā' as a bearer of the *hamza* was later rubbed out; in *suwā'in* (Q 4:149; fol. 1b, l. 5) the Alif was rubbed out; in *'ūtū* (Q 5:5; fol. 2b, l. 14) the Alif al-wiqāyah was added; in *w sh h [d] w '* (Q 5:8; fol. 3a, l. 9–10) the first Wāw and the second one were rubbed out and the word was corrected as in the standard text *shuhadā'a*; in *ṣirāṭin* (Q 5:16; fol. 3b, l. 13) the Yā' to spell the long *ā*[67] was later erased; in *al-ghurābi* (Q 5:31; fol. 4b, l. 5) the Alif was later added; in *jazā'ū* (Q 5:33; fol. 4b, l. 10) the final Wāw-Alif was added; in *maghlūlatun* (Q 5:64; fol. 6a, l. 9) the final Lām and Tā' marbūṭah were later corrected; in *yā-banī* (Q 5:72; fol. 7a, l. 10) the first Yā' was later added; in *wa-rabbī* (Q 5:72; fol. 7a, l. 11) the Wāw was rubbed out and the word was corrected as in the standard text *rabbī*; in *yaqūlū* (Q 5:73; fol. 7a, l. 14) the Alif al-wiqāyah was rubbed out and a Nūn was added, so the word was corrected as in the standard text *yaqūlūna*.[68]

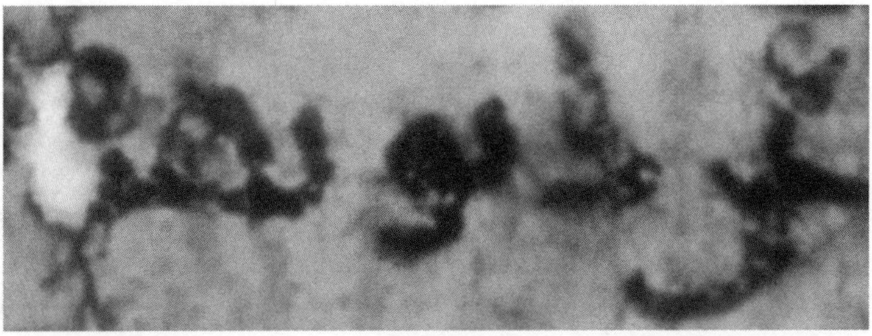

Fig. 11: A. Perg. 2, Österreichische Nationalbibliothek, verso, l. 8

THE ERROR: UNINTENTIONAL AND DELIBERATE

The aim of this paper is to try to deepen the analysis of the constitution and writing of Qurʾānic text, rather than to analyze the meaning of the variant *lectiones*. The Tradition reports some of the variant readings—only a small number—that we can see in these two palimpsest leaves. It is extremely important to find those variants in a manuscript and not just in later quotations. Some of these variants are of no importance, such as the order of words, some of them are omissions, other are additions or "explanatory glosses on the ʿUthmanic text, an expansion,"[69] and sometimes these variants are synonyms.[70] The Tradition reports that "in the early days many of the Companions made for themselves copies of the Qurʾān in which they inserted for their own private edification many explanatory additions, synonyms for words that they did not fully understand, and such like annotations."[71]

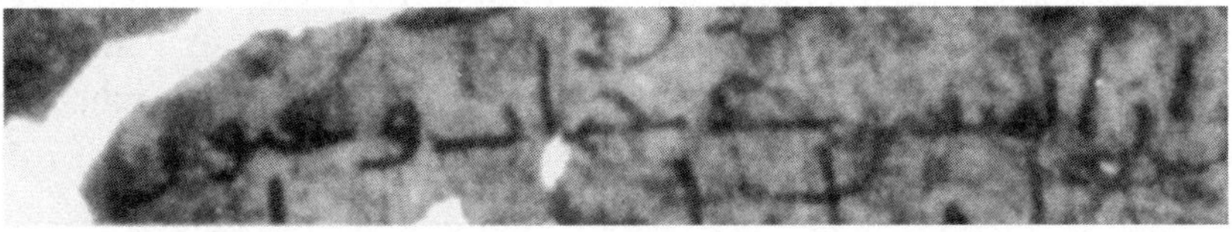

Fig. 12: A. Perg. 213, Österreichische Nationalbibliothek, f. 2 recto, l. 4

Thus, there is nothing strange about *fa-ʾarsala* instead of the standard *fa-baʿatha*, "And God sent Messengers"—they are synonyms. It should be noted (fig. 6, line 12 on recto in Fogg's manuscript) that the use of a different ink reveals that the above synonym was later corrected by the standard word (see table 2).

One should not disregard the traces of the earlier writing and transcription process.

Minor Omission?

I wish to bring a variant reading of lesser importance to attention: the omission of one expression. In line 3 on the recto of Bonhams' manuscript (fig. 1), it is possible to read the *scriptio inferior* as the phrase *fa-ʾḥkum baynahum*, "judge between them" (Q 5:42), *fa-ʾin jāʾūka* is missing. The words *fa-ʾin jāʾūka* are present in the standard reading, but they are missing in the *scriptio inferior* of the palimpsest. The standard text is: *fa-ʾin jāʾūka fa-ʾḥkum baynahum*, "If they do come to thee, / Either judge between them."

Table 2: Q 2:213, Fogg, recto, line 12

Fogg, *scriptio prima*	النبيين	الله	ارسل	فـ	وحدة	امة	الناس	كان
Fogg, *scriptio secunda*			بعث					
			⇧					
Standard Text	النبيين	الله	بعث	فـ	وحدة	امة	الناس	كان

Although the *scriptio prima* is deleted and amended by the insertion of the standard text, the erased Alif, Sīn, and Lām of the original version are still visible.

Fa-ʾin jāʾūka is a basic element in the two adulterers' story.[72] In Mālik's *Muwaṭṭaʾ* the narrative element of the Jews who came to Muḥammad to resolve the problem is a basic element.[73] In the life of Muḥammad, the Jews send the man and the woman to Muḥammad so that he can decide: "they brought the pair to Muḥammad."[74] The story's construction in the biography is parallel to the story of the adulteress in the Gospel (according to Saint John). Someone spoke about a transfer, an imitation, "une impression d'un quasi-décalque opéré à partir de Jean par le Hadith quant au thème et à sa structuration littéraire."[75] The *Muwaṭṭaʾ* version consists of the older draft of the story without the additions of the Sīra. The omission of "if they come to you" in the palimpsest should also call into question the basic elements of the story, provided that the variant reading is not simply a *lapsus calami*, but a deliberate omission. One should suppose that in a different Qurʾānic manuscript there was no narrative element of the Jews who came to Muḥammad. It was added later, and it was a transfer from the Gospel into the Sīra. In the Gospel, the Scribes and Pharisees ἄγουσιν ("lead") the woman to Jesus. However, it does not mean that the *scriptio inferior* is the prestandard text.

Deliberate Omission?

The most interesting variants in Fogg's palimpsest are the omissions. They might attach a different meaning to the text. In Q 2:217, *ḥattā yaruddūkum*,[76] "until they turn you back," is not the same as the standard *ḥattā yaruddūkum ʿan dīnikum*, "until they turn you back from your faith." Furthermore, *wa-man yartadid minkum*, "and if any of you turn back," is not the same as *wa-man yartadid minkum ʿan dīnihi*, "and if any of you turn back from their faith."

It should not be forgotten that the expedition of Nakhla aroused controversy[77] because it was fought in the holy month of Rajab.[78] If the error was not unintentional, the variant could be a sign of the construction process of the Qur'ānic text. In different times, the Qur'ān had to reflect different historical contexts. Therefore, it was necessary to justify the fight, and the word *dīn* was added or was an attempt to join the controversy on the sanctity of Rajab.[79]

CONCLUSIONS

The story of the manuscripts of Ibn Mas'ūd that al-Nadīm reported in the *Fihrist* has never been proven by any written evidence. Arthur Jeffery himself examined about 170 volumes[80] and compiled his *Materials* only on the basis of quotations.

The *scriptio inferior* in the palimpsest of Fogg and his print of the past words in Q 2:222, *(wā-lā taqra)bū al-nisā'a fī maḥīḍihinna hattā yataṭahharna*, the same *lectio* that the Tradition traces to Ibn Mas'ūd, are intriguing: it is evidence of a variant reading. However, it is groundless to say that it is a fragment of one of the manuscripts of Ibn Mas'ūd, who refused to destroy his copies of the Qur'ān in accordance with 'Uthmān's order.

The nonstandard *lectio* found in the palimpsest is not to be considered as proof of the pre-'Uthmānic period, because it was just in the fourth century that Abū Bakr b. Mujāhid (d. 324/936) accepted only the readings based on a fairly uniform consonantal text and he chose seven well-known Qur'ān teachers of the second century and declared that their readings all had divine authority that the others lacked.

This theory was made official only in the year 322/934 when the scholar Ibn Miqsam was forced to retract his view that the consonantal text could be read in any manner that was grammatically correct.[81] In the following year another Qur'ān scholar, Ibn Shanabūdh, was similarly condemned and forced to renounce his view that it was permissible to use the readings of Ibn Mas'ūd and Ubayy.[82] Such evidence, and all the other pieces of evidence found in manuscripts—particularly in palimpsests—is of great importance for all the scholars in Qur'ānic studies, with all their prejudices of a mentality modeled by writing and printing. However, any evidence of a variant reading dissolves and disappears into the words:

"Ne prenez-pas (n'apprenez pas) le Coran de ceux qui ne font qu'en copier des exemplaires!"[83] (Don't take [don't learn] the Qur'ān from those who are only making copies of copies!)

NOTES

1. B. Dodge, ed., *The Fihrist of al-Nadīm, a Tenth-Century Survey of Muslim Culture* (New York, 1970), pp. 57–58.

2. Regarding the exciting journeys of Mrs. Agnes Smith Lewis and her sister Margaret Dunlop Gibson, "The Giblews," see A. Whigham Price, *The Ladies of Castlebrae* (London, 1964).

3. The finding of this manuscript is not as intriguing as the tale that Professor G. Khan told me about the discovery of the palimpsest of the Gospel of St. Mark in Syriac. About the slab of butter slapped by the monks on a grubby old fragment of manuscript, see A. Whigham Price, ibid., pp. 8–9.

4. F. 11, see N. Tchernetska, "Greek Oriental Palimpsests in Cambridge: Problems and Prospects," in *Literacy, Education and Manuscript Transmission in Byzantium and Beyond*, ed. C. Holmes and J. Waring [Medieval Mediterranean 42], (Leiden, 2002), pp. 243–56 and N. Tchernetska, *A Hand-List of the Greek Palimpsest in Cambridge Libraries*, in http://www.cus.cam.uk/~nt208/hand-list.htm.

5. London, 1902.

6. The vellum leaves of the six quires, smoothed out and separated, have been set within strong paper ones. These new leaves have a new format (e.g., the paper page 89a coincides with vellum pages 149a–152b that were in turn a former page in vertical format). The expert binders—it is possible to read their name on the last page—mended the parchment with strips of transparent white gauze.

7. A. Mingana and A. Smith Lewis, eds., *Leaves from Three Ancient Qurâns, Possibly Pre-ʿOthmânic, with a List of Their Variants* (Cambridge, 1914) with a preface by A. Smith Lewis, pp.V–X; an introduction by A. Mingana, pp. XI–XLII, and the transcription of the Qur'ānic text, pp. 1–75, containing Q 7:139–68; 9:18–79; 11:20–39; 13:18–43; 14:1–8; 15:85–99; 16:1–41, 80–128; 17:1–57; 24:17–29; 28:41–51; 29:17–30; 40:78–85; 41:1–20; 44:38–59; 45:1–20.

8. Another disappearance lasted for a longer time. The collection of photostats of early manuscripts of the Qur'ān collected by Bergsträsser and Pretzl were claimed to have been bombed in Munich during the Second World War (see A. Jeffery, *The Qur'ān as a Scripture* [New York, 1952], p. 103). However, they are now kept in the Freie Universität of Berlin.

9. It is still kept in the University Library of Cambridge (the present classmark is Or. 1287.13) where I was kindly allowed to examine the manuscript.

10. The gripping story is handed down from the words handwritten on the first page of the book bound by Eyre & Spottiswoode.

11. "It was at first thought that Dr. Mingana's find in the palimpsest leaves published by him in 1914, *Leaves from Three Ancient Qur'ans Possibly Pre-ʿOthmanic*, with a list of their Variants, might provide us with fragments of one of these earlier Codices. Closer examination, however, has shown that neither they nor the curious variants found by him in Syriac in a manuscript of Barṣalibi (see *An Ancient Syriac Translation of the Ḳur'an Exhibiting New Verses and Variants* [Manchester, 1925]), have any relation to the text of these Old Codices with which we are here concerned" (A. Jeffery, *Materials for the History of the Text of the Qur'ān. The Old Codices* [Leiden, 1937], n. 1, pp. 14–15).

12. "Avec une certaine témérité . . ." Blachère wrote (R. Blachère, *Introduction au Coran* [Paris, 1947], p. 36), though the authors were cautious: "possibly pre-ʿOthmânic" (the title), "we leave the professional palaeographers to assign a definite and final date to these various scraps of parchment. The opinion that some portions of them may date from the very beginning of the VIIIth century is probable" and "a categorical answer, affirmative or negative, would be, on our part, only premature" (*Leaves*, introduction, p. XLI).

13. Some conclusions are unfounded: "We therefore cannot imagine anyone attempting the useless task of writing out a text like ours, after the time of ʿOthmân. Putting all the facts together, as they are known to ourselves, or as they have been handed down to us by a credible tradition, we think that these vellum leaves, now happily my property, were amongst those whose destruction was ordered by ʿOthmân and was incumbent on all true believers in Islâm" (A. Smith Lewis, *Leaves*, preface, p. VII) and "It is evident that if we find a manuscript of the Qurân presenting various readings of consonants and of complete words, and more specially if this manuscript offers some interpolations and omissions, it would not be too rash to suppose that it goes back to a pre-ʿOthmânic period" (A. Mingana, *Leaves*, introduction, p. XXII).

14. "C'est seulement quand les variantes relevées par Mingana auront été confirmées par un nouvel examen du palimpseste . . . qu'il sera permis de conclure que ces fragments représentent bien une autre tradition que notre Vulgate" (R. Blachère, *Introduction au Coran* [Paris, 1947], p. 37).

15. One century later, with an ultraviolet lamp and not only "with a magnifying glass, and sometimes by means of a fresh touch with the re-agent," "painting up its margins with the reagent," a more precise analysis casts new light on the Qur'ānic text of the palimpsest and reveals that some of Mingana's readings are wrong.

16. "Prof. Rev. Mingana, held by some as 'a great scholar of Arabic,' has in fact a shaky grasp of the subject at best," "Mingana's Attempted Distorstion of the Qur'ān, in M. M. Al-Aʿẓamī, *History of the Qur'ānic Text from Revelation to Compilation* (Leicester, 2003), pp. 311–13. The author speaks about blunders, incompetence, incredible dishonesty, inability to read, trick, and creativity.

17. Mingana lists the Qur'ānic variants and number 12 of the second group is *lā yahdā li-qawmi* instead of the standard text *lā yahdā al-qawma* (Q 9:37; ms. 60a, l. 8, p. 32a). The notes of Al-A'ẓamī are: "It is no secret that early scribes occasionally dropped vowels (Alif, Wāw, and Yā') in their copies, and here the writer dispensed with the final vowel in *yahdā* because it is silent. Once again Mingana takes advantage, this time through an absolutely ludicrous transposition. He separates the Alif from *al-qawm* and places it after *lā yahdā*, creating a new ungrammatical phrase that is bereft of all meaning. This is analogous to taking the phrase 'tigers hunting' and converting it to 'tiger shunting'" (*Leaves*, p. 313).

The reading of Mingana is absolutely wrong, but it is not necessary to criticize "linguistic gymnastics" with more linguistic gymnastics. It is true that Mingana separates the Alif from *al-qawm* and places it after *lā yahdā*, but the reason is not the Arabic orthography during the early centuries of Islam. Mingana simply did not see the Yā' before *al-qawm*, therefore he places the Alif of the article of the following word instead of the Yā'.

In 2005, using an ultraviolet lamp, it is possible to read *lā yahdā al-qawma*, with no variants. In regard to the variants of this palimpsest, it should be noted "auch sind einige ihrer Lesungen äußerst unwahrscheinlich. So bedarf die Ausgabe einer Nachprüfung von sachverständiger Seite" (G. Bergsträsser und O. Pretzl, *Geschichte des Qorāns, III. Die Geschichte des Korantexts* [Leipzig, 1938], p. 53, n. 3).

18. A. Jeffery, *Materials for the History of the Text of the Qur'ān. The Old Codices* (Leiden, 1937).

19. The terminology is various: reading, variant, variant reading, *qirā'ah*, multiple reading (see M. M. Al-A'ẓamī, *History of the Qur'ānic Text*, pp. 151–64).

20. Ibid., p. 160.

21. A. Jeffery, *Materials*, pp. 14–15.

22. R. Blachère, *Introduction*, p. 196.

23. In 1919 the conclusion of Mingana about variants and Qur'ānic manuscripts is: "There are in public libraries of Europe many Qur'ānic mss of high antiquity, the oldest dating probably from the 2nd Islamic century, but, apart from some anomalies of spelling due to the rudimentary character of the early Arabic orthography, no real variant can be detected in them. This conclusion is borne out by Nöldeke, who examined some such mss, and by the present writer, who for the purpose of this article consulted three of them preserved in the John Rylands Library. To our knowledge, therefore, the only extant ms which offers slight variations is a palimpsest in the possession of Mrs. A. S. Lewis," in J. Hastings, ed., *Encyclopaedia of Religion and Ethics*, vol. 10 (New York, 1919), pp. 538b–50, s.v. Qur'ān (and in http:// www.dabar.org/Religion/Hastings/JH-ERE-Qur'an.htm).

24. The project is named after Michele Amari, see F. Déroche and S. Noja Noseda, *Introduction to Les manuscrits de style ḥiǧāzī:* Volume 1*: Le manuscrit*

arabe 328(a) de la Bibliothèque nationale de France (Lesa, 1998), pp. XI–XII and Volume 2, *I: Le manuscrit Or. 2165 (f. 1 à 61) de la British Library* (Lesa, 2001), pp. XX–XXIII.

25. The aim of the Amari Project is to publish the facsimiles of all earliest manuscripts of the Qurʾānic text, and to put them at every scholar's disposal. The first volume of the series, *Sources de la transmission manuscrite du texte coranique* is *Les manuscrits de style ḥiǧāzī:* Volume 1*: Le manuscrit arabe 328(a) de la Bibliothèque nationale de France* (Lesa, 1998) and the second one is *Les manuscrits de style ḥiǧāzī:* Volume 2, I*: Le manuscrit Or. 2165 (f. 1 à 61) de la British Library* (Lesa, 2001). The next volume *Les manuscrits de style ḥiǧāzī: Volume 5, I* will contain fragments of manuscripts scattered among various libraries: e.g., in the Dār al-Kutub in Cairo (ms. 731); the Staatsbibliothek of Berlin (ms. or. fol. 4313); the University Museum in Philadelphia, Pennsylvania (E 16269D, E 16269); the Biblioteca Apostolica Vaticana (vat. ar. 1605); the Österreichische Nationalbibliothek (A. Perg. 213, A. Perg. 2); the Oriental Institute of the University of Chicago (A. 6959, A. 6990, A. 6988); see S. Noja Noseda, *Note esterne in margine al 1° volume dei "Materiali per un'edizione critica del Corano," Rendiconti dell'Istituto Lombardo, Accademia di Scienze e Lettere* 134, no. 1 (2000): 3–38, and F. Déroche, *Les manuscrits du Coran en caractères higâzḥ. Position du problème et eléments préliminaires pour une enquête*, s.v. "Quinterni I" (Lesa, 1996).

26. A. Jeffery, *Materials*, pp. 8–9.

27. The source of the details of the two fragments reproduced in this paper is the volume *Les manuscrits de style ḥiǧāzī: Volume 5, I.* For the kind permission to reproduce the images there I thank both Mrs. Claire Penhallurick of the Islamic department at Bonhams and Ramsey Fendall, department head of Asian and Islamic Manuscripts and Works of Art; Sam Fogg and Sam Fogg in person.

28. The writer Jamāl al-Ghīṭānī in an interview with S. Noja Noseda said that he is a besieger in his project (al-Ghīṭānī, "*hunāka makhṭūṭāt majhūlah*," *Akhbār al-Adab* 478 [September 8, 2002]: 18).

29. Sam Fogg, *Catalogue 27, Islamic Calligraphy* (London, 2003), pp. 6–11. It was sold at Sotheby's in the sale of October 22–23, 1992 (lot 551); see the description attached to the parchment for the sale: *A highly important early Qurʾān leaf in hijazi script from the period of the "Rashidun" caliphs.* See also F. Déroche, *Manuel de codicologie des manuscrits en écriture arabe* (Paris, 2000), p. 48. The third important Qurʾānic fragment—in private hands—was sold at a sale in Sotheby's on October 22, 1993; see the Catalogue: *Oriental Manuscripts and Miniatures.* Day of Sale: Friday, October 22, 1993, in the Main Galleries, 34–35, New Bond Street, London, lot 34. *Qurʾān section: an important early Qurʾān section in hijazi script*, pp. 26–29. These leaves are published in *Les manuscrits de style ḥiǧāzī: Volume 5, I.*

30. The parchment has been sold in Bonhams' Islamic Sale of October 11,

2000, *lot 13*. See the Catalogue: *Islamic and Indian Works of Art. Auction: Wednesday 11th October 2000. Bonhams Knightsbridge, Montpelier Street, Knightsbridge, London*, lot 13.

31. A. Jeffery, *Materials*, p. 128; ʿAbd al-ʿĀl Sālim Makram, Akhmad Mukhtār ʿUmar, *Muʿjam*, II, p. 27.

32. *The Holy Qurʾān, Meanings Translated by* Abdullah Yusuf Ali (Beirut, 1934).

33. Should it be possible to dare reading the *qirāʾah* of Ibn Masʿūd *ghulẓāʾa*, (with three strokes: *Lām, Ẓāʾ*, Alif)? (A. Jeffery, *Materials*, p. 39; ʿAbd al-ʿĀl Sālim Makram, Aḥmad Mukhtār ʿUmar, *Muʿjam al-qirāʾāt al-Qurʾāniyya,* al-Kuwait 1402–1405/ 1982–85, II, p. 35; see the review by S. Noja Noseda, in *AIUON* 58, nos. 1–2 [1998]: 289–91).

34. See C. J. Robin, "La réforme de l'écriture arabe, à l'époque du califat médinois," in IV *International Conference on codicology and paleography of middle-eastern manuscripts* (Bologna, 2002).

35. G. Khan, "Standardisation and variation in the orthography of Hebrew Bible and Arabic Qurʾān Manuscripts," in *Manuscripts of the Middle East, V: The Role of the Book in the Civilisations of the Near East* (Leiden, 1990–1991), pp. 53–58; S. Noja Noseda, "A Third Koranic Fragment on Papyrus: An Opportunity for a Revision," in *Rendiconti dell'Istituto Lombardo, Accademia di Scienze e Lettere*, 137, no. 1 (2003): 313–26; S. Noja Noseda, *Introduction to Sources de la transmission manuscrite du texte coranique, I. Les manuscrits de style ḥiğāzī, 2, I. Le manuscrit Or. 2165* (Lesa, 2001), pp. XXVIII–XXX.

36. Ms. or. fol. 4313 (ff.1–7), see W. Ahlwardt, *Die Handschriften-Verzeichnisse der Königlichen Bibliothek zu Berlin*, Verzeichnis der Arabischen Handschriften (Erster Band: Berlin, 1887), pp. 110–11; R. Sellheim, *Arabische Handschriften, Materialien zur arabischen Literaturgeschichte, Teil I* (Wiesbaden, 1976). I am grateful to Dr. Hartmut-Ortwin Feistel of the Staatsbibliothek for giving me the permission to insert some photos of details of this manuscript. It will be published with the other fragments in *Sources de la transmission manuscrite du texte coranique*, 5, I.—Ms. or. fol. 4313 (ff. 1–7) is part of the same codex as the facsimile, plate 44, in B. Moritz, *Arabic Palaeography. A Collection of Arabic Text from the First Century of the Hidjra till the Year 1000* (Cairo, 1905).

37. The long *ā* may be written with Yāʾ in final position (Alif maqṣūrah), but also in middle position: see R. Blachère, *Introduction au Coran* (Paris, 1947), p. 91; C. J. Robin, *La réforme*. Many other examples are in the same manuscript of Berlin (e.g., 2a, l. 11, Q. 4:176, *rijālan* and 7a, l. 13, Q. 5:73, *ʾilāh: wa-mā min ʾilāhin ʾillā ʾilāhun wāḥidun*, the first one written in *scriptio defectiva* and the second one with a Yāʾ). C. J. Robin says that "d'un point de vue chronologique, toutes les graphies avec un yāʾ pour noter le *ā* dans un mot remontent incontestablement à la période où le *alif* n'était pas encore utilisé, c'est-à-dire avant 40 h."

I would like to stress the interesting observation about the use of the Alif in G.-R. Puin, "Observations on early Qurʾān Manuscripts in *Ṣanʿāʾ*," in S. Wild, ed., *The Qurʾan as Text* (Leiden, 1996), p. 109: "On the other hand, does *k-y-l-ḏ-ī=ka-lladhī* imply that the second letter *Yāʾ* should not be pronounced at all?" and Puin, "Neue Wege der Koranforschung, II. Über die Bedeutung der ältesten Koranfragmente aus Sanaa (Jemen) für die Orthographiegeschichte des Korans," *Magazin Forschung* I (1999): 40.

My conjecture is that the Yāʾ to spell the long *ā*, be it in the middle position or in the final position, is due to the influence of the Avestan writing, where "the Avestan letter *ā* is also derived from the Pahlavi script, where this sign was used for *ʾy* at the end of a word (already in the Istanbul sarcophagus inscription). However, as early as in Middle Persian inscriptions from the third century AD, *ʾy* was used to represent the final *-ā* of foreign names" (K. Hoffmann, "Avestan Language I. The Avestan Script," in *Encyclopædia Iranica III* [London, 1989], pp. 47–51), also online at http://iranica.com/articlenavigation). About the origin of the Arabic writing, see S. Noja Noseda, "From Syriac to Pahlavi: The Contribution of the Sassanian Iraq to the Beginning of the Arabic Writing," in K.-H. Ohlig and G.-R. Puin, eds., *Die dunklen Anfänge. Neue Forschungen*, or in this volume.

38. With regard to the Alif of the article written defectively, see G.-R. Puin, *Observations on Early Qurʾān*, pp. 108–109. It should be noted that in the manuscript of Berlin (5a, l. 15) the word *bi-l-qisṭi* (Q 5:42) is written with Alif, but it was later rubbed out, see below, my "Error and corrections."

39. See, e.g., Q 2:213, the synonym *fa-ʾarsala* instead of the standard *fa-baʿatha* (fig. 6).

40. ʿAbd al-ʿĀl-Sālim Makram, Aḥmad Mukhtār ʿUmar, *Muʿjam*, I, p. 310; A. Jeffery, *Materials*, pp. 30 and 316.

41. ʿAbd al-ʿĀl-Sālim Makram, Aḥmad Mukhtār ʿUmar, *Muʿjam*, I, p. 315: *wa-lā taqrabū al-nisāʾa fī -l-maḥīḍihinna wa-ʿtazilū-hunna hatta yataṭahharna* is the reading of Ibn Masʿūd and ʾAnas, whereas A. Jeffery reports only *yataṭahharna* as a variant of Ibn Masʿūd and Ubayy b. Kaʿb, (A. Jeffery, *Materials*, pp. 30 and 121).

42. See A. Fedeli, "*A. Perg. 2: a non palimpsest and the corrections in Qurʾānic manuscripts*," in *Manuscripta Orientalia* 11, no. 1 (2005): 20–27. I have conjectured that the remains of the supposed "alte Schrift" on the margin of this parchment (A. Perg. 2) are corrections to the text written by another copyist. The same portion of Qurʾānic text has been written three times, because it was a writing exercise by two scribes.

43. A. Gacek, "Technical Practices and Recommendations Recorded by Classical and Post-Classical Arabic Scholars concerning the Copying and Correction of Manuscripts," in F. Déroche, ed., *Les Manuscrits du Moyen-Orient* (Istanbul, Paris, 1986), pp. 51–60.

44. See the analysis of the orthography in A. Jeffery and I. Mendelsohn, "The Orthography of the Samarqand Qur'ān Codex," *Journal of the American Oriental Society* 62, no. 3 (1942): 175–95 and the frequent remarks such as "and in any case would be a scribal error without textual significance" (p. 183), or "this is probably merely a scribal error, if not due to a mistake on a paper patch in the folio" (ibid.) or "there is no known variant here, so possibly this is to be taken as a mistake" (p. 184) and also "it must be merely a scribal error" (p. 185) and "the words are omitted by the scribe, obviously by error, thinking he had already written them" (ibid.).

45. The corrections in Qur'ānic text hand down from the tradition: "Les gens corrigeaient leurs exemplaires du Coran (*maṣâḥifahum*) selon sa récitation" (as quoted in G. Schoeler, *Écrire et transmettre dans les débuts de l'Islam* [Paris, 2002], p. 40).

46. With regard to mistakes, it is interesting to quote this point of view: "One of the gateways for an Orientalist assault on the Qur'ān is distortion of the text itself. In my estimate there are over 250,000 copies of the Qur'ān in manuscript form, complete or partial, from the first century of Hijra onwards. Errors are classified in academic circles into the dual categories of deliberate and unintentional, and in this vast collection of manuscripts it is a certainty that many copyists must have committed unintentional errors. Scholars who deal with this subject know very well what fatigue or a momentary lapse of concentration can engender" (M. M. Al-Aʿẓamī, *History of the Qur'ānic Text*, p. 151).

47. As to what concerns corrections due to different variants of Qur'ān, see, e.g., Q 2:222 above mentioned and my lecture *Pre-othmanic Variants in Manuscripts?* at the 29th Deutscher Orientalistentag, *Barrieren–Passagen* (Halle, September 2004), pp. 20–24.

48. C. J. Robin, *La réforme*. Furthermore, an example of this kind of correction is in the manuscript kept in the Bibliothèque Nationale du Paris, 328a, see Y. Dutton, "An Early Muṣḥaf according to the Reading of Ibn ʿĀmir," *Journal of Qur'ānic Studies* 3, no. 1 (2001): 72–74.

49. See also, as to what concerns the orthography of early Arabic papyri and papers (and inscriptions), some examples of scribal lapses, dittographies, haplographies, etc. in S. Hopkins, *Studies in the Grammar of Early Arabic, Based upon Papyri Datable to Before AH 300/AD 912* (Oxford, 1984), pp. 60–61.

50. See above, p. 308a.

51. A. Jeffery, *Materials*, pp. 116–17; see G. Khan, *Standardisation and Variation*, p. 56.

52. M. M. Al-Aʿẓamī, *History of the Qur'ānic Text*, p. 134.

53. The intriguing story of this manuscript (E 20) that was bought by I. Iu. Krachkovsky is narrated by E. Rezvan, *The Qur'ān of ʿUthmān* (St. Petersburg, 2004), pp. 17–18 and Rezvan, "The Qur'ān and Its World: VI. Emergence of the Canon: The Struggle for Uniformity," *Manuscripta Orientalia* 4, no. 2 (1998): 23.

54. E. Rezvan, *The Qur'ān of 'Uthmān*, p. 66 and table 11. See also S. Noja Noseda, *Introduction to Sources de la transmission manuscrite du texte coranique, I. Les manuscrits de style ḥiǧāzī, 2, I. Le manuscrit Or. 2165* (Lesa, 2001), pp. XXVIII–XXX, as regards the Alif maḥdhūfah.

55. Or. 8264, see S. Noja Noseda, "A Third Koranic Fragment on Papyrus: An Opportunity for a Revision," *Rendiconti dell'Istituto Lombardo, Accademia di Scienze e Lettere* 137, no. 1 (2003): 313–26.

56. Noseda, ibid., p. 315.

57. See also Puin, *Observations on Early Qur'ān*, p. 109.

58. It is not so unusual to come across the same word written in two different ways in the same page, see M. M. Al-A'ẓamī, *History of the Qur'ānic Text*, p. 132.

59. As regards forms of *verba mediae infirmae*, see S. Hopkins, *Studies in the Grammar of Early Arabic*, p. 83 and the interesting remark about the long and short forms that may even occur together in the same text.

60. In line 7, an Alif was added and we can see the remains of the former ligature of a Lām with the Qāf. In line 13 there are the traces of the former Alif.

61. The manuscripts "présentent une orthographie qui paraît erratique et contradictoire" because of "l'embarass des scribes": see C. J. Robin, *La réforme*.

62. See the Catalogue: N. Abbott, *The Rise of the North Arabic Script and Its Qur'ānic Development, with a Full Description of the Qur'ān Manuscripts in the Oriental Institute* (Chicago, 1939), p. 60 and plates VIII–IX.

63. The standard text is *shurakā'u*, without the *Wāw*. The tradition does not report the different spelling; see 'Abd al-'Āl Sālim Makram, Aḥmad Mukhtār 'Umar, *Mu'jam*. N. Abbot noted the difference and reported to have found no comment on this, but she did not mention the former spelling *sh r k w* and the added Alif.

64. Vat. Ar. 1605. 1; see the Catalogue, G. Levi Della Vida, *Frammenti coranici in carattere cufico, nella Biblioteca Vaticana* (Vatican City, 1947), pp. 1–2 and plate I. The page following this one is in the Collection of Nour Foundation, see *The Nasser D. Khalili Collection of Islamic Art. Vol. I:* F. Déroche, *The Abbasid Tradition. Qur'āns of the 8th to the 10th centuries AD* (London, 1992), p. 32 and plate I. Both fragments will be published in *Sources de la transmission manuscrite du texte coranique, 5, I.*

65. One should presume that the former text was *mā 'anzala 'ilay-ka*, and later the word *allahu* was added. Two words were rewritten in the space of one word.

66. The folio marked as 6a is the verso, not the recto.

67. See note to Q 5:44 in Bonhams' palimpsest regarding the Yā' to spell the long *ā*.

68. Another interesting detail about the corrections is the correction of characters shape in the fragment A. Perg. 2 (see A. Fedeli, *A. Perg. 2*, p. 24). On the flesh side, line 8, the shape of the 'Ayn in *'an dhunūbihim* was later corrected, as the shape

written the first time looks like Syriac writing and the shape added above the main line is the more rounded form preponderant in Arabic (fig. 11). In the same line, the *Dhāl* of *dhunūbihim* was amended with an added vertical stroke (fig. 11). The former shape is similar to the half circle of the *Dalath* in Syriac writing, without the vertical stroke. The corrected types—in a dark ink, different from the one used by hand A—and the characteristic shape of the Alif with a tail on the left, such as the one in line 5 in the word *kamā* or in line 9 in the word *al-dunyā*, reveal the shape of the Syriac writing. About the Syriac origin for the writing and the Syriac influence on the written transmission of the texts, see S. Noja Noseda, "Parerga to the Volumes of Sources de la Transmission manuscrite du Texte coranique thus far published and in course of publication," *Proceedings of the First World Congress for Middle Eastern Studies, University of Mainz* (September 8–13, 2002), forthcoming; S. Noja Noseda, "La mia visita a Sanaa e il Corano palinsesto," *Rendiconti dell'Istituto Lombardo, Accademia di Scienze e Lettere*" 137, no. 1, pp. 48–52; F. Briquel-Chatonnet, "De l'araméen à l'arabe: quelques réflexions sur la genèse de l'ecriture arabe," in F. Déroche and F. Richard, eds., *Scribes et manuscrits du Moyen-Orient* (Paris, 1997), pp. 135–49; J. Sourdel Thomine, "Aspects de l'écriture arabe et de son développement," *Revue des Études Islamiques* 48, no. 1 (1980): 9–23; G. Troupeau, "Réflexions sur l'origine syriaque de l'écriture arabe," in A. S. Kaye, ed., *Semitic Studies, in Honour of Wolf Leslau* (Wiesbaden, 1991), pp. 1562–70; F. Déroche, *Le livre manuscrit arabe. Préludes à une histoire* (Paris, 2004), p. 15.

69. A. Jeffery, *Materials*, p. 16.

70. An example is in A. Perg. 213, Österreichische Nationalbibliothek (2a in *Sources de la transmission manuscrite du texte coranique, 5, I*): in line 4, Q 52:17 *'inna al-muttaqīna fī jannātin wa-ʿuyūnin* (fig. 12) instead of the standard *'inna al-muttaqīna fī jannātin wa-naʿīmin* "As to the Righteous, / They will be in Gardens, / And in Happiness."

71. A. Jeffery, *Materials*, p. IX.

72. A. L. de Prémare, "Prophétisme et adultère. D'un texte à l'autre," *Revue du Monde Musulman et de la Méditerranée* 58 (1990) = *Les premières écritures islamiques,* pp. 101–35.

73. Ibid., p. 102.

74. Ibid., pp. 102–104; A. Guillaume, *The Life of Muhammad. A translation of Isḥāq's* Sīrat rasūl Allāh, *with introduction and notes* (London, 1968), p. 266.

75. A. L. de Prémare, *Prophétisme*, p. 124.

76. The *lectio ḥattā yaruddūkum* is a conjecture because of the correction *ʿan dīnikum*, later added (fig. 5).

77. L. Caetani, *Annali dell'Islam, II, 1, 2 a.H.* (Milan, 1907), pp. 463–66.

78. "When the month of Rajab came, we used to stop the military actions, calling this month the iron remover, for we used to remove and throw away the iron

parts of every spear and arrow in the month of Rajab" (Bukhari, vol. 5, 59, 661 in http://www.usc.edu/cgi-bin).

79. Regarding the most controversial practices of Rajab and the incessant struggle of the orthodox scholars against the practices of Rajab, see M. J. Kister, "'Rajab is the month of God . . .' A Study in the Persistence of an Early Tradition," reprint in *Studies in Jāhiliyya and Early Islam*, variorum reprints (London, 1980), pp. 191–223, (XII).

80. M. M. Al-Aʿẓamī, *The History of the Qurʾānic Text*, p. 155.

81. See R. Baalbaki, "The Treatment of *Qirāʾāt* by the Second and Third Century Grammarians," in A. Rippin, ed., *The Qurʾān: Formative Interpretation* (Aldershot, Brookfield, USA, Singapore, Sydney, 1999), pp. 159–80.

82. See A. T. Welch, "History of the Ḳurʾān after 632," in *Encyclopaedia of Islam* (CD-ROM Edition v. 1.0), (Leiden, 1999); A. Jeffery, *The Qurʾān as a Scripture*, pp. 96–103; E. Rezvan, *The Qurʾān and Its World: VI. Emergence of the Canon*, pp. 13–54.

83. G. Schoeler, *Écrire et transmettre dans les débuts de l'islam* (Paris, 2002), p. 40: "Abū Ḥâtim al-Sijistânî, et d'autres encore, déconseillaient fortement à leur disciples de les (*muṣḥafiyyûn*) prendre comme source de leur connaissance du Coran"; M. J. Kister, "Lā taqraʾū l-qurʾāna ʿalā l—muṣḥafiyyīn wa-lā taḥmilū l-ʿilma ʿani l-ṣaḥafiyyīn. Some Notes on the Transmission of Ḥadīth," *Jerusalem Studies in Arabic and Islam* 22 (1998): 127–62: "Do not read the Qurʾān to people who rely on Qurʾān codices, and do not carry further the *ḥadīth* knowledge which you obtain from people who use scrolls." For the reluctance to put in writing the text of the Revelation, see S. Noja Noseda, *From Syriac to Pahlavi* in this volume.

9

LEUKE KOME = LAYKAH, THE ARSIANS = ’AṢḤĀB’AL-RASS, AND OTHER PRE-ISLAMIC NAMES IN THE QUR’ĀN: A WAY OUT OF THE “TANGLEWOOD”?[1]

Gerd-R. Puin

The uncertainty of the writing of *’al-’Aykah* or *Laykah* in the Qur’ān is the point of departure for the present investigation, namely, whether the Qur’ān does not contain still further elements of an extrabiblical saga from pre-Islamic Midian. The following names will be discussed: *Laykah / ’al-Ḥawrā’ / Leuke Kome*; *’al-Rass / Arsae*; *Yanbuʿ / Yabbuʿ / Tubbaʿ / Iambia*; *’al-’Aḥqāf / ’al-’aʿmāq*; and *Wabār / Banubari*.

One group of personal and place-names that are mentioned in the Qur’ān are connected with the so-called Punishment Stories (*Straflegenden*).[2] In these passages the faithful are warned not to neglect the duties of humanity with regard to God, because were they to do so, they would be destroyed like certain disobedient peoples in the past. For example:

> *Then We destroyed them, a complete destruction. And* Noah’s folk, *when they denied the messengers, We drowned them and made of them a portent for mankind. We have prepared a painful doom for evil-doers. And (the tribes of)* ʿĀd *and* Thamūd,[3] *and the dwellers in* Ar-Rass . . . (sura 25:36–38)[4]

> The folk of Noah *denied (the truth) before them, and (so did)* the dwellers at Ar-Rass *and (the tribe of)* Thamūd, *and (the tribe of)* ʿĀd, *and* Pharaoh,

> *and* the brethren of Lot, *and* the dwellers in the wood, *and* the folk of Tubbaʿ: *every one denied their messengers, therefore My threat took effect.* (sura 50:12–14)

> *And* the dwellers in the wood *indeed were evil-doers. So we took vengeance on them. . . . And* the dwellers in Al-Hijr[5] *indeed denied (Our) messengers. And We gave them Our revelations but they were averse to them. And they used to hew out dwellings from the hills, (wherein they dwelt) secure. But the (Awful) Cry overtook them at the morning hour.* (sura 15:78–83)

> The folk of Noah *before them denied (their messenger) and (so did the tribe of)* ʿĀd, *and* Pharaoh *firmly planted, and (the tribe of)* Thamūd, *and* the folk of Lot, *and* the dwellers in the wood: *these were the factions. Not one of them but did deny the messengers, therefore My doom was justified. These wait for but one Shout, there will be no second thereto.* (sura 38:12–15)

> The dwellers in the wood *(of Midian) denied the messengers (of Allah). When Shuʿayb said unto them: Will ye not ward off (evil)?* (sura 26:176–77)

Further, other place-names are mentioned in the same vein, including *ʾIram*[6] (sura 89:7), *Madyan*[7] (sura 7:85; 9:70; 11:84, 95; 29:36), and *ʾal-Ḥijr*/Egra,[8] as well as the names of peoples (*ʿĀd* and *Thamūd*), of persons (*Nūḥ* / Noah, *Firʿawn* / Pharaoh, and *Lūṭ* / Lot), and of divine messengers (*Hūd, Ṣāliḥ*, and *Shuʿayb*). Our interest in this paper is restricted to *ʾal-ʾAykah, ʾal-Rass, Tubbaʿ*, and *ʾal-ʾAḥqāf,* as well as the non-Qur'ānic *Wabār,* which is nonetheless to be included in this enigmatic group of names from pre-Islamic Arabian geography, and which has continually offered scholars good cause to seek after their identifications. The map included in this work clarifies the locations of the places with regard to one another; however, we must also point our readers to the two presentations of Arabia following Claudius Ptolemaeus, given in the atlas of W. C. Brice, p. 14 (see bibliography).

ʾAṣḥāb ʾal-ʾAykah, the "People of the Tanglewood"?

The word *ʾaykah* / ايكة is occasionally used in poetry, meaning "*numerous, luxuriant* or *tangled* or *dense*, trees" (Lane), mainly as doves' domicils.[9] As

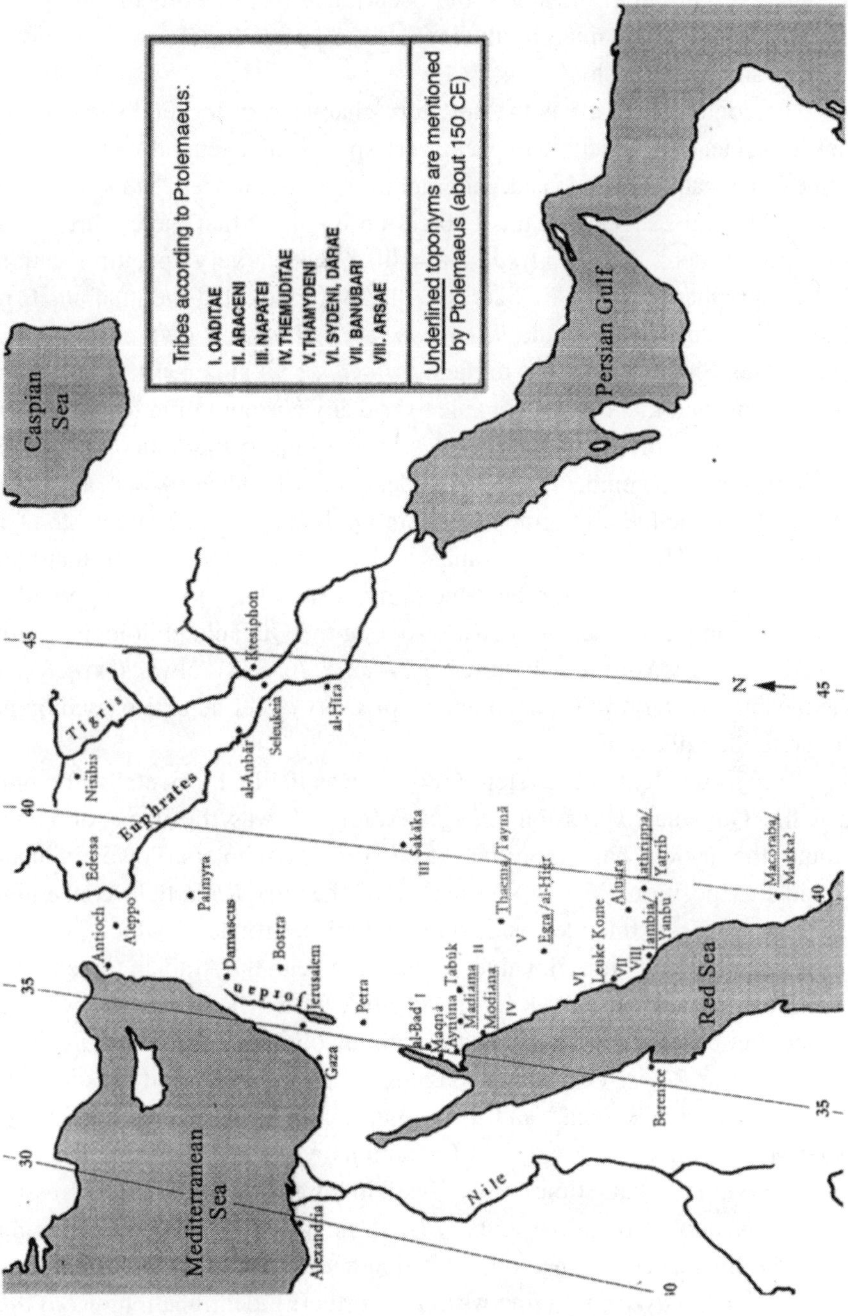

Important Places and Tribes of Early Islam according to Ptolemaeus.

we shall see in detail, however, the occurrence of the word in the Qur'an cannot easily be explained by the recourse to poetry for the two reasons of context and orthography.

The context, as well as the hortatory character, of the Punishment Stories would lead the reader to expect a very specific and generally well-known name of a location, or at least a geographic area. And indeed, a few traditions within Muslim exegesis of this expression do show that there were initial attempts to identify *(')l(-')aykah* / (ا)لـيكة [10] with a very specific location. The geographer Yāqūt (570–626/1179–1229) reports that the inhabitants of Tabūk claimed that the name *'al-'Aykah* referred to their own city, and that the prophet Shuʿayb was sent to them (*Muʿjam*, s.v. 'al-'aykah); Yāqūt comments, however, that he was not able to find any corroboration for this report in the books of the Qur'ānic exegetes. According to the lexicographer al-Jawharī (4th/10th century), one can understand *'al-'aykah* / الـيكة as a "tanglewood," while the orthographic variant *Laykah* لَيْكَة can be understood as a place-name. He reports that some scholars were of the opinion that both versions of the word meant the same thing, just as *Bakkah* was supposed to have been only a variant of *Makkah*. Among the Qur'ānic philologists, only Abū ʿUbayd al-Qāsim b. Sallām (ca. 154–224/770–838) (always?) preferred the meaning of *Laykah* (?) as the name of a city,[11] but he also passed on no concrete identification.

To my knowledge, Wetzstein (1865)[12] was the first Orientalist to argue that the Qur'ānic expression *'al-'Aykah/Laykah* was the name of Leuke Kome, the ancient harbor on the Red Sea. Later scholars, however, abandoned this position. Moritz, the author of the first *RE* article concerning Leuke Kome, cast this idea aside on philological grounds[13] which, incidentally, are completely questionable. In the same year, the Arabian traveler von Maltzan[14] argued with verve for the identification of Leuke Kome with the ancient Iambia (Yanbuʿ); he based this opinion on Mannert's *Geographie der Griechen und Römer* (VI:1), "although Ritter disagrees with it [this identification] and, with Borchart and d'Anville, holds that Leuke Kome and the Auara of Ptolemy and Stephanus Byzantinus were one and the same location." Around the same time, Alois Musil, in his discussion of the expression *'al-'aykah,* quoted from the entry *'al-'ayk* in Ibn Manẓūr's lexicon *Lisān*; however, his inaccurate method of citation betrays his intention to bring the meaning of *'al-'aykah* into line with his (northern) identification of *Laykah.* To quote from Musil: "The word al-Ajka means thicket and Lajka a *neigh-*

boring settlement"; however, the word "neighboring" is not supported at all by the article in the *Lisān*. Musil writes: "Lajka recalls the Greek *leuke*, λευκή, meaning white; and the part of the ruins of Madian [NB: Musil sees these as the ruins of Ḥawrah and the necropolis Maghāyir Shuʿayb, south of the current oasis of al-Badʿ and northeast of Maqnā, on the coast of the Gulf of ʿAqaba] *bordering* on the thickets is still called Ḥawra—which also means white."[15] Musil, then, does not identify the antique Leuke Kome with the name of a city Laykah, of which he is aware from the *Lisān* entry, but rather holds more strongly to the traditional "thicket" meaning.

More recently, A. F. L. Beeston,[16] who did not at all question the meaning of *'al-ʾaykah* as "tanglewood, undergrowth of plants," has come to the astounding conclusion "that the expression *aṣḥāb al-aykati* enshrines a Meccan folk-memory of the ancient cult of Dusares," or (in Arabic) Dhū 'l-Sharā, "in his Dionysiac character as god of vegetation and the vine." C. E. Bosworth[17] agrees with Beeston but also with others who have concerned themselves with *'al-ʾAykah*; he is convinced of the thicket[18] that Musil came across in the lower portion of the Wādī 'l-ʾAbyaḍ, and he does not treat at all of the problem of the differing writing (i.e., with the uncertain orthography) in the Qur'ān.

'Al-ʾAykah or Laykah in the Qur'ān?

The four Qur'ānic verses in which this expression appears, as they are in the Cairo edition as well as in other editions and readings, are suggestions that the reading *'al-ʾaykah* should be abandoned in favor of the place-name *Laykah* (as the *lectio difficilior*).

In the Cairo edition of the Qur'ān, the expression *ʾaṣḥābu 'l-ʾaykati* appears as two orthographic variants. Twice one finds the full form (considered to be "correct") أَصْحَـٰبُ الأَيْكَةِ (15:78; 50:14), and in two other places one finds the "defective" form اصحبُ لـَيْكَة (26:176; 38:13), by which qualifier is meant that the Alif of the article is missing. It is clear from the contexts in question that both forms mean the same thing.[19] The Muslim exegetes find themselves here in a delicate position, for they have to admit that, in terms of the "correct" form لأيكة, there is at least one orthographic mistake in the "incorrect" form; that is, the missing Alif of the article, if not in fact two, if one considers the missing Alif of *ʾaykah* as well. They explain the problem as a phenomenon of varying pronunciations among dialects; as a comparison they mention the (non-Qur'ānic) term *laḥmar* in place of the correct term *'al-'aḥmar*. However, nothing is actually clarified with this comparison in the question of how a dialectical pronunciation could—as an exception in orthography—gain such abnormal influence over the way a word was written.

When one turns from the Cairo edition and consults other streams of transmission, as well as the literature giving variant readings, one finds a more differentiated picture (see the table on the following page). Indeed, examinations of individual manuscripts would also provide a wealth of information, but this investigation cannot be pursued here.[20] Nonetheless, I should mention that I found the "defective" version in a Muṣḥaf from Ṣan'ā', a manuscript written in the archaic "Ḥijāzī" script. The defective writing occurred at a place where the Cairo edition has the "correct" version, and this observation was actually the point of departure for my interest in this topic. In two other Qur'ānic transmissions ("riwāyahs"), namely, *Warsh 'an Nāfi'*[21] and *Qālūn 'an Nāfi'*[22] (see the table on the following page in the gray fields), the word does appear in the two places in which it is vocalized "defectively" in the Cairo edition as لَـيْكَةِ (i.e., as a thing); in these texts it is also written defectively, but it is vocalized as *laykata* لَـيْكَةَ (i.e., as a diptotic name). Notably, the reverse situation does not occur. If one consults the four verses in the *Mu'jam al-Qirā'āt al-Qur'āniyyah* (MQQ),[23] one finds a similar vacillation. In sura 15:78 and in 38:13, the readers Nāfi' et al., defend the "defective" reading ليكة against the الايكة of the Standard Text; in the same way, an anonymous reader prefers the defective reading in sura 50:14.

As one might expect, one also sees differences when it comes to the pronunciation of the ending. In the Standard Text of verses 26:176 and 38:13, the "defectively" written versions لـيكةِ are vocalized with a Kasrah to indicate the genitive. By this means the word is to be understood as a "normal" Arabic noun, indicating a thing (just like the full form الايكة) and not a personal name. At the same time it is implied that, in the case of these "defective" writings, there must be an error present, for the word had to have been written الأيكة. In these places, on the other hand, according to MQQ and the two Qur'ān editions mentioned below, at least Nāfi' et al. are cited with the reading *Laykata* instead of *Laykati*. With this reading they imply that they understand *Laykah* as a diptotically inflected (place-) name, and that therefore there is no error in play concerning the "defective" writing of the word. The editors of the MQQ write at length on the problem of pronunciation:

'Al-ʾAlūsī [died 1270/1853–1854, in his Tafsīr (exegesis) *Rūḥ 'al-Maʿānī*, 30 parts] 19/117 mentions that [the philologist] ʾAbū ʿUbaydah [110–209/ 728–824/5] reported, "In a work of exegesis, we found that *Laykah* is the name of the place (*li-l-qaryah*) and *'al-ʾAykah* the name of the whole region, just like (in the case of) *Makkah* and *Bakkah*. I have seen them (both variants) in the *ʾImām*, the Muṣḥaf of ʿUthmān (. . .): In (sura 15) *'al-Ḥijr* and (sura 50) *Qāf* one reads الأيكة ; in (sura 26) *'al-Shuʿarā'* and (sura 38) *Ṣād*, however, one reads لَيْكَة . The (copies of the) Qur'ān (sent) to (other) centers agree completely (in this matter), and they do not vary (from it)." In the Kashshāf [by the Qur'ānic exegete 'al-Zamakhsharī, 467–538/ 1075–1144], it says: "Whoever reads (the 'defectively' written version ليكة) with the ending *-a* [i.e., *laykata* and not *laykati*] and claims that ليكة—pronounced like ليلة (*laylah*)[24]—is a place-name, is fantasizing (*fa-yatawahhamu*), deceived by the written appearance of the Muṣḥaf, as though ليكة were a non-declinable noun."—He ['al-Zamakhsharī] continues, saying that this is a groundless claim. . . . According to [the exegetical text] *'al-Baḥr 'al-Muḥīṭ* [of ʾAbū Ḥayyān 'al-Gharnāṭī, 654–745/1256–1345], however, 'al-Zamakhsharī rejects the validity of the reading *Laykata,* nearly considering it as apostasy from the faith—may God prevent it![25]

Sūrah: Verse	Standard Text	Other transmissions ("riwāyah"s) of the Qur'ān		Variant Readings according to the MQQ		
	(printed in Cairo + al-Madīnah) *Ḥafṣ ʿan ʿĀṣim*	(printed in Cairo + Tunis) *Warsh ʿan Nāfiʿ*	(printed in Ṭarābulus + Ṣanʿāʾ) *Qālūn ʿan Nāfiʿ*	Nāfiʿ, Warsh	ano-ny-mus	Nāfiʿ, Ibn Kathīr, Ibn ʿĀmir, Abū Jaʿfar
15: 78	اصْحٰبُ الأَيْكَةِ … 'l-ʾaykaẗi	… الأَيْكَةِ … 'l-ʾaykaẗi	… الأَيْكَةِ … 'l-ʾaykaẗi	… لَيْكَة		
26: 176	اصْحٰبُ لـيْكَةِ … l'aykaẗi	… لَيْكَةَ … Laykaẗa	… لَيْكَةَ … Laykaẗa		..لَيْكَةِ	… لَيْكَةَ … Laykaẗa
38: 13	اصْحٰبُ لـيْكَةِ … l'aykaẗi	… لَيْكَةَ … Laykaẗa	… لَيْكَةَ … Laykaẗa			… لَيْكَةَ … Laykaẗa
50: 14	اصْحٰبُ الأَيْكَةِ … 'l-ʾaykaẗi	… الأَيْكَةِ … 'l-ʾaykaẗi	… الأَيْكَةِ … 'l-ʾaykaẗi		..لَيْكَة	

Upon observing the word's stark orthographic and semantic uncertainties, I have concluded that the "defective" variant, being the *lectio difficilior*, is relatively older than the "correct" version, and that the "correctness" of the writing with an Alif can be traced back to a subsequent imposition on the text as it appeared (*rasm*), an imposition intended to illuminate a passage no longer understandable. The older, "defective" writing apparently reflects the original pronunciation *Laykah*, for further investigations of the other possible readings (given the *rasm*)—*lab*[*a*]*kah*, *lat*[*a*]*kah*, etc.—make no sense at all. We will proceed, then, from the original pronunciation of *Laykah* and its meaning as a place-name. The location that corresponds to this name is none other than *Leuke Kome*, the Greek name of the Nabataean harbor on the Red Sea—what else could it be?

However, the problem of the location of this place is not yet solved. Two geographic positions are under discussion: the first concerns Khuraybah near ʿAynūnah in northern Madyan, on the coast of the Red Sea; the other concerns the current Umm Lajj, four hundred kilometres south thereof. Both possibilities derive from varying interpretations of the earliest sources for Leuke Kome. The first comes from the description of the expedition of the Roman Aelius Gallus in the years 25–24 BCE; this expedition began in Egypt and proceeded through the Nabataean kingdom toward south Arabia and back again. The second, more southerly, possibly comes from the *Periplus of the Erythraean Sea,* deriving from either the first[26] or second[27] century CE. Unfortunately, Claudius Ptolemaeus does not mention a place called Leuke Kome in his *Geographia* (second century CE), but there may be an illuminating explanation for this omission.

The Northerly Localization of Leuke Kome

One of the arguments for the northerly possibility is the place-name Ḥawrah حَوْرة, which Musil identified with the ancient place [!] Madyan; he made this identification because the Aramaic / Arabic word *ḥawrā,* when translated, means "white" and therefore corresponds to the Greek *leuke*. This apparently led him to think of *Leuke Kome,* although the latter is actually a seaport and not an inland location like Ḥawrah = Madyan.

Even if one were to consider the notion that the port city should bear the same name as the inland capital (e.g., Modiana = Madiama in Ptolemaeus), it seems hardly plausible that the name of the seaport (Ḥawrah / Ḥawrāʾ = Leuke) should have been adopted for the capital, with the result that the prior name *Madyan* should have been totally forgotten. In Musil's reconstruction, the same would have happened to the name of the harbor itself (Ḥawrah / Leuke), with the result that its contemporary ruins should be called Khuraybah! In a relatively recent publication, Henry Macadam concluded in favor of the northern possibility: "In one explicit statement Strabo notes that the expedition [NB: of Aelius Gallus] arrived at 'Leukē Komē in Nabataean territory.' . . . The site of Leukē Komē, long disputed, now seems to be satisfactorily identified with the site of ʿAynūnah, directly east of the mouth of the Gulf of ʿAqabah" (see M. L. Ingraham et al., *Atlal* 5 [1981]: 76–78; L. I. Kirwan, *Studies in the History of Arabia* 2 [1984]: 55–61 and maps 5 and 58).[28] In the Ingraham article[29] mentioned by Macadam, however, the author says merely that, in the face of the number and historical depth of materials discovered in ʿAynūnah and Khuraybah, "our recent findings at ʿAynūnah suggest that this area is more likely Leuke Kome than other places suggested by other scholars. . . . The abundance of Nabataean / Roman surface pottery . . . at ʿAynūnah in contrast to the few sherds found at al-Ḥawra[30] . . . is convincing in itself . . ." (p. 78ff.). The conclusion to which Macadam comes based on the number of Roman artifacts seems rather tenuous, however, especially when these artifacts are brought into conversation with the description of Aelius Gallus's expedition.[31]

One does not have to be a general to recognize that it does not make sense to sail north from the Egyptian harbor of Berenikê in order to make landfall at the harbor of ʿAynūnah / Khuraybah, only to then march back south to Yemen and eventually to retrace one's steps entirely! Casson, the editor of the *Periplus*, after an extremely extensive discussion of the location of Leuke Kome, also came to the amazing opinion that the port city was to be identified with ʿAynūnah / Khuraybah.[32]

The Southerly Localization of Leuke Kome

Although the question of the northerly or southerly localization of the Nabataean seaport is only of subordinate significance for the present investigation, a southern location for Leuke Kome fits much better in a generalized conception of pre-islamic Midianite geography than any other solution to the problem. According to Strabo, who may have accompanied Aelius Gallus on his expedition, the area of the Nabataeans' influence stretched to the south as far as Leuke Kome.[33] Von Wißmann defends the same perspective and correspondingly argues for a location in the south, in Yanbuʿ itself or in its vicinity.[34]

A heretofore unintroduced argument in favor of the southern location is that in sura 15:79f., verses that mention the *ʾaṣḥābu ʾl-Ḥijr* ("the people from 'al-Ḥijr"), follow directly upon those that mention of the *ʾaṣḥābu ʾl-'aykah* (or better: *'aṣḥābu Laykah!)*. This proximity does not surprise us, for 'al-Ḥijr, the *Egra* of antiquity and the southern capital of the Nabataean kingdom, would naturally have stood in close geographical proximity to its port city of Leuke Kome.

Leuke Kome = 'al-Ḥawrā'

If it is possible, the Ptolemaic material actually does bear one trace that leads us to 'al-Ḥawrā'. While Ptolemaeus indeed does not mention Leuke Kome, he does point to a place—on the correct line of latitude, but displaced a bit eastward and inland—called *Aluara*. If only the name he preserved had been *Alaura!* Then its identification with 'al-Ḥawrā' would be airtight, and it would be clear that Ptolemaeus used the Aramaic translation of the place-name instead of the Greek version which one would expect. As it is, in view of the other arguments that speak in favor of such an identification, I believe the transposition of the two letters to be merely an error of transmission. Incidentally, von Maltzan used the argument of a double naming to argue for the identification of Leuke Kome with Iambia: "The circumstance that Ptolemaeus, who otherwise was so well-educated about Arabia, should not have mentioned Leuke Kome at all, appears to indicate satisfactorily that this name was merely a second name, a [neutral] epithet, for another place-name which the Alexandrian [Ptolemaeus] did include."[35] But the argument works much better for the identity of *Aluara = Alaura = 'al-Ḥawrā'= Leuke (Kome)* than for Iambia!

No other archaeological traces have been found of the ancient city of Leuke Kome. Should one want to search, though, for where the seaport of 'al-Ḥijr / *Egra* possibly would or necessarily must have lain, then one finds a harbor by the name of 'al-Ḥawrā' ("the white") which served as a way station for pilgrims from Egypt until the beginning of the twentieth century. This harbor lay between 'al-Wajh in the north and Yanbuʿ in the south! Since around 414/1023, the place has been known as a walled "city on the coast of the Wādī 'l-Qurà." Although its water is notorious for its salt content, the ships which are going to the Ḥijāz draw their drinking water from there. A Moroccan pilgrim of the nineteenth century reported that the name 'al-Ḥawrā´ did not fit the pitiful circumstances of the place at that time—a statement that allows one to conclude that the name 'al-Ḥawrā' did not derive from the location's miserable condition but rather was inherited from another location which once lay in its surrounding area. This pilgrim further noted that the fishermen who lived on the island of 'al-Ḥassānī, just off the coast from 'al-Ḥawrā', "now and then go diving in the area and find valuable jewelry."[36] This observation is also an indication that the port city disappeared because of a seaquake. This explanation would not be surprising in a region of strong seismic activity like the Red Sea and the northern Ḥijāz; further, it could explain both why Leuke Kome was no longer mentioned after the end of the third century CE[37] and why, much later, the name of the city no longer had any meaning for the Qur'ānic exegetes.

'Al-Ḥawrā' is apparently a name still known on a regional basis; it may be that this knowledge no longer refers to the old, lost city but rather of the coastal region where that city lay and which the aforementioned Moroccan pilgrim experienced. In their catalog of pilgrim way stations, which apparently derives from field research work, Ali al-Mughannum et al. introduce 'al-Ḥawrā' in the following way: "This is 25° 08' N and 37° 12' E, 45 km southeast of the Bir Al-Amarah site, and 7 km north of the city of Ummluj [sic] on the Red Sea coast. . . . A medium-sized site, it comprises several sandy hills with architectural units built of coral and gypsum. Surface collections . . . included a large quantity of islamic pottery sherds, and a few steatite sherds."[38]

Finally, there are also religious implications bound up with Laykah / 'al-Ḥawrā'. In the article on "Qawdam," Yāqūt[39] expressly mentions 'al-Ḥawrā' as the location where a certain ʿAbd 'al-Dār b. Ḥudayb, of the tribe of Juhaynah, wanted to erect a "competition" temple (*bayta*^{n}) in order to draw as many Arabs as possible away from the cultus centered on the Kaʿbah in Mecca. A story such as this could only have occurred in the pre-Islamic period, and if it does contain a kernel of truth, then the location of 'al-Ḥawrā' was of such import that it seemed ideal for the founding of a religious center.

The Qur'ān may contain still more texts that relate to *Laykah = 'al-Ḥawrā',* as, for example: *wa-s'alhum ʿani 'l-qariyati 'llatī kānat ḥāḍirata 'l-baḥri 'idh yaʿdūna fī 'l-sabti . . .* (Pickthall's translation: "Ask them . . . of the township that was by the sea, how they did break the Sabbath. . . .)" (sura 7:163). Thus begins the story of the (Jewish) group of people about whom no more is known but who were turned into apes as punishment for breaking the commandments concerning the Sabbath. In addition, there are dozens of verses that praise God for the wonder of sea travel,[40] even though the locations of the founding of Islam all supposedly lie far inland. It is hardly imaginable that such verses should have arisen in the world of caravan handlers who, on account of the climate, used to follow a route along the *eastern* slope of the Ḥijāz mountain range!

ʾAṣḥāb ʾal-Rass, the "People of the Fountain"?

The identifer *ʾaṣḥāb ʾal-rass,* "the people of the fountain," is just as non-specific as "the people of the tanglewood" and consequently just as ill-suited, in terms of its content, to serve as a warning example for God's punishing judgment. James A. Bellamy named off the exegetical legends about the ʾAṣḥāb ʾal-Rass and then courageously made the following paleographic argument: "Alas, all in vain! Al-Rass is really nothing but Idrīs misspelled. The *rāʾ* was written too close to the *dāl*, which was then read as a *lām* . . . So, Q.E.D.: Idrīs and al-Rass both go back to Esdras, and ʿUzayr goes back to Ezra, and in the apocryphal tradition Esdras and Ezra are the same."[41] Unfortunately, his paleographic argumentation is generally unconvincing, as is also the case here, chiefly if we accept that in early Islamic times the Qur'ān was written in the Ḥijāzī style of script: In it, it is simply impossible to confound a *rā'* with a *dāl*, and to misinterpret this letter subsequently, reading a *lām* instead of the *dāl*!

The earliest information we have concerning a toponym *ʾal-Rass* was transmitted by the Yemenite polymath ʾal-Hamdānī (d. 334/945 in Ṣanʿā').[42] According to his information the term refers either to a *wādī* or to a *sayl* in the region of Jabal Raḍwà, the mountains between Medina, the port of Laykah / ʾal-Ḥawrā' in the north, and that of Yanbuʿ farther south. This report is confirmed by the geographer Yāqūt, who wrote concerning the Ḥusayniyyīn, the tribalized descendants of Muḥammad, that they lived in this valley (*Muʿjam* II:790, s.v. Raḍwà); the Zaydi dynasty of the Rassids of Ṣaʿdah in Yemen have their heritage from this group. According to ʾal-Hamdānī and Yāqūt, then, the valley of *ʾal-Rass* lay north of Yanbuʿ. Ḥamad ʾal-Jāsir, the famous Saudi scholar of the twentieth century, published an article on ʾal-Rass, in which he collected many small bits from the Arabian tradition but did not come to a definite conclusion concerning its location. He did express hope, however, that archaeological work would one day find the solution.[43] Since then, the catalog of pilgrim routes by Ali al-Mughannum et al. has given a specific reference to the location of ʾal-Rass, as mentioned above.[44]

A look at Ptolemaeus's presentation of Arabia, which was written ca.

150 CE, shows a people named *ARSAE*, who lived directly north of *Iambia vic.*, the Yanbu' of today. For this reason Sprenger and Glaser have concluded that the "Arsians" were the inhabitants of Yanbu'.[45] The part of the name which bears its meaning is *ARS;* the remainder is merely an ending corresponding to the demands of Greek and Latin grammar. The Semitic equivalent of the letter sequence *ARS* would be *'-r-s*, and the "natural" pronunciation of that sequence would be /ars/ or /aras/. It is only a short step from here to a word like 'ar-Rass, which would have been understood as Arabic and thus provided an assimilated article.

Qawm Tubba', the "People of the Tubba'"?

In sura 50:14 the "people of Laykah" are followed by the "People of the Tubba'" (*qawm Tubba'*). This group is normally identified with the troops of a Yemenite king who is reported to have invaded northern and central Arabia, an action that resulted in catastrophic consequences for himself. One should not simply reject this interpretation (the "Pharaoh" referred to in the Punishment Stories is never given a name, and Qur'ānic "Kisrà" for the Persian Khosrow also remains nonspecific), even if the word *tubba'*, doubtless a Yemenite expression, may not be used here very correctly.[46] On the other hand, it is both legitimate and well within the sense of the Punishment Stories to look for the "People of the Tubba'" in a place that is concrete and not too far away, as in the case of Laykah and 'al-Rass.

Ptolemaeus's *Iambia vic.* could be just such a location. The current location of *Yanbu'* is, in fact, identical with the ancient *Iambia*, and in similar ways the pre-Arabic names of the other locations in the area are still recognizable in their later, Arabic names (OADitae = 'Ād, THEMUDitae = Thamūd, NAPATei = Nabaṭ, MADIAMa = Madyan, IATHRIPPa = Yathrib, ARSae = 'al-Rass, etc.). This does not mean, however, that the ancient names were completely "Arabic," and that they must therefore agree entirely in the smallest details. We have made the proposition here to show how ARS became 'al-Rass and that, in the case of Leuke Kome, 'al-Ḥawrā' is even the translation of the name into another language entirely! The pre-Arabic name can, therefore, also correspond to a name similar to the Arabic, one like the Aramaic *naba'* ("spring"), whose Arabic equivalent reads *yanbu'* or *yanbū'* (also "spring"). One can also imagine an Aramaized form of the Arabic (if we accept that the names given by Ptolemaeus were also "Old Arabic"): the Arabic Yanbuʿ would, in Aramaic form, assimilate the *nūn* and thus read Yabbuʿ. It is even possible that the place bore both names for quite a long time—*'Allahu 'aʿlam*! The decisive factor is that both Nabaʿ and also Yabbuʿ give the same *rasm* as the Qur'ānic Tubbaʿ. That means that a "regional" reading نبع or يبع is possible, over against the traditional (and actually quite improbable) reading of تبع .

It must be admitted that the philological / paleographic identification of Tubbaʿ with Nabaʿ or Yabbuʿ is not as immediately obvious as that of Laykah with Leuke and 'ar-Rass with Ar(a)s; nonetheless, it does have the advantage that it concerns a known location and fits in the Midianite landscape. The map of the places and peoples mentioned in the Punishment Stories stretches from the Dead Sea in the north (Lūṭ / Lot, and two places not mentioned in the Qur'ān, namely, Sodom and Gomorrah), through 'al-Ḥijr / Egra and its port city Laykah / Leuke Kome, over the Raḍwà mountains with the 'al-Rass / ARSae who lived there, as far as the southernmost location, the Nabataean port of Yanbuʿ / Yabbuʿ / Iambia. What is more, Ptolemaeus knew of the peoples of ʿĀd (OADitae) and Thamūd (THEMUDitae, THAMYDeni). In addition, he called the capital of the ʿĀd *Aramaya*, a name which appears in the Qur'ān as *'Iram* (sura 89:5ff.). The Qur´ān notes concerning the ʿĀd that the messenger Hūd was sent to them by God (sura 7:65; 11:50, 58, 60); in sura 7:65 and in 11:50, he is called "the brother of ʿĀd."[47] The Qur'ān reports about him that in vain he warned his people "in the sickle-dunes"—*bi-'l-'aḥqāfi*—concerning their destruction.

'Al-'Aḥqāf, the "Valleys of Midian" or the "Dunes of Ḥaḍramawt"?

In Madyan / Midian?

If the ʿĀd lived in Madyan / Midian, then the *'aḥqāf* must also be sought in this area. According to the geographer 'al-Bakrī, who based his work on the authority of the Qur'ānic exegete Mujāhid,[48] the reference is to the rocky region of Ḥismā in the land of Judhām,[49] which belongs to Madyan. Yāqūt says of Ḥismā that it lies west of Tabūk and includes therein the large Jabal 'Iram, and Musil adds the interesting information that "the name Aḥḳâf (Ḥaḳâf) has been preserved to the southwest of al-Bedʿ (Madian)."[50] However, Musil does not mention what is to be understood by the name "Aḥḳâf

(Ḥaḳâf)" as to its local population; in general, though, this information fits well with the assumption of an identification in Madyan / Midian.

In Ḥaḍramawt or Oman?

Nevertheless, Islamic tradition identifies the ʾAḥqāf with the sand dunes between Yemen, Ḥaḍramawt, and Oman. This identification, however, is absurd, as "dunes" are not a location against which or on which people gather, least of all dunes in the Empty Quarter![51] The legend itself forms the third part of ʾal-Bakrī's (cf. bibliography) article concerning *ʾal-ʾAḥqāf,* immediately after which he writes about its acceptable localization in the land of Judhām and then cites various authorities who argue that the location is in the dunes of Shiḥr ʿUmān and Ḥaḍramawt:

> Based on the authority of his sources, [the genealogist] ʾIbn ʾal-Kalbī [died 204/819] reports, following ʾal-ʾAṣbagh b. Nubātah:
>
> "We were together once with ʿAlī b. ʾAbī Ṭālib in the time of the caliphate of ʿUmar. At that time he asked a man from Ḥaḍramawt, ʿDo you really know everything about Ḥaḍramawt?ʾ He answered, 'You may as well have asked me for the location of Hūd's grave!' ʿAlī said that he was right. Then the man said, 'When I was still a very young boy, I accompanied a few others as we went to seek his grave, because he was so famous. We traveled a few days through the Wādī ʾl-ʾAḥqāf—one of our party already knew the location—until we came to a red sand dune which contained caves. That (well-informed) man led us to one of these caves, which we then entered. We investigated everything thoroughly, and we came to two stones, of which one lay above the other in such a way that only a slender person could squeeze through the gap between them. There I saw a man sitting on a throne, with rough skin and a thick beard. Sitting on the throne, he was dried out, and as I touched a part of his body, I noticed that he was stiff. Over his head there was something written in Arabic: "I am (the prophet) Hūd, who believes in God; I am in mourning concerning the ʿĀd, because they were unbelievers. Against God's will there was no opposition."' Then ʿAlī said, 'I heard exactly this from ʾAbū ʾl-Qāsim [i.e., the prophet Muḥammad]—may God bless him and grant him salvation!'"

This little tale illustrates how and in which circles the transfer of names took place, when the exegetes sought for textual explanations in the metropoles.[52] From a more hermeneutically suspicious perspective, this is a notable example of how a place-name, mentioned in the Qur'ān but no longer identifiable, could be usurped if it lay just far enough away from the early centers of Islam. (Not that it is the only one, of course; cf. above concerning 'al-Rass, or the "migration" of the ʿĀd to southern Arabia!) The localization of *'al-ʾAḥqāf* in Ḥaḍramawt is an example of a "derived geography," a phenomenon of which there are many examples in the Islamic tradition. Just to mention a few, the most well known popular pilgrimage sites and places of devotion in Yemen are the tombs of Ṣāliḥ and Shuʿayb, and in Ḥaḍramawt it is the Qabr Hūd above all.

Or in Madyan after all?

Thus, the position of the *ʾAḥqāf* in the region of Madyan is not in doubt. The Qur´ānic passage (sura 46:24) reads in Pickthall's translation: "Then, when they beheld it as a dense cloud (*ʿāriḍ*) coming toward their valleys, they said: Here is a cloud bringing us rain." According to information in the Qur'ān, then, the ʿĀd lived in valleys; however, that lifestyle was not normal for cattle breeders (seminomadic Arabs of the tribe of ʿUdhrah?),[53] but it was normal for the (Aramaic-speaking) farmers in the oases. Speaking purely paleographically, it would not be a problem at all to bring the "Kūfic" version, *bi-'l-ʾaḥqāf*, into agreement with one written in Aramaic. The Aramaic alphabet does have a few "false friends" that could lead a person astray who was reading one bit of writing as "Arabic" rather than as Aramaic. The written text, then, as written in Aramaic but spoken in Arabic, could therefore have looked like this: ܒܐܠ ܥܡܩ (or ܒܐܠܥܡܩ);[54] it would have then been read in Arabic as *bi-'l-ʾaʿmāq* (= "in the deep places"), that is, "in the valleys." Misread as Arabic—a phenomenon attested in the Qur'ān[55]—it would give, among other possibilities, بالاحقٰف / *bi-'l-ʾaḥqāfi*. With such a meaning we step quite definitely onto less-secure ground, for the variant literature does not mention this possibility here. The advantage of such speculation, however, consists in that we do not then have to leave the Midianite landscape. Musil's information (cf. n. 50), according to which the word *ʾaḥḳāf* is current in the region of al-Badʿ, would be even more valuable in this connection if he had reported that people in that area use that word to indicate valleys (whether dry or with water); unfortunately, as I have noted, we do not know what they mean by the expression.

Wabār, the "Atlantis of the Desert"?

As we have seen, Qur'ānic exegesis in general placed the enigmatic *'aḥqāf* with its prophet Hūd on the edge of the imaginable world—on the one hand, in a specific place, but on the other hand, still in a mythical land—"nowhere." The fate of *Wabār,* however, was to end up totally in myth. It was a name that did not receive the honor of being mentioned either in the Bible or in the Qur'ān.[56] It was a part of the Midianite extrabiblical saga, which I mention here because it provides Wabār with a similar narrative setting as was given to 'al-'Aḥqāf, and because it also left behind a trace in the work of Ptolemaeus.

Traditionally, Wabār is assumed to be "between 'al-Shiḥr and Ṣan'ā'," or still more diffusely, "in the region between Yabrīn and 'al-Yaman"—that is, in the same wide desert area where the exegetes reported that *'al-'Aḥqāf* lay! As a matter of curiosity, it must be mentioned that scholars were able to find, after a great deal of technical effort, the remains of a settlement in southern Oman. This location was identified quickly and sensationally as Wabār, the "Atlantis of the Sands."[57] Scholars began archaeological digs, but these revealed not a city, but only a building. On the other hand, *Wabār* is considered in the genealogies of the Arabians to be the son of 'Iram b. Sām b. Nūḥ, or alternatively his great-grandson (Wabār b. 'Umaym b. Lawdhān b. 'Iram; Wabār is thereby a descendant of Aramaic speakers). In addition, the geographer Yāqūt (*Mu'jam,* s.v. Wabār) places Wabār's position within the earlier region of the 'Ād and Thamūd: "When God destroyed the 'Ād and Thamūd, he settled the *jinn* in their region, that is, in Wabār."

One could simply stop with a localization in northwest Arabia, but one could go even further. A look at a map of Arabia based on Ptolemaeus reveals a BANUBARI north of the ARSAE. The first part of the word doubtless refers to the tribal identifier *banu/ū;* the second part, *Bari* or *Ubari*, then stands for the actual name of the region or the people. Sprenger wrote very perceptively that "if one looks at plain similarities of names, then it could be the Banû-Bahrâ. But still more similar is Banû-Barra."[58] Unfortunately, this proposal does have a slight blemish, in that both proposed tribal names would trace back to women. For this reason as well I believe the *Ubari* of antiquity to be identical with the *Wabār* of the Arabian legend.

Philologically, *'Ubar* and *Wabār* are not different from one another. Initial *u*'s in Arabian place-names are often written either as an Alif with

Ḍammah or else—especially in dialects—as a Wāw with Ḍammah. For example, the Yemeni regions *Wuṣāb* وصاب and *'Uṣāb* اصاب are the same. This phenomenon also appears in the Qur'ān, for example, in sura 77:11 where it reads *'uqqitat* instead of *wuqqitat*. With this knowledge one no longer has simply to argue for the identification of *Wabār* with *Ubār(i)*, but one can even prove it: the historian of the city of Medina, 'al-Samhūdī (844–911/1440–1506), noted that *'Ubār* and *'Ubayr* ("little *'Ubār*") belonged to the wādīs of 'al-'Ajrad, one of the two mountains of Juhaynah, and that both wādīs went into Yanbu'.[59]

Conclusions

The exegetes of the Qur'ān interpreted the word ليكة as "tanglewood," which is not very convincing because in that case one must admit to errors of writing in two places in the text of the Qur'ān. The other position is that the word is actually a (place-) name, one that had not entirely disappeared; the memory of the exact location to which it could refer, however, seems to have been lost. It is only with a look at the depiction of Arabia given by Ptolemaeus that one comes to the surprising realization that by ليكة the Qur'ān not only handed down the name of the ancient port city of Leuke Kome, but that it also, as providing a means of confirmation, gave the names of other places in the Nabataean kingdom. As a result, it is clear first of all that the written Qur'ānic text contains material that is older than the oral tradition of the text, that is, that it contains *pre-Islamic material*; second, it is clear that occasionally the oldest written transmission preserved this older text, even if the later exegetes, in their time of need, had to reach far too widely to offer their explanations or "corrections." Generally speaking, then, it will be worthwhile to work out the oldest conceivable textual structure and to pay attention to the fact that, in terms of its interpretation, the text is indeed adequate in its content.

NOTES

1. I formulated the foundational ideas of this article in Jerusalem on July 4, 2000, in the paper "Leuke Kome in the Qur'ān: A Way out of the 'Tanglewood'?" as a part of the Eighth International Conference, "From Jāhiliyya to Islam," July 2–7, 2000.

Special attention has been paid in this article to the transcription of Arabic because part of the argument is directly related to the question of how certain words are written in the Qur'ān. Thus, Alif-Waṣlah is always represented by <’>, Hamzah on Alif or Yā' or Wāw by <ʾ>, and Hamzah without carrier as <'>. ʿAyn is, as usual, <ʿ>.

2. On this topic, cf. Aloys Sprenger, *Das Leben und die Lehre des Mohammad* (*Nach großtentheils unbenutzten Quellen bearbeitet*), 2nd ed., 3 vols. (Berlin: Nicolaische Verlagsbuchhandlung, 1869), I: 459–504, 505–25; cf. also Josef Horovitz, *Koranische Untersuchungen*, (Berlin and Leipzig: de Gruyter, 1926).

3. Alois Musil, *The Northern Ḥeǧāz: A Topographical Itinerary*, American Geographical Society Oriental Explorations and Studies, no. 1 (New York: American Geographical Society, 1926), 291f.

4. These translations are those by Pickthall; emphases are my own.

5. Musil, *Northern Ḥeǧāz*, pp. 299–301. Musil is of the opinion that the harbor called Egra / 'al-Ḥijr bore the same name as the Nabataean city of Egra / 'al-Ḥijr, which lay far inland. This situation would then be analogous to that of the city Madyan and its harbor which bore the same name.

6. Ibid., pp. 273f., 312.

7. Ibid., pp. 278–87, 313; Hermann v. Wißmann, "Madiama und Modiana (Madyan, Midian)," in *Paulys Real-Encyclopädie der classischen Altertumswissenschaft, Suppl. Bd.* XII (1970), pp. 525–52.

8. See, e.g., John Healy, "The Nabataeans and Madā'in Ṣāliḥ," *Atlal: The Journal of Saudi Arabian Archaeology* 10 (1406/1986): 108–16 and plates 107, 108, 109 (maps). See also Daifullah Al-Talhi et al., "Preliminary Report on al-Hijr Excavations during the First Season 1406/1986," *Atlal: The Journal of Saudi Arabian Archaeology* 11 (1409/1988): 47–57.

9. ʿAntarah p. 41 l. 19: *a-fa-min bukā'i ḥamāmatin fī ʾaykatin* . . . and al-Nābighah p. 10 l. 14: *tajlū bi-qādimatay ḥamāmati ʾaykatin* . . . according to Albert Arazi, *Six Early Arab Poets*. New ed. and Concordance (Jerusalem, 1999). See also the entry ايك in E. W. Lane, *Arabic-English Lexicon*. I–VIII (London, 1863), repr. in USA, 1955.

10. Unfortunately, the usual Arabic character sets do not provide a Hamza written upon the connecting line between two letters, although this is not rare at all for Qur'ānic quotations. As a substitute for this Hamza in this article, the words which appear in Arabic script will be written with a special long character (*taṭwīl*); however,

the transliteration of this kind of a Hamza is unequivocal, appearing always as <ʾ>, whether the Hamza is placed over a connecting line or without a "carrier" altogether.

11. Murtaḍà al-Zabīdī, *Tāj al-ʿarūs*, s.v. *ʾayk*; Ibn Manẓūr, *Lisan al-ʿarab*, s.v. *ʾayk*.

12. J. G. Wetzstein, "Nordarabien und die syrische Wüste nach den Angaben der Eingebornen (Fortsetzung)," *Zeitschrift für allgemeine Erdkunde* 18 (1865): 441.

13. Moritz in *RE*, vol. XII (1925), col. 2262: "Wetzstein's identification . . . with al-Aika of the Qurʾān, is nothing other than a idea which is linguistically impossible, because λευκή [*leuke*] would be transferred into Arabic as *lûka* or *lûḳa*, as Σελεύκεια [*Seleukeia*] became *Salûḳîya*."

14. Heinrich Freiherr v. Maltzan, *Meine Wallfahrt nach Mekka: Reise in die Küstengegend und im Innern von Hedschas*, 2 vols. (Leipzig: Dyk, 1865; reprint edition, Hildesheim: Olms, 2004) I:16–24; concerning the place here called "Auara," see below, in the section entitled *"Leuke Kome = ʾal-Ḥawrāʾ."*

15. Musil, *Northern Ḥeǧāz*, p. 280. Musil's association reminds one of the equation of Bakkah and Makkah in the exegesis of the Qurʾān.

16. A. F. L. Beeston, "The "Men of the Tanglewood' in the Qurʾān," *Journal of Semitic Studies* 13 (1968): 253–55.

17. C. E. Bosworth, "Madyan Shuʿayb in Pre-Islamic and Early Islamic Lore and History," *Journal of Semitic Studies* 29, no. 1 (Spring 1984): 53–64.

18. In the "thicket," that is, I have myself experienced tribespeople living among thick trees in the immediate vicinity of al-Maṭammah in the Wādī Madhāb, in Yemen. Sitting in that thicket I talked about the neighboring settlement, built from neat multistory clay houses, which an old man laconically commented thus: "Hāwlā buyyāʿ, nastaḍʿifhum" ("Those are dealers [on weekly markets], 'weak ones' in our eyes"). This means that the inhabitants of the houses exist under the protection of the tribespeople living in the thicket. However, one imagines the ʿĀd and the Thamūd much more in rock dwellings or stone houses rather than in a thicket!

19. In the two other transmissions of the Qurʾānic text, as well as in Nāfiʿ's variants (see the table below, in the grayed boxes), a differentiation appears to be made between the thing ("tanglewood" = الأيكة) and the place-name ليكة . This would mean that the varying way of writing the *rasm* has destroyed the identity of both forms.

20. Concerning sura 15:78 I have seen only the two facsimile editions of the manuscripts Paris BN Ms. ar. 328 (a), p. 229, line 20, and London BL Or. 2165, p. 140, l. 21; these manuscripts do not contain the other three texts. Both manuscripts show the "correct" text of the Cairo standard edition. Concerning these facsimiles cf. Sergio Noja Noseda and François Déroche, *Sources de la transmission manuscrite du text Coranique, I: Les manuscrits de style ḥiǧāzī*, vol. 1, *Le manuscript arabe 328(a) de la Bibliothèque nationale de France* (Lesa: Fondazione Ferni Noja Noseda, 1998) and vol. 2:1, *Le manuscript Or.* 2165 (f. 1 *à* 61) *de la British Library* (Lesa: Fondazione Ferni Noja Noseda, 2001).

21. *'Al-Qur'ān 'al-Karīm*. Taṣmīm Muḥammad ʿAbd 'al-Raḥmān Muḥammad, 'al-Qāhirah: Dār al-Muṣḥaf 1383/1964. (*'al-Qur'ān 'al-Karīm* [in the original without a title]). Khaṭṭ 'al-Tijānī 'al-Muḥammadī (AH 1365) (Tūnis: Maktabat 'al-Manār, no year [ca. 1995]).

22. *Muṣḥaf Sharīf*, bi-riwāyat 'al-ʾimām Qālūn bi-'l-rasm 'al-ʿuthmānī. ʾIʿdād Maktabat 'al-Yaman 'al-Kubrā, Ṣanʿā', no year (after 1983). This work was not published in Yemen, but rather in Libya, as the appendix on pages iii–vi reveals. In Zaydi Yemen, however, the transmission following Qālūn is widespread, too. For curiosity I quote its page iv: "The committee [of editors] began its work on Monday, the 27th of Rabīʿ 'al-ʾĀkhar (of the year) 1390 *after the passing of the Prophet* [this being the new era introduced by Muʿammar al-Qadhdhāfī!]—God bless him and grant him salvation!—which corresponds to March 2nd, 1982 AD. It was the anniversary of the first proclamation of the [Libyan] Jamāhiriyyah, the establishment of democratic power, and the announcement of the historical document in which the Muslim Libyan Arabic people made known that the honorable Qur'ān would be the law of society in the Arabic Libyan Socialist People's Jamāhiriyyah. On the blessed Night of Destiny [i.e., on the 27th] of the honored Ramaḍān of the year 1392 after the passing of the Prophet—God bless him and grant him salvation!—which corresponds to June 7th, 1983, a huge religious festival was celebrated in the Mawlāy Muḥammad mosque in Ṭarābulus [Tripoli], on which occasion the Brother in Religion and Revolution, General Muʿammar al-Qadhdhāfī, leader of the Glorious Revolution, officially wrote the last [Qur'ānic] word والناس in the Muṣḥaf al-Jamāhiriyyah, to the cries of "*'Allāhu 'akbar!*" and "*lā 'ilāha 'illā 'llāh!*" of thousands of Muslims." (My additions in [brackets]).

23. ʿAbd 'al-ʿĀl Sālim Makram (wa-) Aḥmad Mukhtār ʿUmar (ʾIʿdād), *Muʿjam 'al-Qirā'āt 'al-Qur'āniyyah, maʿa muqaddimah fī 'l-qirā'āt wa-ʾash-har 'al-qurrā'*. I–VIII. al-Kuwayt: Dhāt 'al-Salāsil, 1402–1405/1982–1985.

24. 'Al-Zamakhsharī argues that "Laykah" should not be read like "laylah," but rather as "l'aykah," that is, with a Hamza after the Lām, because the Alif is not written but still must be taken into consideration in pronunciation. He seems to be thinking here of the two places in which الايكة is written fully.

25. *MQQ* IV, pp. 324f., n. 2.

26. 40–70 CE: Lionel Casson, ed., *The Periplus Maris Erythraei: Text with Introduction, Translation, and Commentary* (Princeton: Princeton University Press, 1989), pp. 6f. and n. 7.

27. 95–130 CE: G. W. B. Huntingford, ed., *The Periplus of the Erythraean Sea by an Unknown Author, with Some Extracts from Agatharkhidēs' 'On the Erythraean Sea'* (London: Hakluyt Society, 1980), p. 12. Wißmann, "Madiama and Modiana," in *RE Suppl.* (1970): col. 542, dated the text even later, "around and after 210 CE."

28. Henry I. Macadam, "Strabo, Pliny the Elder, and Ptolemy of Alexandria:

Three Views of Ancient Arabia and its Peoples," in *L'Arabie préislamique et son environnement historique et culturel: Actes du Colloque de Strasbourg 24–27 juin 1987,* ed. T. Fahd (Leiden: Brill, 1989), p. 299. (The whole article can be found on pp. 289–315.)

29. Michael Lloyd Ingraham et al., "Saudi Arabian Comprehensive Survey Program: c. Preliminary Report on a Reconnaissance Survey of the Northwestern Province," *Atlal: The Journal of Saudi Arabian Archaeology* 5 (1401/1981): 59–79 and plates 62 and 67 (= Contour Map of ʿAynūnah, with Khuraybah).

30. Ali al-Mughannum, Salah al-Helwa, and Jamal Mursi, "Catalogue of Stations on the Egyptian (Coastal) and Syrian (Inland) Pilgrimage Routes," *Atlal: The Journal of Saudi Arabian Archaeology* 7 (1403/1983): 46 (the entire article comprises pp. 42–75).

31. Strabo, Plinius, and Dio Cassius all described this expedition, led by the Roman Aelius Gallus in the years 25/24 BCE from Egypt into the lands of the Nabataeans, allies of the Romans at this time; Eduard Glaser, in his *Skizze der Geschichte und Geographie Arabiens und von den ältesten Zeiten bis zum Propheten Muhammad,* vol. 2 (Berlin, 1890; reprint edition, Hildesheim: Olms, 1976), pp. 45–73, has translated and commented upon these three sources comprehensively. Cf. also the works of Wißmann given in this essay's bibliography, as well as Kai Buschmann's article "Motiv und Ziel des Aelius-Gallus-Zuges nach Südarabien," *Die Welt des Orients* 22 (1991): 85–93.

32. Casson, *Periplus*, pp.143f.; cf. also p. x with reference to "identification of Leukê Komê" by Laurence Kirwan.

33. Musil, *Northern Ḥeǧāz,* p. 310.

34. Wißmann, "Madiama and Modiana," in *RE Suppl.* vol XII (1970).

35. Maltzan, *Meine Wallfahrt,* I: p. 116.

36. Cf. Ḥamad 'al-Jāsir's article on 'al-Ḥawrā' in his *al-Muʿjam al-jughrāfī li-'l-bilād al-ʿarabiyyah 'al-saʿūdiyyah, Shamāl 'al-mamlakah,* Qism I-III ('al-Riyāḍ: Dār 'al-Yamāmah, [1st ed.] 1397/1977), pp. 1463–68.

37. Thus Jawād ʿAlī, *'Al-Mufaṣṣal fī taʾrīkh 'al-ʿarab qabla 'l-ʾislām* (Baghdād: Makt. al-Nahḍah 1970–73; ʾIʿādat 'al-ṭabʿ Bayrūt: Dār 'al-ʿIlm li-l-Malāyīn, 1978, 1980), VII:272, following the *Handbuch der geographischen Wissenschaften,* I: p. 114. Cf. also Kenneth W. Russell, "The Earthquake Chronology of Palestine and Northwest Arabia from the 2nd through the Mid-8th Century A.D.," *Bulletin of the American Schools of Oriental Research* (BASOR) 260, pp. 37–59.

38. Al-Mughannum et al., "Catalogue of Stations on the Egyptian (Coastal) and Syrian (Inland) Pilgrimage Routes," see above n. 30.

39. *Muʿjam al-buldān.* The original report can be found in Hishām b. al-Kalbī, *K. 'al-ʾAṣnām,* ed. Aḥmad Zakī ('al-Qāhirah: Dār 'al-Kutub, 1324/1924); there is also an unaltered reprint edition from (al-Qāhirah: 'al-Dār 'al-Qawmiyyah,

1384/1964), p. 45. Cf. M. J. Kister's article "Ḳuḍā'a" in the second edition of the *Encyclopaedia of Islam*, p. 315.

40. Cf. W. W. Barthold, "Der Koran und das Meer," *Zeitschrift der Deutschen Morgenländischen Gesellschaft* 83 (1929): 37–43.

41. James A. Bellamy, "Textual Criticism of the Koran," *Journal of the American Oriental Society* 121, no. 1 (2001): 1–6.

42. 'al-Ḥasan b. 'Aḥmad 'al-Hamdanī, *Kitāb Ṣifat Jazīrat 'al-'Arab* (in the edition of David Heinrich Müller, *Geographie der arabischen Halbinsel* [Leiden: Brill, 1884–91; reprint edition, Amsterdam: Oriental Press, 1968]), p. 218, l. 24; p. 230, l. 24; and p. 251, l. 9.

43. Ḥamad 'al-Jāsir, "'al-Rass' fī 'l-Qur'ān 'al-karīm wa-'ārā' 'al-bāḥithīn ḥawlah," (*Majallat*) *'al-'Arab* 5 (1390/1970): 1–12., n. 38.

44. Al-Mughannum et al., "Catalogue," p. 45, see above n. 30.

45. A. Sprenger, *Die alte Geographie Arabiens: Als Grundlage der Entwicklungsgeschichte des Semitismus* (Bern, 1875; reprint edition: Amsterdam, Meridian, 1966), p. 31; Glaser, *Skizze,* pp. 104, 232.

46. Cf. Beeston's skeptical article "Tubba'" in the second edition of the *Encyclopaedia of Islam.* Cf. also Yūsuf M. 'Abd Allah's article "tubba'" in *'al-Mawsū'ah 'al-Yamaniyyah* (Ṣan'ā': Mu'assasat 'al-'Afīf 'al-Thaqafiyyah, 1412/1992) (tanfīdh Bayrūt: Dār 'al-Fikr 'al-Mu'āṣir). There is more comprehensive information on *tubba'* in the genealogy of the South Arabians: Werner Caskel's *Jamharat an-Nasab: Das genealogische Werk des Hišām Ibn Muḥammad al-Kalbī*, 2 vols. (Leiden: Brill, 1966), II:66–72.

47. This expression means that he was not a member of the tribe, but rather that he came from outside, as Muḥammad did to Medina and as, still today, many families of tribal leaders do on the Arabian peninsula (Yemen, Saudi Arabia, Qatar, Kuwait, Bahrain). According to a version mentioned by Wahb b. Munabbih, God revealed the Arabic alphabet to the prophet Hūd, an alphabet "with its 29 letters" *(K. 'al-Tījān,* Ḥaydar-Ābād: Maṭb. Majlis Dā'irat 'al-Ma'ārif 'al-'Uthmāniyyah 1347, p. 35). Because only the Arabic alphabet contains 28 letters, plus the ligature Lām-Alif, which is counted as a letter, Wahb clearly means this fuller alphabet. The only other alphabet showing the ligature Lām-Alif at the outset as well as at the end of a word is the Syriac one, which makes clear that there is at least a link between both alphabets. Because "Hūd" appears in the Qur'ān as a term referring to the Jews (nine times it appears as "Yahūd," three times as "Hūd"), the prophet "Hūd" serving possibly as a general personification of the Jews. Wahb's legend would then have as its historical kernel that the Arabs received their alphabet from Jews who wrote in Syriac. Why not?

48. Mujāhid b. Jabr 'al-Makkī, 21—ca. AH 104 ; cf. the article "Mudjāhid" in the second edition of the *Encyclopaedia of Islam.*

49. *Muʿjam,* s.v. "aḥqāf." Cf. W. Montgomery Watt's article "Iram" in the second edition of the *Encyclopaedia of Islam.*

50. Cf. Musil, *Northern Ḥeǧāz,* p. 316.

51. Cf. Sprenger, *Die alte Geographie,* p. 199: "It is very doubtful that, at the time of Muḥammad, al-Aḥqâf, 'rolling hills of sand,' was a proper name; he may have meant the Nefûd of Ḥismà. . . . If there is some historical foundation to these reports, it is that the ʿÂdites lived north of Mecca."

52. On this genre of literature which reaches back into the Umayyad period, cf. Raif Georges Khoury, "Kalif, Geschichte, und Dichtung: Der jemenitische Erzähler ʿAbīd Ibn Šarya am Hofe Muʿāwiyas," *Zeitschrift für arabische Linguistik* 25 (1993): 204–18.

53. Cf. G. Lévi Della Vida's article "ʿUḏhra" in the second edition of the *Encyclopaedia of Islam.*

54. This could be the case *if* the Alif of the article fell out after the particle, something that happens regularly after a Lām and also sometimes after a Bā' or a Kāf (cf. بسم الله, and quite frequently in old manuscripts), and *if* the small stroke at the left of the Aramaic Mīm was overlooked.

55. In my opinion this has happened in the suras Ṣād (no. 38) and Qāf (no. 50), whose "secret letters" ص and ق are different in Arabic but both derive from an Aramaic ṣade; if this letter is "read" as an Arabic one (more precisely, in the Ḥijāzī style of script), then it would be interpreted either as a Ṣād (correctly) or as a Qāf (incorrectly). The same is true for the *ʿamma (yatasā'alūn)* at the beginning of sura 78 which is certainly not different from the *Ḥā-Mīm* letters at the beginning of some other suras.

56. In his major work *Das Leben und die Lehre . . . ,* Aloys Sprenger reported and treated critically both the "Punishment Stories" (I:459–504) and the narratives concerning ʿĀd and Thamūd (I:505–25).

57. As far as I know, two books appeared in connection with the Wabār of Oman: Ranulf Fiennes, *Atlantis of the Sands: The Search for the Lost City of Ubar* (London: Bloomsbury, 1992); and Nicholas Clapp, *The Road to Ubar: Finding the Atlantis of the Sands* (Boston and New York: Houghton Mifflin, 1998). Clapp's argument in favor of the localization of Wabār in Oman rests chiefly on Ptolemaeus's naming of the IOBARitae, which Clapp then identifies with ʾUbār / Wabār.

58. Sprenger, *Die alte Geographie,* pp. 30f.

59. From his *Wafā' 'al-Wafā',* cited by Ḥamad 'al-Jāsir, *Bilād Yanbuʿ: Lamaḥāt taʾrīkhiyyah jughrāfiyyah wa-'nṭibāʿāt khāṣṣah* ('al-Riyāḍ: Dār 'al-Yamāmah, no year given [ca. 1970]), p. 158. Concerning the person and work of 'al-Samhūdī, cf. Bosworth's article "Samhūdī" in the second edition of the *Encyclopaedia of Islam.*

BIBLIOGRAPHY

ʿAlī, Jawād. *'al-Mufaṣṣal fī ta'rīkh 'al-ʿarab qabla 'l-'islām*. Juz' I-X. Baghdād: Makt. 'al-Nahḍah 1970–73; 'Iʿādat 'al-ṭabʿ Bayrūt: Dār 'al-ʿIlm li-l-Malāyīn, 1978, 1980.

'al-Bakrī, 'Abū ʿUbayd ʿAbd 'Allah. *Muʿjam mā 'staʿjam min 'asmā' 'al-bilād wa-'l-mawāḍiʿ*. Juz' I-IV. Taḥqīq Muṣṭafà 'al-Saqqā. 'al-Qāhirah: Lajnat 'al-Ta'līf, 1364/1945.

Brice, William C., ed. *An Historical Atlas of Islam*. Leiden: Brill, 1981.

Casson, Lionel, ed. *The Periplus Maris Erythraei: Text with Introduction, Translation, and Commentary*. Princeton: Princeton University Press, 1989.

EI² = *The Encyclopaedia of Islam, New Edition Prepared by a Number of Leading Orientalists*. 11 vols. Leiden: Brill, 1960–.

Glaser, Eduard. *Skizze der Geschichte und Geographie Arabiens und von den ältesten Zeiten bis zum Propheten Muhammad*, vol. 2. Berlin, 1890. Reprint edition, Hildesheim: Olms, 1976.

'al-Hamdānī, 'al-Ḥasan b. 'Aḥmad. *Kitāb Ṣifat Jazīrat 'al-ʿArab*, edited David Heinrich Müller *(Geographie der arabischen Halbinsel)*. Leiden: Brill, 1884–1891. Reprint edition, Amsterdam: Oriental Press, 1968.

Huntingford, G. W. B., ed. *The Periplus of the Erythraean Sea by an Unknown Author, with Some Extracts from Agatharkhidēs' 'On the Erythraean Sea.'* London: Hakluyt Society, 1980.

'al-Jāsir, Ḥamad. *Bilād Yanbuʿ: Lamaḥāt ta'rīkhiyyah jughrāfiyyah wa-'nṭibāʿāt khāṣṣah*. 'al-Riyāḍ: Dār 'al-Yamāmah, no year given (ca. 1970).

________. *'Al-Muʿjam 'al-jughrāfī li-l-bilād 'al-ʿarabiyyah 'al-saʿūdiyyah, Shamāl 'al-mamlakah*, Qism I-III. 1st ed. 'al-Riyāḍ: Dār 'al-Yamāmah,1397/1977.

________. "'Al-Rass' fī 'l-Qur'ān 'al-karīm wa-'ārā' 'al-bāḥithīn ḥawlah." *(Majallat) 'al-ʿArab* 5 (1390/1970): 1–12.

v. Maltzan, Heinrich Freiherr. *Meine Wallfahrt nach Mekka: Reise in die Küstengegend und im Innern von Hedschas*. 2 vols. Leipzig: Dyk, 1865. Reprint edition, Hildesheim: Olms, 2004.

Musil, Alois. *The Northern Ḥeǧāz: A Topographical Itinerary*. American Geographical Society Oriental Explorations and Studies, no. 1. New York: American Geographical Society, 1926.

Noja Noseda, Sergio, and François Déroche. *Sources de la transmission manuscrite du text Coranique, I: Les manuscrits de style ḥiǧāzī*. Vol. 1, *Le manuscript arabe 328(a) de la Bibliothèque nationale de France*, and vol. 2:1, *Le manuscript Or. 2165 (f. 1 à 61) de la British Library*. Lesa: Fondazione Ferni Noja Noseda, 1998, 2001.

RE = *Paulys Real-Encyclopädie der classischen Altertumswissenschaft. Neue Bearbeitung*. Stuttgart, 1893–.

Sprenger, Aloys. *Das Leben und die Lehre des Moḥammad (Nach größtentheils unbenutzten Quellen bearbeitet)*. 3 vols. 2nd ed. Berlin: Nicolaische Verlagsbuchhandlung, 1869.

________. *Die alte Geographie Arabiens: Als Grundlage der Entwicklungs-geschichte des Semitismus*. Bern, 1875. Reprint edition, Amsterdam: Meridian, 1966.

v. Wißmann, Hermann. "Madiama und Modiana (Madyan, Midian)." In *Paulys Real-encyclopädie der classischen Altertumswissenschaft, Suppl. Bd.* XII (1970), pp. 525–52.

________. "Ōphīr und Ḥawīla (Maʿmal und Ḫaulān)." In *Paulys Real-encyclopädie der classischen Altertumswissenschaft, Suppl. Bd.* XII, pp. 906–80.

POSTSCRIPT

The sporadic mention of persons, peoples, or places is a typical feature of the Qur'ānic style, and the want for more details is certainly one reason for the development of the so-called *Isrā'īliyyāt* genre of popular biblical stories in the early times of Islam. However, the interest in such details is not restricted to the Orientalists' questions of provenance, dependency, or influence, but it has risen also among modern Muslim exegetes. The "father of the literary exegesis of the Qur'ān" is renowned to be the Egyptian Amīn al-Khūlī (1895–1967), whose ideas have been further developed by Muḥammad Aḥmad Khalaf Allah, Bint al-Shāṭ', and today by Naṣr Abū Zaid. In his outline of an exegesis* of the Qur'ān, al-Khūlī mentions explicitly the places and peoples that we have dealt with in this article:

> As long as we mention al-Ḥijr, al-Aḥqāf, al-Aykah, Midyan, the homes of Thamūd and the camps of ʿĀd, without knowing about these places more than these casual indications we are not entitled to say that we have understood what the Qur'ān tells about them or about their peoples nor that we have grasped the intention of what the Qur'ān tells about them. Thus, the lesson of this narrative cannot become manifest, nor can the requested wisdom and guidance become beneficial and effective. (transl. G.-R. P.)

Apart from the religious motive behind al-Khūlī's curiosity to know more about the like Qur'ānic details, there is no doubt that both the believer and the unbeliever have, first of all, an interest in finding facts acceptable for all. In this respect perhaps my article is of help.

* Amīn al-Khūlī : *Manāhij tajdīd fī'l-naḥw wa-'l-balāgha wa-'l-tafsīr wa-'l-adab*. Al-Qāhira 1961, p. 311.—I owe the quotation to Katrin Speicher, "Einige Bemerkungen zu al-Ḫūlīs Entwurf eines tafsīr adabī," in Stefan Wild (Festschrift), *Encounters of Words and Texts. Intercultural Studies in Honor of Stefan Wild*, ed. Lutz Edzard and Christian Szyska (Hildesheim: Olms, 1997) (Arabistische Texte und Studien, Band 10), 3–21.— The German translation of the quotation is there on p. 10.

10

SYRIAN AND ARABIAN CHRISTIANITY AND THE QUR'ĀN

Karl-Heinz Ohlig

The region of "Syria"—a cultural term, not a political one—reaches from the Palestinian coast of the Mediterranean to the other side of the Tigris and from the Persian Gulf to northern Mesopotamia. Historically, the majority of the population was ethnically Semitic and shaped by the Aramaic language and culture. For one-and-a-half millennia, in the time of the Babylonians and the Assyrians, Semitic political empires developed. After this period, eastern Syria stood under Persian, Greek, Parthian, and Sassanian rule, with western Syria under the government of the Romans (and Byzantines).

THE POLITICAL, CULTURAL, AND RELIGIOUS REGION OF SYRIA

Political History—A Short Outline

After a short interlude in the late third millennium BCE (the time of the Akkadians), Mesopotamia, which (at the risk of oversimplification) had until that time been Sumerian, was taken over by the Semitic empires of the Babylonians, the Assyrians, and (beginning in the late seventh century BCE) again by the Babylonians. At the same time, small, and still somewhat automous Semitic states had remained for quite a long period on the eastern coast of the Mediterranean. During the sixth century BCE at the latest, however, these states were integrated into the Neo-Babylonian Empire.

Beginning probably around 1000 BCE, the Aramaic language slowly developed, and it later became the *lingua franca* of this area. In the sixth century it even pushed out the Hebrew language, so that Jesus' mother tongue was Aramaic. This language, first called "Aramaic" and later "Syriac," survived all the politico-cultural overlapping and the occasional repression in its region, and, even into the eighth century CE, when the Arabization of the area had already begun, it was the language of the people, their business, their culture, and the Christian liturgy.

By the eighth century BCE, the Medes ruled over a huge amount of territory north of the Babylonian Empire, from current eastern Turkey to the region around the Indus River; their kinspeople, the Indo-European Persians, then followed them into this area. These latter people, who settled on the Persian Gulf, were for a long time vassals of the Median kings, until they founded their own large empire under Cyrus II (d. 529 BCE), beginning in the middle of the sixth century. To this empire belonged the previous Median Empire, the Babylonian Empire, Asia Minor (Lydia), and later also Thrace and Egypt. A further attempt at conquests in Europe was hindered by the Scythians and the opposition of the Greeks.

Beginning at that time, the Persian language and culture became and remained an important factor in the region under consideration here, although beginning in the middle of the fourth century BCE, even government documents were published in the Aramaic language and script. Also at this time, the Zoroastrian religion (Zarathustra, d. ca. 553 BCE?), which had begun around 600 BCE, acquired religious power that would last into the Islamic period, even though it was not spread via missionaries under the Persian kings. Rather, they preferred to allow the regional religions and priesthoods to remain; Cyrus II, for example, approved of the Babylonians and their priests as servants of the Babylonian city-god Marduk, and Cyrus was hailed as a messianic figure in the (Hebrew) Old Testament.

In the fourth century BCE (beginning in 334), the powerful Persian Empire and the Indus River valley were conquered in only a few years by the Macedonian king Alexander (d. 323); by means of this conquest, Hellenistic culture and Greek language and education spread throughout the area. Hellenistic influence established itself even more strongly during the subsequent period of the empires of the Diadochi. The largest of these, the Seleucid Empire, included the entire Near Eastern region from the west coast of Asia Minor (but not central Anatolia) to the Gulf of Oman. Armenia fell to the Seleucids under Antiochus III (223–187), only to be later conquered by the Romans in 192. Further, although Palestine had initially belonged to the Ptolemaic Empire, it too fell to the Seleucids under Antiochus III; however, the Seleucids' rigid policies of Hellenization in Israel gave rise to the revolt of the Maccabees.

After the death of Alexander, the Parni nomads (from the steppes near the Caspian Sea) migrated south and founded the Parthian Empire, which was at first a vassal state of the Seleucids. In 238 BCE Arsaces I (ca. 297–211 BCE), king of the Parthians, declared his people's independence from the Seleucids. Just fifty years later, the Parthians were able to conquer Persia and Mesopotamia, an event that brought the Seleucid Empire to an end. Beginning in 66 BCE, the Parthians stretched their authority toward northern Mesopotamia; in the west, on the Euphrates, their empire bordered on the sphere of influence of the Roman Empire. In the period following, both the Parthians and the Romans sought to expand their areas of power; however, despite occasional military victories and temporary acquisitions of land, for the most part the Euphrates remained the border between the two.

From the beginning of their imperial reign, the Parthians preserved the governmental structures of the Seleucids. Greek remained the official language, and consequently Hellenistic traditions remained in force for a longer period than the Hellenes themselves. In the first century BCE, though, the central power of the state weakened, and the Parthian Empire became a feudal state with regional principalities. Beginning in this period, Hellenism was repressed, and Persian influences moved to the foreground.

One of the feudal states, Persia, declared itself independent under Ardashir I (ruled 220–240 CE), who was the founder of the Sassanian dynasty; as a result of this move, Persia was able to support the Parthian dynasty, which had been weakened as a result of its battles with the Roman Empire. From this period onward, eastern Syria belonged to the Sassanian Empire. The Sassanians pursued aggressive policies toward their western neighbor, the Roman Empire, but the former spheres of influence remained largely unchanged. It was only in the time of Khosrau I (531–579), who was temporarily able to possess Antioch and who drove the Christians out of Yemen, and under Khosrau II (591–628), who conquered Palestine and Egypt, that the conflicts with the Byzantine Empire reached their apex. The Sassanian army was utterly destroyed in 622 by Emperor Heraclius of Byzantium.

The Sassanian Empire was a strongly centralized state, with a social system marked by divisions resembling castes. Despite the Hellenistic traditions present in the empire, the Persian influences were stronger, and Zoroastrianism was the state religion. Manichaeism, which had arisen in the third century CE following the teaching of Mani (d. 274 or 277 CE), was repressed as a heresy.

Emperor Heraclius, however, structured the Byzantine empire after 622 in a different way. West Syria and Palestine no longer belonged to a province of the empire; rather, they were turned over to Arab princes who were more or less confederated and were responsible for the paying of tribute. Only a few years after its defeat at the hands of the Byzantines, the Sassanian Empire fell apart as the result of a civil war. Here again, Arab-dominated powers took hold of the resulting situation, as large empires developed under Arab leadership, first under the Umayyads and then, after 750, under the Abbasids.

Islamic literature of the ninth century connected the development of Arabic sheikdoms and empires with the expansion of Islam. However, the historical sources from this period (coins and inscriptions) show that these empires were strongly influenced by Christianity for quite a long time.[1] An analysis of the Christian Syriac literature of the period also demonstrates these findings.[2]

CULTURAL INFLUENCES IN SYRIA AND PERSIA

The name "Syria" does not refer to a region that was homogenous, either ethnically or culturally. Above all, Hellenism left behind deep roots in many cities in east Syria beginning with the conquest of Alexander and the period of the Seleucids, but also in the Parthian period. In addition, Persian influences strongly affected east Syrian culture. West Syria, on the other hand, belonged to the Roman Empire as early as the pre-Christian period, and it remained so in the time of the Roman emperors and up to the reign of (the Byzantine) Emperor Heraclius.

Despite these Hellenistic and Persian influences, which were also supported or pushed through by political means over long stretches of time, the Syro-Aramaic tradition, patterns of thought, and language made their mark on the foundational dynamics of this region. The Syrian language and script remained alive and active; they were used for centuries after the beginning of the Common Era by emigré Arabs in the regions they ruled as the language of culture, business, liturgy, and literature. Large portions of the population employed Aramaic as their everyday language. In Nabataea, Palmyra, and Mesopotamia, different dialects of Syriac ("east Syriac") were spoken, while in the West the dialects that were spoken are called "west Syriac." Syriac was the language of the Christianity that was establishing itself in east Syria, as well as of its liturgy and its theological literature. The missionary work of these Christians reached Mesopotamia through Antioch and Edessa. "Edessa's importance for Syrian Christianity ultimately reveals itself in that the Aramaic dialect of the city, what we call 'Syriac,' became the authoritative language of Scripture and liturgy for this branch of Christianity."[3] This connectedness of mentality and language even seems to have remained determinative of east Syrian Christianity in west Syria, for which Greek served as the language of church and theology but in which the Aramaic language remained alive in everyday life. Further, the writings of west Syrian ("Antiochene") theologians were often read—in Aramaic translation—in east Syria.

From this evidence it is clear that Syrian Christianity was primarily shaped by the Aramaic language and manner of thinking; however, there were also other influences, among which Hellenistic theology was primary but which also included Persian/dualist ideas.

CHRISTIANITY IN SYRIA

Christianity made its home in Syria quite early. Many of the writings of the New Testament originated in the Hellenized, bilingual west Syrian region; as was appropriate, given that this region belonged to the Roman Empire, these texts were written in Greek. In Antioch, a Hellenistic city founded circa 300 BCE by Seleucus I that was the later cultural center of west Syria, the followers of Jesus were first called Christians.

Soon, in the second century CE, Christianity seems to have spread further to the east, namely, through Edessa into Mesopotamia, perhaps even to the area east of the Tigris.[4] Most likely, the people playing a role in the missionary work from Palestine into the East included those Palestinian Jewish Christians called "Ebionites"; these individuals were declared heretics in the

West around 150 CE because of their Christology, namely, that they said Jesus was "merely human" (*psilos anthropos*). These Jewish Christians likely had either been driven from the area, emigrated, or moved as part of their work as merchants. However, the Christian mission oriented toward the region of Mesopotamia seems to have taken as its point of departure the Aramaic-speaking synagogue communities of the Parthian Empire.[5] This cultural location (in the synagogues), as well as the cultural relationship between the Jewish and Aramaic mentalities and languages, gave rise to the strong influence by Judaism and the Old Testament on the later east Syrian Christianity. This influence stood closer to the Palestinian beginnings of Christianity than Hellenistic Christianity, in which the ideas and thought patterns of a completely foreign culture were appropriated and made Christianity's own. In this connection, it is also important that quite early (an exact date cannot be given at this point in the relevant scholarship) and through a slow process, a Syriac translation of the Old Testament appeared called the "Peshitta." The Gospels were read until the fifth century in the Syrian form of the "Diatessaron," a gospel harmony put together by Tatian in the second half of the second century. Also, episcopal structures developed quite early, in the second half of the third century.[6]

Christians came into the Parthian Empire, and even more prominently into the Sassanian Empire which followed, by still another path. The military conflicts that broke out again and again in this period resulted, after (usually) short-term land gains by the Persians, in deportations of portions of the population, including Christians who then established their own congregations in east Syria. "These deported Christians, insofar as they consisted of Greek-speaking congregations, do not appear to have been integrated into the local Christian population until the fifth century, for reports of the time speak of divided churches and of two hierarchies with Greek and Syriac/Aramaic as their respective liturgical languages."[7]

The Syrian Christian mission also reached tribes of Arabians quite early, at first in the northern part of the Arabian peninsula, but above all Arabian kingdoms and tribes in Palestine and Mesopotamia, especially in the Euphrates River valley. Henri Charles conjectures that the fourth century was the time of the missionary work among these peoples, or if not, then certainly the fifth.[8] From the characteristics of the Qur'ānic material, however, earlier periods, namely, the third or fourth century, should be accepted, as I will shortly demonstrate.[9]

There will be more to say later concerning the theological influences on the communities of Syrian Christians. What is important here first is that, for approximately three hundred years, there existed a Hellenistic Christianity right alongside Syrian Christianity; indeed, Hellenistic influences are recognizable in the area as a whole for an even longer period. These Hellenistic influences as well as the Persian influences in the area help to explain that, even early in the Christian period, Gnostic movements were quite at home in the region of Syria. For example, Marcionism spread into Syria and Osrhoene from the end of the second century onward.[10] In addition, both the *Odes of Solomon* and the gnostic *Gospel of Thomas* appeared in Syria in the second century, as well as the "Song of the Pearl" in the apocryphal acts of Thomas and most likely also the *Gospel of Philip*. Further, both *Books of Jeu*, in which Seth plays an important role, as well as Sethian Gnosticism and the related Barbelo Gnosticism (transmitted in the *Apocryphon of John*) should be ascribed to this region. This is certainly also true of the Mandaeans (from *manda*, "gnosis" or "knowledge"), who appeared in southern Iraq and Iran, and of their literature; these Mandaeans used the name "Nazoreans" as a marker of self-identification, and they are called "Sabians" in the Qur'ān. Manichaeanism appeared in the third century in Persia and spread eastward to central Asia and westward as far as northern Africa and Italy.

"Gnosticism" was a phenomenon of syncretistic Hellenism, in which an "understanding" of the basis of being, an important soteriological concept for Hellenists, was bound up with an ethical and cosmogonic dualism more or less radical, in this case one strongly influenced by Persian traditions.[11] The negative valuation of the material and/or bodily was often (e.g., in Marcionism) connected with a Christological Docetism; the divine Logos only took on the *appearance* of a body, which he gave up again before the crucifixion. This dualism reveals strongly anti-Jewish impulses among the Gnostic movements in east Syria. These impulses derived from the region's widespread belief in the Old Testament creation story, that is, the story of a good creator and a good creation, against which Gnosticism had to array itself. This context may have been influenced by Jewish communities; however, because the conflicts primarily concerned *Christian* gnosis, it was most likely Syrian Christianity, in which the reception of the Old Testament was very developed, that called forth this polemic on the part of the Gnostic groups.

Along with Gnostic perspectives (whether bound up therewith or independent therefrom), radical ascetic (and sometimes anti-Jewish) ideas were widespread. Already in the second century, there were encratistic streams of thought in Edessa and the surrounding region. Tatian the Syrian was not far from these, as he advocated a strong demarcation for Christians from the Greek culture, which he held to be "lascivious." In addition, Bardaisan (Bardesanes, d. 222), who created 150 anti-Marcionite songs or psalms, should be included here, as well as the later congregation of the deacon Audi (ca. 325 in Edessa) and the Messalians and stylites of the fifth century.

This amazingly colorful landscape of Gnostic and ascetic ideas should not lead one, though, into thinking that "more orthodox" forms of Syrian and Greek Christianity were not able to establish themselves even further, or that they were not determinative for the Christianity of the region. Around the end of the second century, groupings of "orthodox" Christians under the leadership of a certain Palut were known. Further, the Abgar legend of Addai (the *Doctrina Addai*) appeared in the third century, possibly against an early form of Gnosticism in the area. This text claimed the apostle Thomas as the founder of Christianity in Edessa and Syria; in 349 his supposed remains were brought to Edessa, and in 394 they were formally installed.[12] In the course of the third and fourth centuries, a moderate Christianity came to the fore, one no longer dualistic or radically ascetic in nature; this Christianity then spread further, both into Mesopotamia and into Persia.

At this time there was no official persecution of Christians in the Sassanian Empire; however, limited local conflicts did occur, usually with Zoroastrian priests. When systematic persecutions of Christians began in the Roman Empire under Emperor Decius in 250, not a few Christians, primarily those from west Syria, fled to Persia; by means of this influx, the Greek-speaking congregations in Persia grew. It was only after the Edict of Milan in 313, and only fully after the elevation of Christianity to the state religion in 380–381, that doubts arose in the Sassanian Empire concerning the loyalty of local Christians, as they could be maintaining relationships with the Roman Empire. This doubt was strengthened through the expectation of the Roman emperor that he had to take care of Christians wherever they might be, even beyond his own borders. As a result, the first national (that is, permitted by the king) persecutions of Christians took place; these resulted in martyrdoms. Around the end of the fourth century, the situation for Christians began again to improve.

Christianity was able to further establish itself even in these periods of persecution. The church in Persia had its own hierarchy; approximately eighty bishoprics were brought together to create ecclesiastical provinces led by metropolitan bishops.[13] Consequently, the importance of the empire's capital, the city of Seleucia-Ctesiphon on the Tigris, grew. In a process quite similar to the development of Constantinople into a patriarchate, Seleucia-Ctesiphon's bishop soon held the leadership of the entire church in the Sassanian Empire under the title "Catholicos."

In 410 a synod was called in the capital city by the Sassanian king Yazdgird I (this was similar to the situation in the West under the Roman emperors); this synod was intended to reorganize ecclesiastical structures in the wake of the persecutions. Here it was decided to be rid of the double hierarchy of Aramaic- and Greek-speaking congregations; from that point forward there was to be only *one* Syrian-Christian hierarchy. The decisions of Nicaea were discussed and accepted; this was likely a requirement for the integration of the "Greeks." To the bishop of the capital city was ascribed the highest office in the consecration of bishops, whereby he (with the agreement of the king) became the "Head of the East Syrian Church."[14] Before the end of the fifth century, he received the title of "Catholicos," and the Syrian church became autocephalous, merely the institutional formalization of a state of affairs already in force.

The reception of the Council of Nicaea proceeded slowly and with some difficulty; this council was followed by other "Greek" synods, which remained without theological import whatsoever in East Syria. Around 400 the Syrian liturgy spread out from Nisibis into the entire region of East Syria; further, the nascent architecture of churches and holy places was independent of the West.[15] Concerning the Christianization of Arabic tribes, "the state of the sources does not allow definite conclusions to be made, mainly because the Arabic and Turkish tribes were nomadic or at least semi-nomadic." However, the presence of an Arabian bishop in Hira is documented beginning in 410.[16] In the fifth century, Christianity was able to make inroads into the upper, Zoroastrian levels of society, a development that occasionally led to difficulties. By the end of this century, perhaps due to the influence of the Zoroastrian obligation to marry, the influence of monasticism was reduced and celibacy was abolished; even some leaders of the east Syrian Church, including the Catholicos Babai and his successor Silas (early sixth century), were married.[17] At the same time, authority structures were taken over from the model of the Byzantine Church, and their apostolicity was claimed; this move indicated a deepening of the east Syrian

Church's autocephaly, not a division from the Greek church. Beginning around 600, monasticism was able once more to gain a foothold in the East, and in the following century it was fully reintegrated into the church.

The east Syrian Church had not supported the condemnation of Nestorius at the Council of Ephesus (431).[18] Following the later testimony of Catholicos Timothy I (780–823), this meant that "in the East the faith remained as it had been."[19] The forced emigration of Nestorian theologians and Christians from the West further strengthened Nestorian influences in the east Syrian ambit.[20]

The period following Ephesus also witnessed a spread of Monophysite theology in east Syria. For example, Rabbula, the bishop of Edessa from 412 to 435, who had taken part in 431 in Ephesus in the ("Nestorian") synod led by John of Antioch, later turned to the Cyrilline Party and fought against Nestorianism. With this step, though, he came into opposition with the theological school of Edessa, whose leader Ibas deposed him as bishop in 435. Ibas, however, translated works of Diodore of Tarsus, Theodore of Mopsuestia, and Nestorius into Syriac. In 486 a synod in Seleucia-Ctesiphon adopted a Dyophysite creed based on the teaching of Theodore.[21] In addition, all further Syrian synods in the sixth century saw themselves in relation to Theodore's theology, while Nestorius did not play such a role.[22]

The school of Edessa, which was at this time the single center of education for the Persian clergy, was closed in 489 by the (Monophysite) emperor of the east Roman Empire. Teachers and students migrated to Persia, where they strengthened their "Nestorian" character. Later, the Council of Chalcedon was accepted in this region (aside from its condemnation of Nestorius), although it was received only superficially; the Syrians were not able to do much with the council's technical definitions. Still another synod in 605 under the Catholicos Mar Gregorius strengthened the "Nestorian" character of the church in the Sassanian Empire.[23]

After the closing of the school of Edessa, many teachers and students settled in Nisibis, so that this city took over a leading role in theological education from that time into the seventh century. Here, as in Edessa, the writings of Diodore of Tarsus, Theodore of Mopsuestia, and (less often) Nestorius played a central role.

In the meantime, Monophysitism had been able to spread even further, primarily in west Syria. The Monophysite Severus succeeded in becoming the patriarch of Antioch in 512, assisted in large measure by Byzantine politics helpful to his cause. However, in 519, under the rule of Emperor Justin I, he had to retire into Egypt, where he died in 538.

With the support of Empress Theodora, who herself was inclined toward Monophysitism, Theodore "of Arabia" was consecrated as bishop in 542 by the exiled patriarch of Alexandria, Theodosius (d. 566); Bosra was entrusted to Theodore as his metropolitan see. Jacob Baradaeus (d. 578) was consecrated in 544 as "Bishop of the Arabs," and he established Monophysitism in east Syria through visitation trips. Later Monophysites would call themselves "Jacobites" after this Jacob.

Thus developed Monophysite Christianity—primarily, but not only, in west Syria. In east Syria there were countless conflicts between the Jacobites and the Syrian Church under its Catholicos, who represented "the majority of Christians in the Sassanide Empire."[24] For example, Babai the Great (d. after 628), who held together the church in the Sassanian Empire during a vacancy in the Catholicate between 608–609 and 628, was a strict Dyophysite and oriented his thinking to that of Theodore of Mopsuestia. In addition, the school of Seleucia-Ctesiphon, about which little is known, was shaped by "Nestorian" theology.

Because of the Syrian mentality's relationship to Jewish ways of thinking, and also because of the use of the same language, namely, Aramaic, there was a growing convergence between Jews and Christians around the year 700. At that time synods forbade Christians from taking part in Jewish festivals. "Such constantly repeated laws indicate that they were not being followed."[25] On the other side, many Jews at this time converted to (Syrian) Christianity.[26] However, the official Syrian Church and its liturgy (even until today) expressed a sharp anti-Judaism.

After the victory of Emperor Heraclius over the Sassanian Empire in the year 622—that is, in the last phase of the Sassanian rule, as well as under the government of Arabic leaders—the Syrian Church was able to develop further, to send missionaries as far as China, and also to found many new cloisters: "Numerous new monasteries were founded, and many writings and anthologies . . . were produced."[27]

During the late seventh century, and into the eighth, east Syrian academic life blossomed. Theological works and commentaries on Aristotle were produced (e.g., by Catholicos Henanisho' I [d. 700]), and Greek writings were translated into Syriac and Arabic. Above all, scholarly and literary activity in diverse cultural centers of east Syria was important from the middle of the eighth century onward. As Baum has said, "The secular scientific and literary work of the 'Nestorians' flourished during the first phase of the Abbasid period," and even medical and philosophical works from ancient Greek literature were translated into Syriac and Arabic.[28]

STRUCTURES AND MODELS OF SYRIAN THEOLOGY AND ITS MENTALITY[29]

Pre-Nicene Theology

Not counting Gnostic fragments, only a few pre-Nicene literary witnesses survive from which one may discern the contours of a specifically Syrian theology. The most likely reason for this state of affairs was the deep cultural intermixing between "Greeks," Jews, and Orientals. Indeed, it must have taken some time before the various specific Christian communities with theologies distinguishable from one another would have developed; one may say the same for the process by which individuals would have arisen from these groups to put these theologies into written forms. Consequently, Syrian theology in the pre-Nicene period did not enjoy a tradition unbroken in terms of literary witnesses; however, there are enough texts—even if they are transmitted only in fragmentary form—that the most important structures are already recognizable. Fundamental to the Syrian world (and comparable to Jewish understandings) is a thought-world oriented above all to history and not, as in the Hellenistic tradition, to "being" or "essence" as such, that is, to the nature of God, humanity, and the cosmos. God acted in history—through the prophets and through Jesus. Humans can find salvation through following Jesus, through proving themselves worthy (*Bewährung*), and not, as in Greek Christianity, through the "divinization" brought about by the God-man Jesus Christ.

The oldest literary witness to Syrian theology is Ignatius of Antioch (d. between 109 and 117); afterward, from the second century onward, there are extant traces from some of the so-called Apostolic Fathers, along with Tatian the Syrian and Theophilus of Antioch (both of the second half of the second century), Paul of Samosata (second half of the third century), Arius (d. ca. 336), and Eustathius of Antioch (d. between 337 and 370), who began his theological efforts before Nicaea but only later put them in a finished literary form.

The earliest representative is Ignatius of Antioch, who was (also?)

Greek-speaking and in whose writings one can detect the beginnings of elements of later Hellenistic ("Alexandrian") Christology. If his letters are authentic, he emphasizes in his antitheses a second "divine" mode of being (*Seinweise*) for Jesus. Nonetheless, one can also see ideas found in Syrian thought. His own soteriological goal is a thoroughgoing "human-ness,"[30] which is achieved in a concrete human life: "The faithful must follow the way of their Lord, that is, an earthly path in a human life, if they are to come to unity with the Lord and with God."[31] In this the Christian can either fail or prove his worthiness. Despite Ignatius's (or his later editors') appropriation of Hellenistic Christological vocabulary, Jesus was for him above all the "new man," who "obeyed [God] all the way to death."[32]

The *Didache*, which most likely arose in Syria, identified Jesus as the "servant of God."[33] The *Martyrdom of Polycarp*, the origin of which is unclear, named God "the father of this beloved and adored servant, Jesus Christ."[34] Both texts see God in monarchical ways and Jesus as the servant of God; these common features argue for a Syrian origin of the *Martyrdom of Polycarp*.

Tatian the Syrian was born in the northern Mesopotamian area of the Syrian world; in Rome he became a Christian and a student of Justin. After Justin's death Tatian left the community in Rome and went to work in his home region. There, after having made strong criticisms of Hellenism in his *Oration to the Hellenes* (ca. 165), he supported encratitic ideas as far as demanding that the wine used in the celebration of the Eucharist be replaced with water (thus the name "Aquarians"). Only the *Oration to the Hellenes* and some fragments of his gospel harmony, the "Diatessaron" (*hèn dià tessáron*), are extant.[35] The latter, originally written in Syriac, was used for a long time in the Syrian Church and was often set alongside other scriptural writings as canonical; it was not forbidden as heretical until the time of the leadership of Rabbula of Edessa (d. 435). However, it was still used into the sixth century before being completely replaced by the Peshitta.

As a student of Justin's, Tatian spoke of the "divine Logos," who was at the same time the *hypostasis* (original foundation) of everything.[36] He came forth, however, "in the beginning" (Gen. 1:1) from God through an act of God's will and was God's "first-born work."[37] In Jesus "God has appeared in human form"[38] (NB: there is here no accompanying conception of an "incarnation" of the Hellenistic order), and humans are born in imitation of the Logos.[39] In addition to these borrowings from Hellenistic thought, however, Tatian also supported Syrian ideas: above all, freedom, the importance for salvation of temporal actions (the human soul is not "naturally" immortal, but only as a result of a correctly-practiced recognition of God),[40] and a definite monotheism. In Tatian's thought, though, many things remain either unclear or simply unimportant; this modern impression may be the result of the paucity of extant source materials.

There is only one writing extant from Theophilus, who became the bishop of Antioch in 169, namely, *Ad Autolycum*, written after 180 and according to which Theophilus came from Mesopotamia. Like his contemporary Tatian, he set himself against Greek culture and philosophy. His book is often truly "disorganized."[41] He, like Tatian, appropriated the Logos teaching of Justin: the Logos came forth from God in the beginning and, under the name of "Spirit," "Wisdom," "Power," and "Son of God," formed the inner constitution of the cosmos. Nonetheless, he is still the firstborn "of all creation"[42] and therefore is a creature.

Nevertheless, Theophilus was the first to use the word "Triad" for God.[43] His fundamental monarchianism, though, did not dissolve through this usage, for the "Triad" is to be understood in terms of salvation history and in a dynamic fashion. Peculiarly, Jesus does not appear in his text; rather, he is hidden away as the one who is quoted, the one who leads us through his gospel to correct life and to salvation.[44] "Scripture" is only that which is later called the "Old Testament."

It is clear, however, that Theophilus was advocating a starkly "historical" mode of thought. Only through correct action, "through the observing of the divine commandment," can we determine whether our souls are mortal or immortal.[45] Further, he explains that the men of God became "like vessels of the Holy Spirit and like prophets inspired and taught" by God, so that they became "tools of God."[46] He says nothing about Jesus Christ, but one can surmise that he considers him to be—surpassingly?—among this group.

The contours of a Syrian theology cannot be discerned with much clarity, even into the third century. The influences on the theological vocabulary were too strong; these came from Greek-Christian directions, above all from Justin, and possibly also through the teaching on the Logos of Philo of Alexandria, the Jewish theologian and contemporary of Jesus. Too strong also was the coexistence of Syrian and Greek communities of Christians in the Syrian region. Nonetheless, the most important ideas of later Syrian theology were apparent: a defense of monarchianism (despite varying teachings on the Logos), and a strong emphasis on the will of God, on the soteriological importance of history, and on temporal actions, so that even essentials of Hellenistic philosophy like the natural immortality of the soul are subordinated to decisions made in time. Time was required before Syrian thought was able to achieve clear contours; this achievement seems to have occurred in the second half of the third century.

The most important representative of Syrian theology before Nicaea was Paul of Samosata on the Euphrates, who became bishop of Antioch in 258 and died in 272. He was condemned at two synods in Antioch (264 and 268) on account of his Christology, which is, consequently, only accessible in quotations by his opponents. This condemnation, which took place on west Syrian soil, shows that the influence of Greek Christianity was quite strong in that area.

Paul worked against a physical interpretation of the New Testament predicate "Son of God" as referring to Jesus, as this description would consequently teach a "bi-theism," a teaching excluded for Paul by his emphasis on the uniqueness of God.[47] He considered the Logos (or "Wisdom") to be an instrument (*organon*) of the one, unique God. In Paul's writings we see clearly the so-called (Syrian) dynamic monarchianism, in which God works outwardly through his *dynameis* ("powers"), the Logos, and possibly also the Spirit or other potencies.[48] The Logos lived in Jesus as in a temple; his connection with Jesus was similar to that involving the prophets, but deeper and more radical. Consequently, Paul rejected a "preexistence" Christology and the descent of the Son of God from heaven;[49] further, he emphasized that Mary did *not* give birth to the Logos. "On the contrary, she gave birth to a human being, one who was like us."[50] The Logos, however, is "greater than Christ."[51]

How, then, is Jesus the Christ? The structures of the Antiochene "Christology of worthiness"[52] are already apparent: "Christ has become great (only) through Wisdom."[53] Or, he is like us, "but better in every way," because of the "grace, which (rested) upon him."[54] Wisdom rested upon him like a prophet, "even more than Moses," and "in many hearts," "but more in Christ as in a temple."[55] Consequently, there was a close connection (*synapheia*) between the Logos, or Wisdom, and Jesus. This connection occurred "in accordance with obedience (learning) and partaking, not according to essence."[56]

The foundations of Syrian theology are recognizable in Paul of Samosata's writings. He taught "that 'the Son' only refers to the human being Jesus, in whom the Wisdom of God took up residence; further, that 'the Spirit' is nothing other than the grace which God . . . granted."[57] God is an undifferentiated, unique being who reveals himself outwardly through his power, his *organon*, the Logos. Jesus is (only) a human being, although better than all other human beings, even than the prophets and Moses, and he is *on account of this* closely bound up with the Logos, a "power" of God. His "Christ-ness" rests in his "worthiness."

This also includes the idea that worthiness is the soteriological goal of all humans, and specifically of Christians; this worthiness is to be made manifest in following after Jesus. Two other prominent views of salvation at the time are not in view here: Paul advocates neither a Hellenistic-Christian divinization through the mediation of the God-man Jesus Christ nor the view of Latin theology of salvation through the sacrifice of Jesus Christ on the cross.

Arius is the next theologian in whose works one can see directions in Syrian theology. He was born around 256 or 260 in a location that remains unclear, although presumably somewhere in the larger region of Syria rather than in Lybia, as is commonly supposed. Whether he was a student in Antioch of the priest Lucian must remain an open question; additionally, little is known with certainty of his life and thought. Later, however, we know that he was active in the region of Alexandria as a presbyter, and that he stood in opposition to Alexander and Athanasius of Alexandria.

Because he was condemned at Nicaea, his writings are only accessible in fragments and often in the quotations of his opponent Athanasius. T. Böhm has judged only three documents to be historically authenticated (a creed, a letter to Eusebius of Nicomedia, and a letter to Constantine). Concerning the *Thalia*, partially transmitted by Athanasius in his *Orations against the Arians*,[58] he suggests that there were later emendations.[59] Nevertheless, one can safely accept that Athanasius reproduces Arius's thought correctly, as follows: because the Logos came into being before the Aeons, but still "in the beginning," he is a creature—the most beautiful of all creation and the Demiurge. He can be called "divine," for lack of a better term, but he is not God. God proper is conceived of as monarchical, following Syrian theological norms; Arius does not advocate any sort of "intra-God" subordinationism.[60] How, though, could the creature "Logos," who later became incarnate in Jesus (with this doctrine Arius remains true to his Alexandrian surroundings) have been created to be so beautiful "in the beginning"? Here he offers a rare construction: because God in his foreknowledge saw that the Logos would later prove himself worthy in Jesus, he gave him this beauty ahead of time. In this way Arius grounds the Hellenistic Logos-teaching in the Syrian "Christology of worthiness."[61]

WEST SYRIAN THEOLOGY AFTER NICAEA[62]

The Council of Nicaea condemned the Arian theses concerning the temporal beginning and the "creatureliness" of the Son of God. The council taught, first using biblical expressions, his full divinity (if still originating from the Father)—"God from God, Light from Light . . ."—adding thereunto the expression *homoousios*, meaning "of like nature."

From that point on, life became more difficult for west Syrian theologians, because in the church of the emperor, one could no longer say that Jesus was the Son of God on account of his worthiness. He was so always, by nature, before all time (notice also: no longer from the "beginning").

Nonetheless, west Syrian theologians were not ready to simply give up their type of Christianity; their challenge was to find ways to formulate this Christianity acceptably under the Nicene definitions. As a result of these mental exertions, a specifically west Syrian theology arose at this time, a theology also called "Antiochene" after the cultural center of the area.

It became important for questions about God and for Syrian Christology to identify the Son of God, or Logos, with God himself as much as possible. In this way, on the one hand, west Syrian theologians could continue to think of God in partially monarchian terms, and on the other hand, the God-Logos (not the Logos alone) and the human Jesus could be thought of separately. They defended a strict Dyophysite conception of Jesus Christ; one naturally had to make distinctions between the God-Logos and the human Jesus. God remained God, and human remained human; there was no intermixing.

They preserved their Christology of worthiness; however, this teaching could no longer affect the title "Son of God," as before Nicaea, when one could say that Jesus was "Son" because of his worthiness, that is, that he was adopted by God ("Adoptionism"). The Logos had always existed, even before Jesus had proved himself worthy. The only thing left to consider was that the (election and) worthiness of Jesus had the result that he was bound up closely with the God-Logos. Jesus' worthiness no longer affected the Christological predicate "Son of God," but rather worked now on the copula "is" in the Christological confession "Jesus *is* the Son of God."

The unity of the God-Logos and the human Jesus (that is, that the one can be predicated of the other) was seen, therefore, as an existential (so to speak) unity; perhaps a better way to describe it would be as the "togetherness" of two subjects. This unity consisted on God's side of the election of Jesus and of grace, on Jesus' side of his obedience *unto* death (not *through* his death); that is, in ethical proof of worthiness.

It quickly became difficult to develop a new way of speaking on this topic. Diodore of Tarsus (d. before 394), originally from Antioch, and Eustathius of Antioch (d. before 337 [or possibly 360?]) both emphasized the full and unsullied humanity of Jesus and rejected any talk of "mixture."[63] Diodore held fast to the Syrian expression "Son by grace" and added to it the Nicene phrase "Son by nature."[64] He said that "the Logos is called 'human' because he dwelled in the Son of Man."[65]

This manner of speaking about a two-fold "Son-ness" was, however, both complicated and unbiblical. In the years that followed, this language was left aside, although it was occasionally taken up in a hidden form in the title "Christ": Jesus became the Christ by proving himself worthy and is consequently closely bound up with the God-Logos. For the most part, though, this language of "doubles" was avoided, and the Syrian "theology of worthiness" was formulated in another way.

The most important west Syrian theologian, Theodore of Mopsuestia (ca. 350–428), presented the Syrian theology of worthiness in a detailed manner. Unfortunately, Theodore's writings are only extant in fragments (some of which are in Syriac) as a result of his posthumous condemnation as a heretic in the controversy over the "Three Chapters" at the Fifth Ecumenical Council of 553 in Constantinople. As Theodore said: "And he (the human Jesus) exerted himself toward a greater possibility of the most perfect virtue . . . this he showed us in an exemplary way, giving us a path which is, therefore, a duty for us." Jesus grew "in grace . . . , exerting himself toward virtue by following his reason and understanding. . . . And he (the Logos) pushed him toward the highest possible perfection and effected in him an overflow of effort, both in the soul and in the body; in this way he prepared for him a unbelievably large and yet effortless perfection of virtue."[66] Because of his worthiness and the good favor of God which he enjoyed, the God-Logos dwelled in him.[67]

Consequently, for Theodore, Jesus is (only) a human. "Jesus is a human. . . . The human Jesus is like all humans, distinguishing himself from other humans, whose nature is like his, only in grace." Or: "The human (Jesus) is like humans in nature, but God is like God in nature." And: ". . . the Son of Mary should not be held to be God, the Word."[68]

The unity between the two natures—for these he uses the Greek expression *prosopon*, meaning "face" or "outer expression"—Theodore imagines to be analogical to the unity of husband and wife in 'one flesh' (Matt. 19:6). "As in the first case (of the unity of husband and wife), the ability to speak of "one flesh" did not damage the number "two," . . . so also here (in the unity of the divine and human natures) the unity in *prosopon* does not damage the distinction of natures."[69]

Syrian Christology could not be expressed more clearly. From this perspective one can understand how Theodore's (likely) student Nestorius (b. after 381; d. 451) found himself in the middle of conflicts when he became patriarch of Constantinople in 428 and was then confronted with a latent Monophysite piety and the veneration of Mary as *theotokos* (the "Mother of God"). He fought against the understanding of Mary as *theotokos*; in his opinion she only bore the human Jesus (she is thus *anthropotokos*), or at the most the (later) Christ (thus *christotokos*). He sharply distinguished between the human Jesus and the God-Logos, and he saw the unity of the two expressed in a relationship of the God-Logos with the human Jesus.[70]

With the condemnation of Nestorius, and the penetration of Monophysitism that followed, the expression of Antiochene theology was repressed in the realm of the emperor. That said, however, in the Chalcedonian Creed of 451, at least the (Antiochene) Dyophysite expression was preserved. The Antiochene model of a unity based on worthiness, however, was not appropriated (except in the expression "of one *prosopon*"), and the (Alexandrian) image of unity of essence was also rejected.[71]

It was quite a long time before Chalcedon was accepted in the Byzantine church; the decisive factor was most often a "Cyrillian" interpretation of the creed, one in which, following the theology of Cyril of Alexandria, the unity of the God-man was expressed strongly and yet latently in terms of essence.

EAST SYRIAN THEOLOGY[72]

Witnesses up to the Beginning of the Fifth Century

In the midst of the east Syrian church, there were indeed smaller Greek-speaking congregations, and some of their more well-informed theologians may have known something of the discussions proceeding in the West. However, these theologians did not stand in direct confrontation with a Hellenistic theology in the majority, as was the case in west Syria. They did not have to defend their own theology or engage themselves with the theological expressions of the other side.

Consequently, one may assume that before Nicaea (and in general in east Syria before the synod of 410) there was no necessity for theologians to concern themselves with a binitarian or Trinitarian conception of God, with a two-nature Christology, or with an incarnational soteriology based on such a Christology (i.e., that humans are saved because of the incarnation of the Logos). Throughout this period, people were able simply to be Christians in the east Syrian way. Those ideas recognizable in Paul of Samosata—besides, that is, their forcedly antithetical components—likely became decisive for many Syrian congregations: a clear monarchianism; a theology of worthiness; and a Christology of worthiness based thereupon, whereby Jesus' worth and importance for salvation rested in his obedience, and that he is consequently ("by adoption") the Son. This theology was often formulated by looking back to the Old Testament in a way that was poetic and full of images. This method avoided "terminological fixation and definition,"[73] for systematic reflection was not typical of the Syrian mode of thinking.

One Syrian theologian, Aphrahat (d. after 345), of whose life little is known, apparently knew nothing of Nicaea and used Old Testament motifs as his primary subject matter. The Spirit of God rested on the prophets and on Jesus Christ; Christians also receive this Spirit at baptism and ought to live according to it.[74]

In a foundational study, Peter Bruns engaged the theology of Aphrahat.[75] He pointed to the imagistic richness of the Syrian language, which sought to express "the form of Christ intuitively" by means of its "rich inheritance of Oriental lyric poetry."[76] In his seventeenth *Demonstration*,[77] Aphrahat argues the thesis that the Messiah is the Son of God and rejects the Jewish criticism concerning his status as the Son of God. He brings forth a plethora of names for the Christ—indeed, the sheer number of terms forces the individual expressions in their exact meanings to fade a bit into the background—and clarifies the aforementioned naming of the Messiah as the Son of God: "For the venerable name of divinity was also granted to righteous people and to those who were worthy of that divinity. The people on whom God had good favor he called 'my children' and 'my friends.'" He mentions Moses, who was to be "as God" for Pharaoh (Exod. 7:1–2) and for Aaron (Exod. 4:16), as well as Israel, which is a "son" (Exod. 4:22–23; Hos. 11:1–2; Isa. 1:2; Deut. 14:1). He continues: "He said of Solomon, 'He will be for me a son, and I will be for him a father' (2 Sam. 7:14; 1 Chron. 22:10). We also call the Christ the Son of God, through whom we have come to recognize God, as also he [God] named Israel 'my first-born son,' and as he said of Solomon, 'He will be for me a son.' We have named him [Jesus] God, as he also identified Moses with his own name."[78]

Here, Syrian thought has been formulated with great clarity: the title "Son of God" is a title of honor—one of many—and no "essential" name as at Nicaea; rather, it is to be understood in terms of salvation history. God granted Jesus this name as a result of his own favor: "For the name of divinity is given for greater honor in the world, and God has given it to that one on whom he has had favor."[79] D. W. Winkler agrees with Bruns[80] here and summarizes thus: "The name 'Word of God' is meant to express that side of God which is turned toward the world, as God's speech of revelation, embodied through Christ. The 'Son of God' is that one through whom God becomes recognizable."[81] The incarnation is thought of in terms of "enrobing" or "enclothing,"[82] an idea that was apparently valid not only for Jesus but also for other great players in the drama of salvation history.[83]

The special meaning of Jesus in his role as Logos and/or "Son of God" found its basis for Aphrahat in Jesus' own special condescension and humility: "Although he [Jesus] was rich, he made himself poor. Although he was exalted, he degraded his own magnitude. . . . Although he was the one who could bring all the dead to life, he gave himself over to death on the cross. The one who makes us alive has displayed for us all this humility in himself."[84]

Aphrahat's writings reveal the Syrian "dynamic monarchianism" and its accompanying Christology of worthiness. Because of this Christology, then, we also find our salvation through proving ourselves worthy: "Therefore, we also humble ourselves, my beloved. . . . Nothing else will be demanded of us, than that we make our temples beautiful. As soon as the time is fulfilled and he [that is, the Spirit of Christ] returns to his father, he will praise us, because we have given him honor."[85]

Alongside Aphrahat one finds Ephrem the Syrian (ca. 306–373) among east Syrian theologians of great import, in that he anticipated future developments by taking up expressions from Hellenistic-Christian teaching into his own Syrian Christianity. This teacher and author, highly honored in the Syrian Church, left behind an important body of work written in Syriac—exegetical, dogmatic, and poetic texts. Ephrem's works, and above all his songs, had an important role in the later Syrian Church.

"He is the most elegant and greatest of all Syrian authors; he understood how to express his theological insights in poetic language."[86] Ephrem was born and grew up in Nisibis but later moved to Edessa, which belonged at that time to the Roman Empire. There his thought-contexts included Nicaea, a binitarian-Trinitarian terminology, and the conflicts with Arianism. Consequently, his writings and hymns contain indirect references to the incarnation, the divine Logos, and a binitarian theology, although these ideas are not expressly reflected. As a result, one must count him—terminologically, at least—as part of post-Nicene "orthodox" Christianity (in the Greek conception). However, his "Trinitarian and Christological expressions" remain "unclear and opaque," and his teaching on the Trinity balances precariously between "Sabellian modalism and subordinationist tri-theism," with the result that he was "taken up in later periods by Monophysites and Nestorians equally."[87]

As a result of Ephrem's multiple "orthodoxies," it must be considered that a reconciliation of terminology between Syrian and Nicene teachings on God and Christ is impossible on systematic grounds—or that it would lead to conceptions like those of Arius. At a later time, the Hellenistic conception overtook the Syrian, or at least (in an "Antiochene" form) repressed it. Ephrem was able, therefore, if he had wanted to be seen as correct in the eyes of both sides, to remain "unclear" in his language. He achieved this by means of a lack of terminological definition and by his poetic ways of expression. This systematic problem, however, was not the only factor in play, for the uniqueness of the image-rich Syrian mode of thinking was also involved. For example, Ephrem used a number of titles and images for Jesus; for him, though, the goal was not clarity of definition, but rather a glorification of God by means of images. "In Aphrahat and Ephrem, the two early Syrian classical writers, . . . this image-theology comes to full development. It shows us what a Semitic Christianity might have looked like, had the circumstances of history and theology not pushed it aside."[88]

The Reception of Antiochene Theology Beginning in the Fifth Century

Thanks to the reception of Nicaea at the synod of 410, the tendency grew stronger in the Syrian world to speak of a Logos who is God and of the incarnation. Consequently, beginning in the fifth century, one finds in this Syrian region a few churches consecrated to the "Triad." It remains unclear whether the expression "Triad" was understood with monarchian overtones, as one finds, for example, in Theophilus of Antioch. Similarly, one can read an inscription in a church in Dar Kita from the year 418, that speaks of "One God, his Christ, and the Holy Spirit."[89] There are also extant citations of the Matthean Great Commission clearly understood in terms of a dynamic monarchianism.

It has become customary to describe the church in the Sassanian Smpire after the Council of Ephesus as "Nestorian."[90] It must certainly have wounded this church greatly to accept the condemnation of Nestorius. This condemnation was acknowledged, but only later, after the slow acceptance of Chalcedon. Nonetheless, it is clear that his ideas were held to be entirely correct, and his writings were certainly read.

When one looks more closely at the situation, however, one realizes that the works of Diodore of Tarsus and, above all, Theodore of Mopsuestia were far more important. It would be better, it seems, to call this nascent theology in Syria "Antiochene."[91] Even after the Council of Nicaea, the important ideas for these theologians and in this area were a monarchian doctrine of God and a Dyophysite Christology, in which Jesus' worthiness played a large role. While the Logos was called—by necessity after Nicaea—"God by nature,"[92] the associations raised by this statement remained unclear. This disinterest in speculative reflection on the part of Syrian theologians, as well as their lack of a sharp controversy with argumentative opponents (Alexandrian theology), left the specific expressions in question unfocused.

What remained, however, was a continually strong use of the Old Testament and its topoi, as well as an inclusion of Jesus in the historic line of the prophets, whose spiritual gifting he even surpassed because of his worthiness. In addition, the massive work of translating ancient Greek philosophical and medical texts seems not to have affected the foundations of Syrian theology.

Later Developments: An Overview

The foundational structures of the doctrine of God in play up to this point, as well as the attendant historical understanding of soteriology and Christology, remained definitive in the period that followed. However, the straightforwardness of this concept soon—already in Ephrem, for example—became less clear through the reception of Nicaea and its accompanying binitarian (and later Trinitarian) topoi and a Christology which was formulated using terminology of "essence."

This reception took place immediately, as with Ephrem, by means of the Syrian poetic tradition and imagistic language. Through these the sharp contours of its contradictions were lost, and the theology was rendered consequently less clear.

The Syrian acceptance of the Nicene creed at the synod of 410 represented an early instance of inculturation, by which Hellenistic rubrics (*homoousios*, "incarnation") were taken up into the quite different, metaphor-rich understanding of the Syrians. The condemnation of Nestorius in Ephesus led to the result that Antiochene theology spread also into the East, where Theodore of Mopsuestia became the most important point of reference.

Nonetheless, the Syrians do not seem to have immediately been drawn into the characteristic argumentative style of these Antiochenes; rather, like Narsai the poet (d. ca. 502), for example, who founded and led the school of Nisibis, they remained in the tradition of Ephrem while also taking up a few directions of Theodore's theology. The synods of the fifth and sixth centuries did not deal with the controversies raging in the West; rather, they defended a Dyophysite Christology on the basis of Theodore's writings. "The teaching of Nestorius . . . had no meaning for the official (Syrian) church."[93] Formally, writers did speak of belief in the Trinity.

Through the condemnation of Theodore of Mopsuestia in the "Three Chapters" controversy, this Antiochene theologian became "normative from then on for the east Syrian Church. By the end of the sixth century, the name of Theodore had become synonymous with east Syrian orthodoxy."[94]

In the once extensive but now only partially extant literary works of Babai the Great (d. 628), one sees that by the early seventh century, west Syrian theology and Christology had become extremely influential. The doctrine of the Trinity and a Dyophysite "two-nature" Christology were accepted. Nonetheless, it is interesting that Babai strongly emphasizes the unity of God even as he stresses equally God's three-ness. Like Augustine,[95] Babai accepts for God "only one divine will, one divine substance, one divine nature."[96] Above all, it is concerning the single will—which is also the seat of God's action—that he tends to think of God as a subject and in monarchian ways; as opposed to Augustine, Babai sees the incarnation not as the work of God but rather as especially of the Logos—an unexamined opinion, perhaps?

However, one should notice that, despite all this reception of Diodore of Tarsus and, especially, Theodore of Mopsuestia, their most important idea was no longer understood and also not discussed. This particular idea was their emphasis not only on the difference between the God-Logos and the human Jesus, but also on their (existential) connection, by means of an inter-subject model of unity. The typical identification of God and Logos faded in favor of an independence of the Logos (an idea inadmissible according to Theodore), and the foundation of Christological unity in the (election and) worthiness of Jesus was rarely defended any more, and certainly not with either clarity or passion.

Thus, from here on, Syrian theology was marked at its foundation by "Byzantine" Trinitarian and Christological ideas, even if these were interpreted through an "un-Cyrillian" and "Antiochene" lens. The work of Babai became the model for this theology. Consequently, ideas that were originally distinguished for their monarchianism and Christology of worthiness were hidden by the appropriation of foreign vocabulary. It is only in the emphasis on the unity of God despite a Trinitarian structure, as well as in the clean division of divinity and humanity in Jesus Christ, that the minimum standards of authentic east Syrian and Antiochene theology were preserved. In other words, around the year 600, Syrian theology, at least in its terminology, became Hellenized.

THE INFLUENCES OF A SYRIAN-ARABIC CHRISTIANITY ON THE QUR'ĀN[97]

The Syrian-Christian Shaping of the Qur'ān

From a historical-critical point of view, it is incomprehensible to argue that, of the theological problems and ideas communicated in the Qur'ān, those which had quite a long history in the Qur'ān's Christian milieu were "discovered" anew, so to speak. It is much more the case that they were taken over and appear in the Qur'ān text in the proclamations that connect quite consciously with the "Book" (the Old and New Testament), those that confirm this "Book," and those that want to establish its correct interpretation against that of other "People of the Book." In large parts, the Qur'ān seems to want to be something like a new, Arabic-Christian Deuteronomy. Just like Moses—the most-mentioned informant in the Qur'ān—the preacher continually impresses correct teaching and correct standards of behavior upon his audience.

His hearers/readers appear to know the "Book," for in many places the Qur'ān indicates that its statements are familiar to the audience. The text addresses itself to those who know the traditions of the Bible, and it wants to hinder or reverse the ways in which these traditions lead people in the wrong direction.

The various Christian traditions that obtained in the east Syrian region and that contended with one another (often for long periods of time) have left traces behind in the Qur'ān. For example, the polemic of Syrian theology against Jacobite-Monophysite conceptions is reflected in the Qur'ānic rejection of a Trinity made up of God, Jesus, and Mary (sura 5:116–117). Similarly, encratitic traditions may be visible in the Qur'ānic rejection of the enjoyment of wine (SS. 5:91; 2:219; for the other position, see S. 16:67), in rigid commandments concerning fasting, in the restrictions on women, and in radical ideas of criminal law. Further, the opposition to the Jews is likely an inheritance of Christian anti-Judaism, and so on. Many points remain to be discussed, including how much the rejection of the crucifixion of Jesus, the claim that the crucifixion was a sham, and the claim that Jesus was simply translated to heaven (SS. 3:55; 4:156–159)—despite the fact that his death is elsewhere acknowledged (S. 5:117), and even his death and resurrection (S. 19:33)—go back only to Gnostic-docetic ideas.[98] Do these ideas also have roots in Arabic conceptions of protection, which an employer (in this case, God) must give to his employee (cf. the Punishment Stories)? Another possible source is the beginning of the development of conceptions of a translation to heaven (cf. S. 3:52–54)—as in the Shia—so that Jesus was whisked away and his substitute (Muhammad or Ali) took over his role.

Salvation by means of the cross does not appear in the Qur'ān in any form. Is this phenomenon an Islamic peculiarity—a demarcation from Christianity—as it often has been and will continue to be understood?[99] Is the cross then, as it appears from S. 4:156–159, a point of controversy as a symbol of *Christian* salvation, so that the Qur'ān becomes a non-Christian, even an Islamic book?

One must consider, however, that there had always been, from the beginning of Christianity, varying models of soteriology. For Hellenistic Christianity, for example, the most emphasized fact was that God became human, by which action we ourselves, following antique ideas of exchange, become divinized.[100] Consequently, the incarnation is the central *datum* of salvation, while the cross shows clearly how deeply human God indeed became. In the Latin West, on the other hand, and in European Christianities until today, the saving death of Jesus on the cross stands in the foreground, through which our guilt was taken away and we were "saved" and/or justified.[101]

It was still otherwise in the Syrian theology of worthiness. Strongly related to Jewish-Christian thought, this theology placed *discipleship* and *ethics* at the fore.[102] Jesus is the Christ because the Word of God or the Spirit of God rested upon him more than on the prophets or Moses, so that he proved himself worthy *as far as* the death on the cross (not *through* this death). To do the same is what is demanded of all Christians. To say it another way, it is a truncation of Christian thought on salvation to limit it to the Latin/Western pattern. Syrian Christianity was indeed Christianity in all its ways, even if it emphasized different matters in its soteriology; this same is also true for the concepts in the Qur'ān.

Recently, many authors have defended the opinion that most of the theological statements in the Qur'ān—for example, the conception of God, Christology, and eschatology—arose from Syrian traditions of Christianity. Jesus was taken seriously, as in Syrian theology, in the historical role that he took up in the larger mission of God. It has been observed for a somewhat longer period, for example, that at least the Meccan portions of the Qur'ān express foundational ideas which correspond to (Syrian) Christian missionary preaching: "These foundational ideas remind one most especially of the pattern of an ancient Christian missionary preaching, as for example Paul's speech at the Areopagus as narrated in Acts 17. Because of this, Tor Andrae put forward the attractive hypothesis that Muhammad once heard a Christian missionary sermon, and that this experience provided his decisive motivation."[103] Here it is not only some theological statements but rather the concept at the core of the Qur'ān that is traced back to Christian models.

Consequently, one must accept that the reception of the Old Testament and/or its apocrypha and topoi also occurred by the mediation of Syrian Christianity, less so from Jewish communities themselves. All aspects of this reception that could be presumed to come from a Jewish-Christian influence are also to be found in Syrian Christianity, with its strong affinity to the Old Testament, its preference for the pattern of Moses and the prophets, and so on.

As a result of the Qur'ān's rough rejection of Trinitarian ideas and Jesus' identity as the Son of God, many scholars have argued the thesis that Qur'ānic passages in this line have been shaped by Nestorian conceptions.[104] First of all, however, these scholars overlook the fact that, after the Council of Ephesus in 431, Nestorian influences are recognizable in the east Syrian region, but that it was the writings of Diodore of Tarsus and, above all, Theodore of Mopsuestia, that were read, accepted, and commented upon in the centers of learning for Syrian theology. Consequently, it would be better to speak of an "Antiochene" theology. Secondly, these scholars also do not note that even this influence of Nestorian thought waned after 600, as the central Trinitarian and Christological terminology of the tradition of the Greek councils was taken on and adapted—a "Hellenization" of east Syrian Christianity. These ideas were neither reflected upon nor discussed as in the Hellenistic theological tradition; rather, they were simply passed on. It is only in the Dyophysite interpretation of these ideas that the old Antiochene conceptions lived on. Thirdly, these scholars overlook the fact that the Antiochene theology of Diodore, Theodore, and even of Nestorius did not contest either a predication of divinity for the Logos—*homoousios*—or the acknowledgement that Jesus Christ was the Son of God or the Logos; in contrast, they wrote mostly of the "God-Logos." They contested "only" an *essential* unity of the Logos and Jesus and presented "only" another model of unity: a connection of the two on the grounds of election and worthiness (in short, the "acceptance" of Jesus by God)—an "existential" unity. In most places in the Qur'ān, on the other hand, and in contrast with Antiochene theology, a binitarian conception of God appears; only once is there a Trinitarian depiction to be found. Consequently, and bound up with this, the predication of Jesus as the "Son of God" is sharply denied. To sum up: the Qur'ān is neither Antiochene nor Nestorian, even if it has been shaped by Syrian theology.

THE PRE-NICENE SYRIAN FORM OF QUR'ĀNIC THEOLOGY

How should the aforementioned peculiarities be explained? Many passages in the Qur'ān seem to represent an early form of Syrian theology. There is indeed a pre-Nicene Syrian theology present in the Qur'ān, a theology that was defended against the Syrian theology of the seventh and eighth centuries, that of the "People of the Book" contemporary to the Qur'ān. Nicaea does not appear in the Qur'ān; if it is there at all, it is seen only in a negative light in the positions of those being led astray; that is, of the Syrian theology of the seventh and eighth centuries.

This pre-Nicene Syrian theology was still being defended in the East shortly before the middle of the fourth century in the person of Aphrahat. It was present until the year 410 in the entire east Syrian Church, except for Edessa (see Ephrem the Syrian), which belonged at that time to the Roman Empire. Finally, it was present among the common people and in the regions lying outside the ambit of the ecclesiastical and theological centers for at least decades longer.

"Pre-Nicene" Syrian theology defended a decisive monarchianism on the question of God: (the one) God alone has authority. This concept is directed polemically in the Qur'ān against the developments current at the time of its appearance, for God shares power with no one at all. This unitarian monotheism, defined by concerns about power and authority, also excludes the conception of a "Sonship of God" that is "physical," an idea that had developed in east Syria (at the latest) in the seventh and eighth centuries.

Paul of Samosata, who lived in an Antioch that was at his time fully Hellenized, and west Syrian theologians working after Nicaea, shared a common challenge, namely, the developments that occurred in Hellenistic Christianity. However, early Syrian theology had to confront these challenges even before them, dealing with the "simple" New Testament statements that Jesus is the Son of God and that he is the incarnate Logos.

Syriac Christians before Nicaea had understood “Son of God” and “Logos” as “powers” of the one God—the so-called dynamic monarchianism. The Logos, Wisdom, the Spirit, and so on—for the Syrians gathered many such names together—did not compromise the uniqueness of God, but rather *they are he himself in his actions and works*, no separate “hypostases.” In this respect one finds no Arian echoes in the Qur'ān—*contra* Günter Lüling, et al.—because Arianism saw the Logos as time-bound and creaturely, but nonetheless as its own “hypostasis” and as the Demiurge. The theology represented in the Qur'ān is also *pre-Arian*, or at least not touched by Arianism.

There are a few passages in the Qur'ān, from which one can proceed directly to a dynamic monarchianism. One surprising sentence—that is, one that does not fit in its context—is S. 17:85: “The Spirit is the Logos of my Lord. But you [pl.] have retained only a little knowledge.” This passage fits nicely with pre-Nicene Syrian theology, in that the Spirit is explained as the Logos, but as the Logos “of my Lord”—like a *dynamis* of the Lord. Even more closely aligned is S. 16:2: “He sends the angels down with the Spirit of his Logos upon the one whom he chooses from among his servants.” These heavenly beings are to announce to humanity that “there is no other God besides me.” Here the Logos and the Spirit become like angels that represent God's actions outwardly, following the Jewish angelology that had been taken over into Christianity[105] (e.g., Clement of Alexandria [d. before 215] described the Logos and angels as one thing[106], and Origen [d. ca. 250] explained the two cherubim [i.e., angels] on the Ark of the Covenant as the Logos and the Spirit[107]). They are known purely for their function: these aforementioned powers of God come down to humans with the assignment to speak to humans in the place of God.

Sura 40:15 also reflects pre-Nicene Syrian theology: “He sends the Spirit of his Logos upon the one whom he chooses from among his servants.” The Logos and the Spirit were the most important powers for describing God's actions to humans. This is clear from S. 10:3, which describes God as taking his seat on his throne after the six days of creation “in order to direct the Logos.” The Logos seems—as in early Christian theology—to be the more important character, with the Spirit a bit subordinate; as was common in this early period, angels were mentioned along with them. One may compare here S. 19:17: “And we sent our Spirit to her [Mary].” The Logos, the Spirit, and the angels are “powers” of the one and the same God. These passages, and others, show that pre-Nicene dynamic monarchianism came to expression in the Qur'ān, and that it was preserved by the Qur'ān's redactors. Consequently, the Qur'ān criticizes later formulations that defend binitarian and Trinitarian ideas.

It was also necessary in the Qur'ān, as it had already been in earlier Syrian Christology, to reject any notion that Jesus was "physically" or "materially" the Son of God. The idea that Jesus was only a human being, of course, differed from that of the Syrian Christianity contemporary with the Qur'ān. As it says in S. 3:45: "[At that time] when the angels said, 'Mary! God is announcing to you a word [ed. note: "Logos"] from himself, whose name is Jesus Christ and who is the Son of Mary.'" Sura 4:171 calls Jesus the "Word of God" and the "Spirit of/from him." Here, though, the text seems only to refer to the special election and mission of Jesus, in the sense of Syrian Christology (God's Logos and Spirit rested upon him); these ideas revealed themselves already in the virginal birth and were the basis on which Jesus proclaimed the Gospel. Many texts in the Qur'ān contend mightily with the claim that Jesus was the Son of God. Jesus is (only) one sent by God (e.g., S. 5:75).

In addition, the Qur'ān also reflects a unique form of an even earlier Syrian Christology, namely, the confession that Jesus is the "servant of God." One sees this idea in S. 72:19 (which Paret, in his German translation of the Qur'ān, falsely connected to Muhammad), as well as in S. 19:30, a self-referential statement of the Christ-child: "I am the servant of God." It is possible that the Qur'ānic rejection of an "adoption" or "acceptance" of Jesus as the "Son of God" should be understood in this connection (cf. SS. 2:116; 10:68; 18:4; 19:88–91; 21:26; 23:91; 72:3).[108] In pre-Nicene Syrian theology (see here, e.g., the usage of Aphrahat), the expression "Son of God" was not used exclusively as an honorific title for Jesus, as it was later (and even in Syrian theology), so that there was no reason to take hold of the later Antiochene model of unity based on an "adoption" (with only Jesus as the Son). Appropriate to its pre-Nicene time frame, it was not yet required, as it would be in later west Syrian Christology, to reflect a model of unity deriving from a theology of worthiness.

A Christology of worthiness finds expression in the Qur'ān insofar as Jesus has meaning in the proclamation and completion of the will of God; for example, he says at S. 3:51, "God is my and your Lord. Serve him! That is a straight path." In addition, all of us come to salvation as we prove ourselves worthy; that is, as we fulfill our duties (an idea found throughout the Qur'ān; cf. S. 3:57: "To those, however, who believe and do what is right, he [that is, God] will give their full reward").

There are other aspects of the Qur'ān that point to early Syrian influences. The importance of the Old Testament is quite apparent in the Qur'ān. From time to time one can surmise that the Preacher, who is most often spoken to by God with the pronoun "you," sees himself typologically as Moses (who was also an orphan, was at one time "on a false path," and was needy; see S. 93:6–8). Indeed, the term "Muhammad" is mentioned only four times in the Qur'ān, always in Medinan suras, and seems to be an honorific title (the "highly honored one") whose connection with regard to a specific person is often difficult to discern in the Qur'ān—does it relate to Jesus, Moses, or the Arabian prophet? Further, the Qur'ān, or as H. Busse writes, Muhammad, "apparently knows nothing of a fourfold gospel."[109] In east Syria, at least into the sixth century, the Diatessaron was still in use. Is the accusation that Christians have falsified the Scriptures directed against the repression of the Diatessaron in favor of the four gospels of the Peshitta?

THE ARABIZATION OF A PRE-NICENE SYRIAN CHRISTIANITY

That pre-Nicene Syrian theology is still to be found in the Qur'ān in the seventh and eighth centuries shows clearly that *Arabs had already accepted Christianity in an earlier period.* Apparently, the originally nomadic or seminomadic tribes did not give up this foundation in the later periods. As the Qur'ān clearly shows, they did not go along with the later, post-Nicene development of Syrian Christianity (which was forced upon it through its contacts with Byzantine Christianity, despite all its autocephaly),[110] although they did continue to use the Syrian language in their worship services, at least until the linguistic Arabization of the early eighth century. They remained in their original religion, in the Christianity of their beginnings, and they stood by its concerns and defended them aggressively against Jews and Christians "who had been led astray." This was true even after the victory of Heraclius over the Sassanians in 622, when they themselves became politically independent and were able to build larger and larger empires. It was only their own interpretation of the text that was unquestionably a product of revelation. From this point of view it becomes plausible that the Byzantine-leaning theologian John of Damascus (d. 735)[111] would have described the "Ishmaelites"—that is, those Arabs who saw themselves as connected to suras of the prophet Muhammad—as Christian heretics.[112]

The Christianization of Arabs in the Syrian and Arabian regions was rarely—as in the urban milieu of early Christianity—a matter of the conversion of individuals or even multiple individuals. As was appropriate, given the social structure of the time, tribal leaders and their tribes decided to take this step together; one may compare here the Christian mission among the German tribes. Consequently, one cannot avoid admitting, in terms of the sociology of religion, that in this situation many old, Arabian, "pagan" traditions would have lived on under the cover of a Christianity that was binding on an entire tribe and was therefore superficial. In this connection one finds many examples in the Qur'ān: the belief in jinn, sorcery (cf. SS. 113 and 114), and lesser gods and goddesses (cf. S. 53:19–20); inherited societal norms (cf. concerning the relationships between men and women or legal statutes [e.g., the *lex talionis*]); tales from the homeland (see, e.g., in a part of the Punishment Stories or the notes concerning a certain female camel);[113] or even memories of important places like Mecca or Yathrib.

It also appears that the originally nomadic and semi-nomadic tribes practiced their Christianity as a "lay religion," that is, without a noteworthy clerical class; if so, this would point to a very early period of Christianization. The only exceptions to this in the Qur'ān are the traces left behind by monasticism. From this set of circumstances, one can more readily understand the foundationally "folk" nature of the remembrance and editing of biblical and apocalyptic material in the Qur'ān. There were no "specialists" at work here.[114] When Arabs visited Christian worship services, these were carried out entirely by priests who were ethnically Syrian. This context may help explain the "flattening out" of the Syrian theology of worthiness to a "payment for services rendered" ethic, as can be found in the faith of common people in Christian churches even until today.

The uniqueness of the reception of Syrian Christianity, however, makes clear the following, my most important observation on the Qur'ān. These Christianized tribes apparently brought with them into their Christianity a very strong conception of legal structures (rulership and obedience, the legitimation of authority) and contract-related regulations. Through this conception, the considerable humane (with regard to content) and often thoroughgoing reflection of biblical and Syrian theological traditions was withdrawn in favor of formal and structural schemata of order. One's relationship to Allah was expressed as *din*, that is, as a contract,[115] in agreement with the Scripture (Islam). As the Qur'ān shows, this concept, expressed thusly, was polemically set up in the seventh and eighth centuries against the other variants of Judaism and Christianity as the correct path. Insofar as this Arabian (non-Monophysite) Christianity, for which the (late) Qur'ān presents simply the only source, was foundationally shaped by the rubrics and expressions of pre-Nicene Syrian Christianity, it nonetheless betrays a quite unique, even "Arabian," form, one that was oriented toward structures and matters of justice. It then became the bedrock of the ideology of the tribe, and soon the empire, as Arabian authority reached wider and wider.

LATER ADDITIONS

It appears that, as time progressed, other passages also entered into the Qur'ān, passages that quite clearly no longer represented an early Syrian-Arabian Christianity, but rather reflected the beginnings of another religion, a new religion, namely, Islam. Texts of this kind are not particularly numerous, but they are present nonetheless, and they have been of great import in terms of their effects. They should perhaps be reckoned to the end of the eighth century or the beginning of the ninth; that is, to or just prior to the time of al-Mamun.

An empirical answer to this question is difficult, primarily because the oldest extant and datable manuscript of the entire text arises from the later ninth century, while the earlier texts—mostly fragmentary editions—have not been satisfactorily published and certainly have not been investigated from the perspective of textual criticism (for example, must one see them as fragments?). Consequently, the questions must remain open in this area; they can be answered only in the future. At the present time one has recourse only to the many observations arising from the histories of spirituality, culture, and religion. These studies, however, make it necessary to accept that later additions were made.

NOTES

1. Cf. the essay by Volker Popp in this volume, chapter 1.

2. A detailed investigation of the literature in question would extend beyond the realm of this study. I would like to mention only that Syriac Christianity blossomed in the eighth century under Arabian rule; many cloisters and churches were built, and missions as far as China were undertaken. A good deal of literature is extant, including chronicles, saints' lives, cloister legends, and theological treatises. It is remarkable that Islam does not appear in this literature, except in John of Damascus, who speaks of the Christian heresy of the "Ishmaelites" and knows a few suras. It must be borne in mind that the mention of "Saracens" does not necessarily, on its own, refer to Islam. Is it possible that a Christian population should be subjugated by an Islamic authority without this experience finding literary expression anywhere? In her recently published dissertation ("Die jüdisch-christliche Auseinandersetzung unter islamischer Herrschaft, 7.–10. Jahrhundert," *Judaica et Christiana*, no. 21 [Bern: Lang, 2004]), Simone Rosenkranz did not bring to light a single source before the beginning of the ninth century which mentions Islam in conflicts between Jews and Christians; after this period, though, the situation changes.

3. Dietmar W. Winkler, "Ostsyrisches Christentum: Untersuchungen zur Christologie, Ekklesiologie und zu den ökumenischen Beziehungen der Assyrischen Kirche des Ostens," *Studien zur Orientalischen Kirchengeschichte* 26 (Münster: Lit, 2003): 19.

4. Cf. W. Stewart McCullough, *A Short History of Syriac Christianity to the Rise of Islam* (Map of the Sassanian Empire reprinted from the *Cambridge Ancient History*, vol. 12) (Chico, CA: Scholars Press, 1982), p. 34.

5. Cf. Dietmar W. Winkler, "The Age of the Sassanians: Until 651," in *The Church of the East: A Concise History*, ed. Wilhelm Baum and D. W. Winkler (London and New York: Routledge Curzon, 2000), pp. 8–9.

6. Concerning this topic cf. Winkler, *Ostsyrisches Christentum*, p. 9.

7. Ibid., p. 19.

8. Henri Charles, SJ, *Le Christianisme des Arabes nomades sur le Limes et dans le Désert syro-mésopotamien aux alentours de l'Hégire* (Paris: E. Leroux, 1936), pp. 55–61.

9. The Christianization of the Arabian tribes has not yet been satisfactorily studied. However, it is becoming ever clearer that already in "pre-Islamic times" many Arabian tribes were Christianized, both in Arabia itself and even more in Mesopotamia and into the West as far as Palmyra. Despite the fact that these groups spoke Arabic in everyday life, they celebrated the Christian liturgy in Syriac. Cf., e.g., J. Spencer Trimingham, *Christianity among the Arabs in Pre-Islamic Times* (New York: Longman, 1979).

10. Cf. McCullough, *Short History*, p. 26.

11. In this connection cf. the present author's *Religion in der Geschichte der Menschheit: Die Entwicklung des religiösen Bewusstseins* (Darmstadt: Wissenschaftliche Buchgesellschaft, 2002), pp. 216–24 (and the literature cited there). See also Ulrike Stölting, "Die Gnosis: Herausforderung des Christentums," *Imprimatur* 38 (2005): 11–14 and 61–64.

12. Cf. A. F. J. Klijn, *Edessa, die Stadt des Apostels Thomas: Das älteste Christentum in Syrien* (Neukirchen-Vluyn: Neukirchner Verlag des Erziehungsvereins, 1965), p. 10.

13. Cf. Wolfgang Hage, *Syriac Christianity in the East*, Moran 'Ethno' Series no. 1 (Kerala, India: St. Ephrem Ecumenical Research Institute, 1988), p. 7.

14. Winkler, *Ostsyrisches Christentum*, p. 26.

15. Howard Crosby Butler, *Early Churches in Syria, Fourth to Seventh Centuries*, Princeton Monographs in Art and Archaeology (Princeton, 1929), p. 3.

16. Winkler, *Ostsyrisches Christentum*, p. 35.

17. Ibid.

18. Hage, *Syriac Christianity*, p. 8.

19. Ibid., p. 11.

20. Seely J. Beggiani, *Early Syriac Theology, with Special Reference to the Maronite Tradition* (Lanham, NY: University Press of America, 1983), p. xiii.

21. Winkler, "The Age of the Sassanians," p. 29.

22. Ibid., p. 30: "The teachings of Nestorius seem to have no significance for the official Church."

23. McCullough, *A Short History of Syriac Christianity*, p. 151.

24. Winkler, "The Age of the Sassanians," p. 39.

25. Rosenkranz, *Die jüdisch-christlichen Auseinandersetzung*, p. 47.

26. Ibid., p. 48.

27. Wilhelm Baum, "The Age of the Arabs: 650–1258," in *The Church of the East*, ed. W. Baum and D. W. Winkler, p. 44.

28. Ibid., p. 65.

29. For a more complete treatment, see the present author's *Fundamentalchristologie: Im Spannungsfeld von Christentum und Kultur* (Munich: Kösel, 1986), chiefly pp. 198–229. The texts which follow (cited in the original in German and here as "TzT 4:1") come from K.-H. Ohlig, ed., *Christologie I: Von den Anfängen bis zur Spätantike*, Texte zur Theologie, Dogmatik, no. 4:1 (Graz: Verlag Styria, 1989); the original sources of these quotations are given there.

30. Cf. Rom. 6:2.

31. Piet Smulders, "Dogmengeschichte und lehramtliche Entfaltung der Christologie," in *Mysterium Salutis*, ed. J. Feiner and M. Löhrer, III:1, *Das Christusereignis* (Einsiedeln: Benziger, 1970), p. 402; the whole article comprises pp. 389–476.

32. Ibid., p. 403.

33. *Didache* 10:2 (*Die Apostolischen Väter* [Greek-German parallel edition], ed. Andreas Lindemann and Henning Paulsen [Tübingen: Mohr/Siebeck, 1992], p. 15).

34. *Martyrdom of Polycarp* 14:1 (ibid., p. 275).

35. Following Klijn, *Edessa, die Stadt*, p. 96, the Diatessaron was very important for Syrian Christianity, because "the words of Jesus had been transmitted only orally in Syria before Tatian."

36. *Oration to the Hellenes* 5:1 (in German, TzT 4:1, no. 59).

37. Ibid.

38. Ibid., 21:1.

39. Ibid., 5:6.

40. Ibid., 13.

41. P. Dilhofer's word is "verworren," in "Theophilus von Antiochen," in *Lexikon der antiken christlichen Literatur*, ed. S. Döpp and W. Geerlings (Freiburg: Herder, 1998), p. 603; the whole article comprises pp. 602–608.

42. *Ad Autolycum* II:22 (in German, TzT 4:1, no. 60).

43. Ibid., II:15.

44. E.g., ibid., III:14.

45. Ibid., II:27.

46. Ibid., II:9 (in German, TzT 4:1, no. 60).

47. He claims that "two gods would be proclaimed, if the Son of God were preached as God" (from the *Letter to Hymenaeus* 3 [in German, TzT 4:1, no. 97]).

48. Apparently, the conception of an active God would generally have been sufficient for the Syrians. However, Paul was forced also to engage (Hellenistic) matrices of meaning derived from the New Testament (e.g., the "pre-existence" Christology of the Philippian hymn, the "Logos" teaching in the prologue to John's gospel, and the descriptions of Christ's mediation of the creation process in the deutero-Pauline letters).

49. Fragments from the synodal letter of 268 (the question of this letter's authenticity has not yet been finally decided), 3b (in German, TzT 4:1, no. 88).

50. Ibid., 5.

51. Ibid., 4.

52. Translator's note: The author repeatedly uses in this work phrases based on the German word *Bewährung* ("proof, probation, proving oneself, etc.")—Bewährungstheologie, Bewährungschristologie, Bewährungssoteriologie, etc. While the phrase does appear to be at least marginally current in German scholarly circles, I have not found any English version of it, nor even a technical term which approaches the breadth of meaning given to it by the present author. Consequently, and for lack of a better option, I have chosen to translate the phrase in different ways,

all centering around the idea of "worthiness" and "proving oneself worthy," which seem to be the dominant conceptions in the author's mind.

53. Ibid., 4.

54. Ibid., 5.

55. Ibid.

56. Ibid., 13.

57. Karl Baus, *Von der Urgemeinde zur frühchristlichen Großkirche*, 3rd ed., Handbuch der Kirchengeschichte, ed. Hubert Jedin, no. 1 (Freiburg: Herder, 1965), pp. 293–94.

58. *PG* 26 (1887), pp. 11–526.

59. T. Böhm, "Arius," in *Lexikon der altchristlichen Literatur*, p. 52. Specifically, his primary argument is this: in the authentic documents the Logos is a "fully-developed creature," but one that "came into being before the Aeons"; in the *Thalia*, however, the Logos "appeared *in* time." The argument is not convincing, however; the Logos, following the Logos-teaching since the apologists, did come into being "in the beginning"—indeed "before the Aeons," but still in time—and then effected the creation.

60. This conception of a temporal beginning for the Logos had been circulating since the second century. Just as Arius would later, Origen of Alexandria (d. 253/254) had already held this conception to be false, for if the Logos is temporal, then he cannot be divine. However, because Origen held that the Logos must truly be God (which Arius did not do), he pushed back the begetting of the Son and the emergence of the Logos into the eternity of God, and he formulated for the first time the teaching of the so-called "immanent Trinity." Within the Godhead Father, Son, and Spirit have a varying "fullness" of essence—an "intra-God" subordinationism. On this topic cf. the present author's *Ein Gott in drei Personen?: Vom Vater Jesu zum "Mysterium" der Trinität*, 2nd ed., (Mainz: Matthias-Grünewald Verlag, 2000), pp. 60–62.

61. Athanasius quotes from Arius' *Thalia*: "For, he (Arius) says, because God had seen ahead of time that he (the Word) would be good, therefore he gave him this beauty, which he would later achieve as a human by his virtue, so that God caused it come to pass already in his pre-existence because of his (later) works, which God foresaw" (TzT 4:1, no. 91).

62. For finer distinctions concerning the following section, see the present author's *Fundamentalchristologie*, pp. 210–29.

63. Extant in Syriac fragments (in German, TzT 4:1, nos. 108–10).

64. Ibid. (TzT 4:1, no. 111).

65. Ibid. (TzT 4:1, no. 112).

66. Greek fragment from *De incarnatione* (in German, TzT 4:1, no. 117).

67. Ibid.

68. Another fragment from *De incarnatione* (TzT 4:1, no. 118).

69. Still another fragment from *De incarnatione* (TzT 4:1, no. 120).

70. Cf. here the texts in TzT 4:1, nos. 124–27.

71. Cf. the present author's *Fundamentalchristologie*, pp. 270–91.

72. Cf. here primarily Winkler, *Ostsyrisches Christentum.*

73. Ibid., p. 44.

74. Cf. here Beggiani, *Early Syriac Theology*, pp. 16–17.

75. Peter Bruns, *Das Christusbild Aphrahats des Persischen Weisen*, Hereditas, no. 4 (Bonn: Borengässer, 1990).

76. Ibid., p. 66.

77. Aphrahatis Sapientis Persae Demonstrationes, no. 17. In German, Peter Bruns, ed., *Aphrahat: Unterweisungen (aus dem Syrischen übersetzt und eingeleitet)*, Fontes Christiani, nos 5:1 (*Unterw.* 1–10) and 5:2 (*Unterw.* 11–23) (Freiburg: Herder, 1991).

78. Aphrahat, *Demonstration* 17:3–4 (German: Fontes Christiani 5:2, 419–20).

79. Ibid., 17:5 (German, ibid., p. 420).

80. Bruns, *Das Christusbild Aphrahats*, p. 139.

81. Winkler, *Ostsyrisches Christentum*, p. 47.

82. Ibid.

83. This idea of "enrobing" also plays a role in west Syrian Christology; cf. the present author's *Fundamentalchristologie*, pp. 217–19 (author's note: at that time I falsely attributed the conception to Hellenistic thought).

84. Aphrahat, *Demonstration* 6:9–10 (in German, Fontes Christiani 5:1, 197–98).

85. Ibid., 6:10 (in German, ibid., pp. 198–99).

86. Winkler, *Ostsyrisches Christentum*, p. 49.

87. Peter Bruns, "Ephraem der Syrer," in *Lexikon der antiken christlichen Literatur*, p. 194 (the whole article can be found on pp. 191–94).

88. Winkler, *Ostsyrisches Christentum*, p. 55.

89. Butler, *Early Churches in Syria*, p. 51.

90. Friedrich Heiler, in his *Die Ostkirchen* (edited posthumously) (Munich: E. Reinhardt, 1971), p. 303, groups the information about the east Syrian church under the heading "The East Syrian (Nestorian) Church."

91. Thus Winkler, *Ostsyrisches Christentum*, pp. 42–43, 80.

92. One sees this in, for example, the Syrian teacher Narsai (d. 502), who denied the Holy Spirit the ability to be recognized as God; cf. here Beggiani, *Early Syriac Christianity*, pp. 5–6.

93. Winkler, *Ostsyrisches Christentum*, p. 69.

94. Ibid., p. 77.

95. Cf. here the present author's *Ein Gott in drei Personen?* pp. 86–95.

96. Winkler, *Ostsyrisches Christentum*, p. 91.

97. English translations of the Qur'ān in the following section are my own; the citations refer to Rudi Paret's translation, *Der Koran* (Stuttgart: Kohlhammer, 1979).

98. It is to be noted here that the Qur'ān contains no docetic conceptions or interests whatsoever. The statement that Jesus was only *apparently* crucified should be seen only metaphorically or positivistically, as it would be in Syrian theology—an idea of the religious tradition that was simply taken over unreflectively.

99. For example, even Joseph Henninger, "Die Kirche des Ostens und die Geburt des Islam," in *Islam und Abendland: Begegnung zweier Welten: Eine Vortragsfolge*, ed. Muhammad Asad and Hans Zbinden (Olten: Walter, 1960), p. 52, claims that there has existed "from the beginning onward an unbridgeable gap between Christianity and Islam" because of the lack of or controversy concerning the idea of Jesus' ability to save humanity through the cross. More recently, one sees this idea in the book (unfortunately not well-informed concerned the history of theology and that of Islam) of the praiseworthy exegete Joachim Gnilka, *Bibel und Koran: Was sie verbindet, was sie trennt*, 4th ed. (Freiburg: Herder, 2004), esp. pp. 178–85.

100. Cf. the present author's *Fundamentalchristologie*, II: 135–302.

101. Cf. ibid., III: 343–512.

102. One sees this already in Matthew's gospel, in which the cross's meaning for salvation appears only in the quotation of Jesus' words at the Last Supper.

103. Henninger, "Die Kirche des Ostens," pp. 49–50.

104. Cf., for two examples among many, Claus Schedl, *Muhammad und Jesus: Die christologisch relevanten Texte des Korans, neu übersetzt und erklärt* (Vienna, Freiburg, and Basel: Herder, 1978), pp. 562–66, and G. Quispel, *Makarius, das Thomasevangelium, und das Lied von der Perle*, Supplement to Novum Testamentum (Leiden: Brill, 1967), p. 118.

105. Cf. the present author's *Ein Gott in drei Personen?* pp. 24–25, 41–42.

106. Clement of Alexandria, *Paidagogos* (ca. 203), I.59.1.

107. Origen, *Commentary on Romans*, in the comment on Rom. 3:25.

108. Cf. here the present author's *Weltreligion Islam*, pp. 85–86.

109. Heribert Busse, *Die theologischen Beziehungen des Islams zu Judentum und Christentum: Grundlagen des Dialogs im Koran und die gegenwärtige Diskussion*, Grundzüge, no. 72 (Darmstadt: Wissenschaftliche Buchgesellschaft, 1988), p. 116; cf. pp. 116–40.

110. This was not true for, above all, the Monophysite Ghassanids, who were concentrated in the west Syrian region. Consequently, the theology of the Qur'ān derives from *east* Syrian, primarily south Iraqi Arabs.

111. Cf. on this point Alfred-Louis de Prémare's contribution in this volume.

112. John of Damascus says that the Ishmaelites honor a stone (*On the Here-*

sies, Liber de haeresibus opera polemica, in *Die Schriften des Johannes von Damaskus*, vol. 4, ed. by Bonifatius Kotter, PTS, no. 22 [Berlin and New York: Walter de Gruyter, 1981], heresy no. 100 [in its entirety, pp. 60–67], p. 64, Z. 87–94). I will not take up a full and exact discussion of the passage here; however, I will say that the current interpretation that John is speaking here of the honoring of the black stone in the Ka'ba, is completely off the mark. Theodore Abû Qurra (d. 820/825) was the bishop of Harran in Iraq from 795–812. In a tractate on the worship of images written after 799, he accuses the Jews of worshiping "dead things, such as the stone on the Temple Mount (*even shetîya*) in Jerusalem" (Rosenkranz, *Die jüdisch-christliche Auseinandersetzung*, p. 75). Is there a mix-up here? In any case, the numismatic discoveries from the eighth century show that the Christian Arab authorities had coins minted with the symbol of a stone thereupon; on this topic see Volker Popp's contribution in this volume.

113. This female camel appears in numerous places in the Qur'ān itself, unfortunately with no further explanation. John of Damascus, however, was of the opinion that the tales of this camel (he concerned himself far more with the details) were to be found in a single sura (*graphê*) (heresy 100 [in the above-mentioned edition, p. 65, Z. 114]). These Arabian tales of a female camel and its equally female children can be read (in a version fuller than that in John of Damascus) in A. Sprenger, *Das Leben und die Lehre des Mohammad nach bisher grösstentheils unbenutzten Quellen*, 2nd ed., vol. 1 (Berlin: Nicolaische Verlagsbuchhandlung, 1869), pp. 518–25.

114. Cf. here the present author's *Weltreligion Islam*, p. 91.

115. The translation of *din* as "religion" is false in that the overarching term "religion" developed only as a result of the European Enlightenment and primarily in the nineteenth century. It is more correct to understand the term with ideas like "contract," contract relationship," etc.

CONTRIBUTORS

ALBA FEDELI is Lecturer of Arabic at the University of Milan and was Director of the Fondazione Ferni Noja Noseda in Lesa, Italy, until the untimely death by accident of Sergio Noja Noseda on January 31, 2008. Her main interest continues to be research on the earliest manuscripts of the Qur'ān.

CLAUDE GILLIOT is Professor of Arabic Language and Civilization at the University of Aix-en-Provence. His publications include a number of Qur'ān-related articles and also *Exégèse, langue et théologie en islam: L'exégèse coranique de Ṭabarī* (Paris, 1990) and another article on the capability to read and write in early Islam in *Schlaglichter*, ed. Markus Gross and Karl-Heinz Ohlig (2008).

IBN WARRAQ (pseudonym) is an independent researcher at the Center for Inquiry in Western New York. He publishes collections of articles, including *The Origins of the Koran* (1998), *The Quest for the Historical Muhammad* (2000), *What the Koran Really Says* (2002), and *Defending the West: A Critique of Edward Said's* Orientalism (2007).

PIERRE LARCHER teaches Arabic Linguistics at the University of Provence in Aix-en-Provence. His most recent publications include *Les Mu'allaqât: Les Sept poèmes préislamiques* (2000), *Le Système verbal* *de l'arabe classique* (2003), and *Le Guetteur de mirages: Cinq poèmes préislamiques* (2004).

CHRISTOPH LUXENBERG (pseudonym) lives in Germany and is a Semitics scholar and researcher of the Qur'ān. Chief among his publications is the monograph *Die syro-aramäische Lesart des Koran: Ein Beitrag zur Entschlüsselung der Koransprache* (Berlin, 2000; 2nd ed., 2004; 3rd ed., 2005). The English (enlarged) translation *The Syro-Aramaic Reading of the Koran: A Contribution to the Decoding of the Language of the Koran* was published in 2007 by Verlag Hans Schiler, Berlin. Luxenberg has published articles on other examples of Syro-Aramaic traces in the Qur'ān in *Der frühe Islam*, ed. Karl-Heinz Ohlig (2007), *Schlaglichter*, ed. Markus Gross and Karl-Heinz Ohlig (2008), and *Vom Koran zum Islam*, ed. Markus Gross and Karl-Heinz Ohlig (2009).

SERGIO NOJA NESEDA (1931–2008) was Professor Emeritus of Arabic Language and Literature at the Università Cattolica in Milan and President of the Fondazione Ferni Noja Noseda in Lesa, Italy. He was the editor of the facsimile series *Sources de la transmission manuscrite du texte coranique*.

KARL-HEINZ OHLIG is Professor Emeritus of Religious Studies and the History of Christianity in the Faculty of Philosophy of the Universitaet des Saarlandes, Saarbruecken, Germany. He has published many works, but concerning Islam the most important is *Weltreligion Islam: Eine Einführung* (Mainz and Lucerne, 2000). Other Ohlig articles on Christian religious and early Islamic history have appeared in *Der frühe Islam*, ed. Karl-Heinz Ohlig (2007), *Schlaglichter*, ed. Markus Gross and Karl-Heinz Ohlig (2008), and *Vom Koran zum Islam*, ed. Markus Gross and Karl-Heinz Ohlig (2009).

VOLKER POPP is an Orientalist and numismatist in Bernkastel-Kues. He has published works on Sassanian epigraphy and early Islamic coins. Other Popp articles on early Islamic history have appeared in *Der frühe Islam*, ed. Karl-Heinz Ohlig (2007), *Schlaglichter*, ed. Markus Gross and Karl-Heinz Ohlig (2008), and *Vom Koran zum Islam*, ed. Markus Gross and Karl-Heinz Ohlig (2009).

ALFRED-LOUIS DE PREMARE (1930–2006) was Professor Emeritus of Arabic History and Civilization at the University of Provence in Aix-en-Provence. Among his most recent publications are *Les fondations de l'Islam* (Paris, 2002) and *Aux origines du Coran* (Paris and Tunis, 2005).

GERD-R. PUIN is a retired researcher at the Universitaet des Saarlandes, Saarbruecken, Germany. From 1981 to 1984 he was responsible for a Cultural Aid project in Sanaa, Yemen, financed by the German Foreign Office, titled "Restaurieren und Katalogisieren arabischer Handschriften / Restoration and Cataloguing of Arabic Manuscripts." Other Puin articles on Qur'ānic orthography have appeared in *Schlaglichter*, ed. Markus Gross and Karl-Heinz Ohlig (2008), and *Vom Koran zum Islam*, ed. Markus Gross and Karl-Heinz Ohlig (2009).